THE PRINCIPLES
AND PRACTICE
OF AUDITING

THE PRINCIPLES AND PRACTICE OF AUDITING

George Puttick

BCom (Hons) (Cape Town), CA (SA)
Senior Lecturer in the Department of Accounting,
University of Cape Town

Sandy van Esch

CA (SA)
Associate Professor, School of Accountancy,
University of the Witwatersrand, Johannesburg

Consulting Editor:

Suresh Kana

MCom (Witwatersrand), CA (SA)
Deputy CEO, PricewaterhouseCoopers

Eighth Edition

JUTA

First published in 1963
Eighth edition 2003
Second impression 2003
Third impression 2004

© Juta & Co. Ltd 2003
P.O. Box 24309, Lansdowne 7779

ISBN 0 7021 5691 4

Cover design: Welma Odendaal
Editor: Mariaan Nel
Proofreader: Ethné Clarke
Indexer: Cecily van Gend
Typesetting and design by Mckore Graphics, Panorama
Cover photograph: PricewaterhouseCoopers
Printed by Creda Communications

Preface

Information is the lifeblood of the capital markets. Recent scandals and business failures have undermined investors' confidence in those responsible for the content and quality of the information on which businesses report. Those responsible include business executives, boards of directors, independent auditors, third-party analysts and other information distributors. To restore public trust, every participant in the chain must embrace and practise a spirit of transparency, a culture of accountability and individual integrity. Independent auditors are no exception. Having robust auditing is a fundamental cornerstone of modern corporate governance.

Audit methodologies have evolved in recognition of developments in corporate governance, information technology and risk management strategies. The eighth edition of this standard reference for students and practitioners has been completely revised and restructured for these developments. The new edition includes commentary on the most recent South African Auditing Standards, South African Auditing Practice Statements and Audit and Accounting Guides, the audit implications of relevant South African Statements of Generally Accepted Accounting Practice, and the 2002 King Report on Corporate Governance for South Africa.

Whilst the opening chapters trace the historical development of auditing much as they did in previous editions, the discussion has been expanded to include the present and proposed structure of the profession in South Africa, the nature and objectives of auditing, the accounting profession's Code of Professional Conduct, and the auditor's responsibilities. Later chapters cover the Revised Code of Corporate Practices and Conduct, matters applicable to the audit of limited companies, the auditor's duty towards group financial statements, profit forecasts and prospectuses, and the auditor's report on annual financial statements, other reports and other reporting issues.

The text addresses the auditor's understanding of the business, risk assessment, internal control and computerized information systems which the auditor may encounter at a client entity and the implications of these for the audit approach. The COSO control framework, used in the King Report on Corporate Governance for South Africa 2002, underpins the approach to the strategic business objectives, strategic business risks including information technology, and risk and control activities that management implements to manage its business processes.

The text is significantly enhanced to:

- provide guidance on assessing control risk and tests of controls in line with leading current practice;
- separate detection risk and the design of substantive tests;

- reflect a business process analysis approach which identifies process objectives and their core and sub-processes, process level business risks, critical success factors and key performance indicators used by management to manage risks and control significant classes of transactions and balances;
- reflect the effect of the process level business risks and their potential financial statement impact on the audit approach, and the auditor's response by way of tests of controls and substantive procedures;
- cover the content of important new auditing standards and statements issued since 1998;
- include guidance on the New Code of Conduct issued by The South African Institute of Chartered Accountants; and
- include, for each chapter, outcomes-based learning objectives to guide the reader and student of auditing.

It is fitting in the fortieth year in which this book is in print, to acknowledge early contributions and collaborations. The first four editions, the first published in 1963, were co-authored by Ian Taylor and Leon Kritzinger. George Puttick provided assistance for the third and fourth editions, published in 1975 and 1980 respectively, and became acknowledged as a co-author from the fifth edition in 1983. The writing partnership ended after publication of the sixth edition on the retirement of Taylor and Kritzinger. Puttick and Sandy van Esch co-authored the revised sixth edition, Puttick being solely responsible for the seventh edition. This, the eighth edition, has been co-authored by Puttick and Van Esch, with assistance provided by Suresh Kana, the consulting editor.

Finally, the authors sincerely thank all those who assisted in ensuring that this text reflects current best practice and for permissions granted to use copyright material, in particular:

- PricewaterhouseCoopers and KPMG for access to education material, guidance regarding international audit methodologies, and constructive critiques of this manuscript;
- the Public Accountants' and Auditors' Board, and the South African Institute of Chartered Accountants for the use of material from their publications; and
- the Institute of Directors for permission to use extracts from the King Report on Corporate Governance for South Africa 2002.

The authors express their thanks to Professor Hansja Theron and colleagues at UNISA for advice during the writing of this text. Not least, our appreciation to the editorial and production team at Juta Academic.

George Puttick
Sandra D van Esch
Suresh P Kana

Cape Town, November 2002

Contents

13. Auteur Expenditure Transactions and Balances 419

14. Auteur Production/Inventory Transactions Balances 480

LIST OF TABLES AND DIAGRAMS

1

Introduction

Learning objectives

After studying this chapter you should be able to:
1. Outline, briefly, the origins and history of auditing.
2. Explain the development of the auditing profession in South Africa.
3. Explain the different responsibilities and functions of the South African Institute of Chartered Accountants and the Public Accountants' and Auditors' Board.
4. Describe the structure of the membership levels of the South African Institute of Chartered Accountants and the rationale behind it.

1.1 THE ORIGIN AND HISTORY OF AUDITING

The *Concise Oxford Dictionary* defines 'account' variously, including 'answer for', and the 'reckoning of money held in trust'.

In these senses of the word, traces of accounting can be found in the histories of the earliest civilizations, even those in which the art of the recorded word was little known. Accounting in those far-off days could only have taken place orally.[1] The steward in charge of the cattle, goods and other forms of wealth would, from time to time, produce to his master the wealth with which he was entrusted and give an account of his stewardship, reciting from memory the goods and chattels acquired, those disposed of and those still in his possession. The master would listen to this recital of the steward's transactions and question him thereon. The master was the listener, the auditor. So the word 'auditor' (derived from the Latin word *audire*, to hear) acquired a secondary meaning: 'one who satisfies himself as to the truth of the accounting of another'.

With the advent of writing and the acquisition of the art by the more literate of the population, some form of written record was kept by the steward, and

---

[1] See the Bible – Matthew, chapter XXV, and Luke, chapter XVI.

the master, or his delegate, examined the record. So there evolved, side by side, the art of bookkeeping and the practice of auditing, the latter no longer being confined to a mere listening to an account of stewardship.

In ancient Egypt and Babylonia, the practice of checking records was well established. The Greeks and Romans had very complete systems of auditing public accounts. The Greeks, for instance, considered accountability of officials of such importance that everyone connected with government or public administration had to render his account.[2] The practice of rendering accounts appears to have been taken seriously and, by the many references in Greek literature to charges of embezzlement brought against men holding public positions, proved most necessary.

The Greek and Roman practice of accounting and auditing finds its echo in the early records of English public life. In 1285, during the reign of Edward I, the following statute was passed:

> 'It is agreed and ordained that when the Masters of such servants ("Concerning servants, bailiffs, chamberlains, and all manner of Receivers, which are bound to yield Accompt") do assign auditors to take their Account (Accompt), and they be found in arrearages upon the account, all things allowed which ought to be allowed, their bodies shall be arrested and by the testimony of the auditors of the same account, shall be sent or delivered into the next gaol of the King's in those parts.'[3]

It will be appreciated that despite references to accounting and auditing in those bygone days, trade was then extremely simple and records were the crudest, the latter complicated by the use of cumbersome Roman numerals. It was not until the fourteenth century that Arabic notation came into use in Britain and it was, at first, almost as confusing as the Roman.[4]

In the fifteenth century, the phenomenal growth of trade, first in Italy and later in other European countries, brought in its train bookkeeping complexities and problems. It is therefore not surprising that the first printed reference to the double-entry system should appear in Italy. In 1494 a treatise on double-entry bookkeeping by Frater Luca Pacioli was published.[5] Other treatises on the subject followed in quick succession and concurrently with a growing demand for persons capable of recording mercantile transactions.

There is a sixteenth century reference to an order for the auditors of the Pewterers' Company:

> 'Also, it is agreed that there shall be foure Awdytours chosen every yeare to awdit the Crafte accompte and they to paruse it and search it that it be parfect. And also to accompt it, correct it, and allowe it so that they make an ende of the

---

[2] A H Woolf *A Short History of Accountants and Accountancy* 149.
[3] Woolf op. cit. 152.
[4] L Frankland *The Evolution of the Science of Bookkeeping* 17.
[5] *Suma de Arithmetica, Geometria, Proportioni et Proportionalita data.*

awdit thereof between Mighelmas and Christmas yearely and if defaute be made of ffenishinge thereof before Christmas yearely every one of the saide awdytours shall pay to the Crafte boxe vj. s. viij. d. a pece.'[6]

About this time (1543), Hugh Oldcastle's treatise on double-entry book-keeping was first published in England. In 1588 a new and augmented edition of this book appeared, in which reference is made to calling over (chapter 21):

'First deliver unto your fellow the Journall and hold yourself the leager. Then request your fellow that hath the Journall to begin with the first parcell of the said Journall and that hee tell you the name and thing and in what leafe of the leager it standeth in Debitor and Creditor so that you may perceive to what leafe hee sendeth you. And when you have founde the parcell by the shewing of him that hath the Journall then marke and make a token in the said leager in the same parcell with a pricke uppon the pound. – So it be no blemish to the book, that done say to hime that hath the Journall that he therein also make a pricke or signe of your concordance. And beware that none of you without consent of the other make any parcell by reason whereof might grow grevious labours to reforme the correction again of the same. For the parcells discreetly persued and so marked testifyeth a due examination and this examination is to be used in making of accompte between you and any other person before that you deliver it from your hands. – And note also that every parcell in your Journall must for the concordance have two prickes because it ought to accorde with two parcells in the leager, one in dare another in habere.'[7]

In view of the fact that the father of double-entry bookkeeping, Luca Pacioli (date of birth between 1445 and 1450, and date of death probably shortly after 1514),[8] was an Italian, it is no wonder that Italy also claims the honour of being the first country to give birth to a society of accountants, the *Collegio dei Raxonati*, founded in Venice in 1581.[9] It is interesting to note that prospective accountants had to serve 'articles' for six years. After the formation of this society others followed and, by the middle of the eighteenth century, most of the societies in Italy were carried on under the auspices of the state. The societies were entirely private institutions and, in fact, from time to time resisted attempts at state interference.[10]

With the appearance of the joint stock companies and the impetus given to this form of association by the Industrial Revolution in England, it was imperative that those directing a business should account clearly and honestly to the owners, that is to say, the shareholders. The employment of an auditor to act as agent for the shareholders became a necessity, and out of this need grew the profession of accounting and auditing as we know it today.

---

[6] Woolf op. cit. 154.
[7] Frankland op. cit. 35.
[8] Ibid. 26 – 7.
[9] Woolf op. cit. 162.
[10] 'History of Accounting Italy' *Accountants Magazine* 1902, page 554.

The first British society of accountants to be incorporated by royal charter was formed in Edinburgh on 23 October 1854, thus giving birth to the 'Chartered Accountant'.[11] Shortly afterwards followed the establishment of the other Scottish accounting bodies.

The Institute of Chartered Accountants in England and Wales was formed in 1880, followed five years later by the Society of Incorporated Accountants. Members of these accounting bodies became interested in the profession in South Africa and they contributed materially to its advancement.

1.2 THE DEVELOPMENT OF THE AUDITING PROFESSION IN SOUTH AFRICA

As in the United Kingdom, the growth of joint stock companies in South Africa, accompanied by a series of Companies Acts, led to statutory recognition of the South African accounting and auditing profession.

In 1894 the first professional accounting body in South Africa was formed in the (then) Transvaal under the name of The Institute of Accountants and Auditors in the South African Republic, followed, in 1895, by The Institute of Accountants in what was then Natal.

An important advance was made in 1904 when a provincial ordinance was passed which provided for the formation of The Transvaal Society of Accountants. It confined practice to members of the Society. The Natal Society of Accountants came into existence in 1909, as a result of similar legislation. No such legislation was passed in the (then) Cape Province or in the (then) Orange Free State, but societies were voluntarily formed there – the Cape Society of Accountants and Auditors in 1907, and The Society of Accountants and Auditors in the Orange Free State shortly afterwards.

Following upon union in South Africa, many attempts were made to secure uniform legislation. The first such attempt was in 1911 when the four recognized bodies of accountants in the provinces held conferences which resulted in an attempt, in 1912, to introduce a Union Accountants' Registration Bill for this purpose. A select committee reported that the preamble to the Bill had not been proved to its satisfaction and stated that the decision had been arrived at because a majority of the committee did not approve of the compulsory principle.[12]

The next attempt was in 1923 when another Bill was introduced to bring all chartered accountants under one body. This Bill was referred to a select committee and was amended to such an extent that the promoters decided to withdraw it. After this attempt the four South African bodies cooperated more closely and, following the Companies Act of 1926, promoted a short Bill which was passed by Parliament as 'The Chartered Accountants' Designation

---

[11] History of the Chartered Accountants of Scotland 20.
[12] See H Paul, J Bowman and R Ball, *A Pilot Study presented to the Department of Accounting, University of Cape Town*, 1978.

Act (1927)', which authorized members to use the designation 'Chartered Accountant (South Africa)' or 'CA (SA)'.[13]

In 1934 Dr Hjalmar Reitz introduced a private member's Bill to provide for the registration of accountants in the Union; the Bill did not proceed beyond the first reading. He made a second attempt in 1936. In the same year the late Minister Klasie Havenga, then Minister of Finance, instigated the appointment of the Accountancy Profession Commission to enquire into, advise and report upon

> '[w]hether it is advisable to place the profession of accountancy and auditing . . . on a unified basis by incorporation of a representative body having control over the whole profession, and keeping a register in which should be inscribed the names of all qualified members of the profession and, if so, the method by which such register should be established and controlled.'[14]

The Commission recommended the unification of the four provincial societies, the establishment of a register of accountants, the limitation of the right to practice to persons who were members of one of the four societies, and the establishment of an accountancy board to control examinations. The control and discipline of the profession were to be vested in the four societies. It further considered that training under articles was essential. The Commission's Bill was, however, not taken any further.

Based on the Commission's Bill, Mr P V Pocock introduced a private Bill in 1938, which was referred to a select committee, passed its second reading and was discussed in the House in the committee stage on 23 February 1940. It was not completed on that day and was not proceeded with because of the intervention of the Second World War.

In 1945 the four provincial societies held a conference in Cape Town to consolidate the profession, the outcome of which was the coming into being of 'The Joint Council of Chartered Accountants' on 1 January 1946.

On the initiative of the government, the proposals outlined above were renewed in November 1946. A conference, attended by representatives of societies and bodies of accountants, was held in Bloemfontein on 16 and 17 April 1947. From this conference emerged a draft Bill which was based on the Accountancy Commission Bill. However, the government felt that this Bill did not provide adequate protection of public interests. The government in turn produced a draft Auditing Act on 30 November 1949 which would have placed control in the hands of government officials and put the auditor in the position of informer and destroyed the fiduciary relationship between the auditor and the client.

On 22 March 1950 the Minister of Finance received delegates who reported that a draft Bill had been agreed upon and it was requested this draft Bill be

---

[13] The Afrikaans equivalent, 'Geoktrooieerde Rekenmeester (Suid-Afrika)' or 'GR(SA)', was overlooked. The Act was changed in 1971 to protect this designation.
[14] *Accountancy Profession Commission Report.*

introduced at that session of Parliament. The final conference in this long saga, which had lasted almost 40 years, was held on 24 November 1950, and from this the Bill in its final form emerged for discussion with the government law adviser and submission to Parliament. The Bill was enacted on 18 June 1951 and so The Public Accountants' and Auditors' Act 51 of 1951 came into operation on 1 November 1951.

Although the Act provides statutory uniformity in that only persons registered in terms of the Act may 'practise as an accountant or auditor or hold himself out or allow himself to be held out as an accountant or auditor in public practice',[15] the unification of the four provincial societies remained a pipe dream. In 1966 the 'Joint Council' changed its name to 'The National Council of Chartered Accountants (SA)', but this brought no change in the existence of the four provincial societies. In 1970 the National Council appointed Mr E Bowsher of Cape Town to investigate the issue. His report was not accepted. In 1976 the National Council and the Public Accountants' and Auditors' Board appointed a Commission of Enquiry into the Accountancy Profession. The Commission's report was tabled on 31 January 1980 and reported, *inter alia*, that:

> '46. At present the profession in South Africa comprises one layer of qualified persons organized in 22 regional associations, 4 separate provincial societies, the National Council of Chartered Accountants (SA) and the Public Accountants' and Auditors' Board. This complicated structure which has come about for reasons now largely historic has led to confusion in the mind of the layman, but more importantly there is evidence of some duplication of effort and there is a need to present a unified front on the international scene.'

The report explains the reasons for the lack of unification as follows:

> '... There have been several attempts at unifying the profession in the past but these have failed because of reluctance to dispense with the provincial societies, or because of fears of centralized domination, or that the well-tried administrations of the provincial societies would be replaced by a markedly less efficient national administration ...'

However, in 1979 a further move was made towards unification by the creation of a National Institute (the South African Institute of Chartered Accountants) from 1 January 1980 without the immediate dissolution of the provincial societies, which merely achieved a separate legal status (and crest). Financial security was also assured for the National Council, something it had not enjoyed up to that point.

The Institute was duly formed and although the Commission of Enquiry recommended that '. . . the proposed National Institute . . . and the PAAB should set up a joint committee for the purpose of considering their unification', a circular[16] stated that:

---

[15] Section 22, Act 51 of 1951.
[16] COE 2, dated November 1982, Johannesburg.

'... [t]he Board and the Institute are not in favour of pursuing this recommendation at the present time. Consequently, the preparation of further material, including a synopsis of the advantages and disadvantages for submission to the Councils of the Provincial Societies, the Board and the Institute, has been deferred.'

1.2.1 The Institute and the Board – Current functions and responsibilities

An overview of the various functions and responsibilities of the South African Institute of Chartered Accountants (the Institute or SAICA) and the Public Accountants' and Auditors' Board (the Board or PAAB) follows:

Chartered Accountants

To use the designation Chartered Accountant (South Africa) – besides the necessary qualifications and completion of training requirements – one needs to be a member of SAICA. To engage in public practice as an auditor, one needs to register as a member in public practice (RAA) with the PAAB.

Traineeships

Audit firms providing practical training to trainees have to register with the PAAB as a Registered Training Office and all trainees' contracts require registration with the PAAB.

Education

Changes envisaged in the draft Registered Accountancy Act have seen the PAAB taking on a more regulatory role in the past three years, leading to a significant change in the focus of the PAAB's responsibilities for the education and training of RAAs – from direct responsibility for the accreditation, monitoring of education service providers and training offices, to the recognition and monitoring of Institutes and their academic, core assessment, education and training programmes. The PAAB appointed a new Director of Education in 1999 and established a new Education Committee charged with the responsibility of developing and implementing a recognition model and monitoring processes to monitor compliance by those Institutes recognized by the PAAB, whose members will be eligible to write the Professional Practice Examination (the PPE) in the Auditing Specialism. Currently SAICA is the only Institute recognized, however, it is anticipated that in the future other Institutes may seek recognition for their educational programmes and for their members to be admitted as RAAs. As the regulatory body for the auditing profession, the PAAB Education Committee retains responsibility for the setting and adjudication of the Professional Practice Examination (PPE). Success in this examination and completion of a training contract entitles a member of SAICA to register in public practice as a RAA.

As a result of these changes, in 1999, the then Director of Education and staff in the education division of the PAAB, as well as its existing Education Committee transferred to SAICA to form a new education division, EDCO. It retained direct responsibility for the setting of syllabi and accreditation and the monitoring of its education service providers and training offices, leading to the qualification of a chartered accountant and associate general accountant. EDCO retained responsibility for the academic programme (CTA or equivalent); the setting and adjudication of the core assessment programme, the 'Qualifying Examination'; the education programme for the Auditing and Financial Management Specialism fields catering for trainee accountants serving their training contracts in or out of public practice, namely TIPP or TOPP; and the recognized training programme (currently training contracts administered by SAICA and registered with the PAAB are recognized); and finally, the setting and adjudication of the Financial Management Specialism examination.

More recently SAICA's education division has taken on responsibility for a number of educational initiatives at the secondary and tertiary educational levels, described later in this chapter, designed to promote career opportunities in the accountancy profession and aimed at increasing significantly the number of black chartered accountants in the profession.

The requirements for persons wishing to become chartered accountants or registered accountants and auditors are discussed in chapter 3.

Accounting and auditing standards

The Institute has an Accounting Practices Committee which is responsible for establishing accounting standards. Once decided upon, such accounting standards are approved by the independent Accounting Practices Board.

Prior to January 2002, SAICA's Auditing Standards Committee was responsible for the setting of auditing standards, which were endorsed by the PAAB. As with the changing roles of SAICA and the PAAB in education-related aspects, the responsibility for the setting of auditing standards has been relocated to the PAAB with the appointment of a Director of Auditing in 2001, the transfer of the SAICA Auditing Standards Committee to the PAAB at the beginning of 2002, and the establishment of a new, independent Auditing Standards Boards in 2001. The Auditing Standards Committee is responsible for developing South African statements of auditing standards (SAAS). These are based on International Auditing Standards issued by the IAAS and adapted for local conditions. Following due exposure process, consideration of comments received and consensus by members of the Auditing Standards Committee, the proposed SAAS are submitted to the Auditing Standards Board for approval and issue as South African Auditing Standards or Practice Statements.

Professional conduct and disciplinary proceedings

The Public Accountants' and Auditors' Act vests in the Board the power to prescribe Disciplinary Rules and establish a Code of Professional Conduct, both of which it has done. The Board has a Disciplinary Board which considers complaints against registered accountants and auditors and has the power to take disciplinary action against such persons, the most severe of which is to deregister a registered accountant and auditor. Because the Public Accountants' and Auditors' Act and the Board regulates only those members of the accounting profession registered with it, the South African Institute of Chartered Accountants has adopted a parallel Code of Professional Conduct that applies to all members and associates of the Institute. The Institute also has a Disciplinary Committee to hear complaints against its members. See chapter 3.2.5.

Practice review programme

To ensure that users of financial statements can rely on audit reports to add credibility to disclosures in such statements, it is important that the accounting and auditing profession monitor and that it be seen to be monitoring the standard of work performed by its members. To that end, the Public Accountants' and Auditors' Board has in place a programme of audit practice review. See chapter 3.6.

Other Institute functions

Apart from the matters already mentioned, the South African Institute of Chartered Accountants assumes responsibility for the following more important aspects:

Continuing professional education:

Under the auspices of the Institute, courses, seminars and workshops are presented by experts in various fields relating to matters relevant to accountants and auditors. See chapter 3.7.

Technical support and journal:

The Institute, through its well-qualified permanent staff, provides advisory services to members in respect of professional technical and ethical matters and so assists members requiring assistance to adequately fulfil their professional responsibilities. It also publishes a monthly journal, *Accountancy South Africa*, which addresses technical matters and current affairs of interest to professional accountants.

Liaison with Government:

The Institute is responsible for nominating suitable individuals out of its membership to sit on the various advisory committees and boards of Government, ensuring meaningful contribution from the accounting profession to the deliberations of such bodies.

Public relations:

The Institute has fulfilled this role in the past by mounting advertising campaigns to promote the image of the profession as a whole. From time to time the Institute issues press releases concerning matters relevant to the profession, such as developments, appointments to prominent positions within the profession, and responses to statements made about the profession that are thought not to be wholly justified.

1.3 BACKGROUND: STANDARDS SETTING

There are five bodies playing an important role in the establishment of accounting and auditing standards, namely:

- International Federation of Accountants;
- International Audit and Assurance Standards Board;
- International Accounting Standards Board;
- Accounting Practices Board; and
- International Forum for Accountancy Development.

These are discussed below.

1.3.1 International Federation of Accountants (IFAC)

On 7 October 1977, during the International Congress of Accountants held in Munich, an agreement was entered into between 63 accounting bodies representing 49 countries. The broad objectives of IFAC are 'the development and enhancement of a coordinated worldwide accountancy profession with harmonized standards'. To this end IFAC established a standing committee with the specific responsibility and authority to issue exposure drafts and guidelines on auditing.

1.3.2 International Audit and Assurance Standards Board (IAASB)

The standing committee established by IFAC to issue guidelines on auditing was called the Auditing Practices Committee (IAPC). In 2002, the committee was reconstituted as the International Audit and Assurance Standards Board. After January 1980 several International Auditing Guidelines (IAG) were issued. In July 1994, after some revision of the guidelines, their status was changed to that of International Auditing Standards (ISA) and it became a requirement that auditors in countries which had not developed their own auditing guidelines or standards but had adopted the international ones conduct audits in accordance with such standards.

Prior to 1994 the South African Institute of Chartered Accountants, through its Auditing Standards Committee, developed and released its own statements on Generally Accepted Auditing Standards. Whilst these statements often bore similarity to the International Auditing Guidelines they were not aligned to the international pronouncements. In 1994 the Board of the South African Institute of Chartered Accountants approved a proposal that statements of South African Auditing Standards (SAAS) should be based on the International Standards on Auditing (ISA). To implement the decision, the so-called Harmonization and Improvements Project of the local Auditing Standards Committee was undertaken with the objective of aligning statements of South African Auditing Standards (SAAS) with the International Standards, but with improvements and adaptations relevant to the South African context. Any differences in basic principles and essential procedures are referred to in an explanatory paragraph at the end of each South African Auditing Standard.

In January 2002, the responsibility for setting auditing standards was transferred from the South African Institute of Chartered Accountants to the Public Accountants' and Auditors' Board and an Auditing Standards Board was formed, which approves South African Auditing Standards based on the recommendations of the Auditing Standards Committee responsible for developing the standards.

1.3.3 International Accounting Standards Board (IASB)

In 1966 the President of the Institute of Chartered Accountants in England and Wales initiated the establishment of a three-nation study group (Accountants International Study Group, AISG), comprising his own Institute and those of America and Canada. The objective was to make and publish comparative studies of the accounting problems in the three nations. During the six years leading up to the International Congress of Accountants in Sydney in October 1972, the AISG published a number of studies. At the Congress the bodies involved proposed that an international committee be set up to formulate international accounting standards, this became known as the International Accounting Standards Committee (IASC of IFAC). By 29 June 1973 the leading accounting bodies in 10 Western countries had committed themselves to this venture as founder members and undertook to support the development of accounting standards internationally. After that bodies from a large number of other countries (including South Africa) were admitted as associate members. The Committee issued its first statement in January 1975 and has issued numerous since then. This committee has also recently been reconstituted as the International Accouting Standards Board (IASB). South African Statements on Generally Accepted Accounting Practice are based on International Statements.

1.3.4 The Accounting Practices Board (APB)

With the coming into force of the Companies Act 1973, a new phase was introduced by section 286(3) of that Act. In expressing an opinion on the financial statements of a company, the auditor is required to state whether the financial statements fairly present the state of affairs 'in conformity with generally accepted accounting practice'. The function of laying down what constitutes 'generally accepted accounting practice' in South Africa was entrusted to the Accounting Practices Board.

The APB communicates its authoritative opinion by means of statements. To provide an opportunity for as wide an audience as possible to express an opinion on any proposed statement, a subcommittee of the SA Institute of Chartered Accountants (Accounting Practices Committee or APC), and with the approval of the Executive Committee, first issues an 'exposure draft'. After consideration of comments and objections, a final statement is prepared for approval by the APB. If approved, the statement becomes official. Whether compliance with these statements constitutes compliance with the requirements of the Companies Act 1973 is addressed in a circular 8/99 issued by the South African Institute of Chartered Accountants in December 1999. The content of the circular is discussed in chapters 3.2 and 18.

SAICA has for a considerable period of time aimed to obtain legal backing for the Statements of Generally Accepted Accounting Practice. This is likely to become a reality during 2003. During 2002 a Financial Reporting Bill was circulated for comment. The Bill proposes amendments to the Companies Act and its scope is to provide for the:

- setting of financial reporting standards for the preparation and presentation of financial statements by entities that are required by statute to prepare and present their financial statements in conformity with the financial reporting standards;
- setting of general and limited purpose financial reporting standards;
- establishment and functions of the Financial Reporting Standards Council ('the Council'), the main function of which will be the developing and setting of financial reporting standards; and
- supervision and enforcement by the Financial Services Board ('the Board') of compliance by designated entities with the financial reporting standards.

The main objects of the Financial Reporting Bill are as follows:

- The removal of any uncertainty as to what constitutes generally accepted accounting practice by providing for the setting of uniform financial reporting standards by the proposed Council and to afford legal backing for such financial reporting standards by providing for the supervision and enforcement of compliance with those standards. This approach will inevitably result in a more objective, credible, consistent and fair representation of an entity's financial statements.

- The financial statements of an entity should be meaningful and reliable to users of financial statements. It is the object of the Bill to instil confidence into both local and foreign users of financial statements to rely on the information contained in an entity's financial statements.

However, as an interim measure until the Bill is promulgated into legislation, SAICA and the JSE have established a panel of specialists, called the GAAP Monitoring Panel (GMP), to ensure that listed companies comply with South

African Statements of Generally Accepted Accounting Practice. Complaints received by the JSE of alleged non-compliance will be referred to the GMP. The chairman of the GMP will refer the matter to a review committee selected from the panel. They will report their findings to the JSE Listings division, which will use its existing structures to address the matter and consider further action. Actions may include requiring companies to re-issue their financial statements and the imposition of penalties.

1.3.5 International Forum for Accountancy Development (IFAD)

Recently, the Asian crisis has raised questions about the quality of accounting and auditing in the affected countries. Some have suggested that the accounting and auditing profession may not have fulfilled its professional responsibilities in those countries. As evidence, such critics cite incomplete financial information, lack of transparency and inappropriate accounting standards and inconsistent application of those standards as factors contributing to the seriousness of the crisis or to the delay in identifying and responding to it.

The International Forum for Accountancy Development (IFAD) is an initiative of the International Federation of Accountants and the World Bank. The objectives of IFAD are to:

- promote understanding by national government of the value of transparent financial reporting, in accordance with sound corporate governance, by various parties served by the accountancy profession;

- assist in defining expectations as to how the accountancy profession, both in the public and private sectors, should carry out its responsibilities to support the public interest;

- serve to bring pressure on government to focus more directly on the needs of developing countries;

- help harness funds and expertise to build accounting and auditing capacity in developing countries;

- promote cooperation between government, the profession, the international financial institutions, regulators, standard setters, capital providers and issuers; and

- contribute to a common strategy and framework of reference for accountancy development.

1.3.6 General

IFAC has established two further standing committees: an Ethics Committee and an Education Committee. Both committees have issued guidelines and, as a member of IFAC, the South African Institute of Chartered Accountants undertakes to give consideration to these in developing its own ethics and educational standards.

It should be appreciated that it is not possible for any one of the accounting bodies, national or international, to issue immediately a complete set of statements and/or guidelines to cover all aspects and areas where there is a perceived need. The Institute and the APB in South Africa are no exceptions. However, this does not mean that the auditor has carte blanche in areas for which no statement or guideline has been issued. The profession's Code of Professional Conduct sums up as follows the position that the auditor should adopt:

'A practitioner should maintain his professional knowledge and skills. This requires a continuing awareness of developments in the accountancy profession including relevant national and international pronouncements on accounting, auditing and other relevant regulations and statutory requirements.'

1.4 THE STRUCTURE OF MEMBERSHIP LEVELS OF THE SOUTH AFRICAN INSTITUTE OF CHARTERED ACCOUNTANTS

1.4.1 Introduction

In January 1994 the Council of the South African Institute of Chartered Accountants (SAICA) commissioned a study, known as the FAESA Project, to consider the restructuring of the Institute to facilitate broader membership entry into the Institute and, at the same time, to meet the public's expectations concerning membership growth without a lowering of standards. As part of this process, in April 1995, a proposal was submitted to Council outlining a model that would provide for different levels of membership with multiple entry points for aspirant accountants. An Ad Hoc Committee was formed to address and make recommendations to Council on this issue. To this end, the Ad Hoc Committee issued Discussion Paper 14, entitled 'Structure of The South African Institute of Chartered Accountants', to elicit the views of members of the Institute on its proposals. The discussion paper provided background on the need for change, as well as particular proposals for such change. Identified changes and strategic proposals, as outlined in the discussion paper, follow here.

1.4.2 The need for change

Change was seen to be necessary in the light of a changing South Africa, which was democratizing and seeking to empower people to realize their economic potential through affirmative action programmes and the RDP. The Institute was perceived by many to be a white elitist organization in spite of a black advancement programme which had been given high priority for some years by then. Concrete strategies were needed to enable blacks more easily to qualify as accountants and so put to rest the perception of the Institute as a white elitist organization.

Further, the Department of Education had issued a White Paper on Education and the National Qualification Framework Bill (NQF), setting out how Government saw the future of education and training in South Africa. In terms of this, a South African Qualifications Authority (SAQA) was established to provide guidelines and assist relevant bodies in establishing education and training frameworks that fitted into the broader picture. The South African Institute of Chartered Accountants recognized that it needed at an early stage to take a proactive stance and be involved in the process to ensure that all necessary checks and balances were in place to maintain appropriate standards.

As set out in the White Paper, the proposed model for the restructuring of the South African Institute of Chartered Accountants promoted the following key elements:

- Recognition of prior learning;
- Competency-based education and training;
- Portability of qualification; and
- Liberalization of entry requirements.

1.4.3 Strategic proposals

Since it was recognized that the adoption of a strategy was necessary to ensure sustainable long-term growth of the accountancy profession in South Africa, accordingly a strategy was proposed that would:

- facilitate broader entry for accountants in public practice and those in the commerce and industry constituencies;
- allow for three levels of membership, recognizing that, in time, more specialized levels could be added;
- use this structure to facilitate upward mobility towards chartered accountancy in an orderly managed and controlled process; and
- make provision for the introduction of commercial and industrial training contracts.

It was also proposed that the South African Institute of Chartered Accountants should provide additional entry points for aspirant accountants to broaden its membership base, provide access to the accountancy profession for all those with ability and, at the same time, increase its relevance to the public sector, commerce and industry. Four levels of membership were envisaged:

- Chartered Accountants;
- General Accountants;
- Accounting Technicians; and
- Student Accountants.

It was intented that the Institute establish the education and training requirements for the new levels of membership in accordance with the White Paper. In addition, it would establish its own education and training processes for chartered accountants, as well as run appropriate support services for all student membership.

A further important point was that the Institute would take cognizance of the need of members to move from one level to another in the accountancy hierarchy without having to duplicate education and training requirements.

Following on the publication of Discussion Paper 14, meetings were held throughout the country to discuss issues relating to the proposals. These, in turn, were followed by a referendum in which the repositioning proposals received overwhelming support from the members of SAICA. On 22 October 1996, the Council of SAICA approved of the package of proposals based on the structure proposed in Discussion Paper 14. Implementation of the proposals began on 1 January 1997; it was from that date that associates could apply to be admitted into SAICA's new structure. The structure incorporates three colleges, one college of membership and two colleges of associates. These are discussed below.

1.4.4 Colleges of membership

The College of Chartered Accountants

The education and training of chartered accountants continues in much the same manner as before except that credit is given for experience gained at lower levels and for courses passed at General Accountant level, in accordance with South African Qualification Authority standards.

In addition, approved training offices were established in commerce and industry and in the public sector, because it was thought likely that audit practice offices would not be able to meet the demand for persons wanting to qualify as chartered accountants in future. Furthermore, to some candidates the alternative routes would be more attractive, since they would not be required to spend time in an audit office. Such new training offices would also provide a mechanism through which candidates from the General Accountant level would be able to achieve Chartered Accountant status by completing a three-year training contract in public practice or commerce and industry. Training at universities, known as 'academic articles', continues.

Candidates who do not obtain a degree at a university have to complete a five-year training contract, as has always been the case.

Chartered Accountants qualifying through offices in commerce and industry or the public sector do not qualify to register with the Public Accountants' and Auditors' Board (PAAB) and so are not entitled to engage in public practice providing audit services.

Whether a candidate trained in an audit practice, commerce and industry or in the public sector, he or she is entitled to use the Chartered Accountant (SA) designation after completion of the relevant examinations in the Auditing or Financial Management Specialism.

All candidates write two examinations. The first is written at any stage of the training contract after the prescribed academic requirements have been met, and all candidates write this examination. The second examination is a practical one, written in the final year of the training contract. Candidates training in a professional practice (TIPP) write an Auditing Specialism Examination and those training in the commerce and industry and the public sector (TOPP – training outside public practice) sit the Financial Management Specialism Examination. These qualifications are of equivalent standards. Those wishing to engage in public practice have to register with the PAAB once they have met the necessary requirements.

The College of General Accountants

This level incorporates graduate accountants who have a B.Comm. degree, or equivalent, from an approved educational institution, and who have three years' approved practical experience.

All candidates holding a certificate in the theory of accountancy, or equivalent, from an accredited university, have to write a qualifying examination approved by SAICA. This is required to ensure appropriate standards are met.

Most general accountants work in commerce and industry and in the public sector, mainly in middle level accountancy positions. Some of them practise as accounting officers offering accounting, consultancy and taxation services to the public.

General accountants have to gain three years' practical experience at approved training offices in practice, commerce and industry, or the public sector, under the supervision of an approved training officer who would either be a chartered accountant or a general accountant. Recognition is given to some of the time spent in training to become an accounting technician. General accountants wishing to progress towards the Chartered Accountant level are given credit for some experience gained in training to become a general accountant.

The College of Accounting Technicians

Accounting technicians work mainly as support staff in commerce and industry and the public sector, although some may train and work in audit practicing firms. These persons carry out clerical functions, such as those relating to accounts receivable and payable, wages and salaries and other support functions.

Education and training are largely carried out using Competency-Based Education and Training (CBET) techniques in corporations, the public sector and in audit practice offices. Candidates meeting the CBET criteria do not have to write formal examinations. However, passing accredited examinations at technikons and universities count towards meeting the requirements.

While most students progress by demonstrating competence, there is a minimum three-year practical experience requirement.

Training is carried out at registered training offices in commerce and industry, or the public sector, and supervised by approved training officers who would be chartered accountants or general accountants.

Accounting technicians who wish to train to become general accountants are given credit for training received to become accounting technicians. Accounting technicians are also given certain exemptions towards the academic requirements for the purpose of becoming general accountants. These exemptions are determined in accordance with the SAQA standards.

1.4.5 TOPP

Fundamental to the repositioned SAICA is the concept of Education and Training Outside of Public Practice (TOPP), which refers to education and training in the field of commerce, industry or the public sector. This alternative route to obtaining the CA(SA) designation focuses on financial management rather than auditing.

Research showed that there was a need for financial managers trained in commerce, industry and the public sector. These persons receive an advanced financial management education and are exposed to various financial management and related techniques in their training. Another reason for introducing TOPP into South Africa was that the existing chartered accountant training processes, namely RTOs, would be unlikely to cope with the demand for chartered accountants in the future.

1.4.6 NQF and SAQA

The repositioning, as described above, is in harmony with the National Qualifications Framework (NQF) implemented by the South African Qualifications Authority (SAQA). The NQF is Government's vision regarding education and training in South Africa, a vision that SAICA supports.

Fundamental to the vision are the following aspects:

- *Linking of education and training:* There should be a 'seamless' joining of education and training.
- *An emphasis on outcomes:* Emphasis is placed on an individual's ability to successfully carry out a job as opposed to entry requirements.
- *Equivalencies:* If an individual's knowledge and abilities are equivalent to the requirements set down, his or her knowledge and abilities will be accepted as of equal value to the particular requirements specified.
- *Mobility:* Horizontal and vertical mobility are promoted and prior learning is recognized.

1.5 CURRENT DEVELOPMENTS IN THE LOCAL ACCOUNTANCY PROFESSION

These are numerous, but to conclude this chapter attention is drawn only to two important aspects. These being:

- The Draft Accountancy Profession Bill, 2001; and
- The Education Upliftment Project.

A brief discussion of each follows.

1.5.1 The Accountancy Profession Bill

The Accountancy Profession Bill has, a year after its publication, not yet been promulgated into legislation. The major reason for this is the lack of consensus by interested parties on two issues, these being: the Bill allows for accreditation as auditors (given that certain conditions are met) of persons who are members of professional bodies other than the South African Institute of Chartered Accountants; and the proposed membership composition of the various boards and structures to be created under the proposed Act.

Under current legislation, only persons who are qualified Chartered Accountants and who are members of the South African Institute of Chartered Accountants and who have registered with the Public Accountants' and Auditors' Board may be appointed as auditors of companies.

The Draft Accountancy Profession Bill 2001 provides for the establishment of a Representative Council of Accountants (RCA), which is responsible for the coordination, promotion, representation and development of the accountancy profession. It provides also for the establishment of a Regulatory Board of Auditors (RBA), and two related structures, namely:

- The Independent Standard-setting Board for Ethics (ISBE); and
- The Independent Standard-setting Board for Auditing (ISBA).

To become a registered auditor (should the Bill be enacted into statute), written application must be lodged with the RBA. The RBA will only grant registration if it is satisfied that the applicant;

(a) 'has been certified by a professional body accredited by the RBA, and of which the applicant is a member, to have complied with the education and training requirements for a registered auditor;

(b) has been certified by a professional body accredited by the RBA and of which the applicant is a member, to have made adequate arrangements for continuing professional education;

(c) is a fit and proper person;

(d) is not less than 21 years of age; and

(e) where a period of more than five years has elapsed between the date of complying with the education and training requirements for a registered auditor and the date of the application, has the necessary competence to practise as an auditor.'[17]

In terms of section 3(3) of the Bill only the South African Institute of Chartered Accountants is considered to be accredited by the RBA (once it commences its functions). In terms of section 3(2), 12 professional accounting bodies (as listed in schedule 1 to the Bill) are considered to be professional bodies accredited by the RCA, the South African Institute of Chartered Accountants being one of these.

It is conceivable that in the future one or more of the 11 professional bodies accredited by the RCA, but not the RBA, might meet the accreditation requirements of the RBA and thus be accredited by it. Should this happen, members of professional bodies, other than members of the Institute of Chartered Accountants, may register as auditors with the RBA.

Section 3(5) of the Draft Bill sets out the accreditation requirements as follows:

'In order to be accredited, a professional body must demonstrate, to the satisfaction of the accrediting structure that —

(a) it complies with the requirements for the development and achievement of professional competence determined by the accrediting structure;

(b) its qualifications are registered at and meet the requirements of the applicable level of the NQF as determined by the relevant accrediting structure;

(c) it has appropriate mechanisms for ensuring that its members participate in continuing professional education;

(d) it has appropriate mechanisms to ensure that its members are disciplined where appropriate;

(e) it is, and is likely to continue to be, financially and operationally viable for the foreseeable future;

(f) it keeps a register of its members in the form determined by the relevant accrediting structure;

(g) it has in place appropriate programmes and structures to ensure that it is actively endeavouring to achieve the objective of being representative of all sectors of the South African population; and

(h) it meets any other requirement determined by the accrediting structure from time to time.'

Part II of the Draft Bill covers aspects relative to the Representative Council of Accountants under the following headings: objectives; powers and duties; and composition. Part III covers these same aspects relative to the Regulatory Board for Auditors.

---

[17] Draft Accountancy Bill 2001, Section 12(2).

When the Bill is enacted as the Accountancy Profession Act, it will replace the Public Accountants and Auditors Act (PAA Act). Accordingly, it covers aspects currently dealt with in the PAA Act, such as:

- the registration of auditors;
- the powers and duties of registered auditors;
- the establishment of disciplinary committees and procedures for discipline investigations and hearings;
- quality control practice reviews of registered auditors;
- offences and penalties in regard to registered auditors;
- procedural and administrative matters to enable the RCA and RBA to fulfil its statutory responsibilities; and
- aspects relevant to the transition process as a result of the PAA Act being repealed and its replacement by the Accountancy Profession Act.

1.5.2 The Education Upliftment Project

Leaders within the accounting profession in South Africa and others had for some time been concerned about the relatively low numbers of Chartered Accountants from marginalized groups in the country. In the mid 1980s, a landmark Statement of Principles was negotiated between the Association for the Advancement of Black Accountants, the Public Accountants and Auditors Board (PAAB) and the South African Institute of Chartered Accountants (SAICA). As a result of these initiatives, in 1987, the Eden Trust was established in an attempt to address the problem.

Audit firms, companies and individuals made contributions toward establishing an endowment fund, the interest from which is now used to grant bursaries to enable blacks to qualify as Chartered Accountants. As the interest from the Eden Trust Fund allows only for the granting of three bursaries on an annual basis, many accounting firms and companies have taken on the responsibility of personally funding bursaries for students they adopted.

Departments of Accounting at most Universities in South Africa mount academic support programmes to assist students coming from disadvan-taged schooling backgrounds. Whilst the number of Blacks qualifying as Chartered Accountants has increased each year, these numbers are still unsatisfactory given the demographics of the South African population. Realizing that inappropriate educational processes lie at the root of the problem, the South African Institute of Chartered Accountants has mounted what it terms 'The Education Upliftment Project'.

Because of the lack of resources and particularly funding, and because SAICA has been working with Fort Hare, the project is focused initially in the Eastern Cape. It involves two aspects, namely, upliftment programmes at school and tertiary education levels, and an extensive career awareness programme to bring to the attention of blacks the opportunities that a career in the accounting profession offers.

At the school level, the project involves mounting clinics for grade 12 students, initially covering accounting and mathematics literacy issues and following a practical, problem solving approach. The intention is not to re-teach topics but rather to instil in students the ability to apply knowledge. Teachers are encouraged to attend, and accounting professionals are approached to make career opportunity presentations at such clinics.

A further aim of the project at the school level is termed the teacher's enrichment programme. The target group for this programme extends beyond teachers of accounting and mathematics, as it is felt that all persons involved in education should be in a position to pass on to students knowledge of such matters as: personal financial management; budgeting; investment and finance; estate planning; basic computer skills; and basic accounting and internal control principles.

The National Skills Fund has approved funding for this project for a three-year period, which is renewable. Donations have also been received from accounting firms and others. Study guides and other teaching material have been finalized and a timetable agreed with the Department of Education. Selected learners, of which there are approximately 9 600 split equally between mathematics and accountancy learners, are bussed to four clinic venue centres, these being Umtata, Alice, East London and Port Elizabeth.

The intention is that in five years the teachers who attended the programme will be able to run it on their own with the assistance of distance teaching technology. The project will also be extended to other regions in the future.

The second leg of The Education Upliftment Project is aimed at ensuring that the standard of the Bachelor of Commerce degree at the University of Fort Hare (UFH) compares favourably to similar degrees obtained from the historically white institutions. To this end, it was decided that an alliance partner with the necessary expertise was needed to assist UFH in developing and delivering its B.Comm Accounting programmes. Rand Afrikaans University (RAU) and UFH have entered into such an alliance by which RAU assists UFH in the presentation of their B.Comm (Accounting) and B.Comm (Public Finance) programmes as a four-year degree. Academics from RAU do the initial instructing, with tutorial follow up being handled by UFH. Through the further partnership of the South African Institute of Chartered Accountants, B.Comm graduates from UFH will enrol at RAU for their postgraduate qualification, a prerequisite for becoming a Chartered Accountant. The project commenced in February 2002. Its estimated cost over the initial four years is R17 416 000. This funding will come from Government and donors.

2

The Nature and Objectives of Assurance Engagements

Learning objectives

After studying this chapter you should be able to:

1. Outline the framework within which statements of South African Auditing Standards are issued in relation to the services that may be performed by auditors.
2. Describe the various categories of service engagements and the levels of assurance the auditor can give for each such engagement.
3. Describe the major branches or types of audits other than audits of financial statements.
4. Describe the main objective of an audit of financial statements.
5. Describe the consequential objectives and advantages of an audit of financial statements.
6. Describe the scope and terms of an engagement to audit financial statements.

2.1 ASSURANCE ENGAGEMENTS

2.1.1 Introduction

In addition to issuing an opinion on the fair presentation of annual financial statements prepared by companies, which is a statutory requirement, auditors are often engaged to audit and report an opinion on other subject matter. In addition, auditors may be engaged to review financial or non-financial subject matter and report a conclusion based on their review. Engagements to perform an audit or a review are termed assurance engagements. Alternatively, auditors may be engaged to perform agreed-upon procedures and report on factual findings or compile financial statements based on information in the client's accounting records. The South African Institute of Chartered Accountants has issued standards addressing aspects relevant to these various different engagements. In this chapter the different categories of engagements are identified and assurance engagements, with particular emphasis on the audit of financial statements, are discussed. Agreed-upon procedures and compilation engagements are discussed in detail in chapter 19.

SAAS 100 – which at paragraph one is referred to as a Statement of South African Assurance Engagements Standards, but is entitled Assurance Engagements – was issued by the South African Institute of Chartered Accountants in December 2000. The Standard realigns the classification of engagements as set out in SAAS 120 to the extent that audit and review engagements are classified as assurance engagements, whilst agreed-upon procedures and compilation engagements remain classified as related services.

The stated purpose of SAAS 100 is as follows:

- 'to describe the objectives and elements of assurance engagements intended to provide either a high or moderate level of assurance (paragraphs .04 – .30);

- to establish standards for and provide guidance to professional accountants in public practice for the performance of engagements intended to provide a high level of assurance (paragraphs .31 – .74); and

- to act as a framework for the development by the IAPC of specific standards for particular types of assurance engagements.'[1]

The Standard does not apply to an audit or review of financial statements because these two categories of engagements already have existing standards, these being for audit of financial statement engagements, Standards 200 through 800, and for review engagements, Standard 910. The objectives and elements of assurance engagements intended to provide a high level of assurance are discussed here, whilst the standards and guidance for the performance of engagements to provide a moderate level of assurance, or no assurance, are discussed in chapter 19.

2.1.2 Objectives and elements of an assurance engagement

Assurance engagements performed by professional accountants and auditors enhance the credibility of information prepared by one party and so can be accepted with more confidence by another party, the intended user of the information. SAAS 100 defines the objective of an assurance engagement as follows:

> 'The objective of an assurance engagement is for a professional accountant to evaluate or measure a subject matter that is the responsibility of another party against identified suitable criteria, and to express a conclusion that provides the user with a level of assurance about the subject matter.' [2]

---

[1] SAAS 100, paragraph .01.
[2] SAAS 100, paragraph .04.

The subject matter of assurance engagements may be financial or non-financial. These engagements may be in the private or public sector and may involve internal or external reporting. Such engagements provide high assurance in the case of an audit and moderate assurance in the case of a review. Examples of these include environmental reporting, health and safety reporting.

Five elements are necessary for a particular engagement to be classified as an assurance engagement:

- 'A three party relationship involving:
  - a professional accountant;
  - a responsible party; and
  - an intended user.
- A subject matter.
- Suitable criteria.
- An engagement process.
- A conclusion.' [3]

Each of these elements are briefly discussed:

A three party relationship

The responsible party and the intended user of the subject matter and assurance report thereon are often from separate organizations, for example, a company and its bankers. However, it might be that the two parties are within the same organization, for example, the directors of a company may require assurance on information provided by a division within the company.

The responsible party is the person, or persons, who prepared the subject matter. For external reporting the responsible party usually engages the professional accountant. For internal reporting the professional accountant is usually engaged by a party other than the responsible party, for example, the board of directors. External intended users of assurance reports may request or impose a requirement for an assurance engagement.

The intended user is the party for whom the assurance report is prepared. In the case of the audit of annual financial statements engagements, the intended users are established by statute, these being the shareholders of a company to whom the report is addressed and, in terms of common law, other potential users such as financial institutions, regulatory authorities, creditors and potential shareholders. Other intended users might not be established by law but rather by agreement between the professional accountant, the responsible party or those engaging the professional accountant, or the initial intended user.

---

[3] SAAS 100, paragraph .08.

In circumstances where the engagement is for a specific purpose, the professional accountant may restrict the use of the report to specific users. This is done by including a statement in the report that others not identified as users may not rely on it.

The term professional accountant includes persons who are members of the South African Institute of Chartered Accountants and who are registered with the Public Accountants' and Auditors' Board in public practice providing statutory audit services and other services, as well as members who are not registered with the Board and may therefore not issue statutory audit reports on companies, but are employed in industry, commerce, the public sector or education.

Subject matter

In the case of financial information, the subject matter may be financial statements and, in the case of non-financial information, it may be the implementation and operation of internal control.

> 'The subject matter of an assurance engagement is to be identifiable, capable of consistent evaluation or measurement against suitable criteria and in a form that can be subjected to procedures for gathering evidence to support that evaluation or measurement.' [4]

SAAS 100 places such subject matter into three broad categories, being:

- 'Data (for example, historical or prospective financial information, statistical information, performance indicators).
- Systems and processes (for example, internal controls).
- Behaviour (for example, corporate governance, compliance with regulation, human resource practices).' [5]

Criteria

Without accepted criteria against which subject matter can be measured, a reporting accountant cannot add credibility to the subject matter on which the assurance report is based. This is because the criteria form the basis against which the subject matter is evaluated or measured. These criteria need to be suitable and known to intended users. Criteria are suitable if they enable reasonably consistent evaluation or measurement of the subject using professional judgement. This requirement is met if different competent professional accountants using the same evaluation or measurement criteria would reach similar conclusions.

In order for criteria to be known to the intended users, they are either criteria which have gained general acceptance (for example, South African

---

[4] SAAS 100, paragraph .21.
[5] SAAS 100, paragraph .20.

Statements of Generally Accepted Accounting Practice in the case of financial information drawn up on such a basis) or, if the criteria are not generally accepted, they need to be disclosed in the subject matter or the assurance report. This would usually be the case where the subject matter is non-financial or financial but drawn up according to a framework other than Generally Accepted Accounting Practice.

Some examples of assurance reports on non-financial subject matter and suitable criteria as set out in SAAS 100 are:

'When reporting on the way in which an entity is organized or managed, or the extent to which its objectives have been achieved, generally accepted criteria for a particular industry may be used. When reporting on internal control, the criteria may be an established internal control framework or stated internal control criteria. When reporting on compliance, the criteria may be the applicable law, regulation or contract. Criteria may also be developed for specific users, for example, a party to a contract who wants assurance that other parties to the same contract are complying with the contract terms.' [6]

Engagement process

The engagement process involves the professional accountant obtaining sufficient appropriate evidence to express an appropriate conclusion using professional judgement. The extent of the engagement process depends on the assurance being sought from the reporting accountant's report. It would usually be the case that the greater the assurance required the more extensive the process and vice versa. The terms of the assurance engagement thus dictate the extent of the process and these terms need to be agreed upon by the party engaging the reporting accountant and the reporting accountant, as well as possibly other parties such as the intended user or users and the party preparing the subject matter. Given the agreed-upon terms of the engage-ment, the accountant uses professional judgement considering engagement risks and materiality when planning and conducting the engagement. Risk and materiality are discussed in chapter 5.

Conclusion

Having gathered sufficient evidence to draw a conclusion that the subject matter conforms in all material respects with the suitable known criteria, the professional accountant can express such a conclusion.

Where the subject matter contains an assertion by the responsible party, the engagement is termed an attest engagement. In such a case, the professional accountant's conclusion relates to the assertion. Assertions are representa-tions or conclusions about the subject matter based on identified suitable criteria. Where the professional accountant reports directly to a particular party, the professional accountant expresses a conclusion on the subject

---

[6] SAAS 100, paragraph .23.

matter based on suitable criteria, regardless whether or not the responsible party has made a written assertion on the subject matter.

In discussing the levels of assurance provided by the professional accountant's conclusion the Standard has this to say:

> 'In theory, it is possible to provide an infinite range of assurance from a very low level of assurance to an absolute level of assurance. In practice, it is not ordinarily practicable to design an engagement to provide such fine graduations of assurance or to communicate the level of assurance in a clear and unambiguous manner. In addition, absolute assurance is generally not attainable as a result of such factors as the use of selective testing, the inherent limitations of control systems, the fact that much of the evidence available to the professional accountant is persuasive rather than conclusive, and the use of judgement in gathering evidence and drawing conclusions based on that evidence. Therefore, professional accountants ordinarily undertake engagements to provide one of only two distinct levels: a high level and a moderate level. These engagements are affected by various elements, for example, the degree of precision associated with the subject matter, the nature and timing and extent of procedures, and the sufficiency and appropriateness of the evidence available to support a conclusion.

> 'The expression "high level of assurance" refers to the professional accountant having obtained sufficient appropriate evidence to conclude that the subject matter conforms in all material respects with identified suitable criteria. In rare circumstances, the professional accountant may be able to provide absolute assurance, for example, where the evidence available is conclusive and reliable because the subject matter is determinate, the criteria definitive and the process applied comprehensive. However, because of the limitations of the engagement process, a high level of assurance is ordinarily less than absolute. The professional accountant designs the engagement to reduce to a low level the risk of an inappropriate conclusion that the subject matter conforms in all material respects with identified suitable criteria.

> 'The expression "moderate level of assurance" refers to the professional accountant having obtained sufficient appropriate evidence to be satisfied that the subject matter is plausible in the circumstances. The professional accountant designs the engagement to reduce to a moderate level the risk of an inappropriate conclusion. The professional accountant designs the report to convey a moderate level of assurance regarding the conformity of the subject matter with identified suitable criteria.' [7]

SAAS 100 includes as an appendix a diagram showing the relationship between it and the existing statements of South African Audit Standards and South African Auditing Practice Statements. It also includes an indication of possible future standards or statements that may be developed. The diagram is reproduced here.

---

[7] SAAS 100, paragraphs .28, .29, .30.

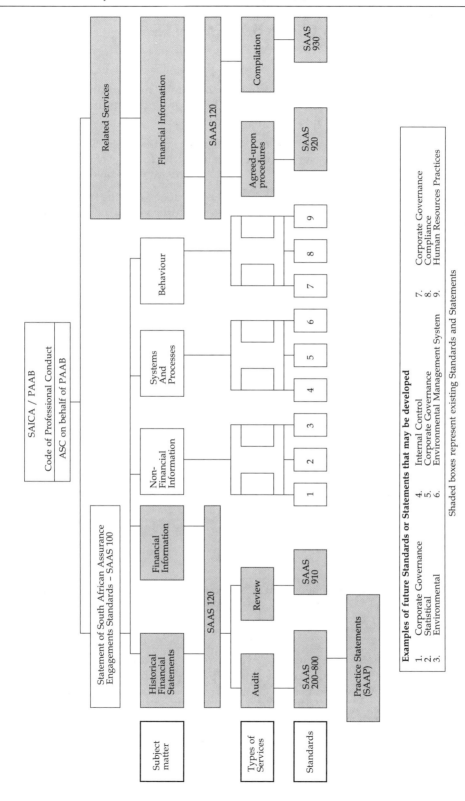

Figure 2.1 The relationship between the statements of South African Audit Standards and South African Auditing Practice Statements

2.2 CATEGORIES OF ENGAGEMENTS

2.2.1 Introduction

The auditor's report on information prepared by an entity increases the credibility of such information. In other words, the auditor's involvement adds audit assurance to information disclosed.

> 'Assurance refers to the auditor's satisfaction as to the reliability of an assertion being made by one party for use by another party. The level of assurance taken from a report should be the same as that expressed by the auditor.' [8]

The assurance the auditor can express is influenced by the auditability of the information, the nature and extent of the procedures performed and the results of those procedures.

Information is auditable if it can be reasonably and consistently estimated or measured for evaluation against criteria which have substantial support or are clearly stated in the information being reported on. For example, annual financial statements or components thereof are measured against generally accepted accounting practice, royalty payments are measured against a royalty agreement.

Generally speaking, with regard to procedures performed and audit findings, the more work done and evidence gathered confirming compliance with the criteria underlying the preparation of the information, the greater the assurance that may be given by the auditor's report, and vice versa.

2.2.2 Framework

SAAS 120, 'Framework for South African Standards on Auditing and Related Services', presents the following diagrammatic illustration of the framework.

	AUDITING	RELATED SERVICES		
Nature of service	Audit	Review	Agreed-upon procedures	Compilation
Comparative level of assurance by the auditor	High, but not absolute assurance	Moderate assurance	No opinion expressed	No opinion expressed
Report provided	Positive assurance on assertion(s)	Negative assurance on assertion(s)	Factual findings on procedures	Identification of informa- tion compiled

Table 2.1 Framework for South African standards on auditing and related services

---

[8] SAAS 120, paragraph .06.

In an audit engagement the auditor expresses a positive opinion at a high but not absolute level:

> 'Absolute assurance is not obtainable as a result of such factors as the need for judgement, the use of testing, the inherent limitations of any accounting and internal control system, and the fact that most of the evidence available is persuasive, rather than conclusive, in nature.' [9]

A review engagement enables 'an auditor to state whether or not, on the basis of procedures that do not provide all the evidence that would be required in an audit, anything has come to the auditor's attention that causes the auditor to believe that the financial statements are not prepared, in all material respects, in accordance with an identified financial reporting framework'.[10] A similar objective applies to a review of information other than financial statements which has been prepared in accordance with appropriate criteria. The level of assurance given in a review report is lower than that given in an audit report and is often termed negative assurance.

For agreed-upon procedures engagements the auditor does not express any assurance but reports factual findings instead:

> 'Users of the report assess for themselves the procedures and findings reported by the auditor and draw their own conclusions from the auditor's work.' [11]

Related service engagements are discussed further in chapter 19.

2.3 TYPES OF AUDITS

2.3.1 Introduction

Auditing constitutes a major part of the activities of a registered accountant and auditor. Auditing has been defined as:

> '... the independent examination of financial information of any entity, whether profit-orientated or not, and irrespective of its size or legal form, when such an examination is conducted with a view to expressing an opinion thereon'.[12]

However, the meaning of the word 'auditing' has become more generic in nature as the audit process is being applied to other areas of financial and business activities. At present auditing literature covers the following major branches:

- independent auditing;
- internal auditing;
- operational auditing;

---

[9] SAAS 120, paragraph .13.
[10] SAAS 120, paragraph .14.
[11] SAAS 120, paragraph .09.
[12] Internal Auditing Guideline No. 3.

- management auditing;
- comprehensive auditing;
- forensic auditing; and
- public sector auditing.

In South Africa, only persons registered in terms of the Public Accountants' and Auditors' Act may practise as independent auditors engaged to report on annual financial statements.[13] 'Auditors' in the other five branches need no specific statutory qualification. They also differ in respect of responsibilities assumed and their independence of the audited entity. The branch discussed in depth in this treatise is the independent audit of annual financial statements. Brief descriptions of the other branches follow.

2.3.2 Internal auditing

Inter alia, management is responsible for the adoption of sound accounting practices and for maintaining an adequate and effective system of internal controls to ensure the safeguarding of assets and the production of reliable financial statements. In large organizations it is common practice to employ internal auditors to check whether the systems and control procedures designed and introduced by management are properly adhered to and carried out. Initially, internal auditors were concerned with the following aspects:

- evaluation of internal control systems and procedures;
- checking compliance with the laid-down internal control procedures;
- ensuring that the assets of the enterprise were protected; and
- performing special investigations.

Over time management realized that internal auditors could make a useful contribution by also using the knowledge gained during their duties to 'audit' and evaluate the enterprise's management systems and operational functions. The latter two branches of auditing are commonly referred to as 'operational auditing' and 'management auditing'.

2.3.3 Operational auditing

As indicated above, the application of internal auditing to an operational function rather than a financial area is known as *operational auditing*. In their book *Operational Auditing*, Lindberg and Cohn define the term more formally as:

> 'a technique for regular and systematically appraising unit and function effectiveness against corporate and industry standards ... with the objective of assuring a given management that its aims are being carried out and/or identifying conditions capable of being improved'.

---

[13] Section 14, Act 80 of 1991.

2.3.4 Management auditing

This branch of auditing covers an evaluation of the enterprise's management systems, whether such systems are operating effectively, and resultant risks if they are not. In North America, management audits are required by law. For example, in the United States, House Bill 1256 requires public utility commissions to ... 'initiate a full and complete management audit once every five years by a competent, qualified and independent firm'.

2.3.5 Comprehensive auditing

The term 'comprehensive auditing' refers to the performance of a management and operational audit in addition to the traditional independent (or external) audit.

2.3.6 Forensic auditing

A forensic auditor is an investigative accountant or fraud auditor, utilizing a combination of accounting, auditing and investigative skills to search for evidence of criminal conduct and the monetary consequences thereof. A forensic auditor may also be required to assist in the determination, or rebuttal, of claimed damages. The forensic auditor is required to analyse, interpret, summarize and present complex financial and business-related issues in a manner that will be suitable for and understood by users of the forensic auditor's report. This information is used as a basis for discussion, debate and, ultimately, the resolution of the matter. A forensic auditor's duties will often involve the following:

- Investigation of financial and other evidence.
- Analysis and presentation of financial evidence.
- Communication of findings in the form of reports and supporting documentation.
- Assistance in legal proceedings, including testifying in court as an expert witness.

2.3.7 Governmental auditing

In the public sector funds are raised by means of direct and indirect taxes at municipal, provincial and central government levels. The funds are raised to provide for, inter alia, the maintenance and building up of the infrastructure for public services and all the activities which by law resort under the various levels of government. All these authorities produce annual budgets from which they can establish the funds required and determine how and from whom the 'taxes' can be raised. Once the taxes have been determined and the budget has been approved, there are two major areas of activity involving financial records, namely, the revenue and the expenditure. In the public sector the auditing of the various authorities resides under the office of the Auditor-General (a public servant). With regard to the central government finances, the Auditor-General reports to Parliament. At local authority level the Auditor-General may and has delegated some audit responsibilities to practising chartered accountants. Although the auditor will report to the local authority, a copy of the report will go to the Auditor-General. Auditing in the public sector is discussed in chapter 22.

2.4 THE AUDIT OF ANNUAL FINANCIAL STATEMENTS

2.4.1 The main objective of an audit of financial statements

Originally an independent audit was confined to proving whether or not the responsible party had accounted for all receipts and payments – what is known as a cash audit. Today auditing goes far beyond this. SAAS 200, 'The Objectives of and General Principles Governing an Audit of Financial Statements', describes the objective of an audit as follows:

> 'The objective of an audit of financial statements is to enable the auditor to express an opinion as to whether or not the financial statements fairly present, in all material respects, the financial position of the entity at a specific date, and the results of its operations and cash flow information for the period ended on that date, in accordance with an identified financial reporting framework and/or statutory requirements.' [14]

To that end an auditor is required to obtain sufficient appropriate audit evidence to be able to draw reasonable conclusions on which to base the audit opinion. Audit evidence comprises source documents and accounting records underlying the financial statements and corroborating information from other sources, for example, representations from management, advice of experts and confirmations from bankers and others. The crux of the matter is thus the sufficiency and appropriateness of the audit tests. This requires an auditor to probe into the activities of the undertaking on which the records are based, and into the controls over these activities and records. The probe would then lead to an assessment of the risk of error, on which rests the decision regarding the nature and extent of audit tests required, thus providing the auditor with sound logical grounds on which to base the audit opinion.

The auditor does not guarantee the accuracy of the financial statements. There are, as a general rule, many balances comprising the financial statements that rest on the basis of opinion, and so it is virtually impossible for anyone to say with truth that the financial statements are correct. Again, it is impracticable for the auditor, especially the auditor of a large concern, to check every single item and, even if this was done, there are no means of being absolutely certain that every transaction which should be recorded has been so recorded.

A further caution for users of the audit report is that they cannot assume that an unqualified audit opinion is an assurance as to the future viability of a

---

[14] SAAS 200, paragraph .02.

company, nor does it indicate that management has conducted the affairs of the company efficiently or effectively.

2.4.2 Consequential objectives and advantages of an audit of financial statements

2.4.2.1 Detection and prevention of errors and fraud

It has already been stated that the auditor's function is to be satisfied that the financial statements fairly present, in all material respects, the state of affairs of the undertaking. Out of this arise two possible further objectives, namely:

- the detection of errors and fraud; and
- the prevention of errors and fraud.

The auditor is not and cannot be held responsible for the prevention of fraud and error. This responsibility rests with management who discharges this responsibility through the implementation and continued operation of adequate accounting and internal control systems.

The detection of errors made innocently or fraudulently is incidental to the auditor's main duty of reporting on the financial statements. If the auditor discovers a material error, the financial statements cannot be a fair presentation and the auditor must ensure that they are rectified accordingly. If the circumstances make it apparent that there has been a deliberate concealment of an asset, it is not enough for the auditor to accept a subsequent presentation of the asset. For example, where the auditor is presented with cash on hand of an amount equal to the balance according to the cash records and the auditor later detects an error in the cash records which inflates the book figure of cash on hand, it is not enough for the auditor to accept further cash presented to make up the difference: the auditor must also inquire why the cashier had not previously revealed the fact of an excess of cash. There are many cases of this kind where what may, at first, appear to be an innocent error is later shown to conceal defalcations of cash or other assets.

The auditor needs to consider how such a fraud affects the work necessary to be satisfied that there are no other fraudulent entries. There is no simple answer to this question. It is for the auditor to exercise skill, sense of proportion and, above all, to be honest in deciding the steps to be taken before reporting on the financial statements. In short, the auditor must exercise professional scepticism.

It must be stressed at this point that the audit of financial statements is not mainly directed towards the detection of fraud or error. However, this is not to say that fraud or error will not be detected. The reader is referred to SAAS 240 paragraph .13, which sets out the South African Institute of Chartered Accountants' viewpoint of the profession's responsibility in detecting fraud.

Errors may be classified as shown in the diagram and are discussed accordingly.

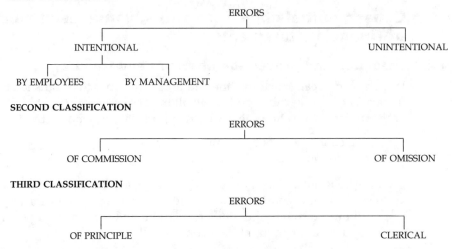

FIRST CLASSIFICATION

```
                              ERRORS
            ┌───────────────────┴───────────────────────┐
       INTENTIONAL                                  UNINTENTIONAL
   ┌────────┴────────┐
BY EMPLOYEES    BY MANAGEMENT
```

SECOND CLASSIFICATION

```
                              ERRORS
         ┌────────────────────┴────────────────────┐
   OF COMMISSION                               OF OMISSION
```

THIRD CLASSIFICATION

```
                              ERRORS
         ┌────────────────────┴────────────────────┐
   OF PRINCIPLE                                  CLERICAL
```

Note: The errors dealt with in one classification are inclusive of those dealt with in the others.

Figure 2.2 Classification of errors

First classification

Errors may occur *unintentionally* through carelessness or lack of knowledge, or may be made with intent to defraud. As a general rule, unintentional errors are made only by the employees, as for example, where an employee enters an amount of a sale incorrectly in the purchases record, or allocates the amount of obsolete plant sold to sales account instead of to plant account. On the other hand, *intentional* errors may be made by both employees and management.

Intentional errors by employees are nearly always accompanied by the misappropriation of some asset, usually cash. For example, a cashier may make an entry in the cash records for a fictitious payment in order to conceal a misappropriation of cash, or an employee may, for a consideration, enter in the records a credit note for a fictitious return of goods in order to cancel the recorded indebtedness of a customer.

Intentional errors by the management are seldom made to conceal misappropriations of assets but are for the purpose of manipulating income statement accounts in order to present an over- or understatement of profits earned to achieve some benefit. The following are examples of these potential circumstances:

● Where the manager of a business is entitled to a commission based on the profits as shown in the income statement, such a person may deliberately inflate the recorded profits on which the commission is based.

- The directors of a public company may deliberately overstate or understate the profits shown in the financial statements for the purpose of increasing or reducing the market value of the company's shares.
- The owner of a business, or the directors of a company, may understate the profit shown in the financial statements for the purpose of evading taxation.

Numerous methods can be employed to falsify the income statement, but one of the common methods is the overstatement or understatement of inventories at the close of the financial year. Other methods include the omission of purchase invoices, but the inclusion of the relevant items in the inventories; and entries for fictitious sales towards the close of one year followed by entries for fictitious returns in the subsequent year.

An effective system of internal control should greatly minimize the risk of any serious errors by the staff, but no such system can guard against the deliberate distortion of the financial statements by the management. It may be said that only the auditor is in a position to discover such malpractices.

Second classification

An error of *omission* arises as a result of a transaction being omitted entirely from the accounting records.

An error of *commission* may occur in one of the following ways:

- an amount entered incorrectly in the accounting records;
- an amount allocated to a wrong account; or
- an incorrect addition of the accounting records.

There are errors of commission which arise at the point of original entry which will not affect the balancing of the trial balance, for example, when the amount of a sale is entered wrongly in the records. But not all errors of original entry are of this type. There may, for example, be an error on one side of a journal entry which will affect the balancing of the trial balance.

An error in allocating an amount to an account in the general ledger may affect the balancing of the trial balance – for example, R10 000 allocated as R1 000, or allocated to the wrong side of the account. However, some errors may not affect the trial balance – for example, an allocation to the correct side and of the correct amount but to the wrong account.

An error in the addition of the accounting records will usually affect the balancing of the trial balance, but not in all cases, as for example the incorrect addition of a bills receivable record, where an accounts receivable control account is maintained in the general ledger.

It is also possible that two errors of commission of equal amount but with opposite effect may be made so that the trial balance balances but is incorrect. These are known as compensating errors.

It is clear from the above that there are many types of errors which do not affect the balancing of the trial balance. An auditor must appreciate the limitations of the trial balance as an instrument for detecting errors. If the trial balance is out of balance it indicates the existence of one or more errors. If the trial balance is in balance, however, it is not at all certain that no errors have occurred. Other means must also be used to satisfy the auditor that the figures presented are fair and reasonable.

The routine tests carried out by the auditor, coupled with a scrutiny of the trial balance, should reveal errors of commission. If the tests bring to light a considerable number of such errors, the auditor should extend the scope of tests and report the matter to the management, as it is apparent that the system of internal control is inadequate.

Where the record of a transaction is completely omitted from the records, the likelihood of detecting it depends greatly upon the nature of the transaction. In the case of transactions relating to expenditure, the routine checking, coupled with an intelligent scrutiny of the ledger accounts, should usually bring to light any such omissions. In the case of transactions relating to income, however, there are cases where no amount of checking by the auditor is likely to bring omissions to light in the absence of an effective system of internal control. For example, if goods have been sold and no record of the sale is made, it would appear that, normally, the auditor has no means of detecting the omission. All the auditor can do in this case is to be satisfied that the system of sales and inventory control is such that omissions are unlikely to occur. There may, however, be cases of omission of income which can be detected by the auditor, as for example the omission of a month's rent (where rent is received monthly), detected by a scrutiny of the rent receivable account.

Third classification

Errors maybe divided into *clerical errors* and *errors of principle*. A clerical error arises through carelessness, whereas an error of principle is due to lack of knowledge. What has been said regarding errors of commission in the second classification applies equally to clerical errors. Poor internal control contributes to an excess of such errors.

Where the error is one of principle, it is indicative of insufficient knowledge on the part of the person committing the error. If the auditor detects such an error, even where the effect on the financial statements is insignificant, the matter should be followed up by questioning the individual and scrutinizing other entries of the same type, as it is very likely that the wrong principle has been applied throughout the period under audit.

A person may, for example, allocate a charge for spare parts for the repair of a machine to the asset account instead of to the repairs account. This may be a clerical error (due to carelessness) or it may be one of principle. The reason for the mistake can only be discovered by questioning the individual responsible. If the auditor discovers that the allocation had been made deliberately, because the person was under the impression that it was the correct thing to do, common sense dictates that the machinery and repairs account should be thoroughly examined, together with the invoices in respect of the relevant entries.

Note that although the error in the above example affects the recorded profit, there may be errors of principle which do not do so, as for example administrative salaries charged to selling expenses account.

2.4.2.2 Distinction between error and fraud

In the above discussion of the classification of errors, no clear distinction was drawn between 'error' and 'fraud'; in the authors' opinion the distinction is a legal one. For an 'error' to be classified as 'fraud' it is necessary, amongst others, to prove intention on the part of the perpetrator(s). Some accounting bodies have issued statements (or guidelines) on 'Fraud and Error'[15] in which the distinction between 'error' and 'fraud' (or 'irregularities') is based on intent. The first classification, as described above, distinguishes between 'error' and 'fraud'. Any of the types of errors which fall within the second and third classifications may consequently be classified as 'fraud', on condition that it can be proved that there was intention to 'defraud'. When the auditor discovers an 'error', circumspection is required. The auditor should thoroughly investigate all the aspects of the 'error' before concluding that the intention behind the 'error' was to defraud. Whether the 'fraud' should be described as 'theft', 'misrepresentation', 'falsification' or by some other legal term is not for the auditor to decide. The circumstances, evidence and acts which should be present to get an accused convicted of any of these misdemeanours should be left to the judiciary to examine.

If satisfied that an 'error' discovered is indeed a case of 'fraud', the auditor may have an added responsibility to report the matter to the management in terms of section 20(5) of the PAA Act. (See chapter 3.3.) The auditor's responsibility for the detection of fraud and error is discussed further in chapter 3.3.

It has been said previously that, as a general rule, it is impracticable for the auditor to check every item in the records and that, even if it were possible, there are no means of making absolutely certain that every transaction has been recorded. Every auditor must rely to some extent on the directors and management of the business for information, and the extent of this reliance depends greatly on the effectiveness of the system employed within a business to safeguard the assets of the entity and to ensure the maintenance of adequate accounting records. Such a system should operate as automatically as possible and is known as internal control.

It is axiomatic that the sounder the internal control (see chapter 9), the more reliance the auditor can place on the records produced. The auditor should,

[15] See, for example, the SAICA's Statement SAAS 240: 'Fraud and error'; and Statement on Auditing Standards AU 327, issued by the AICPA.

therefore, spend considerable time and care in assessing the control environment, particularly the investigation of the system of internal control. In the case of the first audit, the auditor should be satisfied that there is an effective check on all work which has a bearing on the records.

Any weaknesses identified should be reported to the management and the auditor should ascertain what steps have been taken to improve the administration of the internal control in the direction indicated. In this manner, the auditor can reduce the burden of detailed checking considerably and still be reasonably satisfied that the records substantially reflect the facts. At the same time, the auditor is adding value to the client by helping to reduce errors and closing the door to the perpetration of fraudulent practices by the employees.

2.4.2.3 Other advantages

In addition to the foregoing objectives and advantages of an audit, there are other advantages, of which the more important are summarized below.

- The financial statements which have been reported on as 'fairly presenting the state of affairs' by an auditor, are accepted as reliable by interested parties – for example, banks and others who have been approached by a client for a loan usually demand sight of the most recent audited financial statements.

- As a general rule the inland revenue authorities accept, with less questioning, audited financial statements as a basis for the calculation of taxation.

- The audited financial statements provide a reliable basis for the valuation of a business (or shares in a limited company) for estate duty and other purposes.

- The audited financial statements are a sound basis for the settlement of claims. Examples are the claim by a retiring partner or the executor of a deceased partner; an insurance claim for inventories destroyed, based on estimated inventory on hand, and for consequential loss.

- The auditor is in a position to advise the client of improvements which may be made in the accounting system.

- The auditor's knowledge of business and finance generally may be invaluable to a client. Suggestions made by the auditor may point the way to increased efficiency and larger profits.

2.5 THE SCOPE OF AN AUDIT OF FINANCIAL STATEMENTS

The scope of an audit may depend on the instructions received from the client or on the terms of the statute which may govern the audit.

In the case of a sole trader or partnership, it is up to the owners to decide how extensive the audit should be and the auditor must make clear to the client the limit of the auditor's responsibilities and obligations and insist on written confirmation of instructions, or confirm in writing with the client the instructions which were given verbally. The written agreement between the auditor and client is the subject of SAAS 210, 'Terms of Audit Engagements'. In such cases the auditor's report should indicate any limitation of the audit, otherwise the client may seek to recover damages from the auditor for loss suffered through the fraud of an employee which the auditor did not detect because of the limitations of the audit.

Where instructions have in the past been given to the auditor (for example, where the client is a partnership), the auditor should bring to the client's notice any matters discovered during the course of the audit which may affect the client's decision regarding an extension of the auditor's duties in future.

Where the audit is governed by statute, as in the case of limited companies, an engagement letter should still be sent to ensure that the client is fully aware of the scope and limitations of the statutory audit and of the client's responsibility for maintaining proper records and adequate control over them, and over the assets of the undertaking. The letter should be addressed to the directors. Any instructions of the company (or similar undertaking) cannot reduce the auditor's obligations as required by statute, even if every member of the company agrees, but instructions may be issued to increase the auditor's obligations. In such a case, where the auditor is requested to undertake additional work, the precise terms of obligations to be undertaken should be obtained in writing. An engagement letter should be issued by the auditor not only for each new appointment, but should also be issued from time to time for existing appointments (though not necessarily as frequently as annually) and especially so where a change in the scope of the work takes place.

There may be cases where the professional accountant is requested to prepare financial statements from records which are not to be the subject of either complete or partial audit. What has been said above with regard to any limitation of the audit applies equally here. In this regard, readers are referred to chapter 19.

2.6 TERMS OF ENGAGEMENT

2.6.1 Introduction

South African Auditing Standard 210, 'Terms of Audit Engagements', provides guidance on:

- agreeing with a client the terms of the engagement to be undertaken;
- drafting an appropriate form of engagement letter relating to audits of financial statements, as well as other related services; and
- the auditor's response to a request by a client to change the terms of an engagement to one that provides a lower level of assurance.

As already pointed out in the previous section of the chapter, the auditor and the client should agree on the terms of the engagement. In the case of statutory appointments, such as the audit of incorporated companies, the objective and scope of an audit and the auditor's obligations are established by law. Thus the auditor may not accept engagement terms which are in any way restricted, but may accept terms of engagement which go beyond the statutory audit requirements. Such terms might include tax, accounting or management consulting services.

Once agreed upon, the terms should be recorded in an engagement letter or other suitable form, such as a contract. The engagement letter, preferably sent before the commencement of the engagement, helps to prevent misunderstandings surrounding the engagement. To this end, the engagement letter documents confirm the auditor's acceptance of the appointment, the objective and scope of the audit, the extent of the auditor's responsibilities to the client, and the form of any reports.

2.6.2 Content of engagement letters[16]

The form and content of audit engagement letters may vary for each client, but they would generally include reference to the following:

- the objective of the audit of financial statements;
- management's responsibility for the financial statements;
- management's responsibility to implement and maintain internal control systems to prevent errors and irregularities, including fraud and illegal acts;
- the scope of the audit, including reference to applicable legislation, regulations or generally accepted auditing standards;
- the form of any reports or other communication of results of the engagement;
- the fact that, because of the test nature and other inherent limitations of an audit, together with the inherent limitations of any system of internal control,
- there is an unavoidable risk that even some material misstatement may remain undiscovered; and
- access to the records, documentation and other information requested in connection with the audit.

The auditor may also wish to include in the engagement letter:

- arrangements regarding the planning of the audit;
- expectation of receiving from management written confirmation concerning representations made in connection with the audit;
- description of any other letters or reports the auditor expects to issue to the client;

---

[16] SAAS 210, paragraphs .06, .07, .08.

- the basis on which fees are computed and any billing arrangements; and
- request for the client to confirm the terms of the engagement by acknowledging receipt of the engagement letter.

When relevant, the following points could also be made:

- arrangements concerning the involvement of other auditors or experts in some aspects of the audit;
- arrangements concerning the involvement of internal auditors or other client staff;
- arrangements, if any, to be made with the auditor's predecessor, in the case of an initial audit;
- any restriction of the auditor's liability when such possibility exists; and
- a reference to any further agreements between the auditor and the client.

2.6.3 Audits of components

When the auditor of a parent entity is also the auditor of its subsidiary, branch or division (component), the factors that influence the decision whether or not to send a separate engagement letter to the component include the following:

- who appoints the auditor of the component;
- whether or not a separate audit report is to be issued on the component;
- legal requirements;
- the extent of any work performed by other auditors;
- degree of ownership by parent entity; and
- degree of independence of the component's management.

2.6.4 Recurring audits

On recurring audits, the auditor should consider whether or not circumstances require the terms of the engagement to be revised and whether or not there is a need to remind the client of the existing terms of the engagement.

The auditor may decide not to send a new engagement letter each period. However, the following factors may make it appropriate to send a new letter:

- any indication that the client misunderstands the objective and scope of the audit;
- any special or significant changes in the terms of the engagement;
- a recent change of ownership or of management, including board of directors and audit committee;
- a significant change in the nature, size or structure of the client's business; and
- a recent change of legal requirements or the introduction of new legal requirements.

It may be appropriate to remind the client of the original letter when the auditor decides a new engagement letter is unnecessary for any period.

2.6.5 Acceptance of a change in engagement[17]

If, before the completion of the engagement, an auditor is requested to change the engagement to one that provides a lower level of assurance, the appropriateness of doing so should be carefully considered.

A request to change the engagement may result from:

- a change in circumstances affecting the need for the service;
- a misunderstanding as to the nature of an audit or related service originally requested; or
- a restriction on the scope of the engagement, whether imposed by management or caused by circumstances.

The auditor should ascertain the reason for any request to change an engagement before agreeing to such a change. A change in circumstances that affects the entity's requirements, or a misunderstanding concerning the nature of service originally requested, would ordinarily be considered a reasonable basis for requesting a change in the engagement. In contrast, a change would not be considered reasonable if it appeared that the change relates to information that is incorrect, incomplete or otherwise unsatisfactory. For example, in the case of a non-statutory audit engagement, if the auditor was originally engaged to express an opinion and a change to report on agreed-upon procedures is sought so as to avoid a qualified opinion.

Before agreeing to change an audit engagement to a related service, an auditor who was engaged to perform an audit in accordance with generally accepted auditing standards would consider, in addition to the above matters, any legal or contractual implications of the change.

If the auditor concludes that there is reasonable justification to change the engagement, and if the audit work performed complies with generally accepted auditing standards applicable to the changed engagement, the report issued would be appropriate for the revised terms of engagement. In order to avoid confusing the reader, the report would not include reference to:

- the original engagement; or
- any procedures that may have been performed in the original engagement, except where the engagement is changed to an engagement to undertake agreed-upon procedures, when reference to the procedures performed is a normal part of the report.

Where the terms of the engagement are changed, the auditor and the client should agree on the new terms.

The auditor should not agree to a change of engagement where there is no reasonable justification for doing so. An example might be an audit

---

[17] SAAS 210, paragraphs .12 to .19.

engagement where the auditor is unable to obtain sufficient and appropriate audit evidence regarding receivables and the client asks for the engagement to be changed to a review engagement to avoid a qualified audit opinion or a disclaimer of opinion.

If the auditor is unable to agree to a change of the engagement and is not permitted to continue the original engagement, the auditor should withdraw and consider whether or not there is any obligation, either contractual or otherwise, to report to other parties, such as the board of directors or shareholders, the circumstances necessitating the withdrawal.

There are two appendices to statement SAAS 210. The first sets out an example of an engagement letter, for use as a guide in conjunction with the principles as outlined in the statement. The second contains examples of additional paragraphs that might be added to the standard engagement letter given particular circumstances, for example, where services over and above audit services are to be rendered, such as the preparation of financial statements or taxation returns and company secretarial assistance.

3

The Auditing Profession and the Auditor

Learning objectives

After studying this chapter you should be able to:

1. Outline, briefly, the qualifications and regulations of registered accountants and auditors.
2. Describe the objectives and fundamental principles underlying the profession's Code of Professional Conduct.
3. Describe the application of the Code's objectives and fundamental principles to the various aspects and/or situations covered by the Code.
4. Outline the auditor's responsibilities in respect of:
   – reporting an audit opinion;
   – conducting the audit with due professional care;
   – maintaining an independent attitude;
   – reporting material irregularities;
   – detecting and reporting fraud and error; and
   – detecting contravention of laws and regulations.
5. Outline the historical perspective and current position regarding the establishment of South African Auditing Standards.
6. Describe the objectives of quality control policies and the procedures to achieve these, both at an overall audit firm and individual audit assignment level.
7. Outline the needs for, the operation, and the advantages of the profession's practice review programme.
8. Outline the operation of the profession's 'Awareness Self-Appraisal Programme'.
9. Describe in basic terms the auditor's exposure to legal liability and the major areas in which legal action for negligence may be brought against chartered accountants, and steps which might be taken to reduce the risks.

3.1 THE QUALIFICATIONS OF THE REGISTERED ACCOUNTANT AND AUDITOR

In terms of sections 15(2)(b) of the Public Accountants' and Auditors' Act (the Act) it is a requirement for registration as a registered accountant and auditor (RAA) that the applicant has passed the prescribed examination and served under a training contract for the prescribed period.

The PAAB has, in terms of sections 19(1), prescribed that the Public Practice Examination (PPE) be passed by those wishing to qualify for registration as an RAA. Following the establishment of the recognition model for the education of accountants and auditors, the PAAB has determined the successful completion of the following admission requirements for entry to the PPE:

- A *recognized academic programme*, currently the CTA or equivalent offered by universities accredited by SAICA for purposes of admission to Part I of the Qualifying Examination.
- A *recognized core assessment programme*, currently the Part I Qualifying Examination of SAICA.
- A minimum of 18 months of a *recognized training programme* that is registered with the PAAB, currently training contracts administered by SAICA and registered with the PAAB.
- A *recognized education programme*, currently the Auditing Specialism Courses accredited by SAICA which are valid for a period of five calendar years commencing after the calendar year in which the education programme was successfully completed.

Recognition principles

In anticipation of the more independent regulatory role of the PAAB and in light of the establishment of SAQA, the PAAB has established a recognition model for the education of registered accountants and auditors. Recognition is a partnership between the PAAB and professional institutes based on a collaborative quality improvement process that tolerates and encourages diverse and coherent learning programmes, which are not prescriptive. They aim to provide access to and mobility and progression to all who have the ability and desire to register as a RAA whilst achieving, maintaining and enhancing high standards in programmes along the learning path to a RAA. Recognition expects RAAs to be professionally competent individuals, capable of adapting to change and committed to a process of lifelong learning that will enable them to make a meaningful contribution to the profession and society throughout their professional lives. Furthermore, as South Africa continues to participate in a competitive, global economy, the standard of programmes should be on a par with international standards. To achieve this, the PAAB has established the components of the learning path, namely, the recognized programmes indicated above, and has also defined the objectives to be met in each of the components, the standards for the granting and maintenance of the recognition of the programmes of professional institutes and the procedures for monitoring these.

Recognition is the status granted by the PAAB to the academic, education, training and core assessment programmes of professional institutes that meet and continue to meet the recognition standards defined by the PAAB. Currently, the programmes of SAICA are recognized, and it is anticipated that other professional institutes may apply for recognition of their programmes in the future. Recognition is not an assurance that the required standard is achieved in the delivery of a recognized programme, although it implies that the programme contains the minimum requirements necessary for the achievement of the objectives of the programme. Accordingly, the required standard will be assessed by means of the prescribed examination, namely the PPE. The maintenance of recognition status of an institute is dependent upon the recognized programmes continuing to meet the recognition standards of the PAAB, and so a continuous monitoring process over the activities of the accredited professional institute has been implemented by the PAAB.

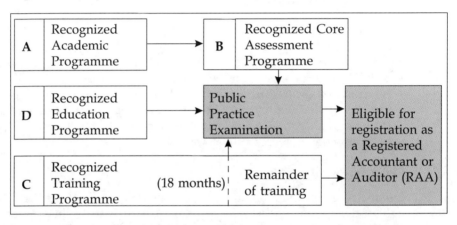

Table 3.1 Programmes in the learning path to registration as a RAA
(Source: PAAB Manual of Information, Section 2, pages 2–7.)

The Public Accountants' and Auditors' Board, established under the Act, conducts the qualifying examination for entry into the auditing profession in South Africa. The prerequisites of candidates for the qualifying examinations are the serving of training contracts (for a period of five years or such lesser period for graduates as the Board may decide) currently three years, and the obtaining from a university in the Republic such a degree, diploma or certificate as the Board may determine. It may therefore be said with confidence that the registered accountant and auditor are well qualified professionally.

Such a person would have gained a thorough knowledge of the theory and practice relating to auditing, financial accounting, management accounting, finance, taxation and other legal matters.

But professional qualifications are not the whole story. If an accountant is to be an asset to the profession and to the community served, other qualities and abilities are required. These may be summarized as follows:

- A person possessing an inquiring mind, so that intelligent questions may be raised on points which affect the audit and technical issues to resolve these are understood and acted upon.

- A person of high integrity and of a character that will not succumb to the forceful personalities of client management likely to be encountered. In the English Court of Appeal, Lord Justice Lindley had this to say of the auditor:

  'Such I take to be the duty of the auditor: he must be honest – that is, he must not certify what he does not believe to be true and he must take reasonable care and skill before he believes that what he certifies is true.'[1]

- A person who realizes that training and education are a continuing process and who, by reading professional journals and attending seminars, keeps abreast of developments in the business world and in the profession. In particular, knowledge of new statements of Generally Accepted Accounting Practice (GAAP) and statements of South African Auditing Standards (SAAS) is required.

- A person who is *au fait* with the requirements of the Public Accountants' and Auditors' Act and other relevant legislation and regulations, which apply to all services provided in the multidisciplinary public practice environment.

- A person who exercises professional duties with courtesy and tact. More can often be gained by a tactful and pleasant approach than the assumption of belligerent authority.

No amount of formal training can endow a person with all the attributes required to make a competent auditor. These are gathered by confronting difficulties and solving them to the best of one's ability, and only the passage of time will develop that indefinable flair of the successful professional accountant.

3.2 THE REGULATION OF CHARTERED ACCOUNTANTS AND REGISTERED ACCOUNTANTS AND AUDITORS IN SOUTH AFRICA

3.2.1 General

The public registered accountant and auditor (RAA) performing audits and issuing reports on annual financial statements is one who must be registered with the Public Accountants and Auditors Board (PAAB). Such a person

---

[1] In re *London and General Bank* (No.2) [1895] 2 chapter 673.

must also be a member of the South African Institute of Chartered Accountants (SAICA). The registered public accountant and auditor is subject to the provisions of the Public Accountants' and Auditors' Act and regulations thereunder, to the rules of the SAICA, and to the pronouncements of the Accounting Practices Board and Auditing Standards Board. In addition, the auditor is also governed by any law or regulation relating to the audit of a specific kind of legal entity, the most usual being the limited company.

A survey of the provisions of the Public Accountants' and Auditors' Act (and regulations thereunder) and of the pronouncements of the SAICA, the Accounting Practices Board and the Auditing Standards Board is given below.

3.2.2 Regulation of auditors under the Act

The Public Accountants' and Auditors' Act may be divided broadly into five important areas. These are:

- The constitution and composition of the PAAB and delegation of powers and duties thereto, including disciplinary powers (sections 2–13 and 23–26).
- Registration of accountants and auditors (including non-residents under specified conditions) and prohibition of unregistered persons practising as such (sections 14–17).
- Training contracts and examinations (sections 18 and 19).
- Powers and duties of auditors, including the furnishing of information as to identity (and changes thereto) to the PAAB and to clients and practice review (sections 20–22A).
- Offences by a public accountant and auditor and prescribed penalties (section 27).

The powers delegated to the Public Accountants' and Auditors' Board have been exercised by the Board mainly in the following areas:

- Regulations made (and notes thereto) concerning conditions for and registering of training contracts and training of those under contracts.
- Regulations relating to qualifying examinations and the scope of subject matter.
- Rules governing the conduct of the registered accountant and auditor. These are in two parts, entitled:
  - Disciplinary Rules; and
  - Code of Professional Conduct (see below).

The introductory paragraph of the Code of Professional Conduct states that breaches of these rules may be considered by the Board as improper conduct coming within the ambit of the Act (section 23) or the Disciplinary Rules (Rule 2.1.20). Section 27 of the Act reads as follows:

'The board may investigate or cause to be investigated and if necessary hear any allegation or charge of improper conduct, whether prescribed or not, of which a person who is or was registered in terms of this Act is alleged to have been guilty while he was so registered …'

Disciplinary Rules 2.1 and 2.1.21 taken together state that:

'… any practitioner shall be guilty of improper conduct if he conducts himself in a manner which is improper or discreditable or unprofessional or dishonourable or unworthy on the part of a practitioner or which tends to bring the profession of accounting into disrepute.'

It is evident that the PAAB has unrestricted power to enquire into any act (or omission) which it finds improper, whether or not specified in the Act or Rules.

Other regulations made by the Board relate, *inter alia*, to audit reports and certificates, and to designations of registered accountants and auditors.

3.2.3 The PAAB's Statements of South African Auditing Standards

These statements of generally accepted auditing standards, referred to as South African Auditing Standards (abbreviated to SAAS), codify best practice and are to be applied in the audit of financial statements. SAAS are also to be applied, adapted as necessary, to the audit of other information and to related services. Statements of SAAS contain the basic principles and essential procedures (identified in bold lettering), together with related guidance in the form of explanatory and other material, which provide guidance for their application. Audit standards should be adhered to in engagements to audit financial statements, as well as other engagements, where an adaptation of them might be necessary. Any deviation from these might require justification by the auditor where any accusations of negligence arise. The historical perspective and the current circumstances for setting South African Auditing Standards, as well as their authority, are discussed in section 3.4 of this chapter.

3.2.4 The Accounting Practices Board's Statements on Generally Accepted Accounting Practice

As indicated in chapter 1, the Accounting Practices Board (APB) is responsible for issuing statements of Generally Accepted Accounting Practice (GAAP) in South Africa. Some uncertainty existed as to whether or not non-compliance with the requirements of GAAP statements in the preparation of annual financial statements constituted a breach of Section 286(3) of the Companies Act. Section 285(3) reads as follows:

'the annual financial statements of a company shall, in conformity with generally accepted accounting practice, fairly present the state of affairs of the company and its business as at the end of the financial year concerned and the profit or loss of the company for that financial year and shall for that purpose be in accordance with and include at least the matters prescribed by Schedule 4, in so far as they are applicable, and comply with any other requirements of this Act.'

To clarify this uncertainty, the APB took senior counsel's opinion in 1977 and again in 1987 on the meaning of generally accepted accounting practice in the context of Section 286(3). Senior counsel's opinion was that whilst compliance with a Statement of GAAP meets the requirements of the Companies Act to conform with generally accepted accounting practice, non-compliance may constitute a contravention of the Act, but would not necessarily do so.

GAAP statement AC 101 acknowledges that there may be extremely rare circumstances where management, in preparing financial statements, might conclude that compliance with a requirement in a statement would result in misleading financial statements, and therefore that departure from a requirement is necessary to achieve fair presentation. In such a circumstance AC 101 paragraph .14 requires financial statements to disclose:

'(a)   that management has concluded that the financial statements fairly present the enterprise's financial position, financial performance and cash flows;

(b)   that it has complied in all material respects with applicable Statements of Generally Accepted Accounting Practice except that it has departed from a statement in order to achieve a fair presentation;

(c)   the statement from which the enterprise has departed, the nature of the departure, including the treatment that the statement would require, the reason why that treatment would be misleading in the circumstances and the treatment adopted; and

(d)   the financial impact of the departure on the enterprise's net profit or loss, assets, liabilities; equity and cash flows for each period presented.'

Where statements of GAAP are deviated from, compliance with paragraph 5 of Schedule 4 of the Companies Act is required. This paragraph reads as follows:

'If it appears to the directors of a company that there are reasons for departing from any of the accounting concepts stated in Statements of Generally Accepted Accounting Practice approved by the Accounting Practices Board, where such appropriate Statements exist, in preparing the company's financial statements in respect of any accounting period they may do so, but particulars of the departure, the effects and the reasons for it shall be given.'

The reference to concepts in paragraph 5 caused some confusion as to how the paragraph should be interpreted, one interpretation being that the required disclosure of departure from statements of Generally Accepted Accounting Practice was only required if such departure was fundamental. Accordingly, in September 1999 the South African Institute of Chartered Accountants (SAICA) sought legal opinion on the interpretation of paragraph 5 of Schedule 4. This opinion was as follows:

'On the evidence available to us, paragraph 5 of Schedule 4 requires disclosure whenever the financial statements of a company depart from any of the Accounting Practices Board (APB) Statements.'

In December 1999, SAICA issued Circular 8/99, 'Compliance with Section 286(3) and Paragraph 5 of Schedule 4 to the Companies Act, 61 of 1973 and Statements of Generally Accepted Accounting Practice'. The stated objective of the circular was:

'To assist directors of companies to meet their obligations in respect of financial reporting in terms of Section 286(3) and paragraph 5 of Schedule 4 of the Companies Act and Statements of Generally Accepted Accounting Practice (GAAP). This circular is also intended to provide guidance to auditors concerning their audit responsibility in this regard.'

The circular reported the legal opinions described above and introduced the concept of there being two financial reporting frameworks, namely, gaap (referred to as little gaap) and GAAP (referred to as big GAAP). Paragraph .07 of the Circular reads as follows:

'In South Africa, at present, there are therefore two financial reporting frameworks, the one based on generally accepted accounting practice (gaap) and the other based on Statements of Generally Accepted Accounting Practice (GAAP). This situation arises because of the wording of S.286(3) of the Companies Act as explained in paragraphs .02 and .04 above. The essential differences between these two bases of accounting are:

- Statements of GAAP are those accounting standards and practices which have been codified by the responsible standard setting body in South Africa, namely the Accounting Practices Board. These accounting standards are based on internationally accepted standards, and compliance therewith would therefore ensure fair presentation in the financial statements and compliance with S.286(3), and

- Generally accepted accounting practice includes those accounting practices which are uncodified, but are regarded as being generally accepted due to their being followed by a number of companies. These practices may or may not comply with Statements of GAAP, but would be the minimum required to meet the requirements of S.286(3), provided fair presentation is achieved.'

With regard to the director's responsibility, the circular suggests that the directors of a company should select either 'big GAAP' or 'little gaap' as the primary basis of accounting for the preparation of financial statements. Where little gaap is the basis used, resulting in a material departure from one or more statements of GAAP, they are required to disclose the particulars of, the reasons for, and the effect of the departure in the financial statements.

If 'big GAAP' is the basis selected, compliance with AC 101 paragraph 12 is required. This paragraph states that:

'An enterprise whose financial statements comply with Statements of Generally Accepted Accounting Practice should disclose that fact. Financial statements should not be described as complying with Statements of Generally Accepted

Accounting Practice unless they comply with all the requirements of each applicable Statement and each applicable approved interpretation.'

Section 301 of the Companies Act requires the auditor to report on whether or not the financial statements being reported on fairly present the financial position and results of operations in the manner required by the Act. In meeting this requirement, the auditor must be satisfied that the requirements of section 286(3) and paragraph 5 of the Fourth Schedule have been complied with. Accordingly, if the basis of preparation of financial statements is 'little gaap', the auditor needs to be satisfied that this basis is appropriate in the circumstances and that the necessary disclosure of the departure from statements of Generally Accepted Accounting Practice has been made. Should this be the case, the circular indicates that the auditor should modify the audit report by drawing attention in it to the non-compliance with statements of GAAP and the disclosure thereof in the financial statements.

Should the auditor disagree with the departure from statements of GAAP, and this departure has resulted in material misstatement in the financial statements, the auditor cannot report that such financial statements show fair presentation in all material respects. The audit opinion expressed in the audit report would thus need to be modified. A modification of the audit opinion might also be necessary where the auditor agrees with the decision to depart from the requirements of statements of GAAP, but adequate disclosure of such departure is not made in the financial statements. Audit reports are discussed in detail in chapter 18.

3.2.5 The profession's Code of Professional Conduct

3.2.5.1 Introduction

It is generally accepted that professionals have an obligation to those to whom they provide services, to their profession, as well as to themselves and fellow professionals. This obligation involves, amongst others, acting with due professional care in the performance of their duties, as well as conducting themselves in accordance with acceptable ethical behaviour, and flows from the need to maintain the confidence of the users of professional services. Any substandard services provided, or unethical behaviour on the part of a professional, is likely to undermine the reputation of the profession and could ultimately lead to a diminished demand for the services provided.

So what is ethical behaviour? The *Concise Oxford Dictionary* defines 'ethics' as:

'... set of principles or morals ..., moral principles, rules of conduct ...';

and 'moral' as:

'concerned ... with the distinction between right and wrong; ... virtuous in general conduct'.

Ethics are thus a set of ideals, which may take the form of rules of conduct that provide the distinction between right and wrong behaviour.

The need to give guidance on ethical behaviour to practising members of the accounting and auditing profession was recognized when the Public Accountants' and Auditors' Act was passed by Parliament in 1951 (now Act 80 of 1991).

The Act, together with its accompanying rules, entrenched a code of professional conduct which included also a disciplinary procedure for its enforcement. The Code consisted of Disciplinary Rules, extended by a set of Rules of Professional Conduct which were further extended by an Interpretation. The Disciplinary Rules and Rules of Professional Conduct dealt with the matter from a negative point of view, that is, they described acts which would constitute improper behaviour, and provided penalties for such behaviour. The Interpretation addressed the concept of professionalism by stating:

> 'It is basic to the concept of a profession that a code of conduct be observed amongst its members which is over and above the requirements of law. Such a code governs the relations of the members of a profession amongst themselves and with the community at large. Self-imposed discipline distinguishes a professional man from members of a trade or other calling.'

Because the PAA Act regulates only those members of the accounting profession who are registered under the Act as practising members, the South African Institute of Chartered Accountants (at that time National Council) adopted a parallel Code of Professional Conduct that applies to all chartered accountants.

The status of the board's Code is described in a earlier section of this chapter. The Institute's Code status derives from paragraph .21 of the Institute's bylaws, which sets out acts and practices deemed to be offences and which, if committed by a member, render him or her liable to penalties. Subparagraph (1) of paragraph .21 reads as follows: 'if a member conducts himself in a manner which, in the opinion of the Investigating Committee or the Disciplinary Committee, is discreditable, dishonourable, dishonest, irregular, or unworthy or which is derogatory to the Institute, or tends to bring the profession of accountancy into disrepute'. If a complaint is lodged against a member of the Institute, the Disciplinary Committee, when forming its opinion, will be guided by the Code.

3.2.5.2 Outline of the Code of Professional Conduct

The Code is divided into four sections. The first sets out objectives and fundamental principles of a general nature and are therefore not intended to be used to solve a chartered accountant's ethical problems in specific instances. The other three sections provide detailed guidance as to the application of the objectives and fundamental principles to a number of typical situations likely to be encountered. The latter three sections are identified as Part A, which is applicable to all members of the Institute, Part B, which is applicable only to members in public practice, and Part C, which is applicable to members in commerce and industry.

As the sections on objectives and fundamental principles are clearly and succinctly set out in the Code they are quoted verbatim in this overview, while the content of Part A, B and C are dealt with by way of a summary of important principles and guidance.

3.2.5.3 Objectives and fundamental principles

The Code recognizes that the objectives of the accountancy profession are to work to the highest standards of professionalism, to attain the highest levels of performance and generally to meet the public interest requirements set out above. These objectives require four basic needs to be met:

- *Credibility.* In the whole of society there is a need for credibility in information and information systems.
- *Professionalism.* There is a need for individuals who can be clearly identified by clients, employers and other interested parties as professional persons in the accountancy field.
- *Quality of services.* There is a need for assurance that all services obtained from a member are carried out to the highest standards of performance.
- *Confidence.* Users of the services of members should be able to feel confident that there exists a framework of professional ethics which governs the provision of those services.

In order to achieve the objectives of the accountancy profession, members have to observe a number of prerequisites or fundamental principles. These are:

- *Integrity (see section 2).* Integrity is essentially an attitude of mind. Adherence to certain standards of conduct and moral behaviour consistently practised will ensure integrity.
  A member should be straightforward and honest in performing professional services.

- *Objectivity (see sections 2 and 3).* Objectivity is essentially the quality of being able to maintain an impartial attitude. It requires a member to be fair and not to allow prejudice or bias or influence of others to override objectivity.

- *Professional competence and due care (see section 4).* A member, in agreeing to provide professional services, implies that there is a level of competence necessary to perform professional services and that the knowledge, skill and experience of the member will be applied with reasonable care and diligence. Members should therefore refrain from performing any services which they are not competent to carry out unless advice and assistance is obtained to ensure that the services are performed satisfactorily.

A member should perform professional services with due care, competence and diligence and has a continuing duty to maintain professional knowledge and skill at a level required to ensure that a client or employer receives the advantage of competent professional service based on up-to-date developments in practice, legislation and techniques.

- *Confidentiality (see section 5).* A member should respect the confidentiality of information acquired during the course of performing professional services and should not use or disclose any such information without proper and specific authority or unless there is a legal or professional right or duty to disclose.

- *Professional behaviour (see sections 6–10).* A member should act in a manner consistent with the good reputation of the profession and refrain from any conduct which might bring discredit to the profession. A member should conduct him-/herself with courtesy and consideration towards clients, third parties, other members of the accountancy profession, staff, employers and the general public.

- *Technical standards (see sections 11–19).* A member should carry out professional services in accordance with the relevant technical and professional standards. Members have a duty to carry out with care and skill, the instructions of the client or employer in so far as they are compatible with the requirements of integrity, objectivity and, in the case of members in public practice, independence (see section 11). In addition, they should conform with the technical and professional standards promulgated by the Institute, relevant authorities and relevant legislation.

3.2.5.4 Part A of the Code, applicable to all members

Section 1: Joint and vicarious liability

1. A member may be held responsible for contraventions of the Code on the part of persons who are:

   - employees of the member;
   - under the member's supervision;
   - partners of the member;
   - fellow shareholders in, or directors or employees of, a company controlled by the member or the member and partners;
   - fellow members in or employees of a close corporation controlled by the member or the member and partners.

2. Members may not use partnerships, companies, close corporations or other separate legal persona to act in a manner in which they would not be permitted to act as individuals.

3. Members may not permit third parties to act on their behalf in a manner which would constitute a contravention of the Code.

Section 2: Integrity and objectivity

1. This section emphasizes integrity and objectivity and the concepts of fairness, honesty and freedom from conflicts of interest, prejudice and bias.

2. Members should avoid personal relationships or interests which may threaten integrity or objectivity.

3. Members should not accept or provide gifts or similar favours.

4. Reasonableness should prevail in identifying relationships that could impair integrity and objectivity.

Section 3: Conflicts of interest as regards integrity, objectivity and independence

1. Members should be alert to the possibility of a conflict of interest and should consider surrounding facts and circumstances before accepting an engagement or continuing in a position.

2. Examples of conflicts of interest include:

   - pressure from an overbearing supervisor, manager, director or partner;
   - family or personal relationships which could give rise to pressure;
   - being asked to act contrary to technical and/or professional standards;
   - divided loyalty as between the member's superior and the required professional standards;
   - the publication of false, misleading or misrepresenting information.

3. An honest disagreement is not, in itself, an ethical issue.

4. Conflicts of interest should be disclosed immediately.

5. Members should decline to act if a material conflict of interest exists.

6. If it is possible for a member to act objectively, notwithstanding a conflict of interest, the nature of the conflict must be explained to all parties and all parties must agree in writing that the member may act.

7. If a member, not in public practice, is unable to resolve an ethical conflict through normal organizational structures, the following should be considered:

   - Review the problem with the immediate superior.
   - If the superior is involved in the problem, raise the issue with the next higher level of management.
   - Consult the executive committee, board of directors, non-executive directors, trustees, partners or shareholders.
   - If considered necessary, advice should be sought from a senior member of or the Advisory Panel of the Institute.

- If the ethical conflict still exists, the member should resign from the employing organization, and submit a memorandum setting out the reasons for resigning to an appropriate representative of that organization.

Section 4: Professional competence

1. Members should not undertake or continue with any professional services which they are not competent to carry out.

2. Where necessary, members should seek technical advice from experts such as other members, lawyers, actuaries, engineers, geologists, valuers.

3. Members must keep up to date in whatever fields of activities they are engaged in, whether in public practice, commerce, industry, academic life or the public sector.

4. Members should maintain professional knowledge and skill and should participate in continuing professional education.

Section 5: Confidentiality

1. Confidentiality must be observed unless:

   - disclosure is authorized;
   - disclosure is required by law; or
   - there is a professional duty or right to disclose.

2. Members should ensure that their staff maintain confidentiality.

3. Members should not use confidential information for personal advantage.

4. Disclosure is required, where necessary:

   - as evidence in legal proceedings;
   - as disclosure to the appropriate authorities – examples are:
     (i) a Revenue inspection; and
     (ii) reporting an irregularity under section 20(5) of the PAA Act;
   - in compliance with technical or ethical standards;
   - in compliance with the Institute's quality review;
   - in response to a disciplinary enquiry or investigation.

5. Where a member is required to disclose information about a client's or employer's affairs, the client or employer must be advised thereof.

6. Where required, disclosure should be confined to such information as is strictly necessary.

Section 6: Tax practice

1. A member should not imply that tax returns prepared and tax advice offered are beyond challenge.

2. A member should advise clients or employers that the content of returns rests primarily with the clients or employers.

3. A member should record tax advice or opinions of material consequence given.

4. A member should not be associated with any return or communication if there is reason to believe that it:

   - contains a false or misleading statement;
   - contains statements or information furnished recklessly; or
   - omits or obscures information required to be submitted.

5. A member is associated with a return if the member has consented to the use of his/her or the firm's name in connection with the return.

6. Returns including estimates are permitted provided the member is satisfied that the amounts reflected are reasonable.

7. A member may rely on information provided by clients or employers provided the information appears reasonable, but members are encouraged to ensure that supporting documentation is provided.

8. When completing tax returns, a member:

   - should refer to previous returns;
   - must make reasonable enquiries; and
   - is encouraged to make reference to supporting records.

9. If a member learns of a material error or omission in a tax return for a prior year, or of the failure to file a required tax return, the member should advise the client or employer thereof and recommend that disclosure be made to the Receiver. The member is not obliged to inform the Revenue authorities, nor may this be done without permission.

10. If the client or the employer does not correct the error, the member should:

    - inform the client or the employer that it is not possible to act for them;
    - consider whether continued association with the client or employer in any capacity is consistent with professional responsibilities; and
    - refer to the section on ethical conflicts above (section 3).

11. If a member continues a professional relationship with a client or employer, reasonable steps should be taken to ensure that past errors are not repeated in future.

Section 7: Discrimination

Members should not practise discrimination based on race, colour, religion, sex, marital status, age or origin.

Section 8: Cross-border activities

Members working in other countries should adhere to local ethical requirements.

Section 9: Publicity, advertising and solicitation

1. Publicity and advertising is permitted, but members are personally responsible to ensure that this section of the Code is complied with.

2. Material used for publicity and advertising should be in good taste and consistent with the dignity of the profession.
   Examples of a lack of good taste include material which tends to shock or sensationalize, or is racist; the trivialization of important issues; excessive reliance on personalities; deriding of public figures; disparagement of educational attainment; odious comparisons; strident, hectoring or extravagant material; comparison with or belittling of competitors, testimonials or endorsements.

3. Advertisements should conform with accepted norms of legality, decency, honesty and truthfulness.

4. Advertisements should not state hourly or other charging rates.

5. Solicitation through direct mailing is permitted unless the member has been requested not to do so.

6. Solicitation through cold calling is allowed for members not in public practice.

7. Solicitation through cold calling is not allowed for members in public practice for professional work.

Section 10: Responsibilities to colleagues

1. Members should consider the welfare of the profession as a whole, should assist fellow members to comply with the Code and should cooperate with disciplinary proceedings.

2. A member should display complete candour if testifying as an expert witness, regardless of the obvious reluctance to give evidence which may be damaging to a colleague.

3. A member should not criticize another member irresponsibly and should not act in a manner which reflects negatively on fellow members.

4. Members should not seek to displace other members in client relationships by means which would lessen technical performance.

5. Members should ascertain if there are any reasons why appointment as accounting officer of a close corporation should not be accepted.

6. On resigning as accounting officer of a close corporation, a member should advise the corporation and each member of the corporation, in writing, of the reasons for resignation.

7. A member who accepts appointment as accounting officer of a close corporation, should inform the outgoing accounting officer thereof in writing.

3.2.5.5 Part B of the Code, applicable to members in public practice

1. Members should be free of an obligation to or interest in clients and should be independent in both fact and appearance – 'be and be seen to be independent'.

2. The following matters could impair a member's independence and objectivity:
   - direct or indirect financial interest in clients;
   - fiduciary interests in clients;
   - loans to or from clients or any officer, director or principal shareholder of client companies;
   - holding a financial interest in a joint venture with a client or employee(s) of a client;
   - financial interest in a nonclient that has an investor or investee relationship with a client;
   - appointments in client companies – for at least the preceding two years;
   - performance of management functions;
   - the same staff member carrying out the accounting and attest functions;
   - personal and family relationships;
   - fees from one client, or group of clients, which form the substantial part of gross income;
   - fees which remain unpaid;
   - acceptance of goods, services or undue hospitality;
   - relationships with clients where a former partner of the member has accepted appointment at the client and also retains a relationship with the practice; and
   - actual or threatened litigation between the member and a client.

3. The following are not normally considered to impair independence:
   - holding of securities in a public company in which the securities are widely held, provided that holding is not material to the member or the company;
   - making deposits with, or accepting loans from clients which are registered as financial institutions on the same terms as are available to the general public;

- making investments in loan stock of public utility corporation clients or municipal clients;
- making indirect investments in clients through the holding of units in mutual funds, insurance policies or retirement funding investments; and
- indebtedness arising out of normal trading transactions on the same terms as are available to the general public.

Section 12: Fees for professional services

1. This section relates to fees for professional work.

2. Agreeing on an acceptable fee is principally a matter for negotiation and consideration may be given to market factors.

3. Fees charged should be a fair reflection of services rendered and the following factors should be taken into account:
   - the skill and knowledge required;
   - the level of training and experience required;
   - the time taken;
   - the degree of responsibility; and
   - the level and extent of investment in technology.

4. The basis on which fees are charged should be explained to the client, preferably in writing.

5. Clients should not be misled concerning fees which are likely to be substantially increased.

Commissions

6. Members should not pay commissions to obtain clients, or accept commissions from third persons for referring products or services to clients, unless the client has prior knowledge of the arrangement.

7. The prohibition on commissions to obtain clients includes referral fees between members in public practice where no work is done by the referring accountant, but excludes such referral fees for work done.

8. The payment of a share of fees to the previous owners of an accounting practice is not regarded as a commission.

Contingent fees

9. Members may not perform work related to the attest function, nor prepare an original or amended tax return, for a contingent fee for any client.

10. In practice, certain work can only be charged for on a contingency basis. Examples include management buyouts; the raising of capital; assisting clients with acquisitions; and circumstances where the client's ability to pay the fee is contingent upon the success of the venture.

11. Fees may only be charged on a contingency basis if objectivity and integrity are not compromised.

12. Where work is done on a contingency basis, the member's capacity and the basis of remuneration should be clarified in any related documents issued by the member. This requirement is in contemplation of third-party reliance.

'Lowballing'

13. Lowballing refers to the quoting of fees significantly lower than those charged by others.

14. Members should be aware that lowballing may affect independence.

15. The same resources must be allocated as would have been to other work of a similar nature.

16. Fees should still be based on skill, level of training, time, etc.

17. Clients should not be misled concerning the range of services covered by the fee and the level of fees anticipated for the future.

Section 13: Signing of reports or certificates

A member may not delegate to any person who is not a partner the power to sign audit or other reports expressing opinions, or certificates, except in cases of grave emergency. In these cases, the circumstances are reported both to the client and the PAAB.

Section 14: Stationery and letterheads

1. Stationery should be of an acceptable professional standard and may reflect the names of all partners; the names of professional assistants registered with the PAAB; the names of other professional assistants, provided that it is clear that they are not registered with the PAAB; and the names of persons, firms and organizations with whom the member is associated.

2. Members should note section 14 and section 27(1) of the PAA Act which provide, *inter alia*, that:

   - no person may hold himself [sic] out to be an accountant or auditor in public practice unless registered with the PAAB, and
   - professional letterheads must reflect the names of partners.

Section 15: Activities incompatible with the practice of public accountancy

Members should not engage in activities which impair integrity, objectivity or independence or the reputation of the profession.

Section 16: Relations with other members in public practice

Accepting new assignments

1. A member in public practice should not attempt to restrict in any way the client's freedom of choice.

2. The services or advice of a member in public practice having special skills may be sought in one or other of the following ways:

   * by the client

     after prior discussion and consultation with the existing accountant; on the specific request or recommendation of the existing accountant; or

     without reference to the existing accountant

     by the existing accountant with due observance of the duty of confidentiality.

3. When a member in public practice is asked to provide services or advice, enquiries should be made as to whether the prospective client has an existing accountant.

4. In cases where there is an existing accountant who will continue to provide professional services, the receiving accountant should:

   * limit the services provided to the specific assignment;
   * take reasonable steps to support the existing accountant's current relationship; and
   * not express any criticism of the professional services of the existing accountant.

5. Before accepting any appointment, the receiving accountant should advise the client of the professional obligation to communicate with the existing accountant and should immediately do so, preferably in writing.

6. Circumstances sometimes arise when the client insists that the existing accountant should not be informed. In such cases, the receiving accountant should decide whether the client's reasons are valid.

7. The receiving accountant should:

   * comply with the instructions received from the existing accountant or the client; and
   * ensure that the existing accountant is kept informed of the general nature of the professional services being performed.

8. The existing accountant should maintain contact with the receiving accountants and cooperate with them in all reasonable requests for assistance.

Superseding another member in public practice

9. Clients have an indisputable right to choose their professional advisers.

10. Members should ascertain if there are any professional reasons why an appointment should not be accepted.

11. In the absence of a request, the existing accountant should not volunteer information about the client's affairs.

12. The extent to which an existing accountant can discuss the affairs of the client with the proposed accountant will depend on whether the client's permission to do so has been obtained.

13. Before accepting an appointment involving continuing professional services previously carried out by another member in public practice, the proposed accountant should:

    • explain to the prospective client the duty to communicate with the existing accountant;
    • ascertain if the prospective client has advised the existing accountant of the proposed change and has given permission, preferably in writing, to discuss the client's affairs fully and freely with the proposed accountant;
    • on receipt of permission, ask the existing accountant, preferably in writing, to provide information on any professional reasons which should be known before deciding whether or not to accept the appointment; and
    • if permission is not granted, consider declining the assignment unless exceptional circumstances exist.

14. The existing accountant, on receipt of the communication referred to, should:

    • reply, preferably in writing, advising whether there are any professional reasons why the proposed accountant should not accept the appointment; and
    • if there are any such reasons or other matters which should be disclosed, ensure that the client has given permission to give details of this information to the proposed accountant; or
    • if permission is not granted, the existing accountant should report that fact to the proposed member in public practice.

15. Matters to be reported to the proposed accountant should ideally include all information of which the proposed accountant should be aware in order to decide whether or not to accept the appointment.

16. The fact that fees have not yet been paid is not a reason why a new member should not be appointed.

17. Once the change in appointment has been effected, the existing accountant should make available to the receiving accountant all client records, unless there is legal reason for withholding them.

Section 17: Recruiting

Visits to schools and universities

1. Recruiting at schools is best done on an institutional basis, and members may not visit schools for the purpose of recruiting staff.

2. Where facilities are made available by university authorities, members may recruit staff on university campuses.

Educational institutions

3. Members may offer bursaries and prizes for students at educational institutions, and may allow the bursaries and prizes to be named after themselves or their firms.

4. Members may endow a chair at a university and may allow their or their firm's sponsorship to be acknowledged publicly by the university.

Competitors' staff

5. Members should not, directly or indirectly, offer employment to employees of other members without first informing the latter.

Section 18: Inclusion of the name of a member in public practice in a document issued by a client

1. Where a client intends to publish a report by a member, the member should take steps to ensure that the context in which the report is published is not such as might result in the public being misled.

2. This applies to other documents proposed to be issued by a client which contain the name of the member, but does not apply to the annual report.

3. Where a member is associated with an organization in a private capacity, the organization may use the member's name on its stationery. However, the member should ensure that this does not lead to any public misconception concerning the member's professional capacity.

3.2.5.6 Part C of the Code, applicable to members in commerce and industry (C&I members)

Sections 20 to 23

1. C&I members have a duty of loyalty to their employers and should support their employer's legitimate and ethical objectives. However, as employees, they cannot be required to break the law, breach professional standards, lie to or mislead the auditors, or be associated with misrepresentation.

2. Differences in accounting judgement or ethical issues should be resolved within the employer organization – with higher levels of management if necessary. If such difficulties cannot be resolved, the C&I member may have to consider resignation. Confidentiality would normally preclude the C&I member from communicating the issue to others.

3. A C&I member holding authority should consider the need for subordinates to develop and hold their own accounting judgement and should deal with differences in opinion in a professional manner.

4. When given specific tasks, a C&I member should not mislead an employer as to his/her degree of expertise or experience.

5. A C&I member is expected to present information fully, honestly and professionally.

3.3 THE AUDITOR'S RESPONSIBILITIES

The auditor has many responsibilities. The major ones are commented on below.

3.3.1 To report an opinion

The auditor's primary responsibility is to give a written opinion on the financial statements or other information that are the subject of audit.

As a general rule, the auditor is concerned with the annual financial statements of businesses, most of which are in limited company form, but of course there are others, sole traders, partnerships, cooperative societies, to name but a few. The provisions of section 20 of the Public Accountants' and Auditors' Act which relate to audit reports apply to the audit of all businesses, be they subject to other statutes (as in the case, for example, of limited companies) or not.

The form of the report the auditor may encounter in the various circumstances is treated in chapters 18 and 19.

Section 20(4) of the Public Accountants' and Auditors' Act provides that an auditor shall give an audit report within a period of four months after the audit assignment was completed.

3.3.2 To conduct the audit with due professional care and competence

As indicated in section 3.1 of this chapter, the auditor has a duty, firstly, to be honest and, secondly, to use reasonable care and skill in conducting an audit and reporting on the subject matter. Failure to do so may result in liability for fraud or negligence.

3.3.2.1 **Liability for fraud or negligence**

With regard to the duty of honesty, it is clear that where an auditor makes a statement which is to be published, and knowing it to be false (which includes the deliberate omission of a material fact necessary to convey the truth), the auditor will be liable for fraud to any party who acts thereon. Fraud may also exist where negligence is so gross as to be tantamount to dishonesty, that is, making a statement with reckless disregard for its being true or false – for example, giving an unqualified report, having done nothing to ascertain the facts. The auditor who is found guilty of fraud will be subject to the sanction of the Public Accountants' and Auditors' Board and is unlikely to remain for long a registered accountant and auditor.[2]

Further, under the Companies Act, the auditor is criminally liable:

- for making a false statement, knowing it to be false, in any report, return, etc., required by the Act (section 249);
- for concealing, destroying or falsifying any book, record, or financial statement of the company (section 250); and
- for making or circulating any report, certificate, etc., in relation to the company's affairs which is false in any material particular unless the auditor can show that reasonable care was exercised (section 251).

With regard to the duty to take reasonable care, the auditor may be liable for negligence:

- to the client; or
- to a third party,

where loss has been suffered as a result of the negligence. Liability to the client arises from either a breach of contract, there being an implied condition in the contract between client and auditor that the latter will act with the care and skill of a reasonable auditor, or from delict as a consequence of breach of duty of care owed to the client. The client has the choice of actions.

Liability to third parties is based on delict. Until March 1982 it was not clear how far the auditor's liability to third parties extended, a situation that was becoming intolerable for accountants and auditors who have, by the nature of their duties, a constant exposure to this liability. Accordingly, an amendment to the Public Accountants' and Auditors' Act was passed which spelt out the limits of liability to third parties.[3]

To summarize, the position now is that where negligence is proved against an auditor, liability to a third party for loss suffered as a result of the negligence arises *only* if it is proved that the auditor:

---

[2] See the Public Accountants' and Auditors' Act, section 13(1)(h).
[3] Sections 20(9), 20(10) and 20(11) of Act 80 of 1991.

- knew or could have been expected to know that the auditor's report, certificate, etc., would be used by the client to induce the third party to act (or refrain from acting) in a particular way; or
- knew or could have been expected to know that the third party would rely on the report, certificate, etc., for the purpose of acting (or refraining from acting) in a particular way; or
- in any way represented to the third party that the report, certificate, etc., given by the auditor was correct while at that time the auditor knew or could have been expected to know that the third party would rely on such representation to act (or refrain from acting) in a particular way.

Because of the importance of this matter to practising accountants and auditors, the PAAB issued, in June 1983, an explanatory memorandum by Professor S J Naudé which is reproduced as appendix 2 to this book.

Where, as is usual, the audit is conducted by the auditor's staff, the auditor is liable for any material failure on the part of staff.

The auditor should appreciate the consequences which may flow from failure to conduct an audit with due care and skill and these should act as a spur to ever-increasing competence in professional work. This represents what may be called the negative approach to an audit – the avoidance of liability.

3.3.2.2 The positive approach

It is a poor auditor, however, who views professional responsibility in this light only. The auditor should cultivate the positive approach of providing the highest standard of service to clients (and to others) and to use best endeavours to improve that capability in the changing circumstances of the business and professional world. In this regard, paragraph 13(c) of the Institute's Code of Professional Conduct is worth repeating here:

> 'A member [of the Institute], in agreeing to provide professional services, implies that there is a level of competence necessary to perform professional services and that the knowledge, skill and experience of the member will be applied with reasonable care and diligence.'

3.3.3 To maintain an independent mental attitude

Independence in this context means freedom from influence of clients or other interested parties who might attempt to exert pressure on the auditor to report in a manner which is to their advantage.

There are two main aspects of auditor independence.

The first of these is the auditor's responsibility to come to an unbiased opinion on matters faced and to have the strength of character not to be led by forceful personalities who may be encountered to accept statements with which the auditor is not completely satisfied. This may be called the internal aspect, that which is known only to the auditor and cannot be the subject of rules imposed by some other authority.

The second, the external aspect, is the face the auditor presents to the world, the environment created or allowed to be created which surrounds professional work. This should be such that it is likely to promote the quality of independence and give others further assurance that their reliance on the auditor's audit report is not misplaced. There are some acts and relationships of the auditor which are likely to erode independence or appear to others to do so. It is not practicable to give an exhaustive list of these, but the following are probably the more important:

- investments in clients;
- indebtedness to clients;
- trusteeships associated with clients;
- acceptance of gifts from clients;
- personal relationship with client personnel; and
- disproportionate fee income from one client.

Any of the foregoing may cause bias in the auditor's mind or give that appearance to others, and accordingly, rules of behaviour have been laid down by both the SAICA and the PAAB in an attempt to prevent or reduce the incidence of such occurrences.[4]

In brief, independence should be practised and be seen to be practised by the auditor. The SAICA's and the PAAB's codes of professional conduct which, *inter alia*, address independence issues have already been discussed.

In November 2001, the International Federation of Accountants (IFAC) issued a revised Code of Ethics for Professional Accountants. Part B, which is applicable to professional accountants in public practice, at section 8 addresses independence in considerable detail. Paragraph 8.12 of the section reads as follows:

> 'This section provides a framework of principles that members of assurance teams, firms or network firms should use to identify threats to independence, evaluate the significant of those threats, and, if the threats are other than clearly insignificant, identify and apply safeguards to eliminate the threats or reduce them to an acceptable level, such that independence of mind and independence in appearance are not compromised.'

As a member of IFAC, the South African profession is committed to aligning its pronouncements to those of IFAC. Accordingly, the Independent Board of Ethics (IBE) of the PAAB is currently considering how to incorporate the changes contained in the IFAC Code into the PAAB's Code. To that end, the IBE has called for comment on the Code and its effective date of application in South Africa. As it is likely that the section on independence will be

---

[4] See Codes of Professional Conduct.

adopted in the PAAB's and SAICA's Codes of Ethics, an overview of the first part of the section is given below.

Section 8, on independence, consists of two parts. The first provides a framework, built on principles for identifying, evaluating and responding to threats to independence. The second, by way of examples, describes specific circumstances and relationships that may create threats to independence and the safeguards that may be appropriate in the specific circumstances. There is a caution that the examples presented are intended to illustrate the application of the principles and should not be viewed as an exhaustive list of all the circumstances that may create threats to independence. Further, it is not sufficient for auditors to merely comply with the examples presented; rather, they should apply the principles set out in the section to the particular circumstances they face.[5]

Threats to independence potentially stem from the following:

- self-interest;
- self-review;
- advocacy;
- familiarity; and
- intimidation.

' "Self-interest Threat" occurs when a firm or a member of the assurance team could benefit from a financial interest in or other self-interest conflict with, an assurance client. Examples of circumstances that may create this threat include, but are not limited to:

(a) A direct financial interest or material indirect financial interest in an assurance client;

(b) A loan or guarantee to or from an assurance client or any of its directors or officers.

(c) Undue dependence on total fees from an assurance client;

(d) Concern about the possibility of losing the engagement;

(e) Having a close business relationship with an assurance client;

(f) Potential employment with an assurance client; and

(g) Contingent fees relating to assurance engagements.'[6]

' "Self-Review Threat" occurs when (1) any product or judgment of a previous assurance engagement or non-assurance engagement needs to be re-evaluated in reaching conclusions on the assurance engagement or (2) when a member of

---

[5] IFAC Code of Ethics for Professional Accountants, paragraph 8.7.
[6] IFAC Code of Ethics for Professional Accountants, paragraph 8.29.

the assurance team was previously a director or officer of the assurance client, or was an employee in a position to exert direct and significant influence over the subject matter of the assurance engagement.

Examples of circumstances that may create this threat include, but are not limited to:

(a)   A member of the assurance team being, or having recently been, a director or officer of the assurance client;

(b)   A member of the assurance team being, or having recently been, an employee of the assurance client in a position to exert direct and significant influence over the subject matter of the assurance engagement;

(c)   Performing services for an assurance client that directly affect the subject matter of the assurance engagement; and

(d)   Preparation of original data used to generate financial statements or preparation of other records that are the subject matter of the assurance engagement.'[7]

'"Advocacy Threat" occurs when a firm, or a member of the assurance team, promotes, or may be perceived to promote, an assurance client's position or opinion to the point that objectivity may, or may be perceived to be, compromised. Such may be the case if a firm or a member of the assurance team were to subordinate their judgment to that of the client.

Examples of circumstances that may create this threat include, but are not limited to:

(a)   Dealing in, or being a promoter of, shares or other securities in an assurance client; and

(b)   Acting as an advocate on behalf of an assurance client in litigation or in resolving disputes with third parties.'[8]

'"Familiarity Threat" occurs when, by virtue of a close relationship with an assurance client, its directors, officers or employees, a firm or a member of the assurance team becomes too sympathetic to the client's interests.

Examples of circumstances that may create this threat include, but are not limited to:

(a)   A member of the assurance team having an immediate family member or close family member who is a director or officer of the assurance client;

(b)   A member of the assurance team having an immediate family member or close family member who, as an employee of the assurance client, is in a position to exert direct and significant influence over the subject matter of the assurance engagement;

---

[7] IFAC Code of Ethics for Professional Accountants, paragraph 8.30.
[8] IFAC Code of Ethics for Professional Accountants, paragraph 8.31.

(c) A former partner of the firm being a director, officer of the assurance client
     or an employee in a position to exert direct and significant influence over
     the subject matter of the assurance engagement;

(d) Long association of a senior member of the assurance team with the
     assurance client; and

(e) Acceptance of gifts or hospitality, unless the value is clearly insignificant,
     from the assurance client, its directors, officers or employees.'[9]

' "Intimidation Threat" occurs when a member of the assurance team may be
deterred from acting with objectivity and exercising professional skepticism by
threats, actual or perceived, from the directors, officers or employees of an
assurance client.

Examples of circumstances that may create this threat include, but are not
limited to:

(a) Threat of replacement over a disagreement with the application of an
     accounting principle; and

(b) Pressure to reduce inappropriately the extent of work performed in order
     to reduce fees.'[10]

When threats other than insignificant ones are identified, appropriate
safeguards should be applied to eliminate the threats or reduce them to
appropriate levels. The threats identified and measures taken to eliminate or
reduce them should be documented.

'Safeguards fall into three broad categories:

(a) Safeguards created by the profession, legislation or regulation;

(b) Safeguards within the assurance client; and

(c) Safeguards within the firm's own systems and procedures.'[11]

'Safeguards created by the profession, legislation or regulation, include the
following:

(a) Educational, training and experience requirements for entry into the
     profession;

(b) Continuing education requirements;

(c) Professional standards and monitoring and disciplinary processes;

(d) External review of a firm's quality control system; and

(e) Legislation governing the independence requirements of the firm.'[12]

---

[9] IFAC Code of Ethics for Professional Accountants, paragraph 8.32.
[10] IFAC Code of Ethics for Professional Accountants, paragraph 8.33.
[11] IFAC Code of Ethics for Professional Accountants, paragraph 8.36.
[12] IFAC Code of Ethics for Professional Accountants, paragraph 8.37.

'Safeguards within the assurance client, include the following;

(a) When the assurance client's management appoints the firm, persons other than management ratify or approve the appointment;

(b) The assurance client has competent employees to make managerial decisions;

(c) Policies and procedures that emphasize the assurance client's commitment to fair financial reporting;

(d) Internal procedures that ensure objective choices in commissioning non-assurance engagements; and

(e) A corporate governance structure, such as an audit committee, that provides appropriate oversight and communications regarding a firm's services.'[13]

'Safeguards within the firm's own systems and procedures may include firm-wide safeguards such as the following:

(a) Firm leadership that stresses the importance of independence and the expectation that members of assurance teams will act in the public interest;

(b) Policies and procedures to implement and monitor quality control of assurance engagements;

(c) Documented independence policies regarding the identification of threats to independence, the evaluation of the significance of these threats and the identification and application of safeguards to eliminate or reduce the threats, other than those that are clearly insignificant, to an acceptable level;

(d) Internal policies and procedures to monitor compliance with firm policies and procedures as they relate to independence;

(e) Policies and procedures that will enable the identification of interests or relationships between the firm or members of the assurance team and assurance clients;

(f) Policies and procedures to monitor and, if necessary, manage the reliance on revenue received from a single assurance client;

(g) Using different partners and teams with separate reporting lines for the provision of non-assurance services to an assurance client;

(h) Policies and procedures to prohibit individuals who are not members of the assurance team from influencing the outcome of the assurance engagement;

(i) Timely communication of a firm's policies and procedures, and any changes thereto, to all partners and professional staff, including appropriate training and education thereon;

---

[13] IFAC Code of Ethics for Professional Accountants, paragraph 8.38.

(j) Designating a member of senior management as responsible for overseeing the adequate functioning of the safeguarding system;

(k) Means of advising partners and professional staff of those assurance
clients and related entities from which they must be independent;

(l) A disciplinary mechanism to promote compliance with policies and
procedures; and

(m) Policies and procedures to empower staff to communicate to senior levels
within the firm any issue of independence and objectivity that concerns
them; this includes informing staff of the procedures open to them.'[14]

'Safeguards within the firm's own systems and procedures may include
engagement specific safeguards such as the following:

(a) Involving an additional professional accountant to review the work done
or otherwise advise as necessary. This individual could be someone from
outside the firm or network firm, or someone within the firm or network
firm who was not otherwise associated with the assurance team;

(b) Consulting a third party, such as a committee of independent directors, a
professional regulatory body or another professional accountant;

(c) Rotation of senior personnel;

(d) Discussing independence issues with the audit committee or others
charged with governance;

(e) Disclosing to the audit committee, or others charged with governance, the
nature of services provided and extent of fees charged;

(f) Policies and procedures to ensure members of the assurance team do not
make, or assume responsibility for, management decisions for the
assurance client;

(g) Involving another firm to perform or re-perform part of the assurance
engagement;

(h) Involving another firm to re-perform the non-assurance service to the
extent necessary to enable it to take responsibility for that service; and

(i) Removing an individual from the assurance team, when that individual's
financial interests or relationships create a threat to independence.'[15]

3.3.4 To report on material irregularities

A further responsibility imposed on the auditor in South Africa is that of
reporting on material irregularities.

The Public Accountants' and Auditors' Act provides for the auditor to report
to the person in charge of the undertaking any material irregularity which
the auditor has reason to believe has taken or is taking place and which has

---

[14] IFAC Code of Ethics for Professional Accountants, paragraph 8.41.
[15] IFAC Code of Ethics for Professional Accountants, paragraph 8.42.

caused or is likely to cause loss to the undertaking, its members, or its creditors; furthermore, if the matter is not rectified within 30 days of sending the report, the auditor is required to furnish the Public Accountants' and Auditors' Board with copies of the report, any reply thereto and any other relevant particulars.[16]

It is not easy to decide what acts or omissions fall within 'material irregularity'. Clearly the breach of a statute or established common-law rule, other than some minor technicality, would come within the term, as would the breach of the constitution of the undertaking (for example, a company's memorandum and articles). How much more the term may encompass, is a moot point.

The question of loss which has been incurred, seems fairly straightforward, though even here it may be noted that the section implies any loss. 'Materiality' refers to the irregularity, not to the loss. What should the auditor's attitude be where there has been a gross breach of statute, but from which flowed some trivial loss only? The real difficulty arises with the phrase: '... or is likely to cause financial loss ...'. How strong must a probability be to become a likelihood and how is the auditor to read the future?

The reader is referred to counsel's opinion by S J Naudé given to the Board on 2 December 1981 (and circularized to registered members), and which is reproduced as an appendix to this book. See also chapter 19, where these and other matters are discussed at some length.

The following points arising from section 20(5) bear stressing:

- The only person obliged to report is the auditor – not, for example, a professional accountant employed only to prepare financial statements from given data.
- The auditor must have reason to believe that a material irregularity has taken or is taking place – not necessarily discovered while conducting the audit; the wording appears to cover events which may have happened far in the past, even before the present auditor was appointed.
- The material irregularity must have caused loss or be likely to do so. If no loss has arisen or is likely to arise, the auditor has no duty under the section.

A particular matter which has been the cause of some perplexity to auditors is the circumstance of clients trading when factually, rather than commercially, insolvent.

The mere fact that the client continues to trade when liabilities exceed assets, fairly valued, is not considered to be in itself a material irregularity, but it creates a situation which is susceptible to reckless, or even fraudulent, behaviour, both of which are without doubt material irregularities.

---

[16] PAA Act, section 20(5).

The reader is referred to *Audit and Accounting Guide: Trading whilst Factually Insolvent*, issued by the Institute, in which the matter is discussed at some length.

3.3.5 To detect and report fraud and error

SAAS 240, 'Fraud and Error', establishes standards and provides guidance on the auditor's responsibility to consider the risk of fraud and error in an audit of financial statements.

3.3.5.1 The nature of fraud and error

The statement defines fraud as 'an intentional act by one or more individuals among management, those charged with governance, employees, or third parties, involving the use of deception to obtain an unjust or illegal advantage. Examples are:

- manipulation, falsification or alteration of records or documents;
- misappropriation of assets;
- suppression or omission of the effects of transactions from records or documents;
- recording of transactions without substance; and
- misapplication of accounting policies.

The auditor is concerned with fraudulent acts that cause material misstatement in the financial statements.

Errors, on the other hand, are unintentional mistakes in financial statements. Examples of such errors are:

- mathematical or clerical mistakes in the underlying records and accounting data;
- oversight or misinterpretation of facts;
- omission of the effects of transactions from records; and
- misapplication of accounting policies.

Errors are thus distinguished from fraud by the absence of intent to misstate financial information. Intent, however, may be difficult to determine, particularly in areas involving accounting estimates. For example, the understatement or overstatement of a provision for doubtful debts may result from unintentional bias or an intentional attempt to misstate financial information.

Misstatements in financial statements relevant to the auditor's consideration of fraud either flow from misstatements resulting from fraudulent financial reporting, or from misappropriation of assets. The former, usually perpetrated by management, are typically referred to as 'management fraud' and the latter, usually perpetrated by employees, as employee fraud. This is not to say that management may not be responsible for the misappropriation or misuse of an entity's assets.

3.3.5.2 The differing responsibilities of the auditor and those charged with governance and management

As directors of a company are regarded in law as acting in a fiduciary capacity in relation to the property under their control, it is they who ultimately are responsible for the prevention and detection of fraud and errors. This responsibility may be fulfilled by those charged with governance and management in a combination of different ways, such as by:

- setting the proper tone by creating and maintaining a culture of honesty and high ethics;
- identifying risks faced and appropriately managing them by establishing an effective control environment;
- instituting and operating appropriate accounting and internal control systems, including authorization and monitoring controls, segregation of duties and physical controls over assets; and
- in larger companies, establishing an internal audit function and appointing an audit committee.

The auditor's responsibility is to plan and perform audit work and evaluate audit findings in such a way that there is a reasonable expectation of *detecting* material misstatements that result from fraud and error, and that distort fair presentation of financial statements. The auditor has no responsibility to *prevent* fraud or error.

As an audit is subject to the inherent limitations of reliance on the effectiveness of internal control and the use of selective testing, it provides reasonable, but not absolute, assurance that material misstatements will be detected. Further, fraud usually involves attempts to conceal material misstatement, such as collusion, forgery, deliberate failure to record transactions, or intentional misrepresentations made to the auditor. As a result, a properly executed audit may not necessarily detect material misstatements arising from fraud or error. The subsequent discovery, therefore, of material misstatements in the financial statements may not in itself be proof that there has been inadequate planning, performance or inappropriate judgement by the auditor.

3.3.5.3 How the auditor should go about discharging responsibilities

An audit, in accordance with South African Auditing Standards, should be planned and performed with an attitude of professional scepticism, recognizing that conditions or events may be found that indicate that fraud or error may exist that cause financial statements to be materially misstated. To this end, the auditor assumes neither that management is dishonest, nor that it is unquestionably honest. Rather, the auditor recognizes that evidence gathered needs to be objectively evaluated to determine whether or not the financial statements appear to be free of material misstatement. At the planning stage, when determining the audit approach, the auditor should assess the risk that fraud or error may cause the financial statements to contain material misstatement. This fraud and error risk assessment should begin by members of the audit team discussing factors that could contribute to the susceptibility of material misstatements in the financial statements. This allows all persons involved in the audit to better understand the potential for misstatement, particularly in the specific area of work assigned to them, and how audit findings in one area may impact on other areas of the audit.

A fraud risk assessment done at the planning stage of the audit should involve making enquiries of those charged with governance and management. In this regard, SAAS 240 paragraph .22 reads as follows:

'When planning the audit, the auditor should make inquiries of management:

- to obtain an understanding of:
  - management's assessment of the risk that the financial statements may be materially misstated as a result of fraud; and
  - the accounting and internal control systems management has put in place to address such risk.

- to obtain knowledge of management's understanding regarding the accounting and internal control systems in place to prevent and detect error;

- to determine whether management is aware of any known fraud that has affected the entity or suspected fraud that the entity is investigating; and

- to determine whether management has discovered any material errors.'

The more important aspects that might be discussed with management include:

- Management's assessment of fraud risk factors faced and how these are being managed.
- Risks of errors occurring within the business processes that could result in material misstatements in the various classes of transactions and account balances.
- The internal audit activity and in particular any serious weaknesses in the control systems, as well as any frauds identified by internal audit.
- How management communicates to employees its view on responsible business practices and ethical behaviour.

The nature, extent and frequency of management's risk assessment, and how these risks are managed by the control systems in place, influence the auditor's judgement of which classes of transactions and account balances are susceptible to material misstatement caused by fraud, perpetrated by employees, or errors.

Discussions with those charged with governance (the directors) may provide useful information to the auditor concerning the risk of material misstatement in financial statements resulting from errors and management fraud. Aspects that might be discussed include:

- Concerns regarding management's assessments of risks faced and implementation of control systems to prevent or detect fraud or error.
- Management's failure to rectify the reported material weaknesses in internal controls.
- The auditor's evaluation of the control environment, particularly regarding the competence, commitment and integrity of management.
- How management's risk management policies and procedures affect the auditor's approach and scope of the audit, including additional audit work deemed necessary where such policies and procedures appear to the auditor to be inadequate.

Appendix 1 to SAAS sets out examples of risk factors that could contribute to misstatements in financial statements as a consequence of fraud. The factors are grouped under two headings, namely:

- Fraud risk factors relating to misstatements resulting from fraudulent financial reporting; and
- Fraud risk factors relating to the misappropriation of assets.

The fraud risk factors that relate to fraudulent financial reporting are split into three categories, as follows:

- Management's characteristics and influence over the control environment.
- Industry conditions.
- Operating characteristics and financial stability.

The more important factors listed under these headings are set out below:

Fraud risk factors relating to misstatements resulting from fraudulent financial reporting

Fraud risk factors relating to management's characteristics and influence over the control environment

- There is motivation for management to engage in fraudulent financial reporting. Specific indicators might include the following:
  - A significant portion of management's compensation is represented by bonuses, share options or other incentives, the value of which is contingent upon the entity achieving unduly aggressive targets for operating results, financial position or cash flow.
  - There is excessive interest by management in maintaining or increasing the entity's share price.
  - Management has an interest in pursuing inappropriate means to minimize reported earnings for tax-motivated reasons.
- There is a failure by management to display and communicate an appropriate attitude regarding internal control and the financial reporting process.

- Non-financial management participates excessively in, or is preoccupied with, the selection of accounting practices or the determination of significant estimates.
- There is a high turnover of management, counsel or board members.
- There is a strained relationship between management and the current or predecessor auditor.
- There is a history of securities law violations, or claims against the entity or its management alleging fraud or violations of securities laws.
- The corporate governance structure is weak or ineffective.

Fraud risk factors relating to industry conditions

- New accounting, statutory or regulatory requirements that could impair the financial stability or profitability of the entity.
- A high degree of competition or market saturation, accompanied by declining margins.
- A declining industry with increasing business failures and significant declines in customer demand.
- Rapid changes in the industry, such as high vulnerability to rapidly changing technology or rapid product obsolescence.

Fraud risk factors relating to operating characteristics and financial stability

- Inability to generate cash flows from operations while reporting earnings and earnings growth.
- Significant pressure to obtain additional capital necessary to stay competitive, considering the financial position of the entity.
- Assets, liabilities, revenues or expenses based on significant estimates that involve unusually subjective judgments or uncertainties, or that are subject to potential significant change in the near term in a manner that may have a financially disruptive effect on the entity.
- Significant related party transactions, which are not in the ordinary course of business.
- Significant, unusual or highly complex transactions (especially those close to the year-end) that pose difficult questions concerning substance over form.
- An overly complex organizational structure involving numerous or unusual legal entities, managerial lines of authority or contractual arrangements without apparent business purpose.
- Unusually high dependence on debt, a marginal ability to meet debt repayment requirements, or debt covenants that are difficult to maintain.
- Unrealistically aggressive sales or profitability incentive programmes.
- A threat of imminent bankruptcy, foresclosure or hostile takeover.
- A poor or deteriorating financial position when management has personally guaranteed significant debts of the entity.

Fraud risk factors relating to misstatements resulting from misappropriation of assets

Fraud risk factors that relate to misstatements resulting from misappropriation of assets are grouped in the following two categories:

- Susceptibility of assets to misappropriation.
- Controls.

Fraud risk factors relating to susceptibility of assets to misappropriation

These fraud risk factors pertain to the nature of an entity's assets and the degree to which they are subjected to theft.

- Large amounts of cash on hand or processed.
- Inventory characteristics, such as small size combined with high value and high demand.
- Easily convertible assets, such as bearer bonds, diamonds or computer chips.
- Fixed asset characteristics, such as small size combined with marketability and lack of ownership identification.

Fraud risk factors relating to controls

- These fraud risk factors involve the lack of controls designed to prevent or detect misappropriation of assets.
- Lack of appropriate management oversight (for example, inadequate supervision or inadequate monitoring of remote locations).
- Lack of procedures to screen job applicants for positions where employees have access to assets susceptible to misappropriation.
- Inadequate record keeping for assets susceptible to misappropriation.
- Lack of an appropriate segregation of duties or independent checks.
- Lack of an appropriate system of authorization and approval of transactions (for example, in purchasing).
- Poor physical safeguards over cash, investments, inventory or fixed assets.
- Lack of timely and appropriate documentation for transactions (for example, credits for merchandise returns).
- Lack of mandatory vacations for employees performing key control functions.

Appendix III to SAAS 240 identifies circumstances that indicate the possibilities of fraud or error. Some of the more important of these are set out below:

- Identification of important matters not previously disclosed by management.
- Significant difficult-to-audit figures in the accounts.
- Conflicting or unsatisfactory evidence provided by management or employees.

- Unusual documentary evidence, such as handwritten alterations to documentation, or handwritten documentation which is ordinarily electronically printed.
- Information provided unwillingly or after unreasonable delay.
- Seriously incomplete or inadequate accounting records.
- Unusual transactions, by virtue of their nature, volume or complexity, particularly if such transactions occurred close to the year-end.
- Transactions not recorded in accordance with management's general or specific authorization.
- Significant unreconciled differences between control accounts and subsidiary records or between physical count and the related account balance which were not appropriately investigated and corrected on a timely basis.
- Significant differences from expectations disclosed by analytical procedures.
- Fewer confirmation responses than expected, or significant differences revealed by confirmation responses.
- Evidence of an unduly lavish lifestyle of officers or employees.
- Long outstanding account receivable balances.

The auditor's preliminary assessment of risk of material misstatement should influence the audit approach in such a way that the planned audit procedures will provide reasonable assurance that material misstatements arising from fraud and error will be detected, if indeed they have occurred.

As the auditor may only become aware of the existence of fraud if informed of it by a client, the auditor should make enquiries of management concerning any fraud or significant error that has been discovered and their response thereto.

The application of audit procedures may bring to light facts or information that should cause the auditor to suspect that material misstatement exists. Some examples are:

- Inquiries from management.
- Analytical review procedures disclose significant differences from expectation. For example, an achieved gross profit percentage which is not in line with known facts might indicate theft of stock or under-recording of sales.
- Significant unreconciled differences between reconciliations of a control account and subsidiary records are not appropriately investigated and corrected on a timely basis.
- Requests for confirmation of balances from third parties disclose significant differences.
- Transactions selected for testing are not supported by appropriate evidence.
- Audit tests detect errors that were apparently known to the client, but were not voluntarily disclosed to the auditor.

- Managers and/or employees have lifestyles beyond their apparent means.

When such conditions or circumstances exist, the planned scope of audit procedures should be reconsidered and other audit evidence gathered to refute or confirm the suspicion of material misstatement.

SAAS 240, at paragraph .49, recommends that the auditor document fraud risk factors identified and his or her responses thereto. Auditors should thus record, in the audit working papers, the following:

- risks identified that could lead to material misstatement in financial statements;
- their assessment of controls implemented by the entity to mitigate these; and
- depending on risks identified and how these are managed, audit procedures planned, and performed, to detect material misstatements in financial statements.

Management representations are an important component of evidence gathered by auditors in drawing conclusions on the fair presentation of financial statements. Paragraph .51 thus states that the auditor should obtain written representation from management that:

- 'it acknowledges its responsibility for the implementation and operation of accounting and internal control systems that are designed to prevent and detect fraud and error;

- it believes the effects of those uncorrected financial statement misstatements aggregated by the auditor during the audit are immaterial, both individually and in the aggregate, to the financial statements taken as a whole. A summary of such items should be included in or attached to the written representation;

- it has disclosed to the auditor all significant facts relating to any frauds or suspected frauds known to management that may have affected the entity; and

- it has disclosed to the auditor the results of its assessment of the risk that the financial statements may be materially misstated as a result of fraud'.

The detection of fraud and error by the auditor might have implications for other aspects of the audit. For example, the auditor might need to reconsider the inherent risk assessment, as well as the control risk assessment, if non-prevention or detection of fraud was as a result of management overriding the internal control system. Similarly, the auditor's detection of errors in accounting information processed by a system where the auditor had assessed control risk as medium to low, would necessitate a reassessment of such risk. A further consideration relates to the reliability of management representations. This would certainly be brought into question in circumstances where management is involved in fraud.

3.3.5.4 **Reporting of fraud or error**

The auditor should report to management, preferably in writing, any detected instances of fraud, notwithstanding that its potential effect on the financial statements is immaterial. All frauds and significant errors known to exist should be reported. Where the auditor suspects fraud, this suspicion too should be reported. The auditor would ordinarily report such frauds to a level in the organizational structure of the entity above that responsible for the persons believed to be implicated. For example, should fraud have been perpetrated at a clerical level in the accounting department of an entity, a report to the chief accountant might suffice. However, should the chief accountant be implicated, a report to the financial director would be appropriate.

Should the auditor report detected or suspected fraud and significant error to management and the report is then disregarded by management, the auditor should report the matter to those charged with corporate governance, namely, the audit committee and the board of directors.

Where the auditor has reported misstatements to management and it decides not to make adjustments to the financial statements, based on their judgement that such misstatements are immaterial, the auditor should inform those charged with corporate governance of the aggregated uncorrected misstatements.

If the auditor suspects that members of the board of directors are involved in a fraud, the matter should be reported to the entity's audit committee, if one exists. In the absence of an audit committee, the auditor may need to seek legal advice on the steps that should be taken if:

- senior members of management, including members of the board of directors, are involved in fraud, or the condoning of fraud; and
- the report to the board is being disregarded, or the auditor suspects that it will not be acted upon; or is unsure to whom the report should be made.

If the auditor concludes that known fraud or error has a material effect on the financial statements and has not been properly reflected or corrected in the financial statements, the audit report would need to be modified by the auditor in order to express a qualified or adverse opinion.

In some circumstances the auditor might suspect fraud or error, but is precluded by the entity – usually the board of directors and its management – from obtaining sufficient evidence to evaluate whether or not fraud or error that may be material to the financial statements, has or is likely to have occurred. In such a case, the auditor should express a qualified opinion or a disclaimer of opinion on the financial statements. This is on the basis of the limitation on the scope of the audit.

The reader is referred to chapter 18 for an in-depth discussion on the form of audit reports appropriate to particular circumstances.

Fraud or errors should not be reported to third parties unless the auditor has a duty imposed by the courts or by statute. Such disclosure is precluded by the auditor's ethical and legal duty of confidentiality. In the case of fraud, the auditor would need to consider reporting a material irregularity reporting to comply with the requirements of section 20(5) of the Public Accountants' and Auditors' Act 80 of 1991.

3.3.5.5 Withdrawing from engagement

Where, during the course of the audit, the auditor has detected or suspects fraud, the auditor may need to consider withdrawing from the audit engagement. This decision is only likely where the auditor knows or suspects that senior management and directors are implicated, or no remedial action was taken concerning the fraud reported, or the auditor has significant concerns regarding the competence or integrity of management or those charged with corporate governance. Should the fraud detected be a material irregularity as defined (see section 3.3.4 of this chapter), the auditor would need to report such material irregularity before withdrawing from the audit engagement. Section 280 of the Companies Act requires an auditor, on resigning, to notify the Registrar of Companies in writing that the auditor is unaware of any material irregularity other than those already reported.

SAAS 240, at paragraph .70, which is headed 'Auditor unable to complete the engagement', sets out the position as follows:

> 'If the auditor concludes that it is not possible to continue performing the audit as a result of a misstatement resulting from fraud or suspected fraud, the auditor should:
>
> - consider the professional and legal responsibilities applicable in the circumstances, including whether there is a requirement for the auditor to report to the person or persons who made the audit appointment or, in some cases, to regulatory authorities,
>
> - consider the possibility of withdrawing from the engagement; and
>
> - if the auditor withdraws:
>   - discuss with the appropriate level of management and those charged with governance the auditor's withdrawal from the engagement and the reasons for the withdrawal; and
>   - consider whether there is a professional or legal requirement to report to the person or persons who made the audit appointment or, in some cases, to regulatory authorities, the auditor's withdrawal from the engagement and the reasons for the withdrawal.'

3.3.6 To detect contraventions of laws and regulations

SAAS 250, 'Consideration of Laws and Regulations in an Audit of Financial Statements', establishes standards and provides guidance on the auditor's responsibility to consider laws and regulations in an audit of financial statements.

The structure and basic principles regarding management's responsibilities and that of the auditor, as set out in the statement, are very similar to that of SAAS 240, 'Fraud and Error', which was discussed earlier in the chapter. The similarities are briefly set out below in point form, followed by guidance specific to the consideration of laws and regulations.

- It is the responsibility of management to ensure that an entity's operations are conducted in accordance with all laws and regulations applicable to it.

- The auditor should obtain sufficient audit evidence regarding compliance with those laws and regulations recognized to have an effect on the determination of material amounts and disclosures in financial statements. Stated differently, the auditor has a responsibility to perform procedures that should detect non-compliance by the entity with those laws and regulations where non-compliance would materially affect its financial statements.

- The auditor should plan and perform the audit with an attitude of professional scepticism, recognizing that the audit may reveal conditions or events that would necessitate questioning whether an entity is complying with laws and regulations.

- The auditor should obtain representations from management that it has disclosed all known actual or possible non-compliance with laws and regulations, and consider the effects of non-compliance when preparing financial statements.

- When the auditor becomes aware of a possible instance of non-compliance, the auditor should obtain information to evaluate the possible effect on financial statements.

- Possible instances of non-compliance should be reported to and discussed with management.

- If, in the auditor's judgement, detected instances of non-compliance are intentional and material, these should be reported without delay.

- If the auditor suspects that members of senior management, including members of the board of directors, are involved in non-compliance, the auditor should report the matter to the audit committee, if one exists.

- If the auditor concludes that non-compliance has a material effect on the financial statements, which has not been properly reflected in the financial statements, the auditor should express a qualified or an adverse opinion in the audit report.

- If the auditor is precluded by the entity, usually its management, from obtaining sufficient evidence to evaluate whether non-compliance that may be material to the financial statements has or is likely to have occurred, the auditor should express a qualified opinion or a disclaimer of opinion.

- If the auditor is unable to determine whether non-compliance has occurred, because of uncertainty imposed by the circumstances rather than the entity, the auditor should modify the audit report by setting out the circumstances in an emphasis of matter paragraph in the audit report.

Guidance specific to consideration of laws and regulations, as set out in SAAS 250, may be categorized into matters relevant to management and those relevant to auditors.

As already stated, the responsibility to prevent and detect non-compliance with laws and regulations relevant to an entity lies with its management. The statement identifies certain policies and procedures which may assist management in meeting its responsibilities. These are as follows:

- Identifying and monitoring legal requirements and ensuring that operating procedures are designed to meet these requirements.
- Instituting and operating appropriate systems of internal control.
- Developing, publicizing and following a Code of Conduct.
- Ensuring employees are properly trained in and understand the Code of Conduct.
- Monitoring compliance with the Code of Conduct and acting appropriately to discipline employees who fail to comply.
- Engaging legal advisers to assist in identifying and monitoring legal requirements.
- Maintaining a register of significant laws with which the entity has to comply within its particular industry and a record of complaints of non-compliance.

In larger entities, these policies and procedures may be supplemented by assigning appropriate responsibilities to:

- an internal audit function; and/or
- an audit committee.

As far as the auditor's responsibilities are concerned, there is no duty to prevent contravention of laws or regulations, and there is a qualified responsibility to detect such contraventions. The reasons are as follows:

- Entities may be affected by many laws and regulations that apply more to their operations than to the accounting and financial aspects of their business, for example, environmental and health and safety regulations. The auditor cannot be expected to examine an entity's compliance with laws and regulations in every aspect of its operations. The auditor usually takes into account only those laws and regulations that are generally recognized as having an impact on the form and content of financial statements. Accordingly, the further removed a contravention of law or regulation is from evidence and transactions ordinarily reflected in financial statements, the less chance the auditor will have of detecting the irregularity.

- The auditor's knowledge of an entity and of the industry in which it operates may result in the auditor detecting non-compliance with laws and regulations. However, because the auditor is not a legal expert, instances of non-compliance may go undetected.

The auditor does have a duty to perform procedures that should identify instances of non-compliance with those laws and regulations where non-compliance would have a material impact on financial statements. To this end, the auditor should obtain a general understanding of the laws and regulations applicable to the entity and its industry. In particular, the auditor should recognize that non-compliance with certain laws or regulations may have dire consequences for the entity. For example, non-compliance with a franchise or licensing agreement may force the entity to cease its operations.

Apart from using existing knowledge of the entity and the industry in which it operates, the auditor, in obtaining or updating a general understanding of laws and regulations applicable to the entity, should:

- enquire of management as to the laws and regulations that may be expected to have a fundamental effect on its operations;
- enquire of management regarding the entity's procedures to ensure compliance with laws and regulations, as well as procedures adopted for identifying, evaluating and accounting for litigation claims and fines or other penalties.

To identify instances of non-compliance with those laws and regulations where non-compliance would have material effect on financial statements, the auditor should – when performing normal procedures aimed at gathering sufficient audit evidence for the purposes of reporting on financial statements – be alert to the fact that such procedures might indicate incidences of non-compliance. Such procedures include reading the minutes of directors' meetings, performing tests on transactions and balances, and directing enquiries to management and legal representatives. Other procedures aimed directly at identifying instances of non-compliance are: specific enquiries of management and the entity's legal representatives of any knowledge on their part of material contraventions, as well as inspection of any correspondence with relevant licensing or regulatory authorities.

Other responsibilities, which are not directly related to the audit, are discussed below.

3.3.7 To register with the PAAB all training contracts and to provide trainees with adequate training

3.3.7.1 Training contracts

A firm wishing to engage trainees is required to make application to the PAAB to become accredited as a training office. An individual within the firm is designated as the training officer and is responsible for monitoring and recording the core training and practical experience exposure of trainees. Such core training and experience is required to cover at least 360 hours in the case of a three-year training contract.

The Act requires the PAAB to register every training contract, which it will do only when it is satisfied that the firm engaging the trainee is accredited as a training office, and on production of evidence that the trainee has the necessary educational qualifications as laid down by the Board.

The contract period is five years or such lesser period as the Board prescribes for trainees holding a recognized university degree, currently three years. The reduction in length of contract and the recognized degrees are set out in the Board's regulations on training contracts.

The Board prescribes the maximum number of trainees a firm may engage at any one time.

Provision is made for the Board to record the satisfactory completion of training contracts, for their cancellation on the grounds of the trainee's misconduct and, with the Board's consent, for the transfer of a trainee to another training office.

3.3.7.2 Proper training of trainee accountants

As described above, the Board requires to be satisfied that the professional practice of the firm applying to register a training contract is such as can provide satisfactory training and experience. But whether satisfactory training is, in fact, provided is another matter. The Board's regulations provide for the termination of the training contract (and the trainee's transfer to another training office) on evidence submitted that proper training is lacking. What the Board has done is to emphasize, in its notes to the regulations, the contractual duty to train the trainees.

The South African Institute of Chartered Accountants' SAAS 220, 'Quality Control', in an appendix to the statement, sets out some of the matters that are relevant to training by giving guidance to practising members in three main areas:

- supervision and review of work done by assistants;
- all forms of training in addition to formal university education, while under training contract, by way of formal lectures, sessions or any other means; and
- on-the-job training, which covers professional training given while the staff member is engaged on particular assignments.

The reader is referred to section 3.5 of this chapter for further discussion on the matter.

3.3.8 Conduct which is befitting a member of the profession

Although one might be forgiven for taking this for granted, the Public Accountants' and Auditors' Board goes to great lengths to insist upon fitting conduct. It deals with the matter from a negative point of view, that is, in its disciplinary rules it describes behaviour constituting improper conduct and provides penalties for such behaviour.

The reader is referred to paragraph 2.1 of the Disciplinary Rules for the lengthy list of acts constituting improper conduct. All of these, with the exception of the last item, describe specific acts.

The last item (item 2.1.21) is very general. Its wording is repeated below and should be taken to heart:

> '[An auditor shall be guilty of improper conduct if he (sic)]:
>
> 2.1.21 conducts himself in a manner which is improper or discreditable or unprofessional or dishonourable or unworthy on the part of a practitioner or which tends to bring the profession of accounting into disrepute.'

3.4 AUDIT STANDARDS AND STANDARD SETTING

Having considered the auditor's responsibilities, the question arises as to how proper implementation of these responsibilities and duties can be judged.

3.4.1 The historical perspective

In South Africa, prior to 1964, it was left very much to the individual auditor to decide how to interpret professional responsibilities. As a result, the attitude of auditors to their duties ranged from the very strict to the casual.

The then National Council of Chartered Accountants in South Africa attempted to remedy the situation by issuing statements on auditing, commencing in April 1964 with the statement on auditing principles and standards (A1). These were by no means mandatory, as is shown by the following contained in the opening paragraph of A1:

> 'The object in issuing statements on the subject is to give some guidance to Chartered Accountants (SA) on what experience has suggested may be the minimum standard which the profession as a whole would wish to attain.'

This position obtained until 1976 when National Council (now the Institute) issued the first of a series of generally accepted auditing standard statements (GAASS) which were binding on the South African auditor. Paragraphs .08 and .09 of GAASS AU 001 read as follows:

> '.08 The auditor has a responsibility to comply with generally accepted auditing standards, and he is subject to discipline by the appropriate professional bodies.

'.09 Section 26 of the Public Accountants' and Auditors' Act (1951) [now section 20 of PAAA 1991] deals with the powers and duties of auditors, and gives the Public Accountants' and Auditors' Board the right to inquire into the conduct of a registered accountant and auditor in the performance of his duties.'

When setting standards, the South African Institute of Chartered Accountants, as a member of the International Federation of Accountants (see chapter 1.3), undertook to follow so far as was practicable, the guidelines of the International Auditing Practices Committee (IAPC). Paragraph 5 of the Preface to *International Auditing Guidelines* (issued July 1979) reads as follows:

'The Authority Attaching to the Guidelines

International Auditing Guidelines issued by IAPC do not override the local regulations referred to in paragraph 3 above governing the audit of financial information in a particular country. To the extent that the International Auditing Guidelines conform with local regulations on a particular subject, the audit of financial information in that country in accordance with local regulations will automatically comply with the International Auditing Guideline in respect of that subject. In the event of local regulations differing from, or being in conflict with, International Auditing Guidelines on a particular subject, member bodies, in accordance with the Constitution of IFAC, should work towards the implementation of the Guideline issued by IAPC, when and to the extent practicable.'

During 1993, Council of The South African Institute of Chartered Accountants decided that South African Auditing Standards should be more closely based on the International Auditing Standards issued by the International Federation of Accountants. This decision was motivated by the following:

- the anticipated international investment in South Africa as a result of the change in political dispensation, with the African National Congress replacing the National Party in government, and the consequent lifting of international economic sanctions against the country; and
- the endorsement of the international auditing standards by the International Organization of Securities Commissions representing 60 countries.

The so-called Harmonization and Improvements Project was undertaken to implement the decision. Its stated aims were threefold, namely:

- the revision of the South African Standards in order to align them in all material respects with International Auditing Standards;
- to effect improvements considered appropriate; and
- to improve the use of such standards by the accountancy profession.

The following guiding principles were applied throughout the project:

- The revised statements of generally accepted auditing standards are referred to as South African Auditing Standards (SAAS).
- Basic principles and essential procedures contained in these statements are identified in bold type.

- To prevent retrospective application of the statements, they contain the effective date from which they are to be implemented. In addition, reference is made in each new statement to the existing statement or statements it replaces.
- To the extent that South African standards differ from international standards, an explanatory paragraph explains these differences.
- A public sector perspective is incorporated into the statements where appropriate.

The usual procedure leading to approval of the new statements was followed, that is to say, the proposed statements were issued as exposure drafts for comment by interested parties before final approval.

3.4.2 The current position

From the beginning of 2002, the responsibility for the setting of auditing standards passed from the South African Institute of Chartered Accountants to the Public Accountants' and Auditors' Board (PAAB). In terms of section 10(1) of the Public Accountants' and Auditors' Act, Act 80 of 1991, the PAAB established an Auditing Standards Board which has the authority to approve pronouncements. These are either statements of South African Auditing Standards (SAAS) or South African Auditing Practice Statements (SAAPS).

The working procedure remains much as before. In order to ensure consistency between South African and International Standards and Practice Statements, as far as this is possible, the following procedures are followed:

- When the International Auditing and Assurance Standards Board (IAASB) issues exposure drafts, these are issued in South Africa with a comment date earlier than the international exposure draft comment date.

- Comments received are collated and a summary is submitted to IAASB.

- Once the international pronouncements are approved, they are considered by the PAAB's Auditing Standards Committee. Whilst being committed to adopting international pronouncements, the committee may include in the South African exposure draft more prescriptive requirements or additional guidance pertinent to local legislation and circumstances.

- After considering comment on the South African exposure draft, and making any changes that might be thought necessary, the local Audit Standards Committee submits to the Audit Standards Board for their approval the proposed South African pronouncement. Any differences between the International and South African pronouncement are explained in the pronouncement.

At the time of writing, 35 statements of Generally Accepted Auditing Standards, referred to as South African Auditing Standards (SAAS) have been issued. A list of these is given in appendix 1. The subject matter of these is discussed in the relevant sections of this text.

With regard to the authority attaching to statements of South African Auditing Standards, SAAS 000, 'Preface to South African Auditing Standards and Related Services', has this to say:

> 'In the opinion of the PAAB's legal adviser a court of law, when considering the adequacy of the work of an auditor, is likely to seek confirmation that in the performance of the audit work, the auditor has complied in all material respects with the statements of SAAS. In the event of significant deviation from the guidance on specific matters contained in the statements of SAAS, the auditor may be required to demonstrate that such deviation did not result in failure to achieve generally accepted auditing standards.'[17]

Statements of South African Auditing Standards (as in the case of International Standards) set out basic principles and essential procedures in bold type. Explanatory and other material within these, set out in normal print, provide guidance for the interpretation and application of these principles and essential procedures. Auditors are accordingly cautioned to understand and apply the basic principles and essential procedures, including the explanatory and other material contained therein. As already mentioned, should an auditor not comply with the Standards, particularly those aspects set out in bold print type, the auditor may be called upon to justify such deviation and this possibly to a court of law or the disciplinary committees of the PAAB and SAICA.

In addition to statements of SAAS, the PAAB issues practice statements (SAAPS). These are intended to promote good practice and provide assistance to auditors in complying with SAAS. SAAPS do not have the authority of Statements of SAAS for they merely provide guidance on the attainment of standards, but again any deviation from such guidance might need to be justified by the auditor.

3.5 QUALITY CONTROL

It is essential that professional accounting and auditing firms establish quality control policies and procedures to ensure effective and quality audits, as well as other professional services, for all their clients.

SAAS 220, 'Quality Control for Audit Work', establishes standards and provides guidance on the quality control policies and procedures that should be implemented by an audit firm to ensure that all audits are conducted in accordance with South African Auditing Standards. It also provides guidance on quality control procedures regarding the work delegated to assistants on individual audits.

---

[17] SAAS 000, paragraph .14.

In the body of the statement, the objectives of quality control policies that should be adopted by an audit firm are set out as follows:

QUALITY CONTROL POLICIES AND PROCEDURES	
Professional requirements	Personnel in the firm are to adhere to the principles of independence, integrity, objectivity, confidentiality and professional behaviour.
Skills and competence	The firm is to be staffed by personnel who have attained and maintained the technical standards and professional competence required to enable them to fulfil their responsibilities with due care.
Assignment	Audit work is to be assigned to personnel who have the degree of technical training and proficiency required in the circumstances.
Delegation	There is to be sufficient direction, supervision and review of work at all levels to provide reasonable assurance that the work performed meets appropriate standards of quality.
Consultation	Whenever necessary, consultation within or outside the firm is to occur with those who have appropriate expertise.
Acceptance and retention of clients	An evaluation of prospective clients and ongoing review of existing clients is to be conducted. In making a decision to accept or retain a client, the firm's independence and ability to serve the client properly, and the integrity of the client's management are to be considered.
Monitoring	The continued adequacy and operational effectiveness of quality control policies and procedures is to be monitored.

Table 3.2 Quality control policies and procedures

An appendix to the statement sets out a comprehensive listing of illustrative examples of quality control procedures. These are set out under the quality control objectives as headings. This should prove to be useful, particular in view of the South African auditing profession's mandatory practice review programme. This aspect is covered in the next section.

A summary of the contents of the appendix to SAAS 220 follows.

EXAMPLES OF QUALITY CONTROL PROCEDURES (APPENDIX TO SAAS 220)	
Professional requirements	Assign an individual or group to provide guidance and to resolve questions on matters of integrity, objectivity, independence and confidentiality: • Document individual issues raised and their resolution. Communicate policies and procedures regarding independence, integrity, objectivity, confidentiality and professional behaviour to personnel: • Provide personnel with an entire listing of the firm's clients (and associates) and notify them of changes. Monitor compliance with policies and procedures relating to independence, integrity, objectivity, confidentiality and professional behaviour: • Obtain, at least annually, written representation from personnel covering their familiarity with the firm's policies and procedures and containing a statement that no prohibited investments were or are held and no prohibited relationships exist.
Skills and competence	Maintain a human resources programme designed to obtain suitable personnel: • Assign an individual or group to take responsibility for the human resources programme. • Plan for the firm's personnel needs at all levels and establish hiring objectives based on current clientele and anticipated growth, personnel turnover and promotion within the firm. • Monitor the effectiveness of the human resources programme. Establish hiring policies by setting qualifications and guidelines for evaluating potential personnel at each professional level: • Identify desirable personal attributes, and required qualification and experience. • Establish procedures for obtaining background information about potential employees. Obtain written documentation, such as copies of diplomas or degrees, curriculum vitae and previous employer references and conduct interviews.
Professional development	Establish guidelines and requirements for a continuing professional education and development programme: • Assign responsibility for the development programme to an individual or group. • Specific courses (programmes) should be acquired or developed and reviewed by suitable individuals. • Courses should be evaluated by attendees and valid responses acted upon. • Course instructors should be adequately trained. • An orientation programme for new employees, giving insight into the firm's particular audit philosophy, audit approach and working paper standards and format, is of particular importance. • Other courses (programmes) should be developed and be appropriate to different responsibility levels within the firm, or continuing professional education programmes presented by persons outside the firm should be utilized. Records should be maintained of attendance at such programmes. • Provide, particularly, for the knowledge levels of designated specialists within the firm to remain abreast of developments.

	• This may be achieved through a firm's own courses, attendance at external education programmes and conferences, membership and participation in particular interest group activities, and the distribution of technical literature.
	Distribute to personnel or make available (by way of an in-house library) information about technical and professional developments.
Advancement	Establish qualifications necessary for the various levels of responsibility within the firm:
	• Guidelines should be prepared describing responsibilities, qualifications and expected performance at each level. These should be communicated to personnel.
	• Criteria should be established for evaluating individual performance. Such criteria may include technical knowledge, analytical and judgemental abilities, communication and leadership skills, and professional bearing.
	Evaluate performance and advise personnel of their progress:
	• Assign evaluation responsibilities and the timing of these.
	• Document evaluations, for which a standard form may be useful.
	• Evaluation documentation should be placed in personnel files.
	• Evaluators should review their evaluations of personnel with them.
	Counsel personnel as to their progress and career opportunities within the firm:
	• Review periodically with personnel the evaluation of their performance. This process should cover, apart from an evaluation of performance, the individual's career objectives, his or her assignment preferences and a projection of career opportunities within the firm.
	• Document the results of review and file these in personnel files.
	• The performance of individual partners should also be evaluated by a senior partner or peers to ensure that they are still able to fulfil their responsibilities.
	Assign responsibilities for making advancement and termination decisions:
	• Base advancement and termination of employment decisions on performance and counselling data collected, as well as the particular needs of the firm.
	• Monitor whether or not individuals meeting established criteria are indeed assigned increased degrees of responsibility.
Assignment	Establish (and document) the firm's approach to assigning personnel so as to achieve a balance between human resources requirements, effective individual personnel development, and effective utilization of available personnel resources:
	• Identify on a timely basis staffing requirements for all the firm's specific audits to establish the firm and office personnel needs.
	• Prepare time budgets for these to determine manpower requirements and to schedule audit work.
	Identify an appropriate person or persons to be responsible for assigning personnel to audits. The following should be considered when assigning personnel:
	• audit size and complexity;
	• special expertise required;
	• planned supervision and involvement by supervisory personnel;
	• personnel availability;

	• timing of the work to be performed;
	• continuity and periodic rotation of personnel; and
	• opportunities for on-the-job training.
	Provide for approval of the scheduling and staffing of audits:
	• Submit for approval the names and qualifications of personnel to be assigned to audits.
	• Consider the experience and training of assigned personnel in relation to the complexity of the audit, and the extent of supervision to be provided.
Delegation	Provide for adequate planning procedures to ensure appropriate direction is provided:
	• Assign the responsibility for planning to appropriate personnel.
	• Develop knowledge of the client or review prior-year working papers, and update information for changed circumstances.
	• Specify matters to be included in the overall audit plan and the audit programme, such as the following:
	– consider current economic conditions and their potential effect on the conduct of the audit;
	– develop proposed audit work programme;
	– determine manpower requirements including the need of specialized knowledge; and
	– prepare estimates of time required to complete the audit.
	Provide procedures for maintaining the firm's standards of quality of work performed:
	• Provide adequate supervision at all levels, considering the training, ability and experience of personnel assigned.
	• Develop guidelines for the form and content of working papers.
	• Utilize standardized forms, check lists and questionnaires that might be appropriate.
	• Provide procedures for resolving differences of professional judgement among personnel.
	Provide on-the-job training during the performance of audits:
	• Involve personnel in as many portions of specific audits to which they are assigned.
	• Discuss with assistants the relationship of the work they are performing to the audit as a whole.
	• Encourage personnel to train and develop their subordinates.
	• Monitor assignments to determine that personnel gain experience in various areas of audits in various industry sectors, and work under different supervisory personnel.
Consultation	Specify areas or specialized situations requiring consultation. Examples include:
	• application of newly issued technical pronouncements;
	• industries with special accounting, auditing or reporting practices; and
	• complex subject matter, such as sophisticated computerized systems and taxation.
	Designate individuals as specialists and define their authority in consultative situations.
	Specify the extent of documentation to be provided of the results of consultation:

	• Assign responsibility for the preparation of documentation. • Maintain subject files containing the results of consultation for reference purposes. Maintain or provide access to adequate reference libraries: • Assign responsibility for maintaining a reference library. • Maintain technical manuals and issue technical pronouncements to personnel. • Maintain consultation arrangements with outsiders to supplement the firm's resources.
Acceptance and retention of clients	Establish procedures for evaluation of prospective clients and for their approval as clients. Such procedures should include the following: • Review available financial statements. • Make enquiries of predecessor auditors, covering their understanding as to the reasons for change in auditors, such as disagreements between them and management, and any information they possess that might have a bearing on the integrity of management. • Evaluate the firm's independence and ability to serve the prospective client, such as available expertise and personnel. • Determine that acceptance would not violate codes of professional conduct. • Provide for documentation of information and the acceptance decision. • Assign an individual or group at an appropriate management level to make acceptance or rejection decisions. Evaluate existing clients upon the occurrence of specified events to determine whether or not to continue the relationship. Events specified could include: • the expiration of a time period; • a change in one or more of the following: management, ownership, legal advisers, financial condition, litigation status, scope of engagement and nature of the client's business.
Monitoring	Determine the monitoring procedures necessary to provide reasonable assurance that the firm's quality control policies and procedures are operating effectively: • Prepare instructions and review programmes for use in monitoring activities. • Prepare guideline instructions to cover the extent of review and the criteria for selection of engagements for review, and the frequency and timing of such reviews. • Establish levels of competence for personnel to participate in monitoring activities and the method of their selection. Provide for the reporting of findings to appropriate management levels: • Discuss selected engagement findings with engagement management personnel. • Report general and selected engagement findings and recommendations to the firm's management, together with corrective action taken or planned. • Determine that planned corrective actions were taken.

Figure 3.3 Quality control procedures

3.6 PRACTICE REVIEW PROGRAMME

In 1993, members of the South African Institute of Chartered Accountants (SAICA) were advised in a newsletter that the Public Accountants' and Auditors' Board (PAAB) and SAICA had assessed the need for a programme of practice reviews and had agreed in principle to the implementation of an audit practice review programme in South Africa.

A further newsletter on the subject was issued by the same two bodies. It set out:

- the perceived need for such a review programme, including the international perspective;
- the proposed operation of the review programme; and
- the advantages which should flow from the introduction of the programme.

The practice review programme has been implemented and is the responsibility of the PAAB. Background to its creation and implementation follows.

3.6.1 The need for the Review Programme

Self-regulation is one of the cornerstones of a profession and is a privilege which is often taken for granted. However, there have recently been indications of a tendency for a greater degree of supervision and control to be exercised by government over self-regulatory bodies such as the auditing profession. In some overseas countries the right to self-regulate has already been lost. If the governing bodies of the auditing profession do not monitor and enforce the rules and standards they lay down, the profession incurs the risk of losing important privileges, including self-regulation.

The aim of self-regulation is to ensure that the accounting profession is seen to be monitoring and enforcing the high standards which it promulgates. To this end, a process is needed which will provide the profession with a means of identifying those practitioners who are ignorant of certain of their professional responsibilities and/or perform substandard work.

South Africa is not alone in facing the problem of substandard auditing work, yet South Africa is one of the few countries which has not yet undertaken some form of practice or peer review of its practising members.

The World Bank investigated the existence of practice review programmes in Africa and suggested that all professional accountancy bodies should implement such programmes as a matter of urgency, for without these foreign investment would be inhibited.

Further, the International Federation of Accountants (IFAC) recommended the establishment of quality review programmes in all member countries. A practice review programme is therefore needed if the South African profession is to conform with worldwide practice in this regard.

3.6.2 Operation of the Review Programme

The document proposed that the programme would operate as follows:

1. It would apply only to the attest function.

2. Every practitioner would be reviewed once every five years.

3. The reviews would be undertaken by a combination of full-time and part-time reviewers who would be experienced practising auditors.

4. The identification of practitioners and clients would be restricted to the reviewers only.

5. The programme would operate on a self-financing basis, with the costs of the review being recovered from the practitioner on a representative charge-out basis.

6. The results of reviews would be referred to an Audit Practice Review Committee of the Public Accountants' and Auditors' Board.

7. Practitioners whose work is judged to be unsatisfactory may be referred for follow-up review or for continuing professional education.

8. Where gross breaches of the standards are found, practitioners would be identified and referred to the investigation committee of the Public Accountants' and Auditors' Board.

3.6.3 Advantages of the Review Programme

The following six advantages were identified:

1. Standards are likely to be adhered to as a result of the presence of the programme, as it would serve to focus the attention of members on their duties.

2. It should identify and discipline where appropriate those practitioners who do not conform to the profession's standards.

3. The review programme should provide an important base for an educational and supportive system for those who need practical guidance and advice.

4. The programme should be the means of preserving self-regulation as a cornerstone of the profession and would enhance the reputation of the profession both locally and internationally.

5. It should lead to improved public acceptance and confidence in the work of the members of the profession.

6. Indications are that practitioners should be able to negotiate more favourable terms for professional indemnity insurance cover, particularly if compulsory insurance were introduced.

3.7 CONTINUING PROFESSIONAL EDUCATION

As mentioned earlier in this chapter, it is fundamental to the continued existence of a profession that its members maintain a high level of professional knowledge and skills. In the modern world the knowledge needed to function as a chartered accountant has expanded and changed at a rapid rate and this trend is likely to continue. Given these developments, it has become increasingly difficult, if not impossible, for members of the accounting profession to keep up-to-date in all the areas traditionally considered relevant to chartered accountants.

With this as background, Council of the South African Institute of Chartered Accountants approved a programme for Continuing Professional Education, which is designed to assist members in keeping abreast with developments and trends relevant to their specific needs. The details of the programme were set out in a circular issued by the Institute in 1992.

In contrast to Institutes elsewhere, which have introduced compulsory Continuing Education Programmes, the South African Institute adopted what it has referred to as an 'Awareness Self-Appraisal Programme'. This is a method whereby chartered accountants assess their own knowledge and skills in those areas that are relevant to them in carrying out their particular professional activities. In order to do this, the Awareness Self-Appraisal Programme requires that chartered accountants:

- identify those areas of professional knowledge that are relevant to the performance of their own particular professional activities;
- assess, as objectively as possible, their own level of awareness needed for each of the relevant areas;
- consider and assess for each topic whether or not their level of awareness is adequate; and
- if the awareness assessment is inadequate, decide upon what action needs to be taken to improve their awareness.

The circular suggested that awareness could be improved by taking one or more of the following actions:

- attending courses provided by the Institute;
- attending other courses;
- studying relevant documents;
- reading journal articles and other publications on the relevant topics;
- attending discussion group sessions provided by the regional associations of the South African Institute of Chartered Accountants; and
- seeking advice from colleagues.

The circular contained an appendix, designed to assist members in the evaluation of their own knowledge levels by listing in column 1 of the appraisal form a wide range of topics that are likely to be relevant to members whether they are in public practice or in commerce or industry. Space is provided to add additional topics, which would vary according to factors such as the nature of work carried out by the registered accountant and auditor and the industry in which his or her company or client is involved. The second column of the appraisal form is to be used for the assessment of the degree of relevance of each topic to the particular professional activities engaged in. Topics have to be rated as high, medium, low or not applicable. The next two columns allow for the assessment of the level of awareness and , if necessary, the action that will have to be taken to address inadequate awareness.

From time to time chartered accountants may be required to demonstrate that they have kept up to date. For example, special expertise may have to be demonstrated before a particular appointment is made or in the defence of a legal action or disciplinary hearing. For this reason, the Institute recommends that all members complete an awareness form, irrespective of their fields of activity, and that this should be done at least annually.

3.8 MANAGING PROFESSIONAL LIABILITIES

3.8.1 Introduction

There are many areas of a registered accountant's and auditor's (RAA's) work that expose the professional accountant to the risk of a claim for damages as a consequence of allegations of negligence in performing the work. The South African Institute of Chartered Accountants accordingly issued, early in 1996, a circular which identified the major areas in which actions for negligence may be brought against chartered accountants by clients or third parties and suggested steps that may properly be taken to reduce the risk of such claims. A further stated purpose of the circular was, partly, to advise members on ways of reducing misunderstandings about the extent of liability that chartered accountants assume in giving advice or expressing audit opinions. This is because claims sometimes arise not out of any inherent defect in the professional work performed but, rather, due to misunderstandings regarding the scope of or responsibilities for that work.

The circular dealt only with the potential liability for professional negligence that may be incurred because of an alleged act or default that results in financial loss to a person to whom a duty of care is owed. It did not deal with liability arising from criminal acts or breaches of statute. For the purposes of the circular, negligence was defined as some act or omission that occurs because a registered accountant and auditor had failed to exercise the degree of care and skill that is reasonably expected of an auditor in the circumstance of each case.

3.8.2 Defining the scope and responsibilities of the engagement

This section of the circular dealt with the following:

- identifying the terms of the engagement;
- defining the specific tasks to be undertaken;

- defining the responsibilities to be undertaken by the client; and
- specifying any limitations on the work to be undertaken.

3.8.2.1 Identifying the terms of engagement

A registered accountant and auditor should ensure that, at the time of accepting appointment, there is agreement on the terms of contract with the client. An engagement letter should be prepared, setting out in sufficient detail the terms of the engagement, including the actual services to be performed, the sources and nature of any information to be provided, and to whom any report should be addressed and supplied. These terms should be accepted by the client, by signing and returning a copy of the engagement letter, so as to minimize the risk of disputes regarding the duties assumed. If the client subsequently asks a member to carry out any additional duties, or in any other way varies the terms of the engagement, the changes should also be defined and agreed by the chartered accountant and the client, once again preferably in writing.

3.8.2.2 Defining the specific tasks to be undertaken

Besides reporting in terms of the Companies Act 1973 and other statutes, registered accountants and auditors are called upon to give opinions and advice in connection with many matters and to undertake a great variety of assignments. The letter of engagement should make clear the extent of the responsibilities the registered accountant and auditor will assume; make particular reference to any information supplied to the RAA and relied on, for which the client or others are responsible; set out in detail the specific tasks to be undertaken; and, where appropriate, exclude those tasks that are not to be undertaken.

Registered accountants and auditors should only accept engagements involving responsibilities they are confident can be met. Should the chartered accountant, during the course of the engagement, ascertain that the responsibilities originally undertaken cannot be met, often because of matters outside of the accountant's control, a variation in the terms of engagement should be obtained. Failure to do this might result in claims for breach of contract, since responsibilities originally agreed to will not be fulfilled. In any event, the report should state precisely which tasks have and which have not been undertaken. Registered accountants and auditors should also ensure that in any invoice sent to clients, the description of the work done is consistent both with the terms of the engagement letter (as well as any subsequent variation thereof) and the report.

3.8.2.3 Defining the responsibilities to be undertaken by the client

A registered accountant and auditor should make it clear in the engagement letter where responsibilities are to be undertaken by the client – for example, annual financial statements or a report or statement prepared by a chartered accountant for issue by the client in circumstances where the chartered accountant can reasonably expect the client to check it for completeness or accuracy before any use is made of it involving third parties. Financial statements prepared for the purpose of submission to Inland SA Revenue Services for the assessment of taxation frequently, although not invariably, fall within this category. Ensuring that clients are aware of their responsibilities should help to protect the registered accountant and auditor from any subsequent disputes. In such cases, the effective cause of any loss suffered by a third party may be reliance on a document which is the responsibility of the person in whose name it was issued, and who ought to have checked it. Therefore, if the registered accountant and auditor considers that some matter needs to be checked by the client, this should be made clear to the client.

3.8.2.4 Specifying any limitations on the work to be undertaken

It may be appropriate to alert the client to limitations or restrictions on the scope of the chartered accountant's work in response to risks unique to a particular engagement. The most common example is where the client requires an immediate answer to a complicated problem. In such circumstances, the registered accountant and auditor should consider whether or not it is appropriate to accept the engagement, and consider also the value to the client of the work that can feasibly be carried out. If the engagement is accepted, the registered accountant and auditor should make it clear in the engagement letter (or at the very least in the report) that the problem is a complex one, that limited time was available in which to study it, that further time is required in order to consider it in depth, and that the opinion or advice tendered might well be revised if further time were available. The engagement letter or report should also state clearly the client's responsibility for the accuracy and completeness of the information supplied to the accountant. In all cases, the client should be warned about the risk of acting on the advice tendered before the recommended further investigation is carried out.

Registered accountants and auditors are sometimes requested to report on profit forecasts. Because of the significant risk inherent in reporting on any prospective financial information, particular care should be exercised in determining whether or not, and if so, under what terms to accept such engagements. On acceptance of engagements, the clients must be made aware that they (the directors) are responsible for the assumptions underlying any profit forecast and that such financial projections are by their nature not susceptible to audit and accordingly no opinion can be expressed as to the possibility that such projections will be achieved.

Other examples of situations in which it may be appropriate to alert the client to limitations or restrictions are:

- an engagement to report based on the performance of agreed-upon procedures, particularly where the parties acknowledging responsibility (that the procedures are sufficient for the purposes), may not fully comprehend the limited nature of the work that they have requested;

- an engagement to report on financial information in which there are significant uncertainties likely to be resolved in the near future – in which case it would be appropriate for the registered accountant and auditor to point out that there is no responsibility to update a report for subsequent events; and

- an engagement to report on a presentation which was prepared to conform with the requirements of a contractual agreement or a regulatory provision, particularly where there are indications that third parties may have differing views – in which case it would be appropriate to state that no representations are being provided with regard to legal interpretation.

Properly worded statements, and warnings of the kind listed above, are not exclusions or restrictions of liability but definitions of the work undertaken and statements as to the extent to which the client can rely on the report. They will help to protect a registered accountant and auditor from a claim from a client or others for negligence based on the contention that the scope of the engagement should have been different or more extensive.

3.8.3 Defining responsibilities to third parties

The definitions of scope of work or any limitations on that work contained in an engagement letter will not be binding on any third party unless they have had proper access to, and have seen, the engagement letter or report in which the work is defined. Registered accountants and auditors should therefore ensure that they set out in their reports, possibly by including a copy of the particular engagement letter, precise details of the work that has been carried out, its purpose and, as far as possible, define the work that has not been carried out, together with any limitations on the work undertaken. If such matters are clearly set out in any report to which a third party may have access, registered accountants and auditors will be afforded some protection in relation both to the existence and scope of any duty of care owed to third parties who claim to have relied on the report. Where registered accountants and auditors are aware that specific third parties will have access to their report, they should also consider requesting the third party to sign a copy of the engagement letter to indicate acceptance of the terms. If this is not possible, registered accountants and auditors should make it clear that they make no representations to third parties as to the sufficiency of the procedures adopted.

A registered accountant and auditor may be able to restrict his or her liability to a client by clearly restricting the use to which a report may be put. The restriction should be included in the engagement letter and should identify the purpose for which the work has been requested. Appropriate wording and its efficacy will depend on the circumstances of each individual case. The following is an example only:

'This report/statement is intended solely for the information and use of the boards and managements of X Limited and Y Limited in connection with the proposed sale of Y Limited to X Limited and should not be used for any other purpose.'

Where financial material is prepared or reported on by a registered accountant and auditor for some particular purpose, liability to an unknown third party who relies on it for any other purpose than for which it was intended, is unsuitable. In such cases, the registered accountant and auditor would usually have no reason to suppose that such reliance would be placed upon it.

The implications of the duty of care to third parties are important for all chartered accountants who produce or report upon financial statements or provide reports of various other kinds that may be relied upon by persons other than those for whom they were originally prepared. By their nature, some documents are inevitably subject to general publication, such as auditors' reports under the Companies Act, and may not be restricted as to their use. In other cases, however, it may be possible for a registered accountant and auditor to reduce exposure to the claims of third parties by restricting the use of the report to named parties.

It can be made a term of the contract between a registered accountant and the client that the report or statement may not be circulated to third parties without prior written consent. If the client does circulate the document without prior written consent, then the client will be in breach of contract.

In addition, the reports or statements may appropriately contain a section specifically restricting circulation. For example:

'Confidential

This report (statement) has been prepared for the private use of X (the client) only.'

When a document is so marked, but is nevertheless relied upon by a third party without the registered accountant and auditor's consent, the registered accountant and auditor will still be able to resist liability on the basis that the third party was not a person whom the accountant had in mind as being likely to suffer loss as a consequence of possible negligence. Such a section should be introduced only where the circumstances warrant it, as it would tend to be devalued by indiscriminate use in connection with documents that, by their nature, must receive a wide distribution.

3.8.4 Limiting or excluding liability to the client

Section 247 of the Companies Act renders void any provision in a company's articles or any contractual arrangement purporting to exempt the auditor from or to indemnify the auditor against any liability for negligence, default, breach of duty or of trust. Thus any attempt to exclude or limit liability in the case of statutory audits of limited companies would prove futile. For all other engagements, however, such as non-statutory audits or engagements to provide non-audit services, registered accountants and auditors should consider the need to negotiate a limitation on the monetary amount of any liability to the client. It is important to realize that any exclusion or restriction of liability will not generally avail the registered accountant against a third party unless that party has notice of the exclusion or restriction.

This being the situation, it may be appropriate to obtain indemnities from clients in respect of claims from third parties arising from the contents of a report or directly from third parties. These indemnities, known as 'hold harmless' clauses, obligate the client or third party to indemnify the registered accountant from third party claims, but do not limit the third parties' ability to assert their claims.

Indemnities may not be practical in situations where a report can be expected to receive wide circulation, such as in the case of accountants' reports in listing particulars or in an acquisition circular. Where use of the report is restricted, however, or where there is no requirement that a public statement about the auditor's involvement be made, it may be reasonable to include an indemnity against any claims or other losses that the auditor may suffer from actions by third parties, including the costs of defending such actions.

It must be remembered that an indemnity does not prevent a claim from being brought against the indemnified party. It merely gives them the right to pass on a liability to the indemnifier. It follows, therefore, that if the indemnity is in some way ineffective or the indemnifier does not have adequate resources to meet the liability, the indemnified party will be left unprotected.

In concluding, the circular reminds registered accountants and auditors that, notwithstanding their best endeavours to ensure that they adopt all the relevant matters as set out in the circular, they may still be exposed to legal claims from clients or third parties. Whether or not these claims have merit, registered accountants and auditors should ensure that they have established proper procedures to deal with all claims promptly, to notify their insurers and to seek appropriate legal advice.

4

The Audit Process and Approach

Learning objectives

After studying this chapter you should be able to:

1. Identify and describe, in broad terms, the major stages of an audit of annual financial statements.
2. Define audit risk and describe its component elements and how they interrelate and affect the auditor's audit approach.
3. Outline, briefly, how the approach to the audit of annual financial statements has changed over time.
4. Describe the factors to be considered by the auditor in selecting an appropriate audit approach in a computerized accounting environment.

4.1 THE AUDIT PROCESS[1]

The audit process entails the auditor performing a series of procedures and activities. These procedures and activities may be divided into four clearly identifiable stages, namely:

- pre-engagement activities;
- planning;
- tests of controls and substantive procedures; and
- evaluating, concluding and reporting.

In turn, each of these four main stages have substages, which are identified and briefly explained below.

---

[1] This section is based on GAASS AU 015, 'The Audit Process'. Although the statement is not a Statement of South African Auditing Standards, it was included in the SAICA Members' Handbook (1996) and provides a good description of the stages of an audit and is as relevant today as when the document was published.

4.1.1 Pre-engagement activities

There are three main pre-engagement activities:

* *Perform new client investigation or consider change in circumstances of existing client.* The reason an auditor performs some investigation of a prospective client, or considers change in the circumstances of an existing one, which might lead to a decision to resign, is to reduce the auditor's business risk to acceptable levels. Business risk is defined in the literature as the risk of potential loss to an auditor's professional practice as a result of events unrelated to the auditor's adherence to professional standards in the conduct of the audit. Association with a client of dubious moral standards, and particularly where motivation exists to misstate disclosures in financial information or indulge in doubtful business and reporting practices, is likely to render the auditor's business risk unacceptable. In these circumstances the auditor should decline appointment. Factors that should be considered during the investigation include the business reputation of the client and any changes in the entity, including changes in ownership or management. Quality control procedures regarding acceptance and retention of clients are set out in chapter 3.

* *Determine skills and competence requirements.* Before accepting an audit engagement, the auditor should determine whether or not the necessary skills and resources are available to complete the work with professional competence. This would involve an assessment of the intricacy of the audit assignment and the estimated time, in hours, required to complete the work. In certain circumstances, if the auditor or audit firm does not itself possess all the skills necessary to complete the assignment, external specialists could be used.

* *Establish terms of engagement.* If a new client is accepted, or it is decided to continue to serve an existing client, the services to be provided by the auditor should be established or reaffirmed. An engagement letter[2] provides the clearest record of the terms of the engagement and is therefore a requirement. Terms of engagement and engagement letters are discussed in chapter 2, section 2.6.

4.1.2 Planning

The planning stage of the audit process involves a number of distinct substages. These are:

* *Obtaining a knowledge of the entity's business.* It is inconceivable that the auditor can plan to conduct an audit in accordance with South African Auditing Standards without a knowledge of the entity's operations and the industry within which it operates. This aspect is discussed in detail in chapter 5, section 5.2.

---

[2] See SAAS 210, 'Terms of Engagements'.

- *Making a preliminary judgement of materiality.* At the conclusion of the audit the auditor reports an opinion that financial statements 'fairly present'. In other words, an unqualified audit opinion implies that financial statements are not materially misstated. The auditor needs to make a judgement of materiality in order to plan the audit in such a way that sufficient evidence is gathered to draw such a conclusion. This judgement is referred to as 'planning materiality' and is usually quantified. The amount is best arrived at by selecting an element of the financial statements which is representative of the size of the entity and expressing materiality as a percentage, or percentage range, of that element.

The financial statements on which the auditor is reporting are usually not available at the planning stage of the annual audit. Planning materiality will therefore of necessity be based on interim financial statements, budgets, or financial statements of one or more prior periods. Materiality is discussed at length in chapter 5, section 5.3.

- *Consideration of inherent risk.* Inherent risk is the intrinsic susceptibility of the occurrence of errors which could be material to the financial statements as a whole, before considering the effect, if any, of internal controls. The auditor's assessment of inherent risk has a direct bearing on the procedures the auditor should plan to perform to gather evidence sufficient to support the audit opinion. Relatively speaking, a low overall assessment of inherent risk relating to an item disclosed in the financial statements would justify a reduction in the substantive audit procedures necessary to verify the fair presentation of that item. Substantive procedures are tests performed to obtain audit evidence to detect material misstatements in financial statements. An auditor may choose not to assess inherent risk where the effort required would exceed the potential benefit to be derived from reducing other auditing procedures. In these circumstances inherent risk should be assumed to be at a maximum. Aspects which bear consideration when assessing the likelihood of misstatement in financial statements may be conveniently grouped into three environmental categories, namely, business, management and accounting aspects. Factors underlying these aspects are discussed in chapter 5, section 5.4.

- *Obtaining an understanding of the accounting system and related controls.* The purpose of obtaining this understanding is to make a preliminary assessment of control risk. Control risk is the risk that a material error which could occur will not be prevented or detected timeously by the internal controls. The knowledge obtained should therefore enable the auditor to identify whether or not internal controls exist which could affect the accuracy of the client's financial statements. If good controls exist, the auditor may plan to place reliance on them as a basis for the preparation of reliable financial information. If the systems of controls are such that the auditor concludes that no reliance may be placed on controls to prevent or detect material errors, the auditor should determine what type of errors or irregularities could occur and should then design appropriate substantive tests with which to detect material errors or irregularities if they have indeed occurred.

• *Formulating an audit approach.* The audit approach is the overall plan the auditor designs to accomplish the primary audit objective of reporting on a client's financial statements at an acceptable level of audit risk. Audit risk is the risk that the auditor will unknowingly express an inappropriate opinion on the financial statements. Inherent and control risks are constituent elements of audit risk which are uncontrollable by the auditor. The third element of audit risk is detection risk. This is the risk that an auditor's procedures will fail to detect errors which could be material to the financial statements. Detection risk is controllable by the auditor in that it relates directly to the auditor's procedures. An increase in the extent of substantive audit procedures will reduce the detection risk and vice versa. The level of detection risk the auditor can accept is influenced by the assessment of inherent and control risks taken together. For example, the lower the auditor's combined assessment of inherent and control risks, the higher the detection risk can be to achieve an overall acceptable level of audit risk. In other words, detection risk should bear an inverse relationship to inherent and control risk.

Should the auditor plan to place reliance on assessments of inherent and control risks so as to reduce the extent of substantive auditing procedures necessary to achieve an acceptable overall level of audit risk, the auditor should gather audit evidence in support of such assessments.

• *Making an assessment of internal controls on which reliance is intended.* Where the planned approach is based on a judgement that reliance on specific internal controls could be an effective and efficient way of achieving audit objectives. This involves the auditor:
  - enquiring into the detailed working of the accounting system and its related controls;
  - recording a description of the system;
  - confirming that the record is an accurate description of the system; and
  - making a preliminary evaluation of the internal controls.

The planning stage of the audit process is concluded by the auditor preparing a written audit programme setting out the nature, timing and extent of the audit procedures necessary to implement the planned audit approach. Such a programme should contain sufficient detail to serve as an adequate set of instructions to those who are to perform the tests of controls and substantive procedures.

4.1.3 Tests of controls and substantive procedures

The purpose of tests of controls is to obtain evidence that the design of the controls are effective to the extent that they will prevent or detect errors and that controls, on which audit reliance is intended, worked effectively throughout the period of intended reliance. If tests of controls indicate that internal controls are not operating effectively, the planned audit approach should be modified. This would involve the performance of increased substantive procedures to achieve a level of detection risk which will result in an acceptable level of audit risk relating to assertions within financial statements.

4.1.4 Evaluating, concluding and reporting

The final stage of the audit process involves evaluating and drawing conclusions on the fair presentation of the financial information and the drafting of the audit report. During this stage the auditor considers the sufficiency of the evidence gathered in support of financial statement assertions. Assertions are the representations of management that are embodied in financial statements. These relate to the individual components of financial statements and may be broadly categorized as existence, occurrence, completeness, rights and obligations, measurement and valuation.

The auditor, when deciding on the fair presentation of assertions, should evaluate the differences between amounts included in the financial information and amounts supported by audit evidence – these differences are referred to as misstatements. For this purpose, the auditor should establish a final estimate of materiality. Qualitative considerations also influence an auditor in concluding whether or not misstatements are material.

If, after consideration of all the evidence, the auditor concludes that the financial statements are materially misstated, management should be requested to make appropriate adjustments. If adjustments are not made, the auditor should consider the effect on the audit opinion and report accordingly. Audit reports on financial statements are discussed in chapter 18.

4.2 THE AUDIT APPROACH

4.2.1 The balance sheet audit approach

An audit as we know it, directed at the expression of opinion on financial statements, consists of three major components. The first involves obtaining, or updating, a knowledge of the client – including its organizational structure and business objectives, strategies and processes – and in doing so, identifying the client's risk exposure and control procedures implemented to monitor these. The second is the assessment of the reliability of the accounting and control systems; the third is the verification of the fair presentation of the financial statements.

This was not always so. Initially the modern-day audit was dominated by the so-called balance sheet audit approach, which involved procedures directed at substantiating that assets and liabilities had been correctly disclosed in the balance sheet. The accounting systems which produced the financial information were largely ignored, the testing of the accuracy of transaction recording being limited mainly to capital items. This is not surprising when one looks at the historical development of auditing in the United Kingdom and the United States of America.

In the United Kingdom audit reporting on the income statement became mandatory only on the passing of the Companies Act of 1947, whereas auditing provisions covering the balance sheet had appeared in the Joint Stock Companies Act of 1844. It is of interest to note that this Act required one or more shareholders to examine balance sheets prepared by the directors.

In the United States of America mandatory audits were introduced only after the enactment of the Securities Act of 1933 and the Securities Exchange Act of 1934, which created the Securities and Exchange Commission. Companies registered with the Commission (SEC) were required to produce audited financial statements with the auditor's report covering both the balance sheet and the income statement. Prior to this mandatory audit requirement, however, the balance sheet audit approach was largely followed, as the users of auditors' services were mainly creditors, particularly banks, whose primary concern was with the solvency of businesses and not their income-earning potential.

The following may be identified as the reasons why the balance sheet audit in itself cannot be sufficient in forming an opinion on the fairness of the financial statements:

- Although the auditor is able, without resort to all the client's detailed accounting records, to verify the existence and ownership of disclosed assets and that liabilities disclosed are in fact owed, there can be no certainty or substantial probability that all assets and liabilities of the client have been included in the financial statements. The auditor's tests for understatement of assets and liabilities must be drawn in part from evidence in the accounting records and therefore depend on the reliability of the accounting system.

- The appropriate valuation of assets under the historic cost convention is largely dependent on reliable accounting records. The valuation of manufactured inventory illustrates the point. The checking of physical quantities, and extensions and additions of the inventory sheets, prove little if the auditor does not check that appropriate unit costs were obtained from reliable accounting records.

- In time, users of audited financial information, in addition to their concern with solvency, directed their attention to achieved earnings and income-earning potential of companies. The focus of auditing thus extended to the income statement and its components. The accuracy of the individual components of the income statement cannot be determined from a balance sheet audit. While the auditor's analytical review procedures directed at the verification of assets and liabilities may cover some components of the income statement, much of the auditor's opinion on the fair presentation of revenue and expenses is based on the assessment of the reliability of the accounting records.

For the reasons mentioned above and because statutory provisions required it, auditors began to conduct procedures other than those aimed specifically at verifying assets and liabilities. Initially these procedures involved checking the clerical accuracy of the accounting records. There was no attempt to evaluate the accounting systems for reliance thereon and verification procedures on the year-end balances were not linked to the audit work done on the accounting records. The procedures usually involved a combination of the following:

- checking the arithmetical accuracy of the books of prime entry;
- checking the postings from the books of prime entry to the relevant general ledger accounts; and
- selecting entries in the books of prime entry and confirming correct recording of transaction amounts and their allocation by reference to underlying source documents.

The balance sheet verification procedures involved:

- checking the arithmetical accuracy of the general ledger accounts;
- checking the balances in the trial balance against those in the general ledger;
- checking that the trial balance balanced and that amounts were appropriately disclosed in the financial statements; and
- verifying the assets and liabilities at the year end.

The verification of assets and liabilities was, at this stage of the development of auditing, little more than acceptance of the book figures after checking the arithmetic and postings. Gradually, however, auditors began to seek external evidence. This development was given impetus as a result of the notorious McKesson and Robbins case in 1939, involving an overstatement of approximately $21 million dollars of stocks and debtors, which led to the extension of American audit procedures to include confirmation of accounts receivable and the observation of stocktaking. These procedures became general practice elsewhere in the world. The focus was for some time mainly on fraud detection.

In the late 1940s there was a gradual shift away from the major concern of fraud discovery to the wider objective of giving an opinion on the overall fair presentation of the financial statements, and emphasis was placed by the profession on the fact that the auditor was not a guarantor of the accuracy of the financial statements. This shift was given impetus by the increasing size of companies, which made it impracticable to check all or even the bulk of the accounting entries. So, to justify the relatively small tests of recorded transactions, auditors turned their attention to the evaluation of the reliability of the accounting systems as the main basis on which to found their opinion on the fair presentation of financial statements.

The extensive development of internal control systems that occurred as a concomitant of increased company size greatly improved the reliability of accounting records and made it possible for auditors to gain the requisite reliance from clients' systems of control.

4.2.2 The systems-based approach

The primary objective of a systems-based audit approach is to assess the effectiveness of the accounting and internal control system so as to decide the reliance that may be placed on it to produce reliable financial statements. In theory, the examination of the system could be approached in two different ways. One could evaluate an accounting system through an examination of transactions processed and recorded by the system or by an analysis of the structure and design of the system itself. The former approach looks at the product of the system and was once the most commonly employed approach throughout the auditing profession. The latter approach involves an examination of the mechanics of the system and if it is designed with appropriate controls, checks and balances to prevent or detect errors, then this would be a good indication that the accounting information produced by the system is reliable.

As far as the primary objective of supporting an audit opinion is con-cerned, either approach has some validity. Following the transaction approach, the auditor draws a conclusion about the whole population based on an examination of a part of it; in the systems approach the auditor makes an inference about the accuracy of the accounting records based on a knowledge and examination of the system which produced those records.

In practice today auditors employ a combination of the two approaches. Generally accepted auditing standards require it and it is logical. The auditor evaluates the effectiveness of internal control as a basis for determining the nature and extent of audit tests, and the question is merely one of relative proportions between systems evaluation and testing the accuracy of transaction recording.

Traditionally, auditors have focused primarily on financial statement accounts when studying and evaluating internal control systems. This is evidenced by the fact that questions in internal control questionnaires were usually drawn up under the account headings of Sales, Purchases, Debtors, Creditors, Fixed Assets, Stocks and so on. Recognizing that the accounting for most transactions entered into by a business flow through the accounting system following a few homogeneous cycles, auditors began analysing controls as a whole within these so-called transaction cycles. This approach has been termed the transaction flow or transaction cycle audit approach.

4.2.3 The transaction flow or cycle approach

The concept of focusing on a small number of cycles through which a large number of transactions are processed into a large number of accounts has been widely adopted by audit firms within the profession.[3]

The following are the four main transaction cycles found in most commercial and industrial enterprises:

- Revenue/receipts;
- Expenditure/payments;
- Production/inventory; and
- Finance.

A fifth cycle, the financial reporting cycle, may be identified and includes such activities as preparing journal entries and postings to the general ledger (to the extent that such functions are not performed within other cycles), selecting generally accepted accounting policies that should be applied, and preparing financial statements and other financial reports. This cycle does not relate directly to the processing of original transactions; rather, it summarizes the activities and transactions of the other cycles for the preparation of financial reports.[4]

A transaction cycle may be identified whenever similar repetitive transactions occur within a business. The number and nature of the cycles will thus differ between entities engaged in different business activities. Further, the five cycles mentioned above may well be inappropriate for specialized undertakings, such as banks and insurance companies. The fact that cycles vary requires, as a first step, that the auditor define the cycles that are operating within the business entity being audited.

Focusing upon transaction cycles does not mean that the general ledger accounts are ignored, for the accounts are where processed transactions are summarized and recorded, and thus where the transaction flow within a cycle ends. It is also important to note that any one transaction may be processed through a number of different cycles before final recording in the general ledger. Stated in another way, the Rand balances in some general ledger accounts result from transactions processed through more than one cycle. For example, the cash balance in the ledger reflects the net result of transactions processed through three different cycles, receipts from debtors being a product of the revenue/receipts cycle, receipts from share and debenture issues a product of the finance cycle, and payments to creditors a product of the expenditure/payments cycle.

---

[3] It has been said that the approach adopted by systems analysts when introducing computerized accounting systems had a significant influence on the development of the cycle approach.

[4] Where accounting records are computerized, a further cycle, the 'integrity cycle', has been identified to pay particular attention to the control aspects of data processing. It is beyond the scope of this book to consider all the aspects of computerized accounting records.

An important aspect of evaluating controls following the transaction cycle approach is the specification of control objectives for each cycle. In the past auditors have focused their attention on control techniques in use rather than on the reasons why they are necessary. Systems were evaluated by comparing control techniques in operation with lengthy check lists of control features, auditors to a large extent relying on their intuition to identify the important ones. The transaction cycle approach involves identifying specific control objectives that should be achieved by internal control techniques exercised within each of the transaction cycles. These objectives provide guidelines against which existing control techniques can be measured. If the control objective is not met, both management and the auditor can focus on the risks of such non-achievement. Management must decide whether the cost of instituting further control techniques is justified and the auditor must assess the impact of the risk of error occurring and going undetected on the nature and extent of audit procedures.

The steps to be taken by the auditor when following the transaction cycle approach to evaluate internal control may be summarized as follows:

- The business activities of the entity must be analysed to identify significant categories of similar transactions that are processed. In this way the relevant cycles which are operating are identified.
- The functions that are performed within each cycle to authorize and record transactions and safeguard assets must be identified.
- The internal control objectives for each cycle must be specified.
- Internal control techniques in use must be identified and evaluated as to whether they achieve the specified control objectives.

The auditor accordingly makes a judgemental decision as to whether the control objectives are achieved, partly achieved or not achieved at all. This is an important phase of the decision on the overall audit approach for it determines the nature and extent of the audit tests to be performed. If the assessment is that the control objectives are wholly or mainly achieved, the auditor designs tests of controls to gain assurance that the control techniques on which reliance is intended are operating and have operated effectively throughout the period under audit. If the control objectives are not achieved or only partly achieved, the auditor must assess the risk that material errors or irregularities could occur and go undetected in the processing of transactions. The risk definition stage is important, for, by identifying the type of error that could occur, that is, the risk faced, the auditor is able to design appropriate substantive tests to search for such errors and should thus detect material errors if these have occurred.

A useful approach is first to define an audit objective which relates to each control objective specified. For example, a control objective of the revenue/receipts cycle might be that there should be an efficient method for determining the amount and terms of credit to be granted to each customer; the related audit objective would be to gain satisfaction that approval was obtained for the granting of credit for customers' orders before goods were dispatched. The auditor can meet the audit objective either by assessing the control objective as having been achieved and accordingly confirming the operation of underlying control techniques by performing tests of controls or, if it has not been achieved, by considering what could possibly go wrong that could affect the fair presentation of the financial statements and then to design substantive tests accordingly. In the example given, this could possibly be that goods are delivered to customers who will never pay for them. This in turn would result in an overstatement of accounts receivable in the financial statements. The auditor must accordingly design extended substantive tests to gain satisfaction as to the recoverability of accounts receivable at the year end.

The following are some advantages which flow from the adoption of the transaction cycle approach to evaluating internal control systems:

- The transaction cycle approach combines a standardized systematic approach with a flexibility that accommodates basic differences between the business activities of diverse companies and the many alternative control techniques that may be instituted by management to meet overall internal control objectives.

- The approach simplifies the review of controls in a complex system environment, as the reviewer avoids being overwhelmed by the details of individual control techniques relating to transaction recording in numerous individual general ledger accounts by focusing on the overall controls which regulate the recording of similar transactions that flow through the cycle and impact on several different ledger accounts.

- The approach simplifies the identification of offsetting strengths where a good control feature in one function compensates for a weakness in another. For example, the weakness arising from the lack of division of duties that exists where the buyer also receives goods supplied is negated by the control requirement that cheques are only prepared once suppliers' statement balances are reconciled to invoices and goods received advices prepared and signed by warehouse or store staff.

- The auditor concentrates on systems of control and related transactions that materially affect the entity's financial statements.

4.2.4 Risk-based audit approach[5]

The definition of audit risk and its analysis into three distinct constituent elements has had a far-reaching effect on the auditor's approach in recent

---

[5] Different terms for the approach have been coined by certain professional firms. Two examples are 'specific risk analysis' and 'transaction risk audit approach'.

times.[6] The distinguishing feature has been the realization that the auditor's assessment of inherent risk (the intrinsic susceptibility of financial information to material error) impacts on the nature and extent of the auditor's other auditing procedures necessary to reduce overall audit risk to an acceptable level. Stated in another way: should inherent risk be assessed at less than maximum, the evidence gathered in support of that assessment provides support (audit assurance) for the auditor's opinion on the fair presentation of the financial statements.

AUDIT APPROACH	AUDIT ASSURANCE		
	Inherent	Control	Substantive
Balance sheet			*
Systems-based/transaction cycle		*	*
Risk-based	*	*	*

Table 4.1 How audit assurance is obtained for different audit approaches

Traditionally, a risk-based audit approach involved the auditor identifying internal and external factors that could result in material errors occurring at an overall financial statement level and then relating such factors to their potential impact at an assertion level in respect of balances or classes of transactions contained in financial statements. Assertions are representations by management, explicit or otherwise, that are embodied in financial statements. For example, underlying assets disclosed in financial statements are the assertions that such assets exist and are owned by the entity; that they have been appropriately measured and valued; and that all assets are accounted for – termed completeness.

A more recent approach being adopted by some auditors is to consider the risks in relation to an entity's business processes and how these risks are identified and managed by the directors and management of the entity. The principle remains the same, which is for the auditor to identify risks of material misstatement and to concentrate audit effort in such risk areas, but the means of achieving this has changed.

Broadly speaking the business risk analysis approach involves the following steps:

- Obtaining a thorough knowledge of the entity, which would include its directors, management and organizational structure, as well as its strategic objectives and business processes.

---

[6] The first official document by the auditing profession worldwide on the topic was an exposure draft issued by the American Institute in December 1982, 'Materiality and Audit Risk in Conducting an Audit'.

- Considering the directors' and management's assessment of the potential risks faced by the entity that could result in material misstatements in the accounting for the activities of an entity's various business processes.

- Considering how the directors and managers of an entity manage these risks. This involves the auditor seeking answers to the following questions:
    - Have the directors and management adequately identified the risks within the entity's business processes that could lead to material misstatement in the financial statements?
    - Are there adequate policies and procedures in place to manage and control such risks? Factors to consider in this regard are the design and implementation of sound internal controls, including the presence of an effective internal auditing activity; the reports produced by the accounting activities, the accuracy and sufficiency of such reports; and the adequacy of management's review of and response to disclosures in such reports.

- Should the auditor conclude that the risks have been adequately identified and are apparently being appropriately managed or monitored, the auditor gathers evidence regarding the operation of such monitoring and control procedures. Once the auditor is satisfied that the monitoring and control procedures have been adequately carried out, the auditor is justified in concluding that the risk of material misstatement is low. This conclusion, in turn, justifies the auditor's performance of minimal tests of a substantive test nature, normally mainly of an analytical review nature.

- Alternatively, should the auditor conclude that the risks have not been adequately identified or appropriately managed or monitored, the auditor responds by designing and performing extended substantive tests, normally mainly tests of detail which should detect material misstatement if indeed such misstatements have occurred.

The audit approach described above has been referred to as a top-down approach: after having obtained or updated a knowledge of the client's business, the auditor interviews the directors and senior management to obtain from them their views on the entity's business objectives, its business processes, the risks faced by the business and how these risks are managed. The auditor will then follow up by gathering evidence of the operation of the control monitoring procedures and thereafter with the substantive evidence gathering phase focused on account balances and classes of transactions and the assertions underlying them. Following this approach more audit assurance is derived – by way of obtaining a greater understanding of the client's business processes and risks and how these risks are identified and controlled by management – than has traditionally been the case. In the more traditional audit risk-based approach, the focus falls more on the financial functions and typical accounting controls when assessing risks and gathering audit evidence.

Focusing on a client's business objectives and processes, risks, and controls enables the auditor to 'add value' to the client by identifying risks the client might not have perceived, by recommending control techniques to mitigate these, and by suggesting improvements to existing control structures. These recommendations, if implemented, should result in an improvement of the client's operations, controls and reporting. On the other hand, if found to be satisfactory by the auditor, this provides comfort to the directors that control mechanisms are adequate and are functioning properly. The approach provides an opportunity for the auditor to give insight to the directors, those charged with corporate governance responsibilities, as to how well, in the auditor's opinion, they are meeting their responsibilities in terms of the delivery of transparent and reliable communication in an entity's financial statements.

The major benefits to the audit firm following this business process focused audit approach are:

- Heightened appreciation by the client of the service being provided by the auditor in the form of recommendations that add value to the client.
- An effective and more efficient audit process with better audit risk management. Audit risk is the risk that the auditor gives an inappropriate audit opinion when the financial statements are materially misstated.
- The capability of better spreading the timing of the necessary audit work and therefore fewer problems in meeting audit reporting deadlines at year end.
- A more interesting audit experience as a result of the auditor's focus on business and control issues, thus leading to greater staff satisfaction within an audit firm.

The audit of the main business processes, following the approach outlined above, is discussed in chapters 12–17. The format for each chapter is, broadly, as follows:

- planning the audit of each business process, including risk identification and audit objectives;
- describing control risks and activities to mitigate these, and tests of controls;
- describing substantive tests to achieve stated audit objectives.

The reader is referred to chapter 5, section 5.4 where audit risk and the risk-based audit approach are discussed in detail.

4.3 THE AUDIT APPROACH IN A COMPUTER ENVIRONMENT

It would be unusual today to find that an entity's accounting records are not computerized. In general, there are two audit approaches which may be available where an entity's accounting records are computerized. These two approaches are respectively termed 'auditing around the computer' and 'auditing through the computer'. The term 'auditing with the computer' has also been coined. In the sense that it refers to the auditor's use of the computer to access computer-generated files in order to verify the information stored thereon or to perform calculations on data stored on file for analytical review purposes, it is not an audit approach in itself, but refers rather to techniques which may be used by the auditor.

4.3.1 Auditing around the computer

When auditing around the computer, the auditor ignores the data processing function and focuses attention instead on source documents, which form the basis for input to the computer, and printouts produced by the computer. The computer is treated as a 'black box' that accepts input and produces output. The auditor obtains satisfaction regarding the accuracy of data processing by comparing source document data with computer-produced printouts and vice versa.

To audit around the computer all the following conditions must be met:

- Transaction data must be captured on source documents.
- Source documents must be controlled and filed in a manner that makes it possible to locate specifically selected transactions for audit purposes.
- Computer-produced printouts must be in sufficient detail to enable the auditor to trace individual transactions from, or to, source documents.

These conditions were usually met when computers were first utilized for accounting purposes, as computers were originally used primarily to perform simple computational tasks. Technological developments, such as on-line data entry, the elimination or reduction of printouts and real-time file updating, have tended to render this approach obsolete.

4.3.2 Auditing through the computer

In this approach the auditor focuses on all phases of the electronic data processing function, including the data processing phase, ignored when auditing around the computer. To this end the auditor studies and evaluates the overall control environment in which computerized accounting applications are developed, maintained and executed, as well as the specific application controls in place to ensure that only authorized transactions are processed and that all authorized transactions are accurately processed and recorded.

The auditor's decision to audit around or through the computer is influenced by three considerations, namely the necessity, possibility and desirability of auditing through the computer. Where there is no available audit trail allowing the auditor to match computer produced outputs (reports) to manually produced inputs, the auditor is of necessity required to consider the computerized accounting environment and relevant controls. This is true also where the auditor, in deciding on an appropriate audit approach, chooses to rely on controls within an entity's computer systems, such as logical access controls in the form of log-on IDs and passwords, and input validation controls such as alpha-numeric code checks, field presence and length checks, and reasonability checks. Alternatively, the auditor may plan to rely on manual checks, the effectiveness of which depend on the accuracy of computer produced information, which requires the auditor to establish that the computer produced reports are reliable.

Regarding the auditor's capability of auditing through the computer, the two major considerations are the availability of suitable programs to assist the auditor in meeting audit objectives, termed Computer Assisted Audit Techniques (CAATS), and the availability of expertise within the audit firm to use these. The availability of time on the client's computer system and how to control the use of CAATS, in practice, often present problems.

The last consideration, the desirability of auditing through the computer, requires the auditor to bear the following in mind:

- The use of CAATS might (and usually does) result in improved efficiency and effectiveness.
- Client confidence in the competence of the service provided by the auditor, as well as an improved value-added service in terms of recommendations regarding the client's computer related activities.
- A more stimulating experience for audit staff and thus greater audit staff satisfaction and commitment.

5

Audit Planning and Control

Learning objectives

After studying this chapter you should be able to:

1. Identify the aspects that need to be considered in planning an audit of financial statements and describe the principles and procedures relevant to these aspects. These aspects are:
    - knowledge of the business;
    - planning materiality considerations;
    - inherent risk assessment;
    - understanding the accounting system and related controls (control risk assessment); and
    - formulating an audit approach to reduce audit risk to an acceptable level.
2. Describe the effects and benefits of appropriate planning.
3. Describe the need for and aspects relevant to the control of the conduct of an audit.

5.1 INTRODUCTION

The auditor must obtain sufficient evidence to support the audit opinion given on the client's financial statements. This evidence-gathering phase of the audit, often called the fieldwork phase, involves four main activities, namely:

- Planning;
- Development of the audit programme;
- Execution of the programme, which includes audit supervision and control; and
- Evaluation of evidence.

The conduct of an efficient and effective audit requires that the work be planned, executed and supervised in an organized manner.

In practice, neither planning nor development nor execution can be treated in isolation; planning is an ongoing process and the finding of errors during the execution stage of the audit may necessitate changes in the audit approach and procedures, either in substance or in emphasis.

Nevertheless, for the purpose of exposition it is convenient to consider the evidence-gathering phase of an audit under the broad heads of planning and control of the conduct of the audit (see 5.6 and 5.7 of this chapter).

Since obtaining or updating knowledge of the client's business is a prerequisite to planning, and because the auditor also considers materiality and audit risk during the planning stage, these concepts are dealt with prior to the detailed discussion of planning.

5.2 KNOWLEDGE OF THE BUSINESS

Inter alia, SAAS 310, 'Knowledge of the Business', states the following as a mandatory requirement:

> 'In performing an audit of financial statements, the auditor should have or obtain a knowledge of the business sufficient to enable the auditor to identify and understand the events, transactions and practices that, in the auditor's judgement, may have a significant effect on the financial statements or on the examination or audit report.'

'Auditor', in the context of this quote, extends to all personnel involved in the audit, from partner in charge through supervisors to assistants.

The task of acquiring knowledge of a business naturally requires more effort and time in a first-time audit of a client as opposed to successive audits where the auditor merely has to update knowledge of any changes in the business. For this reason, audit fees for the time spent in acquiring knowledge of the business in the initial audit are often spread over two or three years.

The knowledge level obtained by the audit partner and supervisors should be comprehensive and thorough; knowledge levels of assistants might be more limited, but at least sufficient for an adequate performance of delegated tasks. For example, audit assistants assigned the task of checking the propriety of cash payments and receipts would not ordinarily be expected to have a thorough knowledge of the industry within which a client operates, nor of legislation or regulatory requirements applicable to it – aspects with which more senior personnel should be familiar.

With this as a caveat, the auditor's knowledge of the client's business should extend to at least the following matters:

- *Knowledge of the industry within which the client operates.* Most businesses, other than conglomerates, operate within an industry sector which may be vulnerable to economic change or have its own unique practices and risks. These aspects have an effect on businesses within the industry and should therefore be known by the auditor. Some important examples of such matters are:

- the state of competition and ease of entry;
- the susceptibility of products to obsolescence as a result of technological or fashion changes;
- the nature of cyclical or seasonal activities;
- an expanding or declining industry; and
- specific industry regulatory requirements, for example those pertaining to banks and the arms and ammunition industry.

● *Knowledge of the client's business operations.* The auditor needs an in-depth knowledge of what the entity does and how and where it operates. Aspects to consider are:
  - *The nature of the entity's business,* for example, manufacturer, wholesaler, retailer or a combination of these. If the client is a manufacturer, the auditor would require an understanding of the particular manufacturing processes, including raw material, labour and production facility (including machinery and energy) inputs into finished goods.
  - *Major suppliers of products and services.* Aspects of relevance are the stability of supply, including any contractual commitments on the part of suppliers, whether local or overseas, order lead times and payment arrangements.
  - *Markets and marketing strategies.* The auditor should know the customer base, including major customers with contractual obligations. Other aspects under this heading are market share and major competitors, the reputation of the entity's products, any warranties, pricing policies (in particular profit margins) and the buoyancy of the market, including recent sales trends and committed orders placed by customers.
  - *The location of factories, warehouses and selling outlets.* The auditor would need to know, in particular, where significant quantities of inventories are stored.
  - *Legislation and regulations applicable to the entity.* From an employment perspective aspects such as minimum wage levels, trade union contracts, pension and medical aid commitments are of importance. Other important matters are the existence of any licensing arrangements, patents, trade marks and royalty and/or franchise contracts.

● *Knowledge of ownership, capital structure and financial performance.* The auditor needs to know details of the owners of the entity – because the audit client may be a subsidiary or associate of another company – as well as of the existence of related parties. These relationships may result in external influences on management when preparing annual financial statements and in transactions being effected at other than 'arm's length' terms. Factors concerning the entity's financial condition and profitability are the debt to equity ratio (the relative proportion of assets funded by capital and by way of loans), liquidity, activity and profitability statistics, such as achieved margins and net profitability. Sources and methods of financing and any change therein are also important. The auditor needs to be aware of trends in these statistics.

- *Knowledge of organizational structure and management characteristics.* Apart from being familiar with the organizational structure from board of directors, through senior to lower management, and down to operational level, the auditor needs to be aware of the overall objectives of senior management and its strategic plans, capabilities, management style and manner of remuneration. Aspects to be aware of are:
    - *Board of directors.* The composition of the board, the presence of both executive and non-executive directors, their individual skills and experience, and business reputation should be noted. Further aspects to note are an adequate diversity of skills such as technical, marketing and finance/accounting, and that decisions are taken based on a majority view or consensus without a suggestion of dominance of the board by one or a few directors. The frequency of board meetings is also important.
    - *Operating management level.* Again, an adequate cross-section of skills and experience is important. Other aspects to note are staff turnover, brought about by unreasonable expectations of performance or poor remuneration packages, and a dependence on key personnel, particularly in the technical or financial accounting (computer expertise) areas. Details of remuneration packages should be noted, particularly where lower-than-normal standard packages are offset by performance bonuses which might motivate 'window dressing' of financial statement disclosures.

Other important matters to consider are the presence or absence of a code of corporate practice and policies and procedures to monitor adherence to it; an audit committee and internal audit function and its mandates and effectiveness; and an effective budgeting and forecasting system with adequate procedures for preparation and adjustment, if needed as a result of changed circumstances. Actual performance needs to be monitored against budgets and, where actual performance is not in line with expectation, the deviation should be investigated by management to ascertain the reasons therefore. These reasons are either one or a combination of the following:

- unrealistic budgets;
- substandard performance;
- errors in the accounting processes;
- theft of assets; or
- fraud.

Unrealistic budgets should be adjusted taking into account more realistic assumptions concerning future expected conditions and events. The reasons for substandard performance should be established and changes made where necessary, and possible, to prevent similar occurrences, for example, changing operating procedures or personnel. The cause of errors in the accounting processes would also need investigation. Such errors might indicate weaknesses in, or a breakdown of, the internal control systems which would need to be rectified. Similarly, the theft of assets or the detection of fraud might raise questions regarding the effectiveness of the internal control systems. In the case of theft or fraud, management should attempt to recover any loss from the perpetrator(s), terminate their employment, and possibly initiate legal action.

The auditor should be satisfied that the reasons for actual performance deviating from budgets are adequately investigated by management and that appropriate remedial action is taken; this aspect is an important part of business risk management, which in turn influences the auditor's audit approach.

A knowledge of the client's business may be obtained from a number of different sources. Some of the more important sources are:

- people within the entity, for example, discussions with directors, senior operating personnel, audit committee members or internal auditors;
- management, strategic plans and policy manuals, documents produced within the entity, for example, accounting and systems of control manuals, monthly management accounts and budgets, minutes of meetings and internal reports by internal auditors and operating personnel;
- people outside the entity, for example, discussions with legal and other advisers to the entity, other auditors and acknowledged industry experts;
- industry publications, for example, trade journals and the financial pages of the press; and
- inspection of the entity's premises and facilities.

5.3 UNDERSTANDING THE ACCOUNTING SYSTEM

5.3.1 Introduction

South African auditing standards require that the auditor should obtain an understanding of the entity's accounting system and related internal controls in order to assess their adequacy as a basis for the preparation of financial information and to assist in designing auditing procedures. This understanding should provide the auditor with a general knowledge of how accounting information relating to transactions is captured, processed, recorded and reported, and should enable the auditor to identify the existence of internal controls which affect the accuracy of financial information.

These days it would be unusual for such accounting systems not to be computerized. When obtaining an understanding of an accounting system in a computerized environment, the manual and electronic data processing (EDP) controls cannot be considered in isolation. Refer to chapters 9 and 10, where computerized controls are distinguished from manual controls and the classification between application and general controls and the dependence of the efficacy of the former on the latter are discussed. The auditor's informational needs when obtaining an understanding of the system should cover the following elements of any EDP system:

- the computer equipment (hardware);
- systems programs and application programs (software);
- operating procedures; and
- personnel.

A brief discussion of each follows.

5.3.2 Computer equipment

The term 'hardware' describes collectively the equipment necessary to perform all the functions and includes:

- the central processing unit (CPU), which is the heart of the computer and performs arithmetic and logic functions;
- input devices, usually terminal keyboards or magnetic barcode readers, that read certain aspects of documents or price tags – for example, description and price of goods from bar codes affixed to sales products;
- output devices, examples of which are:
  - line printers and graph plotters which prepare copy in a written format;
  - visual display terminals which provide visual output on a terminal screen; and
  - computer microfilm devices which use a photographic process to store output on microfilm.

The auditor needs to be familiar with the equipment used, as each component has its own operational characteristics and control requirements.

5.3.3 System programs and application programs

System programs coordinate and control the use of the hardware, support the use of application programs and the data storage and management systems. Coordination tasks involve the scheduling, monitoring and synchronizing of processing and facilitating the storing and accessing of data and programs. Control tasks involve the protection of programs and data from unauthorized access, and the handling of errors.

Application programs contain the instructions required to perform the tasks necessary for the particular data processing requirements of each business process and transaction cycle. These tasks include functions such as data validation at the data input stage, calculations, comparisons, summarizations, sequencing of transactions, enquiry of data stored on file, error correction, and file updating. The auditor is interested in how these tasks are performed and in the controls built into the programs to monitor their performance.

5.3.4 Operating procedures

Operating procedures cover the preparation of data for input, the proper handling of files, the operation of the computer, control over quality and distribution of output, and the correction and processing of detected errors. Proper operating procedures help assure that processing is accurate and that programs, data files and output are protected from unauthorized access and use.

5.3.5 Personnel

Technical expertise is needed to adequately handle the various specialized tasks involved in the operation of computerized accounting systems. The auditor should be familiar with the organization chart of the entity, including the titles and responsibilities of staff such as systems analysts, programmers, computer operators, user and control groups.

5.4 MATERIALITY

5.4.1 General

It has been said, in chapter 3.1, that the auditor should keep a sense of proportion. One aspect of this is materiality, the other is risk. In statement SAAS 320 (paragraph .02) we read: 'The auditor should consider materiality and its relationship to audit risk when conducting an audit.' It is therefore incumbent on the auditor to understand fully how materiality and risk impinge on all audit activities. The first of these elements is considered here (the second element is dealt with later in the chapter).

The Companies Act, Schedule 4, which requires disclosure of many items, refers repeatedly to the materiality of such items as a basis for deciding whether disclosure is required, and the Public Accountants' and Auditors' Act (section 20(5)) requires material irregularities to be reported. The element of materiality arises continually during an audit.

The primary objective of any audit of financial information is to express an opinion on its fair presentation in all material respects. In most instances, the financial information to be audited will be the financial statements of an entity. Although the auditor does not guarantee the absolute accuracy of the audited financial information, the utility of the audited information would be severely reduced if users could not rely on the information being within acceptable limits of accuracy.

The cut-off point of what is acceptable accuracy is whether or not an error (or a combination of errors) is large enough for users of the information to be influenced by it. It is rational to assume that a user will not be influenced by trifles. On the other hand, it is also rational to assume that something 'material' will influence a decision. From the auditor's point of view it is, therefore, important to judge whether or not the ultimate effect of misstatements discovered during the audit is such as to influence the decision of the user.

Throughout the audit the auditor will have to make judgemental decisions as to whether or not some event or item (or group of items) is material. From a practical point of view it is clear that, should a satisfactory definition of materiality be available, the auditor would be able to test the correctness of a decision against that definition. However, as with all abstract concepts, materiality is difficult to define. Indeed, the elusiveness of beauty which led Shakespeare to place it in the eye of the beholder may well find its equal in materiality. Nevertheless, some attempt must be made to harness this concept so that it may be put to work. This is especially so in view of the alignment of South African Accounting and Auditing Standards with International Standards (discussed elsewhere in this book), the main objectives of which are to:

- narrow the areas of difference in accounting practice; and
- ensure the disclosure of accounting policies (or bases) adopted in situations where the financial statements include material items which depend on judgement.

Attempts have been made to give a short definition of materiality but with little success. The SA Institute of Chartered Accountants, in Statement of Generally Accepted Accounting Practice AC 000, defines materiality as follows:

> 'Information is material if its omission or misstatement could influence the economic decisions of users taken on the basis of the financial statements. Materiality depends on the size of the item or error judged in the particular circumstances of its omission or misstatement. Thus, materiality provides a threshold or cut-off point rather than being a primary qualitative characteristic which information must have if it is to be useful.'[1]

Schedule 4 of the Companies Act (paragraph 4) states that 'material' means anything significant in relation to the circumstances of each company. The auditor is still left to decide what will influence the user and what is significant.

The Financial Accounting Standards Board in the USA sums up the matter succinctly:[2]

> 'The predominant view is that materiality judgement can properly be made only by those who have all the facts. The Board's present position is that no general standards of materiality could be formulated to take into account all the considerations that enter into an experienced human judgement.'

The fact is that there is no one answer as to how the auditor should harness the concept of materiality.

---

[1] Readers are referred to Discussion Paper 6, 'Audit Risk and Materiality', issued by the Auditing Standards Committee of the Institute.
[2] Statement of Financial Accounting Concepts, paragraph 131.

5.4.2 Research efforts

Over the past three decades various approaches have been adopted by researchers on the topic in attempts to arrive at a definitive answer. The reasons why researchers have this quest for a definitive answer are that:

- the credibility of audited information will increase as users of audited information will know the exact parameters of the information;
- defending professional liability cases will be easier; and
- it may lead to reduction of audit fieldwork without increasing the audit risk.

Although these efforts have added some very interesting literature to the body of knowledge, the profession is no closer to an acceptable solution than before. At best, each approach merely confirms that there is no definitive answer. Research on the topic can be broadly classified as follows:

- quantitative guidelines;
- materiality decisions in courts of law;
- whether 'accounting materiality' is the same as 'auditing materiality'
- empirical studies on materiality judgements of various user groups and preparers;
- impact on share prices; and
- reporting materiality to users (in the audit report or financial information).

The authors believe that auditors need to be aware of the more important considerations relating to materiality, as gathered from the literature, in order to substantiate their own cut-off point for materiality.

5.4.2.1 Quantitative guidelines

Newcomers to the topic invariably suggest the apparently obvious solution, namely, for the official accounting bodies to lay down a fixed percentage of some common base, as the problem appears to be nothing more than:

- establishing a number; and
- what to do with the number once it has been established.

For example, why not take 2% of gross profit as a cut-off point for materiality? Every item (or error) smaller than 2% of gross profit will be considered immaterial and, conversely, every item larger than 2% of gross profit will be considered material.

Attempts have been made in, amongst others, the USA, Canada, Australia and South Africa to establish strict quantitative guidelines. However, the practical application of these was not nearly as simple as it at first appeared to be. The following queries emerged:

- Why gross profit and not income?
- What is materiality in the case of loss situations?
- Why not take a percentage of assets?

- If income is used as the base, is it before or after tax?
- Why not use equity as the base?
- Why not use a combination of bases to avoid abnormal situations?
- What base best represents the size of the entity?

Leslie, in his research study,[3] concluded that '... although 5% to 10% of income seems widely accepted as a measure of materiality, the materiality problems facing auditors have not diminished over the past two decades. The main reason is that the incomes of many organizations fluctuate widely from year to year. Should materiality be halved and audit costs increased substantially when net income temporarily dips from $1 000 000 to $500 000 (in other words, higher audit costs to compound already less favourable results)? What should materiality be in a break-even or loss year? It is impossible to have zero or negative materiality.'

5.4.2.2 Materiality decisions in courts of law

Although the courts have given judgements[4] in cases in which 'materiality' was considered, the circumstances and the facts of these cases vary considerably and are thus not really suitable for analysis in order to get closer to a definitive answer.

5.4.2.3 Is 'accounting materiality' the same as 'auditing materiality'?

The literature makes reference to accounting materiality and auditing materiality. 'Accounting materiality' relates to the amount at which errors, or irregularities, become serious enough to affect the 'fairness' of the accounting information and require adjustment to, or disclosure in, financial information. 'Auditing materiality' relates to the degree of audit evidence required to obtain reasonable assurance that the financial information is not materially misstated. It thus influences directly the determination of the nature and extent of audit testing required to obtain satisfaction that the financial information does not contain error which exceeds 'accounting materiality'. It follows therefore that the two materiality measures are the same.

5.4.2.4 Empirical studies on materiality judgements of various user groups and preparers

Studies have shown that materiality judgements vary markedly. Widely varying materiality thresholds were given by both auditors and financial executives in answer to questionnaires containing identical circumstances.

---

[3] Donald A Leslie. 1985. 'Materiality: The Concept and its Application to Auditing'. Canadian Institute of Chartered Accountants Research Study.
[4] *Escott v BarChris Construction Corp* (SDNY 1968).

5.4.2.5 Impact on share prices

Various studies have been done on the impact on share prices of qualified audit reports on accounting information. Although observations of market behaviour could improve one's understanding of what is 'material', it must be borne in mind that the materiality of information released can only be tested after the event. Auditors, of course, make materiality judgements before the event. In addition, there are other factors which concurrently affect the share prices and therefore render this approach not accurate enough for setting guidelines. It must also be borne in mind that there are financial statement users other than investors.

5.4.2.6 Reporting materiality to users

Protagonists of this approach believe that the auditor and known major users of the financial statements of an entity should discuss materiality levels to enable all interested parties to reach consensus on quantitative standards that should be used for audit precision purposes. These agreed standards should be disclosed in the financial information or relevant audit reports.

5.4.3 Considerations in establishing materiality

Although holding no brief for the arbitrary percentages described above which take the initiative from the auditor, the writers view with satisfaction the principle of relating materiality to the size of the entity and/or the value of an item to the value of the group from which it comes. The absolute value of an item is seldom a guide to its significance.

The following represents a summary of the more important considerations in establishing materiality:

- It should be appreciated that there are two major elements of materiality relevant to each item. The first is its amount, the second its special characteristics.[5] Where, for example, all debts are on open account, there is usually no need to disclose separately an item even if it exceeds, say, 10% of the total debts; but where some debts are secured and others not, the special characteristic of security may require a division of accounts receivable if the amount of the secured debts (or it may be unsecured debts) exceeds that limit.

- The absolute amount of an item is unlikely to be of consequence in the context of materiality. The relationship of the amount of the item to the financial information as a whole, or to the total of the group from which the item comes, is the important factor.

- Elements of the financial statements, for example, share capital, assets, revenue or income, may be used as indicators of the size of an entity. The

---

[5] Described as quantitative and qualitative materiality respectively.

materiality amount may be arrived at by selecting an element (or combination of elements) of the financial statements which is best representative of the size of the entity and expressing materiality as a percentage, or percentage range, of that element. Factors that should be considered when selecting the appropriate element(s) are stability over time (for example, turnover is likely to be less volatile than income), and whether or not the balance sheet or income statement elements are the best indicators of size. So in the case of a retailing company, which predominantly leases its warehouse facilities and stores, the income statement elements are likely to be the best indicators of the size of the entity, in contrast to a financial institution, where balance sheet elements are likely to be more appropriate.

- Consideration should be given to the question whether the item is best related to:
  - the overall amount of the financial information; or
  - the total of associated items; or
  - the corresponding item in previous years. For example, should the charge for advertising be related

    to the total expenses per the income statement (or to total revenue), or

    to the total of selling expenses; or

    to the amount of advertising for the previous year; or

    to more than one of these?

- Where the item in question relates to both the income statement and the balance sheet, care should be taken to choose the comparison which is most relevant to materiality. Thus the ratio of bad debts provision to the amount of debts outstanding may be very high, but the provision plus debts written off during the year as a percentage of the net sales which generated these debts may be trivial. The second comparison is even more meaningful in the case of bad debts (written off and provided); this expense relates more closely to sales than provision alone relates to accounts receivable.

- The precision with which an item can normally be computed may have an effect on judging its materiality. For this reason, one expects precision in the case of the bank balance, but may accept a fairly wide tolerance in the case of the estimated provision for doubtful debts.

5.4.4 Materiality and the audit process

The auditor first considers materiality at the planning stage of the audit. As the 'number' must be established in order to determine, inter alia, the extent of the tests to be undertaken, the auditor has to make a preliminary judgement of materiality, termed 'planning materiality'.

As planning materiality needs to be quantified, financial information concerning the entity is required in some form or another. This may be in the form of the most recent interim financial statements available, forecasts and/or budgets for the current period, or the audited financial statements of one or more prior periods. Except in the case of a new client, the working papers of the previous audit should be consulted to ascertain the quantitative guidelines used in that period for the determination of materiality. Consideration then needs to be given to the effects of changes in the circumstances of the client, the industry, or the economy as a whole, since the previous audit.

The quantification of 'planning materiality' assists the auditor in gathering evidence sufficient to support the content of the audit report. During the performance of the audit the auditor may find it necessary to change the planning materiality judgement because of findings regarding the sufficiency of evidence to support or negate management assertions underlying financial information disclosures.

Although auditors use various methods of quantifying planning materiality and of applying it to design procedures to detect errors which, individually or in aggregate, exceed the accepted tolerance, their common aim is to be satisfied that the financial statements under audit are fairly stated and to identify (and report on) any material misstatement. This decision, taken at the final stage of the audit, involves the evaluation of the differences between amounts included in the financial statements and the amounts supported by audit evidence. If differences are material, adjustments to the financial statements are required. The materiality level used for this decision, termed 'final materiality', is usually higher than that of planning materiality because, as a general rule, the auditor sets the latter at a level lower than the expected final level to ensure that audit procedures are based on a conservative materiality judgement.

5.5 AUDIT RISK

5.5.1 Introduction

Statement SAAS 400 (paragraph .03) defines audit risk as 'the risk that the auditor expresses an inappropriate audit opinion when the financial statements are materially misstated'.

The assessment of audit risk enables the auditor to conclude, based on the audit evidence gathered, whether or not the audit risk for an engagement is at an acceptable level. Statement SAAS 400 gives no guidance on what an acceptable level of audit risk is, but merely states that the auditor should use professional judgement to assess audit risk and to design audit procedures to ensure that it is reduced to an acceptably low level. In practice audit risk is expressed in numeric terms or in less precise terms, for example, high, medium or low. It is submitted that the generally accepted auditing standard which requires the exercise of due professional care would preclude the auditor from issuing an unqualified audit opinion where the assessment of audit risk is within the high to medium range. As to how low the auditor's assessment of acceptable audit risk should be, empirical research results published in 1983 by Paul Gronsbell-Luntz in his thesis toward his Master of Commerce degree at the University of the Witwatersrand showed that the great majority of respondents to his questionnaire who utilized statistical sampling accepted a maximum audit risk of 5%.

When assessing audit risk the auditor should consider the individual assertions underlying financial information disclosures. As indicated in chapter 4.1, these are the representations of management that are embodied in financial statements and may be categorized as either general or specific. General assertions relate to the overall presentation and disclosure of financial information, while specific assertions relate to the individually disclosed components of financial statements.

Making general or overall assessments of the audit risk based on individual elements of financial statements is inappropriate, for the various assertions relating to each balance sheet or income statement item may not be at equivalent risk. For example, good control over the custody and recording of inventory movements would ordinarily result in a low-risk assessment relating to the 'existence and ownership' assertions. However, a high-risk assessment of the 'valuation' assertion is likely where the company is operating in a highly competitive industry and particularly one which is subject to rapidly developing technology. In these circumstances, more substantive audit work is necessary on the valuation of inventory than on the existence and ownership assertions to reduce the overall audit risk relating to inventories to an acceptable level.

It must be emphasized that the auditor does not eliminate audit risk completely. To do so would be impractical – requiring enormous amounts of audit effort resulting in unrealistic audit fees – and, in most instances, even impossible. While an auditor may elect to reduce audit risk below an acceptable level by performing more extensive procedures than normally required, the auditor should never accept a level of risk which results in failure to comply with generally accepted auditing standards.

5.5.2 Constituent elements of risk

Audit risk assessment may be facilitated by considering the three constituent elements of audit risk individually. These constituent elements are inherent risk, control risk, and detection risk.

5.5.2.1 Inherent risk

SAAS 400, 'Risk Assessments and Internal Control', defines *inherent risk* as follows:

> 'Inherent risk is the susceptibility of an account balance or class of transactions to misstatement that could be material, individually or when aggregated with misstatement in other balances or classes, assuming that there were no related internal controls.'

The definition of inherent risk excludes the consideration of the effect of internal controls because internal control is evaluated and tested separately after the auditor has assessed the inherent risk of misstatement.

The objectives of inherent risk evaluation are twofold, namely:

- the auditor identifies potentially high-risk areas of the client's business operations that would require particular audit emphasis; and
- the auditor estimates the likelihood of material errors occurring in the financial information under audit.

Aspects which bear consideration when assessing the inherent risk of misstatement in financial information may be conveniently grouped into three categories, namely:

- the business environment;
- the management environment; and
- the accounting environment.

When reviewing the business environment the auditor should consider industry and operational factors as well as financial factors. The client's trading performance and liquidity position relative to previous years and current expectations affect the likelihood of misstatement occurring in the financial statements. In general, unfavourable trading results and a deteriorating liquidity situation leading to severe economic pressures will adversely affect the auditor's evaluation of the client's inherent risk.

The integrity of management is important because the potential for deception and the overriding of internal control is always present. An assessment of management's integrity is difficult. Factors that should be considered, however, are management's business reputation, frankness and willingness to cooperate. A wide range of reasons might tempt management to misstate disclosures in the financial statements, particularly where adverse trading conditions prevail. Indicators of potential increases in inherent risk include situations where the financial statements are to be used to raise loan or equity capital; where management is a substantial shareholder and is dependent on dividend income for livelihood; or where share market pressures tempt management to overstate earnings per share in the case of listed companies. When assessing the integrity of management the auditor should also be aware that management may not even indulge in misstatement of financial statements for any direct personal gain, but will rationalize its actions by claiming 'standard business practice' or 'the best interests of all concerned'.

Some accounting environmental factors the auditor should consider when assessing the likelihood of error are: the competence and commitment of the client's staff, time pressures as a result of unrealistic deadlines being set for reporting dates, apparent lack of cooperation between staff within the accounting department or between accounting staff and operating departments, and a history of detected errors in the past.

The inherent risk of misstatement is increased where Rand values are established by way of complex calculations, and particularly where values are subject to difficult estimation processes, for example, overhead recovery rates included in inventory values or valuation of work-in-progress on long-term contracts in construction companies.

The Rand value of account balances also has a bearing on inherent risk assessment, in that immaterial amounts are generally at less risk than high Rand-value items. This is not to say that there is no inherent risk attached to immaterial amounts since immaterial errors in individual balances may, when aggregated, become material. In addition, an apparently immaterial amount may be materially misstated as a result of the amount being grossly understated.

It must be emphasized that the auditor's assessment of inherent risk is a matter of professional judgement. A measure of objectivity may be introduced into the evaluation process by the use of standardized check lists, or questionnaires, which list factors that should be considered by the auditor when assessing the susceptibility of account balances to misstatement.

With regard to the auditor's approach to assessing inherent risk, SAAS 400 suggests that there are two stages to the procedure, namely:

- in developing the overall audit plan, the auditor should assess inherent risk at the financial statement level, and
- in developing the audit programme, the auditor should relate the assessment to material account balances or classes of transactions at the assertion level.

SAAS 400 lists certain factors the auditor should consider when using professional judgement to assess inherent risk. These are as follows:

'At the financial statement level.

- The integrity of management.

- Management experience and knowledge and changes in management during the period; for example, the inexperience of management may affect the preparation of the financial statements of the entity.

- Unusual pressures on management, for example, circumstances that might predispose management to misstate the financial statements, such as the industry experiencing a large number of business failures or an entity that lacks sufficient capital to continue operations.

- The nature of the entity's business, for example, the potential for technological obsolescence of its products and services, the complexity of its capital structure, the significance of related parties, and the number of locations and geographical spread of its production facilities.

- Factors affecting the industry in which the entity operates, for example, economic and competitive conditions as identified by financial trends and ratios, and changes in technology, consumer demand and accounting practices common to the industry.

'At the account balance and class of transactions level.

- Financial statement accounts likely to be susceptible to misstatement, for example, accounts that required adjustment in the prior period or involve a high degree of estimation.

- The complexity of underlying transactions and other events that might require using the work of an expert.

- The degree of judgement involved in determining account balances.

- Susceptibility of assets to loss or misappropriation, for example, assets that are highly desirable and movable, such as cash.

- The completion of unusual and complex transactions, particularly at or nearer period end.

- Transactions not subjected to routine processing.'

5.5.2.2 Control risk

Control risk, the second element of audit risk, is defined as 'the risk that a misstatement that could occur in an account balance or class of transactions and that could be material, individually or when aggregated with misstatements in other balances or classes, will not be prevented or detected and corrected on a timely basis by the accounting and internal control systems'. [6]

Control risk arises simply because the accounting system lacks built-in internal controls to prevent inaccurate, incomplete and invalid transaction recording, or due to the intrinsic limitations of internal controls. These limitations are due to factors such as:

- the potential for management to override controls;
- collusion circumventing the effectiveness of the segregation of duties; and
- human aspects such as misunderstanding of instructions, mistakes made in judgement, carelessness, distraction or fatigue.

The auditor's assessment of control risk involves two phases:

- A preliminary assessment of control risk is made once the auditor has enquired into the accounting system and identified those controls on which it might be effective and efficient to rely in conducting the audit. The assessment of control risk should be done at the assertion level for each material account balance or class of transactions.

- A final assessment of control risk is made after the performance of tests of controls aimed at determining whether or not controls to be relied upon by the auditor were performed adequately as they were designed, and were applied throughout the period of intended reliance; and that the staff involved in the controls did not have other incompatible functions.

---

[6] See Statement SAAS 400, paragraph .03.

The auditor would assess control risk as being high if controls are insufficient to prevent or timeously detect errors, or tests of controls procedures reveal inadequacies in the actual performance of the client's laid-down control activities. Should adequate controls be in place and tests of control audit procedures provide evidence of the satisfactory operation of these controls, control risk would be assessed as low. In these circumstances the auditor is justified in placing reliance on the system to prevent or detect error.

The extent of such reliance is a professional judgement. The first phase of internal control evaluation, the identification of controls or lack thereof, is a subjective judgement requiring of the auditor a sound knowledge of the basic principles of accounting systems design, including good internal control features, and their practical application. The application of statistical sampling techniques for tests of controls allows the auditor to make a more objective evaluation at the conclusion of the second phase of control risk evaluation, as the risk associated with tests of controls and its complement, the confidence level, are quantified for the statistical sample applications.

Recently, corporate governance issues – and therefore management's responsibility (see chapter 21) – have seen a change in emphasis in how some auditors initially approach the inherent and control risks assessment phases of the audit, particularly in the case of larger clients. This approach focuses on management's risk management procedures. In doing so, the auditor establishes – from management – the entity's business objectives and strategies implemented to achieve these, and their identification of the risks faced and how these are being monitored and controlled by them. Should the auditor seek to rely on such controls to prevent or detect errors in the accounting processes, evidence needs to be gathered of their effective operation.

5.5.2.3 Detection risk

Detection risk, the third constituent element of audit risk, is defined as 'the risk that an auditor's substantive procedures will not detect a misstatement that exists in an account balance or class of transactions that could be material, individually or when aggregated with misstatements in other balances or classes'.[7] It consists of two components commonly termed 'sampling risk' and 'non-sampling risk'.

Sampling risk is the risk that material errors will not be detected by the auditor because of the accepted auditing practice of examining less than the whole of an account balance or class of transactions.

Non-sampling risk is the risk that the auditor will fail to detect material errors due to the selection of an inappropriate auditing procedure, misapplication of an appropriate procedure, misinterpretation of audit results or misrepresentation to the auditor by management or third parties. This may arise because of one or more of the following failings:

---

[7] Statement SAAS 400, paragraph .03.

- Time pressure due to unrealistic budgets.
- Lack of competence and application.
- Failure to consult with senior staff when in doubt.
- Irresponsibility.
- Lack of commitment.
- Personal or emotional stress.

The non-sampling aspect of detection risk may be minimized by proper quality control policies and procedures such as audit staff training, the careful allocation of auditing tasks to those competent to perform the work, and adequate supervision and review of work by experienced audit personnel. Risk arising from misrepresentations of management, or others, can be minimized through the use of alternative auditing procedures aimed at gathering evidence to enhance (or negate) oral evidence supplied by management and others. These procedures are particularly necessary where assessment of representations, with hindsight, reveal inconsistencies, or where assessment of inherent risk has raised doubts about management's integrity or honesty. By its very nature, the non-sampling aspect of detection risk cannot be quantified.

The sampling risk aspect of detection risk relates directly to the nature and extent of the substantive auditing procedures performed and is thus controllable by the auditor. Inherent and control risk differ from detection risk in that they exist independently of the audit. In other words, inherent and control risks are uncontrollable by the auditor; detection risk, on the other hand, relates directly to the auditor's substantive procedures and can therefore be varied according to the auditor's professional judgement of the acceptable overall audit risk for the audit assignment. An increase in the extent of substantive procedures will reduce detection risk and vice versa. The level of detection risk the auditor can accept is influenced by the assessment of inherent and control risks taken together. The lower the auditor's assessment of combined inherent and control risks, the higher the detection risk can be. Conversely, the higher the inherent and control risk assessment, the lower the acceptable detection risk should be. In short, detection risk should bear an inverse relationship to inherent and control risk.

5.5.3 Planning relating to risk

For the purposes of planning auditing procedures, the auditor can either plan to make an assessment of inherent and control risks, or assume these risks to be at a maximum and therefore plan to perform extensive substantive audit procedures that should reduce detection risk to a level which results in the acceptable overall audit risk set by the auditor. The latter approach is only appropriate where the auditor concludes that the effort required to assess inherent and control risk would exceed the potential benefit to be derived from reducing the extent of substantive auditing procedures.

Should the auditor plan to place reliance on assessments of inherent and control risk – so as to reduce the extent of substantive audit procedures necessary to reduce audit risk to an acceptable level – the auditor should gather audit evidence in support of such assessments.

It is impractical, if not impossible, to eliminate audit risk completely. But the level of risk must always be such as to comply with generally accepted auditing standards.

To conclude the discussion on audit risk, it is fitting to consider the risks the auditor is exposed to at each major stage of the audit process, from the approach by a prospective client to the issue of the audit report. These stages are:

- *Pre-engagement activities:*
  - Perform new client investigation or consider change in circumstances of existing client.
  - Determine skill and competence requirements.
  - Establish terms of engagement.
- *Planning activities:*
  - Obtain a knowledge of the entity's business.
  - Consider planning materiality.
  - Consider inherent risk.
  - Obtain an understanding of the accounting system and related controls.
  - Formulate an audit approach.
- Perform tests of controls on internal controls on which audit reliance is intended.
- Perform substantive procedures.
- Evaluate audit misstatements.
- Conclude on the sufficiency of audit evidence.
- Formulate an audit opinion and report accordingly.

The pre-engagement activities are performed to decide whether or not to accept appointment as auditor of a new client or continue to serve an existing one. This decision is important for, as with commercial enterprises, the acceptance of appointment may result in loss. This aspect is the business risk run by the practitioner, the potential loss that may be suffered is the damage to the practitioner's professional reputation and therefore loss of clients as a result of adverse publicity. It is for the auditor to decide, utilizing all the facts available, whether to accept or reject the assignment.

In arriving at a decision, the auditor should also consider:

- availability of both human and other resources of the firm;
- independence of partners and staff in terms of prescribed standards;
- reputation and credibility (integrity) of the prospective client's management; and
- the strategic risks faced by the entity and how well these are controlled.

The risk of accepting a client without having sufficient resources necessarily increases the probability of the audit quality and, consequently, the auditor's opinion, being substandard. The auditor should, therefore, not accept an assignment unless the necessary staff are available. Where specialized knowledge is required which is not available within the audit firm, external experts may be engaged. It is clear that where the auditor does not have the knowledge, the risk of a material error or misstatement going undetected will be greater.

The whole question of independence and the rationale behind it is discussed in detail in chapter 2.3. Suffice it to say that, in the context of risk, should the auditor's independence in relation to a particular assignment be questioned, it will be far more difficult to justify the auditor's actions.

It is generally agreed that there is a higher risk attached to examining financial data for a dishonest client than an honest one. During the course of the audit the auditor needs to obtain explanations and other information from management and where these cannot be relied upon because of the dishonesty of the management, the auditor's task is impossible. Again, bear in mind that the auditor is expressing an opinion on the financial statements prepared by, or under the direction of, management – it is therefore important that the auditor assess the integrity and credibility of the directors and management prior to accepting an assignment.

The decision whether to accept or reject an assignment rests ultimately with the auditor. Because of normal business risk, the auditor may decide to accept some assignments with a higher risk than others.

At the planning stage of the audit, the auditor in the first instance obtains (or updates) a knowledge of the client's business, including knowledge of the industry and economic environment in which it operates. This aspect is discussed in section 5.2 of this chapter. The auditor with insufficient knowledge faces the risk of not appreciating the impact of significant events or transactions on the client's financial statements or of not identifying significant areas requiring audit emphasis. The newsmakers of litigation involving auditors have shown that failure to understand the client's business is often a major contributing factor in audit breakdown.

The ultimate objective of the planning process is the formulation of an audit approach, which, if properly implemented, will result in the performance of an efficient audit and one which reduces audit risk to an acceptable level. Inputs toward the final decision on an appropriate audit approach include:

- establishing planning materiality;
- assessing inherent risk of misstatement; and
- obtaining an understanding of the accounting systems and related internal controls to assess their adequacy as a basis for the preparation of reliable information.

An incorrect decision on the amount of planning materiality (see section 5.4 of this chapter) and/or an incorrect assessment of inherent risk could result in insufficient evidence being obtained to support an unqualified audit opinion. This risk is faced only if planning materiality is set at an abnormally large amount or inherent risk is assessed as low when, in fact, it is not. This is so because both the materiality decision and assessment of inherent risk affect directly the quantum of audit evidence required through the performance of substantive tests. Other things being equal, the higher the materiality and the lower the assessment of inherent risk, the less extensive the substantive tests will be. A planning materiality amount which is abnormally low, and/or inherent risk assessed as high where it is low, would result in audit risk being reduced to levels below that required by generally accepted auditing standards. In these latter circumstances the auditor runs the risk of losing clients because of excessive audit fees charged in order to recover the costs of performing substantive tests in excess of what is required.

The remaining stages of the audit process may be conveniently grouped into two categories for the purposes of analysing the risks faced by the auditor, namely:

- the auditor makes an incorrect assessment of control risk; and
- the auditor fails to reduce detection risk to a level which will result in an overall acceptable level of audit risk.

With regard to the first category, two important points must be stressed: The first is that the auditor cannot expect a system of control which will detect all errors of substantial effect but is disproportionate in cost to the risk it is designed to prevent. On the other hand, the quality of the control should be good enough to reduce to a reasonable level the risk of material errors occurring.

The second point is that although it is obvious that the better the internal control, the less risk there is of material errors occurring, this is only so where the system laid down by management has actually operated throughout the financial period under review. The auditor needs to conduct tests of controls to obtain reasonable satisfaction that the controls on which reliance is placed for audit purposes have operated throughout the period. An incorrect evaluation of the ability of controls to prevent or detect errors, or an inadequate tests of control programme, are the possible causes of an incorrect assessment of control risk, which in turn increases the audit risk of the auditor.

With regard to the second category, the auditor faces a sampling and a non-sampling risk aspect. Sampling risk there will always be, because of the accepted practice of testing less than the total population. The level of sampling risk that is allowable in order to achieve the appropriate level of audit risk is dependent on the auditor's assessments of inherent and control risks taken together. The higher the latter, the greater should be the extent of substantive tests to reduce sample risk to an acceptable level, and vice versa. It follows that where inherent and control risks have been incorrectly assessed as low, the sample risk aspect of detection risk is increased, since insufficient substantive tests will be performed to support the audit opinion. The non-sampling aspect of detection risk can be reduced to a minimum by effective quality control. Sound training, delegation of work to competent persons and effective staff supervision should prevent inappropriate audit procedures and/or misinterpretation of results.

5.6 PLANNING

5.6.1 The importance of planning

Two fundamental requirements of an audit are effectiveness and efficiency. An ineffective audit may bring accusations of professional negligence, and an inefficient audit is likely to result in failure to recover fees and ultimately the loss of clients. Thorough and timely planning provides an organized approach to the audit and ensures the optimum utilization of audit staff, prerequisites of an effective and efficient audit.

5.6.2 Scope

SAAS 300, 'Planning', identifies the following matters which need to be considered by the auditor when planning an audit:

- Knowledge of the business.
- Understanding the accounting and internal control systems.
- Risk and materiality.
- Nature, timing and extent of procedures.
- Coordination, direction, supervision and review.
- Other matters specific to each individual audit client, such as:
  - the possibility that the company may not be a going concern;
  - the terms of the engagement;
  - the nature of and deadline for reports; and
  - previously reported audit findings and recommendations.

At the planning stage of the audit, the auditor should also assess the susceptibility of material misstatements in the financial statements from fraud or error, depending on the circumstances of the client. This aspect is discussed in chapter 3.

Planning is fundamental to all audit assignments, but the extent of planning will vary according to the following factors:

- the size and complexity of the client's operations;
- the sophistication of the client's control systems and accounting processes;

- the auditor's previous exposure to and therefore knowledge of the client's business, including its strategic business objectives, risk exposure and how these are managed;
- the number of audit staff available for the conduct of the audit and their respective levels of competence;
- the degree of guidance available to audit staff, furnished by senior qualified personnel, audit manuals, industry sector knowledge databases or standardized audit programmes; and
- the degree of supervision available.

It is important that considerations and decisions taken at the planning phase of the audit are documented in the audit working papers. The form and extent of the planning documentation will vary with the size and complexity of the audit and particularly with the number of staff who will be involved. The sole practitioner, who plans procedures and executes these, has a limited need for a formal documented plan. This is not to say that a total lack of documentation of planning decisions would be justified in the circumstances. The conduct of a large audit assignment involving numerous staff members requires formal planning and more detailed planning documentation. This documentation is often referred to as a planning memorandum.

5.6.3 Effects and benefits

The effects and benefits that flow from audit planning may be identified as follows:

- early communication between the auditor and the client concerning the auditor's requirements and the needs of the client;
- early identification of potential problems or high-risk areas requiring audit emphasis;
- optimal timing of audit procedures;
- the assignment of appropriate staff competent to handle the work; and
- the use of planning decisions as part of the control mechanism.

These effects and benefits of audit planning are discussed below.

5.6.3.1 Communication between client and auditor

Audit staff working at the premises of a client may be disruptive to the extent that office accommodation is required and audit staff must have access to accounting records and to the client's staff. The planning process will enable the auditor to notify the client of planned periods of attendance and broadly identify what access to records and client's staff will be required. Planning will also allow the auditor to communicate well in advance any audit requirements, such as schedules detailing or summarizing information contained in the accounting records, so that these may be prepared timeously by the client for audit purposes.

Effective planning will require that the auditor ascertain from the client the reporting deadlines, that is to say, when the client would like to have the financial statements ready for issue. This will enable the auditor to plan with the objective of avoiding time pressures, pressures which may result in the auditor compromising on sufficiency of audit evidence gathered to support the audit opinion or making incorrect judgemental decisions.

5.6.3.2 Identification of areas requiring audit emphasis

Audit risk, as referred to in section 5.4 of this chapter, is the possibility that the auditor may unknowingly fail to modify appropriately the opinion on financial statements that are materially misstated. By planning, the auditor seeks to limit this risk to a level appropriate to the exercise of professional judgement when issuing an opinion on the fair presentation of financial statements.

In planning the nature, timing and extent of audit procedures, the auditor assesses the risk that material errors may occur (inherent risk) and whether the internal control systems will detect these errors or prevent their occurrence (control risk). In this manner the auditor identifies significant areas of the client's systems or accounting records which require audit emphasis and, in doing so, reduces the risk that audit procedures will fail to detect material error (detection risk). Generally speaking, should the inherent and control risk taken together be assessed being high, the auditor should plan to do one or more of the following:

- select audit procedures specifically designed to detect the kind of errors that could occur;
- increase the extent of substantive audit tests; and/or
- perform substantive audit procedures, on balance sheet items particularly, as close as possible to the financial year end.

5.6.3.3 Timing of audit procedures

Some audit procedures are subject to critical timing constraints, whereas others may be scheduled based on convenience, staff availability and the coordination of audit time requirements across the full spectrum of clients serviced by the audit firm. For example, the audit work done on the client's system of control and transaction recording need not be performed at any specific time, whereas the auditor has no discretion as to timing when attending at the client's count of inventories. However, the order in which procedures are performed is important. If audit procedures designed to test the operation of the system are performed prior to the evaluation of that system, the auditor may be proving the operation of a system on which reliance cannot be placed, which is a waste of time and effort. Again, if substantive work on the year-end balances is done prior to the evaluation and testing of the client's systems, the auditor may be guilty of over-auditing.

The timing of audit procedures should also take account of the possible need for related items to be examined simultaneously. This need may arise when the client's systems of control are such that manipulation of assets and related accounting records is possible. For example, when a cash count is done, it should include all floats and current cash takings, and at the same time bank accounts should be reconciled with the relevant bank statements and negotiable securities examined. This is particularly important where control over cash is unsatisfactory.

5.6.3.4 Assignment of appropriate staff

SAAS 220, 'Quality Control', states, 'any delegation of work to assistants will be in a manner that provides reasonable assurance that such work will be performed with due professional competence required in the circumstances'. This implies that each staff member is given adequate professional training and experience and that staff are assigned only to those sections of the audit for which their training and experience qualify them.

The allocation of appropriate staff is a function of the inherent complexity of the underlying audit task and the audit risks associated therewith. The more complex the task or the greater the audit risk assessment, the higher the level of auditing skill required. Because effective audit planning involves the identification of audit tasks and the assessment of related audit risks, it should result in appropriate allocation of work to audit staff.

5.6.3.5 Planning as an audit time control mechanism

The product of effective audit planning is the development of strategy to achieve audit objectives. Decisions are taken prior to the commencement of the audit fieldwork regarding the nature, extent and timing of audit procedures and the allocation of appropriate staff to do and supervise the work. Based on these decisions, time budgets should be drawn up, estimating and allocating the amount of time required to complete the various components of the audit. Ongoing comparison of actual times taken and estimated time to complete tasks should result in effective time control of the fieldwork. (However, see section 5.6.4 below.)

5.6.4 Audit planning procedures

A prerequisite of effective audit planning is a thorough knowledge and understanding of the nature of the client's business, its management, organization and methods of operation, and the industry within which it operates. Without this information, it will be difficult to make an intelligent assessment of the work to be done, since the auditor is unlikely to appreciate the impact of significant events or transactions on the client's financial statements or to identify significant areas requiring audit emphasis.

The South African Institute of Chartered Accountants Statement SAAS 310, 'Knowledge of the Business', identifies aspects of the audit which will be facilitated as a result of the auditor's knowledge of his client's business. These aspects may be classified under two stages of the audit, namely, the planning stage and the conduct of the audit. Some of the more important aspects identified are:

At the planning stage:

- assessing conditions under which accounting data is gathered, processed and recorded;
- determining planning materiality;
- assessing inherent and control risk;
- identifying the need to use the work of experts; and
- developing the overall audit plan and the audit programme.

During the course of the audit:

- evaluating the reasonableness of estimates, for example, depreciation, accounts receivable provisions and the like;
- evaluating the reasonableness of management representations used as audit evidence;
- identifying related parties;
- recognizing unusual circumstances, for example, illegal acts or irregularities;
- recognizing unexpected relationships in financial information; and
- making judgements about the appropriateness of accounting policies and the adequacy of disclosures in financial statements.

The auditor who has done the audit previously has knowledge of the client and the terms of the audit engagement. The auditor's concern is the changes, if any, that might have taken place since the previous audit. Enquiries directed to management, a review of the directors' board meeting minutes and the management accounts are sources of information about changed circumstances that may impact on the conduct of the audit.

An auditor who has not performed the audit before, but who has access to the audit working papers of the previous year, can use these as a source of information concerning the client and the conduct of the previous audit. The audit approach followed and procedures conducted, the problems encountered and how they were resolved, the time taken and the calibre of staff who did the work are valuable guides when planning the current audit.

The newly appointed auditor will not have experience of the client and may not have access to the previous auditor's working papers. As a consequence, the auditor will have to spend a substantial amount of time becoming acquainted with the circumstances of the client before the overall audit approach can be planned and the audit programme drawn up. The time needed will vary according to the auditor's knowledge of the industry or commercial segment within which the client operates and on the size and complexity of the client's operations.

Audit planning procedures, in the sequence they are most likely to occur, may be summarized as follows:

- Ascertain the exact extent of duties by reference to instructions from the client, preferably written, in the case of a sole trader or partnership, as well as reference to relevant statute in the case of a statutory audit. Engagement letters specify the auditor's obligations and responsibilities assumed. This subject is discussed in chapter 2.6.

- Become acquainted with the terms of the constitution of the business – for example, by reference, in the case of a partnership, to the partnership deed and, in the case of a limited company, to the memorandum and articles of association.

- Acquire – or, if one is the continuing auditor, update – a knowledge of the client's business. This entails ascertaining what the entity's business objectives are, what business processes are in place to achieve these, the business risks faced and how well management identifies, monitors and controls such risks through its established internal control systems. In broad terms, this would involve the following:
  - Ascertain how management views the business risks faced by the entity, and how management monitors and controls these risks.
  - Obtain, or update, a description of the organizational structure of the entity showing, particularly, the names of the executive directors (those having operational responsibilities) and the operational managers, as well as a summary of their respective duties and authority. Personnel responsible for accounting and control activities should also be identified, as should the extent of such responsibilities.
  - Obtain, or update, an understanding of the accounting and control systems. Such systems comprise two identifiable elements, namely, the control environment and the control procedures. The auditor needs to understand the control environment which comprise the director's and management's commitment to introducing and monitoring good systems of controls, including the establishment of an audit committee and an internal audit function, methods of assigning authority and responsibility, and monitoring the performance of these. Control procedures, on the other hand, are the control techniques introduced to achieve the objectives of valid, accurate and complete accounting for business processes. The auditor needs to understand the methods used in executing, recording and processing accounting information related to transactions entered into in the various business processes. Internal control is discussed in detail in chapters 9 and 10.

- Make a preliminary judgement of materiality. Planning materiality should be quantified. As the decision is usually taken before the financial statements being reported on are prepared, planning materiality should be based on the entity's interim financial statements, budgets or financial statements of one or more prior periods. Due recognition should be given to any changes in circumstances of the entity since the information, on which materiality is being based, was prepared. Materiality is discussed in section 5.4 of this chapter.

- Make a preliminary assessment of inherent and control risks related to material assertions underlying the financial statements. If the auditor does not intend to place reliance on such assessments, inherent and control risks must be assumed to be at a maximum. The reader is referred to section 5.5 of this chapter, where audit risk and its constituent elements are discussed.

- Study and evaluate internal controls where audit reliance on these is intended. This involves enquiring into, documenting and testing for compliance those internal controls the auditor intends relying on to reduce audit risk. Internal control and the procedures the auditor should follow to ascertain and evaluate systems are discussed at length in chapters 9 and 10.

- Perform preliminary analytical review procedures on the latest available management accounts to identify disclosures and amounts which are out of line with expectation and might require further audit investigation.

- Prepare audit programmes specifying the nature and extent of the detailed substantive audit procedures to be performed to limit detection risk to appropriate levels and to the budgeted time for each component.

- Decide on the timing of the significant phases of the audit. Liaison with the client would be necessary in this regard.

- Assign suitably qualified staff to the audit in such a way that tasks are allocated to persons capable of handling them, and ensure that the work is adequately supervised.

5.7 CONTROL OF THE CONDUCT OF AN AUDIT

5.7.1 Introduction

The management of individual audits varies in accordance with the size and complexity of the client, on the one hand, and the audit firm's size, organizational structure and delegation policies and procedures on the other. The task of controlling audit engagements in the case of a sole practitioner should present few problems, for such a person is likely to do much of the more complicated work, or only a few staff members will be involved allowing for easier supervision. The position of partners in larger practices responsible for the conduct of audits is obviously different.

Most firms today assign a group of clients to each partner so that client confidence may be gained and maintained through continuity. There are usually two principal methods of assigning staff to audit engagements: The first is called a 'group' system: all personnel are allocated to a number of different groups, each with a fair mix of qualified and unqualified staff, and each group is responsible for one section of clients and reports to one (or several) partners. The other method of assigning clients to audit engagements is according to a 'pool' system: personnel for each client are drawn from the staff pool, with the result that, at one time or another, a member of staff will work for any one of the firm's partners and with all the other members of staff.

5.7.2 Elements of control

Whatever method of assigning work is adopted, adequate control over the fieldwork is required to ensure that the work is performed in accordance with generally accepted standards of auditing and complies with the firm's own particular laid-down standards of performance. The following three important elements of audit control may be identified:

- clear instructions (directions) to staff in the form of audit programmes;
- supervision of the work as it proceeds; and
- review of the work on completion.

Elements of audit control are discussed briefly below.

5.7.2.1 Audit programmes

Audit programmes are a product of the planning process. Such programmes provide a record of judgemental decisions taken by experienced personnel – concerning the nature and extent of procedures to be followed in gathering audit evidence sufficient to justify the audit opinion – but they also serve to instruct staff on how to conduct the audit. This reduces the risk of necessary procedures being omitted or incorrect procedures being applied by inexperienced staff.

The audit programmes should be completed in sufficient detail to enable the individual doing the work to understand the relevance of each step to the audit objective, the techniques to follow in gathering the evidence, the method of choosing the sample (if less than the total population is being checked) and the extent of such tests. Estimates of time to complete each step (or group of steps) are usually included for control purposes. Provision is also made on programmes for staff who did the work to sign or initial the programme against each step, as and when the work is completed, as evidence of having satisfactorily completed each procedure.

The budgeted time should not be viewed by staff as the maximum time they may spend, or indeed the time they should spend, on any aspect of the audit. These times serve rather as a guide to staff as to the depth of analysis or extent of detail expected in performing any audit step or series of procedures and enable the fairly early identification of possible audit inefficiencies through budget overruns. Failure to meet budget may be as a result of unexpected complications that arise, for example, missing supporting documentation or inaccuracies in accounting records requiring further investigation and rectification. If this is the case, the budgets assist in identifying legitimate reasons for fee increases which may be discussed with the client.

5.7.2.2 **Supervision**

It is normal practice for audit partners responsible for audit engagements to delegate the day-to-day control of an audit to a qualified person, normally referred to as the audit manager, senior or senior in charge. The senior is usually an individual who has experience of the client, having worked on the engagement in previous years, and certainly someone who would have been intimately involved, together with the partner, at the planning stage of the audit. The senior should therefore be in a good position to ensure through supervision that the audit proceeds as planned.

Supervision in this context refers to the on-the-job guidance that the senior is able to give to less skilled or inexperienced staff, for example, in interpreting general planning decisions in the planning documentation, or giving advice on what alternative audit procedures to follow if, as is sometimes the case, choice is allowed in audit programmes. On-the-job guidance (referred to as monitoring in SAAS 220, 'Quality Control for Audit Work') involves ensuring that assistants have the necessary skills to perform delegated tasks, that they understand what it is they have been assigned to perform and that the work was carried out in accordance with the audit programme. Apart from guidance to staff, the supervising senior should monitor the performance of all members of the audit team on the engagement by making regular comparison of actual times spent, estimated times to complete tasks and the budget time, assisting where staff are obviously experiencing difficulties and generally ensuring that staff behave in a professional manner befitting the reputation of the firm.

An essential component of the senior's supervision of the fieldwork is the review of the working papers prepared by staff. The review should reveal whether staff members have adequately performed the work and whether the audit findings have been properly summarized in the working papers.

5.7.2.3 **The audit review**

As a general rule, whenever work is delegated by more senior to less experienced staff, all completed work should be reviewed by the delegator. The reviewer should sign and date the working papers reviewed as evidence of having performed this task.

The two primary aims of the review of work are to minimize the risk of necessary procedures being omitted or incorrect ones being applied and to minimize the risk of incorrect judgemental decisions being taken on the basis of the evidence gathered.

The reviewer should generate a list of queries if any audit deficiencies exist, such as, for example, if insufficient audit evidence has been gathered to support any audit conclusions or the audit working papers were not completed in accordance with the firm's policies.

Audit deficiencies may be more readily detected by the reviewer, who has a feel for the audit as a whole and who is more experienced than staff who did the detailed work. Moreover, individual staff members are often exposed only to isolated aspects of the audit and may not appreciate the relevance of the work in one section to the findings in another.

The depth of the review procedures adopted by the reviewing partner will vary inversely with the competence of the personnel who did the work and also with the experience of the first reviewer, if any prior review was performed. For example, the audit senior is likely to review every working paper in detail to be satisfied that the work was performed in accordance with the programme instructions, that the conclusions are supported by the evidence gathered, and that the working papers have been completed in accordance with the firm's policies, whereas the partner may review only key working papers on which findings and conclusions are summarized. The partner is quite entitled to rely with confidence on the detailed review of a suitably qualified senior.

In conclusion, the audit partner is responsible for giving the opinion on the client's financial statements, but often does not do the audit fieldwork personally. The audit partner would therefore to a large extent place reliance on the review of the completed audit working paper file to gain satisfaction that sufficient audit evidence was gathered to support the opinion. In reviewing the work done, the responsible partner will want to ensure that:

- the audit proceeded as planned;
- staff appeared to understand the procedures included in the audit programmes;
- adequate work was performed;
- significant accounting or auditing questions raised during the audit were satisfactorily resolved, for example, audit difficulties might have necessitated an adjustment to audit programmes and accounting problems were resolved by way of adequate consultation;
- audit conclusions are supported by the working papers; and
- the financial position and profits disclosed in the financial statements appear reasonable.

As a result of having performed the review, the partner will be in a position to:

- make recommendations to assist in planning for the next year's audit;
- approve and finalize the audit comments letter to the client which should contain, inter alia, details of any internal control weaknesses and recommendations for improvement, and any significant errors discovered in the accounting records; and
- sign with confidence the audit report on the financial statements.

Working paper reviews are discussed further in chapter 8.

6

Audit Evidence
– Fundamental Concepts

Learning objectives

After studying this this chapter, you should be able to:

1. Explain the nature of audit evidence and discuss approaches adopted by the auditor to obtain sufficient appropriate evidence.
2. Explain how the financial statement assertions are used to develop specific audit objectives for which audit evidence is sought.
3. Discuss the various types of audit procedures that may be used by an auditor and explain which are most appropriate to achieve specific audit objectives set.
4. Explain how the auditor may use computer-assisted audit techniques (CAATs) for gathering audit evidence in IT environments.
5. Describe the types of corroborating evidence available to the auditor and how their quality and reliability is evaluated.
6. Explain how the electronic data processing systems affect the nature, timing and extent of audit procedures conducted.
7. Discuss matters the auditor needs to consider in gathering appropriate audit evidence regarding the occurrence/validity of recurrent and non-recurrent transactions entered into by different legal entities.

6.1 THE NATURE AND SUFFICIENCY OF AUDIT EVIDENCE

6.1.1 Introduction

The purpose of an audit is to enable the auditor to express an opinion on the fairness of the financial statements being audited. In order to express an opinion, sufficient, relevant, and reliable evidence must be gathered to satisfy the auditor regarding the assertions contained in the financial statements and the compliance of such assertions with the entity's stated accounting policies, applied consistently in accordance with a generally accepted accounting framework (for example, GAAP). These assertions are generally regarded as being:[1]

ASSERTION CATEGORY	NATURE OF BALANCES AND TRANSACTIONS
Completeness	There are no unrecorded assets, liabilities, transactions or events, or undisclosed items.
Occurrence/Validity	All transactions recorded, occurred and are valid transactions of the entity.
Existence	All assets exist and liabilities are properly owed at a given date.
Measurement/Accuracy	Assets and liabilities are recorded at the proper amount and all income and expenses have been accurately recorded in the proper period (in accordance with the entity's accounting policies and in compliance with the applicable accounting framework, for example GAAP).
Valuation	Assets or liabilities are recorded at appropriate carrying values.
Rights and obligations	All assets are beneficially owned and liabilities are properly owed by the entity at a given date. Items are appropriately classified and described in accordance with the applicable financial framework (for example, GAAP).

Table 6.1 Management's assertions in the financial statements

Clearly, gathering and evaluating audit evidence comprises the major part of the time spent on any audit assignment. As client fees are primarily based on time spent, the more efficiently and effectively this process is conducted, the more cost effective and better the service the audit firm is likely to render to its client. Equally, the auditor's reputation will be adversely affected by incorrect audit opinions given. Accordingly, it is incumbent on the auditor to reduce the risk of an incorrect opinion being issued. This will depend to a large extent on the auditor's ability to gather and correctly evaluate audit evidence before issuing the report.

The responsibility of the auditor for gathering audit evidence is expressed succinctly in SAAS 500 paragraph .02, 'Audit Evidence', which states:

> 'The auditor should obtain sufficient appropriate audit evidence to be able to draw reasonable conclusions on which to base the audit opinion.'

---

[1] SAAS 500, paragraph .13.

This standard raises the following key issues, each of which will be discussed in this chapter:

● What constitutes audit evidence?
● How does the auditor obtain audit evidence?
● How does the auditor determine whether the evidence gathered is sufficient?
● How does the evidence gathered support the audit opinion?

Guidance on the specific aspects of audit evidence and the auditor's responsibilities is contained in the following South African Auditing Standards: SAAS 500, 'Audit Evidence'; ED-SAAS 502, 'Enquiries regarding Litigation and Claims'; SAAS 505, 'External Confirmations'; SAAS 510, 'Initial Engagements – Opening Balances'; SAAS 520, 'Analytical Review'; SAAS 530, 'Audit Sampling and Other Selective Testing Procedures'; SAAS 540, 'Audit of Accounting Estimates'; SAAS 550, 'Related Parties'; SAAS 560, 'Subsequent Events'; SAAS 570, 'Going Concern' and SAAS 580, 'Management Representations'. References to these statements are made where appropriate.

6.1.2 What constitutes audit evidence?

SAAS 500, paragraph .04 of 'Audit Evidence', defines the term as follows:

> 'Audit evidence means the information obtained by the auditor in arriving at the conclusions on which the audit opinion is based. Audit evidence will comprise source documents and accounting records (irrespective of their storage medium) underlying the financial statements and corroborating information from other sources.'

The underlying accounting records will typically comprise source documents, the entity's accounting records of original entry, general and subsidiary ledgers, inventory records and fixed asset registers. These accounting records are often in electronic format requiring adequate attention to the accuracy of the underlying accounting data before being able to place reliance on the resultant financial statements. Accounting records in electronic format may only be available at a particular time and may not be retrievable after a specified period if backup files do not exist.

The source documents will depend on the nature of the relevant transaction, but will include both written documents and electronic data generated internally by the business as well as those received from other parties with whom the business deals. These documents, which may comprise written documents or electronic data, may include, *inter alia*:

● Sales delivery notes and invoices, statements to customers and remittance advices from them;
● Purchase orders with goods received notes, suppliers' invoices and statements;
● Wages, clock cards and other time records, weekly and monthly payrolls, individual pay records and personnel files;

- Paid cheques, records of EFT transfers, bank deposit slips and bank statements.;
- Contract documents, such as leases and instalment sales agreements; and
- Journal vouchers and reconciliations of ledger accounts or schedules setting out computations of one sort or another.

The source of the documents and the relative strength of the client's internal controls procedures both have a bearing on the extent of reliance which the auditor can place on the source documents as audit evidence. This is discussed in section 6.2 of this chapter.

Other pertinent information which the auditor may gather will include:

- The results of tests of control and detailed substantive audit tests.
- Responses to inquiries.
- Confirmations from outside parties.[2]
- Written and oral representations from management and staff.[3]
- Information ascertained from physical observation of client control procedures or physical inspection of assets owned by the client, that is, by attendance at inventory count.
- Mathematical evidence from recomputation of calculations.
- Evidence from analytical review procedures.

The nature and extent of information which the auditor may consider pertinent will depend on the judgement of what is relevant to the attainment of the audit objectives. The auditor's judgement will be influenced by the assessment of materiality, the audit risk attaching to the particular assertion, the size of the population, the recurring or non-recurring nature of the transaction and the time and cost benefits sought in the conduct of the audit.

By obtaining the evidence, the auditor is seeking to ensure that the risk of material misstatement in any account, which could lead to a material misstatement in the financial statements on which the auditor is reporting, has been limited to an acceptable level. The auditor gathers evidence from different sources and of differing nature; however, it must be realized that the cumulative evidence which the auditor obtains from the source documents and any other information gathered is seldom absolute but is, by its nature, persuasive and generally seeks to corroborate the reason-ableness of the information recorded in the underlying accounting records. At the same time, it is the cumulative evidence which the auditor finally evaluates in deciding on the audit opinion.

For this reason the auditor seldom relies on a single source to provide sufficient audit evidence, but seeks rather to combine evidence from different sources and of a differing nature, which indicates a consistency of result to

---

[2] SAAS 505 and ED-SAAS 502.
[3] SAAS 505 and SAAS 580.

corroborate the information recorded in the accounting records. If the evidence indicates inconsistencies, which may be material, the auditor should extend the selected audit procedures until the inconsistencies are resolved and necessary assurance is obtained regarding the account balance or class of transactions. Failing this, the auditor will have to consider modifying the audit report.

6.1.3 How is audit evidence obtained?

The procedures which the auditor applies to obtain audit evidence are categorized as follows:

- Inspection;
- Observation;
- Enquiry and confirmation;
- Reperformance;
- Computation;
- Analytical review;
- Vouching;
- Tracing; and
- Computer-Assisted Audit Techniques (CAATs).

Inspection, observation, enquiry, reperformance and computation procedures are used by the auditor in the conduct of both tests of control and substantive testing, while confirmation and analytical review procedures are solely substantive test procedures. A more detailed discussion of tests of controls and substantive testing follow later. The purpose of this section is to define the meaning of the audit procedures for gathering audit evidence and to describe which procedure is most appropriate to support a particular audit objective.

- *Inspection, in tests of controls,* consists of examining accounting data such as documents, records, reconciliations and reports for evidence that a particular control procedure has been applied. In this instance the auditor is invariably looking for the signatures of persons authorized to perform that control as *prima facie* evidence that the particular control has been performed. A typical example is a check stamp on a purchase invoice with sections indicating that the purchase has been authorized, the goods charged for have been received, the prices are correct, the invoice is mathematically correct, the account allocation has been approved and the invoice has been approved for payment. If, in selecting a sample of purchase invoices to inspect, the auditor finds that all sections on all invoices selected have been initialled by the appropriate person, the auditor may assume that the checks to ensure the accuracy and validity of the transaction have been applied and will be in a position to conclude on the reliability of the internal control procedures.

- *Inspection, in substantive testing,* consists of examining records, documents and tangible assets. This is probably the most widely used procedure to gather audit evidence. The inspection of records enables the auditor to assess the authenticity of such records, identify potential errors or irregularities, and identify accounts or amounts requiring more detailed corroborating evidence compared with those which may require little additional audit work. The inspection of documents generally provides the auditor with first-hand information of the terms of a particular transaction or agreement, which will enable the auditor to verify the amount and its allocation in the accounting records. For example, inspecting the terms of a royalty agreement will enable the auditor to check the accuracy of the client's calculations to corroborate the amount of the royalties expense in the income statement. However, if the royalties are, for example, based on sales of particular products, the auditor will need to ascertain whether the client's controls over the completeness, accuracy and validity of recorded sales are sufficiently reliable to provide accurate sales information for the royalty calculation. This may necessitate either analytical review and/or tests of controls within the sales system to obtain the required level of assurance. The physical inspection of tangible assets of the entity will provide the auditor with evidence of the existence and condition of the assets inspected, such as inventory or fixed assets; however, the auditor will have to inspect other documents and accounting records to obtain evidence of the value and ownership of the assets.

- *Observation in both tests of controls and substantive testing* consists of watching a process or procedure being performed. Observation provides strong evidence of the observed operation only at the time of observation. Care must be taken when extending conclusions about the process or procedure to periods not observed by the auditor. An example for tests of control purposes entails observing the despatch of goods from the premises to ensure that the person conducting the gate check dispatches no goods without proper delivery documentation and the consequent signing of the delivery documents. An example for substantive purposes is attendance at a client's inventory count to observe the procedures for ensuring that all inventories physically on hand are accurately counted, control is maintained over all inventory count sheets, goods in the despatch and receiving areas are clearly identified with last document numbers noted, and damaged and unsaleable inventory is clearly marked on the count sheets. If the client has material inventory holdings at more than one location, attendance at only one location will not provide the auditor with any assurance as to the client's count procedures at another location.

- *Inquiry and confirmation* involves the auditor seeking relevant information from knowledgeable persons inside or outside the entity, confirming the application of procedures, providing information or corroborating evidence which the auditor did not previously have. The inquiry may be oral or written. Generally, less reliance can be placed on responses obtained internally and these will invariably require further corroboration. Confirmation obtained from third parties is generally more reliable than that obtained internally, and written confirmations are generally more reliable than oral representations. The mark of a good auditor is the ability to ask the right person the right question to obtain the relevant evidence being sought.

Examples of third party confirmations frequently requested by auditors are requests for confirmation of bank balances or loan accounts and accounts receivable circularization requests. Internal confirmation in the form of a letter of representation may be obtained from management.[4]

- *Reperformance* in a test of controls context involves the auditor reperforming the procedures already performed by the client. Reperforming a procedure and finding no errors provides evidence of the functioning of the controls, but provides conclusive evidence only if the auditor finds that errors were detected and corrected by the established controls. In a computerized accounting environment where the auditor may be seeking to establish that controls built into a particular program are operating, test data containing errors may be deliberately run against the client's program in order to identify and either correct or print out the errors in the form of an error report.

   Reperformance in a substantive testing context involves repeating client procedures to determine whether an amount is correctly recorded, for example, reperforming depreciation calculations to verify the amount of depreciation provided for the year.

- *Computation* consists of checking the arithmetical accuracy of source documents and accounting records or of performing independent calculations. In performing computations, it is the object of the exercise, which distinguishes between substantive procedures and tests of controls. If the objective is to obtain evidence regarding the accuracy of recording, it is by definition a substantive procedure, whereas if the objective is to obtain evidence that an arithmetic computation was an independent check, it is a test of control. In practice, both objectives are met, giving rise to the term 'dual purpose'.

- *Analytical review* consists of the analysis of significant ratios and trends, including the resulting investigation of fluctuations and relationships that are inconsistent with other relevant information or deviate from predicted amounts. Overall and specific analytical review procedures are being used increasingly by auditors in order to reduce the extent of detailed substantive testing which is far more time consuming. This trend has developed due to the availability of generalized computer-assisted audit software to facilitate analytical reviews and the substantial investment by many audit practices in personal computers for use by their audit staff on assignments. A comprehensive discussion of analytical review procedures is to be found later in this chapter in the section on substantive testing.

---

[4] SAAS 505 and SAAS 580.

Although not included specifically in SAAS 500, the following substantive tests of detail, sometimes referred to as directional testing of transactions, are generally performed by an auditor:

- *Vouching* involves the selection of items in the accounting records and obtaining and inspecting the underlying source documentation to gain assurance regarding the occurrence (validity) and measurement (accuracy) of the transactions recorded. This is an important audit procedure for detecting an overstatement in an account balance or duplication of transactions recorded. It is not appropriate for detecting an under-statement arising from the omission of a transaction.

- *Tracing* involves the selection of source documents for tracing to the relevant entries recorded in the accounting records. The direction of testing allows for the detection of entries omitted and therefore provides assurance related to the completeness assertion.

6.1.3.1 Computer-assisted audit techniques (CAATs)[5]

When the entity's accounting records are maintained on electronic media, CAATs may be used to perform many audit procedures both in the tests of controls and substantive tests referred to earlier. The use of CAATs may provide effective tests of control and substantive procedures where there are no input documents or a visible audit trail, where population and sample sizes are very large or where it may not be possible to perform the procedures manually. CAATs may be used in the following ways:

- Tests of details of transactions and balances, for example, the recalculation of interest on savings accounts, or the extraction of invoices above a certain value from computer records.
- Analytical procedures, for example, reperforming a variety of calculations, comparing data against established criteria, stratifying account balances.
- Tests of general controls, for example, testing the setup or configuration of the operating program or access procedures to the program libraries.
- Sampling programs to extract data for testing.
- Tests of application controls, for example, testing the functioning of a programmed control.
- Reperforming calculations performed by the entity's accounting system.

CAATs are computer programs and data the auditor uses as part of the audit procedures to process data of audit significance contained in an entity's information systems. CAATs may consist of package programs, purpose-written programs, utility programs or system management programs. Embedded audit routines are sometimes built into an entity's computer system to provide data for later use by the auditor; this will typically happen in circumstances, such as in a bank, where millions of transactions are

---

[5] SAAPS 1009, paragraph .06 – .09.

occurring on a daily basis. Test data techniques are sometimes used during an audit, however, most clients will not permit such data to be introduced into the live environment due to fears that the test data will not subsequently be completely eliminated from the accounting records. Consequently such test transactions may be used in an integrated test facility.

The increasing power and sophistication of PCs, particularly laptops, which are used extensively by audit staff, have resulted in other tools for the auditor to use. In some instances laptops are linked to the auditor's main computer systems. Examples of such tools are:

- expert systems, for example, used in the design of audit programs, audit planning and risk assessment;
- tools to evaluate a client's risk management procedures;
- electronic audit working papers, which provide for the direct extraction of data from the client's computer records, for example, by downloading the general ledger for audit testing such as extensive analytical review procedures; and
- corporate and financial modelling programs for use as predictive audit tests.

6.1.4 How does the auditor determine whether the evidence gathered is sufficient?

In the first place, to be acceptable as audit evidence, the information obtained by the auditor must be appropriate. Appropriateness in this context means the measure of quality of audit evidence, its relevance to a particular assertion and its reliability.[6]

6.1.4.1 Relevance

The question whether evidence is relevant depends on the extent to which it assists the auditor in achieving the audit objectives. Clearly, the audit objective will be related to the assertion, which is what the auditor is attempting to verify. For example, attendance at an inventory count will provide the auditor with evidence as to the physical existence and condition of the inventory, but attendance will not provide any evidence that the inventory has been correctly valued, is complete, or is beneficially owned by the client. Other evidence such as suppliers' invoices, analytical review procedures and confirmations from lenders to whom the inventory may have been pledged, or consignors in the case of consignment stocks held, will provide further evidence of these other assertions.

6.1.4.2 Reliability

The reliability of audit evidence will be dependent on its source and nature. The auditor obtains evidence from internal sources, from external sources

---

[6] SAAS 500, paragraph .07.

and from evidence developed by the audit staff. Generally speaking, evidence such as analytical reviews and trend analysis developed by the auditor will be more reliable than that provided by the client or third parties. Evidence obtained from external sources is generally more reliable than that produced by the client. For example, bank statements and confirmation of balances will be more reliable than the accounts receivable statements produced by the client's accounting system to send to its customers. When the client has good internal controls, the evidence developed internally will be more reliable than when internal controls are weak or nonexistent.

Similarly, evidence concerning factual amounts which can be objectively corroborated, such as the balance in the bank account on a given date, will be more reliable than that which is judgementally determined, such as a provision for inventory obsolescence, which is based on a number of assumptions about future events which may be difficult, if not impossible, to predict with substantial accuracy.

In circumstances indicating fraud or error that could materially affect the financial statements, the auditor must exercise professional scepticism in accepting explanations from management and employees and evidence generated internally or, purportedly, externally. The auditor should also design substantive audit procedures – which will appropriately determine whether the financial statements have been misstated – and consider the implications of any identified misstatements for other areas of the audit. Suitably qualified staff should be allocated to the audit; if necessary, and after discussion with management to ascertain what steps are being taken to address the fraud or error, the allocation of staff may include those with forensic audit experience.

6.1.4.3 Sufficiency

Audit evidence obtained should be sufficient to restrict the audit risk with regard to each material assertion to an acceptable level.

This will be affected by the auditor's assessment of inherent and control risks attaching to the assertion, as well as the materiality of the amounts and the likelihood of errors occurring. Errors detected in prior audits, in the absence of change, as well as errors detected in the current audit are of relevance in this regard. The auditor will generally obtain some assurance from the review of internal controls and tests of controls and from any analytical review procedures. From this the auditor will need to determine the nature and extent of further detailed substantive evidence required to restrict detection risk to an acceptable level.

More evidence will be required when materiality limits for the entity are set at, say, R20 000 than if they are set at R500 000. Similarly, material account balances or transactions which have been found to contain a number of errors, for example sales and accounts receivable overstated due to pricing errors, will require more substantive evidence than account balances where there is little risk of errors or misstatements, for example, share capital and dividends declared.

Qualitative factors, which should be considered in concluding on the acceptability of audit evidence are:

- its objectivity;
- its timeliness;
- the existence of other corroborating evidence; and
- the relative strength of the system which processed the information.

The auditor exercises judgement as to what constitutes 'sufficient appropriate audit evidence' in particular circumstances. Factors influencing the auditor's judgement will include:

- Knowledge of the client's business and the industry in which the business operates, including management strategies and procedures for managing key risk exposures of the business and the auditor's assessment of the nature and level of inherent risk at the financial statement level related to account balances and class of transactions.
- The auditor's understanding of significant business processes, the existence of complex accounting systems and transactions, reliance on electronic data and information, and assessment of control risk.
- The degree of correspondence of management assertions reflected in the financial statements with the underlying records and audit expectations based on audit evidence obtained.
- The materiality of the items examined, previous experience with the client and results of audit procedures, including evidence of fraud and error detected.
- The source, relevance and reliability of external and internal information available.

Finally, the auditor must be satisfied that the audit objective(s) has been achieved relative to the assertions and that detection risk in respect of each has been reduced to appropriate levels. This is a matter of professional judgement. The reader is referred to a detailed discussion in chapters 10 and 11.

6.1.5 How is the evidence related to the content of the audit report?

By obtaining the evidence, the auditor is seeking assurance that the risk of material misstatement in any account, which could lead to a material misstatement in the financial statements on which the auditor is reporting, has been reduced to an acceptable level.

The auditor gathers evidence from different sources and of differing nature; however, it must be realized that the cumulative evidence which the auditor obtains from the source documents and any other information gathered is seldom absolute but is, by its nature, persuasive and generally seeks to corroborate the reasonableness of the information recorded in the underlying accounting records. At the same time it is the cumulative evidence which the auditor finally evaluates in deciding on the appropriate audit opinion.

For this reason the auditor seldom relies on a single source to provide sufficient audit evidence, but seeks rather to combine evidence from different sources and of a differing nature, which indicates a consistency of result to corroborate the information recorded in the accounting records. If the evidence indicates inconsistencies, which may be material, the auditor should extend the audit procedures until the inconsistencies are resolved and provide the necessary assurance regarding the account balance or class of transactions. Failing this, the auditor will have to consider modifying the audit report as indicated below.

The cumulative audit evidence obtained by the auditor during the audit should support an unmodified report expressing an unqualified opinion on the financial statements. If, however, the audit evidence is not sufficient, the auditor will need to consider the effect of the scope limitation on the audit report. Depending on the materiality of the amounts, a scope limitation or multiple uncertainties would lead to a qualified audit opinion or, in the case of significant uncertainty, a disclaimer of opinion. Alternatively, if evidence has been obtained that the financial statements are materially misstated, the auditor needs to express a disagreement in the audit opinion, issuing an 'except for' or 'adverse' opinion. Reference should be made to the reasons for the modification to the audit report in a separate qualification paragraph.[7]

The reader is referred to chapter 18 for an in-depth discussion of audit reports.

6.2 THE NATURE, TIMING AND EXTENT OF AUDIT PROCEDURES

6.2.1 The nature of audit procedures

6.2.1.1 Tests of controls

Tests of control are defined as follows:[8]

'Tests of control mean tests performed to obtain evidence about the suitability and design and effective operation of the accounting and internal control systems, and their operation throughout the period.'

These procedures are designed to establish that key controls, which the auditor intends relying on, were:

---

[7] SAAS 700.
[8] SAAS 500, paragraph .11.

- performed as they were designed to be performed;
- performed adequately;
- performed by someone who did not have incompatible functions; and
- applied throughout the period under review.

The key controls are those control procedures which will ensure that completeness, accuracy and validity assertions are met in the recording of individual transactions in any class of transactions such as sales, purchases, salaries and wages. An entity will normally have other internal control procedures over its transactions, which, for example, are intended to ensure quality control or client service or provide staff motivation to meet sales or production or productivity targets. These controls are of no consequence to the auditor's objective of gathering sufficient evidence to support the conclusions in the audit report and accordingly no tests need be carried out on such controls. Testing the key controls will enable the auditor to assess the control risk for each objective for different classes of transactions as high, medium or low. This assessment will enable the auditor to design appropriate substantive tests to limit the likelihood of material errors going undetected.

Where the entity maintains its accounting records in electronic format, it may be essential for the auditor to identify and test the general and application controls in order to establish the reliability of the underlying accounting data used in the preparation of the financial statements. The auditor may need to use CAATs for purposes of testing the internal controls and data maintained in electronic format and, depending on the complexity of the data processing environment, may also need to involve staff with IT skills and expertise to conduct such tests of controls.

If not intending to rely on internal controls, the auditor should not conduct tests of controls but should proceed to more extensive substantive test procedures instead. The auditor may decide not to rely on control procedures either because a preliminary review of the internal control system for a particular transaction type indicates that the system cannot be relied upon, or because the volume of transactions of that type is insufficient to justify tests of controls. Before proceeding to detailed substantive testing, analytical reviews should be conducted which will provide a certain level of assurance about the audit objectives. Thereafter any further assurance required to limit audit risk to an acceptable level must be satisfied by means of detailed substantive tests.

Tests of controls involve inspection, observation, enquiry and reperformance techniques and are aimed at determining whether or not controls to be relied upon by the auditor were performed adequately, as they were designed, by someone who did not have incompatible functions, and that they were applied throughout the period of intended reliance. The procedures for obtaining evidence have already been discussed.

The selection of the appropriate procedure depends on the manner in which the control is performed. Due to the limitations of individual tests of controls already mentioned, it will usually be necessary for the auditor to apply a combination of the various available procedures to obtain satisfaction that controls operated effectively.

The reader is referred to the more detailed discussion in chapters 9 and 10 relating to the understanding of the strategic business objectives and processes of the entity; the key internal controls implemented to manage significant risks identified in various data-processing environments; the related control risk assessment and tests of controls.

6.2.1.2 Substantive tests of transactions and balances

Substantive procedures are defined in SAAS 500, paragraph .06 as follows:

> 'Substantive procedures mean tests performed to obtain audit evidence to detect material misstatements in the financial statements, and are of two types:
> – Tests of details of transactions and balances, and
> – Analytical procedures.'

Substantive procedures are designed to reduce detection risk to an acceptable level. In contrast, tests of control provide evidence that is directly related to the operation of the internal controls. Certain procedures are dual purpose in nature in that they provide evidence of both the operation of a control as well as the accuracy of recording.

Substantive tests are divided into two broad categories, namely:
- Analytical procedures; and
- Substantive tests of details of transactions and balances.

Both are designed to provide evidence regarding the validity, accuracy and completeness of transactions and the completeness, accuracy, valuation, existence, and ownership of asset, liability, income and expenditure and capital balances at a particular date.

6.2.1.3 Analytical procedures

SAAS 520, paragraph .03 states:

> 'Analytical procedures mean the analysis of significant ratios and trends, including the resulting investigation of fluctuations and relationships that are inconsistent with other relevant information or which deviate from predicted amounts.'

The detailed tests of controls and substantive procedures discussed in chapter 11 should be preceded by broad checks and analytical procedures on the reasonableness of the figures, which lead to the year-end financial statements. This is done by analysing overall relationships and patterns in and among elements of financial information.

There are two main aspects of the analytical review. One is to provide information on any areas which do not appear to conform to the expected and which may require more rigorous examination by the auditor, for example by enlarging the sample size of the tests to be conducted, or, if the test has already been made, by supplementing it with a further test. The other is to corroborate evidence otherwise obtained that the results recorded fairly represent the facts. It should be apparent that these two aspects are indeed two sides of the same coin. If the figures are not as expected they provide a warning to conduct further investigation; if they do conform they give additional assurance of fair presentation.

The reader is referred to chapter 11 for a more detailed discussion of the setting of detection risk and the nature of substantive tests of detail and analytical review.

6.2.2 Factors affecting the timing of audit procedures

When the various tests are to be performed depends on the following factors:

- The type of audit, that is, whether continuous, interim or final.
- The availability of the data, such as transaction details kept in electronic format.
- The stage which the audit has reached.
- The specific audit objective to be achieved.
- The nature of the test to be performed.
- The needs of the client.

The chronological sequence of the audit process dictates that, if reliance on internal control is intended to reduce audit risk, tests of controls should be done prior to the performance of substantive procedures. This is so because the final assessment of control risk can be made only after an evaluation of the test of control results and this assessment of control risk has a direct bearing on the nature and extent of the planned substantive tests. Should tests of controls reveal that internal control procedures have not operated as designed, the planned substantive test procedures should be extended, such that sufficient evidence is obtained to reduce audit risk to an acceptable level.

Tests of controls will be done after the auditor has completed the preliminary assessment of internal controls and has identified the key controls on which the achievement of the audit objectives will rely. As the auditor must obtain satisfaction that the controls have operated as designed throughout the period of intended reliance, it is usual for auditors to evaluate controls at an early stage of the financial year and, depending on the size of the client, to visit the client on a few occasions during the year for the purpose of performing the planned tests of control.

In electronic data-processing environments certain data, such as transaction details, may only be kept for a short time and may not be available in machine-readable form by the time the auditor needs them. Thus the auditor will need to make arrangements for the retention of data required or, alternatively, alter the timing of the audit tests so that they are conducted when the data is available. This may also occur where the client has changed computer systems during the financial year and the data from the original system hardware and software may no longer be accessible via the new hardware and software programs.

Other matters influencing the timing of auditing procedures, and which should be considered by the auditor, are the possible need for simultaneous examination of items and whether or not an element of surprise is necessary for the satisfactory attainment of an audit objective. For example, negotiable securities should be checked at the time of any physical cash count.

The needs of the client regarding publication of its financial results as soon as is possible after the year-end also influence the timing of audit procedures. Where internal controls are satisfactory, assets and liabilities may be verified at a date prior to that of the year-end. In these circumstances, the year-end procedures will consist mainly of the comparison of year-end balances with those of the previous dates at which verification was performed, and a review and investigation of unusual transactions and significant fluctuations.

6.2.3 Factors affecting the extent of audit procedures

The extent of audit procedures will be determined judgementally by the auditor. Factors which the auditor will need to consider are:

- The materiality of the item.
- The auditor's assessment of the inherent and control risks related to the particular assertion underlying the balance or class of transactions, or related to the entity as a whole.
- The level to which detection risk must be reduced to attain a sufficiently low level of overall audit risk. This in turn depends on the auditor's assessment of inherent and control risks taken together.
- The need to obtain sufficient relevant and reliable audit evidence to support the audit opinion.
- The results of the substantive audit tests already completed which may indicate problem areas requiring further audit evidence.
- Previous audit experience with the client.

In small-entity IT environments the level of general controls may be such that the auditor will place less reliance on the system of internal controls. This will result in a greater emphasis on analytical review procedures and substantive tests of details of transactions and balances, which may increase the effectiveness of certain CAATs, particularly audit software. Where smaller volumes of data are processed, manual methods may be more cost effective. A small entity may not be able to provide adequate technical expertise to the auditor, making the use of CAATs impractical, and certain audit package programs may not operate on small computers. In such circumstances the auditor may decide to audit 'around the computer', vouching the various financial reports produced by the accounting system to the relevant supporting documentation.

There remains the question of just how many items should be chosen for a test or sample, how these should be selected, and how to relate the results of the tests to the total population being tested. The principles applicable to sampling in auditing are discussed in chapter 7.

6.3 CONSIDERATIONS AFFECTING EVIDENCE OF THE OCCURRENCE/VALIDITY OF TRANSACTIONS

6.3.1 Introduction

The entries in respect of transactions recorded in a client's accounting records may be divided into two kinds:

- Those which arise by reason of agreement between the client and another party, for example, purchases, sales, and the consequent settlement of amounts owing. These are normally referred to as classes of transactions.
- Those which arise by reason of internal adjustment within the business of the client, for example, writing off bad debts and provisions for doubtful debts and depreciation.

6.3.2 Transactions between the client and third parties

In order to vouch for the validity of any transaction, the auditor has to be satisfied that the transaction is legally valid, and that:

- both the client and the other party have agreed to the transaction;
- the transaction has, in fact, been carried out; and
- the transaction has been accurately recorded in the accounting records of the client, in the correct account and in the correct accounting period.

6.3.2.1 Evidence of agreement by the other party to the transaction

The agreement by the other party is usually evidenced by some document, for example, a purchase invoice received by the client after delivery of goods by the supplier is evidence of the agreement by the other party to sell the goods to the client. An order for goods to be supplied by the client is evidence of the offer by the other party to buy the goods of the client; the agreement will be concluded with the performance by the client in delivering the ordered goods to the customer. The client will then have the right to invoice and recover the agreed price of the goods from the customer. The receipt from the other party of the relevant document, such as the order or the client's delivery note signed by the customer, is sufficient evidence of that party's agreement and it is not necessary, except in extraordinary circumstances, for the client or his auditor to inquire whether the issue of the document was properly authorized by the other party.

When A deals with B, A is entitled to assume that the internal management of B is properly carried out so that B cannot avoid a contract by pleading lack of authority by the staff member who contracted. This point applies equally where B is a limited company by virtue of section 36 of the Companies Act 1973, which prevents a contract being void merely because the company or any officer has acted *ultra vires*.

Even in those transactions where some documentary evidence might be expected, for example a sales order, the fact that the sales were the subject of a client's invoice and that subsequently the amount was paid by the customer is sufficient evidence of agreement by the customer to the sale.

It is apparent, therefore, that in all transactions where the rights and obligations of both parties have been concluded, no further confirmation of the agreement is required from either party, although proof of the amount to be entered in the accounting records is still necessary. However, where the amounts are still outstanding at the close of the financial period under audit, proof of agreement by the other party is necessary.

With regard to amounts owing for credit purchases by the client, this proof exists in the shape of invoices and statements from the other party, supported by evidence – such as an internal goods received voucher – that the client has received the goods invoiced.

In the case of credit sales by the client, proof is provided by seeing that the debt is subsequently paid, by seeing the delivery note signed by the customer acknowledging the receipt of the goods, or by obtaining from the other party confirmation that the sums outstanding, which have been debited to his/her account in the accounting records of the client, are correct.

In the case of cash sales the passing of cash is *prima facie* evidence of agreement by the other party.

6.3.2.2 Evidence of agreement by the client

The auditor must be satisfied that the client has either directly agreed to the transaction, or that the client has given someone a specific or general authority to agree to the transaction.

Where a staff member has been given a particular duty, it is implied that that person has a general authority to issue, or pass as correct, the relevant documents arising from transactions falling within the limits of the person's authority. Thus, for example, a buyer has the power to pass as correct purchase invoices for goods ordinarily dealt in by the client, and a cashier the power to issue receipts.

The auditor should obtain sufficient information as to the duties of each employee and the system of internal controls before accepting that all transactions entered into by the business are being properly dealt with by the duly authorized staff members. Where transactions involve matters other than the day-to-day business of the client, for example the acquisition of a new plant or land and buildings, the auditor should be sure that appropriate authority for such transactions has been given.

In this connection, the auditor must also consider the manner in which the business is organized from a legal point of view. It may be a sole trader, a partnership or a limited company, and different considerations relating to authority to contract apply in each case.

The sole trader

In the case of a sole trader, the owner can transact any business, provided it is within the law.

From the viewpoint of the auditor, the question of authority for any transaction is merely a matter of being satisfied either that the owner has sanctioned it or has delegated power to a member of staff who in turn has sanctioned the transaction. In the case of unusual transactions, for example, the purchase or sale of plant or immovable property, the owner's direct sanction would normally be required.

The partnership

In the non-statutory audit of a partnership, however, a further consideration arises, namely, the extent of a partner's authority to transact business on behalf of the entity.

A partner is an agent of the partnership for all business which can be considered as the normal activity of the entity, and the entity is bound by the acts of a partner in this instance. But if the partner undertakes a transaction outside the scope of the entity's usual business, the entity and the other partners are not bound, unless they have confirmed the transaction or are stopped from denying the authority of the acting partner after they have become aware of the transaction. Any change or extension of the entity's activities requires the consent of all the partners, in the absence of provision to the contrary in the partnership agreement. The auditor should therefore read the clauses of the partnership deed relating to the type of business to be carried on and the authority required to extend or change it. Where a transaction appears to be outside the normal scope of the entity's business, especially where the amount involved is substantial, the auditor should ascertain whether the necessary authority has been given.

It will be noted that, in the absence of agreement to the contrary in the partnership deed, each partner has authority to deal with the day-to-day transactions and so has power to appoint and instruct staff members.

The limited company

The objects and powers of a company

The power of a company to undertake business is vested in the company by virtue of the 'objects' clause of the memorandum of association. The Companies Act 1973 provides that a company shall have the capacity determined by its main object stated in the memorandum, or by the main business actually carried on at 1 January 1974, the date of the commencement of the Act. It also provides that there shall be included in the capacity unlimited ancillary objects except those expressly excluded by the memorandum. It may be that with the passage of time one of the ancillary objects becomes the main business of the company and the Act provides that should this be the case, such business shall be deemed to be the main object.[9]

Every company has plenary power under the Act to enable it to realize its main and ancillary objects, including the common powers set out in Schedule 2 to the Act, except those which are specifically excluded or qualified by the memorandum.[10]

A company thus has the power to do anything an individual can do provided only that:

- its acts come within the main and ancillary objects; and
- there is no specific restriction in the memorandum.

Specific and general authority given to the board of directors

The power to undertake business is exercised by the company either in general meeting or through the board of directors, to whom authority to manage the business of the company has been delegated by the articles of association. Article 59 of Table A (60 of Table B) delegates such power to the board. As a general rule the board has power to carry on all the ordinary activities of the business, which obviously must include the appointment of staff and the delegation to staff members of such authority as is necessary to carry out their duties.

In the case, however, of transactions other than the day-to-day business of the company, it may be that the authority of the board itself is required or, in exceptional cases, even the prior authority of the company in general meeting.

The auditor should, therefore, study the articles of association and note the relevant clauses delegating power to the board, for inclusion in the permanent audit working papers. (It may be, for example, that the purchase of land or the extension of or change in the location of the business requires the prior authority of the company in general meeting.) The auditor will thus be in a position to decide whether the evidence of authority for a particular transaction would be contained in a minute of the board or whether the authority of a general meeting of the company is necessary to enable the directors to proceed with the transaction.

If the directors should exceed their powers, the resulting contract between the company and the other contracting party is as a general rule still valid,

---

[9] The Companies Act, section 33.
[10] The Companies Act, section 34.

but action may be taken by the company against those directors (one or more) who exceeded their powers.[11]

The Companies Act, sections 221 and 222, relating to the issue of shares and debentures, and section 228, relating to the disposal of a substantial part of the company's business, should not be overlooked.

Specific and general authority given to a single director

It is the practice of many companies to include in the articles a clause authorizing the board to appoint a managing director and to delegate its authority to him at its discretion. Article 61 of Table A (63 of Table B) gives power to the board to delegate authority to a single director.

In some cases the work is divided among several directors so that each has their own particular field and their authority is limited accordingly, for example, works director, sales director, finance director. In such a case the auditor should read the relevant clauses in the articles giving power to the board to delegate authority to individual directors. The auditor should also see the board minutes containing the relevant resolutions and note the extent of authority vested in each director. For example, a works director may have the power to authorize repairs to plant but the purchase of new plant requires a resolution of the board, or the works director's power to authorize the purchase of new plant may be limited to a fixed sum annually beyond which the authority of a board resolution is required. Again, such a director may have complete power to appoint staff in the specific department or such appointments may require confirmation by the board.

As already seen, the common powers of a company set out in Schedule 2 to the Companies Act include the power to borrow, subject to any restrictions contained in the memorandum. In delegating power to the directors, some limitation may be placed thereon. Table A article 60 (Table B article 61) limits the directors' powers to borrow.

Where a company has issued debentures or otherwise borrowed and the memorandum limits the company's power to borrow, or where the loan was raised by the directors on behalf of the company and the articles limit the directors' power to borrow, the auditor should make sure that the total of all sums borrowed is not in excess of that for which power is given.

Any excess borrowing, although as a general rule valid as between the company and the lender, may be the subject of action by the company against those members or directors who voted for the excess borrowing. Where a power has been exceeded the auditor should point out to management the company's right of action against those so acting for any

---

[11] Inherent power exists to borrow and give security, to lend and invest, and to buy and sell movable and immovable property, to name but a few of the common powers.

loss incurred. And where it is evident that material loss is likely to be suffered by the company from such an act, it would appear that the position should be disclosed in the financial statements or directors' report. Further, such an act may be a material irregularity requiring the auditor to take the action prescribed in section 20(5) of the Public Accountants' and Auditors' Act 1991.

Examples of transactions

Three examples of transactions undertaken by a limited company are given to illustrate the evidence, which the auditor requires for assurance that the company has agreed to the relevant transactions. In all cases:

- read the memorandum of association and be satisfied that there is no exclusion of or restriction on the common powers vested by section 34 which vitiates the transaction; and
- read the articles of association and be satisfied that general power to manage the company has been vested in the board of directors.

Example 1

The Y Company Limited borrowed R100 000.

Scrutinize the articles of association for any restriction on the authority of the board of directors to borrow and, where there is a restriction, note from the company's financial records whether the total amount borrowed, including the above R100 000, is within the limit.

If so, a board resolution is sufficient. If not, a resolution of the company in general meeting is required.

Read the relevant minute and note its terms.

Example 2

The X Company Limited purchased new plant costing R200 000.

Where authority to purchase has not been delegated, a resolution of the board authorizing the purchase is required, in which case inspect the relevant board minute and note its terms.

Where authority has been delegated, inspect the relevant article conferring on the board power to delegate and read the relevant board minute delegating authority to purchase plant to another person (for example, a director or manager). Obtain written evidence that the delegate has agreed to the purchase. This may be, *inter alia*, a signature or initials on the relevant invoice or copy of the order.

Example 3

The X Company Limited sold its Port Elizabeth branch as a going concern for R400 000.

Scrutinize the articles of association for any restriction on the board's general powers to manage the company, which may relate to this sale. If there is no such restriction a resolution of the board is sufficient, in which case inspect the relevant board minute and note its terms.

If the board's power to authorize this sale is excluded, a resolution of the company in general meeting is required, in which case inspect the relevant general meeting minute and note its terms.

If the branch represents a major part of the assets of the company, ascertain whether the provisions of the Companies Act section 228 have been implemented.

6.3.2.3 Evidence that the transaction has occurred

The auditor must be satisfied that:

- the charge made by one party is accepted by the other;
- the goods or services relating to the transaction have been provided by the one party and accepted as satisfactory by the other; and
- due settlement of amounts owing has been effected.

Where the transaction results in a charge to the client by the other party without goods being involved – for example, repairs, telephone charges, rent, etc. – the evidence that the transaction has been carried out to the satisfaction of both parties is the invoice from the other party duly passed as correct by the appropriate member of the client's staff.

The question of authority to contract and the delegation of that authority discussed above apply equally here. There may be cases where only the owner, or the board of directors of a company, should pass an invoice or account as correct, as for example on the completion of a building erected for the client.

Where the transaction results in a charge by the client to the other party without goods being involved, there may be no documentary evidence that the other party accepts the charge, but subsequent payment is sufficient proof that the other party was satisfied and also that the transaction has been duly carried out. If the amount is still outstanding at the date of the audit, evidence of the acceptance of the charge may be obtained direct from the debtor. It will be noted, incidentally, that this not only proves that the transaction has been properly implemented, but also that the other party agreed to the original contract and that the amount still remains to be paid.

If the transaction involves the passing of goods, the auditor should also be satisfied that the relevant goods were received by the client, or dispatched to the other party. This is not a matter for a complete detailed check, but the auditor should be reasonably satisfied that the internal control on goods received and issued is sound. This entails:

- an enquiry into, and observation of, the system of receiving and issuing goods, and matching them with the relevant invoices; and
- a test of the records of goods received and issued with the relevant invoices to ensure that the system operates with reasonable efficiency.

If the goods sent to a customer are not acceptable to the customer, he or she will either return the goods or claim a reduction in price. The evidence that the return or the claim has been accepted by the client is the credit note and, if the number and value of credit notes appear to be excessive, the auditor may come to the conclusion that the outward invoices are not reliable evidence of sales and may report to the management accordingly.

In certain cases the auditor, when vouching a transaction, need not be concerned with the question of the receipt of the article at the time when the transaction is vouched. This may be done later when verifying the existence of the assets. An example is the purchase of shares; the number of shares will be recorded in the accounting records and will be checked later when examining the relevant share certificates.

Where the transaction is of the settlement of amounts owing, that is, the passing of cash as a result of a purchase or sale transaction, the auditor's approach will depend on whether cash is being paid or being received by the client. When vouching cash paid, the question of agreement to the transaction falls away, but the auditor must still be satisfied that the cash (or its equivalent) was received by the proper party and that the amount has been debited to the proper account.

On the other hand, when vouching cash received, the auditor must not only be satisfied that cash recorded as received is credited to the proper account, but that all cash received has been recorded. This latter point cannot, in the majority of cases, be proved with any exactitude, but an intelligent enquiry into the internal control will allow the auditor to judge how far reliance can be placed on the records presented to him or her.

6.3.2.4 Proof of proper recording of the transaction

Little comment is required on this point. If the two previous points have been proved to the satisfaction of the auditor, it is a simple matter to trace the information on the relevant documents into the proper accounts, through the accounting records. All that need be said here is that where a charge or a credit relates to some matter other than a purchase or sale of goods, which is normally dealt in by the client, the auditor should observe:

- that the allocation of the amount has been approved by a person with the proper authority;
- that from the information on the invoice etc., the allocation appears to the auditor to be reasonable; and
- that the transaction has been recorded in the correct accounting period.

6.3.3 Internal adjustments and provisions

Where an entry arises by reason of a transaction which is an internal adjustment within the business of the client, the auditor's duty is to ascertain:

- that proper authority was given for the entry;
- that the entry appears justified and reasonable; and
- that it is properly recorded, that is, the entries are allocated to the correct account in the correct accounting period.

The question of authority to contract has already been discussed and the points made apply equally here. For example, the auditor would expect an entry for bad debts written off to be authorized by a senior member of management, certainly not by the clerk who invoices the goods.

Justification for the entry may be obtained by documentary evidence, as for example correspondence with attorneys regarding debtors' accounts, which have been written off as bad. On the other hand, the evidence may simply be the opinion of a responsible official coupled with such other information as may be available, for example, in the case of bad debts, the age of the debt, and, in the case of depreciation, the previous rates used for similar machinery.

It remains for the auditor to be satisfied that the entries are properly authorized and allocated to the correct account in the correct accounting period.

The foregoing represents a general survey of validity and authorization requirements in vouching. Specific matters to which the auditor should direct attention when vouching the validity of entries in respect of a particular type of transaction are dealt with later in the relevant chapters dealing with those classes of transactions.

7

Audit Evidence – Sampling in Auditing

Learning objectives

After studying this chapter you should be able to:

1. Define 'audit sampling' and explain how it may be applied to tests of controls and substantive tests of detail.
2. Differentiate between sampling and non-sampling risk in tests of controls and substantive tests of detail and explain how an auditor manages these risks.
3. Describe the similarities and differences between statistical and non-statistical sampling methods and identify those audit procedures which do not constitute sampling.
4. Determine which sampling technique is most appropriate for tests of controls and detailed substantive tests of detail in various circumstances.
5. Explain the steps in designing and executing a non-statistical or statistical sampling plan for tests of controls and substantive tests of detail.
6. Identify the factors that affect sample size.
7. Explain how the auditor evaluates control risk for the particular assertions tested, based on the results of a non-statistical or statistical sample of tests of control, and how this affects the planned level of detection risk.
8. Discuss appropriate responses by the auditor to internal control weaknesses identified during the performance of audit procedures to the sample selected for tests of control.
9. Explain how the auditor evaluates the potential misstatement from the results of a non-statistical or statistical sample drawn for substantive tests of detail.

7.1 SAMPLING IN AUDITING

7.1.1 Introduction

'Audit sampling involves the application of audit procedures to less than 100% of items within an account balance or class of transactions such that all units have a chance of selection. This will enable the auditor to obtain and evaluate audit evidence about some characteristic of the items selected, in order to form or assist in forming a conclusion concerning the population from which the sample is drawn. Audit sampling can use either a statistical or a non-statistical approach'.[1]

Because of the size and complexity of business entities, many of which have well-established systems of internal control, it is virtually impossible and quite unnecessary for every transaction to be audited. However, the auditor still has to obtain sufficient relevant and reliable audit evidence to express an opinion on the financial statements. To do this, the auditor will invariably adopt an approach of selecting samples to which to apply audit procedures so as to conclude on the reliability and fairness of the information contained in the financial statements.

The methods used by various auditing firms to select and evaluate samples differ greatly. Many auditors lack the skills or decide not to apply statistical sampling techniques, choosing to remain with a tried and trusted judgemental or non-statistical sampling approach. In an article[2] quoting from a research study prepared for the Institute of Chartered Accountants in England and Wales it is stated that the study found that only one third of large firms made extensive use of statistical sampling, and only 10% of medium-sized firms made any use of it all. Nonetheless there are certain general principles applicable to all sampling. A full discussion of these issues is set out in SAAS 530, 'Audit Sampling'. This chapter does not address the detailed application of various statistical sampling plans but rather the general principles of sampling.

7.1.2 Sampling risk

As with all other procedures aimed at gathering audit evidence, sampling contains an element of uncertainty and the results of any sample will merely add to the cumulative weight of evidence gathered from all sources. The auditor is faced with sampling and non-sampling risk in both tests of controls and substantive tests of detail.

Sampling risk is the risk that a sample drawn may not be representative of the population. It is the risk that, based on the sample, a different conclusion might be drawn about the population than if the auditor had examined the entire population. The implications for the auditor in conducting tests of controls and substantive sampling plans are discussed below.

---

[1] SAAS 530, paragraph .03.
[2] G Cosserat. 'Judgemental Sampling Rules O.K.', *Accountancy*, April 1983.

7.1.2.1 Tests of controls

- *Risk of underreliance* – the risk that, although the sample result does not support the auditor's planned reliance on internal controls, the actual deviation rate does support such reliance. This may cause the auditor to extend detailed substantive tests unnecessarily. This risk affects audit efficiency as it leads to unnecessary additional work.

- *Risk of overreliance* – the risk that although the sample results support the auditor's planned degree of reliance on the internal control, the actual deviation rate does not support such reliance. This could lead to the auditor failing to identify a material weakness in the internal control and a consequent material error remaining undetected. This risk affects audit effectiveness and may lead to an inappropriate audit opinion.

7.1.2.2 Substantive tests of detail

- *The risk of incorrect rejection* – namely that on the basis of the sample results the auditor concludes that an account balance is materially misstated when it is in fact not. This can lead to unnecessary time spent on further audit tests to gain the necessary level of audit assurance, and is sometimes referred to as the 'alpha risk'.

- *The risk of incorrect acceptance* – namely that on the basis of the sample results the auditor accepts an account balance as correct when it is materially misstated. This can lead to an incorrect audit opinion being given and is sometimes referred to as the 'beta risk'.

7.1.3 Non-sampling risk

This risk can arise whether the auditor is sampling or using other auditing procedures and is in essence the human error factor. It includes the risk that the auditor:

- may use inappropriate auditing procedures which do not meet the stated audit objectives;
- may fail to recognize an error while examining documents or other evidence; and
- may misinterpret the sample results or evidence obtained from other auditing procedures, thus failing to detect a material error.

Non-sampling risk cannot be quantitatively measured, nor can it ever be completely eliminated. It can, however, be kept at an acceptable level by ensuring that proper planning, supervision and review procedures form part of the normal quality controls implemented by the auditing firm.

7.1.4 Statistical sampling – an overview

Both statistical and non-statistical (judgemental) sampling methods may be applied to a population with the objective of obtaining a representative sample. Both methods require the auditor to use judgement in planning and selecting the sample, carrying out the audit procedures and evaluating the sample results.

However, where non-statistical sample sizes and results are determined judgementally, statistical sampling techniques require both the sample size and the results to be determined statistically. Statistical sampling is based on the theory of probability that an unbiased sample properly drawn and evaluated should be representative of the whole population about which one is trying to determine some characteristic or value. The statistical sampling techniques most commonly used in tests of control and detailed substantive sampling plans in auditing are discussed below.

7.1.4.1 Testing of internal controls

- *Estimation sampling* for attributes is applied to estimate the rate of occurrence of deviations in the control procedure being tested, or how frequently the control procedure does not operate as it is intended.

- *Discovery sampling* is used to prove that an irregularity exists. This technique is designed to find at least one error or deviation in the sample and would be used where the auditor suspects that an irregularity may exist and seeks to find at least one such example.

7.1.4.2 Substantive tests of detail

- *PPS sampling*, otherwise known as probability-proportional-to-size or value-weighted selection or monetary unit sampling, is a form of attribute sampling which can be used to estimate the monetary value of an error or of a balance. The sampling unit is expressed in Rand-value terms rather than as an item in the population. This sampling technique is used in non-statistical sampling plans as well. This technique ensures that audit effort is directed to the larger value items.

- *Variable sampling* techniques may be used when the auditor is trying to detect a possible under- or overstatement in an account balance. It is based on normal distribution theory. The auditor draws a sample and then estimates the projected population value on the basis of the results of the sample. Three methods are used, namely, the mean-per-unit method, the difference method and the ratio method. This sampling technique is sometimes used in verification of inventory valuation schedules. However, as sample sizes are usually large, the technique is seldom used in practice.

7.1.4.3 Procedures that do not constitute sampling

- 100% of items checked.
- Inquiry and observation.
- No audit work performed on an account balance or class of transactions.
- Selecting only those items in a population having a particular characteristic.
- The selection of certain items in a population merely to gain an

understanding of the nature of the activities – for example, a walk-through test to establish the operation of the internal controls system.

- Selection of a few blocks of items in sequence for checking.
- Selection of all items over a certain amount.

7.1.5 Stages in audit sampling [3]

Whichever method of sampling is used, it will involve the following stages:

- Designing of the sample;
- Selecting the items to be tested;
- Testing the items; and
- Evaluating the sample results.

These various stages will be discussed below.

7.1.5.1 Designing the sample

The following factors need to be considered by the auditor in designing an audit sample:[4]

Define the test objectives

The auditor needs to clearly define the test objectives to determine the nature of the evidence being sought and the most appropriate audit procedure to be used. For example, if the auditor wants to establish the audit objective that the transaction is valid by reference to proper authorization at a particular stage, the test procedure will be to examine documentary evidence that particular individuals have signed a certain document indicating such authorization. The auditor would then expect that every such document included in the sample would carry the appropriate signature. The audit test objectives will generally relate to obtaining evidence regarding the financial statement assertions of completeness, occurrence (validity), measurement (accuracy), existence and valuation.[5]

Define the population and sampling unit

The auditor must define the population about which conclusions will be drawn. This could be an account balance or group of balances, for example, the accounts receivable ledger balances, or a class of transactions, for example, wages for the year. If certain balances within this population are excluded, say for purposes of a 100% test of those balances, the sample will be drawn from the remaining balances. This is known as stratification and any conclusion resulting from tests on the sample cannot be applied to such balances excluded, that is, they no longer form a part of the population from which the sample is to be drawn. The sampling unit can be defined as a

---

[3] SAAS 530.
[4] SAAS 530, paragraphs .32 – .42.
[5] SAAS 500, paragraph .13.

customer balance, an invoice, a line item of inventory or any convenient unit in order to draw an efficient and effective sample to meet the audit test objective.

Define what constitutes an error (or deviation)

Assuming the test objective has been set, the auditor must also establish what will constitute an error or deviation, as it is the evaluation and projection of these errors, from the sample to the population, which will determine potential audit adjustments and impact on the audit opinion.

Determine the sample size

Where, as is usual, only a part of a group of transactions or balances (or aspects of them) is to be tested, the auditor must decide how many items to include in the test. In earlier times the judgement of the auditor was based on nothing more than a feeling of what was right and block tests were the order of the day – for example, all items in a particular week or month (or multiples thereof). What was lacking was some logical basis of relating the size of the sample to the risk the auditor was prepared to take. The application of more sophisticated statistical techniques allowed the auditor to focus attention on risk by quantifying it, that is, stating it by percentage; the auditor's judgement is still required to decide what percentage risk is considered acceptable. It is an aid to the auditor, not a definitive answer to the problem, a point not appreciated by some auditors. As a result (and for other reasons), by no means all members of the profession accept the technique as the best means of solving the problem and the debate of non-statistical sampling versus statistical sampling still rages.

It is now recognized that sample sizes may be affected by the following factors:[6]

- the degree of assurance;
- the tolerable error;
- the expected error;
- the population size; and
- stratification.

These terms may be strange to readers and it is important that their meaning is understood, as they form the foundation of the sampling principles.

The *degree of assurance* required from the sample remains the area of auditor judgement. For statistical sampling it is expressed as a percentage, for example, 90% – 95%; for non-statistical sampling it is expressed less formally, for example, as high, medium or low. The auditor's decision will be affected by the extent of reliance to be placed on a particular control procedure, the

---

[6] SAAS 530, Appendices I and II, which set out factors to consider when determining size.

assessment of the inherent and control risks as high, medium or low, relating to the assertion being tested, and the assurance the auditor plans to derive from other substantive procedures.

Tolerable error is the maximum error the auditor will be prepared to accept and still conclude that the test objective has been achieved. As with the degree of assurance, this is often expressed as a percentage, for example, 5% – 10%. In the case of a test of control, this will be the maximum number of deviations acceptable, after which no or reduced reliance will be placed on the control procedure. In the case of substantive test procedures, the tolerable error will be related to the materiality amount set at the planning stage of the audit. As with the degree of assurance, this factor is decided judgementally. The smaller the tolerable error, the larger the sample size will be to achieve the same degree of assurance.

If the auditor *expects errors* to be present, either because of previous experience with the client or based on an assessment of the inherent and control risk, this will increase the risk of sampling error and a larger sample size will be required to draw conclusions within the tolerable error and for the degree of assurance required. Clearly the expected error cannot exceed the tolerable error.

The *population size* has relatively little effect on the sample size unless it is very small.

Stratification of the population is the process of dividing the population into subpopulations so that items within each stratum are expected to have certain characteristics, such as monetary value or risk of error. Appropriate procedures should then be designed for each stratum. When used in substantive tests of detail the same degree of assurance can often be obtained with a smaller sample size.

7.1.5.2 Selecting the sample items

In the past, selection of sequential blocks of items for testing was widely applied. A major fault of this method was that it confined the test to a narrow section of the whole population, failing to appreciate that a check of that section tells the auditor nothing about the remainder, the bulk of the population. The gradual realization of this fault led to the selection of items more representative of the whole group or population. This required the use of selection techniques to allow all items in the population an equal chance of selection. There are a number of techniques available; however, the four most commonly applied are:[7]

- Random numbers may be selected from random number tables or generated by computer from a random number program.
- Systematic sampling from a random point involves selecting every nth item using a constant interval, known as the sampling interval.

---

[7] SAAS 530, Appendix III.

Monetary unit sampling is similar to systematic sampling but uses a monetary value as the interval rather than items in the population (often referred to as MUS or PPS – Probability Proportional to Size sampling).

Haphazard sampling involves the auditor selecting from a population a random sample with no particular bias. The auditor needs to guard against an unconscious bias towards the selection of large or unusual items in applying this method of selection. This selection technique is not acceptable when using statistical sampling.

7.1.5.3 Testing the items

The auditor should document in the audit working papers the details of the sampling plan and the relevant sample finally selected. Thereafter he should perform the relevant tests of controls and/or substantive tests of detail on the sample selected and record the test results for evaluation purposes.

7.1.5.4 Evaluating the sample results

Whatever method or combination of methods the auditor uses to select a sample, the results of the tests performed must be evaluated both in quantitative and qualitative terms. This involves the following steps:

- Analyse the errors detected, if any.
- Use the errors found in the sample as a basis for estimating potential error in the population.
- Draw a conclusion about the population from the sample results.

As shown above, block tests give no information on the population and so any decision of the auditor based thereon is meaningless. Where, however, the sample is representative of the whole population, the auditor must consider the nature and cause of the errors found and make a reasoned judgement of their potential impact on the financial statements. To make a reasonable prediction of the entire population based on the results from the sample selected requires that a representative sample be drawn. For this reason it is important that the auditor should investigate carefully the nature and cause of error.

Evaluating results of tests of controls

In the case of tests of control, deviations from the prescribed system might be as a result of management override of laid-down procedures. There are, therefore, two populations: the first population being transactions processed normally, and the second being those where control procedures have been overridden. If this is so, the auditor would need to establish the frequency of control override and thus the magnitude of its consequences on disclosures in the financial statements. This could be done, for example, by questioning staff whose control procedures have been overridden, or by questioning the perpetrators themselves. The auditor also needs to ascertain whether such errors (deviations) from the internal control procedures, detected during the audit of the items in the sample, indicate a potential for material error or fraud. The possible impact of this on the financial statements of the entity and the auditor's detection risk must be considered and substantive tests of detail adapted accordingly.

If the auditor is able to obtain sufficient appropriate evidence that the error (deviation) arises from an isolated event that does not recur, is not representative of similar errors in the population (an anomalous error), and does not affect the remaining population, the preliminary control risk assessment need not be reassessed. If, however, the auditor is unable to do this, planned reliance on the particular control must be reduced and the extent of relevant substantive tests must increase accordingly.

Another example would be where a control procedure was not performed owing to the absence of the responsible person as a result of sick or annual leave. Here again, there are two populations: the period where the appropriate official was available (which is likely to cover the vast majority of the financial year), and that period where the person was absent. It is only during the period of that person's absence that reliance on an internal control procedure is not justified (assuming that the control procedure was not performed by some other person during that period).

Evaluating results of substantive tests of detail

In the case of errors identified by substantive tests, the auditor needs to project the Rand value of error in the sample to assess the likely error amount in the population as a whole. Similar to what was said in relation to the evaluation of tests of control, if substantive tests reveal any error which can be isolated as not being representative (that is, an anomalous error), it should be excluded from the sample error used to project the likely population error amount.

For example, the auditor may be able to establish that a fraudulent transaction entered into personally by a director of a company, but charged as an expense to the business, was charged as a once-off occurrence. If this particular error is not corrected it must be added to the population projection.

The proponents of statistical sampling point out that the sample results can be projected mathematically to the whole population to provide an estimate of the total number of errors in the record or their total value.

It must be stressed that the statistical technique does not deprive or relieve (depending on how the auditor views personal responsibility) the auditor of the necessity to make a judgement on the matter and come to a conclusion. In drawing a conclusion, the auditor must compare the projected error with the tolerable error set at the planning stage of the sample. If the projected error exceeds the tolerable error, the test objectives will generally not have been met, and the auditor will have to consider the effects of this on the audit approach to the assertion being tested. The auditor will also need to consider the sampling risk and the risk that an inappropriate conclusion may be drawn.

7.1.6 Using computers in audit sampling

The capabilities of computers have seen the development of statistical sampling programs for use by auditors when sampling. These programs calculate the required sample sizes – based on specified criteria – for statistical and non-statistical sampling plans, randomly select samples for audit investigation, and project the likely population condition based on the audited sample results. For example:

- 'A random sample of goods received notes in respect of purchases of inventory and/or delivery notes for sales of inventory for the purpose of testing the internal control procedures on which the auditor wishes to place reliance so that the objectives of completeness, validity and accuracy are met in relation to the purchases and sales of inventory within the entity's business process.'

- 'A random selection of a sample of inventory items from the inventory records for test counting at or near the entity's year-end and/or for substantive testing the basis of measurement of such items in accordance with the accounting policy of the entity.'

Computer assisted audit techniques (CAATs) are also used to sort and stratify populations in accordance with specified criteria. For example: stratification of the accounts receivable ledger balances for the purposes of positive circularization of all balances in excess of a certain amount.

8

Audit Working Papers

Learning objectives

After studying this chapter you should be able to:

1. Explain the purpose of audit working papers.
2. Discuss the nature of matters to be documented in audit working papers.
3. Explain the principles to be followed in the preparation of individual working papers and be able to provide examples of such.
4. Describe the types of working papers that typically may be found in an audit working papers file and how these may be organized.
5. Discuss the different levels of review that might be performed on audit working papers and how these should be evidenced.
6. Explain the legal principles of ownership, custody and confidentiality of audit working papers.

8.1 THE PURPOSE OF WORKING PAPERS

8.1.1 Introduction

Working papers should be kept to provide evidence that the auditor performed the audit with the requisite degree of care and skill, in accordance with statements of generally accepted auditing standards referred to as South African Auditing Standards (SAAS), and to support the audit opinion on the financial statements of the client. SAAS 230, 'Documentation', sets out the principle in paragraph .02 as follows:

> 'The auditor should document matters that are important in providing evidence to support the audit opinion and evidence that the audit was carried out in accordance with statements of South African Auditing Standards.'

SAAS 230, 'Documentation', goes on to explain in paragraph .03 that:

> '*documentation* means the material (working papers) prepared by or obtained and retained by the auditor in connection with the performance of the audit';

and recognizes that

'working papers may be stored on paper, film, electronic media or other media'.

- In addition to the above principle, guidance as to the auditor's responsibilities to maintain sufficient documentation is contained in the following SAAS statements:
SAAS 230 'Documentation' – the full statement;
SAAS 100 'Assurance engagements', paragraph .57;
SAAS 210 'Terms of audit engagements', paragraph .02;
SAAS 220 'Quality control', paragraphs .08 – .17;
SAAS 240 'The auditor's responsibility to consider fraud and error in an audit of financial statements', paragraph .49;
SAAS 300 'Planning', paragraphs .08, .10 and .12;
SAAS 310 'Knowledge of the business', paragraphs .07 and .08;
SAAS 400 'Risk assessments and internal control', paragraph .22;
SAAS 920 'Engagements to perform agreed upon procedures', paragraph .14;
SAAS 930 'Engagements to compile financial information', paragraph .10; and
SAAS 1005 'The special considerations in the audit of small entities', paragraphs .27 – .31.

Should negligence be alleged, audit working papers could provide evidence both for and against the auditor in legal proceedings/court of law. Thus great care must be exercised in their preparation and content. There are certain basic needs fulfilled by the retention of audit working papers. Working papers:

- assist in the planning and performance of the audit;
- assist in the supervision and review of the audit work; and
- record the audit evidence resulting from the audit work performed to support the auditor's opinion.

The audit file content will vary depending on the approach adopted by each professional auditor or firm, the complexity of the engagement and extent of use of microcomputers on the audit.

8.1.2 The use of microcomputers in documenting, planning and performing the audit

Microcomputers or laptops (PCs) are used extensively by auditors to perform various audit engagement tasks in a time-efficient manner and with improved audit effectiveness. The specific tasks that can be performed depend on the audit software programs available (either purchased or developed by the audit firm, as in the large multinational audit firms), the particular computer configuration, processing methods, and the storage media adopted by the client.

PCs are widely used in the preparation of audit working papers and in the performance of audit procedures. Word processing allows for the automation of certain clerical and administrative tasks, such as providing templates of standard documents used by the firm. Examples are engagement letters, working paper lead schedules, audit programmes, audit reports, standard format of financial statements, management representation letters.

The maintenance of audit working papers in an electronic format allows for multiple access by all staff working on the audit which, although it may achieve audit efficiencies, carries with it security risks of unauthorized access and the loss of client and audit information should a PC (laptop) be stolen or become infected with a computer virus. The audit firm must have strict policies and procedures to protect electronic information such as: passwords to limit access to authorized staff, uploading of information to a central server at the firm on regular (daily) basis and the regular saving of back-up copies. One of the advantages of electronic audit working papers is that managers and partners will be able to review the audit working papers and files on-line at their convenience.

Databases are often used to store the firm's *audit manual,* containing its audit philosophy and methodology, for ready reference by audit staff. The database also contains auditing standards and legislative requirements, so that staff accessing the database will be informed promptly of any changes to auditing standards or changes to the firm's philosophy and methodology, including working paper requirements.

8.1.3 Planning and performing the audit

The previous year's working papers are an invaluable source of reference in the planning stages of the current assignment. Time budgets are usually prepared based on actual hours of the previous year and adjusted for any known changed circumstances. They also give guidance as to the calibre of staff required on the job to perform the various tasks competently. Programs are available that match assigned audit tasks, of varying levels of difficulty or complexity, to staff who have been assessed as possessing the necessary skills for those tasks.

PCs may be used very effectively in preparing budgets, recording time spent on the engagement and scheduling work commitments of staff. Regular status reports on work in progress can be produced which compare actual time spent to date, and estimated time to completion, with time budgeted for each component of the engagement. Work-in-progress reports can be obtained for individual engagements and for all engagements controlled by the partner-in-charge of the engagement, thus facilitating the management of time spent, fees earned, billings to clients and fee collections and enabling the analysis of fee income and costs for individual divisions or cost centres of the audit firm.

Audit staff turnover or promotion within the firm frequently results in a lack of staff continuity on client assignments from one year to the next. Working papers communicate information to staff members unfamiliar with the client's operations, the overall audit approach adopted and the detailed procedures performed in the previous years, which provide a basis for current procedures, adjusted where thought necessary or desirable after critical examination by the partner and audit senior(s) assigned to the job. Slavish adherence to previous procedures should be avoided lest some previously undetected audit deficiency is perpetuated.

8.1.4 Control of fieldwork

The audit staff assigned to a client's audit must be adequately instructed and supervised. SAAS 220 'Quality Control', in paragraph .08, states the principle as follows:

> 'The auditor should implement those quality control procedures that are, in the context of the policies and procedures of the audit firm, appropriate to the individual audit.'

This involves informing audit staff of their responsibilities and the objectives of the audit procedures they are to perform. It also involves informing them of the nature of the client's business and possible accounting or auditing problems that might affect the audit.[1] The supervision and review aspects will be dealt with later in this chapter.

8.1.4.1 The audit programme

Audit programmes, which form a substantial part of audit working papers, serve as a useful means of controlling and recording the proper execution of the work. SAAS 300 'Planning' sets out the principles as follows:

> Paragraph 10: 'The auditor should develop and document an audit programme setting out the nature, timing and extent of planned audit procedures required to implement the overall audit plan.'
>
> Paragraph 12: 'The overall audit plan should be revised as necessary during the course of the audit.'

The audit programme will be prepared for each area and would be designed to meet the specific audit objectives. It follows therefore that should the overall audit plan be revised during the course of the audit, the audit programme for the areas affected may likewise be revised. An audit programme serves three main functions, viz.:

- instruction to the audit staff as to the detailed audit work required;
- a link between the evaluation of the client's system of accounting and control, as well as the tests of controls and substantive procedures to be applied; and
- a record of the audit work done in the various areas and the identities of the staff who did the work.

---

[1] SAAS 220, 'Quality Control', paragraphs .10 and 11.

The form of the audit programme, as with the audit working papers, will vary depending on the policies and practices of the individual practitioner or audit firm.

A review of completely signed-off audit programmes should satisfy the audit partner that all required procedures were performed and that findings reached in support of the ultimate conclusions are adequately documented in the working papers.

Carefully designed audit programmes go a long way to reduce the chance of omissions or incorrect procedures being applied by less experienced assistants and provide coherence to the diverse individual procedures comprising the whole audit conducted by any number of individuals.

8.1.4.2 Documenting the review and evaluation of business processes

A description of the client's processes for recording and managing significant classes of transactions is recorded by the auditor either in the form of narrative notes, internal control questionnaires, or by way of flow charts. Word processing facilities are used to modify notes and questionnaires to take account of any changes since the preceding year's audit. Flow-charting software packages facilitate the drawing of process flow charts that record key management controls, on which the auditor may plan to rely, for significant classes of transactions. They are also useful for recording changes in these processes.

Programs have been developed which, for example, automatically flag situations where a client's staff perform incompatible duties that breach internal control principles and indicate the design or implementation of a particular control is ineffective or improperly performed. These assist the auditor in identifying potential misstatements.

8.1.4.3 Obtaining and documenting audit evidence and preparation of financial statements

PCs may be used to communicate directly with client's computer stored data so that selected records can be retrieved and printed out for subsequent audit investigation and analysis. The capability to access the client's records is dependent on the compatibility of the client's computers with the auditor's generalized enquiry programs. Standard format software enquiry programs are available but, in the case of complex client systems, the auditor will require staff with specialized IT knowledge to access the client's records.

Computer assisted audit techniques may be used very effectively to perform analytical review procedures on computerized client data. These techniques range from ratio calculation, ratio comparison and trend analysis with previous years' and industry averages, to regression analysis and projection of potential misstatement. Some analytical review programs not only calculate the ratios and make comparisons, but also indicate potential causes of misstatement should current ratios and trends be out of line with expectations. Areas of misstatement identified can then be investigated more fully. The analytical reviews performed may be printed out, or kept in electronic format, and form part of the audit working papers.

Items disclosed in the financial statements are often made up of a number of individual general ledger account balances which are grouped together for disclosure purposes. Lead schedule is the term used for the auditor's working paper which details the make-up of each disclosed amount. Audit working paper software programs will automatically generate and cross reference lead schedules to the relevant supporting schedules containing the detailed ledger account analyses and may produce these directly from the client's computerized records.

Auditors often prepare and print the annual financial statements for their clients, particularly for smaller clients. Programs with combined enquiry and word processing facilities are used to prepare financial statements from the final balances in the client's records which are presented in a standard format to comply with the applicable generally accepted accounting framework (GAAP). Copies of the draft and final financial statements will be included in the working papers.

8.1.5 Justification of audit opinion

The auditor should have evidence to show the composition of the figures in the relevant financial statements and the audit procedures applied to test their veracity and leading to a reasoned opinion, thus serving the client competently. The audit report must be fully justifiable so that should the question of negligence be raised the auditor's defence rests on readily available information.

To these ends, the audit working papers should contain evidence that generally accepted auditing standards were complied with, that sufficient appropriate audit evidence was obtained, and that the conclusions drawn from the audit evidence support the audit opinion given.

8.2 THE NATURE AND CONTENT OF WORKING PAPERS

With regard to the form and content of working papers, SAAS 230, 'Documentation', has this to say in paragraphs .05 and .06:

> 'The auditor should prepare working papers that are sufficiently complete and detailed to provide an overall understanding of the audit'

and further:

> '... the auditor should record in the working papers information on planning, the nature, timing and extent of the audit procedures performed, the results thereof, and the conclusion drawn from the evidence obtained.'

8.2.1 Types of audit working papers

Audit working papers will usually include, inter alia, schedules, checklists, correspondence, analyses of transactions and balances, a working trial balance and schedule of audit adjustments, audit programmes, extracts from legal documents, and statutory records of the client, details of procedures performed, lead schedules, financial statements and audit reports.

It is common practice for the auditor to prepare and maintain two sets of files for each client – a permanent notes file and a current audit file. The allocation of working papers between these two files varies. Some audit firms prefer to file information of a continuing nature in a permanent file whereas others maintain it instead on carry-forward schedules, which are transferred annually from one year's current file to the next.

In recent times, audit firms often retain both continuing and current audit evidence for each engagement in one file, organized with a table of contents and separate sections that accommodate each of the SAAS statements, requiring audit evidence to be documented (refer to the Introduction to this chapter). For ease of reference examples of both approaches are dealt with in this chapter.

8.2.2 Permanent file

Two main categories of information of relevance to current and future audits may be identified, viz. information of an ongoing nature concerning the auditor's understanding of the client's operations, and information concerning the conduct of the audit. The items of information of continuing audit interest, which are listed below are, where applicable, normally found in the permanent file.

8.2.2.1 Information concerning the auditor's understanding of the client's business

- Extracts of the memorandum and articles and Extracts of minutes of meetings (in the case of a limited company).
- Extracts of partnership deed (in the case of a partnership).
- An organization chart, indicating the status and names of responsible officials and the limits of their authority.
- The nature of its operations, providing a description of the client's significant business objectives, business processes and significant classes of transactions and balances.
- A record of the client's accounting and internal control system, and the monitoring controls and key performance indicators used by management to control the business.
- Copies of previous years' audited financial statements and related audit reports.
- Financial and accounting information.
- Copies of, or extracts from, important contracts or other documents.

8.2.2.2 Information concerning the management of the audit

Copies of the engagement letters setting out the scope of the assignment and responsibilities assumed by the auditor. Chapter 2 covers engagement letters in greater detail.

The record of the audit planning steps, discussed in chapter 5, should show planning decisions made each year, overall audit approach and field work administration matters such as: staffing requirements showing allocation of work between staff grades; time records showing budgets and actual times taken; fee calculations; materiality limits and synopsis of tests performed and their extent.

A record of aspects and characteristics of the client's operations of greatest audit significance, and the most difficult of these to audit.

The permanent audit notes afford easy reference to information with continuing importance for the conduct of each audit of the particular client. The importance of keeping this information up to date must be stressed. Additional information should be added and alterations made in the course of subsequent audits to reflect changed circumstances.

8.2.3 Current working papers

These contain a record of the nature and extent of audit tests decided upon and applied, the auditor's findings, and his conclusions on the subject matter. How the relevant information can best be set out and the results of the tests best summarized depend on the auditor's preference and the circumstances of each particular case.

Two separate current files are usually maintained. The first, the transaction audit file, contains information concerning the client's system, the audit thereof and a record of other transaction audit work performed. The second contains a record of the verification of year-end balances and is normally referred to as the balance sheet or financial statement audit file. The following is the more usual information recorded in each of these files.

8.2.3.1 The transaction audit file

- General planning schedules, which contain a record of decisions taken regarding, inter alia, audit approach, timing of attendances, time budgets and assignment of suitably qualified staff. The more detailed programming of the audit stages, and the extent and nature of tests, may be documented in the planning working papers but are more likely to be an integral part of the audit programmes filed in their appropriate sections.

- A record of the client's internal control systems and the auditor's evaluation thereof. As indicated in chapters 9 and 10, different methods of recording the information may be used, viz. narrative notes, questionnaires (or check lists) and flow charts. The information is divided into sections, examples being purchases/payments transactions, revenue/ receipts transactions.

● A record of the nature and extent of tests of controls performed on the key management controls on which the auditor proposes to rely, and conclusions reached based on the particular findings.

● A copy of the internal control weaknesses report sent to management or the audit committee and its response thereto.

● Evidence of consideration of the work of internal auditors, outsource providers and other experts and conclusions reached regarding the use of their work in the conduct of the audit.

● A record of the analytical (or operations) review findings, conclusions, and their effect on further audit procedures.

● A record of the nature and extent of substantive tests performed comprising a detailed record of the items selected and tested, and conclusions reached as a result thereof. The substantive test audit programmes for each significant class of transactions are usually arranged by asset, liability and income statement components for ease of integration with the financial statement audit file.

● Schedules, which summarize interim audit results and conclusions, such as error listings and evaluations and details of uncleared items. The schedules should highlight potential problem areas of significance to the conduct of the final financial statement audit.

8.2.3.2 The financial statement file

● A copy of the draft financial statements.
● A copy of the audit report on the financial statements.
● A copy of the working trial balance extracted from or checked with the client's general ledger.
● Schedules showing the composition of items appearing in the financial statements, usually referred to as 'lead schedules'.
● A record of the audit evidence gathered by the auditor, usually consisting of:
  – audit programmes showing the nature and extent of verification procedures performed;
  – schedules supporting audit programme steps, showing detail of items selected, tests performed, and the auditor's findings and conclusions;
  – evidence obtained from external confirmations from third parties, supporting the verification of items such as bank certificates, loan confirmation certificates, debtors' confirmation letters;
  – details of computations of estimated liabilities and provisions;
  – copies of communications with other auditors and experts; including procedures applied regarding components whose financial statements are audited by another auditor, for example, subsidiaries or associate companies;
  – a management representation letter.

- Conclusions reached about how exceptions and audit and accounting matters of significance, disclosed by audit procedures were resolved.

8.2.4 Client engagement file

More recently, the larger multinational audit firms *project manage* their audit engagements and no longer draw a distinction between a permanent file and current transaction file or financial statement file. There is a move towards retention of the audit working papers in electronic format, although most firms keep both electronic and hard copy working paper files. Under these circumstances, the firm merely has an engagement audit file that may typically be divided into the following sections and individual working papers numbered with an alpha and sequence number:

Section A – Engagement management: This section may typically contain the following information: Audit checklists; documents identifying significant issues and decisions taken with regard to these; the terms of the engagement; communications with the client; logistical plans for handling the engagement – staffing budgets, etc; evaluation of internal audit, other auditors, service organizations or experts whose work the auditor may wish to use in the course of the audit.

Section B – Reporting: This section may typically contain the following sub-sections: Lead schedules and/or trial balances; current and prior period financial statements, including the audit report; summary of unadjusted differences; final analytical review and results; other reports; GAAP and statutory disclosure checklists.

Section C – Communications from the audit firm: This section contains communications from the audit firm to the client and the audit committee. The nature and content may vary, but will generally advise the client on any shortcomings identified during the audit.

Section D – Strategic business analysis: This section may typically contain details documenting the auditor's understanding of the client's strategic business objectives, identification of strategic business risks and how management is controlling such risks, identification of significant classes of transactions, and core processes for recording the transactions; analytical review procedures at the strategic analysis stage; and a risk analysis and separate analysis of potential fraud risk.

Section E – Standard audit programmes: This section will typically contain audit programmes and details relating to the auditor's responsibilities to gather audit evidence to comply with specific auditing standards such as: fraud and error, SAAS 240; going concern, SAAS 570; related parties, SAAS 550; litigation and claims, ED-SAAS 502, laws and regulations, SAAS 250; and subsequent events, SAAS 560.

Section F – Process analysis and remaining audit procedures: This section will typically contain analyses of core processes, and management controls that the auditor may wish to rely on for significant classes of transactions, audit programmes and details of tests of controls performed; identification of significant classes of transactions and balances; analytical reviews of such transactions and balances; and substantive tests of detail to address any remaining risks of material misstatements.

8.3 WORKING PAPER FORMAT

As noted above, the manner in which the relevant information can be set out in the audit working papers depends on the auditor preference and the circumstances of each particular case. Complete standardization of format would result in inflexibility, inhibit initiative and would not make allowance for the variety of circumstances with which working papers would have to deal. Within any one audit firm, however, general conformity to a certain laid-down format with regard to content, arrangement and indexing of working papers is desirable as this:

- provides an organized approach to the audit, particularly through the use of pre-printed internal control questionnaires and audit programmes;
- permits several staff members to work on one assignment in a co-ordinated manner; and
- provides an efficient means of communicating results of the audit work to reviewers as they will be familiar with the form of working paper layout.

8.3.1 Principles of preparation

Heading: Each schedule should contain the name of the client, a title, describing the content of the schedule, and the balance sheet date or period covered by the schedule if related to transactions.

Signature and dating: On completion of their respective tasks related to the specific working paper, the names or initials of the preparer and reviewer, as well as the date on which the schedule was prepared and reviewed, should be inserted to establish responsibility for the work performed.

Referencing: Each firm will establish its particular sequence and sections in which audit working papers will be filed, in order to group together different aspects of the engagement and to facilitate cross-referencing and review and to evidence compliance with the SAAS requirements for documentary evidence. Consequently every schedule or document should contain a numbered reference – for example, **A1**, **D6**, etc. – indicating where the schedule should be located in the audit working papers.

Cross referencing: Information on one schedule that is taken from another working paper or carried forward to another working paper should be cross-referenced with the reference number of that other working paper. Most PC programs used in the preparation of audit working papers allow for working papers to be electronically cross-referenced and linked. This allows for the automatic updating of linked schedules as the audit progresses. For example, the schedule of audit adjustments would be linked to the working trial balance columns for the adjusting entries and as new adjusting journal entries are noted they will automatically update the working trial balance which will insert the reference to the relevant adjusting journal entry. Similarly, the identification of inherent or control risks may be cross-referenced to the relevant audit programme procedures designed to address the particular risk area.

Audit tickmarks: The tickmarks used on individual schedules relate to the audit procedures performed. Each working paper should contain an explanation of the nature and extent of the procedures performed to support the meaning of each tickmark used.

Audit conclusion: Every section of the work should contain a conclusion regarding the results of the procedures performed and whether they meet the stated audit objectives. This should include conclusions reached about how exceptions and unusual or contentious matters disclosed by the audit procedures were resolved.

Whatever the format adopted, there are certain basic essentials with which working papers should conform, viz.:

- organization;
- completeness; and
- clarity and conciseness.

These are discussed below.

8.3.2 Organization

A normal method of filing, indexing and cross-referencing should be used. A standard index should ensure that all the required schedules have been prepared and are filed in a pre-determined order.

For the purposes of convenience, a system of standard lettering should be used with a particular letter used consistently for each particular working paper item. This means that in the balance sheet audit file each item in the financial statements is given a letter of the alphabet. This letter should be entered on the top right-hand corner of each schedule. The main or lead schedule, which contains a summary of the composition of the item, bears the relevant letter and any supporting schedules are marked with that letter and consecutively numbered. All lead schedules should be cross-referenced to the draft financial statements. Such a referencing system helps reviewers of the file to locate information quickly.

8.3.3 Completeness

Each schedule should clearly indicate its index number or letter, the name of the client, the financial period under audit, the name of the person responsible for its preparation, the date of preparation and a description of the nature of the schedule. The name or signature of the individual who performed the work fixes responsibility and should result in a more effective review, as the work of less experienced staff should be the subject of more thorough scrutiny than that of seniors. The dating of audit working papers is important as it marks the date on which audit procedures were completed, a matter of particular importance should the question of the auditor's responsibility toward some fact or circumstance which occurred in the post balance sheet period be raised.

Working papers should be completed in sufficient detail to be easily understandable to the reviewer without further explanation from the preparer thereof. To this end, they should give details of information obtained and the source thereof, the nature, timing and extent of work done to confirm that information, and conclusions reached as a result of the examination.

8.3.4 Clarity and conciseness

Working papers should be clear and concise. All facts and figures should be precisely identified and all explanations and conclusions kept short and to the point. Clarity can be better achieved through point-form notes than by lengthy narrative. Extracts of salient matters may be more appropriate than photocopies of lengthy documents such as title deeds, accounts receivable and inventory listings. Superfluous working papers and details should be avoided as these add nothing to the supporting evidence available to the auditor and may confuse the reviewer.

8.4 REVIEW AND OWNERSHIP OF WORKING PAPERS

8.4.1 Review by engagement staff

SAAS 220 'Quality Control', in paragraphs .08 to .17, provides guidance as to quality control procedures appropriate to the individual audit. Assistants to whom work is delegated need appropriate supervision and review in order to monitor the progress of the audit and consider whether the assistants have the requisite skills and competence to carry out the tasks assigned, understand the audit directions and that the work is being carried out in accordance with the overall audit plan and the audit programme. The reviewer should become informed of and address significant accounting and auditing questions, by considering their significance and modifying the overall audit plan and the audit programme as appropriate. In addition, any differences of professional judgement between personnel and/or the client should be resolved and, if necessary, the appropriate level of consultation should be considered.

The review should be done by personnel of at least equal competence to consider whether the work has been performed in accordance with the audit programme; the work done and results have been adequately documented; all significant matters have been resolved or are reflected in the audit conclusions; the objectives of the audit procedures have been achieved and the conclusions expressed are consistent with the results of the work performed and support the audit opinion.

The extent of review will obviously differ depending on the size and complexity of the audit and the staffing arrangements. At times the review of the work of junior staff assistants may be done by a senior staff assistant, at other times the review will be undertaken by the audit manager and finally by the audit partner. Review of working papers must be evidenced, generally by the reviewer initialling and dating the relevant audit working paper. A small 'box job' may simply be reviewed briefly by the audit partner prior to signing the audit report on the financial statements.

8.4.2 Peer review

In the case of large complex audits, particularly where significant audit matters affecting the audited financial statements have been identified in the course of the audit, a peer review may be undertaken by another partner in the same firm. This may arise where the appropriate application of certain complex, generally accepted accounting statements (GAAP) appear to be in dispute and where technical advice is required in order to ensure the appropriate audit opinion is expressed.

In addition, the audit firm may have instituted a senior partner review process for selected audit engagements as part of its normal quality control procedures. At times independent peer reviews may be arranged between firms. This practice is not commonly encountered in South Africa.

8.4.3 Practice review

A periodic practice review of individual auditing practitioners is undertaken by the Practice Review staff of the PAAB. This is done in a five year cycle and is provided for in section 22A of the Public Accountants' and Auditors' Act. The primary purpose is to monitor compliance by Registered Accountants and Auditors (RAAs) with appropriate levels of professional standards in the performance of the attest function. The secondary objective is to provide guidance to RAs to assist them to improve their standards.[2] RAA's are subject to practice review at least once in a five-year cycle. Strict confidentiality is observed with regard to the findings of the reviewer.

Where a practitioner is found not to comply, Practice Review refers the matter to the Investigation Committee of the PAAB which, after due inquiry, has the right to take action to discipline the member. Such action may include a re-review within a short space of time, the levying of a fine or, in persistent cases of non-compliance, the extreme step of terminating the practitioner's registration in public practice. Alternatively, the PAAB Practice Review

[2] PAAB Manual of Information 2002 – Section 22A and Section 6: Practice Review.

committee may require the practitioner to attend technical updates in specific areas coupled with re-review after a short period.

8.4.4 Ownership, custody and confidentiality

SAAS 230 'Documentation', in paragraph .13, states that:

> 'The auditor should adopt appropriate procedures for maintaining the confidentiality and safe custody of the working papers and retaining them for a period sufficient to meet the needs of the practice, and in accordance with legal and professional requirements or guidelines for record retention.'

Working papers are the property of the auditor, although portions of or extracts from the working papers may be made available to the entity at the discretion of the auditor.

Circular 6/98 issued by SAICA in November 1998, deals with the retention of audit working papers. Whilst the auditor is not compelled by statute or court decision to compile, collate or retain audit working papers for any specific period of time, the Public Accountants' and Auditors' Act was amended in 1993 to allow the PAAB to review the practice of a registered accountant and auditor. This allowed the reviewer to 'inspect any book, document or thing in the possession or under the control of an accountant and auditor'. The practice is to look at attest functions performed during the most recent 24 months.[3] SAICA has recommended that working papers be retained for a minimum period of five years. Where there are legal or other reasons to retain the working papers for longer periods, for example, if the auditor is aware that litigation is pending where the audit working papers may be required as evidence, such working papers should be retained until the litigation or threat thereof has passed.

The retention of records on computer magnetic tapes, disks or other media is part of the modern business environment. The Computer Evidence Act of 1983 provides that an authenticated computer printout is admissible as evidence in legal proceedings provided it is accompanied by an affidavit made by a person with knowledge and experience of computers. Consequently, such records similarly need to be retained for a minimum period of five years, or longer, if litigation is pending.[4]

Working papers contain a considerable amount of information that should be considered confidential. Consequently, the information contained in the working papers should *not* be disclosed except in the following circumstances:

- When disclosure is authorized by the client or employer in the interests of all parties.

---

[3] Circular 6/98, 'Retention of records and working papers', paragraph .06.
[4] Circular 6/98, 'Retention of records and working papers', paragraphs .07 – .10.

- When disclosure is required by law, in the course of legal proceedings or to disclose to appropriate authorities infringements of the law which the auditor is required to report.

- When there is a professional duty or right to disclose, in order to comply with technical standards and ethics requirements, to protect the professional interests of a member in legal proceedings, to comply with practice review of the PAAB or to respond to an inquiry by the Investigation or Disciplinary Committees of the PAAB or SAICA.[5]

Where there is a change in the auditors appointed, the proposed accountant will usually communicate with the existing auditor before accepting the engagement. In the absence of a specific request, the existing auditor should not volunteer information about the client's affairs. The extent to which the existing auditor can discuss the affairs of the client will depend on whether the client's permission to do so has been obtained and/or the legal or ethical requirements relating to such disclosure.[6]

Should the communication include a request to review the working papers of the existing auditor, this may only be considered with the consent of the client and at the discretion of the audit firm concerned. Access is unlikely to be granted in circumstances where there is a possibility of litigation against the existing auditor.

---

[5] SAICA Code of Professional Conduct, Section 5 – Confidentiality, and IFAC Code of Ethics for Professional Accountants, Section 4 – Confidentiality.
[6] SAICA Code of Professional Conduct, Section 17, paragraphs .15 and .17; PAAB Code of Professional Conduct, paragraphs .15, .18; and IFAC Code of Ethics for Professional Accountants, Section 13, paragraphs .15 and .17.

9

Understanding Risk Assessment, Internal Control and Computerized Information Systems

---

Learning objectives

After studying this chapter you should be able to:

1. Explain the importance of risk management and internal control.
2. Define and discuss internal control.
3. State the limitations of internal controls and explain the roles and responsibilities of management, audit committees, internal auditors and other parties with regard to the internal controls in an entity.
4. Explain how computerization of accounting records affects the business processes and internal controls of the entity.
5. Describe key aspects of general and application controls in an IT environment and how these are linked to the financial statement assertions.
6. Explain the nature and importance of control activities typically implemented by an entity to manage business risks for all significant transaction flows.
7. Explain how the auditor evaluates the internal controls and determines the extent of reliance to be placed on specific internal controls, and how this affects the auditor's decision to perform tests of controls and substantive audit procedures.
8. Explain the methods used by an auditor to obtain and document an understanding of the internal control systems for all significant transaction flows.
9. Discuss the different IT environments and data processing methods that may be encountered and how these may affect the auditor's understanding of the strategic business risks, evaluation of internal controls and the audit procedures adopted.

9.1 INTRODUCTION TO INTERNAL CONTROL

9.1.1 The importance of risk management and internal control

The importance of risk management, which involves the identification of risks faced by business entitites and the implementation of systems to mitigate these, has long been recognized. These aspects feature prominently in the literature and in the reports and recommendations of various national and international commissions appointed to advise on corporate governance and the prevention of fraudulent reporting practices. Among the more important reports have been the National Commission on Fraudulent Financial Reporting (1987, The Treadway Commission Report) issued in the United States, followed by the report of the Committee of Sponsoring Organizations (1992, The Treadway Committee) entitled *Internal Control – an Integrated Framework*. The latter, which became known as the COSO report, was aimed at establishing a common definition of internal control and providing an assessment standard for control systems. Structured to accommodate the guidance contained in the COSO report, SAS55, 'Consideration of the Internal Control Structure in a Financial Statement Audit' (the US equivalent of the South African SAAS 400, 'Risk Assessments and Internal Control'), was issued by the US Auditing Standards Board in 1998.

The US reports were followed by:

- the CICA report of the Canadian Institute of Chartered Accountants, in 1988;

- the Report of the Committee on the Financial Reports of Corporate Governance, known as the Cadbury Report, issued in the United Kingdom in 1992;

- the King Report on Corporate Governance, issued in South Africa in 1994; and the second King Report on Corporate Governance, issued in South Africa in 2002 (referred to hereafter as the King II Report).

The King II Report and its recommendations apply to all public companies listed on the JSE Securities Exchange, banks, financial institutions, insurance companies and public sector enterprises that fall under the Public Finance Management Act. Section 2 of the report deals extensively with the responsibilities of directors and management for risk assessment and internal controls. These aspects are discussed in this chapter whereas other corporate governance aspects of the King II Report are dealt with in chapter 21.

This chapter discusses, *inter alia*, aspects related to risk management, including systems of internal control, and draws on material set out in the King II Report.

Risk management[1] is defined in the King II Report as:

> 'The identification and evaluation of actual and potential risk areas as they pertain to the company as a total entity, followed by a process of either termination, transfer, acceptance (tolerance) or mitigation of each risk.'

Risk management is a process that uses internal control as one of the measures to mitigate and control risk. Some risks cannot be managed through traditional internal control systems, for example, political, technological and legislative risks, and so these have to be managed using flexibility and forward planning. The total process of risk management, which includes a related system of internal controls, is the responsibility of the board of directors (top management); the execution of the risk management process should be the responsibility of every employee.

According to the King II Report recommendations, the board of directors is responsible for ensuring a systematic, documented assessment of the processes and outcomes surrounding key risks undertaken for purposes of its statement on risk management and internal controls in the annual financial report. This risk assessment should at least address the company's exposure to physical and operational risks; human resource risks; technology risks; business continuity and disaster recovery; credit and market risks; and compliance risks. As this responsibility is often delegated to management and internal audit functions, management is accountable to the board and due monitoring processes must be implemented and performed by them on a regular basis. Management may appoint a chief risk officer to assist with the consideration of the risk strategy and policies and implementation of the risk management process.

9.1.2 Internal control: definition and aspects

Risk management is a function of all staff in all daily activities throughout the company. Sound risk management and internal control frameworks tailored to the specific circumstances of the company are a part of daily operational activities and should not be viewed independently of normal business activities. Controls should be established to encompass all management responses to risk. Controls are derived from the way in which management runs the company and should be integrated into all business processes at every level of the company.

The King II Report defines Internal Control[2] as follows:

'*Internal control* is a process designed to provide reasonable assurance regarding the achievement of organizational objectives with respect to:

- the effectiveness and efficiency of operations;
- the safeguarding of the company's assets (including information);

---

[1] The King II Report, page 73.
[2] The King II Report, page 73.

- compliance with applicable laws, regulations and supervisory requirements;
- supporting business sustainability under normal as well as adverse operating conditions;
- the reliability of reporting; and
- behaving responsibly to stakeholders.'

Five essential aspects of control are identified[3] as having to be present in order to implement an effective and efficient internal control system. These are:

- Control environment.
- Risk assessment.
- Information and communication.
- Control activities.
- Monitoring.

Each of these aspects and their related factors are discussed below.

9.1.2.1 Control environment

The control environment sets the tone regarding the company's provision of the necessary discipline and structure for all aspects of risk management and control. It includes such factors as *integrity, ethical values and organizational culture, employee competence, management's philosophy and operating style*, the manner in which the company *assigns authority* and the way in which it develops its people, and the attention and direction given by the board of directors.[4]

Integrity, ethical values and organizational culture

These refer to the principles, norms and standards the company promotes for the guidance and conduct of its activities, internal relations and interactions with external stakeholders. Cultural values and norms may differ among individuals, varying from Western notions of individualism to African notions of participation and inclusiveness. Companies should develop a culture of conduct based on generally accepted behaviour and organizational values as embedded in their mission statements. This involves the identification of ethical principles and standards that will guide behaviour and accountability in the following areas:

- *Responsibilities to share owners* and the financial community, including disclosure, accounting practices, insider trading and conflicts of interest.
- *Relations with customers and suppliers*, including marketing issues and the use of market power, pricing practices, quality and safety of goods.
- *Employment practices*, including equality of opportunity, occupational health and safety and other principles related to employer/employee relationships, for example support for Aids awareness programmes.

---

[3] The King II Report, pages 78–79.
[4] The King II Report, page 78.

- *Responsibility to the community*, including support for community activities, social investment and attention to social and environmental impact. In order to emphasize the importance of integrity and ethical values, the board should formulate and implement a code of ethics in consultation with its various stakeholders which should contain the following core ethical principles: fairness, transparency, honesty, non-discrimination, accountability and responsibility, and respect for human dignity, human rights and social justice.

A recent fraud survey[5] has shown that rampant fraud exists in South African business enterprises. Findings indicated that 88% of respondents believed employees were responsible, while 32% believed management to be the source of fraud. The survey indicated that losses occurred mainly through theft of monetary assets, physical assets and misuse of assets under the person's control. The main causes of fraud were identified as collusion between employees, and between employees and third parties, followed by poor internal controls and management override of controls. Employees involved were invariably found to be living beyond their means and heavily in debt. In terms of SAAS 240, 'Fraud and Error', the auditor needs to consider the risk and significance of possible employee fraud at each audit client, as well as management's actions to mitigate such risks and how this may result in material misstatement, or fraudulent financial reporting, in the financial statements. The auditor will have to adapt the audit procedures accordingly.

Competence of employees

Competence of employees at every level of the organization is important for the achievement of business objectives. This affects the human resources policies and practices of the company. In order to properly perform their duties, staff in both operational and financial areas must have the requisite skills and knowledge. In South Africa, with its need for meaningful transformation and black economic empowerment in the workplace to redress historical social and economic imbalances, there is a skills shortage in many areas, particularly accounting, IT and management. The need for transformation coupled with the need to keep achieving business objectives necessitate achieving a balance between recruitment and retention policies. To this end, new employees are screened with a view to obtaining a mixture of integrity, skills, knowledge and experience levels, as well as the implementation of training programmes for new and existing employees to develop appropriate skills and competencies.

Recent government directives have helped to effect change, for example: the introduction of the Employment Equity Act No. 55 of 1998, obliging companies to develop an Employment Equity Plan; the Skills Development

---

[5] The KPMG Fraud Survey (July 2002).

Act No. 97 of 1998, and the Skills Development Levies Act No. 9 of 1999, which govern the provision of resources for skills development and training by companies.

The auditor should consider whether senior management and staff have the necessary business experience, accounting skills and financial knowledge to deal appropriately with complex transactions, internal control systems and accounting practices. Such considerations also provide opportunities for value added services for the client, with regard to guidance for adjustments to financial records, in IT support and in providing training for the client's accounting staff.

Management's philosophy and operating style

Management's philosophy and operating style will be affected, firstly, by the formal structure of the organization and the way in which authority is exercised; and, secondly, by the characteristics or behavioural aspects and operating styles of the board and management, and their attitude towards responsible risk assessment and internal controls.

Structure of the organization: The composition of the board of directors and the way in which they exercise their governance responsibilities have a major impact on the control environment and organizational integrity of the company. For example, a dominant and autocratic Chief Executive Officer may override controls to serve his/her interests rather than those of the company, but a highly democratic board may become indecisive and fail to take prompt action to manage strategic business risks.

The following all contribute to the quality of the control environment: the level of knowledge, skills, experience and stature of directors; directors' independence from management; the presence of a reasonable number of non-executive directors on the board who exercise oversight responsibilities for the actions of management; and the way such directors engage with internal and external auditors. Furthermore, the existence of an audit committee with an appropriate composition and functions also contributes to the quality of risk management and the financial reporting objectives of the company.

Characteristics of directors and management: The board's and management's approach to the taking and monitoring of business risks is an important characteristic of the control environment. Management's style of communication may take the form of informal discussions with key managers, rather than a more formal communication of policies in writing. The establishment of key performance indicators and error handling procedures, such as exception reports, is also important. The directors' attitudes and actions towards financial disclosure and adoption of conservative or aggressive accounting policies can limit or significantly increase the risk exposure of the business. It is important for directors and senior management to have an awareness and understanding of the risks associated with the company's IT infrastructure and operation, as well as the degree of dependence placed by the entity upon IT systems. In addition, management should have a strategic plan for the potential use of new IT technologies in enhancing the business.

Finally, management's attitudes towards information processing, accounting functions and personnel send a clear message to employees about the significance management attaches to the internal controls of the entity and their implementation of the policies and procedures.

Assignment of authority

Assignment of authority deals with the manner in which the board and management assign responsibility to company employees for all entity activities. For authority to be assigned effectively, all employees need to understand how their work is interrelated to that of others in achieving the objectives of the company. This would relate to the control activities over transaction processes of the company, from authorization at inception and storage of supporting documents, the computerized input, processing, and reporting of business transactions and subsequent monitoring. Responsibility should be delegated in such a way that individuals are clearly accountable for their actions and functions. Employees should understand that their performance will be monitored against the agreed key performance indicators, budgets, etc. A general control consciousness should be established amongst employees. Failure to establish and monitor specific duties, responsibilities and related reporting mechanisms could lead to a lack of accountability, uncorrected errors and undetected fraud in the organization.

If the company depends on significant IT applications, the responsibility for the implementation of appropriate general and application controls must be specified and monitored on a continuous basis. This would include policies for ongoing system developments and training of employees on new applications. Physical and programmed access controls must also be strictly controlled. In addition, formal backup, disaster recovery and business continuity procedures must be put in place and communicated clearly to all relevant staff in the organization.

9.1.2.2 Risk assessment

The risk assessment process involves the identification, evaluation and management of risks that are significant to the achievement of the company's objectives. Where possible, risk assessment should include an estimate of the likelihood of occurrence, the quantification of the impact, and a comparison with available benchmarks for the particular industry or business sector, or as established by the company itself.[6]

---

[6] The King II Report, page 78.

Risk assessment is a continuous process requiring regular review as and when internal and external changes influence the company's strategies and objectives. Circumstances demanding management's close attention include substantive changes to the operating environment, new personnel, new or revamped operating systems, rapid growth, new technology, new products or activities, corporate restructuring, acquisitions and disposals, and changes in foreign operations. Decisions should be taken about the management of each risk, that is, to terminate, transfer, accept or mitigate. Management's risk assessment should include considerations of the risks associated with its IT environment and the company's dependence thereon.

The auditor should obtain an understanding of the significant business risks that could affect the strategic business objectives of the entity and identify the financial statement implications of the strategic business risks for potential material misstatement in the financial statements. The risk analysis should identify significant classes of transactions and balances, as well as key or core business processes. The auditor then considers the effectiveness of the steps taken by management to mitigate the significant risks in running the business, for example, the identification of critical success factors, the use of key performance indicators, and the frequency with which these are monitored by management. Once the auditor has obtained a thorough understanding of the business processes, an appropriate audit strategy can be formulated.

9.1.2.3 Information and communication

Pertinent information arising from management's risk assessment and aspects relating to control activities should be communicated in a form and time frame that enable employees to properly carry out their responsibilities. Information communicated may include accurate, timely and relevant financial and operational data, supported by adequate and appropriate information systems.[7]

All companies should have *information systems* that measure process results against objectives, and *communication* practices to ensure all such information, both positive and negative, is promptly received by senior management. This is important for the effective management of the business.

The accounting system, whether computerized or manual, should provide a complete transaction trail, with account balances and transaction details linked to one another, using a system of coding and cross-referencing to the underlying documentary evidence. In on-line computer systems, individual transactions generally have a unique transaction number to identify the nature and type of the transaction and allowing the source and details to be established. Many computer systems generate the relevant internal documentation and automatically allocate a sequenced transaction number

---

[7] The King II Report, page 79.

to the particular transaction, whether it be sales, purchases, cheque payments or payroll transactions.

Information may be retained electronically and only be accessible at certain times or by means of special inquiry programs for reports. It is essential that accounting systems have clear audit trails, which allow management and employees to deal with queries from, for example, suppliers and customers, and the auditor to select any particular transaction or class of transactions for audit review and verification.

Documentation

Documents are an important aspect of internal control and a source of audit evidence. A variety of documents are encountered in every business. These range from transaction documentation (such as orders, delivery notes or goods received notes, invoices and statements to customers and from suppliers and other service providers, bank statements, cheques and electronic funds transfer forms, payroll slips, journal vouchers, statutory returns to payroll accounts payable and other regulators, correspondence with internal and external parties), to contracts, wage agreements, minutes of meetings of directors, shareholders and management, policy documents and computer and accounting system documentation.

Good source document design for transactions requires that documents should be printed specifically for the organization, display its name and be pre-numbered. Such pre-numbering allows a sequence check to be made and thus establishes a means of ensuring that the completeness of all source documents supporting transactions are accounted for. A check of sequential numbering for different classes of transactions makes it possible to detect any attempt to misuse documents, for example, where unused stationery has fallen into unauthorized hands (manual system), or the company's documents have been forged, or fictitious transactions have been generated using the computer systems. Multiple copies of internally generated documents are frequently encountered to minimize the need to transcribe information from one document to another and to reduce the possibility of transcription error. For example, a four-part document could serve as an order, a delivery note, a customer's invoice and a copy sales invoice to be retained by the company.

Documents should be designed to facilitate the correctness and completeness of recording. To this end, as much information as is possible should be pre-printed on documents and clearly marked spaces provided for the items that have to be entered. Apart from the details necessary to adequately document the information relevant to transactions, space should be provided for the required signatures, or initials, of those who authorize and approve transactions or check the information recorded on source documents. Before transactions are recorded in the accounting records, someone (other than those persons responsible for the preparation of source documents) should check the accuracy of the information and amounts recorded on the documents. The people who perform these checks should sign or initial source documents as evidence of their having performed the tasks. This makes it possible to pinpoint accountability and responsibility for various functions and duties and facilitates the early detection and correction of errors and fraud.

In a computerized accounting system, many of the transaction checks for completeness, measurement/accuracy and occurrence/validity will be programmed into the particular application software to monitor every transaction as it is initiated and recorded. This may take the form of input validation checks, requiring the completion of particular fields by the data capture clerk, and screen formats that prevent a transaction being recorded until all fields have been entered. While transactions are being processed for a particular application, programmed controls would make it possible to detect errors, resulting in *exception reports*. Exception reports are generated by the system to highlight errors and exceptions, for example: a list of missing sequence numbers of delivery notes or goods received notes captured for a sales or purchase run; hours worked exceeding specified maximum limits for a weekly payroll run; a list of inventory items with negative balances appearing in the inventory ledger at the month end.

Records in a computerized accounting system include both master files and transaction files, such as inventory records, sales price master files, fixed asset registers, employees' standing data and cumulative pay records; master files of customer or supplier details as well as ledger accounts with a record of all transactions with the particular supplier or customer; printouts of different classes of transactions and general ledger accounts. In a manual accounting system, records will comprise the books of prime entry, such as a sales journal, purchases journal and cashbook, journals and ledgers and fixed asset register.

Communication ensures that all employees involved in the accounting and financial reporting system understand what they should do and how their activities are interrelated with one another's and with parties external to the organization. Communications include policy manuals, accounting, report-ing and system documentation to guide employees regarding their respective duties and responsibilities. A chart of accounts should be available to facilitate the allocation of transaction amounts to the correct accounts and to ensure the consistent treatment of similar transactions. Such a chart lists all the general ledger accounts and defines transaction types that should be allocated to each account. It will include exception reports and the monitoring processes for action and rectification to ensure the accuracy and reliability of the financial reporting.

9.1.2.4 **Control activities**

These are the policies and procedures established by management as a response to internal and external risks. Control should include a diverse range of activities aimed at enhancing the control environment, including specific and general authorization procedures, delegation of authority, approval processes, verification processes, operating reviews, reporting, and the segregation of duties applied at various levels throughout the organization.[8]

Control activities needed to achieve control objectives should incorporate the following features or characteristics, often referred to as *internal control principles*:

- Segregation of duties.
- Information processing controls:
  - General controls; and
  - Application controls.
- Physical controls.
- Operating reviews.
- Reporting.

Each of these internal control principles is discussed below.

Segregation of duties

Every transaction should be properly authorized, executed and recorded. If one person performs all three aspects it is possible for that person to misappropriate assets and manipulate the accounting records by passing false entries to conceal shortages. Good control requires, therefore, that different individuals or departments should perform the three aspects underlying any transaction. The important principle here is that the persons handling assets, or who have access to them, should not maintain the accounting records for such assets, nor have the authority to initiate transactions involving them.

The obligation to safeguard the assets of an organization requires that transactions be entered into only once the appropriate individual has authorized them, and that each transaction conforms to the terms of its authority. The authority to transact should be delegated to defined individuals so that they may be held accountable for their actions. This delegated authority is either specific or general. Specific authority is distinguishable from general authority in that authorization is required for each and every transaction of a particular type. Typically, specific authority is required for predetermined, unusual, high monetary value or infrequent transactions, such as the purchase or disposal of capital assets. General authority is usually sufficient for routine transactions, such as credit sales to customers at the usual advertised or marked prices where authorized pricing and credit sales policies have been laid down within the organization.

---

[8] The King II Report, page 79.

In the case of computerized accounting systems, there should be a proper segregation of duties within the IT department and between IT departments and user departments. Within the IT department, systems development, operations, data controls and security administration should be segregated, while IT staff should not correct data submitted by users and should be independent of the user departments. The following example of a purchase transaction process will illustrate the difference:

Example

In a manual system:

In a trading company, the buyer may initiate a purchase of inventory, the stores personnel may receive the goods ordered and place them into the relevant store, preparing a manual goods received note to indicate they have received what was ordered. Thereafter, the accounts personnel are responsible for recording the purchase and raising the liability in the general ledger, once they receive the invoice from the supplier, and have ascertained that the purchase was properly authorized and the goods have been received, this is done by matching the details on the invoice with the relevant purchase order and goods received note.

The cashbook personnel may then prepare, and record, the cheque or EFT transfer for signature by the accountant or financial director in order to settle the amount owing to the supplier. Prior to despatching the payment, the accounting personnel would reconcile the creditor's account to the supplier's monthly statement and prepare a remittance advice to send with the cheque payment or EFT transfer to supplier. The payment would then be checked to the relevant monthly bank statement and reconciliation.

Example

In a computerized system:

In the case of a computerized accounting system, the initiation of the order by the buyer may immediately raise the provisional inventory and liability in a temporary file, to which the computer will allocate a distinct purchase order number. On receipt of the goods, the stores personnel will place them in the store and then, instead of completing a manual goods received note, may merely capture the receipt directly into the computer system against the particular purchase order number, which will then automatically transfer the purchase from the temporary file to the inventory and creditor's files in the general ledger. Thereafter, accounts personnel may merely capture the supplier's invoice number to activate an EFT payment to the supplier, where arrangements have been made to pay suppliers 'on invoice'. The accounts personnel will maintain control by reconciling the general ledger printouts containing the creditor's account to the supplier's statement received at the month end. The EFT transfer will be agreed to relevant monthly bank statement and reconciliation.

This is not to say that the segregation of incompatible functions negates entirely the risk of misappropriation, and concealment thereof; as indicated by the findings of the Fraud Survey mentioned earlier, collusion between two or more people is always a possibility. Adequate screening of prospective employees before hiring them and management supervisory checks should minimize this risk, or detect collusion if it has indeed occurred.

Information processing controls

These are the processes put in place to ensure the completeness, measurement/accuracy and occurrence/validity of all transactions initiated, recorded and reported. As most businesses of whatever size use computerized accounting systems, these controls are further categorized between general and application controls, as discussed below.

General controls

The purpose of general controls is to control program development, program changes, computer operations, and to secure access to programs and data. These controls are more pervasive affecting the whole IT environment of the entity rather than specific applications. Whilst weaknesses in the general controls do not necessarily prevent the auditor from seeking to place reliance on and test controls over particular applications for specific classes of transactions, for example, sales or payroll, they may none-the-less affect the auditor's control risk assessment and decision to dispense with tests controls and pursue substantive audit tests instead.

In highly sophisticated and computerized systems where the client's dependence on IT systems is significant, such as SAP integrated databases, banking systems, etc., the soundness of the general controls is more critical for ensuring the security of the system and its capacity for meeting the control objectives for all transactions.

The following general control areas are widely recognized and applied:

- organization and operation controls;
- systems development and documentation controls;
- hardware and system software controls;
- access controls; and
- data and procedural controls.

Each of these areas is discussed below.

Organization and operation controls

These controls revolve around the management philosophy, operating style and business structure discussed earlier. In particular, where the entity is dependent on computerized systems, this relates to the segregation of duties between employees in the IT department to ensure that there are no conflicting duties and responsibilities. Distinctions should be made between an IT manager (or director) with overall responsibility for the IT function and its development; those responsible for the hardware and systems software development and program changes; those responsible for the day to day operations and running of applications, including a separation of functions to support the hardware functioning, network administration and the management and storage of system data; those responsible for the security administration or database administration of the entire system, whether centralized or distributed – including the administration of access controls and monitoring of security breaches.

The IT department should be independent of user departments and report directly to the board of directors. With the changes in technology and introduction of aspects such as e-commerce, senior management may not have the technical expertise to understand the risks and complexities of the IT environment. This makes the employment of appropriately qualified IT staff with integrity of paramount importance for organizations with significant dependence on computerized systems. Significant frauds have been perpetrated using computer systems, and management has to remain alert to the possibility that this could arise in their own organization. Consequently, key performance indicators and security breaches should be monitored very closely in order to detect, investigate and correct any such incidences. Employees at all levels will need to be trained to use the relevant parts of the computer system to which they are granted access and to understand and implement the relevant controls consistently.

In recent years a number of large entities have regarded the IT functions as not forming part of their core business and have downsized large IT departments to outsource significant parts of the IT functions. This poses particular risks (to be addressed later in this chapter), of which the most important is the loss of control by the entity over its own processes. Specific physical and contractual arrangements – in the form of a service level agreement, the specification of internal controls to be implemented and the rights of access to be granted – need to be established with an outsource provider to adequately manage these risks. The auditor will need to consider such arrangements to gain an understanding of the strategic risks of outsourcing the relevant IT aspects of the client's business.

In small organizations and owner-managed businesses it may not be possible to separate these functions, and the auditor needs to recognize the risk of potential error or fraud that may arise in such circumstances. It may also mean that the controls are effectively vested in a few people with incompatible duties and, consequently, limited reliance will be placed on internal controls and a more substantive approach will be taken in the audit.

Systems development and documentation controls

These controls relate to the ongoing development of the entity's computer systems to enable it to meet the business objectives, particularly the information and communication aspects. As a result, these controls relate to the development, review and testing of new hardware and software systems; controls over program changes; proper documentation of the hardware infrastructure, software and database structure; and the network topology to identify all active network points, and any changes thereto.

- *Systems development, review and testing* should involve the initial specification by the IT project team of the requirements, which should be done in consultation with users to define their needs; securing tenders or quotes from potential suppliers for the acquisition of 'off-the-shelf' software and operating systems, and the selection and appointment of these providers; or the appointment of programmers and technical staff if software programs are to be developed in-house; the testing of the new hardware and software in a test environment in consultation with users; the training of users; and management of the project through to implementation. It also involves establishing formal authorization procedures for approval of the new systems or changes to existing systems, prior to implementation.

  The internal and external auditors should, usually, be involved in the project team to advise, amongst others, on appropriate programmed and manual controls to be included. The process should include an implementation plan that allows for conversion from existing systems to new systems whilst maintaining the integrity of the balances transferred. This requires attention, *inter alia*, to the timing of the changes, analyses of data and metadata of the new formats and fields in the new system, installation of new hardware and software and attention to the interface with existing hardware and software.

- *Systems documentation* is very important to both management and the auditor, since it provides a description of the computer processing activities. The documentation provides IT staff and internal and external auditors reviewing the system with a means of detecting weaknesses; it serves as a reference for training users and for dealing with problems and errors encountered in operating the system; and it provides the information for IT staff maintaining the existing systems and for any further IT developments. Systems documentation is likely to include flow charts and descriptions of the systems and programs; operating instructions for the IT staff and users involved in computer processing operations and data storage; control activities to be followed by IT staff and users in order to meet the transaction control objectives of completeness, occurrence/validity and measurement/accuracy; specification of the input documents and processes and any changes thereto, and specification of reports to be generated, their content, frequency and distribution.

  In integrated database systems, changes to systems may affect the location of data elements in the database. Care must be taken in the documentation to ensure that both IT staff and users are made aware of the implications for changes to input routines, controls usually implemented, and changes to definitions contained in the data dictionary or directory.

Hardware and system software controls

Hardware and systems software controls are designed to detect and prevent any breakdowns or disruptions of computer services for critical computer functions due to hardware failure or corruption of software programs. They are also intended to monitor the input, processing and communication of data along the entity's networks to ensure these are not corrupted, so as to maintain the integrity of data in the computer systems.

There are a range of controls to be implemented from organizational policies and procedures regarding the personal use of PCs, the use of unlicensed software, and policies to be followed when travelling with a laptop or using it off the premises. This will also include policies relating to the updating of software programs to ensure the most current version of the software is loaded onto users' computers timeously and, where necessary, simultaneously.

Hardware and communication controls relate to such checks as dual read, parity checks, echo checks and read-write checks to monitor faulty transmissions of data. They may also include physical controls such as secure computer sites, physical security over hardware – for example, PCs chained to desks and with locked cases, security alarm systems, encryption of key files, time-out facilities if a user should leave the PC unattended for any length of time and environmental controls to protect against fire and floods. Uninterrupted Power Supplies (UPS) units should be installed where continuous functioning is critical; in the event of a power failure, the UPS unit will automatically activate and provide an alternate power source for a limited period.

Anti-virus software should be installed to protect the computer systems from viruses introduced via Internet transactions and e-mails, and from attempts by hackers to penetrate the entity's systems. Greater controls are required by organizations that have links to the Internet for on-line access to data and programs from remote sites through telecommunications. For example, firewalls screening all messages entering and leaving the entity's system help to manage the risk of unauthorized access to data and programs.

In database systems, the general controls over the data and database become even more critical, because of data sharing, data independence and other attributes which will be dealt with later in this chapter.

Access controls

Access controls should prevent unauthorized access to hardware and both systems and application software. These controls may take the form of physical controls, programmed controls and control procedures. *Physical controls* have already been mentioned and include: locking unauthorized users out of rooms where computers are located, locking the PCs or terminals themselves, and security guards and surveillance cameras.

Programmed controls

These may take the form of passwords allowing access to the PC or terminal, and computer networks and menus defining the areas of the system accessible to individual users for purposes of their duties or responsibilities. Controls may include a librarian function to access program and data files for transaction runs, the appointment of a database administrator to manage the granting and provision of access definitions to the data and database in accordance with management's policies, and a data dictionary to define and manage data access within the database. Access to program data and files should be limited to IT staff involved in systems development processes and, similarly, require a password access.

Systems that have on-line data entry may have many users with direct access from remote sites. For example, such users must be given a key, card or password and ID that identifies them and grants the approved level of access in accordance with established user profiles. Fingerprint and voice recognition software is being used to restrict access to more sophisticated computerized systems. For example, a bank card with a Personal Identification Number (PIN number) will enable an individual to access, from an electronic banking terminal, his or her bank account, to draw or deposit money, transfer amounts between accounts and pay creditors, print statements and obtain general information regarding other banking services, such as Forex rates, bank charges, etc. Secure access restricts customers' access to only those accounts and operations that are included in their user profile and serviced by the bank. Once enabled by the particular bank, these services may also be provided on-line to a customer from his or her telephone, cell-phone or PC.

Procedural controls over access

These include manual approval and monitoring of access granted, as well as programmed controls to prevent and log unauthorized access attempts. Security personnel should review these logs on a regular basis and action should be taken against persons responsible for a security breach. The degree of security will obviously depend on the sensitivity of the information in the system and the risk of fraud or error that might arise. For example, in the case of a bank where unauthorized access can result in the immediate misappropriation of funds by means of a transfer between bank accounts, the password access granted to bank employees is very strictly enforced and transfers from suspense accounts or other 'high risk' accounts are monitored continuously by security administrators for prompt identification of improper transactions and immediate, appropriate action by management.

Data and procedural controls

These controls, firstly, regulate the daily operations around input, processing and output from application programs and the computerized accounting systems to ensure completeness, and measurement/accuracy of transactions recorded and minimize the risk of processing errors.

Secondly, these controls are intended to ensure the continuity of operations. Such controls would include arrangements for regular backups of data and programs, both onsite and offsite, and formal disaster recovery plans and business continuity arrangements relating to the information systems. In the event of any disaster that might affect the business, such as fire, earthquake, acts of terrorism, or even simple computer failure, such as hard drives crashing, data and procedural controls minimize the risk of a disruption of operations.

The controls around input, processing and output rely on the procedures of different individuals and departments in the entity. The precise nature of the controls will depend on the type of computer processing used, namely batch input and processing, on-line input with batch processing or real-time updating, and whether the client uses stand-alone PCs or a networked system with remote terminals. In essence, the procedures must ensure that all data input is screened and checked for errors before being accepted into the system and, after that, that all data input has been completely accounted for.

The procedures must allow for proper distribution of the delivery-of-reports output, and for tracking these from the particular application run to the designated user. Procedures must also be in place for the review of exception reports and correction of errors. Monitoring processes should also be in place to monitor the nature and incidence of errors, particularly to identify recurring errors that indicate a material weakness or breakdown in controls. Performance measurement reports should enable senior management to monitor the performance of their staff, for example, reports providing comparison to budgets, gross profit margins, production targets and the calculation of commissions payable to staff.

Procedures must be in place to ensure that the correct data files are used for each transaction run to update the previous month's balances with the current month's transactions. Generally, a grandfather-father-son back-up relationship should be maintained in processing the information, to allow for the reconstruction of data when this becomes necessary. The information may be backed up continuously or periodically, to a server or onto removable CDs or stiffie disks. Recovery software and techniques are available for the recovery of data where hard drives crash or are accidentally re-formatted. Where system changes have taken place and new hardware and software are installed, special provision may be needed to allow access to the transactions data on the old system for a period of time, at least until completion of the audit for the year in which the conversion has taken place. A problem commonly encountered is that new software does not enable access to the old records. An auditor therefore needs to make arrangements to ensure that any necessary audit tests can be performed before the old system becomes inaccessible.

Application controls

The purpose of application controls is to establish specific control procedures over the accounting applications in order to provide reasonable assurance that all transactions are *authorized* and recorded and are processed *completely, accurately* and on a timely basis. This involves both manual processes and controls, and computerized processes and controls that may be carried out by IT personnel and users or programmed into the application software. Different controls are implemented at the three stages of recording and processing to achieve the control objectives, which may be presented by the following matrix:

TRANSACTION STAGE	CONTROL OBJECTIVES		
	Completeness	Measurement Accuracy	Occurrence Validity
Input			
Process			
Output			

Table 9.1 Control objectives relate to transaction stages

Input controls

Input controls are those controls that are designed to detect and prevent errors before data capture into the accounting system.

Input controls: Occurrence/validity objectives

Authorization controls establish the validity of the transactions, while physical evidence of delivery or receipt establishes the actual occurrence. Authorization may be either general or specific. General authorization will apply where there are numerous transactions of the same type, for example, credit approval for sales before they are processed. This approval may be given manually or electronically with an automatic reference to the customer master file for established credit limits and current ledger balance owing. If the credit limit is exceeded, the order is not processed. The entity will generally establish a list of approved employee signatories who may authorize particular classes of transactions. A further check will be the existence of master files with approved customer or supplier details that will be checked by the system as soon as a sales or purchase order is captured.

Specific authorization will apply to transactions that do not occur as frequently, for example, the purchase of fixed assets such as factory plant and machinery. These may require formal, minuted approval of the board or capital expenditure committee, as well as signed purchase order, contract and invoice approved by one or more of the directors for payment. The authorization will also affect the correctness of the account allocation or measurement of the transaction, as this approval should be indicated on the source documents by signature of the persons approving the transaction.

Procedures to ensure that only authorized transactions are accepted into the system will generally be linked to authorized signatures on source documents giving rise to the transaction. Such signatures may be manual or electronic; in the latter, the transaction documentation is generated automatically by the system, for example in e-commerce transactions.

Supervision and physical controls over the input terminals ensure that unauthorized persons may not capture transaction data into the system. Passwords and menu levels restrict staff and allow them to record only those transactions which they are authorized to handle. The segregation principles were discussed earlier, namely to separate the functions of custody of the assets from the recording of those transactions, their authorization and management supervision.

Input controls: Completeness and measurement/accuracy objectives:

Controls that will ensure the completeness and measurement/accuracy of transactions at the input stage include the following *Input Validation Tests*:

- *Data capture and preparation procedures* by users or IT staff at central or remote terminals or data capture points in the system.
- *Verification controls* entail that input data from the source document is keyed in by a second person or entered by the data capture clerk twice, followed by a comparison of the results.
- *Matching of ledger codes with master file data*, for example, customer or supplier code and name matched, inventory code numbers and descriptions match.
- *Sequence checks* of source documents or transaction numbers.
- *Batch input control procedures*, such as batch headers and agreement of manually generated batch control totals with computer generated control totals.
- *Missing data checks* by means of a visual review of input data for obvious errors, and screen formats on entry requiring all fields to be completed before the transaction is accepted.
- *Valid character check* done for individual fields whether alpha or numeric characters are recorded as appropriate.
- *Limit and reasonableness checks* to determine whether the captured data falls within pre-established reasonableness limits, for example, total weekly hours worked by an employee cannot exceed a specified maximum number of hours. Attempts to capture the wrong data will result in the entry being rejected at the input stage.
- *Check digits* are algorithms used as part of a particular customer account, supplier account, inventory item or staff ID numbers to ensure that the correct entries are captured. For example, the last three numbers on a

credit card contain an algorithm that validates the credit card number both for the holder and as issued by the particular credit card company.

* *Errors* detected at the input stage should be corrected by the users and the correction resubmitted, immediately if possible; errors detected at the processing stage may be corrected by the IT staff.

Processing controls

Computer processing controls relate to completeness and measurement/ accuracy and are designed to detect loss of data, check arithmetic computation and allocation to ledger accounts. They include controls over data storage, retrieval, updating and maintenance. Processing controls are generally programmed into the relevant application software and include the following:

* Checks to detect loss of data, arithmetic computation and account allocation include record counts, sequence tests, control totals, hash totals and programmed limit and reasonableness tests, cross-adding of analyses of totals and exception reporting.

* Checks to ensure the completeness and accuracy of updating will include checks to ensure the correct generation (grandfather-father-son) of master files is updated by means of manual agreement of computer established totals to original input documents, run to run totals, check of brought forward and carry forward totals, and check of the file set up for the run.

* Data storage and retrieval controls will include file labelling, both internal and external, computer updating procedures, audit trails whether electronic or hard copy, and manual checks by users to source documents, database controls administered by the database administrator.

* Data storage controls related to file maintenance include the reconciliation of file totals, regular review of computer record/balances to physical counts and cut-off checks; review by users of results, such as transaction listings, gross profit margins, comparisons of actual to budget etc.; amendments to standing data such as customer, supplier and employee master file details – checked one-on-one for individual authorized changes processed and batch totals for the total additions/deletions from the master file for the processing period; the accuracy of the details remaining in the standing data file should be reconciled to before and after reports and/or manual control accounts, which could be checked manually in detail and to hash totals on batch input headers.

Output controls

Output controls are designed to ensure the results of the processing are correct. The important aspect of this is the manual review and reconciliation by users of the relevant printouts, the identification of errors or exceptions and error correction procedures.

In addition to error and exception reports, outputs may include:

- *Transaction documents*, such as delivery notes and invoices, weekly and monthly payslips and cheques.
- *Financial information*, such as transaction summaries, weekly and monthly payroll printouts, monthly trial balance, and reports of detailed transactions for the month or period, detailed analyses of trade debtors' and trade creditors' account balances and aged schedules of accounts receivable and payable, changes to standing data for payroll, suppliers and customers, and the interim and annual financial statements.
- *Management information* reports such as monthly or quarterly management financial statements with budgets and year to date figures compared, operational activities, key performance ratios and analyses, and monitoring of control activities for decision making.

IT staff control procedures usually include:

- Controls over the output hardware and storage, such as printers, stiffie disks, CDs, electronic tapes, tape libraries and back-ups.
- Output handling procedures, such as distribution checklists, transmittal sheets, distribution logs, report release forms, and where reports are transmitted electronically, the users' password gives access to download the relevant reports and analyses; and physical access and control of the printouts to maintain the confidentiality of reports.
- Specification of standard report contents, frequency and distribution lists for authorized users.

User control procedures to validate the reports received, include:

- Checking to see that the report received is what was ordered and that it appears complete.
- Review of the printout for any abnormalities against established criteria and norms.
- Reconciling of computer batch totals with manually compiled totals on the batch headers.
- Periodic counts and reconciliation of computer totals with physical assets, for example, inventory printouts agreed to inventory physically on hand, fixed assets counts agreed to fixed asset registers.
- Performance of reasonableness checks, review of key performance indicators and detailed checking back to source documents.
- Higher level reconciliation, supervision and review by supervisors and departmental managers.

Error handling procedures

These are designed to ensure that incorrect items are promptly investigated, corrected and resubmitted, and previous account balances and totals of analyses are adjusted. Error handling procedures by users will include:

- Scrutinizing of rejection lists or lists of missing sequence numbers.
- Checking and controlling rejections and resubmissions.

- Investigation of the cause of exceptions and changes to internal control procedures should this prove necessary.
- Supervisor or management analyses and monitoring of exceptions, the number (incidence of occurrence), presentation, distribution and method of follow-up.

Physical controls

- There should be appropriate physical security measures to protect a company's assets. These measures should ensure that only those with due authority have access to assets.

- In the case of manufacturing or trading operations, which dispatch goods by delivery trucks, there should be only one exit from the company's premises with some gate control to ensure that goods leave only if accompanied by valid delivery or sales documentation. Retailers selling to customers over the counter can exercise a measure of control by positioning cash registers close to the shop's exits, using distinctive wrappings or bags, and by employing floor-walkers and surveillance cameras to detect customers or staff involved in shoplifting.

- Storerooms should have locking facilities with adequate control over keys. They should also have alarm facilities. It is particularly important to restrict access to high Rand-value items more susceptible to theft. The smaller these items are, the more easily they can be misappropriated, and the smaller the risk of detection.

- In a high-volume cash-sales environment, such as a supermarket, cash on hand should be kept to a minimum by regularly clearing tills during the day and banking the takings promptly. If cash is not banked until the day following its receipt (which is often the case in practice), it should be locked in a secure drop safe overnight. Arrangements are often made for a security company to collect the money daily from the drop safe, for depositing at the bank. Rather than expose the entity's own staff to the risk of hijacking and physical harm from thieves, a security company, which is better equipped, takes on the risk. Cash loss insurance may also be taken out to protect the company from loss, in the event of theft of cash takings.

- Computer equipment should be protected by both physical and programmed access controls. Physical controls may include equipment being locked in particular offices or computer centres with access restricted to authorized users by means of keys, or hardware being chained to the desk on which it is situated, passwords for identification, swipe cards with the user's ID, photo and pin number encoded thereon. It may also include, in a PC distributed environment, the use of security guards and surveillance cameras throughout the premises, monitored from a central security point. Programmed access controls would normally be administered by a security administrator and involve the use of passwords to restrict IT staff, and other users, to particular areas of the computer system.

- Apart from the physical controls to protect assets, management control is achieved by regular counts of assets and comparisons of physical quantities with those recorded. The knowledge that apparent shortages will be investigated is likely to discourage misappropriation. Examples are: physical counts of inventory, fixed assets and petty cash and comparison of these to the inventory ledger, fixed assets register and petty cash record respectively.

Operating reviews

Operating reviews differ from the other internal control principles discussed so far. In essence they are higher level controls by management to ensure the effective and continuing operation of the other general and application controls. Operation reviews may involve the following:

- Ongoing monitoring and review, by management at different levels, of the laid-down control procedures to ensure that these are operating as they were designed to, and that delegated responsibilities have been properly discharged.

- Analysing exception reports to ascertain the cause and incidence of errors detected during the input or processing of data, identifying whether these affect the completeness, or measurement/accuracy of the accounting information, and taking remedial action to prevent further similar errors.

- Identification of internal control weaknesses by internal audit staff detected in the course of their audit work in particular departments of the entity.

- Considering changes to the internal control systems in situations where weaknesses have become apparent as a result of errors that have come to light, which were not prevented or detected by the control systems, for example, errors might be found as a result of customer or supplier queries.

- Review of performance reports by operational staff and comparison to key performance indicators for the early identification of problem areas.

Reporting

Printouts of general ledger balances and a variety of other detailed transaction or financial performance reports should be obtained on a monthly or more frequent basis and distributed to the relevant user department or person. There should be frequent (at least monthly) balancing and reconciliation routines to test the accuracy and reliability of the accounting records to the underlying source documents. Corrective action should be taken to rectify errors appearing in exception reports to ensure the accounting records are accurate and will produce reliable financial statements.

The reports may include comparisons of actual current financial year results to budgets and forecasts and prior period amounts, with explanations provided to management for differences identified. Where possible, the financial results should be compared with operational data, for example, revenue from hotel accommodation compared to occupancy rates for the month or other period; gross profit margins compared to the physical quantities sold and revenue earned; returns on investments compared with expectations, to mention but a few key performance indicators. Many others are available for the particular industry segment or business.

Management should review the reports, firstly for indications of corroboration with their expectations, and secondly for identifying potential material misstatement in the financial statements.

9.1.2.5 Monitoring

Management's monitoring procedures involve the assessment of actual performance against that anticipated. Management's anticipation of performance is specified by them in the form of key performance indicators, such as sales volumes, profit margins and the relationship of expenses relative to sales levels. The investigation (monitoring) by management of deviation from the actual to the expected may reveal that these are because of unreasonable expectations or errors. If the latter, this brings into question the effectiveness of the systems of control and thus the risks to which the entity is exposed. The progress of activities aimed at rectifying weaknesses in internal controls or risk management processes should also be monitored.[9]

The board must fully understand the business risk issues and key performance indicators that could affect the ability of the company to achieve its purpose and enhance shareholder value in the long term. Hence, business risk and key performance indicators should be benchmarked against industry norms and best practice. This will assist in evaluating and monitoring the company's performance and in ensuring the effectiveness of its systems of internal control, so that the board's decision-making and the accuracy of its reporting are maintained at all times.

An important constituent in business processes is new technology and IT-based operations and the extent to which the company's information and communication processes are dependent on these. IT-based operations should be subject to the risk-based principles of *validation, security, integrity, availability* and *continuity* applied to both existing systems and new implementations. These will be discussed further in this chapter.

In addition to other compliance and enforcement activities, the board should consider the need for a confidential reporting process, 'whistleblowing', covering fraud and other risks.

---

[9] The King II Report, page 79.

9.1.3 Limitations of internal controls

Whilst an adequate and effective system of internal control should mitigate to an acceptable level the significant risks faced by the company, such a system is designed to manage rather than eliminate the risk of failure, or to maximise opportunities to achieve business objectives, it can only provide reasonable, not absolute, assurance. SAAS 400, 'Risk assessment and internal control', identifies the following inherent limitations of internal controls in paragraph 11:

- *Cost vs. benefit*: This relates to management's usual requirement that the cost of an implemented control should not exceed the anticipated benefit. In circumstances where management has assessed the risk of loss and has decided to 'accept' the risk as insignificant, this could lead to an absence of controls in areas where the auditor may consider them to be very necessary. For example, management may regard cash loss insurance as unnecessary even though a large percentage of the company's turnover is earned from cash sales.

- *Routine vs. non-routine transactions:* Most controls are directed at routine rather than non-routine transaction processes, for example: in a business where thousands of sales transactions occur daily, such transactions are likely to be tightly controlled, with specific approval, processing and monitoring controls in place. On the other hand, infrequent transactions – such as the purchase of fixed assets for high values, usually formally approved by directors' minutes – may not have formalized procedures in place to identify, capture and communicate the transactions and, as a result, the completeness and measurement/accuracy of the recorded transactions may be in doubt.

- *Human error*: This relates to the potential for human error due to carelessness, distraction, mistakes of judgement and the misunderstanding of instructions. Temporary or permanent changes in personnel or in systems or procedures may contribute to human errors. In the last ten years many South African businesses have undergone restructuring and downsizing, leading to retrenchments and therefore to circumstances in which the remaining staff may be unaware of control procedures previously implemented and, further, may be unable to provide satisfactory explanations to the auditors of adjusting entries in the general ledgers.

- *Collusion*: This refers to the possibility that a member of management or an employee colludes with parties inside or outside the entity in order to circumvent internal controls. An example of collusion internally may be found in a payroll situation where there is collusion between, say, a staff member in human resources and one dealing with funds transfers – the human resources staff member adds fictitious employees and/or additional 'employee' bank accounts onto the standing data files of the payroll, and the other staff member then authorizes the electronic funds transfers to these 'fictitious' employee bank accounts. A commonly encountered example of collusion externally is one where the employee in the buying department colludes with an external supplier. For example, the buyer receives kickbacks for purchasing of large quantities from the particular supplier; or a salesperson in the company provides kickbacks to a buyer employed by a large customer with the aim of exceeding the normal sales targets. Collusion, between employees in the same organization and between employees and external third parties, was identified as one of the main causes of fraud in a recent fraud survey.[10]

• *Management override*: This revolves around the possibility that a person responsible for exercising a control could abuse that responsibility, for example, a member of management overriding a control. Respondents to the KPMG Fraud Survey (2002) estimated the source of frauds committed in their organizations as 32% by management, and 88% by employees. The Nel Commission Report (2001) found evidence of fraud at a management level in 70% to 85% of companies that fail and are placed into liquidation in South Africa. Management override may be associated with aggressive earnings policies, personal expenses processed through the business, improper authorization of transactions, deliberate misleading representations to secure financial benefits, for example, loans from an external lender, and may involve fictitious or fraudulent transactions and fraudulent financial reporting. These actions may be associated with deliberate attempts by management to mislead the auditors.

• *Changes in conditions:* This relates to the possibility that procedures may become inadequate due to changes in conditions, and that compliance with control procedures may deteriorate. Examples of these may include: changes in the IT environment, changes in the entity due to large acquisitions, reorganizations, development of new products or services, operations in regions that are economically unstable, application of new accounting standards, off-balance sheet finance, special purpose entities, lack of personnel with appropriate accounting expertise, high degree of complex regulation, and operations exposed to volatile market conditions such as futures trading.

9.1.4 Roles and responsibilities of various parties for internal control

The King II Report indicates that 'risk management and internal controls should be practised throughout the company by all staff, and should be embedded in day-to-day activities'. However, the actual roles and responsibilities differ amongst different parties. For this reason it is appropriate to consider what the roles are and how they complement one another to provide an effective system of risk management and internal control. This is important for the auditor in gaining an understanding of the strategic business objectives, the strategic business risks, risk management and internal control systems implemented by the client.

---

[10] KPMG Fraud Survey, July 2002.

Board of directors

The board of directors is statutorily responsible for the governance of the company. To the board falls the responsibility for setting a tone of control consciousness at the top with regard to the integrity and risk management policies of the company. The directors have the primary responsibility of ensuring that management in the various sections of the business meets its responsibility for establishing and maintaining sound systems of internal control in the day-to-day running of the business. In addition, the directors have a responsibility for monitoring and remaining alert to the possible risk of management override and fraud in the company, and the responsibility for taking prompt action to deal with improper conduct by management, in order to safeguard the assets of the company and prevent the possibility of fraudulent reporting. Currently, in South Africa, a board of directors will comprise both executive and non-executive directors. The chief executive officer (director) and the remaining executive directors have line responsibility for implementation of systems of internal controls, while the non-executive directors will have a role to play in monitoring the performance of the executive directors and holding them accountable for failure to implement effective systems and evidence of material weaknesses and breakdowns in controls.

Management

It is the task of management to design and implement effective systems of internal control to manage the risks of the business and to ensure that all the control aspects are addressed. The systems should be layered down through the operations of the business, with individual department managers taking line responsibility for and being accountable to senior management for the implementation of control activities in their department. Financial managers and IT staff play an important role in the design, implementation and monitoring of the internal control activities. Financial controls are exercised through the development of budgets, strategic plans and key performance indicators and thereafter monitoring the financial reports, analysing results, both financial and operational, against key performance indicators to detect and prevent possible material error, fraud and fraudulent reporting in the financial statements. The results of their analyses should be contained in reports to, *inter alia*, senior management, the board of directors, the audit committee, internal audit department and the external auditors where appropriate.

The audit committee

The first King Report (1994) recognized the importance of the audit committee in ensuring that proper systems of internal control are implemented and monitored, risk areas are identified and managed appropriately, financial information provided to users is accurate and reliable and the company has procedures to ensure it complies with legal and regulatory requirements. The report led directly to a change in the Listing Requirements of the JSE Securities Exchange which required all listed companies to appoint an audit committee comprised mainly of non-executive directors having financial expertise. The Public Finance Management Act contains a similar requirement for the appointment of an audit committee and internal audit function for all public sector entities governed by that Act. The King II Report recommends, *inter alia*, that 'the audit committee should review the functioning of the internal control system and the internal audit department, the risk areas to be covered in the scope of the internal and external audit and any accounting or auditing concerns identified as a result of the internal or external audits'.

Internal auditors

Both the first King Report (1994) and the King II Report (2002) have stressed the importance of an effective internal audit function as 'one of the mechanisms for necessary checks and balances in a company'. The King II Report recognizes that an effective internal audit function should provide assurance that management processes are adequate to identify and monitor significant risks; confirm the effective operation of the established internal control systems; credible processes for feedback on risk management and assurance; and objective confirmation that the board receives the right quality of information from management and that this information is reliable. Whilst the internal audit does not have line responsibility for either the risk assessment or internal controls as such, it should assist the board, directors and management in identifying, evaluating and assessing significant organizational risks to business objectives and provide independent assurance as to the adequacy and effectiveness of related internal controls and the risk management process. It should also assist the directors and management to maintain effective controls by evaluating their efficiency and effectiveness and by developing recommendations for enhancement or improvement.

Independent external auditors

External auditors, in a financial statement audit, have a statutory responsibility to report to the shareholders on the company's financial statements, and to consider statutory requirements and accounting standards for financial reporting. This contrasts with the role of the internal auditor. Through their audit the external auditors may identify weaknesses in internal control or risk management processes, but this is not the main purpose of their audit, and they will examine and test internal controls to the extent considered necessary for reporting on the financial statements. Since the auditor may apply substantive procedures rather than tests of control in order to gain sufficient appropriate audit evidence, the audit opinion on the financial statements does not express any opinion on the efficiency and effectiveness of the systems of internal control. Should such an expression of opinion be required by management, this would form part of a separate related services engagement. Related services engagements are discussed in Chapter 19.

9.1.5 Special considerations in the audit of small entities

The preceding discussion of risk assessment and management control of the business is appropriate to any of the large entities to which the King II Report applies. However, it must be recognized that small and medium sized entities are unlikely to implement either risk assessment strategies or controls in such a formal manner. SAAS 1005, 'Special considerations in the audit of small entities', provides guidance for the auditor in circumstances of the audit of small entities. It is impossible to provide a precise definition of a small entity and both quantitative and qualitative factors must be considered.

SAAS 1005, paragraph .07, for the purposes of the practice statement regards a small entity as any entity in which:

'(a) There is a concentration of ownership and management in a small number of individuals (often a single individual who is a natural person); and

(b) One or more of the following is found:

- Few sources of income,

- Unsophisticated record keeping

- Limited internal controls together with the potential for management override of controls.'

Many small entities ordinarily have few owners and the day-to-day running of the business is managed by the owner – generally referred to as 'owner-managed' entities. The businesses often have a fairly limited range of products or services and operate from a single or limited number of locations.

Such businesses invariably have a limited number of accounting staff and many outsource this function to an accounting firm, which is often also appointed as the auditors of the business. Where accounting staff is employed, they are invariably involved in merely recording the transactions and perform few if any control activities. Accounting records are often very basic and unsophisticated, although many businesses may use branded accounting software packages on a stand-alone PC. In a small, networked environment, the tasks of security administrator, database administrator and network administrator may all be handled by only one or two individuals who are also users of the business applications. To this extent, the task of understanding the business may be a simpler one, but the risk of omission and misstatement of transactions recorded and, consequently, the potential for material misstatement in the financial statements is very real.[11]

---

[11] SAAS 1005, 'Special considerations in the audit of small entities', paragraphs .55–.59.

SAAS 1005, 'Special considerations in the audit of small entities', also indicates in paragraph .40 that 'the documentation of the auditor's knowledge of the business is equally important in all audits irrespective of the size of the entity, however, the extent of documentation depends on the complexity of the audit and the number of persons engaged on the audit.'

Sophisticated internal control procedures are neither necessary nor desirable, and the fact that there are usually very few employees makes segregation of duties impracticable. The owner-manager plays a dominant role in the business and will usually be the person who exercises the overall supervision, review and authorization functions in the business. The owner-manager is effectively responsible for the risk assessment and the exercise of strong supervisory controls, sufficient to prevent fraud and errors or to detect and correct these should they arise. This in itself, however, may introduce other risks, such as management override of controls. Consequently, the auditor should carefully assess the inherent risks, as these may be less than *high* for particular financial statement balances and assertions, and obtain an understanding of the control environment and the overall influence of the owner manager and other key personnel.

Control risk is often assumed to be high and a substantive audit approach is followed, with communication to management of any weaknesses in the design or operation of the accounting or internal control systems which have come to the auditor's attention.[12]

The downside is that the owner-manager will usually have technical expertise in his or her own particular field, but may not have a sufficiently detailed accounting knowledge to recognize, for example, contraventions of GAAP. Such an owner-manager will invariably rely on the auditors, or those providing an accounting service, to detect errors affecting completeness, measurement, valuation and disclosure. The lack of sophisticated internal controls does not in itself imply that fraud or material errors may exist; it does, however, indicate a high risk of these and so it is unlikely that the auditor would follow a test of controls approach on the audit. The potential for override of controls is heavily dependent on the integrity, attitude and motives of the owner. For this reason, the auditor is well advised to exercise professional scepticism, and to refrain from making assumptions about the dishonesty or unquestionable honesty of the owner-manager.

Several thousand small entities exist in South Africa. Some are structured as private companies and are required to have statutory audits; others are structured as close corporations, partnerships, sole traders or trusts, and not required statutorily to have an audit performed. The owner-manager may decide to appoint an auditor, for example, in order to provide audited financial statements to the relevant South African (or another country's) Revenue Services in support of their income tax returns, or at the request of

---

[12] SAAS 1005, 'Special considerations in the audit of small entities', paragraphs .48 – .53.

the bank manager to support the ongoing provision of bank overdraft facilities. In these circumstances, the terms of the engagement must be agreed with the client and the audit report adapted accordingly. See the later discussion of related services engagements in chapter 18.

9.2 UNDERSTANDING BUSINESS RISKS AND INTERNAL CONTROLS

9.2.1 Introduction

In this section the responsibility of the auditor to obtain an understanding of the business risks and internal controls and how this might affect the audit methodology employed are discussed.

SAAS 400, 'Risk Assessments and Internal Control', paragraph .02, states the principle as:

> 'The auditor should obtain an understanding of the accounting and internal controls systems sufficient to plan the audit and develop an effective audit approach. The auditor should use professional judgement to assess audit risk and to design audit procedures to ensure that it is reduced to an acceptably low level.'

Further, in paragraph .15:

> 'The auditor should obtain an understanding of the accounting system sufficient to identify and understand:
>
> - Major classes of transactions in the entity's operations
>
> - How such transactions are initiated
>
> - Significant accounting records, supporting documents and account balances in the financial statements; and
>
> - The accounting and financial reporting process, from the initiation of significant transactions and other events to their inclusion in the financial statements.

And further in paragraphs .16 and .17:

> 'The auditor should obtain an understanding of the control environment sufficient to assess directors' and managements' attitudes, awareness and actions regarding internal controls and their importance to the entity ... [And] the auditor should obtain an understanding of the control procedures sufficient to develop the audit plan.'

'Bottom-up' audit approach

The auditor's main concerns regarding the financial information being examined are:

- that material errors or misstatements may occur in the accounting process; and

- that material errors or misstatements which occur may not be detected by the selected audit procedures.

These concerns resulted in a 'bottom-up' approach, which has been used by auditors for many years. The bottom-up approach focuses on the financial transactions and typical accounting controls to determine whether the control objective related to the financial statement assertions, completeness, occurrence/validity and measurement/accuracy are met for significant classes of transactions. Generally, the review and tests of controls and findings would be concluded by discussions – between management and the partner in charge of the engagement, the audit manager or the audit senior – to communicate identified weaknesses that might lead to material misstatements in the financial statements. Thereafter, the auditor would use substantive audit procedures, both analytical reviews and tests of detail, to detect any remaining errors and misstatements.

'Top-down' audit approach

The collapse of major corporations around the world has led to significant concerns that the traditional 'bottom-up' audit approach is not effective in identifying strategic business objectives and risks or management's processes aimed at managing these. While the traditional audit process has focused on risk identification based on audit objectives – namely the financial statement assertions – to assess audit risk, this 'bottom-up' approach has focused neither on the assessment of the effectiveness of management's processes for identifying the entity's strategic business risks and procedures implemented to manage these. Concerns have been expressed that the 'bottom-up' approach may not be effective for identifying all significant audit risks and therefore may have contributed to an insufficient linkage between the residual risks of material misstatement from fraud or error, for significant classes of transactions and balances, and the design of specific appropriate substantive audit procedures to detect these. The premise is that turning the risk focus around to the 'top-down' audit approach will result in the improved identification of significant audit risks and facilitate the use of the appropriate substantive audit procedures to address these risks.

The King II Report, the revised SAAS 240, 'The auditor's responsibility to consider fraud and error in an audit of financial statements', issued in July 2001, together with the 'linkage project' of the International Audit and Assurance Board of IFAC (the IAASB), indicate a reconsideration of the 'bottom-up' audit approach. The principles stated in SAAS 240 has led to a significant shift in the audit approach of many audit firms, particularly those with clients whose business operations may be more complex from the perspective of their structure, size, accounting policies, business transactions and dependence on sophisticated computerized accounting and information systems regarded as posing a higher audit risk.

The following paragraphs in SAAS 240, in particular, are relevant:

Paragraph .02: 'When planning and performing audit procedures and evaluating and reporting the results thereof, the auditor should consider the risk of material misstatements in the financial statements resulting from fraud and error.'

Paragraph .20: 'In planning the audit, the auditor should discuss with other members of the audit team the susceptibility of the entity to material misstatements in the financial statements resulting from fraud or error.'

Paragraph .22: 'When planning the audit the auditor should make inquiries of management:

- To obtain an understanding of:
  - Management's assessment of the risk that the financial statements may be materially misstated as a result of fraud, and
  - The accounting and internal control systems management has put in place to address such risk.

- To obtain knowledge of management's understanding regarding the accounting and internal control systems in place to prevent and detect error,

- To determine whether management is aware of any known fraud that has affected the entity or suspected fraud that the entity is investigating, and

- To determine whether management has discovered any material errors.'

The 'top-down' approach involves more detailed discussions by the entire audit team with management and employees at the planning stage and during the audit to understand management's strategic business objectives, their perception of business risks faced and the critical success factors and key performance indicators that they use to manage the business and fraud risks.

If management's risk identification processes are appropriate and control activities are shown to be working effectively, this should then provide a higher level of assurance regarding the *completeness, measurement/accuracy* and *occurrence/validity* of significant classes of business transactions and the *completeness, existence, measurement, valuation, rights* and *obligations*, and *presentation* and *disclosure* of significant balances in the financial statements. Where necessary controls are lacking, the auditor needs to focus audit effort on those classes of transactions and balances that may be materially misstated.

Another important shift in the 'top-down' audit approach has been to involve the whole audit team in the engagement planning sessions to ensure that all audit staff understand, contribute and remain alert to the particular risks in the business and opportunities for inquiry from management of the control activities used to manage risks and significant classes of transactions and balances identified, relative to the particular aspect of the business that the audit staff member is involved in auditing.

Whether the auditor applies a 'top-down' or 'bottom-up' approach (or a combination of these) to the audit, in order to plan the audit, it is necessary for the auditor to obtain an understanding of each of the five aspects of control discussed earlier in this chapter and, in particular, to identify significant business risks that might give rise to material misstatement in the financial statements, namely the understanding gained of the *control environment; risk assessment; information and communication, control activities and monitoring*. In the case of a continuing audit engagement, the auditor will have knowledge of these various aspects from the previous year's working papers and will need to update that knowledge by reference to changes and new developments in the business.

Once an understanding of the various aspects is obtained, the auditor needs to assess the control risk for specific assertions in significant classes of transactions and balances in the financial statements and determine what tests of controls, if any, will be performed. This aspect is discussed in chapter 10.

Thereafter, the auditor identifies the remaining risk of significant misstatement in the financial statement balances for specific assertions so as to determine the substantive procedures necessary to reduce detection risk to an acceptable level. This aspect is discussed in chapter 11.

9.2.2 Strategic business objectives and related strategic business risks

In order to identify the *strategic business objectives* the auditor needs to understand the entity's objectives, strategies and aspects of the business. First, the auditor ascertains the nature of the business: the industry or sector in which the entity is operating, management's strategies (plans) for achieving its strategic objectives, such as expanding its markets internationally, becoming a market leader, generating a substantial percentage of its turnover through e-commerce transactions within a specified period of time. This requires discussions with senior management and essentially aims at understanding the strategic management process of the entity.

The auditor also identifies how management plans to operationalize their strategic objectives, that is, by gaining an understanding of the markets, products and services supplied, customers and key alliances and relationships, including key suppliers, distributors and related parties, and ascertaining the processes management follows to manage strategic business risks arising.

External influences

Next, the auditor needs to obtain an understanding of the *external influences* created by the general business environment, specific sector or industry in which the client's business operates, and significant external constituencies that might affect the strategic business objectives and strategic business risks.

External influences may include, amongst others:

- *The political environment* in different countries in which the entity operates that might affect the regulation and continuance of the business and require compliance with laws and regulations.
- *Economic factors* that might impact the entity's operation in local and foreign markets, both for supply or demand of goods and services, or factors which affect significant increases in costs incurred by the business.
- *Social factors* affecting the demand for the entity's products and services including changes in the demographics and spending power of different sections of the population who are the target market of the entity.
- *Technological factors* that might affect the entity's ability to produce its goods at competitive costs or to penetrate new e-commerce markets.
- *The threat of new entrants and bargaining power* of *multiple suppliers* in a sector, as well as *bargaining power of customers* (who are unlikely to remain out of loyalty when there are multiple suppliers in a market) and *substitute products* (often at a cheaper price).

Management may be inclined to manipulate the results of the business for particular stakeholders. It is important that the auditor identify the relationships that management regards as significant and circumstances that might tempt management to misstate the financial statements. Some stakeholders that management may wish to attempt to influence are:

- *Shareholders:* Meeting expectations of investors could lead to deliberate attempts, including fraud, to inflate results and paint a rosy picture for such stakeholders.
- *Suppliers:* These may have concerns about the entity's ability to continue as a going concern or may attempt to impose restraint of trade agreements.
- *Tax:* The complexity of tax laws could lead to unintentional or deliberate misrepresentation in the financial statements to hide a failure by the company to comply with all applicable tax laws.
- *Employees:* Here the focus is likely to be on remuneration levels of management and competitive bargaining for different categories of employees.
- *Bank or other lenders:* Lenders will be interested in whether the entity can continue to service its long-term and short-term debts.
- *Environmental:* The general public will be interested in any significant environmental impact the entity might have and its social responsibility commitments.

Knowledge databases

Knowledge databases have been developed over time by several audit firms. These databases contain a wide range of information to facilitate an understanding of laws and regulations affecting various business sectors, including key performance measurements commonly used; profitability and liquidity statistics of companies in the sector; marketing trends and market share of the major players; competitors in the industry, and new legislation affecting businesses in that sector. These may be used to analyse the client's strategic business risks related to its business objectives; provide current industry information over a wide range of business sectors; record key performance indicators which may be used to evaluate the client's business risk exposure; and identify core business processes and significant classes of transactions. Knowledge databases assist audit staff in gaining an understanding of the client's business and facilitate the identification of potential risks of material misstatement in the financial statements. These databases thus enable auditors to focus audit effort on identified risk areas, and so should result in an appropriate mix of tests of controls, substantive analytical reviews and tests of detail, to gather sufficient, appropriate audit evidence effectively and efficiently.

An understanding of the strategic management process will enable the auditor to identify how the overall direction of the entity is set, how its resources of capital and people are allocated and monitored, and will include the external business environment; opportunities and threats arising; the strategies and capabilities of major competitors; the performance of its own control activities and findings of internal audit in this regard; how formalized the reporting and communication processes are to different levels of management and how effective the communications are in generating a prompt and appropriate response from management; and, finally, how management aligns its process objectives with the entity's strategic objectives.

9.2.3 Significant classes of transactions, balances and core processes

The auditor also needs to obtain an understanding of the core and sub-processes for significant classes of transactions, for example, in the case of a supermarket trading operation the core process of trading may be split into sub-processes such as sales, purchases, cash receipts, inventory in and out, cash payments and distribution costs. Each core process will have sub-processes over which management exercises control activities to achieve its strategic objectives. The breakdown into sub-processes enables the identification of significant classes of transactions and balances that relate to the grouping of similar activities within such sub-processes.

In addition to the trading core process, a second core process may be identified, for example, that of property management, should the company sell its products through numerous stores, which may need to be acquired, leased or built, equipped and maintained for the display and distribution of its products. A third core process, that of cash management, may also be identified. For example, for a major national or international supermarket group the lead time between the cash received, from customers, and the repayment period granted, by suppliers, may result in several billion Rand available on a daily basis and earning interest if invested on call at money market rates.

Underpinning the core processes is the provision of resources, or services, to run and manage the entity, which enable all the core activities of the business. These will include the *financial aspects* of accounting, cash management and financial reporting; *human resources* and the employment and development of suitably qualified staff at all levels; *internal audit* for monitoring the efficiency and effectiveness of control activities and processes; and the development and maintenance of the entity's *IT systems* and capacity.

9.2.4 Financial statement implications of strategic business risks

After obtaining an understanding of all the strategic business objectives and strategic business risks, as well as the effectiveness of management's processes for managing these risks, the auditor needs to identify the strategic business risks remaining, particularly those that management does not appear to be controlling effectively. The auditor will have to consider which of these may lead to a potential risk of material misstatement in financial statements due to errors or fraud.

The potential effects of the risk of misstatement related to core processes and sub-processes must be identified, as well as the particular financial assertions affected, in order to link the audit procedures appropriately to the identified risk.

9.2.5 Core processes, process level business risks and related financial statement risks and controls

The auditor gains an understanding of how each *core process and sub-process operates*. This enables the auditor to make a preliminary assessment of *process level business risks* and related *financial statement risks* and from here identifies the potential financial statement effect and the *relevant assertions* that may be materially misstated.

The auditor considers specific controls or compensating controls that the client has in place to prevent or detect and correct such misstatements. The remaining business process level risk is then evaluated as being *high*, *medium* or *low* for the particular financial statement effect expected and the specific assertions identified as being at risk.

The relevant audit objectives and audit procedures directly related to gathering audit evidence regarding the remaining risk of misstatement in the financial statements, are now determined. Where the remaining risk of misstatement relates to significant balances, the auditor considers:

- *the quality of the information* available to determine whether the accounting treatment is correct;
- *the historical accuracy* of the account balance, judged from previous audits results;

- *the assumptions* used by management to arrive at the balance;
- *the competence* of the accounting personnel in preparing the accounting information and the complexity of any calculations involved; and
- *the potential for management bias* that could lead deliberately to a material misstatement.

9.2.6 Planning: Tests of controls, remaining substantive audit procedures, analytical review and tests of detail

Where the remaining risk of misstatement relates to significant classes of transactions, the auditor considers the particular assertion affected and examines the design of the controls that should prevent or detect and correct the errors, or fraud, and tests whether they operated throughout the period of intended reliance. Where necessary, the presence and incidence of errors is determined by means of substantive tests of analytical review or detail. The tests allow the auditor to gather sufficient evidence – that is, either that there is no material misstatement, or the exact nature and amount of the error – in order to make the necessary adjustment or disclosure in the audited financial statements.

Where the remaining risk of misstatement relates to significant balances, the auditor considers the particular assertion affected and designs appropriate substantive tests – analytical review or tests of detail to gather sufficient evidence to indicate there is no material misstatement or, if there is, to show the precise nature and amount of the error. The auditor then should request the necessary adjustment or disclosure in the audited financial statements.

9.3 DOCUMENTING THE UNDERSTANDING OF THE ENTITY'S BUSINESS AND INTERNAL CONTROLS

SAAS 400, 'Risk assessments and internal control', paragraph .22, requires

'[T]he auditor to document in the working papers:

- The understanding obtained of the entity's accounting and internal control systems, and

- The assessment of control risk. When control risk is assessed at less than high, the auditor would document the basis for the conclusions.'

Various methods may be used to document the understanding of the entity's business and internal controls. The extent of documentation will depend on the size and complexity of the entity and the nature of its internal controls. In the first time audit engagement, extensive documentation will be required to record the strategic business objectives, strategic business risks, significant classes of transactions and balances, and related core processes and sub-processes. In subsequent audits, these records would be available for updating with regard to changes since the preceding audit.

Narrative notes may take the form of brief descriptions of the structure and nature of the business, organization charts and extracts from accounting manuals documenting the client's control environment and control activities. In a large entity, the narrative notes should also address the five control aspects and relevant factors under each heading, namely:

- Control Environment;
- Risk Assessment;
- Information and Communication;
- Control Activities; and
- Monitoring.

Questionnaires may be used. These will typically consist of a series of questions to which a *Yes/No* answer is required; a *No* answer is usually indicative of weaknesses in internal controls procedures affecting either the general controls or controls over specific business processes or applications. The questions will usually be linked to the specific financial statement assertions to link to potential risks of misstatement in the financial statements. Questionnaires are generally standardized pre-printed documents. Firms may have questionnaires adapted for particular industries or business sectors.

Flow charts present graphically the flow of documents through the accounting system or control activities, the sequence of procedures and the persons involved at each stage where key control procedures are performed. This method ensures as far as practicable the completeness of the record, eliminates the need for much narrative and highlights the salient points of control and any weakness therein. It does not, however, necessarily record the physical controls, personnel involved, access controls or general supervisory controls.

Computerized information systems notes should provide reasonable details of the hardware and software used by the entity, an indication of the level of dependence on information systems, the information systems skills and resources in the entity, how information security is managed, including backup, disaster recovery and business continuity procedures, the reliability of the information systems and the degree of change in computer information systems planned or in the process of being implemented; the degree of dependence on external outsource suppliers, and the direction and operation of the computer information systems. In addition, should the auditor decide to adopt tests of controls approach, the relevant general and specific application controls in the computerized systems must be documented in greater detail.

In the 'top-down' audit approach described in this chapter, the documentation to record the strategic business objectives, strategic business risks, significant classes of transactions and balances, related core processes and sub-processes, and key performance indicators will form part of the current audit working papers, with documents carefully linking the related aspects: from the 'understanding of the business' document through the 'risk analysis' document, linking to the financial statement effects and key processes, the process analysis document and process level business risk to the remaining risk of significant misstatement in significant classes of transactions, their controls and balances and specific assertions affected through to the audit objectives to be met and related audit procedures.

9.4 COMPUTER INFORMATION SYSTEMS AND INTERNAL CONTROLS

It is fairly safe to say, and without fear of contradiction, that no other development has had a greater effect on accounting and business systems than electronic processing. It is also certain that in 1812 when Charles Babbage first conceived of the idea of his 'Difference Engine' (believed to be the origin of the development of an automatic digital computer), he could not have foreseen the revolution brought about by computers in so many spheres of life. His 'Analytical Engine' that followed and the subsequent 'Hollerith' machine are history. So, in fact, are the first and second generation computers. Technological advances have allowed hardware to develop to such an extent that processing speeds have been reduced to 'pico-seconds'. In addition to this astronomical advance in processing speeds, modern computers are more robust than their forebears and less susceptible to environmental hazards. For these and other reasons, the costs of hardware have been reduced to a point where even small business can afford to 'get into the computerization act' through micros and minis (PCs) and laptops.

It is highly unlikely that auditors today will encounter more than a handful of clients who do not have some form of computerization in their businesses, and many who have very sophisticated networked systems. The systems may be used in the operational side of the client's business, as well as in the accounting and management information systems.

Consequently, every auditor needs to develop some degree of expertise in the use of computers, the hardware and software aspects, security and control issues, and be at least sufficiently skilled to assess and evaluate the general and application controls of a client with a simple stand-alone PC or small networked environment. The auditor needs to be able to recognize when the system is complex, sophisticated and requiring skilled computer audit staff for review, testing and evaluation. The following pages cover the basic information and aspects with which an auditor needs to be familiar. A qualified accountant is well advised to develop his or her knowledge of computer systems further after qualifying, although this is likely to happen in the context of the work environment and to the extent necessary, either to audit clients' computer systems or as a user of financial and management information systems when employed as a financial manager or director.

9.4.1 Important IT components

The auditor should be familiar with the following:

- Hardware (grouped into the Central Processing Unit (CPU));
- Software (system and application programs); and
- Data organization and processing methods.

Computer hardware

Peripheral to the Central Processing Unit (CPU) are:

INPUT DEVICES	OUTPUT DEVICES	MEDIA
Monitor or display unit	Monitor or display	Hard drives, diskettes, CD Rom, DVD, Tape drives, DLT Drives, Data Warehouses, Computer microfilm devices
Keyboard and mouse	Modem, LAN, WAN	
Scanners	Printers	
Media recognition devices, such as voice and optical character recognition	Electronic telecommunications and wireless links	

Table 9.2 Components of a computer system

Computer hardware is the physical equipment associated with computer systems. The Central Processing Unit or CPU is the nerve centre or control unit containing an arithmetic-logic unit which performs the myriad of calculations. Peripheral to this are the input/output devices, such as screen, keyboard, mouse, hard disk, sound card, communications and mass storage devices.

Computer software

Software programs are what enables the computer to run and comprise two broad categories: system programs and application programs.

System programs include:

- *Operating system software*, such as Microsoft Windows, DOS, UNIX, LINUX. These control the operation of the CPU and its peripheral input and output devices, the execution of programs, main storage and management of files.
- *Utility programs* perform data processing and organization tasks.
- *Compilers and assemblers* translate specific programming language into machine-readable form that can be understood by the computer.
- *Database management systems* control the files, data records and data dictionary for database systems and can make changes to these to accommodate data needs in the database.
- *Security systems* basically control and monitor access to various parts of the computer system, log usage and prevent access to unauthorized users.

Application programs are the software programs that allow the user to perform specific data processing routines, such as:

- Microsoft Office, Lotus Smart Suite and Star Office all provide the following program modules: Word processing, spreadsheets, presentation packages, small database systems and E-mail managers and Internet access.

- Business software, such as ACCPAC, SAP, Oracle, etc., provide financial accounting modules such as: general ledgers, inventory, payroll, sales billings, accounts receivable and receipting, purchases and payments and creditors, master files and transaction files; and anti-virus software programmes, such as Nortons, Trendscan, MacAffee, to name a few.

- Operational software, such as production packages, CAD drawing and design packages (such as AutoCad, Solid Works and Inventor) for the mechanical design and manufacturing market.

- Specialized software, such as that used by the medical profession (for example, sophisticated computerized medical equipment; hospital management systems, medical funds contributions and claims management systems), and the hospitality industry (such as travel bookings, hotel management systems), and music programmes to run MPF music and CDs.

9.4.2 Benefits and risks of IT systems

The benefits and risks that are derived from the implementation of computerized information systems in a business are dealt with in paragraphs .02, .03 and .04 of SAAS 4011, 'Risk assessments and internal control – CIS characteristics and considerations', and include the following:

Benefits

- *Consistency of performance:* Programmed functions are potentially more reliable than manual systems provided all transaction types and conditions that could occur are anticipated and incorporated into the systems.

- *Programmed control procedures:* Computer processing allows for the design of internal control procedures into the program software. These include password access controls, menus access controls, exception and error reporting and reasonableness and limit checks.

- *Systems generated transactions:* Certain transactions may be generated automatically by the information system without the need for an input document. This may greatly improve the capacity and efficiency of the business operations. Authorization for such transactions may come in the form of digital signatures, which are not visible, and the calculation will be based on programmed criteria. An example is the processing of interest on bank savings accounts.

Risks

Organizational risks

- *Concentration of functions and knowledge:* Generally, the number of persons involved in a computerized information system is significantly reduced in comparison with a manual system. This often leads to problems in that there is a lack of segregation of duties. In addition, IT personnel may be the only ones with a detailed knowledge of the input, processing and output functions and, hence, the internal controls and any weaknesses, which might be exploited by them.

- *Concentration of programs and data* Transaction and master file data and programs may be concentrated in one installation, or centrally with a distributed environment throughout the entity. There is an increased potential for unauthorized access leading to unauthorized alteration of programs and data, unless the entity has adequate security controls in place.

Design risks

- *Consistency of performance:* Transaction errors in programs will consistently process the same error for all transactions until detected and corrected. This opens the door for significant fraud where a person in the entity, who has access and the authority to amend application programs, does so in order to benefit personally and directly.

Processing risks

- *Absence of input documents:* Data may be entered directly into the computer system without supporting documents and, in some on-line environments, data entry authorization may be replaced with computerized authorization, for example, automatic granting of credit limits.

- *Lack of visible transaction trail:* Certain data may be maintained on computer files only. In a manual environment it would usually be possible to follow a transaction through the system by examining source documents, books of account and ledger records, files and reports. In an information systems environment, the transaction may be partly in machine-readable form and, in addition, it may only exist and be accessible for a limited time.

- *Lack of visible output:* Certain transactions or results of processing may not be printed, or only summary data may be printed. The lack of visible output may result in the need to access data on computer files.

- *Single transaction with update of multiple or database computer files:* A single input to the accounting system may automatically update all records associated with the input, particularly in a database system. Any errors in inputs may therefore create errors simultaneously in several different accounts.

- *Vulnerability of data and program storage media:* Large volumes of data and the computer programs used to process the data may be stored on portable or storage fixed media which may be vulnerable to theft, loss, or intentional or accidental destruction.

9.4.3 Data organization

Data organization refers to the ways in which data is handled and stored. The first level of data organization is at the file structure level. This will include the security, directory structures and user profiles restricting access to authorized users of particular parts of the file structure.

Two types of files are commonly encountered in accounting systems, namely, transaction files and master files. *Transaction files* will usually contain the details of the particular class of transactions captured during the period, such as sales, purchases, payroll, cash receipts or cash payments; *Master files* will contain up-to-date information about the particular general ledger account balances, such as accounts receivable, accounts payable, inventory or bank.

Some master files will contain *standing data*, such as: *details of approved customers* or suppliers and may include data such as customer or supplier name, account number, delivery and postal addresses, credit limits, discount rates and period of credit granted, and a history of goods purchased from or by the company over a specified period of time. A *sales price master file* will contain all inventory product codes, descriptions and selling prices used for billing customers. *Employee standing data master files* will record the personal details of all employees hired, their rate of pay, tax status, membership of medical aid funds, pension funds, labour unions, etc.

9.4.4 IT environments and data processing methods

With the ready availability of computers, a variety of IT environments may be encountered. These will have different data processing methods, risk profiles, internal control implications and audit implications. The main IT environments that an auditor is likely to encounter, and therefore needs to have some knowledge and awareness of, include:

- Stand-alone personal computers (PCs);
- Database systems;
- On-line computer systems;
- Transactions processed by service organizations (outsourced);
- Electronic commerce; and
- Data warehouses.

Each of these will be dealt with in the following sections and are presented in the context of their implications for the auditor in an audit of financial statements.

9.4.4.1 Stand-alone personal computers (PCs)

SAAPS 1001, 'IT Environments – Stand-alone Personal Computers' provides guidance for stand-alone PC environments. The worldwide proliferation of

PCs and laptops during the past 10 years has found millions produced and sitting on the desks of almost every organization of any size, as well as in homes, schools and universities. PCs may be found in both a stand-alone situation and in a linked networked environment. In addition to multiple other functions, PCs can be used for processing accounting transactions and producing reports that are essential to the preparation of the financial statements.

In stand-alone environments, PCs may be used by a single user or multiple users. Users are frequently not very knowledgeable about programming and tend to simply use 'off-the-shelf' software packages, such as electronic spreadsheets or database applications. Consequently, the security policies and procedures in such environments, both physical and programmed, are likely to be informal and applied on an ad hoc basis. In these circumstances, the owner-manager may be the only effective control. The auditor should be wary of placing undue reliance on controls in such an environment. Where PCs are used in a distributed network environment, there is likely to be more formal security structuring and it may be possible to place reliance on the controls.

Failure to implement appropriate organizational policies and procedures may lead to: the entity using out-of-date programs; errors in the data and the information derived from them; and, an increased risk of fraud. Policies and procedures should include criteria for acquisition, implementation and documentation standards, user training, security, backups and storage guidelines for data and programs, password management, personal usage policies, data protection standards, program maintenance and technical support, an appropriate level of segregation of duties and protection against viruses. A further risk is the use of unlicensed software; the entity must have strict policies regulating this, as well as controls to monitor software usage by staff.

Physical protection will include locking of PCs, locking of offices when not in use, camera surveillance and security guards, insurance to cover loss should theft occur, and the implementation of environmental controls. Physical protection will also extend to security over removable and non-removable media, such as diskettes, CDs, hard drives and laptops. Multiple users will increase the risk of storage media being misplaced, altered or destroyed.

The degree of control and security in PC operating systems and application programs vary, but there are techniques and software to ensure data is processed and read as authorized and accidental destruction is minimized. This is largely achieved by using user profiles and passwords to access the PC, programs and individual files, removable storage media, encryption of sensitive data and access control packages.

Continuity of business in a stand-alone PC environment will be dependent on the general care taken by the user to ensure that backup programs and data files are kept at a secure location away from the PC. In the event of the destruction of the equipment, continuity of business also relies on access being available to another PC at short notice, depending on the use and importance of the underlying systems.

The effect on the accounting system and internal controls will depend on the extent to which the PC is used to process accounting applications and transactions. The potential lack of segregation of duties in a stand-alone PC environment may allow errors and fraud to go undetected for some time. Adequate controls over access to programs and data, combined with controls over input, processing and output of data, may compensate for the weaknesses in general controls. As a minimum, this will include a system of transaction logs and batch balancing procedures and the regular review and reconciliation of significant classes of transactions and balances by senior management.

After obtaining an understanding of the accounting systems, the auditor may decide that it is not cost effective to test controls. In this case, the auditor may decide to proceed directly to substantive tests, using a combination of analytical review and tests of detailed transactions and balances.

9.4.4.2 Database systems

SAAPS 1003, 'IT Environments – Database Systems', provides guidance on IT environments with a database system. A database may be defined as a collection of data that is shared and used by many different users for different purposes. Individual users are generally aware only of the data they each use and are unaware of the entire set of data stored in the database. The IT technology is likely to be complex, linked with the entity's strategic business plans, and will therefore require the involvement of both IT staff and auditors with appropriate, specialized IT skills.

Database systems consist principally of two aspects: the database and database management system (DBMS). The DBMS interacts with other hardware and software aspects of the overall computer system. Database systems are distinguished by two important characteristics, namely, data sharing and data independence and, consequently, they require the use of a data dictionary set up with defined relationships and organized to permit multiple users access in different application programs. Data resource management is essential for maintaining data integrity for the whole organization and includes:

- the *data administration* function, which is responsible for the ownership of data, its meaning and relationship with other data and entity-wide integrity; and

- the *database administration* function, which is primarily concerned with the technical implementation of the database, the day-to-day operations and the policies and procedures governing its access and everyday usage.

More detailed guidance on the data and database administration functions is contained in SAAPS 1003, in paragraphs .15 to .19.

Generally, internal controls in a database environment require effective controls over the database, the DBMS and the applications. In a database system, general controls have a far greater importance than application controls, because of the need to share data between multiple users and applications, which has a pervasive effect on application processing. Of particular importance to the auditor are the general control policies and procedures for the following: a standard approach for development and maintenance of application programs; data model and data ownership; access to the database; segregation of duties; data resource management; and data security and database recovery procedures. Detailed guidance on these aspects is provided in SAAPS 1003, paragraphs .22 to .27.

The effect of a database system on the accounting system and associated risks will depend on the extent to which databases are being used by accounting applications, the type and significance of financial transactions being processed, the nature and structure of the database and the general and application controls in a database environment.

Audit procedures in a database environment will be affected principally by the extent to which the accounting system uses the data in the database. Consequently, should the auditor wish to, or need to, place reliance on the database, he or she will have to gain an understanding of the database control environment and consider the effect of the general and application control policies and procedures on the audit risk as indicated above. If reliance is intended, the relevant controls should be tested.

Whether the auditor uses tests of controls or substantive tests in a database environment, it will generally be more effective to do so using CAATs to extract samples and perform a wide range of analytical review procedures. If the database administration controls are inadequate, the auditor may be unable to compensate for weak controls by any amount of substantive tests and may need to consider the implications for a qualification or disclaimer of his or her audit opinion.

9.4.4.3 On-line computer systems

SAAPS 1002, 'IT Environments – On-line Computer Systems', defines on-line computer systems as computer systems that enable users to access data and programs directly through terminal devices. Such systems may comprise mainframe computers, minicomputers or a network of connected PCs. The IT technology is likely to be complex, linked with the entity's strategic business plans, and require the involvement of both IT staff and auditors with appropriate IT skills. By far the greater number of computerized accounting systems nowadays makes use of on-line computer systems and consequently it is important to understand the implications of these for the audit.

On-line systems allow users to directly initiate various functions, such as:

- entering transactions;
- making inquiries;
- requesting reports;
- updating master files; and
- electronic commerce activities.

On-line systems use many different types of terminal devices. Their functions vary widely and depend on their logic, transmission, storage and basic processing capabilities. Types of terminals that might be encountered are:

- *General purpose terminals*, such as:
  - Basic keyboard and screen for capturing data without any validation within the terminal and for displaying data from the computer system on the screen.
  - Intelligent terminal used for the same basic functions as the keyboard and screen but with the additional functions of validating data within the terminal, maintaining transaction logs and performing other local processing.
  - PCs used for all the functions of an intelligent terminal with additional local processing and storage capabilities.

- *Special purpose terminals*, such as:
  - Point-of-sale devices such as on-line cash registers and optical scanners are used in the retail trade.
  - Automated teller machines used to initiate, validate, record, transmit and complete various banking transactions. Depending on the design of the system, certain of these functions are performed by the automated teller machine and others by the main computer.
  - Hand-held wireless devices for entering data from remote locations.
  - Voice response systems used to allow user interaction with the computer over a telecommunications network, based on verbal instructions given to the computer. Common applications include telephone banking and bill payment systems.

Terminal devices may be found either locally or at remote sites. Local terminal devices are connected directly to the computer through cables, whereas remote terminal devices require telecommunications or wireless communications to link them to the main computer. Users may be within or outside the entity, such as customers or suppliers, and application software and data are kept on-line to meet user needs. Systems resources are shared through LANs and WANs and this has led to a growth in distributed environments. Client/server systems have resulted in applications being split so that processing can be performed across several machines, where the processing occurs on the server and the desktop computer.

Employees, business partners such as group companies and associates, customers and other third parties may obtain access to an organization's on-line applications through electronic data interchange (EDI) or other electronic commerce applications. Programmers may also use the on-line capabilities to develop new programs and maintain existing programs. Support personnel may also have on-line access to provide maintenance and support to users.

On-line computer systems may be classified according to their input, process and output functions as follows:

- *On-line entry/real-time processing:* Individual transactions are entered at terminal devices, validated and used to update computer files immediately. The results are then available immediately for inquiries or reports
- *On-line entry/batch processing:* Individual transactions are entered at a terminal device, subjected to certain validation checks and added to a transaction file that contains other transactions for the period. Later, during a subsequent processing cycle, the transaction file may be validated further and then used to update the relevant master file. For example, journal entries may be entered and validated on-line and kept in a transaction file, with the relevant general ledger master files being updated on a monthly basis. Enquiries or reports generated from the master file will not include transactions entered after the last master file update.
- *On-line entry/memo update and subsequent processing:* This is also known as shadow update and combines on-line/real-time processing and on-line/ batch processing. Individual transactions immediately update a memo file that has been extracted from the most recent version of the master file. Enquiries are made from this same memo file. These same transactions are added to a transactions file for subsequent validation and updating of the master file on a batch basis. For example, a cash withdrawal through an automated teller machine is checked against the customer's balance on the memo file and is then immediately posted to the customer's account on the memo file to reduce the balance by the amount of the withdrawal. From the user's perspective, this will seem no different from on-line/real time processing, since the results of data entered are available immediately. However, the transactions have not been subjected to the complete programmed validation checks which will occur in the subsequent processing and updating of the master file.
- *On-line enquiry:* On-line enquiry restricts users at terminal devices to making enquiries of master files. In such systems, the master files are updated by other systems, usually on a batch basis. For example, the user (sales person) may inquire on-line about the credit status of a customer before accepting an order from that customer.
- *On-line downloading/uploading for processing:* On-line downloading refers to the transfer of data from a master file to an intelligent terminal device for further processing by the user, for example, data at the head office representing transactions of the branch for further processing and

preparation of branch financial reports. The results of this processing and other locally processed data may then be uploaded to the head-office computer.

Applications in an on-line environment may have greater exposure to unauthorized access and update. Consequently general controls will include both physical and programmed controls to mitigate the risk of viruses and prevent unauthorized access. These may include: physical controls, such as the use of key locks, locked computer rooms, inactivity time-outs, controls over passwords, system development and maintenance, transaction logs and firewalls. Programmed controls will include on-line monitors, menus, authorization tables, passwords, files and programs.

Certain application controls are particularly important in an on-line environment, including: pre-processing authorization, terminal device input validation checks and processing routines that check the input data and processing results for completeness, accuracy and reasonableness; input error handling procedures that will comprise both manual and automated routines; cut-off procedures for transactions; file controls to ensure the correct data files are being used; stringent controls over master file changes as these could have a pervasive effect on processing results; balancing routines; and segregation of incompatible duties.

As with the previous computerized environments, the effect of on-line computer systems on the accounting system and internal controls will depend on the extent to which the on-line system is being used to process accounting applications, the type and significance of financial transactions being processed and the nature of files and programs the applications use and, finally, the effectiveness of the entity's security infrastructure in controlling the risks of the on-line system. Factors affecting the potential errors or their reduction are more fully explained in SAAPS 1002, 'IT Environments – On-line Computer Systems', paragraphs .24 – .26.

In well-designed and controlled on-line computer systems, the auditor is more likely to seek to place reliance on the controls and is likely to test both general and application controls. From earlier discussions in this chapter it is clear that should the auditor use a top-down audit approach, the controls selected for testing will be those that management relies upon for managing the strategic business risks and potential risks of errors and fraud, including relevant key performance indicators. On-line applications lend themselves to the use of CAATs, both for the testing of general and application controls and for substantive tests – both analytical review and tests of detail. As the computer systems are likely to be complex, both IT staff and audit staff involved in testing the system will need to have specialized IT expertise, skills and knowledge. More detailed guidance is provided in SAAPS 1002, 'IT Environments – On-line Computer Systems', paragraphs .27 – .31.

9.4.4.4 Transactions processed by service organizations (outsourcing)

There has been a trend for many years by businesses in South Africa to outsource functions not considered as 'core business'. In many instances this has included the outsourcing of IT applications of the business to service providers with expertise in the particular IT area. Most common amongst these has been the outsourcing of payroll processing, maintenance and upgrading of IT systems, outsourcing of treasury functions, pension funds and medical schemes, to mention but a few. The SAICA Audit and Accounting Guide: 'Reports on the processing of transactions by service organizations – Guidance for auditors' (the Guide), published in June 2002, indicates that guidance is provided from two perspectives:

- The first relates to the factors an independent auditor – referred to in this section as the *user auditor* – should consider when auditing the financial statements of an entity that uses a service organization – called the *user organization* – to process certain transactions.

- The second revolves around guidance for an independent auditor – referred to in this section as the *service auditor* – who reports on the processing of transactions by a *service organization* for *user auditors* and *user organizations*.

Risk assessment

When a user organization uses a service organization, transactions affecting the user organization's financial statements are subject to control policies and procedures that are, at least in part, physically and operationally separate from the user organization. Where the user retains control over the related accountability, there is a high degree of interaction between the policies and procedures of both organizations. However, where, the service organization executes the user's transactions and maintains the related accountability, it may not be practicable for the user organization to implement effective control policies and procedures over those transactions. This increases the risk of fraud and error that could adversely affect significant classes of transactions and balances and lead to material misstatement in the user's financial statements. In such circumstances, certain policies, procedures and records of the service organization may be relevant to the user organization's ability to record, process, summarize and report financial data in its financial statements.

Responsibilities of the user auditor

In order to comply with SAAS 400 on 'Risk Assessments and Internal Control', which requires the user auditor to obtain an understanding of the accounting and internal controls sufficient to plan the audit and develop an effective audit approach, the user auditor needs to consider the effect of the service organization on the internal control structure of the user organization and the availability of audit evidence. This knowledge should be used to:

- identify types of potential misstatements;
- consider factors that affect the risk of material misstatement; and
- design substantive audit tests.

Paragraphs .06 to .21 of the SAICA Guide provide a detailed discussion of the user auditor's responsibilities, key aspects of which are dealt with below. In order to determine the significance of the service organization's policies, procedures and records in the planning of the audit, the user auditor should consider the following factors for significant classes of transactions and balances:

- The significance of the financial statement assertions affected.
- The inherent risk associated with the assertions affected.
- The nature of the services provided, whether highly standardized and provided to a large number of user organizations, or unique and used by only a few.
- The terms of the contract between the user and the service organization, and the latter's capability, including record of performance, insurance coverage and financial stability.
- The user auditor's prior experience with the service organization.
- The extent of auditable data in the possession of the user organization.
- The existence of specific regulatory requirements that may dictate the application of particular audit procedures, beyond those required to comply with SAAS.

Information about the service organization's policies and procedures may be in the possession of the user organization and available for consideration by the user auditor. These may include: user manuals, system overviews, technical manuals, and reports on the service organization's policies and procedures, such as those from service auditors, internal auditors or regulatory authorities. If this information is regarded as insufficient, the user auditor has several options: firstly, through the user organization, the auditor could contact the service organization or the service auditor to obtain specific information; secondly, the auditor could request that the service auditor perform specific procedures; thirdly, the auditor could visit the service organization to perform such procedures. The service level agreement between the user and service organizations should make due provision for the appropriate rights of access, but may not necessarily do so. The user auditor will have to consider whether any restriction on access may lead to a scope restriction for the audit of the user organization or whether sufficient evidence can be obtained through other means.

After identifying strategic business risks related to the outsourcing functions, and after gaining an understanding of the internal control structure, the user auditor identifies whether the outsourced functions constitute a significant class of transactions or balances, identifies core processes affected and ascertains management's processes, including key performance indicators and control activities for controlling the risks. These provide the basis for the identification of key controls at the user organization or service organization which the user auditor may wish to test so as to obtain evidence of the operating effectiveness throughout the period of intended reliance, and in order to reduce the extent of substantive testing. The user auditor's final assessment of control risk will be based on the combined evidence obtained from the following sources:

- *Tests of the user organization's controls*, such as the re-performance of controls for selected items in a test environment, or the re-performance of the user organization's reconciliations of output reports with original source documents. For example, where the user organization uses a service organization to process payroll transactions, the user organization may establish internal control structure policies and procedures over input and output data to prevent or detect material misstatements. The user auditor may perform tests of the user organization's controls to establish a basis for assessing control risk below the maximum. In such a case, the user auditor may decide that it may not be necessary or efficient to obtain evidence of the service organization controls over program changes or processing of the payroll.

- *A service auditor's report* on policies and procedures placed in operation and tests of operating effectiveness, or a report on the application of agreed-upon procedures that describe relevant tests of controls (this may be performed in accordance with a specific request from the user auditor). Where the relevant controls are applied only at the service organization, and not at the user organization, evidence of the operating effectiveness at the service organization will need to be obtained either by means of a *service auditor's report* or by *appropriate tests of controls* performed by the user auditor at the service organization.

Should weaknesses in internal controls be identified as a result of the tests of control, the user auditor should communicate these to the user organization's management. The service auditor may also be requested by the service organization to perform substantive tests for the benefit of the user auditor; this may occur in response to a specific request, or in terms of contractual arrangements in the service level agreement.

In using the work of the service auditor, the auditor of the user organization will then have to consider the guidance in SAAS 600, 'Using the work of another auditor', in deciding whether this provides satisfactory evidence that there are no material misstatements in the financial statements arising from the operations outsourced. If the evidence is not considered satisfactory, the auditor will have to consider the audit evidence obtained from other audit procedures; failing this, the auditor will have to consider the effect of the audit opinion on the audited financial statements of the user.

Responsibilities of the service auditor

The responsibilities of the service auditor, key considerations and the types of reports that may be provided to the user auditor or user organization are set out in paragraphs .22 – .24 of the SAICA Guide. The service auditor is responsible for the representations in his or her report and for exercising due care in the application of procedures that support those representations. Although the service auditor should be independent of the service organization, it is not necessary that the service auditor be independent of each user organization.

Consideration of fraud and error

If the service auditor becomes aware of fraud or errors – as defined in paragraphs .03 and .04 of SAAS 240, 'Fraud and Error' – attributable to the service organization's management or employees and which may affect one or more user organizations, the findings should be communicated to the appropriate level of management at the service organization. The service auditor should also ascertain whether this information has been communicated to the relevant user organization and, if management at the service organization has not done so and appears unwilling to do so, the service auditor should inform the service organization's audit committee or top management with equivalent authority or responsibility. If the audit committee does not respond appropriately, the service auditor may consider resigning from the engagement. The service auditor may also need to consider whether any responsibility arises under section 20(5) of the Public Accountants' and Auditors' Act.

Related services engagement

The type of engagement to be performed, and the form in which the related report will be represented, should be established by the service organization. It is generally advisable that this be done in consultation with the user organization and user auditor, so that clarity may be achieved on what is most suitable for the purposes of the user organization's audit (paragraph .51 of the Guide).

Generally, two types of reports are issued by the service auditor in respect of policies and procedures of the service organization, which may be relevant to the user organization's internal control structure and aim of achieving specific control objectives. The two reports are:

- Reports on policies and procedures placed in operation, indicating their nature and content, and how the service auditor would obtain the evidence to support the representations in the report, paragraphs .25 – .37 of the Guide.

- Reports on policies and procedures placed in operation and tests of operating effectiveness, indicating their nature, content and how the service auditor would obtain the evidence to support the representations in the report, paragraphs .38 – .50 of the Guide.

Reports on policies and procedures placed in operation

These reports provide the user auditor with an understanding of the policies and procedures necessary to design effective tests of controls and substantive tests at the user organization. These reports should address the control framework discussed earlier in this chapter, namely, the control environment, control activities, information, and the communication and monitoring processes of the service organization that might be relevant to the user organization. Evidence will generally be obtained through the service auditor's previous experience of the service organization and through procedures such as inquiry of appropriate management and supervisory personnel; inspection of service organization documents and records, and observation of service organization activities and operations. Inquiries would also be made to the service organization about any changes in policies and procedures that might be considered significant by the user auditors or user organization. These could include:

- procedural changes to accommodate new statements of GAAP;
- major changes in an application, for example to permit on-line processing; and
- procedural changes to eliminate previously identified deficiencies.

The report of the service auditor should:

- contain specific reference to the applications, services and products;
- identify the scope and nature of procedures of the service auditor;
- identify the party specifying the control objectives; indicate the purpose of the report, namely, that the service organization's description fairly presents, in all material respects, the policies and procedures relevant to the user, that these were suitably designed and were in operation at the specified date;
- contain a disclaimer as to the operating effectiveness, and the service auditor's opinion regarding the purpose of the report;
- contain a statement of the inherent limitations of the potential effectiveness of policies and procedures at the service organization;
- contain a statement about the risk of projecting these to future periods; and finally
- identify the parties for whom the report is intended.

Furthermore, where the system assumes the user will put in place certain policies and procedures, this should be indicated. Deficiencies apparent in the design of any of the policies or procedures, that prevent the achievement of the specified control objectives, should also be reported.

The report of the service auditor is not intended to provide evidence of operating effectiveness or provide any basis for assessing control risk below the minimum.

Reports on policies and procedures placed in operation and tests of operating effectiveness

These reports relate to whether policies and procedures were suitably designed to achieve particular control objectives, whether they were placed in operation by a specified date, and whether they were operating with sufficient effectiveness to provide reasonable, but not absolute assurance that the related control objectives were achieved during the specified period. In addition to the matters dealt with in the service auditor's *report on policies and procedures placed in operation*, this second type of report must deal with the nature, timing and extent of the tests of policies and the procedures performed. It must also make statements about the period covered by the tests and the results of the tests, and do so in sufficient detail for user auditors to determine the effect on their control assessments. The service auditor should consider whether significant deficiencies in the design or operation of the policies and procedures of the service organizations could adversely affect the ability to record, process, summarize or report financial data without error. In addition, user organizations would not generally be expected to have policies and procedures in place to mitigate and, if these are identified, they should be communicated in the service auditor's report. Such reports may be useful in providing the user auditor with a basis for reducing the control risk assessment below the maximum. The service auditor may also be requested to perform substantive tests of user transactions or assets at the service organization, in which instance the nature, timing, extent and results of the procedures would be included in the service auditor's report or in a separate report.

Management representations

The service auditor should obtain, from the service organization's management, written representations which deal with: acknowledgement of their responsibility for establishing and maintaining appropriate policies and procedures; acknowledgement that the description of the policies and procedures provided to the service auditor fairly present in all material respects aspects relevant to the user organization's internal control structure, and that these had been put in place as of a specified date; acknowledgement that management believes the policies and procedures are suitably designed to achieve the specified control objectives; acknowledgement that any significant changes since the last examination have been disclosed to the service auditor, as have all known illegal acts, irregularities or uncorrected errors, attributable to the management or staff of the service organization, which might affect one or more user organizations; and disclosure of any design deficiencies which management is aware of, including those where the cost of corrective action may exceed the benefits.

9.4.4.5 **Electronic commerce**

SAAPS 1013, 'Electronic commerce – effect on the audit of financial statements', provides guidance to an auditor where the entity being audited engages in commercial activity that takes place by means of connected computers over a shared public network, such as the Internet, that enables communication with individuals and businesses around the world. Such transactions are referred to interchangeably as e-commerce transactions or e-business activities (which may include non-transactional activities). Both terms refer to the increasing use of the Internet for business to consumer, business to business, business to government and business to employee e-commerce, which introduces new elements of risk to the audit of financial statements of these entities.

Obtaining an understanding of the significant business objectives and significant business risks for a client engaging in e-commerce requires the auditor to have the requisite IT and Internet business knowledge to perform the audit. These skills will vary with the complexity of the client's e-commerce strategies and activities and their significance to the entity's business. The auditor's understanding will relate to the entity's e-commerce strategy and activities, the technology used to facilitate these, the risks involved and how management is managing these, including the security infrastructure and related controls affecting the financial reporting process and the dependence of the entity on e-commerce activities and its ability to continue as a going concern.

E-commerce activities may be complementary to the entity's traditional business activities, or they may represent a new line of business. The geographic lines of transit that characterized physical trade of goods no longer apply where goods and services can be delivered via the Internet. Certain industries are more conducive to e-commerce trading than others and may be in a more mature phase of development. Examples of industry sectors transformed by e-commerce include, amongst many others: computer software, securities trading, banking, travel services, books and magazines, recorded music, advertising, news media and education.

SAAPS 1013, 'Electronic commerce – effect on the audit of financial statements', paragraphs .13 – .19, sets out matters that are relevant in considering the entity's e-commerce strategy in the context of the auditor's understanding of the control environment, the extent of e-commerce activities, and the entity's outsourcing arrangements and risk identification. Matters that are relevant include:

- the involvement of those charged with governance in aligning the e-commerce activities with the overall business strategy;
- whether e-commerce supports a new activity, or is intended to make existing activities more efficient or reach new 'global' markets;
- sources of revenue and how these are changing, as well as how management's evaluation of e-commerce affects the earnings of the entity and its financial requirements;

- management's attitude to risk and the extent to which it has identified e-commerce opportunities and risks in a documented strategy supported by appropriate controls; and
- management's commitment to best practice in e-commerce trading and certificates of authentication.

The extent of e-commerce activities usually relates to the entity's understanding of how the Internet can be utilized. Examples may include all or some of the following:

- The provision of information about the entity and its activities that can be accessed by third parties such as investors, customers, suppliers, finance providers and employees.
- The facilitation of transactions with established customers, whereby transactions are entered via the Internet.
- Attempts to gain access to new markets and new customers, by providing information and transaction processing via the Internet.
- The creation of an entirely new business model, introducing new types of risks.

Many entities do not have the technical expertise to establish and operate the in-house systems needed for e-commerce transactions, and may therefore depend on service organizations such as Internet Service Providers (ISPs), Application Service Providers (ASPs) and data hosting companies to provide all or many of the IT requirements for e-commerce. An entity may also use service organizations for various other functions engendered by its e-commerce activities, such as order fulfilment, delivery of goods, operation of call centres, and certain accounting functions. Certain policies, procedures and records maintained by the service organization may be relevant to the audit of the entity's financial statements. The auditor will need to consider, firstly, how management is managing the outsourcing risks and, secondly, assess the effect that the service organization has on the assessment of control risk.

The key business risks arising from e-commerce activities include:

- Loss of transaction integrity.
- Pervasive e-commerce security risks, including virus attacks, and the potentials for fraud by customers, employees and others through unauthorized access.
- Improper accounting policies, ranging from improper capitalization of expenditures such as website development costs, complex contractual arrangements; title transfer risks; translation of foreign currencies; allowances for warranties or returns (when selling in global markets); and revenue recognition issues, such as:
  - whether the entity is acting as principal or agent and whether gross sales or commission only are to be recognized;
  - if other entities are given advertising space on the website how revenues are determined and settled (barter transactions);

- treatment of volume discounts; and
- cut-off issues (for example, whether sales are only recognized when goods and services are delivered, and when delivery is considered to have taken place).
- Non-compliance with taxation and other legal and regulatory requirements, particularly when e-commerce transactions are conducted across international boundaries.
- Failure to ensure that e-commerce contracts, evidenced only by electronic means, are binding in a court of law and, further, determining which court in which country has jurisdiction.
- Over-reliance on e-commerce when placing significant business systems and transactions on the Internet.
- Systems and infrastructure crashes with significant downtime.

SAAPS 1013, 'Electronic commerce – effect on the audit of financial statements', in paragraphs .20 – .21, contains guidance on how the entity should address its e-commerce risks. This is achieved by the implementation of an appropriate security infrastructure and related controls which should include measures to: verify the identity of customers and suppliers; ensure the integrity of transactions; obtain agreement on trade terms (non-repudiation procedures); obtain payment from or secure credit facilities for customers; and establish privacy and information protection protocols.

Legal and regulatory issues are problematic, as a comprehensive framework does not yet exist and e-commerce transactions are conducted in many legal jurisdictions. These issues are dealt with in paragraphs .22 – .24 of SAAPS 1013.

Internal control considerations are important to the auditor and the matters discussed earlier in this chapter apply equally here. In particular, security aspects are critical and the auditor needs to consider how these are being controlled. Should the e-commerce comprise a significant class of transactions for the entity, the auditor will need to evaluate the controls over transactions, the alignment of old and new processes, and the form of audit evidence – all likely to be primarily, if not totally, in the electronic format. Clearly, the auditor will have to use CAATs for performing tests of controls, analytical procedures and detailed substantive tests. Guidance with regard to these can be found in paragraphs .25 – .36 of SAAPS 1013.

9.4.4.6 Data warehousing

Modern businesses depend on information that is reliable and available at the right time, at the right place and in the right form. In order to generate information that is appropriate for decision support purposes, many organizations are undertaking data warehouse projects for the purpose of providing management with easy access to the organization's information resources. These projects entail the extraction and storage of data from operational systems in an integrated, subject-based database. Whilst operational systems contain the transactions of the organization and record its financial information for purposes of producing its financial statements (the main focus of the external auditor), management relies on a wealth of other internal and external information to make important decisions about running the business and managing the strategic business risk exposure. Decision support systems are designed to enable managers to analyse data from the organization's operational systems in order to identify trends, perform demographic analyses and 'what-if' analyses.

The SAICA Audit and Accounting Guide: 'Data Warehousing (the Guide)', published in May 2000, provides guidance as part of the Information Technology Series. This Guide provides guidance in respect of the data warehouse architecture, distinguishing between data warehousing and operational systems; the design and implementation of a data warehouse; data marts and data resource management; the business risks and control and audit implications. The Guide indicates that data warehousing is not a new IT application, but is instead a new IT architecture typically consisting of a set of programs that extract data from operational systems, a database that maintains warehouse data, and systems that provide data to users. When the particular data warehousing strategy has been established, existing operational processing systems continue to operate within their present function or process-orientated data structures.

Data warehouses could include market information about customers' demand patterns on a geographical or economic basis, credit information such as interest rates, industry information about competitor's market share and returns. Such information is then used to make decisions about buying and selling activities, investment in inventory, opening of new markets, money market management, advertising campaigns, capital investment in new product lines, acquisitions and disposals of aspects of the organization, etc. Data warehouses provide a means of collecting and extracting related aspects of the internal and external information needed by management to make important capital investment and trading decisions.

For example, a major South African retailer uses a data warehouse to anticipate the inventory demand of every retail outlet and to manage its product distribution from nine central distribution warehouses to its more than 700 retail outlets in South Africa and other countries in Africa. Other data warehouses may be structured as client relational information databases to enhance the organization's service delivery to customers. A financial institution may use data warehouses to profile the needs of their individual and corporate customers, and to improve services and provide a holistic one-stop service to customers over their lifetime – for example, a range of investment products, savings accounts, cheque accounts, short-term and long-term loan facilities, credit cards, garage cards and foreign exchange transactions, insurance products, on-line and Internet banking, to mention a few. By providing clients with personal bankers at accessible points and a system that allows authorized personnel access to all aspects of a client's portfolio, the bank can provide informed and appropriate advice promptly, and enable banking clients to manage their finances more effectively.

Data warehouse architecture

Defining characteristics of data warehousing are the separation of operational data and decision support data, as well as the separation of processing functions. By separating these very different processing environments, the data warehouse architecture enables both operational and decision support applications to coexist, which allows optimization of data processing time and procedures. The data warehouse architecture consists of six distinct aspects:

- *Operational systems* provide most of the source data for the data warehouse. Data will be sourced from the organization's own operational database, other organizational databases and external databases.

- *Transformation processing* involves the extraction and transformation (filtering, conversion and condensation) of data using transformation software to capture the data needed to populate the data warehouse database. Data extraction entails the scanning and selection of data from the operational databases according to predetermined parameters. To ensure the integrity of the data, synchronization between the different applications feeding the data warehouse must be maintained at all times. The objective is to impact minimally on the operational systems.

- *Database* – the data warehouse can be described as an *integrated, subject orientated, time-variant and non-volatile* collection of data structured in support of management's informational requirements and *accessible* to authorized users who have limited knowledge of the organization's data structures.

    The *integration* defines the organization's key data items and sets out the logical relationships ensuring corporation-wide consistency in usage, in terms of data naming and definition, encoding structures and measurement of variables.

    The second important characteristic of the data warehouse's data is that its design and structure are *orientated* to the important *subjects* (underlying its core processes) of the organization, such as Customer, Supplier, Product, and Vendor – in contrast with its operational systems, which are designed around applications and functions, such as Loans, Savings and Bank Cards, in the case of a financial institution.

    The third defining characteristic is that it is *time-variant* or historical in nature, providing a snapshot at a specific point in time, in contrast with operational data which is accurate at the moment of access.

    The data in the database tends to be static or '*non-volatile*', since it is not updated through the transaction processing cycles.

- *Middleware* can be defined as all the hardware, software and communication facilities that make it possible to access data across server hardware platforms from client workstations. The database of the data warehouse may reside on a mainframe or in the client/server environment. Typically, the middleware software allows a user on a workstation to perform a request via the network for data that is resident on the server's databases.

- *Decision support and presentation processing* consists of the end users' decision support applications, which typically access the data warehouse database through a standard query language (SQL). These include query and reporting spreadsheets and analyses, decision support and executive information systems.

- *Meta data directory* is an essential aspect of the data warehouse architecture. It provides users with a single source or repository of information about the data in the data warehouse, and covers the contents, the source, the data transformation process from the legacy systems, how the data has been summarized and how it needs to be extracted from the data warehouse. The directory contains information to explain what a particular data item means in business terms, and it also provides data about reports, spreadsheets and queries related to that data.

Data warehouse design and implementation

As with any other IT systems development, the design and implementation of a data warehouse is a challenging process involving five major phases: the compilation of a data warehouse data model, the definition of the system of record, the design of the physical data warehouse data base, the design and construction of the transformation programs and the execution of the programs created to populate and maintain the data warehouse's database. Clearly, data warehousing crosses functional lines to look at the core processes to be catered for and involves people in a number of different departments and business functions. The core team will generally involve a project leader, data analysts, business analysts, a database administrator and programmers/analysts responsible for creating the extraction, transformation and end user applications. The development and implementation team and end users need appropriate training. An appropriate development methodology should be employed and a pilot project should be run prior to full implementation.

As data warehouses are usually voluminous, a common approach is to use separate business areas (for example, sales, marketing, etc.) as a subset of the warehouse. These are referred to as *data marts* and contain data specific to the needs of a particular group of users.

Data warehouse management and security

The introduction of data warehouse technology in an environment typified by a number of end users making use of a common warehouse database for various end-user purposes, necessitates the proper resourcing of the data resource management function. Organization-wide data resource management, combining the functions of data administration and database administration, is necessary for enacting standards and promoting data integrity for the organization as a whole. Data administration is responsible for the logical structure and definition of the organization's data, whereas the

database administration is primarily concerned with the technical implementation of the database of the data warehouse, its day-to-day operations,
and the policies and procedures governing its access and everyday usage.

The advanced and more complex utilization of database and client/server
technologies raise several issues and business concerns. The concentration
of data in a central database increases the risk of industrial espionage and
management should be concerned about securing sensitive information
from competitors and other outside parties. If the organization makes
strategic decisions based on the information compiled from the data
extracted from the warehouse database, the integrity of the data's
qualities – pertaining to completeness, accuracy, validity and timeliness –
becomes a critical issue that has to be managed. As the organization's
dependence on the data warehouse and processes to 'conduct business as
usual' increases, the reliability of the data extraction and the integrity of the
meta data, the reliability of the decision support systems applications and
end-user tools must increase proportionally. Accordingly, management
must ensure that appropriate backup, disaster recovery and business
continuity plans are put in place.

In order for users to feel assured of the necessary degree of accuracy, formal
control procedures must exist to ensure that data from operational databases
is identified and retrieved correctly, the data warehouse database is properly
designed, implemented and maintained, and any data warehouse data
retrieved and presented is used wisely. Similarly, the data management
processes must include controls to achieve an effective level of integrity,
including procedures for a standard approach to development and
maintenance of the warehouse database and application, assignment of
responsibilities for data ownership, access control to protect the database
from access by unauthorized users, and the segregation of duties between
users, data and database administrators, systems development and technical
support functions.

The auditor's perspective

The data warehouse is designed to meet the strategic, long-term and
positioning needs of top management and analysts. In addition, the data
warehouse creates no data; all the data in the warehouse's database is
extracted from the organization's operational databases and other external
sources, and in the subsequent summarization and roll-ups – to make
the data usable for effective decision making – the identity of the source
of the data is automatically lost. Consequently, the auditor does not consider
the data warehouse a system of record for financial auditing purposes.
However, during the planning stage of the audit, the auditor should obtain
an understanding of the data warehouse and its database management
systems, the transformation processes, decision support tools and their
relationship to the accounting systems under review to determine whether:

- the data warehouse environment has any impact on the financial statements or financial reporting in any way, for example, providing the basis for decisions made by management with regard to provisions raised or other judgemental areas of the financial information, or

- the warehouse functionality can be used to assist the auditor in performing the audit, for example, by providing the data for a review of the key performance indicators used by management to manage its core business processes, analytical procedures to determine areas of audit significance, and trend analyses using data residing on the data warehouse database.

10

Assessing Control Risks and Tests of Controls

Learning objectives

After studying this chapter you should be able to:

1. Explain the auditor's responsibilities in assessing the effectiveness of the entity's controls to prevent and/or detect and correct material misstatements that might arise from error or fraud, as well as the steps the auditor would follow to do this assessment.
2. Discuss the relationships between the financial statement assertions, potential misstatements, specific audit objectives and tests of controls.
3. Distinguish between the auditor's preliminary and final risk assessments and explain how the preliminary assessment of control risk affects the auditor's decision to follow primarily a test of controls approach, or a substantive approach.
4. Discuss the audit effectiveness of control risk assessments and tests of control in an audit of financial statements.
5. Identify the controls necessary in any transaction process; the potential misstatements where controls needed are not effective, and select controls for testing.
6. Discuss the factors affecting the nature, timing and extent of tests of controls, differentiating between preventative and detective controls, and design appropriate audit procedures to test controls on which the auditor may wish to place reliance.
7. Describe the factors that influence the auditor's decision to place reliance on the internal audit in respect of the entity's internal controls.
8. Describe how an IT environment affects the auditor's assessment of control risk, of general and application risks and controls, and the audit approach to tests of controls.
9. Describe the various computer-assisted audit techniques (CAATs) that may be used in tests of internal controls.

10. Explain how the auditor evaluates evidence from tests of controls for his or her final control risk assessment.
11. Discuss matters to be considered by, and the responsibility of, the auditor in communicating control weaknesses to management.

10.1 ASSESSING CONTROL RISK

10.1.1 Understanding control risk assessment

The auditor's responsibilities for assessing the effectiveness of the design and operation of management's controls over process level risks for significant classes of transactions and balances to prevent or detect and correct material misstatements is discussed in this chapter. The discussion covers factors affecting the auditor's decision whether or not to perform tests of controls to meet the audit objectives related to the *completeness*, *occurrence/validity* and *measurement/accuracy* assertions for significant classes of transactions and balances and the process of selecting tests of controls, and the evaluation of the results of such tests.

Inherent and control risks are generally intrinsically linked, so the concept of the risk of *significant misstatement* results from a combined assessment of inherent and control risks. The evaluation of the results of tests of controls affecting the determination of detection risk and the linkage needed to the design of appropriate substantive tests of analytical review and tests of detail to reduce the residual risk of significant misstatement remaining in the financial statements. Control risks and tests of control are discussed in this chapter and substantive tests in chapter 11.

Guidance regarding the responsibilities of the auditor for the assessment of inherent and control risks is contained in SAAS 400, 'Risk Assessments and Internal Control', where paragraph .18 states the control risk principles as follows:

'After obtaining an understanding of the accounting and internal control systems, the auditor should make a preliminary assessment of control risk, at the assertion level, for each material account balance or class of transactions.'

Further, in paragraph .20:

'The preliminary assessment of control risk for a financial statement audit should be high, unless the auditor:

- Is able to identify internal controls relevant to the assertion that are likely to prevent or detect and correct a material misstatement; and

- Plans to perform tests of control to support the assessment.'

Further, in paragraph .22:

'The auditor should document in the working papers:

- The understanding obtained of the entity's accounting and internal control systems; and

- The assessment of control risk. When control risk is assessed at less than high the auditor would also document the basis for the conclusions.'

Consequently, the auditor would assess control risk as being high if controls are insufficient to prevent or timeously detect errors, or tests of controls reveal inadequacies in the actual performance of the client's laid-down control activities. Should adequate controls be in place and tests of control provide evidence of the effective operation of these controls, control risk would be assessed as low. In these circumstances the auditor is justified in placing reliance on the system to prevent or detect error.

10.1.2 Steps in control risk assessment

With the 'top-down' audit approach, the auditor obtains an understanding of the various aspects of control – the *control environment, risk assessment, information and communication, control activities and monitoring* processes – to identify the core and key processes of the business and then to understand the business process level risks, their effect on the financial statements and potential *significant misstatements*. Figure 10.1 illustrates the 'top-down' approach.

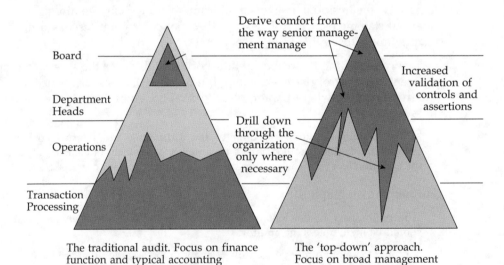

Figure 10.1 Change in the focus of the audit
(Source: PricewaterhouseCoopers)

The change in the focus of the audit is illustrated in Figure 10.1: the areas where audit comfort is derived (shown as dark blue in the diagrams) start at the top, whereas the more traditional audit (shown as light blue) tends to a more bottom-up approach with increased focus on the finance function and financial statement items and transactions, however much the auditor may also try to understand monitoring controls. The diagram also illustrates that although much of the audit comfort is gained at a relatively high level with the 'top-down' approach, the auditor needs to test down at the operations/transactions level where it is not possible to get sufficient audit comfort from validating management's monitoring processes.

With the 'top-down' approach, the auditor identifies control activities and monitoring procedures, those specific controls and key performance indicators implemented by management to prevent, or detect and correct, *significant misstatements* in significant classes of transactions and balances. The 'top-down' approach is used as the basis for this chapter, as well as for chapter 11 and the other chapters discussing the audit of various classes of transactions and balances.

The steps the auditor follows to assess the risk of *significant misstatement* for audit objectives related to the financial statement implications of business risks are summarized below:

- **Step 1:** The auditor obtains a *preliminary assessment* of the risk of significant misstatement by considering the information gathered in obtaining an *understanding of the client's risk management processes* and the *control activities designed and implemented* by management to manage the risks for key processes and the related significant classes of transactions and balances.

- **Step 2:** The auditor, having obtained a thorough understanding of the process level risks (arising from the initiation, processing and reporting of significant classes of transactions and balances), now *identifies* their potential effect on the financial statements and the risk of *significant misstatement* for particular *assertions* and the related *audit objectives*.

- **Step 3:** The auditor identifies the *control activities* used by management and whether these are sufficient to *prevent or detect and correct significant misstatements*.

- **Step 4:** The auditor performs the *tests of controls*, firstly to obtain audit evidence to determine whether the *design* of the controls is appropriate and, secondly, to acquire evidence about the *operating effectiveness throughout the period* under review.

- **Step 5:** Finally, to determine the nature and extent of analytical review and detailed substantive audit procedures to be performed, the auditor *evaluates* the evidence gathered from the tests of controls to confirm or reject the preliminary assessment of *significant misstatement* or the *combined inherent and control risk assessment*.

Where control risk is assessed as high for significant classes of transactions or balances, the auditor should not perform tests of controls but should proceed, instead, to the design of appropriate substantive tests to detect any risk of significant misstatement.

The steps involved in the design of tests of control are discussed below.

10.1.2.1 Preliminary assessment of control risk and audit effectiveness

The previous chapter discussed at some length the auditor's need to obtain an understanding of the client's business. The auditor uses the knowledge gained from the process of understanding the *control environment, risk assessment, information and communication, control activities and monitoring* processes of management, to identify key business processes, process level risks and the effect of such risks on the financial statements. By discussions with the client, the observation of control activities and reading any client documentation, the auditor should be able to identify significant classes of transactions and balances and specific controls on which reliance may be placed to prevent, or detect and correct, potential significant misstatements in those transactions and balances.

If reliance on controls is intended, the auditor needs to perform tests of controls to obtain evidence that such controls operated as they were designed to throughout the financial period under audit.

Should the auditor assess control risk as being at an unacceptable level, obviously no reliance could be placed thereon, and the auditor would thus need to design and perform extended substantive tests to detect, if any, material misstatements.

The audit effectiveness of control risk assessments and tests of controls

In a quasi peer review undertaken in 2000 by the Public Oversight Board's Panel on Audit Effectiveness, a number of problems relating to the audit effectiveness of the auditor's understanding of the control environment and assessment of control risks and tests of controls were identified. These are summarized below:

- Assessment of the *control environment* was performed in all instances; however, the results indicated that a 'more thoughtful analysis and in-depth auditor knowledge' of the entity's control environment, as well as the more extensive use of IT personnel at this stage of the audit, could have resulted in a more effective audit being performed (page 25).

- The in-depth understanding of information systems and controls, the assessment of the risk assessments performed and of the degree of reliance placed on controls varied considerably among engagements even within the same firm (page 26).

- Although IT specialists were used in understanding general and application controls in the more complex computerized systems and in the performance of tests of computer controls, the co-ordination between IT and general audit staff was lacking where an increased understanding would have improved the control risk assessment process (page 26).

- The practice of assessing the control risk below the maximum level and relying on tests of controls to reduce detailed substantive tests was found to be uncommon, particularly for small to medium sized clients, although it was more common for large clients (page 26).

- However, when the auditor planned to rely on tests of controls, the nature, timing and extent of the tests of controls varied considerably. In some cases there appeared to be confusion over what constitutes an internal control over an identified risk, as opposed simply to a procedure for processing a transaction. There also appeared to be some confusion over the identification of controls relevant to the auditor's selection of substantive tests and the nature, timing and extent of appropriate tests of controls in the circumstances (page 26).

- The documentation of the audit team's understanding and assessment of internal control takes different forms, including firm-specific checklists and detailed descriptions of the entity's policies and procedures. Documentation of the control environment was found to be lacking in some instances. In a number of engagements the documentation of the control work in key areas was found to be incomplete or lacking in substance (page 26).

As a result of these findings, the Panel for Audit Effectiveness (2000, at pages 29 – 30) has recommended that audit firms critically examine, *inter alia*, their audit work on internal control; the emphasis placed in professional development training programmes on assessing and testing components of internal control; as well as the need for auditors to have a higher level of technology skills and involvement of IT specialists in large audits.

These aspects should be borne in mind in circumstances where control reliance is intended. Clearly, there is a need to involve the audit team as a whole in different aspects and for the team to include audit personnel with significant audit, industry and technology experience in order to correctly identify the risks of significant misstatement, relevant controls and appropriate tests of controls.

10.1.2.2 Understanding business processes and identifying significant classes of transactions and balances for tests of control

Where the 'top-down' approach is adopted, the auditor identifies the core business processes and the underlying key processes affecting the significant classes of transactions.

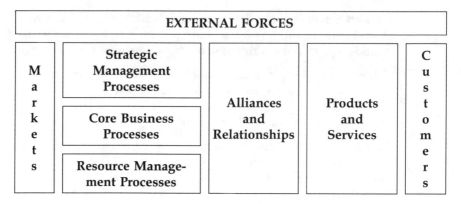

Figure 10.2 Generic business process model
(Source: KPMG)

Figure 10.2 illustrates a business process model used by a large auditing firm. Similar models are applied by most of the large firms as part of their audit methodologies to gain a better understanding of the business and, therefore, the audit risks in their clients in order to perform a more effective audit.

Example

In applying the business process analysis approach in, for example, a large retail trading operation the following core processes may be encountered:

- The first core process may be *trading*, and the related key processes may be the product selection and purchasing of retail inventory, pricing of goods for sale, and inventory management.

- The second core process may be *store planning and image*, involving site selection, property management, store layouts and design, brand advertising and promotion.

- The third core process may be *cash and credit cards management* with the related key processes being the receipt and deposit of cash, the daily investment of surplus funds, money market accounts, with the related interest income, and payment of suppliers.

Underpinning the core processes will be the management of the business resources, namely, the human resource management, finance and treasury management, legal and regulatory management and information systems management that operate to support the core processes of the business.

10.1.2.3 Selecting control activities for tests of controls

Each core process and resource management process, when broken down into the key processes, will have business process level activities such as inputs, activities and outputs, as well as computer information systems that need to be controlled to ensure, amongst other control aspects, the completeness, measurement / accuracy and occurrence / validity of individual transactions recorded on a daily basis. These business process level activities will include a variety of control activities implemented by management.

Where these processes give rise to large volumes of transactions or material amounts, they will comprise significant classes of transactions and, ultimately, significant balances in the financial statements. The understanding of the business risks will enable the auditor to identify the particular assertions in the financial statements affected by each key process that may potentially contain a risk of significant misstatement. The auditor will then identify and focus on specific control activities that management may have put in place to prevent or detect and correct material errors or fraud in the financial statements affecting these assertions. The controls may take the form of manual controls or computerized / programmed controls and may be performed at the input stage, during processing or at the output stage of any transaction process.

10.1.2.4 Tests of the design and operating effectiveness of controls

If the auditor is able to identify those specific controls and key performance indicators used by management to control significant classes of transactions or balances that are likely to achieve the objectives of completeness, measurement / accuracy and occurrence / validity, they may be tested in order to determine whether reliance can be placed on them to reduce the extent of substantive testing required for the specific class of transactions or balances.

Table 10.1 illustrates how a significant class of transactions for one of the core processes in the above example of a retail trading operation, may be used to identify the financial statement effect, related assertions, risk of significant misstatement, the typical controls that may be encountered and the typical tests of controls that the auditor would perform.

SIGNIFICANT CLASS OF TRANS-ACTIONS	FINANCIAL STATE-MENT ASSERTIONS/ POTENTIAL SIGNIFICANT MISSTATEMENT	CONTROL ACTIVITIES	TESTS OF CONTROLS
Trading Core Process Cash sales to retail customers and cash receipts from them.	**F/S Assertions** CVA Cash sales, CVA cash receipts and CVA Output VAT.	**Monthly bank reconciliation** approved by the financial director.	Inspect bank reconciliations during the year to determine if they were performed time-ously and balance to the books and records. Also inspect evidence that the financial director monthly reviews the reconciliation.
	Potential Misstatements Cash sales may not be recorded – CA. Cash receipts may not be banked intact CVA. VAT liability may not be accounted for.	**Inventory shrinkage key performance indicator (KPI)** Stores and stock management monitor shrinkage KPI on a monthly basis to detect any errors in accounting records, including output VAT or physical security.	Inspect inventory shrinkage reports to determine that they are prepared at month end and consider key performance Indicators (KPI) benchmark against norms for the industry and variances followed up.
		Electronic point of sale (EPOS) system config-uration Each day finance / management reconciles the systems sales for each retail store to the cash and credit card receipts per the bank statement. The senior accountant reviews this reconciliation.	Confirm with IT Department that they performed test work related to the original EPOS system configuration design and implementation as part of the post implementation review. Obtain documents to support procedures.
		The audit firm's IT department performed a post-implementation review of the EPOS system two years ago. The review was comprehensive and included the configuration of the bar code readers at the tills and the configuration of sales to the ledger.	Corroborate with client's IT analyst and management responsible for EPOS that configuration has not changed. Perform system query to confirm access levels for changing configurations as per policies manual.
		Inventory count procedures Physical counts of inventory are performed on a cyclical basis and attended by internal audit. Stock management reviews a quarterly report; internal audit reviews their reports.	Observe stock counts in final quarter. Determine whether records were updated and differences investigated by internal auditor. Determine whether internal auditor attended counts during year – inspect reports of stock count summaries.

Table 10.1 Example of significant classes of transactions, related financial statement assertions and significant risk of misstatement, controls and tests of control

Preventative controls versus detective controls

Preventative controls function at the input or processing stage of a transaction to identify and reject the input that does not meet established criteria.

Detective controls, on the other hand, function after the physical and accounting processes are completed. Detective controls may cover, for example:

- *Transactions* for a particular period, such as the human resources manager's review of monthly payroll reports; the marketing manager's review of reports on sales and gross margins analysed on a product or geographic basis; or the inventory manager's review of reports of stock shrinkages in a retail store.

- *Balances* at a point in time, such as reconciliations of accounts payable account balances to the suppliers' statements received; the reconciliation of subsidiary ledger balances to general ledger control accounts; and an age analysis for accounts receivable at month end.

- *Exception reports* from any transaction processing run that indicate errors arising for a variety of reasons and affecting different assertions, for example, a list of missing or duplicated delivery note sequence numbers for a sales transaction run which indicate potential completeness errors.

- *Analysis of key performance indicators* used by management, such as inventory turnover, gross profit margins on particular inventory lines and shrinkage rates. When these performance indicators are not in line with expectations, they alert management to accounting errors or physical losses relating to several different assertions.

Preventative controls normally relate to specific assertions for individual transactions, whereas detective controls address multiple assertions and generally relate to more than one transaction. Another important distinction between preventative and detective controls is the skills competence level of persons responsible for performing the control. The *preventative controls* will generally be performed by clerical staff, such as data capture clerks, salespersons and buyers, who may have a limited understanding of the financial implications of transactions and who may not appreciate or understand the effect of potential errors. The *detective controls* will invariably be performed by more senior staff or the owner manager in a business who have a sound understanding of the business and the implications of potential errors or fraud. Detective controls are also more likely to reveal material misstatements arising from management override of controls or fraud, except, of course, where the staff member performing the control is in fact the person perpetrating the fraud and override of controls. For this reason, it may be more efficient and effective for the auditor to select a number of management's higher level detective controls, rather than selecting preventative controls over individual transactions as a basis for reliance thereon.

10.1.2.5 Evaluating tests of controls and assessing the risk of significant misstatement

Once the auditor has tested the operation of the specific controls on which reliance is intended, the auditor needs to consider the findings. Evidence of deviations from the specified controls is used to evaluate their effectiveness in ensuring the relevant assertions – *completeness, occurrence/validity and measurement/accuracy* – for the class of transactions from which the sample was selected, will be met. In addition, the auditor considers whether the evidence indicates that the controls have operated throughout the period under review. Based on the results, the risk of significant misstatement (combined inherent and control risks) will be assessed as high, medium or low. The considerations supporting the auditor's evaluation of evidence from tests of controls and assessment of control risk are discussed in section 10.4 of this chapter, after the discussion of the tests of controls in an IT environment.

10.2 DESIGNING AND PERFORMING TESTS OF CONTROLS

10.2.1 The nature of tests of controls

SAAS 400, 'Risk assessments and internal control', in paragraph .24 indicates that tests of control are performed to obtain evidence about the effectiveness of both the:

- Design of the accounting and internal control systems, that is whether they are suitably designed to prevent, or detect and correct material misstatements, and
- The operation of the internal controls throughout the period.'

The principle, as contained in paragraph .28, is that:

'The auditor should obtain evidence through tests of controls to support any assessment that is less than high. The lower the assessment of control risk, the more evidence the auditor should obtain that accounting and internal control systems are suitably designed and operating effectively.'

Tests of controls involve:

- *Inspection* of documents, reports and electronic files for evidence of the performance of the control;
- *Observation* of the control being performed, such as observing a stock count, observing screen input or batch input controls at a computer terminal; observing a gate check on goods despatched from the premises;
- *Enquiry* of appropriate entity personnel to ascertain which control procedures are performed and by whom; and
- *Reperformance* of the control to detect whether the system has correctly identified any error in input, processing or output.

These procedures are aimed at determining whether or not controls to be relied upon by the auditor were performed adequately, as they were designed, by someone who did not have incompatible functions, and that they were applied throughout the period of intended reliance. The reader is referred to the more detailed discussion in chapter 6 of the procedures for obtaining sufficient appropriate audit evidence. It must be noted again that, for obvious reasons, evidence obtained from observation is only valid at the time of the observation and should not be assumed to have operated in that way throughout the period of the audit.

The auditor should consider various factors in determining whether the design of the control is appropriate. These factors are:

- What risks is the control designed to mitigate? That is, is the design of the control appropriate to address the particular risk(s)?

- How is the control performed? That is, how frequently is the control performed and, for a manual control, how competent is the person / persons performing it – do they understand why they are performing the control, and performing it sufficiently well to detect any error or fraud? For programmed controls, when are they performed, and is the logic correct and comprehensive – for example, will a programmed 'reason-ableness check' detect all possible errors or only certain errors?

- What is the nature and size of the misstatements the control is intended to detect and correct? What is the cost : benefit trade off? That is, for what aspects has management decided to accept the risk of loss and / or judged it as unlikely to be material? And, as a result of the management's decision, what specific controls are not implemented to prevent the potential risk?

- Who is performing the control – that is, is it someone who does not have incompatible functions?

In the audit of a small owner-managed business, it is unlikely that the control activities will be as formalized as that of a large business, and often the owner manager is the only effective control to ensure the *completeness, measurement/accuracy* and *occurrence/validity* of transactions recorded. It is therefore unlikely that the auditor will seek to test controls and, instead, conduct the audit by performing substantive audit procedures with a combination of analytical review procedures and detailed substantive tests.

If the auditor does not intend to rely on internal controls, tests of controls should not be conducted. In this case the auditor should proceed to perform substantive tests comprising analytical reviews or detailed substantive tests. The auditor may decide not to rely on control procedures either because the preliminary review of the internal control system for a particular transaction type indicates that the system cannot be relied upon, or because the volume of transactions of that type is insufficient to justify tests of controls. Before proceeding to detailed substantive testing, analytical reviews should be conducted which will provide a certain level of assurance about the audit objectives. Thereafter any further assurance required to limit audit risk to an acceptable level must be satisfied by means of detailed substantive tests.

The selection of the appropriate procedure depends on the manner in which the control is performed. Due to the limitations of individual tests of controls, discussed earlier, it will usually be necessary for the auditor to apply a combination of the various audit procedures available to obtain satisfaction that controls operated effectively and to support a final assessment of control risk as *high, medium or low*.

10.2.2 Extent of tests of control procedures

The extent of tests of control procedures deemed necessary to support the degree of reliance the auditor intends to place on an internal control, remains a matter of professional judgement. It is obvious that if no reliance on an internal control is intended, there is no need to perform tests of control procedures, and common sense dictates that the more reliance the auditor seeks from an internal control, the more evidence of its effective operation is needed. It is important to bear in mind the principle that where two or more internal controls are designed to achieve a common objective, it would normally be sufficient to perform tests on only one of them. In these circumstances the control tested is often referred to as a key control.

10.2.3 Period covered by tests of control

The auditor should obtain adequate assurance about the effective operation of an internal control throughout the intended period of reliance. If the tests are conducted at an interim period, the auditor will have to gain assurance about the operation of that control during the subsequent period, which has not been tested. Factors which the auditor would need to consider are the results of earlier audit tests of control; whether the control procedure has been changed during the remaining period; and evidence of the effective operation of that control obtained by other procedures, such as analytical reviews, cut-off and roll-forward tests or other substantive audit procedures.

10.2.4 Using the work of internal auditors in tests of controls

Guidance is provided in SAAS 610, 'Considering the work of the internal audit', on the use of an internal auditor's work in tests of controls, namely, that the external auditor should evaluate and test the work of the internal auditor before placing reliance on it. The external auditor should gain an understanding of the scope of the internal audit activities and the structure and independence of the internal audit function.

The responsibilities of internal auditors in an organization frequently involve reporting on the efficiency, effectiveness and economy of the internal control activities of the entity. The external auditor should coordinate the internal and external audit activities by discussing with the internal auditor the internal control tests and reviews performed during the current financial year and inspect reports regarding important areas recently audited by the internal auditors. Before using the work of the internal auditor in tests of controls, the auditor needs to consider the following:

- the organizational status of the internal auditor;
- the scope of the internal audit function;
- the technical competence of the internal auditor and of the staff performing the tests of controls;
- the effectiveness of reporting lines to management;
- whether the work done is properly planned, performed and documented; and
- whether the audit evidence obtained reasonably supports the conclusions drawn.

10.3 ASSESSING CONTROL RISK IN AN IT ENVIRONMENT

10.3.1 General principles

SAAS 401, 'Auditing in a Computer Information Systems Environment', indicates in paragraph .09 that:

> 'When the IT systems are significant the auditor should obtain an understanding of the IT environment and whether or not it may influence the assessment of inherent and control risks.'

In paragraph .10:

> 'In accordance with the statement of SAAS 400 'Risk Assessments and Internal Control', the auditor should make an assessment of the inherent and control risks for material assertions in the financial statement assertions.'

And further, in paragraph .13:

> 'In accordance with the statement of SAAS 400 'Risk Assessments and Internal Control', the auditor should consider the IT environment in designing audit procedures to reduce audit risk to an acceptable level.'

To address these principles and assess inherent and control risk in a computerized environment, both *general* and *application* controls need to be considered in order to identify whether there are specific controls on which the auditor wishes to place reliance and which therefore need to be tested. As indicated in Figure 10.3 below, controls in an IT environment will comprise manual *user controls* and *programmed controls*.

- A *user control* may be defined as any control where the user is responsible for the completeness, accuracy or authorization of a system's output, and would include users from different departments in a business, as indicated in Figure 10.3.
- A *programmed control* may be defined as any control built into the application system to ensure completeness, accuracy or authorization of transaction recording.

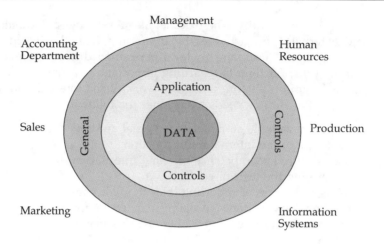

Figure 10.3 Control in an IT environment

Before relying on programmed controls, the auditor needs to ensure that the computer program on which the control depends is operating properly. Programmed controls depend on three components:

- access component
- system development and program change, and
- manual follow-up component.

Inadvertent reliance

Inadvertent reliance occurs when an auditor reduces substantive procedures without properly testing the underlying controls, or uses reports without first establishing an 'audit base' through substantive or compliance testing. Inadvertent reliance can occur as a result of any of the following situations:

- Misidentification of user controls.
- Use of IT generated reports.
- Use of IT generated reports outside of the reliance information systems, such as reports generated from a data warehouse.
- When output from a computer system is accepted as being complete, accurate and valid without first verifying that this is the case.
- A perception that the computer 'does not make mistakes'. It is as well to recognize that the computer does what it is programmed to do, and programmed errors, potentially, will be replicated on every transaction.
- An assumption that programmed controls are correct.
- End-user computing environments where the calculations on spreadsheet applications of users which have not been validated are used as the basis for input to the computer system.

The existence of the IT environment does not change the specific audit objectives, but the methods used to verify the effectiveness of the controls will be affected by the particular system in use. (Refer to chapter 9 for an extensive discussion of the various IT environments that might be encountered.) The auditor can use either manual audit procedures, or CAATs, or a combination of these to obtain sufficient appropriate audit evidence. Two approaches are recognized in the audit of computerized accounting systems: firstly, auditing *'around the computer'* and, secondly, auditing *'through the computer'*.

Auditing around the computer

The assessment of control risks and the selection and performance of tests of controls by *'auditing around the computer'* involves the auditor in testing and assessing the effectiveness of the *manual user controls*. This is the case whether these are general controls or controls over input to and output from particular accounting applications. The purpose of testing and assessing manual user controls is to ensure the *completeness, measurement/accuracy* and *occurrence/validity* of the particular class of transactions or balances. Technological developments such as on-line data entry, the elimination or reduction of printouts and real-time updating have largely rendered this approach obsolete, except for the small stand-alone PC environments often encountered in small to medium-sized owner managed businesses.

Examples of general controls could include evidence of the enforcement of policies and procedures for controlling access to computer systems and data, reviews of exception reports and correction of errors and resubmission of transaction input data. An example of application controls could be manual controls over the submission of batch data for input and subsequent comparison to the printouts resulting from the application run.

Auditing through the computer

It may not be possible to perform some audit procedures manually, because they rely on complex processing or involve huge volumes of data, or for which no hard copy evidence is available. This may occur at different stages in the business cycle:

- Source information may be initiated electronically, such as by voice activation, electronic imaging, or point of sale electronic funds transfer.
- Some transactions may be generated directly by computer programs without any specific authorization, such as interest calculations for clients' investment and savings accounts in a bank.
- A system may not generate a visible audit trail, although programmed control procedures are still performed. The only hard copy evidence of this may be an exception report, for example customer credit limits exceeded.
- A system may not produce detailed hard copy reports but simply summary reports with details maintained in computer files.

In these circumstances, the auditor will need to *'audit through the computer'* in order to gather evidence regarding the effective design and operation of controls. In 'auditing through the computer' the auditor is involved in using CAATs to test the *computerized or programmed controls* – whether general controls, or application controls over input, processing and output from particular accounting applications – in order to assess the effectiveness of the controls and ensure that only authorized transactions are processed and all such transactions are accurately processed and recorded. In other words, the auditor ascertains that computerized or programmed controls meet the audit objectives and assertions of *completeness, measurement/accuracy* and *occurrence/validity* for the significant classes of transactions or balances. Even where the approach is to 'audit through the computer', the auditor may still need to follow up on any manual detective controls around the output from the application processing, such as the review of exception reports and financial reports generated.

Effect of the IT environment on the assessment of inherent and control risk

As indicated earlier, the preliminary assessment of inherent and control risk or risk of significant misstatement as *high, medium or low* depends on whether the auditor is able to identify general or application controls as being appropriately designed and operating throughout the period of intended reliance and for significant classes of transactions and balances on which the auditor wishes to or needs to place reliance, by virtue of the complexity of the IT environment. The principles discussed earlier in this chapter do not change at all. The risk assessment in the IT environment will thus be part of the overall control risk assessment or risk of significant misstatement made for the particular class of transactions or balances.

If appropriate control procedures are identified, the auditor will need to select those he or she wishes to test and perform the necessary tests of controls.

10.3.2 General controls and tests of controls

As discussed in the previous chapter, the general controls include:

- organization and operation controls;
- systems development and documentation controls;
- hardware and system software controls;
- access controls; and
- data and procedural controls.

In sophisticated computerized environments such as integrated database systems with networked topologies and remote access for on-line real-time transactions, the general controls may be critical to ensure that risk of significant misstatement is controlled. In such circumstances, the auditor will need to identify the preventative and detective controls over the different general control areas. This is necessary, since effectiveness of the design and operation need to be tested in order to address the particular risks arising during the period under review, for example: the controls exercised by a security administrator in granting, to personnel, password access to different parts of the database, and procedures to ensure password access is disabled immediately an employee resigns or is fired. The auditor will invariably require the involvement of IT specialists to perform such tests and, where the relevant controls are programmed controls, it may be necessary to use CAATs to perform the tests of controls. Aspects of the general controls will be identified in the course of gaining an understanding of the business, specifically related to the type of IT information systems used by the client.

10.3.3 Application controls and tests of controls

The purpose of application controls is to establish specific control procedures over the accounting applications in order to provide reasonable assurance that all transactions are *authorized* and recorded and are processed *completely*, *accurately* and on a timely basis. This involves both manual processes and controls, and computerized processes and controls, that may be carried out by IT personnel, users or programmed into the application software. Different controls are implemented at the three stages of *input, processing* and *output* to identify the control objectives, which may be presented by the following matrix:

CONTROL OBJECTIVES	Completeness	Measurement/ Accuracy	Occurrence/ Validity
Transaction stage			
Input			
Process			
Output			

Table 10.2 Application controls: Matrix for the input, process and output stages of transactions

Application risks which may be encountered include:

- Weak security
- Unauthorized access to data
- Unauthorized remote access
- Inaccurate information
- Erroneous or falsified data input
- Misuse by authorized end-users
- Incomplete processing
- Duplicate transactions
- Untimely processing
- Communications systems failure
- Inadequate training
- Inadequate support

In order to identify the controls to test for any significant class of transactions or balances, the auditor will need to ascertain:

- which controls are manual versus programmed controls;
- where are the risk points for the particular class of transactions or balances;
- what controls are present at each stage of the application, that is, input, process and output; and
- how is *completeness, measurement/accuracy* and *validity/occurrence* achieved?

Controls that would typically be found in an IT environment and which the auditor may wish to test could include the following:

INPUT CONTROLS		
Completeness	Accuracy/Measurement	Validity/Occurrence

• Sequence checks
• Batch control procedures and reconciliation over number of items captured
• Visual review of source data
• Data capture and preparation controls
	• Screen formats and re-keying of data captured
	• Batch controls over amounts and account allocations
	• Input validation checks:
	  – Code tests
	  – Value tests
	  – Limit tests
	  – Check digit
	  – Echo checks
	  – Reasonableness tests
	• Transaction log for control total and reference lists
		• Terminal Security:
		  – Passwords
		  – Physical restriction
		• Dedicated terminals for data capture
		• Visible evidence of authorization – signatures of authorized personnel
		• Segregation of personnel with incompatible duties, namely as between:
		  – Segregation
		  – Custody
		  – Recording
		  – Authorization
		  – Management supervision
		• Supervisory review

Table 10.3 Controls over input in an IT environment to meet the related assertions

PROCESSING CONTROLS		
Completeness	**Accuracy/Measure-ment**	**Validity/Occurrence**
Controls to detect loss of data: • Record counts • Control totals • Hash totals *Maintenance of data:* • Reconcile file totals after a processing run • Regular comparison of master file balances to physical • Review of results *Standing data amendments and maintenance:* • One on one comparisons of changes • Batch totals • Reconciliation to manual control account • Detailed comparison and vouching of standing data to source documents and files.	*Controls to ensure accuracy of updating:* • Update correct generation of master files • Check file set-up • Check brought forward totals • Manual agreement of computer established totals • Run to run controls • Limit and reasonableness checks • Cross-footing and arithmetic computation • Overflow exception reporting	*Controls over data storage, maintenance and retrieval:* • File labelling – internal and external • Computer updating process • Audit trails • Database controls over access • Administration of database and data directory • Hash totals

Table 10.4   Controls over processing in an IT environment to meet the related assertions

Output Controls

IT outputs from a business process will typically comprise:

• *Transaction documentation*, such as sales invoices, statements, pay slips and cheques.

• *Financial reports*, such as detailed transaction listings, account balances and analyses, for example, a list of accounts receivable, inventory and fixed assets, general ledger printouts, quarterly management accounts, and annual financial statements.

- *Management information reports*, for example, operational reports, production reports, reports on control activities and key performance indicators, and reports supporting decision making aspects, such as budgets, cashflows, etc.

Consequently, the aspects where controls are likely to be implemented relate to the distribution of the output, the higher level reconciliation and review by users, including management, and controls over error handling procedures. Output controls that would typically be found in an IT environment and which the auditor may decide to test could include the following:

OUTPUT CONTROLS		
Output handling procedures	**Manual user procedures**	**Error handling procedures**
Printouts: • Distribution checklist • Transmittal sheets • Distribution log • Report release forms • Passwords • Physical access *Exception reports:* • Specify the number/ frequency • Format of presentation defined • Distribution to persons responsible for inquiring and rectifying errors and exceptions • Method of follow-up specified and persons responsible identified	*Completeness and accuracy / measurement:* • Check that what was received is what was ordered • Ensure the reports received are complete by reference to input data, source documents, cut-off information • Review the printouts for abnormalities • Reconcile computer batch totals with manual compiled totals • Reconcile computer totals with physical source documents and input control sheets • Perform reasonableness tests — key performance indicators	• Ensure that items on exception or error reports are promptly: – Investigated – Corrected – Re-submitted • Adjust previously established control totals • Scrutinizing rejection lists • Checking and controlling rejections • Control, monitor and analyse errors • Investigate reasons for exceptions

Output to electronic media: • Controls over distribution to networked computers • Via Internet to remote sites • Output to printers located at remote sites • Files saved onto hard drives, disks and tapes	• Perform in-depth tests	

Table 10.5 Controls over output in an IT environment

10.3.4 End-user computing controls

The computing power of PCs and the versatility of package spreadsheet programs have rapidly increased the use of spreadsheets by end users for a variety of purposes, many of which may seem to be relatively straightforward due to their widespread use. There are, however, significant risks present in end-user applications where management is relying on spreadsheets for decision-making. Accordingly, the auditor needs to ascertain the extent of end-user usage to assess the risk of material misstatement for any significant transactions or balances. Controls that the auditor would look for as being present to minimize the risks include[1]:

• *Analysis:* understanding the requirements before building the spreadsheet;
• *Design review:* review by peers or system professionals;
• *Documentation:* formulas, macro commands, and any changes to the spreadsheet;
• *Verification of logic:* reasonableness checks and comparison with known outputs;
• *Extent of training:* formal training in spreadsheet design and implementation;
• *Extent of audit:* informal design review or formal audit procedures;
• *Support commitment:* ongoing application maintenance and support from IT personnel.

These controls relate primarily to the spreadsheet design and use. However, the auditor should also consider the effectiveness of established general controls, such as policies and procedures aimed at preventing or curbing, for example, the theft of confidential data; the risk of viruses; time wasted by

---

[1] Gallegos, Manson & Allen-Senft (1999), *Information Technology Control and Audit*, page 174.

employees in devising new spreadsheets when standard spreadsheet files are available; the use of erroneous accounting data (for example, incomplete or inaccurate data downloaded into the spreadsheet for decision modelling); and the risk of inappropriate or insufficient backup procedures.

10.3.5 Computer-assisted audit techniques (CAATs)

When planning an audit, the auditor may consider an appropriate combination of manual and computer-assisted audit techniques. Factors to consider in deciding to use CAATs include:

- the IT knowledge and experience of the audit team;
- the availability of CAATs and suitable computer facilities and data;
- the impracticability of manual tests; and
- the effectiveness and efficiency; and
- the timing.

Before using CAATs, the auditor should consider the controls incorporated in the design of the entity's computer systems to which CAATs could be applied, in order to determine whether CAATs should be employed and, if so, how. CAATs may be used, for example, for performing tests of *general controls*, such as testing the set-up or configuration of the operating system, or access procedures to program libraries, or by using code comparison software to check that the version of the program in use is the version approved by management. CAATs may also be used for performing tests of *application controls*, such as testing the functioning of a programmed control in a particular application.

SAAPS 1009, 'Computerized assisted audit techniques (CAATs)', provides guidance on the nature and type of CAATs, practical considerations in the use of CAATs, steps to be followed in applying CAATs, as well as controlling the application, documentation of the planning, execution and audit evidence, and the use of CAATs in a small entity environment.

SAAPS 1009, 'Computerized assisted audit techniques', in paragraph .05 describes CAATs as 'computer programs and data the auditor uses as part of the audit procedures to process data of audit significance contained in a entity's information systems.' The data may be transaction data on which the auditor wishes to perform tests of controls or substantive procedures (see next chapter), or it may be other types of data, such as the security files relating to access to the program libraries. The auditor can then use CAATs to review and gain evidence of the existence and operation of those programs. The nature and types of CAATs commonly used are described in detail in paragraph .05 (SAAPS 1009). A discussion follows below.

Nature and type of CAATs

CAATs may be package programs, purpose written programs, utility programs and system management programs. Regardless of the origin of the programs, the auditor must substantiate their appropriateness and validity for audit purposes before using them.

- *Package programs* are generalized programs designed to perform data processing functions, such as reading data, selecting and analysing information, performing calculations, creating data files and reporting in a format specified by the auditor. Four leading software packages used by auditors are ACL, DIAL, SAS and IDEA, which can be used on either a mainframe or microcomputer platform.

- *Purpose written programs* perform audit tasks in specific circumstances.

- *Utility programs* are used by an entity to perform common data processing functions, such as sorting, creating and printing files.

- *System management programs* are enhanced productivity tools that are typically part of a sophisticated operating systems environment, for example, data retrieval software or code comparison software.

Audit testing techniques that may be used for tests of controls are discussed below.

Embedded audit routines

Embedded audit routines are sometimes built into an entity's systems to provide data for later use by the auditor. These will generally be used in circumstances where the volumes of transactions are huge and an on-line real-time or batch update environment is in use, such as the use of auto teller machines by banks with their on-line, memo and batch update processing. These include:

- *'Snapshots'* of a transaction as it flows through the computer systems. Audit software routines are embedded at different points in the processing logic to capture images of the transaction as it progresses through the various stages.

- *System control audit review file (SCARF)* involves embedded audit software modules within an application system to provide continuous monitoring of the system's transactions. The information is collected into a special computer file that the auditor can then examine.

Test data techniques

Test data techniques are sometimes used during an audit by entering data into an entity's computer system and comparing the results obtained with predetermined results. The auditor may use test data to:

- test specific controls in computer programs, such as on-line password and data access controls;
- test transactions selected from previously processed transactions to test specific processing characteristics of an entity's information systems; and

- test transactions in an *integrated test facility* where a 'dummy' unit (for example, a fictitious department) is established and to which test transactions are posted during the normal processing cycle.

Invalid and valid data are included and if application controls are functioning properly the client's programs should detect all erroneous data introduced into the test data, for example, invalid codes, negative values and Rand amounts in excess of the amount set for limit or reasonability checks. To be effective, the test data must be designed to test each 'programmed' control the auditor intends to rely on. This requires an intelligent imagination and technical proficiency on the part of the auditor when preparing test data for, say, the inclusion of invalid data so that the test data deliberately tests the design and operation of the controls and its adequacy in detecting the problem.

However, a previously mentioned problem remains: while the test data approach provides information about the design of the particular control at that point in time, it does not provide assurance that the client has run the same programs throughout the period subject to audit. The auditor may have difficulty obtaining satisfaction in this regard, even if the client does have available for audit various computerized operating logs on program runs, controls over program changes and the use of the appropriate application program for any particular transaction run.

The use of test data, and the deliberate entry of invalid data, create the risk that the client's accounting information systems may become corrupted. Consequently, all test data used must be clearly tagged so as to identify the transactions for subsequent removal from the client's systems. For this reason, in most cases the client will not permit the introduction of test data into the live accounting environment and the test data will have to be run in a test environment. In all instances when test data is processed with the entity's normal processing, the auditor must ensure that the test transactions are subsequently eliminated from the entity's accounting records.

Simulation or parallel processing

In simulation or parallel processing the auditor either uses a purpose written program, possibly using a fourth-generation language, or a general-purpose package program, which simulates the client's program being tested. Client-prepared input is processed, using the auditor's program, and if the client's controls have been operating effectively, the client's program should have generated the same exceptions as the auditor's program. Parallel processing is similar to using test data, except that the auditor controls the program rather than the input. As is the case with test data, this approach provides no assurance that the client's programs simulated by the auditor were used throughout the audit period. The technique is further limited by the difficulty of adequately simulating client application programs, particularly in the case of large applications and the substantial costs involved.

Code reviewing and flowcharting

When performing program code reviews and flow-chart checking, the auditor studies the client's documentation supporting computer programs with the objective of determining what controls have been prescribed and how they have been built into the programs.

Code reviews involve the analysis of program code source listings line by line, whereas flowcharting involves the analysis of the diagram, which shows the logic flow through a computer program.

The documentation of programs which depict controls do not provide the auditor with sufficient evidence that the controls shown represent functioning controls in the program and that these are actually being used for processing transaction data. For this reason, reviews of program documentation do not on their own meet the auditor's objective of ascertaining that the controls, on which reliance is intended, functioned effectively throughout the audit period. The technique is useful, however, in obtaining an understanding of purported controls within computer programs and can assist the auditor greatly in designing simulated transaction data that will adequately test controls using the other techniques described above.

Other audit tools

The power and sophistication of laptops have resulted in other tools for the auditor to use. In most of the medium to large firms, all audit staff will be required to have laptops for use on the audit. In some cases these will be linked back to the audit firm's main computer systems and database. Examples of the tools commonly used are:

- *Expert systems*, for example, in the design of audit programs and in audit planning and risk assessment, knowledge databases for different businesses.
- *Tools to evaluate* a client's risk management procedures, including typical key sectors, as well as the firm's audit manual, and performance indicators for a variety of business sectors.
- *Electronic working papers* as discussed in chapter 8, which provide for the direct extraction of data from the client's computer records, for example, downloading the general ledger for audit testing; and standard documentation templates for use on audits.
- *Corporate and financial modelling programs* for use as predictive audit tests.

10.4 EVALUATING EVIDENCE FROM TESTS OF CONTROL AND ASSESSING CONTROL RISK

SAAS 400, 'Risk assessments and internal control', in paragraph .31, states:

'Based on the tests of control, the auditor should evaluate whether or not the internal controls are designed and operating as contemplated in the preliminary assessment of internal control risk.'

Paragraph .36 has the following to say about the final assessment of control risk:

> 'Before the conclusion of the audit based on the results of substantive procedures and other audit evidence obtained, the auditor should conclude whether, or not, the assessment of control risk is confirmed.'

The evaluation of deviations from the laid-down control procedure is important in determining the extent to which reliance can be placed on an internal control. A deviation occurs when an internal control procedure has not been applied correctly, whether or not a quantitative error has occurred. The objective of tests of control procedures is to obtain satisfaction regarding the operation of an internal control, in contrast to a substantive procedure, which provides evidence directly related to a particular assertion. For this reason, the frequency, nature and causes of all deviations from the prescribed procedure and their possible impact on other areas of the audit should be considered by the auditor when considering the extent of reliance to be placed on an internal control, regardless of the amount of error or lack thereof in recording as a result of the deviation.

Careful investigation of deviations might reveal, for example, that deviations detected only occurred while a particular staff member was on annual vacation. Reliance on the effective operation of the control would therefore be justified for the rest of the year. This issue becomes particularly significant in a computerized accounting environment when the failure of a particular internal control built into a computer program could lead to the same error recurring with every transaction processed. Numerous examples of computer fraud perpetrated in this manner are quoted in the literature.

If tests of control procedures reveal that certain controls are not operating effectively, the auditor should consider the types of error or fraud which could arise as a result of the failure of those control procedures, leading to significant misstatement in the financial statements and modify the nature, timing and extent of the planned substantive procedures to reflect not only the lower level of reliance to be placed on those controls (higher control risk), but also to detect any material errors which may have occurred and were not detected or corrected by the system.

In these circumstances the substantive procedures performed should be specifically designed to detect the error or fraud not corrected by the system and should be linked to the relevant financial statement assertion affected. Depending on the assertion affected, the detection of the error or fraud may, for example, involve reperformance of reconciliations of general ledger accounts to underlying source documents or calculations to verify the *completeness* and *measurement/accuracy* of amounts recorded; sequence tests, using CAATs, to identify duplicated or omitted sales or purchase transactions; confirmations of customers to identify erroneous charges – although this is more likely to obtain a response where the error is to the customer's disadvantage.

Tests of control, when they yield satisfactory results, provide evidence that the auditor is justified in relying on the preliminary assessment of control risk. Conversely, substantive tests, which reveal errors, would ordinarily require a reassessment of control risk and inherent risk if these were assessed as low in the preliminary assessment.

This approach recognizes that the auditor's objective in studying testing and evaluating controls is ancillary to the primary objective of reporting on the financial statements and is therefore a means to an end, namely, to obtain sufficient appropriate audit evidence to support the audit opinion. To expend audit effort enquiring into, documenting, testing and evaluating internal controls other than those on which the auditor intends to rely to reduce audit risk and, by implication, the extent of substantive testing required, is effort wasted.

If the accounting system is such that the auditor concludes that no reliance may be placed on controls to prevent, or detect and correct material errors, the auditor should determine what types of errors or fraud could occur as a result of the control weaknesses, and design appropriate substantive audit procedures that would detect such errors or fraud should they indeed have occurred.

10.5 COMMUNICATION OF WEAKNESSES

10.5.1 Communication of weaknesses in internal controls

SAAS 400, 'Risk assessments and internal control', in paragraph .46, indicates that as a result of obtaining an understanding of the accounting and internal control systems and the tests of controls, the auditor may become aware of weaknesses in the systems. The stated principle is that:

> 'The auditor should make management aware, as soon as practical, and at an appropriate level of responsibility, of material weaknesses in the design and operation of the accounting and internal control systems that have come to the auditor's attention.'

There are several important aspects that an auditor needs to consider when communicating weaknesses detected during the preliminary review and subsequent tests of controls performed in the ordinary course of the financial statement audit. Several aspects are discussed below.

Weaknesses identified in the design and operation of controls are likely to relate specifically to the financial statement assertions that the auditor is attempting to gain assurance about through the tests of controls and, consequently, will not necessarily include all general or application control weaknesses present in the particular class of transactions or balances. The auditor will have to address specifically any false expectations of the client that the report deals comprehensively with all controls over particular key business processes and classes of transactions.

The potential impact of such weaknesses, on additional procedures that the client or auditor may need to perform in order to be able to finalize the preparation and audit of the annual financial statements, must be considered and discussed with the appropriate level of management. It may be necessary for additional staff to be assigned to the audit, or for staff with particular skills and expertise to be employed by the client to investigate the weaknesses and perform the additional procedures deemed necessary to rectify errors, and to design and implement more effective controls.

The control weaknesses identified may lead to a suspicion that material fraud may be occurring or that material irregularities exist. Should the auditor's suspicions be roused, in order to comply with SAAS 240, 'Fraud and Error', the matter must be investigated further to ascertain the source, nature and extent of the suspected fraud and, if possible, to identify the parties involved. The auditor may also consider it necessary to involve forensic audit staff in an investigation. Should this situation arise, the auditor should first discuss it with the client at a senior management level, possibly the board of directors or the audit committee. The auditor will then also need to consider whether a material irregularity has occurred or is likely to occur and, if so, the extent of his or her reporting responsibilities in terms of section 20(5) of the Public Accountants' and Auditors' Act.

In circumstances where the client has outsourced certain transactions – for example, payroll processing – and weaknesses are then identified, the auditor should identify whether these are occurring in the client's organization or at the outsource provider. By inquiry and examination of the terms of the service level agreement, the auditor should determine the appropriate action and by whom it should be taken. It may be necessary to request the auditors of the outsource provider to review controls at the outsource provider to establish the precise nature and extent of the weaknesses and potential impact on the client's financial statements.

The weaknesses identified may also present the auditor with an opportunity for value added services to the client. This could take the form of a detailed review and evaluation of the system of internal controls over the particular transactions or key processes, and include the auditor's recommendations for improvements to the client. This comprises a separate related services engagement, however, and care should be taken that the auditor's independence is not compromised. To this end, staff from the auditing firm involved in the related service engagement should not be the same persons as those involved in performing the financial statement audit.

10.5.2 Communication of audit matters to those charged with governance

Matters may come to the attention of the auditor in the course of testing and evaluating management's control activities, and in assessing the risk of significant misstatement in the financial statement that relates to audit matters of governance interest. Paragraph .02 of SAAS 730, 'Communications of audit matters with those charged with governance', states the principle as follows:

> 'The auditor should communicate audit matters of governance interest arising from the audit of financial statements with those charged with governance of an entity.'

Paragraph 06 indicates:

> 'The auditor should determine the relevant persons who are charged with governance and with whom audit matters of governance interest are communicated.'

The form of governance of entities is very diverse, not only from one entity to the other, but also as between one country and another. In order to avoid misunderstandings, the auditor may well reach agreement with management and include in the engagement letter the terms regarding the form of communication, the relevant persons to whom audit matters of governance should be reported and, additionally, any specific aspects which the parties have agreed will be communicated in such report. It must be made clear that audit matters are only those identified in the ordinary course of the financial statement audit, and that the auditor is not required to design specific audit procedures for the purpose of identifying matters of corporate governance.

The King II Report (2002) recommends that an audit committee should be appointed for public listed companies and public sector entities. Where such a committee exists, the external auditor's report may be addressed to, and presented at a meeting of, the audit committee. In other circumstances, the report may be addressed to the full board of directors, or to the owner of a business (in the case of an owner-managed business), or to the board of trustees (in the case of not-for-profit companies). In some public sector entities, such a report may be presented to the auditor-general.

Paragraph .12 of SAAS 730 identifies the following as matters which might be included in such report:

- 'The general approach and overall scope of the audit, including any expected limitations thereon, or any additional requirements.
- The selection of, or changes in, significant accounting policies or practices that have, or could have a material effect on the financial statements.
- The potential effect on the financial statements of any significant risks and exposures, such as pending litigation, that are required to be disclosed in the financial statements.
- Audit adjustments whether or not recorded by the entity that have, or could have, a significant effect on the entity's financial statements.
- Material uncertainties related to events and conditions that may cast doubt on the entity's ability to continue as a going concern.
- Disagreements with management about matters that, individually or in aggregate, could be significant to the entity's financial statements or the

auditors report. These communications include consideration of whether the matter has, or has not, been resolved and the significance of the matter.
- Expected modifications to the auditor's report.
- Other matters, warranting attention by those charged with governance, such as material weaknesses in internal control, questions regarding management integrity and fraud involving management.
- Any other matters agreed upon in terms of the audit engagement.'

The timing of the auditor's communications will depend on the nature of the matters communicated. In normal circumstances, the communication will be made at the conclusion of the audit; in other instances, where a matter is identified as being significant and requiring urgent attention or action, the auditor should communicate it to top management as soon as possible.

The communication may be made orally or in writing. Factors to be considered are:

- the size, operating structure, legal structure, and communications processes of the entity being audited;
- the nature, sensitivity and significance of the audit matters of governance being communicated;
- the arrangements made with respect to periodic meetings or reporting of audit matters of governance interest; and
- the amount of ongoing contact and dialogue the auditor has with those charged with governance.

Where the communication is made orally at a meeting, it is appropriate to follow this up with written minutes of the meeting to record matters reported and management's responses thereto. The communication of the matters in the form of a written report ordinarily are preceded with an initial discussion with management regarding the matters to be included therein, except where the matters relate to questions of management competence and integrity. The purpose of the initial discussion is to clarify facts and issues, and to give management an opportunity to provide further information. Particular laws and regulations may require the external auditor to communicate governance related matters to management and may specify the form and content of such communications.

The auditor should bear in mind the requirements of the Code of Professional Conduct, issued by both SAICA and the PAAB, or existing laws and regulations regarding confidentiality of matters being reported and any potential conflicts of interest that might arise. Where necessary, the auditor may wish to seek legal advice before submitting the communication on audit matters of governance to the entity.

11

Detection Risk and the Design of Substantive Tests

Learning objectives

After studying this chapter you should be able to:

1. Explain the interrelationship between inherent, control and detection risk and how this affects the planned level of substantive tests.
2. Explain how the nature, timing and extent of substantive tests may be varied to achieve the desired level of detection risk.
3. Discuss how the risk of significant misstatement in significant classes of transactions and balances is determined and the factors to be considered.
4. Explain how the auditor links the risk of significant misstatement in significant classes of transactions and balances to the appropriate substantive audit procedures to detect and correct potential misstatements in the financial statements.
5. Discuss the factors the auditor must consider in determining the nature, timing and extent of substantive audit procedures.
6. Discuss the nature of analytical review procedures and factors to be considered in determining their reliability as audit evidence.
7. Discuss the nature of substantive tests of detail of transactions and balances and considerations in determining the timing and extent of such tests.
8. Explain how the auditor uses computer assisted audit techniques (CAATs) to conduct substantive tests of balances and transactions.
9. Discuss the relationships between the financial statement assertions, potential misstatements, specific audit objectives and substantive tests.
10. Describe the nature and uses of audit programmes for substantive tests.
11. Discuss and prepare substantive audit programmes for first-time audit engagements.

12. Describe the considerations for the design of substantive audit programmes for particular circumstances.

11.1 DETERMINING AN ACCEPTABLE LEVEL OF DETECTION RISK

11.1.1 Introduction and principles

Detection Risk is defined in SAAS 400, 'Risk Assessments and Internal Control', paragraph .03, as:

> 'The risk that an auditor's substantive procedures *will not detect a misstatement* that exists in an account balance or class of transactions that could be material, individually or when aggregated with misstatements in other balances or classes of transactions.'

It is clear from this stated principle that detection risk is reduced by the *effectiveness* of the auditor's substantive audit procedures in detecting significant misstatement, in particular assertions contained in transactions and balances reflected in the financial statements. The level to which detection risk must be reduced is dependent on the auditor's combined assessment of inherent and control risks. Such assessments thus influence the nature, timing and extent of substantive tests to be performed to reduce detection risk and therefore audit risk to an acceptable level.

SAAS 400, 'Risk Assessments and Internal Control', at paragraph .39 states as a principle that:

> 'The auditor should consider the assessed levels of inherent and control risks in determining the nature, timing and extent of substantive procedures required to reduce audit risk to an acceptable level.'

In addition, materiality considerations must be taken into account as they directly affect the auditor's decision regarding the significance of the potential misstatements, nature and extent of substantive tests to be performed and the sufficiency of audit evidence obtained. Readers are referred to chapter 5 for a detailed discussion on audit risk and materiality.

Interrelationship between Components of Audit Risk		Control Risk assessed as:		
		High	Medium	Low
Inherent Risk assessed as:	High	Lowest	Lower	Medium
	Medium	Lower	Medium	Higher
	Low	Medium	Higher	Highest
		Acceptable level of Detection Risk		

Table 11.1 The interrelationship between the components of Audit Risk

(Source: SAAS 400, 'Risk assessments and internal control', Appendix.)

The relationship between the assessment of *Inherent Risk (IR), Control Risk (CR)* and *Detection Risk (DR)* is represented above and is referred to as the *Audit Risk Model*. The inverse relationship of the detection risk component may be reflected as follows:

$$DR = \frac{AR}{IR \times CR}$$

There is an inverse relationship between *Detection Risk* and the combined level of *Inherent Risk* and *Control Risk*. For example, when the *Inherent Risk* and *Control Risk* for a significant class of transactions or balances are assessed as *High*, *Detection Risk* needs to be reduced to a *Low* level so as to achieve an acceptable level of audit risk. This principle is stated in SAAS 400, 'Risk Assessments and Internal Control', paragraph .44:

> 'The higher the assessment of inherent and control risk, the more audit evidence the auditor should obtain from the performance of substantive audit procedures.'

What is particularly important here is that the substantive tests performed are appropriately designed to obtain sufficient appropriate audit evidence regarding the financial statement assertions, for the particular class of transactions or balances, where there is potential risk for significant misstatement due to the combined inherent and control risk final assessment.

On the other hand, where both inherent and control risks are assessed as *Low*, *detection risk* can be accepted at a *high* level. This means that the auditor requires only a limited amount of audit evidence from substantive audit procedures in order to support the financial statement assertions. As a consequence, the auditor may perform only analytical procedures on the particular class of transactions or balances to achieve an acceptable level of *audit risk*.

Attempts to allocate numbers or weightings to the various components of the audit risk model have been unsuccessful. The norm is to assess risk using the terms *High, Medium or Moderate, and Low* to denote the risk conditions assessed in the case of *inherent* and *control risks*, and the level of risk acceptable in the case of *detection risk*.

SAAS 400, 'Risk Assessments and Internal Control', paragraph .42, states as a principle that:

> 'Regardless of the assessed level of inherent and control risks, the auditor should perform some substantive procedures on material account balances and classes of transactions.'

In order to limit *detection risk* in circumstances where material misstatements arising through fraud by management are indicated, the auditor needs to design specific audit procedures that will address the risks identified and ensure sufficient, appropriate audit evidence is obtained to mitigate such risks.

Audit strategy or audit approach decisions are taken at the planning stage of the audit when deciding the most effective and efficient means of gathering the audit evidence needed to justify the opinion. An important decision that needs to be taken is the mix between reliance on the systems, requiring the performance of tests of controls and substantive testing. The planned approach or strategy, however, may have to be changed as a result of evidence gathered from the performance of tests of controls. The audit approach or strategy may be revised as follows:

Where tests of controls yield satisfactory results, higher levels of detection risks are acceptable, justifying more audit evidence being gathered from substantive analytical procedures and less from tests of details; or conversely

Where tests of controls yield unsatisfactory results, a lower level of detection risk is required, necessitating more audit evidence from tests of detail and relying less on analytical procedures performed.

Should the auditor be unable to obtain sufficient appropriate audit evidence from the combined tests of control and substantive tests, this may constitute a scope restriction, and depending on the materiality of the potential misstatement, the auditor should consider the impact on the audit opinion. This responsibility is stated in paragraph .44 of SAAS 400, as follows:

> 'When the auditor determines that detection risk regarding a financial statement assertion for a material account balance or significant class of transactions cannot be reduced to an acceptable low level, the auditor should express a qualified opinion or a disclaimer of opinion.'

This leads then to the question of how the auditor assesses the risk of significant misstatement remaining in the financial statements after all reasonable audit procedures have been carried out?

11.1.2 Assessing the risk of significant misstatement

Whilst the preparation of the financial statements on which the auditor is reporting is the responsibility of management, paragraph.13 of SAAS 700, 'Auditor's Report on Financial Statements', requires that the scope paragraph in the unmodified audit report state, *inter alia*, that 'the financial statements are *free of material misstatements'*. In order to limit the auditor's detection risk, the auditor needs firstly to assess the risk of significant misstatements arising through fraud or error remaining in the audited financial statements; then the auditor needs to design specific audit procedures that will address the risks identified and ensure sufficient and appropriate audit evidence is obtained. In this way the auditor manages the risk of expressing an inappropriate or incorrect audit opinion through obtaining sufficient appropriate audit evidence.

In applying the 'top-down' approach to the audit, the risks of significant misstatement will have been identified in the course of gaining an understanding of the key processes and process level risks for the core processes of the business, as discussed in chapters 9 and 10. When making decisions about the substantive procedures needed, for each audit objective the auditor must assess the risk of significant misstatement remaining in the financial statements, arising from key business process level risks for each significant class of transactions and balances. This is necessary if the auditor is to determine the detection risk and nature and extent of substantive audit procedures to be performed.

The following factors provide a useful basis for evaluating, for each audit objective selected, the overall risk of significant misstatements remaining (assessed as *high, medium or low*) for each significant class of transactions and balances arising from key business process level risks. It also provides the means for linking the substantive tests directly to the remaining risk of significant misstatement in the financial statements.

FACTORS	High	Medium	Low
The *residual business risk*, linked to the strategic risk, business process level risks and management's procedures to manage and control the risks.			
The *quality of the information* available, internal or external – is it corroborated, is it factual or based on estimates?			
The *historical accuracy/measurement* – what has been the previous experience with the entity in respect of the particular transaction cycle, account balance and/or assertions?			
The *underlying assumptions used* – for example, whether based on GAAP, industry specific, general business conditions, financial, foreign exchange rates, interest rates, etc.			
The *qualifications and competence of the personnel* involved in accounting and recording, and the *complexity of the estimating process* for the class of transactions or balances involved for the particular assertions affected.			
Any evidence of *management bias* and incentive to misstate, whether due to personal benefits to be derived, market pressures and expectations, and budget pressures from management or group companies.			

Table 11.2 Factors for evaluating the risk of significant misstatement remaining for each audit objective selected for significant classes of transactions and balances arising from key business process level risks

Based on the above analysis, the auditor would document the overall assessment of the potential risk of individual significant misstatements for each of the key business processes, identifying the particular assertions, which could contain significant misstatements. This enables the auditor to establish the critical audit objectives and document the related audit response by setting out the nature and extent of audit procedures, whether by way of tests of controls, substantive analytical review procedures or substantive tests of detail in an audit programme to gather audit evidence to detect and correct any such misstatements.

The auditor considers what level of assurance has been gathered regarding the effectiveness of management's risk management processes, including the entity's control activities, monitoring processes and key performance indicators, which the auditor may have ascertained from his or her understanding of the business, or as a result of tests of controls that justify an assessment of the risk of significant misstatement as low. If there is evidence of management bias, the auditor should also consider the risk of fraud and the deliberate override of controls by management.

Deliberate management override of controls

The risk of deliberate management override of controls depends to a great extent on the attitude, motive and competencies of management. Certain conditions or events identified during tests of controls would influence the auditor's assessment of the risk of remaining significant misstatement; these would, in turn, influence the auditor's decision to perform particular analytical review procedures, or to increase the extent of substantive tests of detail, or to involve forensic audit staff in the audit. Potential indicators of such conditions and events include:

- Management draws no distinction between personal and business transactions.
- Management's lifestyle appears materially inconsistent with the level of their remuneration.
- Unusual transactions, and non-standard journal entries particularly around year-end.
- Parts of the accounting records being unavailable / lost for implausible reasons.
- A significant incidence of material cash transactions without adequate documentation.
- Limitations on the scope of the audit without satisfactory explanation, for example, not being able to contact third parties for confirmation purposes.

These circumstances, if identified, may indicate a risk of fraud affecting the financial statements and require the performance of additional audit procedures, or the involvement of audit staff with particular skills or experience, possibly including forensic auditors or IT specialists to assist with further investigations.

11.1.3 Determining what substantive procedures are appropriate

One of the important issues under debate in auditing at present is how to ensure the linkage between identification of risks of significant misstatement in significant classes of transactions or balances, and the design of appropriate substantive audit procedures that will be most effective in preventing or detecting and correcting such misstatements in the financial statements. At present the move towards a 'top-down' audit approach, using business process analysis to understand the client's business better, and to understand how management is controlling the key risks that affect the financial statements, is intended to address these risks and focus the audit effort more effectively.

An important aspect includes decisions regarding the staffing of the engagement where particular skills or experience is needed to recognize and address the audit risks. Examples of such circumstances include:

- *A client with a highly sophisticated integrated database* with millions of transactions occurring during the year. The audit staff may include qualified computer audit staff to review the programmed and manual controls and to test the information processed to provide evidence of the reliability of the system and to ensure the completeness, occurrence and measurement of transactions from which the financial statement information is produced.

- *A client who is part of a multinational group.* The auditor may need to use the work of other auditors in different legal jurisdictions who have knowledge of the local legal requirements, accounting frameworks and auditing standards applied in those jurisdictions to gather appropriate audit evidence for the principal auditor reporting on the group financial statements.

- *Where there is an indication of material fraud.* Forensic audit staff may be assigned to audit the particular risk areas.

In deciding the nature and extent of substantive tests that are appropriate, the auditor has a choice of performing analytical review procedures or detailed tests of significant classes of transactions and balances. The lower the risk of not detecting significant misstatements from substantive analytical procedures the higher the detection risk can be for substantive tests of detail. The choices and decisions taken by the auditor may represented by the 'decision table' in Figure 11.1:

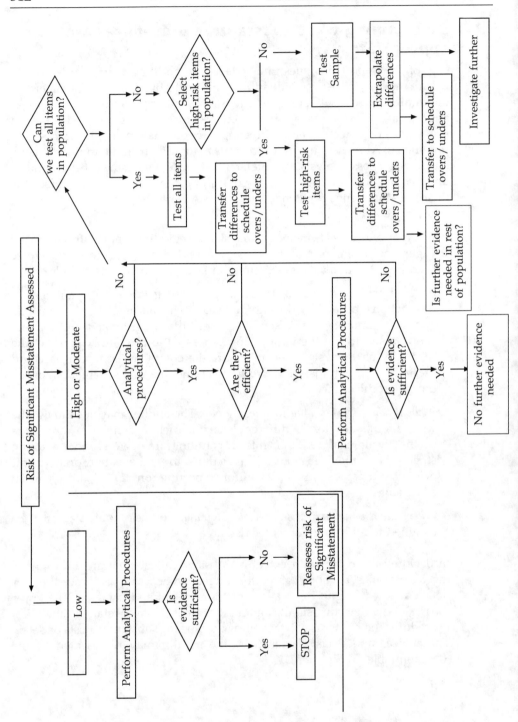

Figure 11.1 Decision table for substantive procedures

(Source: KPMG.)

11.2 DESIGNING SUBSTANTIVE TESTS

11.2.1 Introduction and principles

The nature, timing and extent of substantive audit procedures are a function of the auditor's judgement regarding materiality and audit risk. Having set materiality limits in aggregate and at individual balances level, and having assessed the inherent and control risks, the auditor is in a position to design substantive tests. In the 'top-down' audit approach described in the preceding chapters, the aspects that will guide the auditor in determining the nature, timing and extent of substantive audit procedures will include the following:

- A greater allocation of audit resources to areas of high audit risk, identified in the course of gaining an understanding of the client's strategic business risks, the core business processes, key processes and process-level risks. This will follow the auditor's assessment of the risk of significant misstatement remaining in significant classes of transactions and balances based on the results of tests of control, fraud risk assessment and substantive analytical procedures.

- Significant classes of transactions and account balances should receive more substantive audit attention than immaterial amounts.

- If indicated, from the results of interim substantive audit work or the assessment of the risk of significant misstatement identified during tests of controls or analytical procedures, the auditor may decide to reduce the materiality levels to increase the amount of audit evidence required and the cut-off threshold for proposing audit adjustments for errors detected. For example, if the auditor detects an aggressive revenue recognition approach by management and high risk of overstatement of revenue, materiality may be decreased at the account level and less reliance placed on internally generated audit evidence and more on external audit evidence.

- Where the assessment of control risk for particular classes of transactions, or business locations indicates a significant number of errors, which in aggregate may exceed materiality levels originally set, the materiality at a financial statement level may be decreased to increase the amount of audit evidence required and the cut-off threshold for proposing audit adjustments for errors detected.

- Where fraud indicators are present, materiality levels should similarly be reduced and the high-risk areas potentially affected identified to focus the audit efforts to detect and correct the effects of the fraud on the financial statements, whether attributable to fraudulent financial reporting or the misappropriation of assets of the business. Less reliance will be placed on internally generated audit evidence and more reliance on externally generated evidence. It may also necessitate a forensic element to the audit in areas where the fraud is suspected.

Substantive audit procedures are defined in paragraph .06 of SAAS 500, 'Audit Evidence', as:

> 'Substantive procedures mean tests performed to obtain audit evidence to detect material misstatements in the financial statements, and are of two types:
>
> - Tests of details of transactions and balances, and
>
> - Analytical procedures.'

Tests of controls provide evidence that is directly related to the effectiveness of the design and operation of the control activities and any deviations from these; substantive procedures, by contrast, are directly related to gathering evidence about the monetary amounts contained in individual balances and classes of transactions for specific assertions of management embodied in the financial statements. The assertions form the basis for the *audit objectives* since the auditor needs to gain sufficient appropriate audit evidence that the assertions embodied in the audited financial statements do not contain any remaining risk of significant misstatements.

Management's assertions, and hence the audit objectives, are those generally regarded as attributable to:

- classes of transactions or events for the period under review, namely: *completeness, occurrence/validity* and *measurement/accuracy*; and
- account balances at the period end, namely: *existence, rights and obligations, completeness, measurement/accuracy and valuation, presentation* and *disclosure.*

Consequently, if a high level of assurance is gained from tests of control and substantive analytical procedures, the extent of substantive test of details can be reduced. Conversely, if the auditor finds limited assurance from tests of controls, and control risk is assessed as high for significant classes of transactions and balances, and limited assurance is obtained from substantive analytical procedures, the substantive tests of detail of significant classes of transactions and balances need to be focused and more extensive.

When the 'top-down' audit approach is followed, the auditor will focus on obtaining assurance from the tests of detail for those assertions with the potential for significant misstatement, rather than seeking assurance regarding all possible assertions for the particular balance or class of transactions. The following example illustrates the principle:

Example

Your long-standing client is a fashion retailer with numerous stores situated around South Africa. You have always been satisfied in previous audits with the client's controls over the physical existence, measurement and valuation of inventory. During the current financial year, the client opens five new stores in city centres in Italy and begins to market South African fashions to Italian buyers.

At financial year end 20% of the retail inventory is located at stores in Italy. Sales levels have not met expectations and inventory turnover ratios for the Italian stores are lagging behind those in South Africa. Clearly, in this set of circumstances, due to the export situation and complexities involving costs of exporting and foreign exchange rates, the potential significant risk of misstatement lies in the correct measurement / accuracy of inventory shipped to Italy and the valuation at the year-end of the 20% of inventory located in Italy. The substantive tests of detail should focus specifically on procedures to verify the measurement assertion for a sample of inventory purchases made by the stores in Italy, and the valuation assertion in obtaining evidence regarding the net realizable value of the inventory reflected in the financial statements located in Italy.

In order to link the remaining risk of significant misstatement to appropriate audit procedures and to reduce detection risk to an acceptable level, the auditor needs to understand the nature of substantive analytical procedures and substantive tests of detail in order to determine which is the most appropriate to apply in particular circumstances. The auditor must also be aware of considerations regarding the quality of the audit evidence and the timing and the extent of testing to be performed (refer to the discussion of audit evidence in chapter 6).

11.2.2 Nature, timing and extent of substantive analytical procedures

11.2.2.1 Nature of substantive analytical procedures

Substantive analytical procedures are usually the most cost effective for the auditor. As a result, these would generally be applied before proceeding to substantive tests of detail of transactions and balances. Analytical audit procedures are defined in paragraph .03 of SAAS 520, 'Analytical procedures', as being:

'The analysis of significant ratios and trends, including the resulting investigation of fluctuations and relationships that are inconsistent with other relevant information or which deviate from predicted amounts.'

There are two main objectives of analytical review. One is to provide information on any areas which do not appear to conform to the expected and which may require more rigorous examination by the auditor, for example, by enlarging the sample size of the tests to be conducted, or, if the test has already been made, by supplementing it with a further test. The other objective is to corroborate evidence, otherwise obtained, that the results recorded fairly represent the facts. It should be apparent that these two aspects are indeed two sides of the same coin. If the figures are not as expected, they provide a warning that further investigation is required; if they do conform, they provide additional assurance of fair presentation.

Steps in performing substantive analytical procedures

Any analytical review needs to be effective in throwing into relief significant departures from the prediction or expectation in one or more of the balances comprising the financial statements. To this end, there are five steps to be followed in using substantive analytical procedures. The steps are to:

- develop a prediction or expectation;
- define a significant difference or threshold;
- compute the difference between the actual and the expected;
- investigate significant differences and exercise judgement to conclude; and
- document the basis for the conclusion.

Each of the steps of analytical review are discussed below.

Develop a prediction or expectation

The auditor should use the knowledge gained from understanding the business to develop an expectation of the likely amounts to be recorded for the specific account balances or class of transactions, taking account of management's procedures for establishing these. The rationale behind an auditor's prediction or expectation should be documented and shown to be based on what the auditor observes is occurring and the auditor's knowledge of the nature of the business, budgets and/or effect of the circumstances.

For example, in the audit of a hotel group, hotel occupancy rates would be expected to increase in the Gauteng region during August 2002, as a direct result of the international Earth Summit to be held in Sandton. The documentation or the rationale should include information of any key performance indicators that management uses to monitor amounts or changes in the account balances or class of transactions selected. The data used to develop the expectation may be non-financial, such as operating or industry data, or external information. The latter come from government and industry sources, private forecasting organizations, competitors and other market sources. The usefulness of the data may be limited by several factors, such as age, bias, mismatch with client information, quality and incentive to manipulate results to meet market expectations.

Define a significant difference or threshold

Because the auditor's expectation will often not be identical with the client's recorded amount, it is necessary to define what will constitute a *significant difference or threshold* requiring further investigation. This will depend on the purpose of the analytical review procedures, and on the level of assurance required. The greater the level of assurance required, the lower any acceptable threshold will need to be.

For example, if the information is disaggregated to a particular account balance, such as establishing whether rental expense for the year is reasonable, one would expect very little difference between the rental balance expected and the actual amount recorded. However, when considering the gross profit margin achieved, where the client has numerous line items selling at different mark-ups, the gross profit margin may differ from expectations. In this circumstance, further investigation might be necessary to probe the validity of the reasons.

Compute the difference between actual and expected

This should normally be a simple calculation between the expected and the reported values. Differences between the expected and actual should take account of the threshold defined for the analytical procedures applied to the particular balances or class of transactions. Care should be taken that the auditor's evaluation of the results relates to balances audited so that unaudited balances do not inappropriately influence the auditor's judgement of the sufficiency and appropriateness of evidence obtained.

Investigate significant differences and conclude

Differences *in excess of the threshold* require additional investigation to obtain adequate explanations from management and find appropriate supporting evidence to corroborate these. Care must be exercised, adopting an attitude of professinal scepticism, so that undue reliance is not placed on management's responses. If management is unable to provide an explanation or if such explanation is not considered adequate, other audit procedures to resolve the issue should be applied.

Documentation

The analytical procedures performed and their results should be documented in the audit working papers. Where the results of the analytical review are considered to provide adequate substantive audit evidence, this may eliminate the need for or reduce the extent of the substantive tests of detail required. The rationale behind any such decision should be documented.

Types of analytical procedures

Analytical procedures may take many forms, depending on the nature of the client's business, the information available in the records, and the statistical expertise available to the auditor. The approach may range from simple scrutiny of figures to sophisticated statistical manipulation of figures. No exhaustive description of review methods is attempted, but the following analytical techniques are probably the more significant:

- ratio analysis;
- trend analysis;
- reasonableness testing;
- regression analysis; and
- scanning analytics.

With the top-down approach, the auditor should ascertain which key performance indictors of financial and non-financial data are used by management to monitor the business activities and how effective these are in managing and responding to the strategic and business process risks to which the entity is exposed.

Where a client has established a data warehouse, the auditor should ascertain how the financial data is extracted from the operational systems and the source of non-financial data used to prepare financial models or regression analyses used by the client. This is particularly important where analyses and reports prepared from information in the data warehouse are used by management in an end-user computing environment, for example, to calculate the amount of doubtful debt provisions or inventory write-offs to be recorded in the financial records.

Analytical techniques

Ratio analysis: This is the comparison, across time or to a benchmark, such as industry indices, peer group data of relationships between financial statement accounts (for example, return on equity), and between an account and non-financial data (for example, cost per order, sales per square foot/metre, customer footfalls in a retail store). Other examples may be:

> Where the client operates a standard cost system, a periodic scrutiny of the variances, consideration of the reported causes of any material variances, and investigation if necessary. Special attention should be given to any significant material usage and labour efficiency variances as misappropriation of raw materials or cash (for wages) is likely to give rise to such variances.

> Financial ratios can also be used to test the reasonableness of the balances in financial statements.

Trend analysis: This is the analysis of changes in an account over time. Simple trend or fluctuation analyses typically compare the previous year's account balance (the 'expectation') with the current balance. Trend analysis can also encompass multiple time periods and includes comparing recorded trends with budget amounts and with competitor and industry information. Techniques such as weighted averages, simple linear trends and exponential smoothing may be used to evaluate the trends, and to predict the present balances. These predictions may then be compared with the amounts recorded. Once calculated, the trend in the ratios may also reveal meaningful differences.

Reasonableness testing: This is the analysis of account balances, or changes in account balances between accounting periods. It involves the development of a model to form an expectation based on financial data, non-financial data or both. Examples include the following:

- An expectation for hotel revenue may be developed using a model that includes the average occupancy rate and the average room rate by category or class of room.

- A comparison of expense or income accounts with related balance sheet or income statement accounts – for example, interest paid or received – with the related loan account, or depreciation expense relative to the fixed assets of the entity, to identify any significant departure from the expected pattern.

- The use of gross profit margins to gain assurance about sales, cost of sales and inventory. Where the client can readily verify physical inventory figures at fairly short intervals, for example, by means of continuous inventory records, it is possible to compare periodic (say monthly) sales to cost of sales, or gross profit to sales, and identify any material change in the ratio. In such a case it may not be readily apparent whether the cause of the variance in the ratio is due to the sales or cost-of-sales figure. However, where the auditor is satisfied by adequate checks that the cost of sales is fairly stated month-by-month, the relationship can be used to determine the credibility of the sales figures.

Regression analysis: This is the use of statistical models to quantify the auditor's expectation with measurable risk and precision levels. In regression analysis the amount being investigated is called the dependent variable; the factors to which it is related are called the independent variables. For example, an auditor might form an expectation for sales by performing a regression analysis using model inputs, such as management's sales forecast, commission expense (if applicable and if it is not a fixed percent of sales) and advertising expenditures. Standard software packages such as Microsoft Excel can be used to perform regression analysis. In this example, the variables would be sales and cost of sales.

Scanning analytics: This is the identification of anomalous individual items within account balances or other client data through a periodic scrutiny of ledger accounts, records of original entry or transaction audit trail printouts such as income and expense accounts, adjusting entries, suspense accounts, reconciliations and the investigation of any monthly (or weekly) amount which departs significantly from the norm without an apparent reason. This technique requires an experienced auditor who understands the client's business, who is able to recognize amounts of anomalous individual items, and who can exercise judgement in the selection of specific items for enquiry or detailed testing. In computerized accounting environments, CAATs may be used very effectively for scanning and sorting data in a ledger and printing reports of items which meet specified criteria, that is, those that indicate errors or particular trends.

An example is a wage payment for a particular week (or several weeks) much in excess of the average. It may be due to legitimate causes (for example, unusual levels of overtime) or there may be a misappropriation or error.

11.2.2.2 Timing of analytical review procedures

Analytical review procedures may be used at various stages of the audit. The audit objectives will vary depending on the stage at which it is done. SAAS 520, 'Analytical procedures', paragraph .08, recognizes that analytical procedures may be used at the following stages:

'At the planning stage where a review of management accounts or interim reports may disclose important trends and assist in understanding the business and in identifying the potential risk areas.

As substantive procedures when their use can be more efficient or more effective than substantive test of detail in reducing detection risk for specific financial statement assertions.

As an overall review of financial statements in the final review stage of the audit.'

Overall analytical review, done during the planning stage of the audit, assists the auditor in understanding the client's business. It is intended to highlight unusual trends or amounts which appear out of line with expectations in order to direct the audit effort to areas of high audit risk, thereby affecting the nature, extent and timing of specific substantive tests designed to counter the potential risks.

As *substantive procedures*, used during the conduct of the examination, specific substantive analytical procedures can be effective in determining the reasonableness of account balances or classes of transactions, thereby reducing the extent of detailed substantive testing needed. Such analytical procedures frequently corroborate the results of other substantive audit procedures or identify amounts which require further explanation and specific substantive tests of detail. These procedures are discussed in detail later in this chapter.

At the *conclusion stage* of the audit, overall analytical procedures of the financial statement disclosures provide a final check on the reasonableness of their content, as well as corroborating the cumulative evidence otherwise obtained.

In all these instances analytical procedures provide the auditor with a better understanding of the business and provide a variable level of audit assurance.

Figure 11.2 illustrates the relationship between the assurance, precision, rigour and the purpose of analytical procedures.

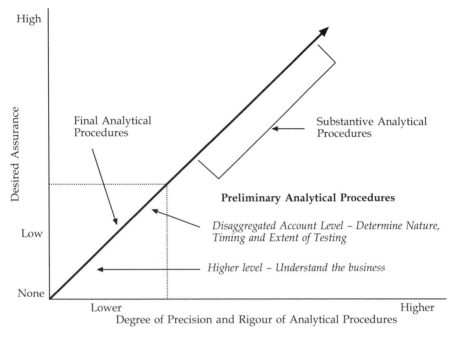

Figure 11.2 Relationship between assurance, precision, rigour, and the purpose of analytical procedures

(Source: PricewaterhouseCoopers.)

11.2.2.3 Extent of analytical procedures

There are two aspects to be considered by the auditor: first, the *extent of analytical procedures* and, second, the *extent of reliance* which the auditor may place on the results of the analytical procedures performed as substantive procedures. Factors that the auditor needs to consider, as identified in paragraphs .12 to .16 of SAAS 520, 'Analytical Procedures', are discussed below.

The extent of analytical procedures to be performed

When deciding to use analytical procedures as substantive procedures, the auditor will need to consider a number of factors, such as:

● The objectives of the analytical procedures and extent to which their results can be relied upon.

● The nature of the entity and the extent to which information can be disaggregated, that is, an analytical procedure may be more effective when applied to individual accounts or sections rather than the entity as a whole.

- The availability of both financial and non-financial information.

- The reliability of the information, that is, its completeness, accuracy and validity – what is the auditor's experience of this historically, and the entity's experience when used, for example, for budgets and key performance indicators?

- The relevance of the information available.

- The source of the information – is it internal or external and from an established and credible source or not?

- Is the information, particularly industry information, comparable? Entities in the same industry may be structured very differently and consequently aspects such as gross margins, level of turnover or investment returns may not necessarily be comparable from one entity to another.

- What is the auditor's experience and knowledge of the client gained in previous audits, the types of problems encountered, and accounting adjustments needed at previous year-ends?

- Other relevant factors arising from the knowledge of the business.

The extent of reliance to be placed on the results of substantive analytical procedures

The extent of reliance placed on the results of the substantive analytical procedures will depend on the auditor's assessment of the risk that the analytical procedures may identify relationships as expected, when, in fact, a material misstatement exists. Consequently, the extent of reliance will depend, *inter alia*, on the following factors:

- The materiality and nature of items involved and their significance relative to the financial statements as a whole. For example, if inventory is a material amount, the auditor should not rely solely on analytical procedures, but might do so for certain income and expense items when they are not individually material.

- Assurance obtained from other audit procedures, directed towards the same audit objective, which support the analytical review results. For example, the review of subsequent receipts from debtors may support an analytical review of the accounts receivable age analysis and decisions about the amount of doubtful debts provisions required in respect of long outstanding accounts receivable balances.

- The accuracy with which the analytical review results can be predicted. For example, if an entity has a consistent mark-up policy to arrive at selling prices, the gross profit percentage anticipated is predictable. (See earlier discussion and Figure 11.2.)

- The auditor's evaluation of the strength or weakness of internal controls, which may necessitate more substantive tests of detail where control risks are assessed as high.

- Whether the auditor can obtain satisfactory explanations for unexpected or unusual relationships identified during the analytical review.

Analytical procedures are a most useful means of obtaining audit evidence effectively and efficiently, and are being used more extensively to facilitate such procedures as computer-assisted audit software has become more accessible to audit firms. Care must be exercised by the auditor, however, to avoid becoming overdependent on analytical procedures to the exclusion of detailed substantive testing procedures.

11.2.3 Nature, timing and extent of substantive tests of detail of transactions

11.2.3.1 Nature of tests of detail of transactions

Substantive tests of detail of transactions are directly related to gathering evidence about specific assertions contained in individual classes of transactions and balances recorded in the accounting records and reported in the financial statements. In applying the 'top-down' audit approach, attention will be directed specifically to those assertions where the remaining risk of significant misstatements are identified.

Substantive tests of detail of transactions are used to gather audit evidence regarding the *completeness, occurrence/validity* and *measurement/accuracy* of individual transactions. These tests are ordinarily applied to samples selected from significant classes of transactions identified from key business processes. Significant classes of transactions for the variety of business entities that might be encountered by an auditor could typically include the classes of transactions and the income statement and balance sheet account balances listed below:

- *Revenue transactions and balances:*
  - sales revenue and accounts receivable balances; and
  - cash receipts and cash (bank) balances.
- *Expenditure transactions and balances:*
  - purchases, operating expenses, depreciation expense and fixed asset balances;
  - payments to vendors and accounts payable balances;
  - payroll expenses and payroll creditors; and
  - cost of sales and inventory balances.
- *Financing and investing transactions and balances:*
  - borrowings, interest expense and other liabilities;
  - lending to others, interest revenue and notes receivable;
  - acquisitions and disposals of financial instruments; and
  - equity capital, reserves, taxation and dividends.

Transactions selected for testing are vouched to or from the supporting documents to the related transaction listings and entries recorded in the relevant general ledger accounts, whatever forms such records may take, that is, whether manual or computerized. In a computerized environment, the different transactions recorded simply become data captured into the computerized accounting system and analysed into the underlying database, so it is the nature of the different legal rights and obligations, evidenced in the type of source documents and authorization processes, that distinguish one class of transactions from another.

Transactions source documents

Typical source or supporting documents that the auditor might encounter in the various classes of transactions include:

- **Revenue transactions and cash receipts:**
  - delivery notes and invoices for sales and credit notes for goods returned, VAT returns, statements provided for credit customers, customer remittance advices, and customer master-file information;
  - receipts, till rolls and till cash count forms, signed credit card forms or electronic slips, bank stamped deposit slips, bank statements for banking transactions, bank reconciliations; and
  - transaction printouts, such as monthly sales and an aged analyses listing of all accounts receivable at each month end.

- **Expenditure transactions and cash disbursements:**
  - *Purchase transactions and disbursements:* purchase orders, goods received notes and suppliers' delivery notes, invoices and statements for purchase transactions, reconciliations of suppliers' accounts and supplier master-file information; cheque requisitions, paid cheques and EFT transfers.
  - *Payroll transactions*: employee communications, including letters setting out the employee's terms of appointment, or letters of dismissal or resignation, comprise the standing data supported by related personnel files and records; weekly clock cards, and signed attendance registers; industry or trade union agreements regarding authorized pay rates applicable, documents and information relating to deductions from employees and payments to 'deduction creditors' such as SARS for PAYE, retirement funding contributions, medical aid returns of employee and employer contributions, contributions to trade unions; and minutes of remuneration committees (particularly for approval of senior management remuneration and benefits); printouts of payslips, weekly and monthly payroll summaries and cash disbursements of net pay, whether by way of paid cheques or EFT bank payments, and annual individual employee gross payroll slips to support IRP5 and IT3 tax certificates.
  - *Fixed asset purchases:* minutes of directors or capital expenditure committees, purchase orders or contracts detailing the terms, such as

a building contract, plant or equipment supply and installation, lease agreements for motor vehicles, depending on the nature of the asset acquired and basis of settlement, invoices from suppliers, cash disbursements and documents evidencing ownership such as title deeds for property acquired, registration and licence papers for vehicles acquired, licence agreements for software purchased. Source documents could also include supplier invoices for property, plant, equipment and vehicle maintenance costs incurred and the related cash disbursements.

– *Property transactions:* lease agreements supporting rental expense, or revenue, depending on whether the client is the tenant or the landlord, supplier invoices for property maintenance expenditures, monthly statements for municipal charges including assessment rates, electricity and water supplied and refuse removal.

- **Financing and investing transactions:**
  - This may include, *inter alia*:
  - loan agreements, granting of bank overdraft facilities and related interest expense charges, cash receipts in respect of loans received and cash disbursements for loan and interest repayments;
  - brokers bought and sold notes in respect of acquisitions or disposals of investments in listed companies and cash receipts and dividends advice notes for dividends received;
  - agreements for derivatives and options traded, commodities purchased, and forward exchange contracts;
  - prospectuses for new share issues, minutes of boards of directors or shareholders approving particular transactions in accordance with companies act requirements or articles of association of the entity.

Types of substantive tests of detail of transactions

The audit procedures performed to gather audit evidence during substantive tests of detail of transactions include:

- *Vouching* the sample of recorded transactions selected to the underlying source documents to detect potential overstatement – errors of commission and unauthorized transactions. Such tests may identify misapplication of accounting policies or GAAP, errors in calculation of amounts recorded, the existence of fictitious transactions, misinterpretation of contract terms, misallocation of amounts to ledger accounts between capital, liability and revenue items or asset and expenditure items, and amounts brought to account in the incorrect period. This will provide evidence related to the *measurement/accuracy* and *validity/occurrence* objectives.

- *Tracing* from a sample of source documents to recorded entries to detect potential understatement – errors of omission arising from errors or irregularities. This is more likely to occur in transactions where expenses incurred have not been brought to account with a resultant understatement of expenditure or assets and liabilities. Problems identified in this area will invariably necessitate the application of specific cut-off procedures by the auditor at year-end. This will provide evidence related to the *completeness and measurement/accuracy and validity/occurrence* objectives.

- *Re-computation* of amounts of selected transactions will provide evidence of *measurement/accuracy*, for example, in invoicing sales – based on the correct inventory items at the correct prices charged to the correct customer account and allocated to the correct general ledger sales account. Similarly re-computation of expenditure transactions will provide evidence of measurement/accuracy of amounts recorded for purchase transactions, payroll amounts paid to employees and payroll creditors, and inventory in accordance with the accounting policies of the entity and in accordance with GAAP.

- *Enquiry* is one of the most important procedures applied by an auditor to obtain a proper understanding of transactions recorded in order to identify errors and irregularities. Enquiries may be made of any member of the client's staff and enable the auditor to form an impression of the competency of the individuals responsible for authorizing and recording transactions and the potential risk of significant misstatement for the relevant class of transactions, whether by way of computational errors, misallocations between accounts, potential fraud and misapplications of GAAP principles. This will provide evidence related to the *completeness and measurement/accuracy and validity/occurrence* objectives.

As tests of detail are usually applied to a sample, the auditor will seek to draw conclusions about the entire population of transactions as a result of the findings from the sample selected. The reader is referred to the discussion of the principles of sampling in auditing in chapter 7.

In a computerized environment, CAATs may be used:

- to select, sort and print all payroll transactions during a particular period where, for example, gross pay is based on hours worked, but these exceed a maximum number of hours for the week;

- to compare employees appearing on weekly or monthly payrolls to the master file standing data of employees, and to print out names that do not appear in both places; and

- to select particular items for detailed vouching, such as selecting all changes to master file details of employees' banking accounts in order to verify that the proper *authorization procedures* were followed. Exceptions identified in the reports would then be discussed with management to ascertain the reasons and, if necessary, the appropriate action taken, or audit adjustments proposed to rectify any errors.

In the case of a forensic audit where fraud is suspected or alleged, sampling is not an option and transactions affected would have to be vouched 100%

and carefully documented as they may be required as evidence in a criminal trial.

In performing the audit procedures, the auditor must bear in mind the audit evidence principles relating to the quality of the evidence inspected – internal versus external, its relevance and reliability – and exercise professional scepticism with regard to explanations provided by management and staff (see the discussions in chapter 6).

For example, if there is a possibility that revenue may be overstated, this may be due to a duplication of transactions recorded, or it may be the result of aggressive revenue recognition policies followed by management. The appropriate audit response would be to select a sample of sales entries for vouching to supporting delivery notes in order to verify the *occurrence/validity* of the transactions. Particular attention will be applied to audit procedures to verify the *cut-off* for sales immediately prior to and after the financial year-end, by vouching a sample of recorded sales transactions to the supporting delivery notes and invoices, or other evidence of the effective date of delivery of the goods and services. In addition, credit notes passed subsequent to the financial year-end may be selected to vouch supporting documentation to determine whether these appeared to be valid or were related to attempts to overstate the sales figures with fictitious entries for the preceding financial year. The audit procedures would provide evidence of both *completeness* and *occurrence/validity* assertions. Enquiries would be made regarding the appropriateness and consistency of application of the revenue recognition policies of the company, given the nature of the sales billings which provide evidence of the *measurement/accuracy* assertions.

11.2.3.2 Timing of tests of detail of transactions

Where detection risk is assessed as high or where the size and complexity of the client necessitates the performance of an interim audit, tests of detail of transactions may be performed during the interim audit – usually several months before the financial year-end. Where detection risk is set as low, as a result of inherent and control risk being assessed as high, the tests of detail of transaction will be performed shortly before and after the financial year-end.

If the auditor decides to perform detailed tests of transactions prior to the year-end, the auditor must have a basis for placing reliance on the effectiveness of the controls for the remaining period so that any significant risk of misstatement would be detected. This means that the auditor may have to select sample items from the period between the interim and year-end audits, thus extending the substantive tests of detail for the remaining period, in order to extend the audit conclusions from the interim audit to the end of the period.

The performance of substantive tests of detail of transactions does not relieve the auditor of the responsibility to verify the relevant account balances arising from the particular class of transactions at year-end. In addition, it is unlikely that the auditor will test all assertions in the tests of details of transactions. Therefore, the auditor will be unable, without further substantive procedures, to draw conclusions about the remaining assertions. For example, tests of sales invoices to verify the *completeness and measurement/accuracy* assertions will not provide evidence of the valuation of accounts receivable at year-end. Figure 11.2 sets out several of the factors that the auditor will need to consider when extending the interim audit conclusions regarding the risk of significant misstatement remaining in the financial statements for significant classes of transactions, namely:

- The effectiveness of the control activities and evidence that these continued to be reliable during the remaining period.
- Any evidence of management bias to misstate the financial statements.
- The existence of large and unusual year-end adjustments affecting the class of transactions and balances.
- The volatility of the account and its predictability ascertained from substantive analytical procedures.
- Whether exception reports from the accounting system are designed to identify and report such fluctuations.

11.2.3.3 Extent of tests of detail of transactions

More evidence is required where detection risk has been set as low than where there is little risk of misstatement and detection risk is set as high. Extent in the case of substantive tests of detail of transactions relates to the number of items being selected for the sample, that is, whether this is 20 or 200 sales invoices or goods-received notes, inventory items for counting at a stock count, accounts receivable balances for circularization, paid cheques for inspection, etc. The sample size is a matter of professional judgement and different firms generally establish a policy regarding the sample sizes they are comfortable to apply. Clearly, sampling principles must still be considered and conclusions may not be drawn about the whole population unless a representative sample is first selected (see discussion of sampling in auditing in chapter 7).

Where the auditor encounters an error prone population in a particular class of transactions or in a particular location of the client's business, extension of sampling procedures to and increased sample size of the relevant transactions will not provide adequate evidence that the potential misstatement from the aggregate of errors found in the sample will not exceed materiality levels set. Having identified the source and nature of the errors arising, alternative procedures will need to be applied, which may necessitate the client employing persons to check the entire transaction population for the period when it is suspected the errors arose in order to identify and rectify errors to the satisfaction of the auditor. The internal or external auditor may be requested to provide staff to assist in this work. Where the errors have arisen due to programmed errors in a particular application affecting every transaction, it may be possible, using CAATs and data mining techniques, to quickly analyse and sort the entire population for the financial year and calculate the adjustments necessary.

A further consideration affecting the timing of tests of detail of transactions in computerized accounting environments is the availability of the underlying data. For example:

- Should the client change computer systems during the year, the previous systems may not be accessible once the conversion to the new systems is implemented.
  - Where applications are outsourced, and the auditor wishes to test a particular run of the application, this may need to be done when the outsource provider is running the application. In addition, unless the service level agreement provides for access, the external auditor may not be granted access to the client's data and information maintained at the outsource provider. In this case, it may be necessary for the auditor of the outsource provider to perform particular audit tests on the external auditor's behalf.
  - In highly sophisticated computerized systems, such as banking systems, the auditor may have to arrange for embedded CAATs to monitor the regularity of transactions as they occur and for such programs to provide for 'audit' exception reports for periodic review by the external auditor.

11.2.4 Nature, timing and extent of substantive tests of detail of balances

11.2.4.1 Nature of substantive tests of detail of balances

Substantive tests of detail of balances are directly related to gathering evidence about specific assertions contained in account balances at a particular date, rather than the detailed entries making up the balance recorded in the accounting records and reported in the financial statements. In applying the 'top-down' audit approach, attention is directed specifically to those assertions contained in significant balances where the remaining risk of significant misstatements are identified. The remaining risk of significant misstatement in a balance will, of course, be *after* the assurance already gathered from audit evidence obtained from tests of controls, substantive analytical procedures and substantive tests of detail of transactions. As with the tests of detail of transactions, the tests of detail of balances are also likely to be time consuming, involve a more experienced level of audit staff and, therefore, be costly to perform.

Tests of detail of balances are used to gather audit evidence regarding the assertions that are generally regarded as being attributable to account balances at the period end, namely: *existence, rights and obligations, completeness, measurement/accuracy and valuation, presentation and disclosure.*

With the focus on gathering audit evidence related to the remaining risk of significant misstatement, it is as well to understand the type of audit evidence that may be sought for each aspect related to particular balance sheet or income statement balances.

The types of procedures which are specifically performed in tests of detail of balances typically include: inspection, observation, enquiry, re-performance and computation procedures used by the auditor in the conduct of both tests of control and substantive testing, while confirmation and analytical review procedures are solely substantive test procedures.

Inspection, in substantive tests of balances, consists of examining records, documents and tangible assets. This is probably the most widely used procedure to gather audit evidence. The inspection of records enables the auditor to assess the authenticity of such records, identify potential errors or irregularities, and identify accounts or amounts requiring more detailed corroborating evidence, compared with those requiring little additional audit work.

- The inspection of documents generally provides first-hand information of the terms of a particular transaction or agreement and enables the auditor to verify the amount and its allocation in the accounting records. For example, inspecting the terms of a royalty agreement will enable the auditor to check the accuracy of the client's calculations to corroborate the amount of the royalties expense in the income statement. However, if the royalties are, for example, based on sales of particular products, the auditor will need to be satisfied that the client's internal controls over the *completeness, measurement/accuracy* and *occurrence/validity* of recorded sales are sufficiently reliable to provide accurate sales information for the royalty calculation. This may necessitate either analytical review and/or tests of controls within the sales system to obtain the required level of assurance.

- The physical inspection of tangible assets of the entity will provide the auditor with evidence of the existence and condition of the assets inspected, such as inventory or fixed assets.

- Inspection of other documents, such as title deeds or confirmation from a mortgage bondholder holding the title deeds, provides evidence of the ownership of fixed property; inspection of vehicle registration and licensing documents provides prima facie evidence of the ownership of vehicles, whereas lease or hire-purchase agreements indicate third parties rights and obligations in respect of such vehicles.

Observation *in substantive tests of detail of balances* consists of watching a process or procedure being performed. Observation provides strong evidence of the observed operation only at the time of observation. Care must be taken when extending conclusions about the process or procedure to periods not observed by the auditor. For example, the *observation* of a stock count will provide the auditor with evidence regarding the physical *existence* of inventory included in the inventory balance at the date of the count and the client's procedures for ensuring the *completeness* of the inventory count.

Other substantive procedures will have to be performed to gather evidence regarding the remaining assertions embodied in the inventory balance.

Re-performance in substantive tests of detail of balances involves repeating client procedures to determine whether an amount is correctly recorded, for example:

Re-performing depreciation and present fair value calculations (to verify the impairment of fixed assets for the year) provides evidence of the *valuation* assertion for the net realizable value of fixed assets reflected in the balance sheet and related impairment expense in the income statement.

Re-performance of bank reconciliations at year-end provides evidence of the *completeness* and *valuation* assertions for the bank balances reflected in the balance sheet.

Computation in substantive tests of detail of balances consists of checking the arithmetical accuracy of source documents and accounting records or of performing independent calculations to support the amount of an account balance. This will generally provide evidence regarding the *measurement/ accuracy* and *valuation* of a particular balance.

Enquiry and confirmation in substantive tests of detail of balances involves the auditor seeking relevant information from knowledgeable persons inside or outside the entity – either providing information the auditor did not previously have, or providing corroborative evidence regarding a particular balance at year-end. The enquiry may be oral or written. Generally less reliance can be placed on responses obtained internally and these will invariably require further corroboration. Confirmation obtained from third parties is generally more reliable than that obtained internally, and written confirmations are generally more reliable than oral representations. Depending on the nature of the confirmation sought, it may provide evidence of any or all of the assertions, namely, *existence, rights and obligations, completeness, measurement/accuracy and valuation* and may also support the *presentation and disclosure* in the financial statements. The mark of a good auditor is the ability to ask the right person the right question to obtain the evidence being sought.

Examples of third party confirmations frequently requested by auditors at year-end are requests for confirmation of bank balances or loan accounts and accounts receivable circularization requests.[1]

Internal confirmation in the form of a letter of representation may be obtained from management.[2]

---

[1] SAAS 505.
[2] SAAS 580.

11.2.4.2 Timing of substantive tests of detail of balances

Substantive tests of detail of balances will usually be performed at the financial year-end. Substantive tests performed prior to year-end will generally be performed only in circumstances where the auditor is satisfied that control procedures are appropriately designed and have operated effectively throughout the period. Where the auditor is not satisfied regarding the effectiveness of the controls, he or she may well insist that the verification of existence, whether by way of stock counts or debtors' confirmation requests, be performed at the year-end. For example, for trading stores retailing fashion wear and accessories, the risk of pilferage (shrinkage) by both staff and the public is very high, and it may only be possible to establish the physical *existence* of inventory on the last day of the financial year and so stock counts would be arranged for that date.

Where detailed tests of balances are performed at an earlier date, cut-off tests of the relevant transaction will generally need to be performed at both the earlier date and at the year-end with *roll-forward* tests in the form of substantive analytical procedures performed on the related transactions occurring between the two dates.

In addition, tests performed at an earlier stage will generally relate only to some and not all assertions affecting the account balances, for example:

- The positive *circularization of debtors' balances*, say, a month prior to year-end provides evidence of the *existence* of the debtor. Confirmations received, which contain information about uncorrected errors in the account balances, may provide some limited but not conclusive evidence regarding the *measurement/accuracy* of the balances at that date and, where receipt of goods are disputed, may provide evidence of the *'non'-occurrence* of transactions comprising the balance circularized. Confirmations provide no evidence, however, of the *valuation* assertion in respect of the balances, and so other year-end or post year-end procedures – such as a review of post balance sheet cash receipts from debtors – will be needed to verify the recoverability of the debtors' balances. In addition, cut-off tests of sales and cash receipts will need to be performed at both the circularization date and the year-end, as will the agreement of the total of the debtor's listing at both dates to the general ledger control account to establish the completeness of the population from which the sample is being selected for confirmation. Any unusual entries or unexpected trends recorded during the intervening period will need to be investigated. The circularization and subsequent confirmation by the debtor will generally not provide any evidence of the rights and obligations between the client and the customer, or any evidence, for example, of factoring or pledge of the book of debtors by the client.

- *Inventory counts* conducted during attendance at the annual stock count (if performed prior to year-end) will provide evidence regarding the *existence* and *condition* of the inventory, but these will also require subsequent detailed substantive vouching of the cost of the individual items selected, re-computation of the total inventory book value and net realizable value tests to determine the valuation of inventory at year-end. As with the debtors' confirmation process, the auditor will need to perform cut-off tests of purchases and 'cost of sales' of inventory at both the stock-count date and the year-end and substantive analytical procedures by way of roll-forward tests from the date of the stock-count to the year-end. Any unusual entries or unexpected trends recorded during the intervening period will need to be investigated. In addition, while the stock count provides evidence of the existence of the inventory at the count location at the time of the count, it provides no evidence of the *rights and obligations* by way of *ownership* of the items which may be held, for example, on consignment, in bond, or may be pledged to secure debts of the client.

In addition to the assurance gathered from tests of controls, substantive analytical procedures and substantive tests of transactions, the combination of substantive tests of detail of balances gathered, prior to, at and subsequent to the year-end should provide the auditor with the cumulative weight of corroborative evidence to support the assertions for individual account balances and the financial statements as a whole. Where this is not achieved, the auditor needs to consider the risk of significant misstatements – actual or projected – remaining in the financial statements and the effect of these on the audit opinion.

11.2.4.3 Extent of substantive tests of detail of balances

As with tests of details of transactions, the principle is that more evidence is required where detection risk has been set as low, than in circumstances where there is little risk of significant misstatement and detection risk is set as high. The extent of substantive tests of detail of balances will also be affected by whether the auditor has decided to follow a mixture of tests of controls, substantive analytical procedures and detailed tests of transactions and balances, or whether the auditor assesses the inherent and control risks as high and decides to obtain all audit evidence from substantive tests of detail of transactions and balances with limited use of substantive analytical procedures.

In applying the 'top-down' audit approach, the extent of substantive tests of detail of balances will focus on obtaining sufficient audit evidence for those assertions embodied in significant balances, where a significant risk of misstatement has been identified. Failure to detect and rectify any such misstatements may directly affect the auditor's liability and possible allegations of negligence in the future. The extent of evidence required in these instances will be directly related to its sufficiency in providing assurance that the significant risk of misstatement has been identified and rectified.

The extent of evidence required for balances where a significant risk of misstatement is not expected will then depend on several factors and must be considered in both quantitative and qualitative terms. In some instances, such balances may have very few transactions occurring during the year and substantive analytical procedures combined with an external confirmation may provide sufficient evidence. Income statement balances that are relatively stable may be corroborated with substantive analytical procedures linked to the related asset or liability balances, such as interest expense or income on fixed period, fixed rate borrowings or loans advanced.

Other balances may involve more complex accounting principles involving calculations and estimations based on a number of underlying assumptions that require a particular level of skill and expertise in auditing the amounts. In these circumstances the auditor will need to assign suitably qualified staff to perform more detailed tests of such balances. The extent of evidence in such circumstances will include audit working papers setting out how the amounts have been calculated, evidence supporting the various assumptions used, which may be based on extracts from agreements, published market related rates to support fair value measurements, and external confirmations. Some of the audit evidence may be generated by complex computer programs or comprise complex macros in spreadsheets and may need to be audited electronically. This may require the involvement of audit staff with appropriate computer skills or external experts, such as actuaries providing actuarial valuations of retirement funds or life insurance funds.

Other balances may affect specific disclosures in the audited financial statements required by the Companies Act or the Johannesburg Securities Exchange Listing Requirements for listed companies, where significant misstatements would not be tolerated, and amounts must be verified as correct, for example disclosures regarding directors' emoluments and benefits.

Substantive tests of detail of balances from significant classes of transactions may involve sampling procedures and, as indicated earlier for the tests of detail of transactions, the number of items being selected for the sample, whether this is 20 or 200 inventory items for counting at a stock count, or the number of accounts receivable balances selected for circularization, the sample size is a matter of professional judgement. Different firms generally establish a policy regarding the sample sizes they are comfortable to apply. Clearly sampling principles must still be considered and conclusions may not be drawn about the whole population unless a representative sample is first selected. The reader is referred to the discussion in chapter 7 on sampling in auditing. The extent of these tests will be discussed in greater detail in the various transaction cycle chapters.

11.2.4.4 Staffing for substantive audit procedures

Various levels of expertise of audit staff assigned to the audit engagement are required to perform substantive audit procedures. This may range from staff assistants performing routine tests of detail on samples of transactions to more experienced staff with knowledge of the client and industry who are able to recognize fraud risk indicators and the potential for significant risks of misstatement in significant classes of transactions and balances. It may require staff with computer skills and expertise to perform substantive tests and analyses using CAATs, or experts to provide confirmations regarding the valuation of particular assets and liabilities.

The firm's quality control policies should provide for an appropriate assignment of staff to any engagement in line with their skills and competencies. The 'top-down' audit approach, in line with the requirements of SAAS 240, advocate a greater involvement of the entire audit staff in understanding the strategic and business process level risks for key business processes which denotes an appropriate mix of experience and inexperience on any engagement. The usual supervision and review processes should be strictly observed to ensure that significant risks of misstatement are not overlooked.

11.2.5 Relationship between the risk components and the nature, timing and extent of substantive tests

It has to be borne in mind that substantive tests are the final line of defence for an auditor against financial statements published containing a remaining risk of significant misstatement that was not detected or corrected. Figure 11.3 below illustrates the relationships discussed in the preceding sections of this chapter and may clarify the position for readers.

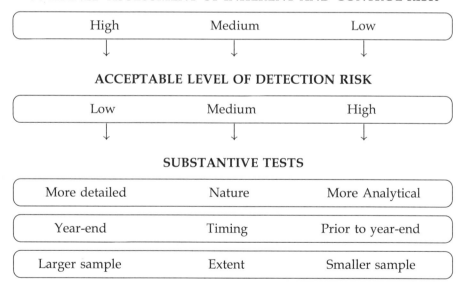

Risk of Significant Misstatement

COMBINED ASSESSMENT OF INHERENT AND CONTROL RISK

High	Medium	Low

ACCEPTABLE LEVEL OF DETECTION RISK

Low	Medium	High

SUBSTANTIVE TESTS

More detailed	Nature	More Analytical
Year-end	Timing	Prior to year-end
Larger sample	Extent	Smaller sample

Figure 11.3 Interrelationship between risk components and substantive tests

11.3 DEVELOPING AUDIT PROGRAMMES FOR SUBSTANTIVE TESTS

11.3.1 Using computerized audit techniques (CAATs) for substantive audit procedures

Where the client has a computerized accounting system, it will generally be more effective to use CAATs in the course of the substantive audit procedures. Typical ways in which this can be done are indicated below:

- *Audit working papers:* The firm's audit working papers may be available on generally accepted audit software packages such as 'Case ware' or packages developed specifically for the audit firm. Thus much of the working papers can be prepared and either printed out in a hard-copy file or retained in electronic format on the firm's main client servers. The working papers would document the audit programmes, and schedules analysing account balances and significant classes of transactions detail. They would, similarly, document samples selected and results of substantive tests performed.

- *Substantive analytical procedures:* CAATs may be used to download information from the computerized accounting records and then, using spreadsheets and modelling programs, the full range of analytical procedures may be performed. In the case of a continuing audit engagement, the auditor may have historical data and analyses from previous years on file to compare with the current analyses to determine trends and fluctuations.

- *Sample selection:* Sampling software can facilitate the selection of random and other samples of source documents or transactions recorded and print these out for the purpose of performing detailed substantive audit tests. Sampling software may be used, for example, to select debtors accounts for circularization and then to print not only the list of debtors selected, but the standard confirmation request letter to be sent to the debtor and the circularization control schedules to record and monitor the responses from debtors.

- *Data sort and analyse and print exception reports:* CAATs may be used to sort data within the computerized accounts according to specifications of the auditor, for example, to analyse and print out the following:
  - *Revenue transactions:* Sales analyses by month or by product line or geographic area, by sales person or by commission payable, by gross margins; to list any duplicated or omitted sales delivery notes or invoices.
  - *Payroll transactions:* Analyses of weekly and monthly gross payrolls; to list master-file changes to standing data for employees for a specified period.
  - *Inventory listings:* These may be analysed and stratified into large numbers of items or items large in value, either for analytical

procedures or to select particular items for detailed pricing or inventory ageing tests of detail.

- *Re-calculation:* Any calculations performed by application software can be automatically re-calculated, for example, calculations of interest payable on loan or current account balances with the bank or other group companies.

11.3.2 Developing audit programmes for substantive tests

The reader is referred to chapter 8 where the principles relating to the preparation of audit programmes and audit working papers are dealt with comprehensively. Historically, standard audit programmes were prepared for the different classes of transactions to cover audit procedures for transactions and balances – whether at the interim or year-end stage of the audit – and incorporated test of controls and substantive procedures, and differentiated primarily between tests to be performed at the interim stage versus those to be performed at or subsequent to year-end.

The move to the 'top-down' audit approach (discussed in chapters 9 and 10) necessitated a very different format of audit programme. The emphasis now falls on understanding the strategic business risks, the identification of core and key business processes, and the documentation of process-level risks that potentially present risks of significant misstatement in significant classes of transactions or balances. Each audit firm will evolve its own particular way of documenting its audit programmes, but one of the imperatives today is to record in the working papers the *linkage* between the *identification of risks of significant misstatement* and *the auditor's response to the risk*, whether by testing and assessing the effectiveness of management's controls or by performing substantive analytical procedures or tests of detail of transactions and balances. An important part of the way in which audit programmes are prepared for this approach, is that potential risk of misstatement, as well as the rationale for the specific audit procedures to be performed, need to be indicated – and if no such procedures are considered necessary, the rationale for that decision must be given as well. This leads to far more comprehensive, qualitative audit programmes focused on the detection and correction of misstatement than would have been prepared in earlier audit methodologies. Undoubtedly the approach has been influenced to some extent by the experiences of several large audit firms in having to defend their actions in litigation suites.

With the 'top-down' approach the purpose of the audit programme may be described as grouping financial statement assertions together into audit objectives and linking the understanding obtained during the process level analysis phase related to the financial statement assertions, to the assessment of the risk of significant misstatement and planned audit procedures. Consequently, the audit programme is now prepared on the basis of the relevant core process with their related key processes and process level business risks. Typically, audit programmes contain the following:

- A *summary of the audit objectives* related to the business process, documenting whether the audit objectives are critical and, upon completion of the audit work, a conclusion with regard to each audit objective specified.

- Identification of the *financial statement accounts affected* by the business process (for example, to continue the earlier example of a large retailer, the core process of trading would include: inventory, debtors, turnover, cost of sales, provisions and contingencies as the financial statement items affected).

- Identification of the *financial statement objectives* combined into each audit objective (for example, the valuation of inventory).

- The *assessment of the risk of significant misstatement* for each audit objective, indicating this risk as *high, medium or low* and *documenting the rationale* for the assessment. For example, using each of the factors mentioned in Table 11.2, namely: the *residual business risk*, the *quality of the information* available, the *historical accuracy/measurement*, the *underlying assumptions used*, the *qualifications and competence of the personnel* involved in accounting and recording, and the *complexity of the estimating process*, any evidence of *management bias* and incentive to misstate.

- *Planned audit procedures* to gain audit evidence *to support the risk of significant misstatement* for each audit objective (that is, considering the effectiveness of management's controls and use of key performance indicators to prevent or detect and correct significant errors or fraud). This will involve discussions with management at appropriate levels, the re-performance of key indicators and the testing of controls to determine whether the auditor's initial risk assessment should change or stand. This part of the working paper should have a space where the timing of the audit procedures may be indicated, as well as for the signature of the person performing the task, and for cross-references to other detailed working papers.

- The response of the auditor to the assessment of *the risk of significant misstatement*. This is done by documenting the *planned audit procedures* by way of *substantive analytical procedures* and *tests of detail of transactions and balances* for the remaining audit work *for each audit objective* for which the *risk of significant misstatement* has been identified. This part of the working paper should have a space set aside where the timing of the audit procedures can be indicated and where the person performing the task can sign it off and cross-reference it to other detailed working papers.

It remains now to look briefly at several special considerations affecting the design of substantive tests.

11.4 SPECIAL CONSIDERATIONS IN DESIGNING SUBSTANTIVE TESTS

11.4.1 External confirmations

The auditor should consider whether it is necessary to use external confirmations in order to obtain sufficient appropriate audit evidence. Guidance with regard to the auditor's responsibilities is provided in SAAS 505, 'External confirmations'. In determining whether external confirmations should be obtained, the auditor should consider materiality, the risk of significant misstatement and how the evidence from other planned audit procedures will reduce detection risk to an acceptably low level for the applicable financial statement assertions. External confirmations may be requested in relation to account balances, terms of agreements or specific transactions of an entity with third parties. Examples where these may be requested include: bank balances and other information from bankers, accounts receivable balances, inventory held by third parties, property title deeds held by lawyers for safe custody or by financiers as security, investments purchased, but not yet delivered, or registered on STRATE, loans from lenders and accounts payable balances.

The reliability of the evidence obtained by confirmation needs to be considered. This may be affected by the control exercised by the auditor over the confirmation process, the characteristics of the respondent and any restrictions imposed by management. Where unusual or complex transactions have been entered into, the auditor may wish to confirm the third party's understanding of the terms, in addition to the inspection of documentation at the client.

Depending on the nature and content of the confirmation sought, external confirmations may provide evidence of any of the assertions, but is unlikely to provide evidence of all assertions; additional evidence will be found through other audit procedures. Thus the wording of the confirmation request should be tailored to the specific assertions. Confirmation requests will usually incorporate management's authorization to the respondent to disclose the information to the auditor.

Confirmation requests may take the form of a positive or negative request, or a combination of these. A positive confirmation request asks the respondent to reply to the auditor in all cases, whereas a negative confirmation asks the respondent to reply only in the event of disagreement with the information provided in the request.

Should management request the auditor not to confirm certain balances, the auditor will have to consider the reason and whether there are valid grounds for such a request. If there are valid grounds, the auditor will seek audit evidence through alternative means. If the auditor does not accept the validity of management's reasons, this amounts to a scope restriction and the auditor will need to consider the impact on the audit opinion.

The confirmation process should be documented and the auditor should maintain control of the process throughout. Non-responses to positive requests should be followed up and if unsuccessful, alternative audit procedures should be applied to provide evidence about the assertions that the confirmation was intended to provide. The auditor should consider the reliability of the respondent, particularly where fraud and collusion with third parties is suspected. Confirmations may be sought by means of e-mail or obtained in an electronic format. Exceptions identified from the responses should be considered and the effect on the auditor's assessment of the risk of significant misstatement in the financial statements revised accordingly. Finally, the results of the confirmation requests must be evaluated together with the results from other audit procedures.

11.4.2 Initial engagements – the audit of opening balances

When an auditor is performing an audit engagement for the first time, additional substantive procedures will be needed to verify the opening balances brought forward from the previous period. SAAS 510, 'Initial engagements – opening balances', provides guidance in this regard.

A first-time audit may arise in the following circumstances:

- the prior period financial statements were audited by another auditor; or
- the prior period had not previously been audited. For example, where an entity had previously operated as a Close Corporation, which does not require an audit of its financial statements, was converted to a company during the financial year under review and consequently now requires audited financial statements.

In such circumstances, SAAS 510 indicates, at paragraph .02, that the first time auditor has the responsibility of 'obtaining sufficient appropriate audit evidence that:

- The opening balances do not contain misstatements that materially affect the current period's financial statements;
- The prior period's closing balances have been brought forward correctly to the current period, or when appropriate have been restated; and
- Appropriate accounting policies are consistently applied, or changes in accounting policies have been properly accounted for and adequately disclosed'.

Opening balances are account balances that exist at the beginning of the period and are based on the closing balances from the previous period and consequently reflect the transactions of prior periods, and accounting policies applied in the prior period.

Factors that will affect the sufficiency and appropriateness of the audit evidence obtained will include the accounting policies followed by the entity; whether or not the prior period financial statements were audited and, if so, whether the audit report was modified for any reason; the nature of the accounts and the potential risk of significant misstatement in the current period's financial statements; and the materiality of the opening balances relative to the current period's financial statements.

Prior period audited by another auditor

Where the prior period was audited by another auditor, the current auditor may be able to obtain sufficient appropriate audit evidence by reviewing, with the client's consent, the previous auditor's working papers – provided the predecessor auditor is willing to grant access to the prior period audit working papers. If the prior period audit opinion was modified, the current auditor would pay particular attention to the reasons for the modification as these present a potential risk of significant misstatement for the current period. Care should be taken to observe the PAAB Code of Ethics in the course of communications with the predecessor auditor.

Prior period not audited

When the prior period was not audited, the auditor would first obtain an understanding of the business and process level risk analysis, paying attention to opening balances which could arise from significant classes of transactions or balances assessed as containing a risk of significant misstatement. The auditor would also consider the evidence obtained from tests of controls, and substantive analytical procedures or tests of detail of transactions and balances for the current period audit. As a first step, this would provide evidence of the reliability of the opening balances versus those indicating a risk of significant misstatement remaining in the opening balances. The next step would be to identify the relevant financial statement assertions affected and devise appropriate audit responses to obtain the necessary audit evidence.

Aspects where significant misstatement might arise may be the *existence* and *valuation* of *inventories* at the start of the current period where the accounting policies may be inappropriate or material errors may have been made – in particular, any attempts made to overstate closing inventories at the end of the previous period. This may necessitate the performance of an interim physical count and valuation of inventories, including the performance of cut-off tests at both the count date and the start of the period, and roll-back procedures comprising substantive tests of detail of transactions to verify the purchases and cost of sales recorded, from the commencement of the period to the date of the count. *Enquiries* of management and inspection of underlying documents, together with the evidence obtained during the current audit, should provide evidence of the *rights and obligations* over the inventory items at the start of the period. Substantive analytical procedures, such as a review of gross profit margins in the current period, may provide additional evidence of the *existence* and *valuation* of inventory at the start of the period.

In the case of remaining current assets and liabilities, such as accounts receivable owing by customers and amounts owing to suppliers, the verification of the current period transactions should provide evidence regarding the *existence, completeness, rights and obligations, and valuation* of those balances through receipts and payments recorded during the current period and verification of the current period closing balances. The current period audit procedures should result in the detection and correction of any remaining risk of significant misstatement in the opening balances.

The opening balances for non-current assets – such as long-term loans owing and provided, and investments – may be verified by means of external confirmations from the relevant third parties. A review of the underlying current period accounting entries and inspection of source documents, such as written agreements, will also provide evidence of the *rights and obligations* at the start of the period.

The opening balance for fixed assets may also be verified largely by substantive tests of detail of the current period movements – additions and disposals, and verification of the *existence, completeness, valuation, and rights and obligations* relating to the current period end balances. Roll-back procedures will then enable the auditor to establish what the opening balances would have been. Enquiries of management and inspection of underlying documentation will provide evidence of rights and obligations at the start of the period and this may be corroborated with external confirmations obtained from third parties, such as lessors and bondholders.

Enquiries of management will provide some indication of the accounting policies applied by the entity in the previous period, which the auditor should be able to verify by inspection of the underlying books and records. Where the accounting policies are considered to be inappropriate or have not been applied consistently, the auditor must ensure that there is compliance, in the current period financial statements, with the requirements of GAAP statement AC 103 with regard to the adjustments, restatement of comparative figures and presentation and disclosure of any change in accounting policies. Opening retained income might be affected materially by any such changes in accounting policies and may need to be restated.

SAAS 510, 'Opening balances', provides guidance in paragraphs .11 – .14 and in the Appendix as to the reporting responsibilities of the auditor in the case of first-time audit engagements. These will be discussed more fully in the section on the auditor's report on financial statements, in chapter 18.

11.4.3 The audit of accounting estimates

Accounting estimates contained in financial statements are often regarded as containing a risk of significant misstatement of balances; after all, they are based on management's assumptions and they are subject to future events or circumstances that are uncertain. To this extent, provisions are judgemental areas where errors of judgement or deliberate manipulation could significantly affect reported results in financial statements. SAAS 540, 'Audit of accounting estimates', contains guidance regarding the nature of accounting estimates and the effect on the audit procedures performed to gather sufficient appropriate audit evidence.

Accounting estimate is defined in paragraph .03 of SAAS 540 as: 'an approximation of the amount of an item in the absence of a precise means of measurement'. Examples included in the statement are:

- 'Allowances to reduce inventory and accounts receivable to their estimated realizable value;

- Provisions to allocate the cost of fixed assets over their estimated useful lives;

- Accrued revenue;

- Deferred taxation;

- Provision for a loss from lawsuit;

- Losses on construction contracts in progress; and

- Provisions to meet warranty claims.'

The nature of accounting estimates

Whether accounting estimates are simple or complex depends on the nature of the particular item. For example, an accrual for rent or municipal charges may be established with reasonable certainty from third party documentation, whereas estimating provisions for slow-moving inventory could become very complex and require careful analyses of current and historical data, as well as assumptions about forecast sales where the entity depends on volatile consumer patterns of demand and does not have signed contracts to support the assumptions. In many instances, estimates are based on formulae evolved over time by the entity; the validity of the underlying assumptions need to be reviewed and reassessed periodically. Estimates may also be routine and generated automatically, such as a provision for warranty claims by a vehicle service division comprising a fixed percentage of sales invoiced and processed as part of the ongoing accounting entries, or non-routine and established only at the period end, such as provisions for doubtful debts. The uncertainty associated with certain estimations may have no objective or established criteria on which to determine their validity, such as provisions for settlement of litigation claims where the court judgment has yet to be given. In such circumstances, the auditor may need to consider a possible modification of the audit report.

The audit of accounting estimates

Where the auditor has determined that the particular accounting estimates comprise a significant risk of misstatement, the auditor should obtain sufficient appropriate audit evidence to detect and correct such misstatement, to establish that the balance is reasonable in the circumstances and, when required, is appropriately disclosed and presented in the financial statements. The assertions about which the auditor will be attempting to obtain audit evidence include *completeness, measurement and valuation, rights and obligations, and presentation and disclosure.*

The auditor needs to gain an understanding of the procedures and methods used by management to make the accounting estimates. The substantive audit procedures may include:

- Reviewing and testing the procedures used by management to develop the estimate, including:
  - *Evaluation of the data and consideration of the assumptions* on which the estimate is based. For example, is the data accurate, complete and relevant? Are the assumptions based on generally accepted industry or government statistics, or are they specific to the entity and based on internal data? Which assumptions are particularly sensitive to variation, subjective or susceptible to material misstatement? Does the complexity of the estimating warrant the use of an expert such as an actuary, engineer or geologist, chemist, etc.?
  - *Testing of the calculations* should be performed for estimates where a significant risk of misstatement is identified, including an assessment of the competence, experience and integrity of client staff involved in preparing and checking the estimates. Where the provisions are calculated using end-user computing facilities and electronic spreadsheets, this may necessitate on-line audit, by staff members with the requisite IT skills, of the relevant macros and calculations used.
  - *Comparison*, where possible, between *estimates made for prior periods* and the actual results obtained, for example, provision for doubtful debts versus actual bad debts written off in the following period.
  - *Consideration* of *management's approval* procedures, including the review and monitoring processes, the level of management involved, and evidence of such reviews in the supporting documentation.
  - In addition, the factors listed in Table 11.2 should be given due consideration in assessing the risk of significant misstatement in the estimates.

- *Using an independent estimate* for comparison with that prepared by management. The auditor may make or obtain an independent estimate and compare it with that used by management.

- *Reviewing of subsequent events* which confirm the estimates made. Transactions and events that may occur after the period end, but prior to completion of the audit, may provide evidence to support the amount and disclosures relating to the reasonableness of the estimate.

- *Involving more senior audit staff* in the audit of complex estimates carrying the risk of significant misstatement in significant balances.

Evaluation of results of audit procedures

Finally, the auditor needs to evaluate the evidence obtained, based on the auditor's knowledge of the business and whether or not the evidence is consistent with other evidence obtained during the audit. Where there are significant differences between the auditor's estimate and that of management, this requires a discussion with management and a decision regarding any proposed adjustment. Where the client refuses to amend the provision, the auditor needs to consider how the misstatement, along with other audit adjustments proposed, may affect the audit opinion.

11.4.4 Accounts involving related party transactions

The auditor is responsible for obtaining evidence regarding the identification and disclosure by management of related parties and the effect of related party transactions that are material to the financial statements. Some of the major risks associated with related parties arise from the fact that the supporting information regarding the identification of the related party and of related party transactions may be uncertain or incomplete. More importantly, related party transactions may not be on an arms-length basis and may lead to deliberate misstatements in the financial statements or attempts to hide fraudulent transactions.

GAAP AC 126 requires the disclosure of related parties and related party transactions in the audited financial statements, and SAAS 550 recognizes that it is management's responsibility to identify and disclose related parties and related party transactions. The existence of related parties may affect the financial statements, for example, the tax requirements for different legal jurisdictions may be different where related parties exist. The reliance placed by the auditor on external confirmations may be reduced where these are obtained from related parties.

SAAS 550, 'Related parties', provides guidance with regard to the auditor's responsibilities and the audit procedures to be performed. The first step is to understand who is a related party and, then, what transactions constitute related party transactions. Related parties and related party transactions are defined in paragraph .04 of SAAS 550, 'Related parties':

- *'Related parties* are considered as related if one party has the ability to control the other party or exercise significant influence over the other party in making financial and operating decisions.
- *Related party transactions* are the transfer of resources or obligations between related parties, regardless of whether, or not, a price is charged.

Also of interest, *control* and *significant influence* are defined as follows in paragraph .06 of GAAP AC 126, 'Related parties':

- *Control* is ownership directly or indirectly through subsidiaries, of more than one half of the voting power of an enterprise, or a substantial interest in voting power and the power to direct by statute or agreement the financial and operating policies of the enterprise.

- *Significant influence* (for the purpose of this statement) is participation in the financial and operating decisions of an enterprise, but not control of those policies. It may be exercised in different ways, usually by representation on the board of directors, participation in the policy-making process, material inter-company transactions, interchange of management, or dependence on technical information ...'

In a reporting entity, related parties may include holding, subsidiary and fellow subsidiary companies, associates, jointly controlled entities; individuals owning directly or indirectly voting interests that gives them significant influence, close family of such individuals; key management personnel, including directors, officers and any close family members; and enterprises where the individuals and key management mentioned previously also hold a substantial voting interest or are able to exercise significant influence in dealing between the two entities (AC 126, in paragraphs. 04 and .07).

Audit procedures to identify related parties

The auditor needs to review the information provided by management as to the identification of all related parties. To address the concern regarding the completeness of the information, the auditor should perform the following substantive audit procedures:

- Review prior year working papers for names of known related parties.
- Review the entity's procedures for identifying related parties.
- Enquire as to the affiliation of directors and officers with other entities.
- Review shareholder records to determine the names of principal shareholders.
- Review minutes of the board of directors and shareholders and the register of directors' interests for evidence of related parties.
- Inquire of other group auditors regarding additional related parties.
- Review income tax returns and other information supplied to regulatory authorities.
- Be fully satisfied regarding the disclosure of related parties in the financial statements.

In reviewing management's information about related party transactions, the auditor should be alert to the possibility of other material related party transactions. While the auditor is seeking to gain an understanding of the business, consideration should be given to the adequacy of control procedures over the identification, authorization and recording of related party transactions. In particular, the auditor should be alert to:

- transactions with abnormal trade terms;
- transactions that lack apparent logic;

- transactions in which substance differs from form;
- transactions processed in an abnormal manner;
- high volumes or significant transactions with certain customers or suppliers in comparison with others (although this does not of itself indicate a related party); and
- unrecorded transactions, such as provision of management services with no charges levied.

The review of identified related party transactions should include ascertaining whether they have been properly recorded and disclosed. Owing to the difficulties in identifying related parties and related party transactions, and where other audit evidence may not be expected to exist, the auditor should obtain written representations from management concerning the completeness of the information it has provided and the adequacy of disclosure in the financial statements.

11.4.5 Subsequent events

The responsibility of the auditor for events occurring after the balance sheet date has long been a vexed issue, and flows from the twin difficulties of pinpointing the timing of the authorization for issue and the actual date of issue of financial statements. The problem is often aggravated by those public companies which tend to press for early release of their results in newspapers and by the financial press presenting abridged 'audited financial results'. When this happens before the audit is fully completed, the management of those companies may then pressure the auditor to refrain from making any significant change which may affect the final, formally published annual report containing the audited financial statements.

The important consideration is the definition of 'events after the balance sheet date' – as contained in paragraphs .02 and .03 of GAAP AC 107, ' Events after the balance sheet date', and paragraph .03 of SAAS 560, 'Subsequent events' – and the distinction drawn between *adjusting* and *non-adjusting* events. The definitions describe:

> '*Events after the balance sheet date* as those events, both favourable and unfavourable, that occur between the balance sheet date and the date when the financial statements are authorized for issue and identifies two types of events:
>
> - Those that provide evidence of conditions that existed at the balance sheet date (adjusting events after the balance sheet date), and
>
> - Those that are indicative of conditions that arose after the balance sheet date (non-adjusting events).'

GAAP AC 107, 'Events after the balance sheet date', provides examples of the recognition and measurement of adjusting events and non-adjusting events, at paragraphs .09, .11 and .21.

In paragraph .01 of SAAS 560, 'Subsequent events', *subsequent events* refer to four stages of events occurring from the auditor's perspective, namely:

- 'After the period end but before the date of the auditor's report;
- After the date of the auditor's report but before the release of the auditor's report to the entity;
- After the auditor's report has been released to the entity, but before the financial statements are issued to users;
- After the financial statements have been issued to users.'

Clearly the risk of significant misstatement remaining in the audited financial statements relates to adjusting events not detected or adjusted, and non-adjusting events requiring disclosure but which are not appropriately disclosed.

Events occurring after the period end but before the date of the auditor's report

In the course of the substantive test of details of transactions and balances described earlier in this chapter, the auditor would already have reviewed subsequent events, for example, to establish the correct cut-off for sales and debtors, purchases, inventory and creditors, and the clearing of outstanding items in bank reconciliations to subsequent bank statements. In addition to these procedures, the auditor may perform the following specific substantive procedures to detect adjusting or non-adjusting events:

- review procedures management has in place to detect such events;
- read minutes of shareholders' and directors' meetings held after period end;
- review the latest draft of the financial statements for the current period;
- extend enquiries of attorneys related to litigation and claims;
- consider external information; and
- enquire of management as to whether subsequent events have occurred that might affect the financial statements, such as new commitments, borrowings, guarantees; disposals of assets or operating units; issues of shares or debentures; assets expropriated or destroyed by floods, etc.; plans to realize assets for less than their carrying value; developments regarding risk areas and contingencies; unusual accounting adjustments and events affecting accounting policies applied.

When the auditor becomes aware of such events, it is necessary to consider whether these have been appropriately accounted for or disclosed.

Facts discovered after the date of the auditor's report but before the financial statements have been issued to users

The auditor does not have any responsibility to perform procedures or to make any inquiry regarding the financial statements after the date of the audit report. In the period between the date of the auditor's report and the date of issue of the financial statements to users, the responsibility to inform the auditor of facts that might materially affect the financial statements rests with management.

When the auditor becomes aware of such a fact, the auditor should consider whether the financial statements need amendment or not, discuss the matter with management, and follow through with the appropriate action.

When management amends the financial statements as a result of such facts, the auditor issues a new report on the revised financial statements; the revised report should not be dated before the amended financial statements are signed and approved. The subsequent review tests would be extended to this new date.

Should management not amend the financial statements, when the auditor believes the statements require amendment and the auditor's report has not yet been issued to users, the auditor should modify his/her report to express a qualified or adverse opinion. Should management ignore the auditor's advice to amend the financial statements, the auditor needs to take action based on the recommendations of the auditor's attorneys, to prevent reliance on the audit report.

Facts discovered after the financial statements have been issued to users

After the financial statements have been released to users the auditor has no obligation to make any enquiries regarding such financial statements. If, after the issue, the auditor becomes aware of a fact that existed at the date of the report and which, if known at that date, may have resulted in a modified audit report, the auditor should consider whether or not the financial statements need revision and discuss the matter with management, and then take the action appropriate in the circumstances. Management has a choice to withdraw the financial statements issued, to revise and re-issue them, or to decide to do nothing.

- *Management revises the financial statements*: The auditor carries out the relevant subsequent review procedures, reviews the steps taken by management to ensure that everyone who received the previously issued financial statements is informed of the situation, and then issues a new report on the amended financial statements. The revised audit report should include an emphasis of matter explaining the reasons for revision of the previously issued audit report.

- *Management takes no steps, does not inform recipients of the situation, and does not revise the financial statements*: If the auditor believes the financial statements require amendment, the auditor should notify management that action will be taken by the auditor to prevent future reliance on the auditor's report. The action taken will depend on the advice of the auditor's attorneys. It may not be necessary to revise the financial statements when the issue of the financial statements for the following period is imminent, provided the appropriate disclosures are made in such financial statements.

11.4.6 Going concern

The going-concern assumption is a fundamental principle in the preparation of financial statements. The risk of significant misstatement arises for the auditor when the going-concern assumption is considered appropriate, when in fact it is not, and the auditor fails to detect the significance of the events or circumstances that cast significant doubt on the entity's ability to continue as a going concern. A further risk is that in the circumstances, material irregularities might occur, requiring reporting in terms of section 20(5) of the Public Accountants' and Auditors' Act, but the auditor fails to recognize these as material irregularities or fails to report them.

Consequently, when planning and performing audit procedures, the auditor should consider the appropriateness of management's use of the going-concern assumption in the preparation of the financial statements. Guidance on management's responsibilities in the assessment of the going-concern assumption, and the auditor's responsibilities in response to indications of going-concern problems, are contained in SAAS 570, 'Going concern'.

The two perspectives are discussed below.

Management's responsibilities

Financial statements should be prepared on a going-concern basis unless management intends to either liquidate the enterprise or has no realistic alternative but to liquidate. GAAP AC 107, 'Events after the balance sheet date', states clearly in paragraph .14 that 'an enterprise should not prepare its financial statements on a going-concern basis if it determines after the balance sheet date either that it intends to liquidate the enterprise, or has no realistic alternative but to do so as the effect is so pervasive that a fundamental change in the basis of accounting is required.' Management is required to state formally in the audited financial statements its assessment of whether the entity is regarded as a going concern for the foreseeable future, which should relate to a period not less than 12 months after the balance sheet date (GAAP AC 101, paragraph .25).

SAAS 570 provides guidance as to the numerous events or conditions, grouped broadly under the headings of *financial, operating and other circumstances*, which, individually or collectively, may cast significant doubt on the entity's ability to continue as a going concern.

The auditor's responsibilities

In planning the audit, the auditor should consider whether there are events or conditions which cast significant doubt on the entity's ability to continue as a going concern.

Throughout the audit, the auditor should remain alert to evidence of events or conditions which may cast significant doubt on the entity's ability to continue as a going concern. If such conditions are identified, in addition to considering the effect on the auditor's assessment of inherent and control risk (the risk of significant misstatement) and the level of detection risk set, the auditor should perform the following additional substantive tests of detail:

- review management's plans for future action based on its going-concern assessment;
- gather sufficient appropriate audit evidence to confirm or dispel whether or not a material uncertainty exists, by carrying out procedures considered necessary, including considering the effect of any plans of management and other mitigating factors; and
- seek written confirmation from management regarding its plans for the future.

The substantive procedures that the auditor performs will involve enquiry of management regarding its future plans, obtaining of external confirmations where appropriate; inspection of cash flow projections and the underlying assumptions made, including their reliability historically, minutes, contracts, enquiries of the entity's attorneys regarding claims and litigation pending, review of events after the balance sheet date to identify any that might mitigate the circumstances, and consideration of whether any additional information has become available since management performed its assessment.

Guidance as to the more detailed audit procedures the auditor would ordinarily perform is provided in paragraphs .25 to .27 of SAAS 570.

Audit conclusions and reporting

Based on the audit evidence obtained, the auditor has to determine whether, in the auditor's judgement, a material uncertainty exists which is related to events of conditions that alone or in aggregate may cast significant doubt on the entity's ability to continue as a going concern. The real difficulty with any going-concern assessment relates to the stage of going concern reached at the particular reporting date. Entities seldom suddenly experience going-concern problems and go into liquidation. There are invariably rumblings for some time, perhaps even several years before the company reaches the point of no return. Accordingly the auditor is generally reluctant to take a strong stand against management should it have plans that might reasonably turn the entity around from a loss situation to a profitable one. This dilemma has been recognized in the literature over many years. While no evidence could be found to support claims that a going-concern qualification in the audit report would ensure the entity's failure – in fact, the contrary has been found in many instances – there remains a perception on the part of management and the public that a going-concern qualification portends the failure of the entity. This problem is recognized in SAAS 570 at paragraphs .28 to .34, dealing with the reporting responsibilities of the auditor, which are identified as follows:

Going-concern assumption appropriate but a material uncertainty exists

- The auditor considers whether the financial statements describe the conditions or events giving rise to the significant doubt and management's plans to deal with these and state clearly that there is a material uncertainty which might cast doubt on the entity's ability to continue as a going concern.

- If adequate disclosure is made in the financial statements, the auditor should express an unqualified opinion and modify the audit report to include an emphasis of matter that highlights the existence of the material uncertainty relating to the event or condition that might cast significant doubt on the entity's ability to continue as a going concern and draws attention to the relevant note disclosures.

Going-concern assumption inappropriate

- If in the auditor's opinion the going-concern assumption is inappropriate and the financial statements have been drawn on the going-concern basis, the auditor has no choice but to express an adverse opinion.

- When the entity's management has concluded that the going-concern assumption is not appropriate and the financial statements are prepared on an alternative authoritative basis, usually referred to as the 'break-up' basis, reflecting the assets and liabilities as far as possible at net realizable values, assuming a sale or liquidation situation. If the auditor is able to validate the alternative basis and this appears appropriate, the auditor may express an unqualified opinion with an emphasis of matter to draw attention to the relevant disclosures.

11.4.7 Management representations

SAAS 580, 'Management representations', addresses the need for the auditor to obtain representations from management and provides an example of the wording of a typical management representation letter. It is recognized that throughout the audit the auditor obtains representations from many parties within and external to the entity being audited. These may be verbal or written and address the range of assertions underlying the financial statements. With regard to representations obtained in writing from management, it is probably true to say that it is a standard procedure by auditors on every audit engagement to request written representations. Such representations generally relate to obtaining evidence that management acknowledges its responsibility for the fair presentation of the financial information in the financial statements in accordance with the relevant reporting framework and has approved the financial statements.

Where sufficient appropriate audit evidence cannot reasonably be expected to exist, the auditor should obtain written representations from management on matters material to the financial statements. It is important to recognize, however, that management representations cannot be a substitute for audit evidence that the auditor could reasonably expect to be available.

If the contents of a management representation letter is contradicted by other audit evidence, the auditor should investigate the circumstances and, if necessary, reconsider the reliability of other representations made by management.

12

Auditing Revenue Transactions and Balances

Learning objectives

After studying this chapter you should be able to:

1. Describe the different sources from which an entity may derive its revenue and discuss how this may affect the rights and obligations between the entity and other parties.
2. Explain why revenue transactions and balances are regarded as a significant class of transactions and specify the accounts involved in revenue transactions and balances.
3. Describe the relationship between the financial statement assertions of management and audit objectives set for the various financial statement assertions contained in revenue transactions and balances.
4. Explain how the auditor's understanding of the revenue process level business risks and consideration of materiality affects the preliminary assessment of the risk of significant misstatement in the financial statements.
5. Discuss how the auditor's understanding of the client's internal control components could influence the assessment of the risk of significant misstatement for revenue transactions and balances.
6. Describe the types of documents, records and typical functions that may be encountered in credit sales, cash receipts and sales adjustments.
7. Discuss considerations applicable to the auditor's evaluation of inherent risks and relevant control activities affecting the various financial statement assertions for credit sales, cash receipts and sales adjustments.
8. Discuss relevant aspects of tests of controls when the auditor plans to assess control risk below the maximum for credit sales, cash receipts and sales adjustments.

9. Explain the principles to be applied and factors to be considered in evaluating the risk of significant misstatement remaining in the financial statements.
10. Explain how the auditor determines acceptable levels for detection risk and the effect on substantive audit procedures for sales and accounts receivable balances to obtain sufficient audit evidence to meet specific audit objectives.
11. Describe analytical procedures that would be effective in identifying accounts likely to contain material misstatements.
12. Design and execute an audit programme for substantive tests of detail of transactions and balances for sales, cash receipts and sales adjustments to achieve specific audit objectives.
13. Explain the use of confirmation procedures in substantive tests of accounts receivable.
14. Describe appropriate audit procedures to evaluate the allowance for irrecoverable accounts receivable.

12.1 NATURE OF REVENUE TRANSACTIONS

12.1.1 Introduction

The revenue transactions of an entity comprise the means by which it earns income from its business activities. This may take many different forms, for example:

TYPES OF BUSINESS	REVENUE SOURCES
A trading operation	A trading operation earns revenue from the buying and selling of goods which may be by way of a large retail operation with numerous stores and sales made to the general public, or as a wholesaler supplying retail outlets from bulk warehouses, or more recently, from the increasing use of internet selling or e-commerce transactions. Trading operations also typically include the small owner-managed trading businesses found in many 'flea markets', cafés, or general dealers in small towns and villages, which are a familiar sight in Africa.
An auto-motive manufacturer	Earns revenue from the supply of vehicles and parts to retail distributors of its particular vehicle brand; retailers in turn earn revenue from the sale of new and used vehicles and, where the vehicle sales outlet includes a petrol apron and vehicle servicing facility, they earn revenue from the sale of petrol to motorists, from the servicing of customers' vehicles and from the sale of vehicle parts to customers.

TYPES OF BUSINESS	REVENUE SOURCES
A manufacturer	Purchases raw materials and uses these in a manufacturing process to produce finished goods for users or for resale by other trading operations.
Advertising agencies	Earn fee revenues from the creative design of adverts and the 'flighting' of the adverts on television or radio and publication in various media, including Internet websites.
A professional practice	Lawyers, medical doctors and other medical service providers, accountants and business consultants earn income primarily from fees or commissions. Medical facilities such as hospitals and clinics bill for services rendered, ranging from the provision of ward accommodation and nursing facilities to bed patients, intensive care facilities, surgery facilities, the provision of drugs to patients, and rentals from consulting rooms occupied by medical practitioners.
IT consultants	Generate revenue by earning commissions on the supply of hardware and software, from service fees for installation and IT support services, by way of call centres provided to their clients, as well as from monthly fees as Internet Service Providers and licensing fees for the use of particular software products.
Investors	Earn revenue in the form of interest and dividends, from profits and losses from buying and selling investments, and from rentals earned from property investments made.
Estate agents	Earn revenue from commissions on property sales structured by them between willing buyers and sellers, and commissions from the management of property let on behalf of owners, usually calculated as a percentage of the rentals collected by them from property letting.
Public sector entities	May generate revenue from billings for services rendered, such as municipal accounts for the provision of water and electricity, and from taxes levied, such as property assessment rates, vehicle and business licence fees.
Schools and universities	Earn revenue primarily from billing fees to students (or their parents) and from government subsidies granted according to established funding formulae based on various criteria.
Banking and financial institutions	Earn revenue from bank charges levied on customers, and finance charges earned from the judicious investment of client's monies with the resultant interest or profits realized.

TYPES OF BUSINESS	REVENUE SOURCES
Insurance companies	Earn income from premiums charged to clients and from the investment of monies held. In the case of short-term insurers, the premiums would be applied for meeting insurance claims and costs of running the business; long-term insurers would be responsible for the investment of the premiums received, after allowing for a contribution from each premium to the costs of running the business, to provide for the retirement and death benefit claims of the persons insured.
Restaurants and fast food outlets	Generate revenue from the sale of food and drinks to patrons, while the farmer earns revenue from supplying produce to the fresh vegetable market and to abattoirs, butcheries and dairies.
Building contractors	Earn revenue from the billing of contract work completed.

Table 12.1 Revenue sources for different business entities

The nature of the business processes of the entity determine the sources of revenues that an entity might earn; this will affect the documentation required and the means of recording of individual transactions. Different GAAP revenue recognition policies may also apply, affecting the measurement of such transactions. Some companies may operate in global markets with multinational entities, others may operate locally and may run their business from their homes.

From the perspective of the financial statement audit, however, no matter how complex or simple the business processes, the audit focus is on management assertions affecting the income statement and balance sheet balances resulting from the revenue transactions. As discussed in the preceding chapters, these are: *existence or occurrence, completeness, measurement, valuation, rights and obligations,* and *presentation and disclosure.*

12.1.2 Audit objectives

To achieve audit objectives requires the auditor to obtain sufficient appropriate audit evidence regarding each significant assertion related to revenue transactions and resultant balances to reduce the risk of significant misstatement in the financial statements to appropriately low levels. Revenue transactions – by their very nature, volume and monetary amount, as well as the fact that they are separately disclosable in the audited financial statements – are usually the most significant figures in the income statement and will give rise to material balances in the balance sheet such as accounts receivable and cash and bank.

As revenue transactions are generated internally they are exposed to the risk of management override of internal controls of accounting processes and deliberate manipulations leading to fraudulent financial reporting. However, because of their volumes and amounts, revenue transactions are also likely to have more formal control activities implemented by management to manage the business risk exposure. Consequently, revenue transactions present an area where the auditor could obtain evidence from tests of controls supporting a medium to low assessment of inherent and control risk and leading to acceptance of a higher level of detection risk which may be addressed to a large degree by analytical procedures and reduced reliance on detailed substantive tests.

The discussion in the rest of this chapter uses a retail operation as a typical example of a business entity which generates revenue transactions, and the considerations affecting the tests of control, substantive analytical procedures and substantive tests of detail. However, the principles apply to many other types of revenue transactions encountered in other types of business operations. It is appropriate to start by indicating the account balances affected by revenue transactions. These are set out diagrammatically below.

REVENUE TRANSACTIONS	ACCOUNT BALANCES DEBITED	ACCOUNT BALANCES CREDITED
Credit sales	Accounts receivable Cost of sales	Sales Output VAT Inventory
Cash receipts	Bank discount allowed	Accounts receivable
Sales adjustments for goods returned or pricing adjustments	Sales returns Output VAT	Accounts receivable
Provision for bad debts	Bad debts expense	Allowance for irrecoverable debts
Bad debts written off	Allowance for irrecoverable debts	Accounts receivable

Table 12.2 General ledger account balances typically affected by revenue transactions for a trading operation

The audit objectives for the audit of revenue transactions and balances are derived from management's assertions and these are used as the basis for the discussion in this chapter. The links between the assertions and the corresponding audit objectives, which were discussed in chapters 9 and 10, can be set out as shown in Table 12.3.

MANAGEMENT ASSERTION	AUDIT OBJECTIVES
Revenue transactions	
Completeness	All sales made during the period have been recorded.
	All cash received during the period has been recorded.
	All sales adjustments during the period have been recorded, including goods returned, discount granted and bad debts written off.
Occurrence/ Validity	All sales recorded represent actual deliveries of goods supplied during the period.
	All cash receipts recorded represent cash actually received during the period.
	All sales adjustments recorded for goods returned, discounts granted and bad debts written off during the period were properly authorized and credits for goods returned relate to goods physically returned.
Measurement/ Accuracy	All sales, cash receipts and sales adjustments were accurately calculated in accordance with the GAAP policies applied by the entity and recorded in the correct accounts in the accounting records.
Revenue balances	
Completeness	Accounts receivable represent all amounts owing by customers at the balance sheet date.
Existence	Debtors, as reflected in accounts receivable at year-end, do exist.
Measurement/ Accuracy	Accounts receivable represent the sum of the balances owing by individual debtors at the balance sheet date.
Valuation	The provision for doubtful debts represents a fair estimation of the amount needed to reduce accounts receivable to net recoverable value at the balance sheet date.

MANAGEMENT ASSERTION	AUDIT OBJECTIVES
Rights and Obligations	Accounts receivable represent valid legal claims for payment that the entity has against its debtors at the balance sheet date. The rights of any creditor in respect of accounts receivable factored or pledged at the balance sheet to secure obligations of the entity have been identified.
Presentation and Disclosure	Turnover correctly discloses the net sales of the entity for the period in accordance with the GAAP policies applied by the entity. Accounts receivable are properly disclosed and classified in the financial statements. Appropriate disclosures have been made with regard to accounts receivable factored or pledged.

Table 12.3 Management assertions and the related audit objectives for revenue transactions and balances

12.1.3 Understanding the client's business

That it is important for the auditor to obtain an understanding of the client's business cannot be emphasized too strongly. It enables the auditor to assess the materiality and reasonableness of significant balances and classes of transactions reflected in the financial statements, and to understand the performance of the client entity relative to the external and internal factors affecting it. The auditor needs to be aware of laws and regulations affecting the client's business, of management's plans for future developments, locally or internationally, and of industry trends affecting that type of business. The auditor also needs to be alert to circumstances or events occurring in the country that may affect the client's revenues positively or adversely, and know what control activities management has in place to manage the risks arising.

Such understanding of the client's business enables the auditor to:

- recognize the potential risk of material misstatement in the financial statements arising from external or internal risks that management has not managed effectively;
- anticipate the total revenues of the business, the different gross profit margins expected for different categories of revenue and related expense accounts, as well as expectations with regard to total debts and debt collection periods that are the norm for the business;

- detect potential misapplications of GAAP, such as aggressive revenue recognition policies and failure to make adequate provision for irrecoverable debts and misappropriations of cash or other assets; and

- determine an effective audit strategy.

Consideration of materiality

The auditor's assessment of the inherent and control risks is done in the context of the *materiality* of any potential risk of significant misstatement. Revenue in a trading operation generally comprises one of the most significant balances in the income statement. Where sales are made on credit, accounts receivable could also comprise a significant balance in the balance sheet. Accordingly, the auditor would regard revenue as material. Where retail sales are made only for cash, cash at bank may be a material figure in the balance sheet. The significant risk of material misstatement then lies firstly in an overstatement of sales and accounts receivable and, secondly, in the risk of cash misappropriated. Auditors frequently base the level of quantitative materiality set on $\frac{1}{2}$% of total revenues for a trading business.

Where there are large volumes of cash sales, the business may well establish a treasury department as a second core process for cash management – generating significant amounts of interest income from the investing of surplus cash on daily or short-term call in money market accounts – until the cash is required for settlement of suppliers' accounts. The audit of this aspect of revenue is discussed in chapter 17.

12.1.4 Analysing revenue process level business risks

The significance of revenue transactions in driving the business and its cash flows makes it likely that management will implement strict controls around all aspects of sales, sales adjustments, cash receipts, and banking. Several key performance indicators may evolve to be monitored by management on a daily or weekly basis.

In applying the 'top-down' audit approach, and using the business model discussed in chapter 10 to obtain an understanding of the key business processes of the client, the auditor makes a preliminary assessment of the risk of significant misstatement in the financial statements and devises appropriate audit strategies.

As discussed in chapter 10, the core processes are analysed according to the various interrelated key processes and process level business risks. For example, the *key process of trading* involves the three main process level business transactions of product selection and purchasing; inventory management; and product pricing and sales – since the business cannot make any sales unless it has inventory on its shelves to sell. Revenue transactions and balances represent one of the process level business transactions. Product selection and purchasing as a process level business transaction is discussed in chapter 13, while inventory management as a business process level is discussed in chapter 14.

Knowledge of the interrelationships within each key process makes it possible for the auditor to build up an expectation of amounts affecting related transactions and balances; this facilitates the auditor's use of analytical procedures to identify material misstatements and reduces the extent of detailed substantive testing required.

An understanding and analysis of the revenue transactions for a trading client enables the auditor to identify the process level business risks and the respective inputs, activities and outputs, because these generally involve the implementation, by the client, of different control activities to manage the process level business risks. In a large retail trading operation, the control activities occur at different stages of the revenue transactions and are frequently performed by different persons. The analysis of the revenue process level business risks for a trading operation would focus on the control activities typically implemented over:

- credit sales to wholesale and possibly retail customers;
- cash sales to retail customers, cash receipts and credit card management; and
- sales adjustments.

In order to demonstrate the auditing principles, the control activities, control risk assessment, tests of controls, substantive analytical and detailed tests of revenue transactions and balances are discussed in view of the three aspects above.

12.1.5 Preliminary assessment of the risk of significant misstatement

The auditor should consider the combined effect of the inherent risk and control risks (the risk of significant misstatement) affecting revenue transactions and be alert to any that could occur in the particular client's business. (See Table 11.2 and discussions in chapter 11 on the evaluation of the overall risk of significant misstatement.) The *inherent risks* specific to revenue transactions and balances, and likely to be encountered, include:

- *Management bias and incentive to misstate revenues*, whether to achieve budgets, increase performance bonuses, inflate earnings for reporting in the financial statements, secure additional funding from banks, attract a potential purchaser for the business, or to affect the share price on the local Securities Exchange.

- The *complexity of the revenues billed*, for example, the possibility of errors of revenue and of VAT collection and VAT payment occurring where the entity has commenced Internet sales during the financial year and management still has limited experience of the problems that might be encountered.

- The risk of *management override of controls* to process fictitious sales around the financial year-end, which are subsequently reversed in the next financial year. Naturally this leads to an overstatement in both sales and accounts receivable.

- *Incorrect cut-off applied*, which means that sales from the next financial period are brought into the current period in error or deliberately. Conversely, sales for the current period may be accounted for in the next period.

- Pressures to *understate the allowance for irrecoverable accounts receivable* balances, particularly where several major customers owing substantial amounts are experiencing financial difficulties, or customers located in foreign countries are encountering difficulties in remitting payment to the client entity that may pose a potential going-concern problem for the client entity in the future.

- The *risk of fraud and theft* is high in a trading operation where a significant part of the revenues are settled in cash or by credit card or cheque.

- *High risk of theft* by staff and robbery attempts. Where a client entity operates multiple tills, for example, a hypermarket, it increases its exposure to problems in respect of security and physical controls over individual tills, the physical handling of large sums of money on a daily basis, and the counting and depositing of millions of Rand from multiple outlets.

- The risks of *irrecoverable amounts* arising from cash sales settled by customers with invalid cheques or stolen credit cards.

- The *risk of errors* occurring, for example:
  - when product barcodes are not updated to reflect new selling prices, the *sales* of a particular item may be recorded at the *wrong price*, affecting the gross margins realized; and
  - with high volume sales, errors often occur when the scanner at the till cannot read the item code, and when cashiers capture the *wrong code* or the *wrong quantity* of items sold, or when they give the *incorrect change* to a customer.

- The risk that, if not tightly controlled, *sales adjustments or returns* may be used by staff to *conceal theft of cash*.

- The *factoring of debts* creates complex rights and obligations that may lead to *classification errors in the balance sheet* and incorrect or inadequate disclosures in the notes to the financial statements.

Given the nature of the inherent risks and the usually high volumes of sales in a large retail operation, management is likely to design numerous control activities, in the first instance to prevent errors, but also to monitor those control activities aimed at the prompt detection of errors and misappropriations, as well as at the implementation of immediate corrective action. Before performing the tests of controls and substantive test procedures, the auditor makes a preliminary assessment of the *risk of significant misstatement for the revenue transactions and balances* in the financial statements. The auditor considers each of the factors listed below and documents the overall assessment as *high, medium or low*. This then influences the auditor's decision to follow a test of controls approach or a mainly substantive approach by way of analytical procedures and specific substantive tests of detail of transactions and balances. The reader is reminded that the risk would be assessed for the following factors, and the reasons for each factor documented:

- *Residual business risk,* that is, those risks remaining after consideration of the strategic and business process level risks and management's procedures to manage and control these risks.

- *Quality of the information* available, whether it is internal or external, corroborated, and factual or based on estimates.

- *Historical accuracy/measurement,* relates to the previous experience of the auditor with the entity in respect of the particular class of transaction, account balance and/or assertions.

- *Underlying assumptions used,* for example, whether based on GAAP, industry specific, general business conditions, financial, foreign exchange rates, interest rates, etc.

- *Qualifications and competence of the personnel* involved in accounting and recording, and the *complexity of the estimating process* involved in the particular class of transactions or balances and for the particular assertions.

- *Management bias* and/or any evidence of a management incentive to misstate, whether the incentive is personal benefit, market pressures and expectations, or budget pressures from management or group companies.

The auditor would seek corroborating information by way of enquiries, inspection of documents or observation of control procedures performed, to support the preliminary assessment of the risk of significant misstatement. The auditor would further identify the effect on the financial statements for particular account balances and design appropriate audit procedures to detect and correct any potential material misstatement remaining.

12.1.6 Consideration of internal control components

The aspects of the internal control components that could affect the assessment of the *risk of significant misstatement of revenue transactions and balances* are briefly considered overleaf. Before making decisions about the tests of controls that need to be performed, the auditor is likely to focus on management's monitoring activities and the design of detective controls, and whether these are appropriate for the objective they are intended to meet.

The related account balances arising from revenue transactions imply that the audit evidence for particular assertions for one balance is met for the corresponding balance as well. For example, if cut-off tests performed on sales and cash receipts indicate these are satisfactory and have been handled correctly, by inference the cut-off on accounts receivable balances will also be satisfactory.

12.1.6.1 Control environment

The control environment includes such factors as integrity, ethical values and organizational culture, competence of employees, management's philosophy and operating style, the manner in which the company assigns authority and the way in which it develops its people, and the direction given and attention paid by the board of directors (see the discussion on the control environment in chapter 9). These factors may positively or negatively affect the risk of significant misstatement of revenue transactions. The possible impact may be reduced if management, in consultation with employees, establishes a code of conduct that sets a zero tolerance for theft and misappropriation of assets and management is seen to be actively enforcing the code at all levels of staff, from the most junior to the most senior, with disciplinary hearings, dismissal of offenders, and legal action to recover assets. Management also displays its integrity in the way it adopts reasonable accounting policies, that is, by not encouraging aggressive revenue recognition attempts.

The human resource policies should allow for the employment of staff with the appropriate skills. In addition, these policies should actively support skills development and training both of new and existing staff members. Not only would this minimize the risk of errors occurring, it would improve the chances of detection and early correction of such errors that do arise. Management's operating style should convey a responsible and ethical approach to the running of the business. Management should be seen to be monitoring the control activities and should avoid deliberate attempts to override controls. Authority should be delegated in such a way that staff are made accountable for their actions, and these processes should be enforced by the monitoring procedures of management. If these various factors are not implemented or managed effectively, the risk of significant misstatement undoubtedly increases.

12.1.6.2 Risk assessment

Management's risk assessment processes related to revenue transactions should identify and evaluate those risks likely to impact most directly on the sales and delivery of goods and services, as well as on cash management procedures, such as handling the receipt, banking and investment of monies received. Management should be seen to implement effective, appropriate controls over aspects where the risks are most significant. Among the risks the management of a trading operation would need to manage, because they directly affect potential revenues, is the management of the related process level business transactions of the selection and purchasing of products to respond to changing consumer demands, and the management of inventory to ensure, at all times, that sufficient inventory levels are maintained to supply customers' needs whilst avoiding overstocking of unsaleable goods. It is important that management show a commitment to mitigating the risks of significant misstatement from revenue transactions.

12.1.6.3 Information and communication

The information and communication requirements within the entity must provide for adequate documentation of the system and of the policies and procedures implemented for all aspects of the entity's revenue transactions. This should include all the inputs, processing and outputs which ensure all revenue transactions are properly captured into the accounting records, which, in turn, result in the correct presentation and disclosure in the financial statements. It should include also the design of documentation for the various functions in the revenue transactions and the way in which cash and credit sales are initiated, evidence of delivery of goods supplied or returned, the recording of the sales and any adjustments, and the receipt and banking of cash (including cheques and credit card slips), debt collection processes, and printouts of the transaction audit trails, including any exception reports generated and account reconciliations performed.

Another important aspect is the IT systems used and the general and application controls (both manual and computerized) implemented over all aspects affecting the revenue transactions. A reminder here that unlike the general controls which are pervasive to the entire business, the application controls are specific to the input, processing and output for revenue transactions and balances – that is, for initiating, performing, recording, and monitoring the sales, sales adjustments and cash receipting and banking aspects.

12.1.6.4 Monitoring

Monitoring processes of particular interest to the auditor are those used by management as *key performance indicators* to monitor the effective functioning of control activities implemented over revenue transactions and designed to detect and correct errors and fraud or other risks that may adversely affect critical success factors for the business. These key performance indicators may address both external and internal risks and range from the monitoring of: bank interest rate changes (which affect management decisions regarding money market investments); daily reports on the total cashiers' takings and amounts banked for all stores around the country, including the highlighting of any unders and overs, allowing for immediate enquiry into the reasons; reports by internal audit on the effectiveness of marketing initiatives aimed at improving or marketing particular product brands; reports on gross margins realized on different product lines; the number of footfalls in each store on different days of the week or month in anticipation of periods of increased consumer volumes and activity requiring the allocation of additional staff; the incidence of customer complaints (for example, with regard to products returned or service received) and the effect on the buyer's decision to stock the particular items or advise the supplier that the items appear flawed.

On more formal reporting levels, monitoring processes include the monitoring of actual monthly or quarterly results against budget and targets set; reports on internal control weaknesses, from the internal and external auditors and from the risk assessment manager or director, identifying strategic or process level business risks, and management's actions in response to problems identified by the key performance indicators.

Due to the volumes and the likelihood that management will implement effective controls over revenue processes, it may well be that the auditor is able to assess control risk as medium or low and perform tests of controls to gather assurance regarding their design and operation throughout the period. The discussion now moves to the control activities in revenue transactions. An overview of the revenue process, which assumes a computerized environment, is set out in Figure 12.1.

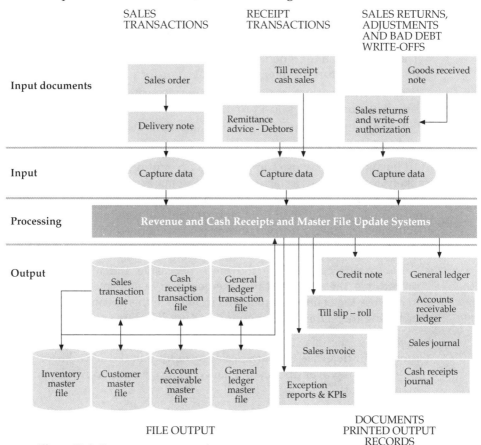

Figure 12.1 Revenue process overview

(Adapted from Boynton WC, Johnson RN and Kell WG, *Modern Auditing* (7 ed.), John Wiley & Sons Inc., USA, 2001, page 576.)

12.2 CONTROL ACTIVITIES AND TESTS OF CONTROL

As indicated in the introduction to this chapter, revenues may be earned by an entity from a variety of sources. The nature of the revenue transactions directly affect the form of documents used, the functions that occur, the recording processes followed, and the control activities implemented by management to ensure the input, processing and output for all *revenue transactions* recorded satisfy management's assertions of *completeness, measurement/accuracy and occurrence/validity*. Additionally, the process must allow for the balances arising from the revenue transactions to satisfy the assertions of management at the period end, namely, that of *existence or occurrence, completeness, measurement, valuation, rights and obligations, and presentation and disclosure*, as shown in Table 12.3.

The control activities for revenue transactions are discussed under the three main functions of credit sales, cash receipts and sales, and sales adjustments.

12.2.1 Credit sales transactions

The revenue transaction process has three major functions:

- The distribution of goods or services to customers in exchange for promises of future payment (credit sales) or for cash (cash sales).
- Receipts from customers for goods or services previously (credit sales) or simultaneously (cash sales) provided.
- Sales adjustments made for goods returned, adjustment of pricing errors, and bad debts written off or allowed for.

Most businesses today use computerized accounting systems and an auditor is likely to encounter a variety of IT systems at a client, as discussed in chapter 9. For purposes of this chapter, a computerized accounting environment is assumed. It is appropriate to remind readers that the effectiveness of the control activities in a computerized environment depend on two aspects, namely:

- *General controls:* These are the more pervasive and affect policies and procedures, the attitude of management and management's actions taken to address the control components to manage their businesses effectively, including the higher level monitoring and detection controls.

- *Application controls:* These are specific to the particular transaction process, in this case the sales, cash receipting and sales adjustments, as well as those over the maintenance of accounts receivable and cash management.

Weaknesses in general controls could mean that application controls which are thought to be appropriately designed and operating effectively, may not be relied upon, although this is not always the case.

12.2.1.1 Common documents and records for credit sales

The documents commonly encountered in the revenue transactions process for credit sales to customers include the following:

DOCUMENTS	NATURE OF DOCUMENT
Customer order	This is an external request, made verbally or in writing. Verbal orders are received over the counter, or conveyed to the salesperson by telephone. Written orders for goods and services to be supplied may be received using the customer's formal purchase order, generated as an Electronic Data Interchange (EDI) order, according to an EDI agreement between the client and the customer, or they may be received electronically in the form of an order placed on the business's website.
	In the case of an EDI or e-commerce order, a formal 'acceptance of order' may be e-mailed to the buyer by the seller to confirm the instructions received and, in addition, to request details such as the buyer's credit card or bank account number, which allows for the immediate charge to their bank or credit card account of the selling price in lieu of a printed and signed contract. In essence, there must be a contractual relationship established between the parties, which commences at this point.
The sales order	This may be generated by the entity to capture the customer's details and request into a format that is acceptable to the particular accounting system. The details may well be captured directly into the computer, forming the data entry which will allow the computer system to generate the rest of the internal documents evidencing the sales transaction, namely, a delivery note and invoice set and subsequent entries to the customer's account and the general ledger accounts.
	The sales order may also represent an acknowledgement of the order and constitute an acceptance of the contract. Sales orders will be pre-numbered. This allows for a sequence check to be performed at a later stage. Any break in sequence would indicate unprocessed orders and thus loss of sales.

DOCUMENTS	NATURE OF DOCUMENT
Delivery document	The form used to evidence delivery of the goods will depend on how delivery is to be made: Local deliveries by the entity to its customers, or collected by customers from the entity's premises, may simply be accompanied by a sequentially numbered *delivery note* or *waybill*. This reflects details of the items purchased by the customer and provides a place for the customer's signature, serving as acknowledgement of receipt of the goods or services. A copy of a delivery document is usually retained by the customer and another is returned to the supplier. Where the goods ordered have to be exported or transported by another carrier, whether by road, rail, air or sea, evidence of delivery may take the form of a *bill of lading*, comprising a variety of *shipping documents* covering costs, insurance and freight. The carrier may be the agent of the seller or the buyer, and this determines when constructive delivery will occur and when rights and obligations will pass from the buyer to the seller. This aspect is important in determining the timing of *revenue recognition* and usually requires a separate indent file for each such shipment, as well as recording in a shipping register.
Sales invoice	This document reflects the amount charged to the customer and provides details of the goods or services supplied, the terms of the sale, and payment arrangements, for example, 30 days, 60 days, etc. The sales invoice also reflects any VAT charged to the customer and zero-rated items to which VAT does not apply.
Monthly statement	Printed at the end of the month for posting to the customer, this document reflects the sales and receipts transactions during the month, as well as any credits (or debits) passed for sales adjustments.
Sales transactions file	All sales made to customers during a particular period are recorded in the sales transactions file. It provides the basis for maintaining sequence controls over invoices that are likely to be numbered automatically by the sales invoicing system. This file would be used during the revenue transactions processing run (batch update basis) to update the accounts receivable ledger and general ledger sales, the accounts receivable

DOCUMENTS	NATURE OF DOCUMENT
	control account, and the inventory account for the quantities and cost of goods sold. In an on-line real-time system the accounts receivable, inventory and general ledger accounts are updated immediately as transactions are captured. The file contents are generally referred to as *current data*, which will be closed off at the end of the financial period.

Table 12.4 Common documents used for credit sales

Computer stationery should be designed distinctively, bearing the entity's details, logos, etc. Its layout should ensure that the nature and purpose of each document is clear to internal users and external third parties and that it meets all legal requirements.

In addition to the above documents, which all arise from the credit sales transactions, the entity will maintain the following computerized accounting records to process revenue transactions applicable to all three functional areas, namely credit sales, receipts and sales adjustments.

COMPUTERIZED ACCOUNTING RECORDS	NATURE OF RECORD
Customer master file or customer relationship file	This file contains the details of approved customers with comprehensive details, including the name, *account number*, delivery address, postal address, telephone numbers and contact persons, *credit limits, payment and discount terms*, and, frequently, a history of sales made by the entity to the customer over a period. New customers added, or deletions, or approved customers who have exceeded their credit limits and who are refused further credit facilities would be flagged in this file. Any changes to this file would normally require senior staff authorization. The file contents are sometimes referred to as *standing data* as changes to the details occur infrequently.
Pricing master file	This file usually contains a complete record of all inventory items available for sale and the authorized selling prices for each item. Once again, as with the customer master file, any changes to this file should require the authorization of senior staff, such as the marketing manager or director, as it is the source of all the prices used to invoice customers. The file contents are sometimes referred to as *standing data* as changes to the details occur infrequently.

DOCUMENTS	NATURE OF DOCUMENT
Accounts receivable master file	This file contains a complete record of transactions with the customer, namely, credit sales, receipts and sales adjustments for goods returned, discount granted, pricing adjustments and bad debts written off. It also reflects the balance owing at any given time by the customer/debtor. Details contained in this file form the basis for an age analysis of the outstanding amount, comprising the balance owing from a debtor and, of course, for an aged analysis listing of all accounts receivable balances at any particular date.
General ledger master file	This file contains the detailed accounts recording the revenue transactions and balances for each financial accounting period. Accounts affected include: the cumulative *sales* transactions account/s, *sales returns, accounts receivable, bad debts written off, allowance for irrecoverable accounts receivable* and *output VAT*.
Inventory master file	This file contains the details of all inventory descriptions and quantities on hand, as well as the date of inventory quantities received, returned or sold. The file would be updated during the *sales processing run* with the products sold and supplied to customers during the period, reducing the balance on hand at the period end. It may well contain a history of sales volumes for the individual product line items.

Table 12.5 Common computerized records for credit sales

In addition to the documents that would be printed by the computer system discussed above, management would obtain other printouts from the accounting records relevant to credit sales transactions that would include the following:

PRINTOUTS	NATURE OF PRINTOUT
List of sales transactions	A monthly list of *sales transactions*, from the *sales transactions file*, which may be analysed by product line, geographic area, by salesperson, or sales outlet. This printout would normally be distributed to the marketing department and the financial management.
Accounts receivable age analysis	A monthly *age analysis of accounts receivable*, as well as a detailed accounts receivable listing reflecting the details of each customer's account and comprising the outstanding balance owing at the date of the listing.

PRINTOUTS	NATURE OF PRINTOUT
General ledger trial balance	*General ledger trial balance* including the balances related to the revenue transactions balances.
Key performance indicators	These may include gross margins on product lines where sales have occurred, turnover of inventory balances and slow moving lines; age analysis by percentage of accounts receivable balances, and outstanding debt recovery periods.
Exception reports	*Exception reports*, for credit sales, could include a list of missing sequence numbers for invoices not yet processed to accounts receivable; a list of debtors who have exceeded their credit limits; gross margins for product lines or categories which do not fall within defined parameters; sales level to major customers; and long outstanding accounts receivable balances.

Table 12.6 Common printouts for credit sales

Certain staff members, such as clerks involved in debt collection and senior sales managers, may be granted access to the details of accounts receivable and inventory pricing files by means of on-line enquiry programs. This enables a clerk to deal with enquiries from particular customers with regard to their accounts, to settle an amount owing, or to query a particular charge levied. This access should not enable the staff to make any changes to account balances without following the normal procedures for processing sales adjustments, or making changes to standing data in master files.

12.2.1.2 Credit sales functions

A series of activities relates to credit sales functions. The revenue transaction process for credit sales begins when an order for goods or services is received. A decision is made, based on the creditworthiness of the customer, to supply on credit or to insist on a cash sale. Goods ordered are supplied or services rendered, the customer is invoiced and the sale is recorded. The revenue transaction process for credit sales is completed when payment is received from the customer in accordance with the terms of sale and the cash received is recorded. Other entries may be made when appropriate, such as those to reflect sales returns or cash discounts, or to write off irrecoverable accounts receivable balances.

The credit sales functions may be subdivided into four distinct functional areas, as follows:

- the initiation and credit control function;
- the dispatch function;
- the invoicing function; and
- the sales and accounts receivable recording function.

In order to meet the basic requirements of an effective system of control over credit sales, the activities under each of the functional areas should be organized and the records prepared in the manner discussed below.

The initiation and credit control function

A credit sale commences with an order received from a customer and requires the acceptance of the order by the entity to constitute a valid contract. This binds the entity (the seller) to supply the goods ordered; in turn, the buyer accepts the obligation to pay for the goods when they are received. Clearly, an order cannot be accepted if the entity does not have the inventory, or if the entity cannot supply the goods, or supply the goods within the delivery period required by the customer. Equally, the entity will not wish to supply a customer if it is unlikely to be paid for the goods supplied. Consequently, most businesses will establish a credit control department. In the case of an owner-managed business, the credit control function may be performed by the owner, who would wish to determine the credit standing of the customer before the order is accepted. Reference should be made to the status of the customer's account and credit limit before orders received are approved for further processing. In the case of verbal orders at the counters, the sales assistant should be able to access the customer's current credit status and limits by means of an on-line enquiry program. Before filling the order, any credit granted in excess of that in the customer master file should be authorized by senior sales personnel or, if one exists, the credit department.

New customers should be required to follow laid-down procedures for the granting of credit. Such procedures would usually include: the completion of a credit application form, requiring details of trade references (companies with whom credit accounts are kept), bankers' references and, in the case of individuals, their current earnings. Based on this information and enquiries to trade referees, the credit department should establish credit limits for customers. This credit rating and detailed information would be captured into the customer master file. Any changes to the customer master file should be authorized by a senior credit controller or by management.

The identification of a customer of a manufacturer or wholesaler is usually fairly simple, since orders are ordinarily received on a customer's formal letterhead or a printed order form. In the case of a large retail business, each customer may be given a customer card (shopping card) with an account number to facilitate identification and encourage the customer to buy from the entity on a regular basis. The production of the card when buying goods is normally accepted as sufficient evidence of identity and credit standing.

These controls are designed to reduce the risk of non-recovery of debts for goods supplied and relate to the *valuation* assertion for accounts receivable. If, in the auditor's assessment, the controls exercised by the credit control at the initiation stage are effective, this may reduce the detailed audit work to be performed later in evaluating the allowance for irrecoverable debts. It also means that adequate information should be available to support the estimate of the allowance required and, if combined with sound debt collection procedures, may result in a lower allowance for irrecoverable debts being required at year-end.

The dispatch function

The dispatch of goods and the preparation of the invoice for each sale should be so arranged that the risk of unauthorized removal of goods from the premises be kept to a minimum. There are various ways of achieving this, depending on whether the goods sold are delivered to customers or taken by customers at the counter.

Goods delivered

Where goods are delivered to customers, the following controls might be implemented:

- All orders, whether received directly from a customer or through a sales representative, in writing or verbally, should be recorded so that every order can be accounted for in a methodical manner. This should be done on pre-numbered sales order forms. In a retail or wholesale business, where goods are sold from inventory, the computerized accounting system will usually automatically and sequentially number a full document set, comprising the sale order, delivery note and invoice, for any sale of inventory. Generally the same number will be allocated to each document to facilitate subsequent follow up and control over the *completeness* of transactions.

- No parcel of goods should be dispatched without a pre-numbered delivery note being attached to it. In some types of business, such as a retail store, it is common practice for the invoice itself to be given to the purchaser, thus also serving the function of a delivery note.

- Where delivery of the goods takes place by the seller's own transport, some evidence that the customer has received the goods should usually be obtained (and where the value is high, that the items delivered are those ordered). This may be done by having duplicate copies of delivery notes, one copy being signed by the customer and returned to the deliverer. Alternatively, the delivery person may obtain the customer's signature opposite the relevant entry in a delivery book. There are cases where evidence of delivery is dispensed with, where the value of the articles delivered is small and it is inconvenient to obtain such evidence, for example, newspaper deliveries.

- Where goods are sent by public transport, the copy of the consignment note signed by the representative of the transport service and returned to the sender acts as evidence of the proper delivery of the goods.

- The delivery notes or their equivalent, signed by the customers, should be filed methodically in sequential order. The dispatch department of the business should capture the dispatch details into the computer system to keep a record of all goods physically dispatched, including:
  - the date of dispatch;
  - the name and address of the customer; and
  - the delivery note number.

- A fairly frequent check of sales *cut-off* should be made by a senior member of staff to determine whether every invoice issued in a particular period is accounted for in the goods outward record in the same period and vice versa. This is especially important towards the close of one financial year and during the first few weeks of the next: an invoice which is charged in one year in respect of goods delivered in the succeeding year (and therefore treated as part of the inventory at the year-end) will wrongly increase the recorded profit; conversely, an invoice charged in the succeeding year for goods delivered in the present one will wrongly reduce the recorded profit. This monitoring procedure will provide evidence of the correct *measurement/accuracy* of the transaction in respect of its allocation to the correct accounting period.

- Prior to dispatch, items should be checked against delivery notes to ensure that the description and quantity of goods correspond. It is a good practice for the dispatch clerk to initial the delivery note as evidence of this check. This control activity will provide evidence of the *completeness* and *occurrence* of the transaction.

- All goods should leave the dispatch department or the company's premises through an authorized exit only. Should the value of goods warrant it, it may be appropriate to have a gatekeeper who checks that only parcels accompanied by a delivery note leave the company's premises. Such procedures are designed to minimize the risk of misappropriation of inventory and of losses due to the omission of sales information affecting the *completeness* and *occurrence* assertions.

Counter sales and deliveries

Where the customer purchases on credit and merely collects the goods from the business premises, for example, a vehicle parts centre, the same delivery and invoicing process and documentation would be prepared as for goods delivered to the customer. Again, the customer would be expected to sign the delivery note as evidence of receipt of the goods supplied, should he or she subsequently default on payment. This provides evidence of the *occurrence* assertion.

Where the sales over the counter amount to 'cash sales', the procedures applicable to the recording of cash sales and receipting would be followed. In this case, the 'invoice' may merely comprise a till slip given to the customer upon receipt of payment for the goods purchased.

In order to guard against the unauthorized removal of goods, it is the practice in many stores to pack goods, which have been invoiced, in wrapping paper or packets bearing the name of the store. Security staff can thus more easily detect any person who leaves a department or the store with what might be stolen goods. Other stores, such as Makro, do not provide any bags and items purchased are merely taken by the customer in a shopping trolley, with security guards checking all the items in the trolley to the customer's till slip before allowing them to be taken from the premises.

The invoicing function

The invoicing of customers should be done in such a way as to ensure that all goods delivered are invoiced (that is, none are omitted); that only goods actually delivered are invoiced (that is, none are duplicated or fictitious); that the goods delivered are invoiced to the correct customer at the correct price; and finally, that all invoiced goods are recorded in the general ledger and accounts receivable ledger in the correct accounting period. This clearly affects all three assertions, *completeness, occurrence/validity and measurement/ accuracy*. Failure to implement adequate control procedures over all of these aspects will greatly increase the risk of a significant misstatement in the financial statements.

A trading company will generally have computerized accounting systems allowing for a number of the control procedures to be programmed into the sales application program, ensuring these assertions are met for every transaction. For example, once the sales order is captured and credit approval given, the system should be programmed to perform the following checks automatically for every credit sales transaction:

- Match the customer name and account number to the *customer master file* to ensure the invoice is allocated to the correct accounts receivable account – meeting the *measurement/accuracy* assertion.

- Match the sales order details with the delivery note and invoice set to ensure the existence of the debtor and occurrence of the transaction.

- Match the description of the goods on the sales order and delivery note with the inventory codes in the *inventory master file* to ensure the correct item is invoiced.

- Match the price quoted on the sales order and that used on the invoice to the *pricing master file* containing the authorized price list to ensure the *measurement/accuracy* assertion is met and items are charged at the correct prices.

- Have programmed checks on the mathematical accuracy of the invoices, both with regard to the amount charged for the items supplied and for the calculation of output VAT to ensure the *measurement/accuracy* assertion is met.

- Separate the preparation of invoices from the dispatch and inventory control departments.

The customer's name and the quantity and description of goods supplied should be obtained from the relevant delivery note and the price from the *pricing master file* or quotation. The delivery note should preferably be a copy of the invoice, thus fulfilling the requirement, in the most direct manner, of ensuring that all goods leaving the business are invoiced out. In a computerized sales system this is generally achieved with the printing of a multiple sales document set, with all documents having the same sequence number and comprising the sales order, delivery note and invoice. Sales staff should scrutinize even computer-generated invoices before uploading these to the customer's account in order to detect apparent errors. If this is done, the person performing the scrutiny should initial the invoice as evidence of the check performed. It should be borne in mind that computers do make errors and where this is due to programming errors, the problem will potentially affect every transaction processed. The auditor should be alert to the possibility that such errors may be deliberate and indicate a fraud.

The revenue recording function

This is the final stage of recording the credit sales invoice from the sales transaction file, into the general ledger – sales, accounts receivable, cost of sales and output VAT accounts – as well as to the individual debtor's account in the accounts receivable ledger. The sales processing run should also update the customer master file, if a history of sales transactions is maintained there, and the inventory master file for the cost of sales and the quantities of goods sold.

The reader is referred to the discussion in chapter 9 regarding the different computerized accounting environments, from relatively basic stand-alone PC systems to sophisticated database applications. The important control activities that management need to have implemented are:

- Controls to ensure that sales recorded relate to transactions that have occurred. The system may allow for the sales invoices to be processed only once the dispatch clerk records the receipt of the signed delivery note acknowledgement from the customer. In many computerized accounting systems the updating of the accounts receivable and general ledger accounts will occur with the sales transaction processing run. Where the computerized system is an on-line real-time system, the updating will occur automatically as the transaction is captured. Controls, whether manual or programmed, that match the invoice recorded to signed delivery notes from the customer will ensure the *completeness and occurrence/validity* of the transactions recorded. It will also provide evidence of the *rights and obligations* between the parties and the *existence* of the debtor recorded in the accounts receivable ledger.

- Programmed sequence controls over the invoices processed should result in an exception report where sequence numbers are missing or are duplicated. There should be evidence of management follow-up and correction or appropriate action taken for all exception reports. This will ensure the *completeness* of recorded sales transactions.

- There should be evidence of data and procedural controls over data, files and programs, such as reconciliation and monitoring controls to ensure that the correct opening balance files are used for the periodic sales processing run to update the general ledger accounts and other master files. In addition, the procedures should provide for the reconciliation of the movement between the opening and closing balances of control accounts, for example the accounts receivable ledger control account is reconciled with the total of the month's transactions recorded for sales, sales adjustments and receipts from debtors. The system should provide for 'run-to-run' totals to be generated and manually checked by accounting staff.

- Regular printouts of the month's sales transactions, as well as key performance indicators and comparisons to budgets and targets set for sales personnel should be reviewed by marketing management to probe any unusual trends and take corrective action.

- A listing of aged accounts receivable balances and movements for the current month should be printed out and reviewed by the marketing manager and the credit controller responsible for debt collections. Marketing management should be held accountable for any bad debt write-offs. The list should show the individual account balances, analysed by the age of the components of the total debt. This aged accounts receivable list is used by the credit control department to identify customers who have exceeded their credit terms and to whom letters of reminder or demand will be sent. There should be a firm policy that the debts of those customers who fail to respond to these letters are handed over to the company's attorneys for collection. The monitoring of the aged accounts receivable list also provides management with information concerning the effectiveness of the credit-granting and debt-collecting procedures.

- The list of accounts receivable balances referred to above is normally produced at the time when the accounts receivable monthly statements are prepared. These statements should be prepared and mailed to customers owing amounts by accounting staff with no involvement in the capturing of sales transactions or recording or approval of sales adjustments or the receipt and depositing of receipts from debtors.

12.2.1.3 Value-added tax

Mention has been made, in the discussion of credit sales, of the responsibility of an entity which is a registered vendor under the Value-Added Tax Act 1991, to recover output VAT from its customers for payment to the South

African Revenue Services (SARS). Appropriate procedures should be put in place to ensure the monthly VAT returns are completed and submitted, and that the output and input VAT amounts are correctly captured into the accounting system from the sales invoicing and expenditure transactions and properly reconciled for submission and payment to or recovery from SARS. Such procedures should ensure that the *completeness, occurrence/validity, measurement/accuracy, and rights and obligations assertions* are met.

It could be that the client's value-added tax inputs exceed the tax outputs for the last VAT tax period for the financial year, in which case SARS should be reflected in accounts receivable in the year-end financial statements. The same is true where the last VAT return submitted reflects a refund due which has not yet been settled. In these circumstances, the auditor needs to agree the balance owing by SARS to the VAT control account in the general ledger and copy of the relevant return submitted. If the amount has been paid over in the next financial period, the auditor should agree the amount owing at the year-end with the refund received.

The auditor should be alert to circumstances where the client appears to have failed to comply with the complex provisions of the VAT Act, for which substantial penalties may be incurred. In these circumstances the auditor may need to discuss the need for a detailed substantive audit of the VAT control account and VAT returns submitted.

12.2.2 Cash sales and receipt transactions

A business entity receives cash from many sources, *inter alia*, cash sales, receipts from debtors, investment income in the form of interest and dividends, rental income, receipts from the disposal of fixed assets and investments, insurance claims, proceeds from the issue of shares, long-term and short-term loans received; intercompany charges levied for services provided. This chapter discusses cash receipts from cash sales and the collection of accounts receivable. The discussion proceeds in chapters 13, 14 and 15 to the audit of cash payments relating to expenditure transactions and production and personnel transactions. Chapters 16 and 17 follow with the audit of cash balances related to investing, financing, securities and cash balances.

12.2.2.1 Documents and records for cash sales and receipt transactions

The documents commonly encountered in the revenue transactions process for cash sales and receipts from credit customers include the following:

DOCUMENTS	NATURE OF DOCUMENTS
Cash summary sheets and cash register tally rolls	From cashiers operating cash registers or point of sale terminals for cash sales. The cash summary sheet will record the *cash, cheques* and *credit card slips* counted by the cashier at the end of each shift and, after deduction of the cash register float, should be agreed to the total of the cash register tally roll or electronic total registered for the particular cash register for the particular cashier's shift.
Remittance advices	Received from credit customers detailing how the amount paid by them has been arrived at. These may not always be received, and when received, may take different forms, from the remittance advice tear-off slip on the customer's statement to a written letter and detailed summary sent by the customer, or simply a cheque received in payment without any explanation. The remittance provides the information for the client entity to allocate the receipt in the account receivable correctly. This is important for the correct ageing of any balance outstanding as errors in allocation may affect the estimate of the allowance for irrecoverable amounts and accordingly the *valuation* assertion.
Remittance diary	Prepared by the person or persons responsible for opening the mail and recording remittances received from credit customers. Every such remittance should be recorded with details of the name of the drawer, the amount and the date of the cheque (to highlight any *post-dated cheques* received that cannot be deposited immediately), and whether any remittance advice is attached to aid in the correct allocation of the receipt against amounts owing by the customer. Where *uncrossed cheques*, payable to the entity, are received through the mail, the cheques should be restrictively crossed immediately, with the words *Not Transferable*. This is to prevent the possible misappropriation and cashing of such cheques by employees who have access to them. Controls in this area affect the *completeness* of cash receipts banked and recorded.

DOCUMENTS	NATURE OF DOCUMENTS
Electronic funds transfer advices received from the bank or customers	For payments made by electronic transfer from customers – generally large customers who find it safer to pay their suppliers in this way rather than mailing cheques and running the risk of theft and misappropriation. Identification of the customer is necessary to ensure the receipt is allocated to the correct accounts receivable, affecting the *measurement/accuracy* assertion.
Photocopies of bank stamped deposit slips	Where customers have made direct deposits to the entity's bank accounts in settlement of amounts owing they may well attach a copy or the original of the relevant bank stamped deposit to their remittance advice in order to facilitate the entity's identification of the customer who has deposited the amount to the entity's bank account. It is necessary to identify the customer to ensure the receipt is allocated to the correct accounts receivable, affecting the *measurement/accuracy* assertion.
Bank stamped deposit slips prepared by the entity	For daily deposits of cash, cheques and credit card slips from cash sales and remittances from credit customers. This provides evidence of the *completeness, existence* and *occurrence* assertions.
Bank deposits	For *electronic credit card or bank debit authorizations:* received from e-commerce transactions on the entity's website on the Internet. These provide evidence of the *completeness, existence* and *occurrence* assertions.
Debit orders tape and printout	Businesses such as Insurers, Medical Aids and Security services – who derive their income from regular monthly insurance premiums or contributions from members or customers – may obtain a signed authorization from the client or member to process a debit order against the individual's bank account. The authorization and client details are loaded onto a tape which is run electronically and instructs the various banks to process the payments from their clients' banking accounts on a particular day each month to recover the relevant amounts owing.

DOCUMENTS	NATURE OF DOCUMENTS
Receipts may be issued to credit customers	On request, as evidence of the payment made. This may take the form of a cash register or point of sale terminal imprint on the remittance advice when the payment was made to the cashier, or a manual receipt may be made out. Not all credit customers will request a receipt, but the amount paid would be credited to their account and should reflect on the following month's statement to the customer.
ACCOUNTING RECORDS	**NATURE OF RECORD**
The cash receipts journal	May be maintained manually or generated electronically from the capture of the detailed bank deposit slips to record receipts from cash sales and remittances from credit customers.
The cash receipts transactions file	Will record all cash receipts captured into the computer systems. During the 'cash receipts' processing run, it will be used to update the general ledger bank balances, the relevant cash sales accounts and individual accounts receivable accounts in the accounts receivable ledger. Where the credit customer has been granted discount for early payment, the discount allowed amount would be recorded in the cash receipts journal and the gross amount would be credited to the customer's account with the net amount deposited into the bank account.

Table 12.7 Common documents and records for cash sales and receipts

12.2.2.2 Cash sales and receipt functions

Cash received by the entity will arise from two main sources: first, from *cash sales and receipts* 'at the tills' and, second, from *remittances from credit customers* usually received 'through the mail', in payment of their accounts receivable balances. These will be dealt with separately below.

The cash sales and receipts functions may be subdivided into the following four distinct functional areas:

- *Cash sales:* recording the distribution of goods or services to customers in exchange for cash;
- *Receipt* of cash, cheques, credit card slips;
- *Depositing* of cash, cheques, credit card slips received into the entity's bank accounts; and
- *Recording* of the cash, cheques, credit card slips received, in the books and records of the entity.

The main risk attaching to cash receipts transactions is the risk of theft before or after the recording of the cash and consequently the main risk of significant misstatement in the financial statement is firstly one of *completeness* and secondly of *occurrence/existence*. Readers will also notice that unlike the credit sales functions, both the receipt of cash and depositing of cash involve primarily manual activities and procedures. The result is that many of the controls over the receipt and depositing functions will involve manual checks rather than programmed controls and it is only once the receipts are recorded that programmed controls will become effective.

Many businesses handle large volumes of cash. For example, a large supermarket or hypermarket may have 30 or more point of sale terminals operating during busy times, with cashiers working in shifts of several hours each. Clearly, in such a business the implementation of strict security controls over cash is necessary. This may include:

- The employment of security guards, within and outside the store, and the use of surveillance cameras at strategic points, monitored continuously from a security centre, to detect shoplifters and monitor cashiers and cash controllers having responsibility for the counting of cash and preparation of bank deposits.

- The use of drop safes. These contain locked cash security boxes in which completed deposit slips are placed for collection by the appointed coin security company, who holds the keys to the drop safe and will take its contents to the bank for depositing. The entity retains a record of all deposit slips placed in the drop safe to compare to the bank stamped slips returned by the coin security company after deposit at the bank.

- Coin security companies. Security companies are, in turn, susceptible to armed cash heists en route to the bank. Since the drop safe security boxes could be stolen, the entity's cash receipts are still exposed to risk of theft even after being recorded. Management will usually carry cash loss insurance to cover this risk, but the entity will need to maintain precise records to prove subsequently what monies were in the locked drop safes handed to the coin security company for transporting to the bank.

By comparison, in a small trading operation, the owner-manager will exercise controls over a few cashiers, or act as cashier himself or herself. The owner is also likely to implement security by way of security guards and surveillance cameras located in various parts of the store to detect shoplifters and to monitor activities of the cashiers and customers at the cash registers or point of sale terminals in the store. Owner-managed businesses may find the use of drop safes and coin security companies too expensive, in which case the owner or trusted employees will handle the banking of the deposits personally. Such trading operations are also exposed to the risk of loss by theft and personal physical injury, which may be fatal.

Readers will notice that in all instances the cash transactions are between the entity and third parties in the form of customers and banking institutions.

This provides an indirect, but independent check, on the accuracy and completeness of receipts recorded, in that customers will eventually complain if payments made by them are not reflected in their accounts, or if debit orders processed by the entity are duplicated, or cash sales are run up incorrectly on a cash register.

Recording cash sales

Effective control over cash sales involves two basic requirements, namely:

- Every cash sale must be recorded in the correct amount.
- There must be an effective comparison of the cash sales amount recorded and the amount of cash received from this source to the cash deposited and recorded in the general ledger and bank accounts.

Most retail trading operations make use of cash registers or point of sale computer terminals for recording cash sales of inventory to customers. In addition, barcode scanners are used at each point of sale terminal; these scan information and the price from the bar coding on the item purchased. This reduces the risk of cash sales being made at incorrect prices. All cash registers and point of sale terminals provide the following to allow for monitoring by the customer of the recording of the sale by the cashier:

- A *visual display* of the amounts being rung up and the final, cumulative amount owing for the goods purchased, which the customer is able to observe as the items are being rung up. Usually, an error made by the cashier will be detected and queried immediately by the customer. The customer, however, is more likely to query an overcharge than an undercharge. This control affects the *completeness, occurrence* and *measurement* assertions and relies on the customer to monitor the items being charged correctly.

- A *printed tally slip* listing all items purchased, the sale price, an indication of whether the item is subject to VAT or is VAT exempt, and the method of payment, namely cash, cheque or credit card. A copy of the tally slip is given to the customer as evidence of the goods sold and settlement received for the goods purchased. This document facilitates control over the *completeness, occurrence* and *measurement* assertions and relies on the customer to monitor the items are charged correctly.

- An internal record, which may be a *tally slip*, is locked in the cash register to be removed, at the end of a cashier's shift, by the cash controller (the key holder) for purposes of cashing up. An internal record may also be in the form of a *computer file or tape*, in the case of computerized point of sale terminals which record every sale in a daily *sales transaction file*, which is then used to update the general ledger record of cash receipts, cash sales and cost of sales when it is uploaded in the sales processing run at the end of each business day.
  - When the customer or the cashier detects that an error has occurred in

the ringing up of goods, the controller will generally be called to authorize the correction of the error. This control affects the *completeness, occurrence* and *measurement* assertions.
- The keys to open the cash registers, or reset the register at the start of a new shift or change of cashier should be under the control of a responsible member of staff, usually a cash controller or floor manager, in the case of a large department store.
- It should be appreciated that the use of such equipment merely reduces the risk of misappropriation of cash by the sales assistants; it does not eliminate the risk. The efficacy of the equipment depends largely on the proper control of the keys thereto and on the reaction of the customers to the wrong amount being recorded.

• *Printed control totals* for all sales rung up on the cash register or point of sale terminal at the end of each day. These are written or printed on a daily *cash summary sheet* by the controller or floor manager, depending on the nature of the operation.

Receipts from cash sale customers

Cash receipts: Where the customer pays *cash*, the cashier is responsible for counting the cash and making sure the correct amount is collected from the customer before ringing up the sale as complete.

Each cashier will normally carry an appropriate level and mix of coins and notes by way of a *cash float* in order to give change to customers. During a shift the cashier may require a fresh supply of certain coins or note denominations for change purposes. In a busy store with numerous till points, it is the job of the cash controller to collect large note denominations from the cashier and exchange these at the cash control centre for the smaller coin or note denominations requested by the cashier.

The experience of the entity over time enables it to anticipate the amount and the denominations of cash supplies that will be needed during a cashier's shift, and in which denominations. Once again, the security aspects will require attention, with the cash control centre preferably situated in an unobtrusive location, well secured by locks and access strictly restricted to those staff members, such as the cash controller and cashiers, and the coin security company staff, who need access.

Cheque receipts: Where the customer pays by *personal cheque*, the entity will usually implement strict controls around the *details to be provided by the drawer*. Generally a rubber stamp on the reverse of the cheque requests details such as the drawer's full names, identity document number, address and telephone number. The cashier will be required to inspect the ID of the customer and verify the accuracy of the information provided before accepting the cheque. The cashier will also, usually, request that a customer cross the cheque restrictively as *Not Transferable* and make it payable to the entity's name. In some instances the customer may be asked to make out a 'cash' cheque, but this increases the risk of misappropriation by the cashier and other staff.

Credit card receipts: Where a customer pays by credit card, an *on-line or manual credit card machine* will be available at the till point. The swiping of the customer's credit card records the settlement of the customer's purchases by means of credit card payment.

The *on-line credit card machine* is linked directly to the host banking institution. The machine prints a credit card slip for the customer to sign, a copy of which is retained by the cashier while a second copy goes to the customer as a record of the charge to his or her credit card account. The credit card slip will be included in the daily bank deposits by the entity.

In the case of a *manual credit card machine*, the cashier has a supply of credit card payment slips, printed in triplicate, which are completed manually and signed by the customer. The customer is then given the top copy for their record of payment, and the second and third copies are retained by the cashier and subsequently attached to a merchant voucher and deposited in the bank along with the rest of the cash and cheques received for the day. Control over the credit card slips and subsequent depositing affects the *completeness, occurrence* and *measurement* assertions.

Depositing the cash received from cash sales

Management should establish strict control policies and procedures to be followed by cashiers when counting and recording their takings and floats at the end of each shift, which they would do on a *cash summary sheet*. Control policies and procedures for cash sales include the following:

- At the end of the shift, the cashier takes his or her till drawer to the cash control point where the contents, cash, cheques and credit card slips are counted, by the cashier and cash controller together, on *standard cash count forms* used to record the count and any overs or unders. These forms would also allow for the signature of both the cashier and the cash controller to acknowledge the amounts as correct and to indicate that the cashier has discharged his or her responsibility for the cash by handing it over to the cash controller for banking after the count.

- The totals of the cash count sheet will then be listed on a daily *cash summary sheet* which also identifies the cashier, till point and shift time. The till float is deducted from the total of the cash, cheques and credit card slips to arrive at the total receipts from sales rung up by the cashier. This amount is then compared by the cash controller to the cash register or point of sale total for the shift and any *unders or overs* are noted and investigated immediately by enquiry of the cashier and review of the sales recorded.

- Staff in the cash control centre will immediately thereafter prepare the relevant bank deposit slip to be placed in a drop safe for collection and depositing at the bank by the coin security company.

Recording the receipt of cash from cash sales

After depositing at the bank, the coin security company staff returns the bank stamped deposit slips to the accounts department of the entity. Here the cash receipts clerk captures the details into the *cash receipts journal and/or the cash receipts transactions file*, which updates the relevant general ledger accounts on a regular basis. The accounts clerk will compare the *bank stamped deposit slips captured* to the daily *cash summary sheet*, the printout of the *cash receipts transactions file* and the *bank statements* received from the bank later. Any discrepancies must be followed up promptly by the clerk and reported to the senior accountant or financial director.

These control procedures will provide evidence of the *completeness, existence* and *measurement/accuracy* assertions.

12.2.2.3 Cash receipts from credit customers

Cash received by the entity *from credit customers* is usually received 'through the mail', in payment of their accounts receivable balances. The functions relating to *remittances from credit customers* may be subdivided into the following distinct functional areas:

- the *receipt and recording* of cash, cheques, credit card slips and electronic funds transfers in the books and records of the entity; and
- the *depositing* of cash, cheques, credit card slips and electronic funds transfers received into the entity's bank accounts.

Effective control over receipts involves three basic requirements, namely:

- All receipts must be *accounted for*.
- All receipts must be *promptly recorded* in the correct amount to the credit of the correct accounts receivable account, the accounts receivable control account, and to the debit of bank.
- All recorded receipts must be *deposited* in the company's bank account, intact and timeously.

The receipt and recording of cash, cheques, credit card slips and electronic funds transfers (EFTs)

Misappropriation of cash or cheques is an obvious threat. It is therefore imperative that management implement strict controls around the initial receipt and depositing of payments from credit customers, and the subsequent recording of the receipts to ensure the allocation to the correct accounts receivable account.

There should be appropriate segregation of duties between those receiving the remittances through the mail and depositing the monies and those responsible for initiating, authorizing and allocating credit notes for processing to accounts receivable. This will prevent the risk of fraud by employees from 'cash rolling', in which cash stolen is substituted with a credit note to disguise the loss of the money and prevent the detection of the misappropriation by the customer and management. Monitoring procedures, such as higher level review and reconciliations of cash received to bank deposits, may also facilitate an effective check on those staff responsible for receiving and recording the receipt of money. Controls include:

- All incoming mail should be opened by or in the presence of responsible senior staff, and cheques and other forms of money contained in the mail should be immediately listed in a *remittances received diary* under the date of receipt, and initialled by the responsible senior staff. Uncrossed cheques and postal orders (rare) should be crossed restrictively as *Not Transferable* for the account of the business at the appropriate bank, immediately on receipt. This would provide evidence of the *completeness* of receipts.

- All accounts receivable remittances, cheques and other correspondence should then be passed to the accounts receivable department or staff responsible for recording the receipt and preparing the bank deposit slip for accounts receivable amounts, who should sign the remittance diary as evidence that they have received all the cheques/payments listed therein.

- The customer remittance, if received, will usually be attached to a copy of the receipt and filed in the accounts receivable department to support the aged listing of accounts receivable. This should be agreed to the relevant deposit entry on the bank statement.

- At times the remittance advices may be accompanied by a bank stamped deposit slip, or EFT payment advice, indicating that the customer has paid the amount owing directly into the entity's banking account. The normal procedures for capturing such receipts into the relevant customer's account receivable should then be followed, with the copy of the receipt attached to the customer's remittance advice and copy deposit slip or EFT payment.

- Where the customer has authorized payment by means of credit card, the entity needs to process a credit card payment voucher and attach the customer's authorization to the slip deposited with the rest of the cheques received.

- In a large trading organization, with the computerization of accounting records, the receipts will usually be captured into the accounting system individually on a *cash register or point of sale terminal* dedicated for that purpose and located in a department in the store or offices of the entity, with staff specifically responsible for receiving accounts receivable payments.

- The capturing of the receipts and cash discount granted should automatically update the *cash receipts transactions file* from which the *cash receipts journal* will be printed.

- The computer system generally provides for an automatic sequential numbering of the receipts, as well as the immediate allocation of the receipt to the customer's account indicating the specific invoices paid, or to the oldest balance outstanding, to enable the correct age analysis of the account to be performed. In an on-line system, the capturing of the receipt automatically updates the general ledger, accounts receivable control account and the company's bank account. In a batch system, the receipts are captured into the cash receipts transactions file, which will be used to update the general ledger and accounts receivable ledger records later when the 'master file update' processing run is performed. These will contain programmed controls that ensure the amounts are allocated to the correct ledger accounts, providing evidence of the *completeness, measurement/accuracy, occurrence* and *existence* assertions.

- Management should perform periodic checks of the copies of the receipts and the composition of bank stamped deposits, in comparison with the information in the remittance diary. Evidence of the review should be provided by means of the initials of management on the relevant pages of the remittance diary. A test of the deposit slips only may be considered sufficient; however, if discrepancies are discovered, a complete check of all the bank deposit slips for the relevant period should be made. This will provide evidence of the *completeness and measurement/accuracy assertions*.

- As payments through the mail are, almost without exception, made by cheque, many businesses have ceased to mail copies of receipts to customers unless requested to do so. The paid cheques on the customer's own bank statement are considered adequate evidence of payment. Further, the receipt will be reflected on the accounts receivable statement sent to the customer by the entity for that month.

- In a small business use may be made of pre-printed sequentially numbered receipt forms that are written out manually and provide the requisite number of carbon copies, as well as bearing the concern's name. All unused books should be kept under strict control by senior management, with some form of stationery register kept to record the books of receipt forms received from the printer and those issued to the cashier.

- Cancelled receipts should be attached to the appropriate copies and the original and all copies clearly marked 'cancelled'. Note: this should not arise where receipts are issued from a point of sale terminal or cash register in a computerized receipting situation.

- The practice of some customers of giving *post-dated cheques* should be discouraged. Where post-dated cheques are accepted, they should be retained in a secure place (locked safe or drawer), by senior management in the accounts receivable department, until due date when they are deposited in the bank. A register should be maintained recording the cheque details, when it was received and due date. An official receipt should not be issued in respect of a post-dated cheque until it becomes due and is deposited in the bank. The entity may acknowledge receipt of such cheques by letter. Care should be taken that the deposit of these cheques is not overlooked.

- Cash sales, if considerable in number, should be the subject of rigorous control (see previous section). If there are only occasional cash sales, it is better to incorporate such sales in the credit sales system whereby invoices are issued, the cash received is treated as payments by accounts receivable, and using a 'Cash Sales' account in the accounts receivable ledger.

- In a large business, the cashier should not have access to accounting records other than the cash records, so that collusion between the cashier and some other person(s) is required before fraud can remain undetected. In a smaller business, the cashier may have to undertake additional duties, in which case the management should exercise care in allocating the work in such a way that the probability of the cashier passing entries to conceal a misappropriation of cash is reduced to a minimum.

- In no case, except in a very small business where the owner exercises personal supervision, should the cashier have access to the accounts receivable ledger or accounting records other than the cash records.

- A daily listing of the *cash receipts journal* from the *cash receipts transactions file* should reflect all *accounts receivable receipts* issued during the day. This listing should include details of the customer account to which accounts receivable receipts have been allocated and an analysis indicating whether the receipts are in the form of cash, cheques, credit cards, direct deposit by customers, or EFT payments.

The depositing of cash, cheques, credit card slips and EFTs received into the entity's bank accounts

- In a large trading operation, such as a supermarket or hypermarket, separate bank deposit forms should be prepared for depositing amounts received from credit customers for credit to accounts receivable accounts, as distinct from receipts from cash sales.

- All cash, cheques and other forms of money received should be deposited in the bank as soon as practicable, usually on the first business day immediately following the receipt of the money. As indicated earlier for cash sales, accounts receivable deposit slips may also be collected by a coin security company for depositing at the bank. The bank stamped deposit slip should be returned to the accounts receivable department for filing.

- Senior staff in the accounts receivable department should manually agree the bank stamped deposit slips to the daily *cash receipts journal* printout, and do so on a regular basis, to ensure that the split between cash, cheques and credit card slips is correctly reflected. They should also agree the direct deposits made by customers and EFT payments to the entity's bank statement when received.

- If a cheque which has been deposited is returned by the bank for any reason, it should be recorded separately in the cash payments journal and should be captured by means of a cash payments journal entry to the debit of the relevant accounts receivable account, even where it is immediately re-deposited. When re-deposited, a separate deposit slip should be used so that the cheque is not merged with the amount of the daily deposit of money received. The re-deposit may be captured by means of a fresh receipt as discussed above. The entries in the cash records for the return and the re-deposit of the cheque will therefore be clear and matched exactly by appropriate entries in the bank statement.

- The bank balance as shown in the general ledger should be reconciled, at least each month, with the balance as shown on the bank statement. A senior accountant should perform the bank reconciliation or, if prepared by the cashier or cash controller, the reconciliation should be scrutinized and checked by the financial manager or financial director. A further monitoring control may be achieved by the periodic preparation of the bank reconciliation by a senior staff member, without previous notice to the cashier, and the performance of cash counts at all tills at the same time. The cash count is an essential feature of the check to detect any possible cash rolling activities by the cashier.

- Any communication from customers raising queries relating to matters under the control of the cashier should be referred to the senior accountant or financial director and not to the cashier. This should help to bring to the notice of management any inefficient or fraudulent practice engaged in by the cashier or by staff handling the mail and recording the remittances received.

12.2.3 Sales adjustment transactions

The sales adjustments functions relate to journal or 'non-cash' entries and may be subdivided into the following three distinct functional areas:

- Cash discounts granted;
- Sales returns and allowances for goods returned or for correction of pricing differences; and
- Bad debts written off.

Sales adjustment transactions are not usually a significant class of transactions, either in terms of large volumes or in terms of significant amounts. However, they may present a risk of errors or fraud, or be used to hide the misappropriation of cash received from cash sales or from credit customers. For example, cash misappropriated may be covered by recording the incorrect discount, or by processing a credit note to the relevant customer's account for the amount of cash taken.

Alternatively, a journal entry may be recorded by a staff member with access to the computerized accounting records and relevant source documents to process journal entries, to write off the amount of the receipt misappropriated against the allowance for irrecoverable accounts. The customer may not detect the defalcation, as the amount paid would still be reflected as a credit on the customer's statement for the particular month, and he or she may assume that the entity merely 'journalizes' its receipts. Of greater concern and more significantly, sales adjustment may be an attempt, often by management, to hide the processing of fictitious sales. This may arise particularly around the financial year-end as management strives to meet budgets and targets set.

The main risk in respect of sales adjustments is clearly that entries may be recorded for *unauthorized transactions* and/or for events that did not actually occur, that is, the *existence* and *occurrence/validity* assertions are those directly affected. The effect of misstatements, however, potentially affect the *measurement* and *valuation* assertions as well.

Consequently, the control activities that management implements to control sales adjustments must include, as a first step, the *segregation of duties* that would require collusion between different persons to defraud the entity. Additionally, management should require a more senior level of *authorization* and formal documentation for individual sales adjustments transactions, and the regular *monitoring* of the incidence and value of such transactions. Enquiries should be made at an appropriate level of management, or possibly by involving the internal auditors, when the incidence of sales adjustments appears to be increasing beyond normal expectations to investigate the reasons for this and rectify the problem.

Cash discounts granted

As cash discounts are usually granted in terms of the repayment arrangements negotiated with the customer, these terms would be contained in the customer master file records. Accordingly, it will be possible for the cash receipts program to recalculate the *cash discount* recorded by reference to the total amount received from the customer, the date of the invoice or balance being paid by the customer, and the rate of discount that the customer is entitled to.

An exception report could then be produced as part of the *cash receipts transaction file* master file update, listing all discount amounts that are not in accordance with the discount rate and payment terms recorded in the customer's master file record. This report should be reviewed on a regular basis by senior accounting staff or the marketing management, but specifically by staff not involved in the receiving or recording of cash receipts from credit customers.

Cash discounts may also be granted when requested by cash customers on cash sales, where they pay by cash rather than by cheque or credit card. The company policies and procedures may require the cashier to call for the cash controller or senior sales staff to authorize the granting of discount on cash sales, which is achieved when the authorized person keys in the access password to activate the cash discount key on the point of sale terminal or cash register. Once again, the *cash receipts program* may provide for the automatic checking of any such discounts granted and the printing of amounts by way of an exception report where the amounts do not meet the programmed criteria.

Sales returns and allowances

A credit note issued for goods returned should not be dispatched to the customer until the relevant goods have been returned and checked by those staff members who are responsible for attending to customers' returns of goods and to warranty claims to establish the condition of the goods and the reasons for the returns. Credit notes for allowances – for example, goods of inferior quality, or incorrect prices charged – should be issued only on authority of a sales management staff member to whom the duty has been allocated – who should be independent of the receipt and recording of receipts from cash sales and remittance from credit customers, and the processing of these to the accounts receivable ledger.

It frequently occurs that damaged goods returned may be exchanged for the same, undamaged, or a different item. In this case, the credit note would be issued with reference to the original invoice and a new invoice would be made out immediately for the replacement item(s) in the normal way, credit or cash sale at the point of sale or cash register till.

Large stores that have a policy of accepting returns from customers may set up a separate department to deal with returns, which makes the monitoring of such transactions relatively easy. In addition, it is generally possible to allocate to the department senior staff supervisors with authority to approve credit notes up to certain limits. Customers may be required to produce evidence of the previously purchased item now being returned; this evidence may be an invoice or a cash till slip showing the amount previously paid for the item. When this evidence cannot be produced, the customer may be required to complete a written 'sales returns' document, providing their name, address and contact telephone number and the reason for returning the goods. This provides evidence of the *existence, occurrence/validity* and *measurement/accuracy* assertions.

Management should monitor the number and value of credit notes issued on a regular basis. If these appear to be excessive, inquiries should be made to determine the reason. Since credit notes may be indicative of inefficiency, and possibly fraud, within the organization, appropriate action should be taken to rectify the situation. This will provide evidence of the *existence, occurrence/ validity and measurement/accuracy* assertions.

If any invoice or credit note has been cancelled, both the original and duplicate(s) should be clearly marked 'cancelled' and filed with the retained copy, so that the numbers run consecutively. If it is practicable, a cancelled invoice or credit note should bear the initials of a person with authority.

In a computerized accounting system, it is insufficient to merely 'cancel' an invoice or credit note by merely writing 'cancelled' on it. The cancellation of an invoice requires the issuing of a credit note to offset the charges made on the invoice and, similarly, the cancellation of a credit note requires the issuing of an invoice to reverse the amount of the credit note. The cancellation will require the authorization of sales management, by way of signature, and the filing of the printed documents in a file of cancelled invoices or credit notes in the sales or credit control department.

Bad debts written off

Every journal entry recorded to write off irrecoverable accounts receivable balances should be approved and initialled by duly authorized senior management, for example, the senior accountant, credit control manager or financial director. This person should not have any involvement in the receipt or recording of cash receipts or remittances from customers, in order to reduce the risk of misappropriation of cash and cover up by means of a journal write off of the amount owing.

A bad debt write off of a customer's balance should be accompanied by supporting documentation of correspondence between the customer and the entity regarding disputed charges, or with debt collection agencies regarding attempts to recover amounts owing by the customer, which support the amounts considered irrecoverable. It may be that the customer cannot be traced, or is illiquid or insolvent and therefore unable to pay. Debts should not be written off simply because there has been no movement on the account for some time, or without due enquiry and attempts made to recover the amount owing. This senior authorization will provide evidence of the *occurrence/validity* and *valuation* assertions.

The reader is referred to a discussion on the auditing of the *allowance for irrecoverable debts* later in the chapter.

12.2.4 Assessing the risk of significant misstatement

The auditor is likely to encounter a wide variety of revenue sources and documents in different businesses with different control environments, a complexity of contractual arrangements and GAAP issues regarding the timing and basis of revenue recognition. Where multiple 'routine' revenue transactions occur, the controls are likely to be more formalized. Hence, there is the possibility of establishing that a control has functioned throughout the period of intended reliance by means of tests of management detective controls. Equally, it should be possible by enquiry and observation to identify aspects of the revenue transactions where material breakdowns of controls have occurred, the reasons for this and what action management has taken to address the problems.

Ultimately, the main risk of significant misstatement (combined inherent risk and control risk assessment) will lie in the *completeness, occurrence/validity and measurement/accuracy* of sales transactions, cash receipts transactions and output VAT transactions and the *existence* and *valuation* of accounts receivable, cash/bank balances and output VAT at the financial year-end.

The risk of significant misstatement will thus be affected directly by:

- incorrect cut-off of sales and receipts or aggressive revenue recognition policies, likely to result in an overstatement of revenue, output VAT and bank balances;
- the possible override of controls by management and consequently an increased risk of fictitious sales and non-existent accounts receivable; and
- an insufficient allowance for irrecoverable debts, similarly resulting in an overstatement of accounts receivable on the balance sheet.

Factors that the auditor will consider in evaluating the risk as high, medium or low are those set out earlier under the preliminary assessment of the risk of significant misstatement. After gaining an understanding of the nature of the business and the control components, and having completed the analysis of the process level business risk for sales and receipts transactions, the auditor would have gained sufficient information to judge the effectiveness of the design of management's controls over the sales, cash receipts and sales adjustments.

For example, circumstances of the rationale the auditor may document in assessing the risk of significant misstatement as *Low* may be as shown in Table 12.8.

RISK ASSESSMENT: LOW	RATIONALE
Residual business risk	The process level risk analysis has identified adequate management control activities that would mitigate the chance of significant misstatement.
Qualifications and competence of the estimator and complexity of the estimating process for the allowance for irrecoverable debts	The credit controller provides information to the financial director on debts which he or she believes are most likely to require provisions against them. The auditor has no reason to doubt the competence of the credit controller who has been performing this role for several years and has an in-depth knowledge of the accounts receivable customers, many of whom are of long standing.
Assumptions on which the estimate is made	The calculation of the estimate is based on a flat percentage of year-end aged debt categories, adjusted for specific debt problems. This basis is consistent with the prior year, and the bad debt write off in the current period is in line with the proper year estimate. The analytical review of sales trends has not identified any significant changes in profiles of sales or customers that would change the risk profile.
Management bias	There is no indication of management override of controls during the period.

RISK ASSESSMENT: LOW	RATIONALE
Quality of information	The system of recording debtors is well controlled. Invoices are raised based on deliveries to the customer, and receipts are recorded when remittances are received. This should provide an accurate record of accounts receivable balances at the year-end. The credit controller maintains a close relationship with individual customers and as such is well informed to make an assessment of any current or imminent problems affecting the estimate of irrecoverable debts.
Historical accuracy	During the year, the previous allowances for irrecoverable debts have proven appropriate and have closely mirrored actual bad debts written off. No significant recoveries of bad debts written off previously have been made.

Table 12.8 Assessing the risk of significant misstatement

The auditor would normally perform audit procedures to support this assessment, such as enquiring about the contact with customers and inspecting communications with customers having long outstanding balances; discussing with the credit controller the historic basis of bad debt write offs and percentages used by aged category and inspecting evidence of management's review of adjustments made for irrecoverable accounts receivable.

12.2.5 Testing controls

12.2.5.1 Gaining an understanding of the business and control components

The 'top-down' audit approach does not require the auditor to test all the controls over the revenue transactions, but rather to gather assurance regarding the effectiveness with which management has managed its control activities to ensure that errors and fraud are detected and corrected and that the risk of significant misstatement will not remain in the audited financial statements. To this end, the most effective of the detective controls and key performance indicators that management has implemented to detect and prevent material error and fraud for each of the areas are the ones that the auditor may decide to rely and test on to establish their effective operation.

The auditor should focus on whether the design of 'higher level' reconciliation and matching controls – performed manually or programmed into the computer system – are producing exception reports that are promptly investigated and actioned by management, rather than exhaustively testing the preventative controls of individual clerks performed at the data capture stage. In addition, the auditor will inquire about the key performance indicators the management uses to monitor the revenue transaction, such as budgeted sales gross margins, average debt repayment period, to mention a few.

The auditor will also consider what assurance can be obtained from analytical procedures and cut-off tests regarding the *existence*, *measurement* and *valuation* of accounts receivable, adequate assurance from such procedures might mean that extensive tests of controls need not be performed.

12.2.5.2 Assessing the risk of significant misstatement and testing controls

Should circumstances allow it and the auditor wishes to assess the combined inherent and control risk (the risk of significant misstatement) as *Low* the important controls, particularly over cash receipting and depositing where there is a high risk of fraud, will need to be tested for their effective operation. As many of the controls over cash receipting and depositing are manual controls, the main audit procedures would include *observation* of the performance of the controls; *inspection* of the daily *cash summary sheets* to see evidence of the signature of the persons performing the matching controls, and enquiry regarding the action taken for any discrepancies identified.

If the controls on which the auditor plans to rely are programmed controls, it will be necessary to obtain evidence about the effectiveness of the design and operation of the relevant *general controls*, controls in the *specific application* (for example, the calculation of discount granted on receipts), and the manual follow up (for example, the matching of the printout of the cash receipts journal to the relevant bank stamped deposit slips), and *monthly reconciliation of the cash receipts journal to the bank statements* received.

In assessing the control risk as low, the auditor needs to take account of all facets of the control components assessed (see section 12.1.6 of this chapter) to be able to conclude that the controls allow for effective management and the detection and correction of errors and fraud.

If the auditor plans to assess inherent and control risk as medium or high, the auditor may simply document the understanding of the control activities and inspect evidence of the control performed while enquiring about the handling of control activities.

Where tests of control are performed at an interim stage, the auditor will need to select several items from the remaining period to test when returning for the year-end audit, in order to establish that the control had continued to operate as designed for the remaining period and that there had not been any material change in the control activities performed in order to place reliance on the controls for the whole period.

RISKS	PROGRAMMED CONTROLS	MANUAL CONTROLS	TESTS OF CONTROLS
Credit control function and initiating credit sales			
Sales may be made to customers who have not been given credit facilities or to customers outside of credit limits	Customer code numbers on orders are matched to accounts receivable master file record code numbers. Current outstanding balances plus sales value of current orders are compared to credit limit. Delivery advices (delivery notes) are only generated if the above two matters are in order.	The credit control function involves reviewing credit applications and supporting information regarding earnings and credit references, approving credit limits and authorizing the opening of new accounts. Appropriate approvals for manual override of credit limit extensions.	Enquiry from staff and inspection of documentation evidencing the performance of these controls.
Dispatch function			
Goods ordered may not be delivered. Goods may be dispatched without approved delivery notes. Goods dispatched may not correspond to the description and quantity of goods recorded on delivery notes. Customers may dispute that goods ordered and delivered were received.	Once the customer's sales order is approved the system produces an order, delivery note and invoice set, the invoice details being held in a temporary file until the physical delivery has been effected and inputted. The computer matches all goods drawn for delivery against the items and quantities on the sales order, and prints an exception report of unmatched items or quantities for back order.	Prior to goods being boxed or parcelled, an independent check is made of goods to the delivery note details. Delivery notes signed as evidence of the above two checks. Sales staff follows up on short deliveries and unfilled orders to expedite delivery to the customer. Security staff checks that goods only leave the premises if accompanied by delivery notes. Customers sign delivery notes as evidence of having received goods and in good order.	Observe the performance of these checks. Inspect delivery notes of the relevant signatures of staff and customers as evidence of delivery. Inspect evidence of review by client staff of the exception report of unmatched items and back orders.
Invoicing function			
Deliveries may not be invoiced.	Regular printouts of invoices in the temporary file and completed deliveries transferred to sales and accounts receivable. Should invoices only be generated after delivery, invoices should be allocated the same sequential number as delivery notes and the system should match invoices to delivery notes using these sequence numbers. Unmatched delivery notes should be printed out on a report.	Printout of invoices in temporary file reviewed and reasons for non-release or non-delivery investigated and resolved. Printouts of delivery notes not yet invoiced are reviewed and resolved.	Inspect printouts for evidence of review by client staff and enquire regarding any apparent problems of non-deliveries and/or deliveries made for which invoices are still held in the temporary file. Inspect printouts for evidence of review by client staff and enquire regarding any apparent problems related to deliveries not invoiced.

RISKS	PROGRAMMED CONTROLS	MANUAL CONTROLS	TESTS OF CONTROLS
Invoices may be generated without valid orders, and dispatch of goods or invoices may be duplicated for valid dispatches.	The system matches invoices to delivery notes using the dedicated pre-numbering system and mismatches are printed out on an exception report.	Printouts of unmatched invoice number and delivery note numbers and sales order and/or duplicate invoices related to delivery notes are reviewed and resolved.	Inspect printout for evidence that discrepancies are resolved.
Incorrect prices may be charged due to the incorrect prices used or incorrect product description and code input for the sales order or delivery note or sales invoice.	Pricing master file changes controlled through logical access controls. Controls allowing only authorized individuals to affect changes thereto. The system checks that the correct version of the pricing master file is uploaded. This by using and checking master file version numbers. The system could check the apparent appropriateness of product code numbers inputted i.e. alpha/numeric checks for code number digits and the use of check digits and matching of the product code and description.	The listing of authorized price changes is compared to the computer procured listing of prices after the changes have been affected and approved. If invoices are manually produced, or if there is no pricing master file, an independent check of prices charged on invoices is necessary.	Inspect documentation to ascertain that appropriate authority was given for pricing changes. Reperformance checks that printouts of changed prices agree to those authorized. This may be done using CAATs. Enquire into general controls over IT processing and application controls over revenue transactions to ensure that the correct version of the pricing master file is used to process invoices. Inspect invoices for the signature of the person responsible for checking prices. Re-perform check by agreeing prices charged to the authorized price listing.
Invoice amounts might be inaccurately calculated.	Programmed controls over pricing, calculations, product codes, product description and customer account codes for every invoice. If computer produced, control of changes to invoicing programs to be monitored and operation controls should be in place to ensure that the current version of the invoicing program is used when processing sales invoices. The program code to be password protected allowing only authorized changes thereto. Regular printout of all program changes made.	If manually produced, independent checks performed on the accuracy of the calculations on invoices, VAT and total amount. All program changes reviewed and approved by senior staff.	Inspect invoices for signatures of those responsible for checks on the accuracy of invoice calculations. Re-perform tests to prove the accuracy of invoices amounts. Enquire into general controls over changes to the invoicing program and operating procedures to ensure the authorized and current version of the programme is used to process invoices. See evidence of review and approval of program changes. IT audit staff to review general and application controls over program changes.

RISKS	PROGRAMMED CONTROLS	MANUAL CONTROLS	TESTS OF CONTROLS
Recording of credit sales			
Sales invoices may be recorded in the incorrect account in the receivable records. Sales invoices may be recorded in the accounting records (omissions).	Check digits incorporated in customer code numbers. The system matches customer codes and delivery address details on orders, delivery notes and invoices with those in the accounts receivable master file. Run-to-run control totals are calculated and matched. This involves a reconciliation of the opening balance of the total accounts receivable amount plus sales transaction amounts for the period being agreed to the master file closing balance once sales invoices for the period have been processed.	Screen validation checks require fields to be corrected before allowing the transaction input to be accepted. Accounting staff inspects the printout and reconciliation of all run-to-run master file totals for the sales invoicing and accounts receivable processing run. Monthly statements are sent to customers and customer queries regarding disagreement with balances reflected on month end statements are investigated and resolved.	Run test data against the sales application programme to test the input validation controls. Inspect evidence that client staff check the reconciliations and balancing of the run-to-run master file totals on the printouts. Inspect the customer queries correspondence file and ascertain the validity and resolution of queries.
Sales invoices may be recorded in the incorrect accounting period.	If invoices are only generated once delivery is affected. The system should produce a printout of un-invoiced deliveries using the dedicated transaction numbers allocated.	Manual sales cut-off procedures performed on a regular basis. The total of the sum of the individual balances in the accounts receivable master file are agreed on to the total of the accounts receivable control account. If invoices are generated simultaneously with orders and delivery notes the printout of invoices in the temporary file is scrutinized for probity. The printout of delivery notes not matched with invoices is reviewed and investigated to ensure that all un-invoiced sales are in respect of deliveries not yet affected.	Inspect the printout and re-perform the sales cut-off functions. Inspect the reconciliations of accounts receivable master file total to the control account total for the signature of the responsible official. Re-perform the reconciliation.

RISKS	PROGRAMMED CONTROLS	MANUAL CONTROLS	TESTS OF CONTROLS
All of the above mentioned.		Management reviews actual performance against key performance indicators, for example – actual sales against budget – achieved gross profit percentage – number of days sales in account receivable – the aged analysis of debts currently outstanding – bad debts written off as a percentage of total accounts receivable outstanding.	Inspect documentation evidencing the adequate identification and resolution of actual performance being out of line with the identified key performance indicators. Enquire as to what management has done to resolve any problems indicated in this regard.
Recording of cash sales			
Cash sales may not be recorded at point of sale.		Cash registers or point of sale tills are situated at or near the exit and display amounts recorded. Printed slips of sales given to customers. Check out points monitored by surveillance cameras.	By inspection of premises, point of sale tills and enquiry of management confirm the adequacy of the physical control over these aspects.
Cash sale taking may not be deposited.	A daily cash sales summary sheet is printed for each till.	Cash takings for each till are counted and reconciled to the relevant sales summary sheet. Independent checks that all cash takings per sales summaries are deposited.	Inspect 'cashing up' records for signatures of those responsible for counting cash and reconciling the amount to the sales summary sheet. Inspect deposit slips and sales summaries for signature evidencing the check. Re-perform the check that deposited amounts correspond to sales summary amounts.

RISKS	PROGRAMMED CONTROLS	MANUAL CONTROLS	TESTS OF CONTROLS
Receipts from debtors through the mail may not be deposited.	Debtor details and amounts received are recorded via a terminal. A deposit slip is automatically prepared and printed.	Post opened by two persons. Any negotiable cheques are restrictively crossed. Mail openers sign the list of amounts received.	Enquire as to and observe that mail opening conforms to the laid down procedures. Inspect list of amounts received for signatures of mail openers.
		If the deposit slip is not automatically prepared at the time of mail opening, the person responsible for preparing the deposit slip to sign the list of cheques received as evidence of having received all amounts.	Inspect the listing of cheques for the relevant signature.
			Inspect the list of cheques and/or deposit slip for the signature of the responsible person.
		Independent check that all cheques listed at mail opening are deposited.	Re-perform the check that the amounts deposited correspond with the listing of cheques.
Receipt of EFTs or direct deposits may not be recorded.		Remittance advices of amounts paid by EFT or direct deposit are compared to daily EFT transfers or direct deposit listings from the bank.	Inspect the listings for the signature of the responsible person.
			Re-perform the reconciliation.
Recording of receipts			
Receipts may be recorded to incorrect accounts receivable accounts.	On entry of the accounts receivable account code number, the name and other details are retrieved from the master file and appear on the terminal screen.	A comparison of the information on screen is made with the remittance advice and/or cheque details.	Enquire into and observe the procedure being followed at mail opening.
		Monthly statements mailed to customers with any queries regarding amounts reflected thereon investigated and resolved.	Inspect query correspondence and ascertain their resolution.
			Enquire as to any major unresolved queries and proposed action.
Recorded receipts to accounts receivable may not be matched by bank deposits.	Accounts receivable accounts are automatically credited at the time of the preparation of the deposit slip at mail opening.	Independent preparation of regular bank account reconciliation.	Inspect reconciliations for the signature of the responsible person.

RISKS	PROGRAMMED CONTROLS	MANUAL CONTROLS	TESTS OF CONTROLS
		Management monitors:	Enquire into these matters.
		Daily cash summary sheets and receipt listings matched to deposit slips.	Inspect records and documentation for evidence of these monitoring procedures.
		Accounts receivable queries and their resolutions.	
		Reconciliation of accounts receivable master file total with control accounts.	
		Reconciliation of bank account balances.	
		Long outstanding amounts reflected on accounts receivable age analysis.	
		Actual performance against identified key performance indicators.	

Table 12.9 Risks, controls and tests of controls – sales and receipts transactions

12.3 DETECTION RISK AND SUBSTANTIVE TESTS OF TRANSACTIONS AND BALANCES

12.3.1 Introduction

The preceding discussion should have provided the reader with a sound understanding of the nature of revenue transactions in a business; the control components and typical control activities encountered over sales, receipts and sales adjustments; and the assessment of control risk and tests of control. It remains to discuss the substantive audit procedures that the auditor will perform to reduce detection risk to an acceptable level for the balances and classes of transactions arising from revenue transactions as reflected in the financial statements.

Paragraphs .42 and .44 of SAAS 400 state that:

'Regardless of the assessed levels of inherent and control risks, the auditor should perform some substantive procedures on material account balances and classes of transactions.'

Further that:

'The higher the assessment of inherent and control risk, the more audit evidence the auditor should obtain from the performance of substantive procedures.'

And finally that:

'When the auditor determines that detection risk regarding a financial statement assertion for a material account balance or class of transactions cannot be reduced to an acceptably low level, the auditor should express a qualified opinion or a disclaimer of opinion.'

Whilst this chapter has restricted the discussion to the main revenue transactions by way of sales, cash receipts, sales adjustments and output VAT, and the resultant balance sheet balances of accounts receivable, allowance for irrecoverable accounts receivable, and Output VAT, the final accounts receivable balance on the balance sheet will undoubtedly include other accounts receivable amounts, such as loans to employees, associate companies, accrued interest on loans, short-term investment of surplus cash, rents receivable from property letting activities, and other sundry accounts receivable. These other accounts receivable balances are beyond the scope of this chapter and are discussed in later chapters in the audit of those other classes of transactions.

With the 'top-down' audit approach the format of audit programmes has become far more descriptive, more qualitative and focused on obtaining sufficient appropriate audit evidence regarding specific assertions/audit objectives for individual balances, by performing specific audit procedures designed to detect any risk of significant misstatement remaining in the relevant financial statement balances. In addition, in documenting the audit procedures to be performed most effectively and efficiently, the auditor firstly considers the sufficiency and appropriateness of the audit evidence obtained from performing substantive analytical procedures, before proceeding to perform tests of detail to achieve the acceptable level of detection risk.

A useful framework for approaching the preparation of any substantive audit programme is given in Table 12.10:

SUBSTANTIVE TESTS FOR EACH CATEGORY	AUDIT OBJECTIVES				
	C	O/E	M/V	R/O	P/D
1. Obtain and document an understanding of the business:	×		×	×	×
Identify the significant streams of revenue transactions for the core business processes and significant accounts receivable balances. – Identify the strategic objectives of management, external and internal risks and critical success factors for the core business processes.					
Obtain trial balance or schedules of revenue transactions and accounts receivable balances: – Agree opening balances for accounts receivable to the previous year's working papers. Cast general ledger and accounts receivable ledger and agree total of accounts receivable closing balances to control account in general ledger.	×		×		

SUBSTANTIVE TESTS FOR EACH CATEGORY	AUDIT OBJECTIVES				
	C	O/E	M/V	R/O	P/D
2. Substantive analytical procedures:	X	X	X		
Recall significant classes of transactions and balances for key processes – credit and cash sales and receipts and key performance indicators used by management to monitor these – so as to develop a prediction or expectation for accounts receivable and sales from knowledge of the core process and sales business process and history of sales and accounts receivable.					
Define a significant difference or threshold – based on materiality at account balance level.					
Calculate ratios and compute the difference between the actual and the expected for the following ratios: • % gross profit margins • number of days sales in accounts receivable • inventory turnover ratios • perform a sales trend analysis • identify unusual items, particularly around year-end.					
Investigate significant differences and exercise judgement to conclude.					
Document the basis for the conclusion.					
3. Tests of detail of transactions:					
Select a sample of transactions recorded and inspect documents which provide evidence regarding the validity, accuracy and completeness of sales, receipts and adjustments.	X	X	X	X	X
Perform cut-off tests of the main transactions flows (e.g. sales, cash receipts and sales adjustments).	X	X			
Inspect subsequent events (e.g. receipts from customers recorded after year-end and credit notes passed).	X	X			
4. Tests of details of balances (Note 1: See 12.3.5 for discussion of substantive tests of details of balances):					
Confirm a sample of accounts receivable balances (positively, negatively or both).		X	X		
Evaluate the recoverability of accounts receivable and adequacy of the allowance for irrecoverable debts.			X		
5. Presentation and disclosure:					
Determine if the presentation and disclosure of accounts receivable and revenue transactions accords with GAAP and is properly classified.				X	X
Determine whether the financial statement notes reflect the rights and obligations of the entity with regard to each class of revenue transactions and balances whether asset or liability and any accounts receivable factored or pledged.				X	X

Table 12.10 Framework for the content of a substantive audit programme to address specific risks of significant misstatement in revenue transactions and balances

12.3.2 **Determining the acceptable level of detection risk**

Detection risk is the inverse of inherent and control risk. So if the combined assessment of inherent and control risk (the risk of significant misstatement) is low, the auditor can accept detection risk at a high level. This will mean that the auditor requires less evidence from substantive tests of analytical procedures and tests of detail of transactions and balances to conclude on whether the audit evidence obtained supports the financial statement assertions for the particular balances, namely: *completeness, existence, measurement/accuracy, valuation, rights and obligations, and presentations and disclosure.* In such circumstances the auditor may limit the substantive tests to merely performing substantive analytical procedures and obtaining confirmations from external third parties and a limited amount of substantive tests of detail of transactions and balances.

However, if the auditor assesses the combined assessment of inherent and control risk (the risk of significant misstatement) as high for particular assertions, detection risk needs to be reduced to a low level requiring more extensive substantive analytical procedures and tests of detail.

12.3.3 **Substantive analytical procedures**

Again, with reference to chapter 11 where the nature, timing and extent of substantive analytical procedures were discussed, a reminder of the principle that substantive analytical procedures are usually the most cost effective for the auditor and would therefore generally be applied before proceeding to substantive tests of detail of transaction and balances.

Chapter 11 identified five steps to be followed in using substantive analytical procedures. The applications of these revenue transactions and balances are:

- *Develop a prediction or expectation:* This relates to expectations for turnover, profit margins and accounts receivable based on the auditor's understanding of the business, market shares and the economy, and history.

- *Compute the difference between the actual and the expected:* This involves the performance of the ratios and comparisons, for example:
    - Observe the trend of monthly (or weekly) totals of sales recorded and compare with those of previous years and budget. Any unexpected fluctuations should be discussed with management and, if necessary, investigated further.
    - Compare the percentage gross profit to sales with that of previous years and budget. If the entity sells product lines at differing mark-ups, as department stores do, make the comparison per product line or group of products with similar margins. Any marked differences should be discussed with management.
    - Calculate the accounts receivable and inventory turnover ratios and compare with prior years. Unexpected changes in these ratios may be

caused by a number of factors including unrecorded sales, the recording of fictitious sales or cut-off problems.

– Scrutinize recorded sales for unusual items, for example particularly large amounts and postings to the sales general ledger account from sources other than sales records. Investigate these. Pay particular attention to unusual sales recorded close to the year-end.

- *Define a significant difference or threshold to conclude:* Ascertain those used by management as key performance indicators and consider the effectiveness of their monitoring procedures.

- *Investigate significant differences and exercise judgement:* Here the auditor analyses ratios relative to the expectations formulated above. Increased tests of detail may be necessary on sales and accounts receivable balances where unexplained differences remain.

- *Document the basis for the audit conclusion:* The auditor concludes on whether the audit evidence gathered supports the assertions/audit objectives that he or she was trying to substantiate.

12.3.4 Substantive tests of detail of sales and cash transactions

The audit work of evaluating internal control, testing its operation, and the substantiation of the correctness of transaction recording will give the auditor some satisfaction that sales revenues, miscellaneous income and receipts have been properly brought to account. It follows that if credit sales and receipts from accounts receivable have been correctly accounted for, the accounts receivable figure (at least with regard to existence and ownership) will be correctly stated.

It remains for the auditor to perform verification procedures on the final accounts receivable amount to be included in the audited financial statements. Conversely, the satisfactory conclusion of these verification procedures provides further evidence that the credit sales and receipts from accounts receivable were properly accounted for during the year. An overstatement of accounts receivable will be accompanied by an over-statement of sales or an understatement of cash, and vice versa. This relationship is of prime importance, because the nature and particularly the extent of the verification procedures to be performed by the auditor on the final accounts receivable and cash balances will be influenced by the auditor's evaluation of the internal control systems within the revenue/receipts cycle and the results of the transaction testing.

Certain tests of detail of sales and cash transactions may be performed during the interim auditing stage. Since the significant risk of misstatement in sales and cash receipt transactions is that sales may be overstated due to fictitious sales transactions recorded and receipts which may have been misappropriated, it would be appropriate to select a sample of sales and receipts from the remaining period to the financial year-end. The auditor would then inspect vouchers in support of transactions and make such enquiries as are necessary to establish the *existence and occurrence* assertions, and the *measurement/accuracy* regarding calculation and the allocation of the amounts recorded as revenue transactions and balances in the general ledger accounts in the correct accounting period.

Cut-off tests of sales and sales returns

At the year-end, substantive test of transactions will be performed on sales, sales returns and cash receipts to obtain evidence that these aspects are accounted for in the current period. These are referred to as cut-off tests and procedures.

Cut-off tests of sales are designed to provide evidence that:

- sales recorded in the current financial year are in respect of goods and services delivered prior to the financial year-end (*completeness* and *occurrence*);

- the corresponding cost of sales entries have been processed in the same period and goods delivered have not been accounted for in inventory at the financial year-end (*completeness* and *occurrence*); and

- the revenue recognition policies of the entity accord with GAAP and have been applied correctly and consistently (*measurement* and *valuation*).

Sales should be recorded in the period when delivery takes place. While the sale of goods from inventory usually provides a clear evidence of delivery once the goods are collected by or delivered to the customer, other sources of revenue may be far more complex to determine. For example, where revenue is derived from construction contracts, the amount of revenue brought to account will depend on the stage of completion of the contract. Revenue from licence fees will depend upon the terms of the licensing agreement. Goods imported or exported may be sold on a FOB (free on board) or CIF (Cost, insurance freight) basis where the carrier will be the agent of the buyer (FOB) or of the seller (CIF) and where constructive delivery is effected once the goods are handed by the seller to the agent of the buyer. The carrier may be a shipping company, airline carrier, and rail or road transport company.

Consequently, before performing the cut-off tests, the auditor should be aware of what constitutes delivery for the particular clients revenue transactions and what documents evidence the date of delivery. In addition, the auditor would ascertain what control procedures management has implemented to ensure the correct cut-off of revenue transactions. In an ordinary sale of inventory, the audit procedure would be to ascertain the last delivery note numbers and to select a sample of delivery notes before and after the year-end to inspect the supporting evidence of when delivery took place, in order to determine whether the transactions have been recorded in the correct period. These tests provide evidence of the *completeness, occurrence* and *existence* of sales and accounts receivable at the financial year-end.

The same procedures used to establish the cut-off for tests of credit notes for sales returns are used for the sales. However, where there is significant risk that fictitious sales transactions may be recorded, the auditor may well extend the sample of credit notes issued after the financial year-end in order to ascertain whether these appear to be genuine or merely reversing fictitious sales recorded prior to the year-end but not actually delivered. The sales returns cut-off will thus also provide complementary evidence of the *completeness* and *occurrence* of the sales transactions.

Cut-off tests of cash receipts

The cut-off tests of cash receipts relate both to cash sales and receipts from customers. The auditor may, if cash holdings are significant, attend to observe, or actually perform, cash counts at close of business on the last day of the financial year. All cash on hand would then be agreed to the relevant cash summary sheets and bank stamped deposit slips on the following business day. In so far as the cash relates to cash sales, the auditor would also compare the amounts to the cut-off tests on sales to ensure that the transactions are brought to account in the same (correct) accounting period.

The procedure for amounts received from credit customers is much the same as that for amounts received from cash sales, viz.: In so far as the cash and cheques on hand at the year-end relate to remittances from credit customers, they would be counted by the auditor, or by the client with the auditor observing the count procedures; the count would be agreed to the cash receipts journal and the last numbers of receipts issued by the close of business at the year-end; and the details would then similarly be agreed to the bank stamped deposit slip on the following business day. The purpose is to gather evidence that all receipts to the close of business at the year-end have been recorded in accounts receivable and bank in the correct accounting period. The procedures similarly provide evidence of *completeness, existence* and *occurrence*.

A further audit procedure is necessary, namely: to inspect the bank statements for the last month of the financial year with the aim of identifying any EFT payments and direct deposits made by customers that have been credited to the entity's bank account prior to the year-end, and to check that the allocation of these receipts to the relevant accounts receivable account occurred in the correct accounting period. These procedures similarly provide evidence of completeness, existence and occurrence.

The reader is referred to the procedures to be followed by the auditor in performing the cash counts at year-end (or any other time) set out in part 12.3.6 of this chapter. The cut-off of cash and bank balances will be verified by the re-performance of the bank reconciliation to the bank statement and confirmations obtained from the bank at year-end. The focus in this chapter is primarily on the cash receiving aspects rather than the cash withdrawals and payments which are discussed more fully in chapters 13 and 17.

12.3.5 Substantive tests of detail for accounts receivable balances

Having obtained a schedule of the accounts receivable balances, or using CAATs to download the accounts receivable balances from the client's accounting records to the auditor's PC, the total amount would be checked to the control account balance in the ledger to determine whether they agree. Tests of the ageing of the balances would have been performed as part of the test of control or during the test of the sample of sales and receipts transactions. Accordingly the remaining substantive procedures left to perform is the confirmation of selected accounts receivable balances and the evaluation of the allowance for irrecoverable receivables. A discussion of each of these follows.

12.3.5.1 Confirmation of accounts receivable balances

The confirmation of accounts receivable involves the direct communication between the auditor and the client's credit customers to obtain external confirmation from them regarding the *existence* and *validity* of amounts owed by the customers. Confirmation of accounts receivable does not provide any evidence of the recoverability of the amount (the *valuation assertion*) and other substantive procedures must be performed to establish this. Whilst requests for external confirmation of accounts receivable balances is not required by SAAS 505 'External confirmations', this procedure is frequently performed by auditors.

In deciding to request external confirmations, the auditor first considers the materiality of the account balances, the assessed level of inherent and control risk and how the evidence from other planned procedures will reduce audit risk to acceptable levels (SAAS 505, 'External confirmations', paragraph .05).

The auditor has no right to go beyond the records and documents in the client's possession to carry out the audit and can therefore communicate directly with the customers only if the client is agreeable to this. Consequently, confirmation requests ordinarily include management's authorization to the respondent to provide the information requested by the auditor.

If management refuses the auditor permission to request confirmation from certain customers, the auditor must exercise professional scepticism in ascertaining the reasons and considering whether the request is justified. Where the auditor considers the refusal of the client is not justified, and is prevented from sending out the confirmation request to that customer(s), the auditor must advise the client that this could present a scope limitation (SAAS 505, 'External confirmations', paragraph .26). If the auditor is unable to gain sufficient audit evidence regarding the particular customer's balance from alternative procedures, for example from the inspection of subsequent receipts and remittance advices from the customer, and where the customers' balances that the auditor is prevented from requesting confirmation of, individually or cumulatively, are material to the financial statements, the auditor should consider the possible impact on the auditor's report on the financial statements, and the auditor should make this clear to the client.

Use of positive and negative confirmations

The auditor may use both positive, or negative, external confirmation requests, or a combination of both. The distinction between the two forms of confirmation request is as follows:

- *Positive confirmation:* is a written request to customers to reply to the auditor indicating their agreement with the balance owing at the confirmation date, as reflected on the monthly statement enclosed with the request letter, or by asking the customer to indicate the balance owing at the confirmation date.

- *Negative confirmation:* involves the inclusion of a sticker placed on the monthly statement sent to the customers inviting them to contact the auditor only when they disagree with the balance as reflected on the statement at the confirmation date.

A response to a *positive confirmation* request to customers is generally expected to provide reliable audit evidence. There is a risk, however, that a respondent may reply without verifying that the information is correct. On the other hand, the fact that a response has not been received to a *negative confirmation* request provides no hard evidence that the customer received the confirmation request or necessarily verified that the information contained therein is correct. Accordingly, *negative confirmation* requests provide less reliable audit evidence than *positive confirmation* requests and the auditor should consider performing other substantive procedures to supplement the *negative confirmation* requests.

Negative confirmation requests may be used to reduce audit risk to an acceptable level when:

- the assessed level of inherent and control risk is low;
- a large number of small balances are involved;
- a substantial number of errors is not expected; and
- the auditor has no reason to believe the respondents will disregard these requests.

Timing and extent of confirmation requests

In deciding to what extent to use external confirmations, and which form of confirmation request should be used, the auditor will consider the characteristics of the environment in which the client operates and the practice of respondents in dealing with requests for direct confirmations.

For example, if the customers comprise mainly other business operations they are likely to have appropriate records of accounts payable and are thus in a position to respond to a positive confirmation request. As a general rule, the auditor of a manufacturing concern or wholesale business, whose customers are mainly other business concerns, is likely to get a reasonable response to a confirmation based on a positive confirmation request.

In contrast, if the client is a retailer to the general public, with numerous relatively small amounts owing by customers who are unlikely to maintain formal records of their accounts, the likelihood of receiving a high level of responses is very low. In this case the review of subsequent receipts and normal payment patterns from customers may be a more effective audit procedure to establish the *existence*, *measurement/accuracy* and *valuation* of accounts receivable. In such circumstances, experience has shown that few people take the trouble to reply to the request unless the balance shown on the statement appears to them wrong and to their disadvantage. In such cases it is logical to use a negative confirmation request.

The auditor may also decide to use both forms of request where the client may have a few individual debtors with very large balances, comprising a significant percentage of the total accounts receivable balance, who would be sent *positive confirmation* requests; and numerous other debtors with smaller balances owing, who would be sent *negative confirmation* requests.

The auditor also needs to consider the type of information the customer is able to confirm in designing the confirmation request. For example, where customers, such as large retail hypermarkets, purchase on an EDI basis (electronic data interchange or B2B basis) and who settle each individual invoice amount owing by means of EFT (electronic funds transfer), rather than paying for the entire month's purchases from one supplier at month end, it may not be possible for them to confirm a balance owing. In this situation the auditor will generally request confirmation of the individual invoices making up the balance outstanding at the confirmation date and will need to provide such a schedule for the customer to confirm.

The auditor would ordinarily confirm accounts receivable regarding amounts owed at the client's year-end. However, given that the entire confirmation process takes some time to complete and the responses to positive confirmation requests are required before the audit is completed, the confirmation request is often sent out a month or two prior to the financial year-end, particularly where the client has set a reporting deadline close to the year-end.

The accounts receivable confirmation process

When confirming accounts receivable the auditor should maintain control over the process of selecting those to whom the request will be sent, the preparation and sending of confirmation requests, and the responses to those requests (SAAS 505, 'External confirmations', paragraph .30).

Procedures to be performed when confirming accounts receivable

- Obtain a list of accounts receivable balances as at the confirmation date, cast the schedule and agree the total to the accounts receivable control account in the general ledger.

- Ensure that there is a statement for every account receivable, other than those mentioned below, by checking the statements with the list of balances. Enquire from management whether any accounts receivable balances are not to be confirmed, for example, those accounts in the hands of attorneys for collection.

- Use CAATs to select the sample required for positive confirmation or negative confirmation and agree the customer's details, including the name and address appearing on the monthly statement with the customer master-file details.
  - There is no apparent means by which the auditor can be certain that the recorded addresses are the correct ones and it may be that a member of the staff has fraudulently altered an address to that of a third party that can be relied upon to accept and destroy the statement or confirmation letter, so that it neither falls into the hands of the genuine debtor nor is returned to the auditor.
  - The auditor may thus consider it necessary to check or at least test the correctness of addresses by, for example, reference to any recent correspondence from the debtor or, if practicable, the telephone directory.

- Enclose the positive confirmation request letter with the customer's statement or affix the auditor's negative confirmation request sticker or stamp to the statement. It should be evident that the effectiveness of confirmation is greatly reduced if the reply is made via the client, due to the opportunity given to members of the client's staff who may be involved in fraudulent practices to suppress the replies intended for the auditor, and settle the matter with the debtor.

- Supervise the mailing of the statements and confirmation letters and provide for envelopes returned as 'address unknown' from the post office to be routed directly to the auditor. The statements and confirmation letters should remain under the control of the auditor between the time that they are checked and the time mailed, so that a member of the client's staff does not have an opportunity to remove any statements and/or substitute others.

- Follow up all queries and complaints by customers relating to their statements and ensure that all necessary steps have been taken to rectify any errors revealed in this way.

- Follow up statements returned by the post office as 'not delivered' by obtaining the correct addresses and reposting, or if no other address is known, reporting the matter to the management and ascertaining whether provision has been made for such debts as irrecoverable.

- Where many credits are recorded for returns and/or allowances in the period between the end of the year and the time of the audit, investigate the matter to ascertain the amount of such credits applicable to sales prior to year-end and whether they are bona fide. If the amount involved is significant, it may be necessary to bring the credits into account at the year-end and so reduce the sales income and accounts receivable accordingly.

- A working paper should be prepared to control the confirmation requests and responses that would typically contain the following details:
  - The details of the basis for selection of accounts for positive or negative confirmation;
  - The specific accounts selected for positive circularization together with an analysis of the responses received to each positive confirmation request and the actual responses received filed in the working papers;
  - Where in the case of positive confirmation a reply has not been received, re-confirm and, if still no reply is received, scrutinize the relevant debtor's account. If it appears as subsequently paid, vouch the receipt. If the debt is still unpaid, ascertain whether the debt was correctly recorded by examining the relevant order forms and delivery notes.
  - The results of enquiries of management regarding the nature of any disagreements expressed by the respondents in their confirmations, that might indicate material errors or misstatement in the accounts receivable balances, and how these were resolved;
  - An analysis of the results of the sample of accounts receivable confirmed to disclose the proportion of errors therein and the projection of the likely rate and amount of error potentially existing in the accounts receivable balance.

- Finally the auditor should evaluate whether the results of the confirmation process, together with the results from any other procedures performed, provide sufficient appropriate audit evidence of the financial statement assertions being audited.

- Where confirmation requests are made at a date prior to the financial year-end, the auditor should obtain sufficient appropriate audit evidence that transactions relevant to the assertions in the intervening period to the financial year-end have not been materially misstated. This may involve the performance of analytical procedures regarding the sales and receipts for the intervening period as well as cut-off tests of sales, cash receipts and sales adjustments performed at both the confirmation date and the financial year-end.

12.3.5.2 Evaluating the recoverability of accounts receivable

Given the satisfactory completion of the above-mentioned procedures, with regard to the *completeness, existence/occurrence* and *measurement assertions*, the accounts receivable can be taken as correct, or reasonably so. It remains for the auditor to decide the fair recoverable value thereof or, to put it negatively, to estimate what portion of the accounts receivable balances is irrecoverable. Accordingly, the following work remains to be done to gather audit evidence regarding the *valuation* assertion:

- Obtain an aged list of accounts receivable balances at the financial year-end and use CAATs to cast and cross-cast the schedule and agree the total to the general ledger control account for accounts receivable. Alternatively, CAATs may be used to extract the schedule.

- Select a sample of the balances and test the ageing of the balances reflected, where possible use CAATs for this purpose. Ascertain the basis used by the entity to age debts in different categories – current, 30 days, 60 days and 90 days and over, whether this is determined by allocating receipts to specific invoices or whether receipts are merely allocated against the oldest amount outstanding.

- Inspect receipts from debtors received subsequent to the financial year-end and up to the time that the auditor performs audit procedures relating to the recoverability of debts. Balances subsequently paid should be marked accordingly on the aged list of accounts receivable.

- Obtain information regarding the terms of credit allowed. This may be standard for all customers or there may be special terms allowed to particular customers. In a computerized information system, this information would normally be kept in the customer master file and the auditor could request a printout of the credit terms for all, or specific debtors.

- Review the aged list for the long-outstanding amounts remaining unpaid and use CAATs to analyse individual accounts to ascertain the composition of the balances and customer payment history. Inspect any correspondence with the debtor, or debt collectors that provides evidence as to the recoverability of the balance. This may include information obtained for the accounts receivable confirmations indicating disputed charges. Enquire whether long outstanding amounts are attributable to disputed charges, requiring the issue of a credit note, or whether they indicate an inability of the debtor to meet its payment obligations.

- The tendency for the balance to increase out of proportion to the net sales to the customer may be evidence of a debtor's growing inability to meet its obligations. A scrutiny of the successive monthly balances on such accounts for the year under audit may therefore be useful. This applies especially to debtor's paying round sums instead of settling particular invoices. The auditor in this scrutiny should also have regard for any entries in the ledger accounts, which may indicate that a debt is not worth its face value, for example, the renewal of bills receivable, cheques received but not met and subsequently reversed. Again, there may be notes on the ledger accounts, or in the records kept by a credit control department, to the effect, for example, that the debtor cannot be traced. Generally speaking, the auditor should, while inspecting the evidence, be alert for any signs that indicate the likelihood that debt will be irrecoverable in whole or in part.

- Should any customers be situated in other countries, consider not only the debtor's ability to pay but also whether the exchange regulations of the foreign country permit the debtor to remit payment to South Africa. Some countries prohibit, or at least restrict, the outflow of money to other countries. In such circumstances the auditor may, if the sums involved are material, have to consider whether a special provision is required to cover probable losses arising as a result of this.

- Ascertain the basis used in prior years to compute the allowance for irrecoverable debts and review management's calculation of the provision for the current year for consistency. Enquire about any change in the basis of the calculation and consider the justification for this. Ascertain the adequacy of the provisions in prior years by reference to the amount of bad debts written off in the current period. Recalculate the allowance for irrecoverable debts for each ageing category and compare this to the provision raised by management for the current financial year. Thereafter, discuss the list of long-outstanding accounts receivable balances with the appropriate management (usually the credit controller or financial manager) to decide on the reasonableness and adequacy of the amount to be provided as an allowance for irrecoverable debts.

- The allowance for irrecoverable debts is an accounting estimate, the amount of which is decided upon based on both objective evidence and the judgement of the client and the auditor regarding the probable outcome of future events. The reader is referred to the discussion on the audit of accounting estimates in chapter 11 for matters requiring consideration. In coming to a conclusion regarding the adequacy of the provision, and the sufficiency and appropriateness of the audit evidence obtained, the auditor will also take into account the effectiveness of the client's controls over the granting of credit to customers, the debt collection process and the entity's history of bad debt write-offs.

Bad debts recovered

As a general rule a firm of attorneys or a debt-collecting agency handles these matters. The auditor should examine the statements and correspondence from the attorney or debt-collecting agency and so vouch the cash received. Deductions for fees and expenses should be journalized as an expense, the gross sum collected thus being recorded as bad debts recovered. The auditor should satisfy himself that all sums so recorded have been written off previously as irrecoverable.

12.3.6 Substantive tests of detail for cash and bank balances

The revenue/receipt transactions are completed when amounts received from accounts receivable, cash sales or miscellaneous income are deposited in the bank. Control features to ensure that all amounts received are banked and the audit procedures to test that the system was adhered to and amounts received correctly accounted for, are explained above. It remains for the auditor to be satisfied that the cash and bank balances recorded in the accounting records are correct. It follows that if there is satisfactory internal control and audit tests of transactions have proved accurate recording of cash receipts and payments (see chapter 17), the cash and bank balances will be correctly reflected. Conversely, the satisfactory verification of cash and bank balances confirms that cash receipts and payments transactions were correctly recorded during the period under audit.

12.3.7 Presentation and disclosure

Refer to GAAP statement AC 111, 'Revenue', which prescribes the accounting treatment of *revenue* arising from the sale of goods, the rendering of services and the use by others of enterprise assets. In particular, the statement provides the criteria for the timing of revenue recognition, as well as the measurement and disclosure requirements.

Accounts receivable and cash are regarded as financial assets in terms of paragraph .09 of GAAP AC 133, 'Financial Instruments: Recognition and Measurement', which defines a *financial asset* as including: '(a) cash and (b) a contractual right to receive cash or another financial asset from another enterprise'; and *fair value* as the amount 'for which an asset could be exchanged, or liability settled, between knowledgeable, willing parties in an arm's length transaction'.

The amount owing by customers for accounts receivable less the allowance for irrecoverable accounts receivable reflects accounts receivable at their *fair value* and should be disclosed in the current asset section of the balance sheet. The allowance for irrecoverable accounts receivable need not be shown separately, being a provision for diminution in value of a current asset. Depending on the nature of the concern's business, it may be appropriate to show trade and non-trade accounts receivable separately. For example, included in accounts receivable may be a substantial debt due from the sale of fixed assets. Failure to show such non-trading debts separately, if material, would distort the accounts receivable turnover ratio. Many businesses, however, do not make this distinction.

Where the amounts involved are material, credit balances in the accounts receivable should be included in accounts payable, and debit balances in accounts payable included in accounts receivable.

GAAP also requires the current and non-current portion of accounts receivable to be separately disclosed, and details to be provided in the notes to the financial statements of any accounts receivable balances that have been factored or pledged as security for liabilities of the entity.

13

Auditing Expenditure Transactions and Balances

Learning objectives

After studying this chapter you should be able to:

1. Describe the nature of expenditures that might be expected to arise directly from the core processes of a variety of businesses and distinguish these from the nature of the expenditures encountered in the resource management processes of any business.

2. Explain which expenditure transactions and balances could be regarded as significant classes of transactions and specify the accounts affected by these.

3. Describe the relationship between the financial statement assertions and audit objectives for expenditure transactions and related balances.

4. Explain how the auditor's understanding of the process level business risks related to various expenditures, and consideration of materiality, affects the preliminary assessment of the combined inherent and control risk (the risk of significant misstatement) in the financial statements.

5. Discuss how the auditor's understanding of the client's internal controls could influence the assessment of the risk of significant misstatement for expenditure transactions and related balances.

6. Describe the types of documents, records and typical functions that may be encountered, for expenditure transactions and related balances.

7. Discuss considerations applicable to the auditor's evaluation of inherent risks and relevant control activities affecting the various financial statement assertions for expenditure transactions and related balances.

8. Describe tests of controls that are necessary where the auditor plans to assess control risk below the maximum for expenditure transactions and related balances.

419

9.   Explain how the auditor determines acceptable levels for detection risk and how this affects substantive audit procedures for expenditures and related balances to obtain sufficient audit evidence to meet specific audit objectives.
10. Describe substantive analytical procedures that would be effective in identifying expenditure transactions and related balances likely to contain material misstatements and in obtaining audit evidence supporting expenditures and related balances.
11. Design an audit programme for substantive tests of detail for significant classes of expenditure transactions and accounts payable and bank balances.

13.1 NATURE OF EXPENDITURE TRANSACTIONS

13.1.1 Introduction

Expenditure transactions of entities comprise expenditure on goods, services and the acquisition of fixed assets used directly or indirectly to generate revenue it earns from its business activities. Certain of these expenditures will be related directly to the production of income from the core processes of the business, whilst others will form a part of the entity's resource management expenditures, which provide the infrastructure for the core business processes to occur.

An entity's expenditures vary greatly in nature, amount and incidence. This chapter focuses on the control activities and audit of significant classes of transactions and balances relating to the purchase of goods and services and the payment of accounts payable and cash disbursements. The control activities over expenditures and payments arising from the purchase and management of inventory and payroll expenditures are discussed in chapters 14 and 15 and those relating to fixed asset acquisitions and investments in chapter 16.

Business entities will need premises from which to operate. The costs involved usually constitute a significant balance in the income statement where premises are rented and may also reflect as significant balances in the balance sheet where properties are owned by the entity.

In addition to expenditure on business premises and human resources, expenses incurred as part of core business processes frequently result in significant classes of transactions, and should thus be subjected to more formal control activities to prevent, or detect and correct, errors and fraud. Examples of these expenses include advertising and promotion costs, research and development cost, and other costs associated with operating a business such as rates, electricity, telephone and other municipal levies. Other expenses may occur less frequently and have less formal control activities implemented over them, such as legal expenses or other professional fees incurred.

The business processes of different business entities introduced in Table 12.1 in chapter 12 will determine the nature of the different types of expenses incurred by them. Whilst certain expenditures are fundamental to all business entities, the specific nature and their quantum are diverse and peculiar to the core processes of different entities. Examples of expenditures, other than on business premises and human resources, are provided in Table 13.1 below.

TYPE OF BUSINESS	TYPICAL EXPENDITURES ARISING FROM CORE BUSINESS PROCESSES
A trading operation	Product selection and purchasing, inventory management, the provision of customer services, advertising and promotion and maintenance of quality standards.
An automotive manufacturer	The acquisition of the equipment and tooling needed for a vehicle assembly line; the design costs and manufacturing expenditures for different vehicle models or royalties for licensing rights to assemble internationally branded vehicle models; purchasing and inventory management for vehicle components, paints and consumables such as grease and oil used in the assembly of vehicles (this may also include shipping and clearing charges and forex gains or losses for imported components). Expenses may be incurred in safety testing, weighing and registration of engine and chassis numbers for newly assembled vehicles and distribution costs in delivering vehicles to the appointed vehicle distributors.
A manufacturer	The acquisition of equipment used in the manufacturing process; purchasing and inventory management of raw materials, consumables and finished goods; marketing and distribution costs of finished products to consumers or retailers and administration expenses.
Advertising agencies	Advertising fees paid to publishers and other media for 'flighting' their client's adverts on television or radio and publication in various media, including Internet websites. Expenses will also be incurred on creative design and photographic materials.
A professional practice	The expenses of lawyers, accountants and business consultants will include items such as printing and communications; travelling costs of staff to clients, acquisition or leasing of office furniture, equipment, including computers and vehicles, provision of library and research facilities.

TYPE OF BUSINESS	TYPICAL EXPENDITURES ARISING FROM CORE BUSINESS PROCESSES
Medical service providers	Specialized medical equipment and drugs for use in the practice; travelling expenses to patients or conferences, and delivery and insurance of medical equipment used in the practices or purchased or manufactured for supply to other service providers.
Medical facilities	Hospitals and clinics may have several core processes and incur expenses providing ward accommodation for bed patients, trauma facilities, consulting rooms for medical practitioners and facilities for X-ray departments. In particular, cleaning and medical waste removal costs to maintain the germ-free hospital environment; expenditures in catering facilities for bed patients and nursing staff; acquisition of sophisticated equipment for operating theatres and furniture and equipment for different wards and reception areas of the hospital. A further core business may be the operation of a pharmacy within the hospital premises with related purchasing and inventory management.
IT consultants	The supply, assembly and installation of various configurations of computer equipment to customer specifications; the purchase and inventory management of computer components, network cabling; of hardware and software supplied to customers or retail service outlets; travelling, accommodation and communication expenses, and royalties and licensing fees for software distribution rights, expenditures in IT servicing and support services to customers possibly from call centres or help desks.
Investors	The acquisition of share investments, and payment of broking fees and taxes on transactions, or in the selection and acquisition of investment properties and management of those properties for tenants; in interest payments on loans obtained to finance the property purchased; legal expenses will be incurred in handling property transfers and drawing lease agreements.

TYPE OF BUSINESS	TYPICAL EXPENDITURES ARISING FROM CORE BUSINESS PROCESSES
Estate agents	Acquisition of office equipment; advertising of properties for sale, travelling expenses in taking potential buyers to inspect properties; communication costs; commissions payable to agents arising from property deals and legal expenses in drawing contract documents for facilitating complex property deals such as turnkey projects. Estate agents involved in property letting and management for clients, or their own account, will incur property maintenance expenses, which may be recoverable from the property owners.
Public sector entities	Provision of the infrastructure for delivery of the particular services the entity is directly responsible for, such as the provision of infrastructure, water and electricity, roads, rail services, airports and shipping ports, health care facilities such as hospitals and clinics, housing for lower income groups, income tax services, government pensions and social security services.
Schools and universities	Expenses related to the *core process of teaching* and *research*; providing classroom and research facilities; the provisioning of libraries, printing of course materials; purchase of teaching materials; provisioning of computer, scientific, engineering and medical laboratories; conference expenses for staff and researchers; sports facilities and equipment. Residential universities may have a separate core process of *student affairs*, incurring expenses on marketing and student enrolment services, expenses arising from student accommodation and catering facilities; the provision of bursaries for needy students; student counselling centres and medical facilities.
Banking and financial institutions	Expenditures related to the core processes will include specialized secure computer networks and equipment for the provision of banking and autobank teller facilities, interest paid on deposits from customers, charges from other banks, security expenses over cash, and cash in transit activities, and internet banking facilities; customer relationship expenses, including sponsorships of sporting and cultural events and marketing expenses.

TYPE OF BUSINESS	TYPICAL EXPENDITURES ARISING FROM CORE BUSINESS PROCESSES
Insurance companies	First core process will be selling of insurance policies and the assessment and payment of claims. Expenditure incurred on office furniture and equipment and vehicles; commissions payable to brokers and agents involved in selling policies; fees to claim assessors and settlement of claims and benefits. Insurance claims paid by short-term insurers will relate to insurable losses incurred by the parties insured. In the case of long-term insurers, benefits paid will relate directly to payments of annuities and lump sums on retirement to the insured persons or in respect of death benefits paid to executors of deceased estates or nominated beneficiaries. Insurance companies may well have a *second core process*, namely *asset management*, assuming responsibility for the investment of premium income in short-term and long-term financial instruments, property development and other investments. The entity may incur expenses for property maintenance and periodic upgrading, where properties are acquired for resale or letting; and for the collection of investment income in the form of rentals, interest or dividends.
Restaurants and fast food outlets	These are often run as franchise operations. Expenditure relates to the core process of supplying food. This will include the acquisition of catering equipment, the furnishing of restaurant facilities in accordance with specific décor and layout of a particular franchise brand, e.g. Wimpy, Steers and MacDonalds. In addition, the business will incur expenses relating to the purchase of meat and fish, fresh produce and tinned or frozen foodstuff for catering; cold-drinks, alcohol, wines and malts for bar services supplied to customers; royalties and advertising expenses may be payable to the franchisor.
Building contractors	Expenses on direct labour and building materials, the hire or acquisition of construction equipment and site equipment, tools, payments to subcontractors, short-term insurance premiums and security costs to cover accidents and prevent theft on sites, municipal site deposits and clearance certificates. Further expenditures are likely to include travelling expenses to building sites, communications, accommodation and food for construction site employees on out of town building sites.

Table 13.1 Typical expenditures arising from core business processes

13.1.2 **Audit objectives**

To achieve the audit objectives requires the auditor to obtain sufficient appropriate audit evidence regarding each significant assertion related to expenditure transactions and related balances to reduce the risk of significant misstatement in the financial statements to appropriately low levels. While revenue is clearly the most significant amount in the financial statements of a *retail operation*, the aggregate expenditures of such an entity will also be significant.

Individual expenditure transactions and balances directly related to the core activities of a business are likely to be regarded as significant, such as purchases of goods for resale and payments of accounts payable, whereas other expenses, although material in amount (for example, property rental) may carry a low risk of misstatement, while others may be immaterial quantitatively but significant from a qualitative perspective (for example, directors' emoluments or other items that require separate disclosure in the financial statements).

The discussion in the remainder of this chapter continues using a *retail operation* to illustrate typical expenditure transactions and related balances reflected in financial statements, as was done in chapter 12 for revenue transactions. The principles covering tests of controls, substantive analytical procedures and substantive tests of detail are applicable also in the audit of other business entities. The account balances affected by expenditure transactions are set out in Table 13.2 below:

EXPENDITURE TRANSACTIONS	ACCOUNT BALANCES DEBITED	ACCOUNT BALANCES CREDITED
Purchases of inventory for resale Various expenses Various assets acquired	Purchases or inventory Other expenses Input VAT Prepaid expenses Fixed assets	Accounts payable
Accruals of expenses at period end	Other expenses Input VAT	Accounts payable
Payments to suppliers by cash, cheque, and EFT	Accounts payable	Cash Discounts receivable Bank

Table 13.2 General ledger account balances typically affected by expenditure transactions for a trading operation

Regardless of the diversity of expenditure or complexity of accounting or legal requirements, in formulating an opinion on the financial statements, the auditor needs to gather sufficient appropriate audit evidence regarding management assertions relating to expenditure transactions reflected in income statement and related balance sheet balances.

The link between management's assertions in financial statements and the corresponding audit objectives for expenditure transactions and balances are set out in Table 13.3.

MANAGEMENT ASSERTION	AUDIT OBJECTIVES
Expenditure transactions	
Completeness	All purchases and payments made during the period have been recorded.
Occurrence/ validity	Recorded purchases have been properly authorized and represent goods, services and assets actually received during the period.
	All payments recorded represent valid payments made.
Measurement/ accuracy	All purchases and other expenditures have been correctly calculated, allocated and recorded in the correct accounts in the general ledger in accordance with the GAAP policies applied by the entity.
	All payments made, after deduction of all supplier discounts claimed, are recorded in the correct accounts payable account.
Expenditure balances	
Completeness	Accounts payable represent all amounts owing to suppliers of goods and services at the balance sheet date.
Existence	Recorded accounts payable and accruals represent amounts owing by the entity at the balance sheet date.
Measurement/ accuracy and valuation	Accounts payable are stated at the correct amount at balance sheet date, determined in accordance with the GAAP policies applied by the entity.
	Related expenditures reflected in the income statement and assets reflected in the balance sheet have been similarly determined in accordance with these GAAP policies applied consistently by the entity.

MANAGEMENT ASSERTION	AUDIT OBJECTIVES
Rights and obligations	Accounts payable represent valid legal claims for payment against the entity by its suppliers at the balance sheet date.
	The rights of any secured creditor in respect of inventory pledged or property mortgaged at the balance sheet to secure obligations of the entity have been identified.
Presentation and disclosure	Accounts payable and related expenditures are properly disclosed and classified in the financial statements in accordance with GAAP policies applied consistently by the entity.
	Appropriate disclosures have been made with regard to pledges or mortgages of entity assets to secure liabilities of the entity, and of contingent liabilities, commitments and related party transactions.

Table 13.3 Management assertions and the related audit objectives for expenditure transactions and balances

13.1.3 Understanding the client's business

That it is important for the auditor to understand the client's business cannot be emphasized too strongly. It enables the auditor to assess the materiality and reasonableness of significant balances and classes of transactions arising from expenditures of the entity, that are reflected in the financial statements and to understand the performance of the client entity relative to external and internal factors affecting it. For example, from the different gross profit margins expected for different categories of revenue, the auditor should be able to anticipate the reasonableness of the cost of sales and expectations with regard to other expense accounts arising from the core business processes that are the norm for the business and industry.

The expenditure items regarded as significant classes of transactions and related balances will usually be those related to the core business processes. The auditor thus needs to identify the core processes and process level business risks in order to make a preliminary assessment of the *risk of significant misstatement* of expenditure transactions and related balances.

The auditor needs to be aware of the strategic business risks faced by a client arising from external factors, such as laws and regulations, that could affect the strategic and operational risks of the client, or that might affect particular expenditures by the client or require specific disclosure in the financial statements. Internal factors that affect the client's purchasing processes business risks are supplier alliances and relationships, the quality of products and services available and at what cost. Knowledge of the control activities management has in place to manage these risks is also necessary.

Consideration of materiality

The auditor's assessment of the inherent and control risks is done in the context of the *materiality* of any potential risk of significant misstatement. Purchases in a large trading operation will generally comprise one of the more significant balances in the income statement namely, for goods sold *cost of sales*. Goods unsold at year-end, *inventory*, and purchases made on credit and not settled, *accounts payable* are balances which are usually material to balance sheet disclosures.

The risk of significant misstatement, in the absence of adequate controls to ensure the *completeness, occurrence/validity and measurement/accuracy* of purchases and cash payments are:

- firstly, an understatement of purchases and accounts payable, for purchases made and received, but not recorded in the current period; and
- secondly, an overstatement of purchases and accounts payable, where purchases are recorded in the current period, but in respect of which the goods are only received in the next.

In considering the materiality of purchases of inventory and accounts payable, the auditor will initially determine a quantitative materiality amount. The reader is referred to the discussion on materiality in chapter 5 for guidance on the bases that might be applied.

With regard to other expenditure transactions and balances affecting items appearing in the income statement or balance sheet, the auditor, in considering the risk of significant misstatement and determining the appropriate audit procedures to be performed, will have regard to both quantitative and qualitative materiality factors, such as any GAAP or Companies Act requirements for specific or separate disclosure of such items in the financial statements and the possibility of fraud or error. This may result in a lower quantitative amount being set for materiality for expenditure items.

13.1.4 Analysing expenditure process level business risks

The analysis of process level business risks may best be illustrated by the following example of a large trading operation with numerous retailing outlets.

Example: Case 13.1

The process level business risks relate to the *completeness, occurrence/ validity* and *measurement/accuracy* of product selection and purchasing of products for resale and consumables used in the core business processes and related payments made to suppliers. Management may regard the critical success factors and key performance indicators to control product selection and purchasing and payments of accounts payable as:

CRITICAL SUCCESS FACTORS	KEY PERFORMANCE INDICATORS
Timely, relevant information is received by management to determine purchase requirements.	Number of stock-outs.
Purchases made ensure inventory levels are maintained at appropriate levels.	Number of stock-outs and individual inventory items turnover statistics.
Payments are made to suppliers within agreed payment terms.	Percentage of supplier complaints due to late payments. Accounts payable days outstanding. Liquidity ratios.
Supplier discounts claimable are maximized.	Average purchase price per unit or discounts received as a percentage of total purchases.

Table 13.4 Example of critical success factors and key performance indicators

Applying the top-down audit approach, the auditor would need to ascertain management's response should actual performance be out of line with the identified key performance indicators. Management would have documented their means of investigating and establishing the cause of such deviations. An appropriate response might require improvement over control activities to prevent, or detect and correct errors or fraud, that might arise affecting the *completeness, occurrence/validity and measurement/ accuracy* of recorded purchases from, and payments to, suppliers.

The auditor would ascertain whether or not those responsible did the checks to ensure that delivery times and product quality standards were met, percentage stock-outs were minimized, and that any queries from suppliers or unexpected changes to liquidity ratios were promptly investigated and resolved by management. That the auditor is satisfied with these matters will provide evidence that the risks are being appropriately managed. Apart from management's monitoring procedures, the auditor would ascertain the other control activities in place. These would include:

- An exception report being generated from a three-way match of the purchase order, invoice and goods received document that reflects:
  - daily unmatched deliveries for review by *inventory management* and enquiry from the buying department to confirm whether or not an order was placed; and
  - price differences between those reflected on purchase orders and invoices for follow up by *accounting personnel,* who refer to *inventory personnel to confirm receipt of the goods, and subsequent liaison with the supplier* regarding pricing differences.
- Internal audit staff review the exception reports from the inventory management system on a monthly basis to ensure appropriate resolution of problem items.

The auditor may conclude that management's review of the key performance indicators and design of the control procedures are sufficient to ensure the *completeness, occurrence/validity and measurement/ accuracy* of the purchasing of products for resale and consumables used in the core business processes and the related payments made to suppliers. In this case the auditor would make a preliminary assessment of the risk of significant misstatement in the transactions and balances as low.

This preliminary risk assessment will be confirmed should tests of controls provide evidence that:
- exception reports generated were adequately reviewed and any problems resolved;
- appropriate investigation and explanations were obtained where actual performance deviated from laid-down key performance indicators; and
- key control techniques within the purchases and payments systems operated as designed.

In these circumstances, limited substantive tests would be necessary for expenditure classes of transactions and related balances. These would consist mainly of substantive analytical review procedures on the various expenditure classes of transactions and attendance at the client's inventory count and follow up (see chapter 14) and a check of the reconciliation of selected amounts payable balances to provide evidence of the accuracy and rights and obligations in respect of inventory and accounts payable respectively.

The inter-relationships within each key process make it possible for the auditor to anticipate an expectation of amounts affecting related transactions and balances. This facilitates the auditor's use of analytical procedures to identify material misstatements, or confirm fair presentation, and accordingly justifies a reduction to the extent of detailed substantive tests required.

An understanding and analysis of the expenditure transactions of a client enables the auditor to identify the process level business risks and the respective inputs, processing activities and outputs, because these will generally involve the implementation by the client of different control activities to manage the process level business risks. Control activities are usually performed by different persons involved in the processing of expenditure transactions, which occur at two stages, namely:

- purchases of goods and services or assets from suppliers; and
- payment to suppliers and other creditors and petty cash expenditures.

Functions, control activities, control risk assessment, tests of controls and substantive analytical and detailed tests of purchases transactions and balances related to these two aspects are discussed below.

13.1.5 Preliminary assessment of the risk of significant misstatement

The auditor should consider the combined effect of the inherent risk and control risks (the risk of significant misstatement) affecting expenditure transactions and related balances and be alert to any that could occur in the particular client's business which might distort fair presentation of the financial statements.

Following the recent collapse of major corporations, both locally and internationally, there is anecdotal evidence that indicates a large scale of deliberate misapplication of GAAP and fraud by management and employees. Methods used include:

- Capitalization of expenditure and subsequent impairment of the asset that should ordinarily have been expensed immediately. This has the effect of increasing reported profits and inflating reserves in the current financial year.

- Raising of excessive provisions to be held in reserves, which are then released as income as and when management wish to do so, effectively 'smoothing' income. Conversely, failure to make adequate provision for obligations existing at the year-end, or failure to reduce the carrying value of assets to recoverable amounts.

- Use of special purpose entities to move liabilities 'off balance sheet' or to create 'fictitious income streams' by virtue of charges between related parties.

- Complex tax schemes to defer or hide income tax or VAT liabilities.

- Charging of personal expenses to the business, and cases of senior management treating business funds as their own personal slush funds.

The *inherent risks* of material misstatement possibly encountered that are specific to expenditure transactions and related balances include:

- *Management bias and incentive to misstate expenditures*, whether to achieve budgets, increase performance bonuses or understate expenditures and liabilities for reporting in the financial statements; to secure additional funding from banks, or attract a potential purchaser for the business or mislead shareholders affecting the share price on the local Securities Exchange; or for personal gains by charging personal expenditures to the business.

- The *complexity of the expenditures incurred* where the entity has, during the financial year, started operating sales outlets in a foreign country where management has limited experience of problems that might be encountered, including the level of competence to process the business transactions correctly. This could result in errors in expenditure allocation and translation of foreign currencies, as well as errors in estimating provisions.

- The risk of *management override of controls* or *fraud by employees* in collusion with third parties to process personal expenditures as business expenditures and the possible duplication of payments, in error or intentionally, by personnel with the ability to process payments to accounts payable.

- *Incorrect cut-off applied*, so that purchases of goods or services received during the current financial period are recorded in the next, in error or deliberately. Conversely, purchases might be recorded in the current period, but the goods or services received only in the next. Where the entity imports goods for resale and these are in transit at the period end, but ownership has already passed, that is, FOB imports where the carrier is the agent of the purchaser, the understatement of goods in transit is at risk.

- Management may be under pressure to reflect higher levels of earnings and working capital. Accordingly, they may be tempted to *understate accounts payable* balance and provisions involving estimates for inventory and accounts receivable write downs, or guarantees provided on goods sold.

- Where the entity *imports goods for resale* errors may arise in recording the purchases as a result of using inappropriate currency exchange rates. The complexities of recording foreign exchange transactions where forward cover may have been taken out or transactions hedged could also lead to errors in recording profits and losses on foreign exchange and on the hedging instruments, with a consequent error in accounting for the cost of inventory imported. A further risk is the failure to allocate to inventory all costs of importation, such as freight, insurance and customs duty costs.

- The inherent *risk of fraud and theft* related to expenditures is high in a large *retail operation*, due to the volume and diversity of purchases of goods, services, fixed assets and payments, complexity of transactions, and misappropriation of goods, both by staff and customers. The risk is increased where accounting staff responsible for the preparation and capturing of payments may have access and are able, for example, to load new accounts to the accounts payable master file records, in this way processing fictitious transactions.

- Late payments to suppliers may result in *discounts receivable*, to which the entity is entitled, not being claimed – or, if claimed, being disallowed and increasing expenditures unnecessarily.

- Changed cost of inventory purchases may not be appropriately identified for the purposes of valuing inventory on a FIFO basis and consequently *inventory* and *cost of sales* may be incorrectly accounted for.

- Rights and obligations that are not recorded might lead to *classification errors in the balance sheet* and incorrect or inadequate disclosures in the notes to the financial statements.

Given the nature of the inherent risks and usually high volumes of purchases of goods and services, management of a large retail trading operation is likely to implement adequate control activities to prevent or detect errors and fraud. As management might be motivated to overstate profits, the understatement of expenditures and accounts payable would be the auditor's major concern. The risks are thus the omission of transactions, incorrect cut-off and misallocations between capital and revenue expenditure, which affect the following assertions: *completeness, occurrence/existence* and *measurement/accuracy*.

Before performing tests of controls and substantive test procedures, the auditor makes a preliminary assessment of the *risk of significant misstatement for the expenditure transactions and related balances* in the financial statements. The auditor considers risk factors and documents the overall assessment as *high, medium or low*. This assessment influences the auditor's decision on an appropriate audit approach. The reader is reminded, as discussed in preceding chapters, that the *risk of significant misstatement* needs to be assessed for each of the following factors, and justification documented for each assessment:

- The residual business risk.
- The quality of the information available.
- The historical accuracy/measurement.
- The underlying assumptions used.
- The qualifications and competence of the personnel involved in accounting and recording and the complexity of the estimating.
- Any evidence of management bias and incentive to misstate.

These aspects are discussed later in the chapter.

In order to make a preliminary assessment of significant misstatement, the auditor should obtain an understanding of the controls over purchases and payments. This would be achieved by the review of prior year audit working papers, observation of the controls being performed, enquiry of management and staff and inspection of documents and printouts. The inspection of documents and printouts provides evidence of reconciliations to suppliers' statements and bank statements, that error reports are reviewed and that appropriate corrective action is taken.

13.1.6 Consideration of internal control components

The five internal control components, discussed in chapter 9, which affect the auditor's assessment of the *risk of significant misstatement* are considered below in relation to expenditure transactions and related balances. These are the *control environment, risk assessment, information and communication, monitoring and control* activities. The control activities discussed relate to the two significant classes of transactions arising from expenditures, namely:

* purchases of goods and services, or assets; and
* payment to suppliers and other creditors, and petty cash expenditures.

Before making decisions on which tests of control to perform, if any, the auditor is likely to consider management's monitoring activities and the design of detective controls, and whether these are appropriate for the objectives they are intended to meet.

13.1.6.1 Control environment

The control environment discussed in chapter 9 included such aspects as integrity, ethical values and organizational culture, competence of employees, management's philosophy and operating style, the manner in which the company assigns authority, the way in which it develops its people, and the attention given to control aspects by the board of directors.

These factors may affect the risk of significant misstatement of expenditure transactions both positively or negatively. The possibility of theft or the unauthorized use of assets is reduced where management establishes a code of conduct, in consultation with employees, that sets a zero tolerance for theft or unauthorized use of assets and where management is seen to actively enforce the code at all levels, from the most junior to senior of staff members. This means that, in the event of transgressions, disciplinary hearings should be followed by dismissal of offenders and legal action to recover assets. A critical aspect in relationships between the entity and its suppliers is the adoption of policies and procedures that prevent the acceptance of bribes and kickbacks by buyers, or management, from suppliers anxious to increase their levels of supply to the entity.

Management also displays its integrity in the way it adopts reasonable accounting policies. That is to say, management should discourage the misallocation of expenditures to deferred expenditures, it should not capitalize expenditure to manipulate net income results, or raise excessive provisions to reserves in good trading periods to reduce tax liabilities and smooth income.

The human resource policies of an entity should cater for the employment of staff with the appropriate skills. In addition, these policies should actively support the training of its staff to develop the necessary skills. This should minimize the risk of errors occurring and improve the chances of their detection, and early correction should they arise. Management should be seen to be monitoring the control activities and should avoid attempts to deliberately override controls. Delegation of authority should be done in such a way as to make staff accountable for their actions and the monitoring procedures of management should enforce these processes. If these various factors are not implemented or managed effectively, the risk of significant misstatement undoubtedly increases.

Given the generally high levels of inventory shrinkage in retailing businesses, strict physical and other controls over an entity's inventories is necessary. This aspect is discussed in chapter 14.1.

13.1.6.2 Risk assessment

Management's risk assessment processes related to expenditure transactions should identify and evaluate those risks that impact most directly on the purchases of goods and services and other expenditures, and the settlement of accounts payable balances. Management should implement effective appropriate controls over aspects where significant risks are apparent.

The process level business risks that management of a trading operation would need to manage in respect of purchases of goods and services and payment of suppliers are the following:

- The establishment and management of *alliances with suppliers* to ensure continuity of supplies of quality at best prices and at desired delivery times. This will affect all aspects from ordering of goods to acceptance of delivery, prompt settlement of amounts invoiced and prompt resolution of any account queries.

- The selection of suppliers and products purchased so as to respond to changing consumer demands. Buyers should continuously be looking for innovations in products available in order to retain and build the customer base.

- The monitoring of stock-outs, and the reasons therefor, so as to limit these as far as it is possible.

- The monitoring of cost prices and comparison of these with prices of other potential suppliers.

- The monitoring of mark-ups to provide the most competitive prices to the customers.

- The management of payments to suppliers to prevent duplication of payments, unauthorized payments to non-approved suppliers and failure to deduct discounts to which the entity is entitled.

- The effective management of inventory so as to maintain inventory at appropriate levels to supply customers' needs whilst avoiding excessive inventory holdings. This aspect is of particular importance where products have a limited shelf life or are subject to fashion changes or technical obsolescence.

- The risks of the entity's information systems not being equipped to handle the complexities of the purchasing and payments transactions for the volumes generated by the business.

Having obtained an understanding of the way in which these risks are addressed by management's monitoring and control activities, the auditor should be able to determine the likelihood of any risks of material misstatement remaining undetected or uncorrected by management and use this understanding to decide upon the audit strategy for auditing purchases and payments.

13.1.6.3 Information and communication

The information and communication requirements within an entity must provide for adequate documentation of the system and the entity's policies and procedures regarding all aspects of the expenditure and payments transactions. This should include the inputs, processing and outputs that ensure all expenditure transactions are properly captured into the accounting records, which in turn will result in the correct presentation and disclosure in the financial statements. This should include also the design of documentation which evidences the various functions in the purchases of goods and services transactions from the way in which these are initiated; evidence of receipt of goods; and any returns of faulty or incorrect goods supplied; the recording of purchases and any adjustments, and the initiation and recording of the payments to suppliers; and printouts of transaction audit trails, including exception reports generated, and account reconciliations performed.

Of importance is the reliability of the IT systems which involve the general and application controls, both manual and computerized, implemented over all aspects affecting the expenditure transactions. A reminder here that unlike general controls which are pervasive to all applications, the application controls are specific to the input, processing and output for expenditure transactions and balances, that is, for initiating, performing, recording, and monitoring the purchases of goods and services, purchases adjustments and payment aspects (refer Figure 13.1).

13.1.6.4 Monitoring

The setting of key performance indicators so as to match actual performance against these is vital to management's monitoring procedures. In respect of purchases, *key performance indicators* may address both external and internal factors and could range from the monitoring of: stock-out reports; reports on gross margins realized on different product lines or geographic areas; reports on sales trends of products for each store to anticipate periods of increased consumer activity which may require additional inventory holdings to meet the demand; reports monitoring the incidence of customer complaints, for example, with regard to products returned, as this may affect the buyer's decision to stock the particular items or advise the supplier that items appear flawed.

Monitoring processes include also comparison of actual monthly or quarterly results against budget; reports on internal control weaknesses from the internal and external auditors and from the risk assessment manager or director identifying strategic or process level business risks and management's action in response to problems identified.

The importance of related account balances arising from expenditure transactions should not be overlooked in the monitoring process as evidence regarding particular assertions for one account balance implies that the assertion is also met for a corresponding balance. For example, if cut-off tests performed on purchases and accounts payable indicate these are satisfactory and have been handled correctly, by inference the purchases cut-off on inventory balances arising from goods received will also be correct.

The discussion now proceeds to the control activities over expenditure transactions. An overview of the purchases process, which assumes a computerized environment, is set out in Figure 13.1.

13.2 CONTROL ACTIVITIES AND TESTS OF CONTROL

13.2.1 Purchases of goods and services

As indicated in the introduction to this chapter, depending on an entity's business processes, expenditure transactions may be diverse. The nature of the expenditure transactions will directly affect the form of documents used, the functions that occur, the recording processes followed, and the control activities implemented by management to ensure the input, processing and output for all *purchase and payment transactions* recorded to satisfy management's assertions of *completeness, measurement/accuracy* and *occurrence/ validity*. Additionally, the process must allow for the *balances* arising from the *expenditure transactions* to satisfy the assertions of management at the period end, namely, that of *existence or occurrence, completeness, measurement, valuation, rights and obligations* and *presentation and disclosure* as shown in Table 13.3.

The control activities for expenditure transactions are discussed under the two main functions of:

- Purchases of goods and services, or assets; and
- Payments to creditors and petty cash expenditures.

Most businesses today use computerized accounting systems and an auditor is likely to encounter a variety of IT systems at a client, as discussed in

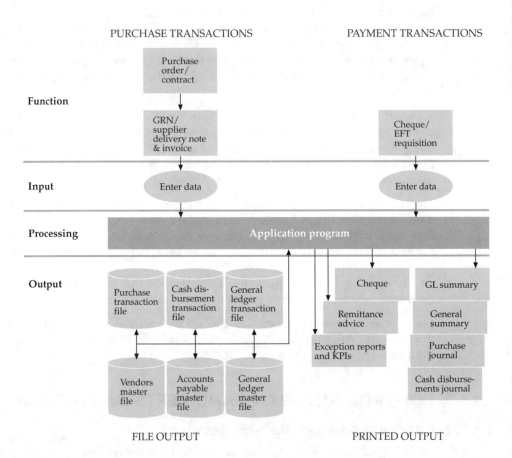

Figure 13.1 Expenditure process overview

chapter 9. For the purposes of this chapter, a computerized accounting environment is assumed. A reminder that the effectiveness of the control activities in a computerized environment depend on two aspects, namely:

- *General controls:* These are pervasive and include organization and operational controls, systems development controls, access controls and disaster recovery plans.

- *Application controls:* These are specific to the particular transaction process, in this case purchases of goods and services and payments to suppliers and other creditors, as well as the maintenance of accounts payable records and cash management.

Weaknesses in general controls could mean that application controls which are thought to be appropriately designed and operating effectively may not be relied upon, although this is not always the case.

13.2.2 Common documents and records for purchases of goods and services

The documents commonly encountered in the expenditure transactions process for purchases of goods and services include the following:

DOCUMENTS	NATURE OF DOCUMENT
Purchase requisition (PR)	This is the initial internal request from the person or department of the organization to the buyer or buying department to initiate a purchase order for goods or services. The requisition may be verbal or in the form of a printed document, or e-mail or electronic request in an EDI or B2B environment. It may also be generated automatically by the inventory system monitoring the re-order levels of all inventory items and would be for the economic order quantities inventory master file for each item and may indicate the approved supplier. In small to medium sized organizations it may be dispensed with entirely.
Purchase order (PO)	This is the *formal written authorization* from the entity to the supplier: specifying the supplier, the goods to be supplied, the prices to be charged and discount and payment terms and the delivery address. Depending on the size and complexity of the business and its computer systems, the purchase order may be prepared manually and later captured into the system (batch input and update processing), or the purchase order details may be captured directly into the computer system by the buyer to generate a pre-numbered Purchase Order (PO) document which is printed out and a copy dispatched to the supplier (on-line system).
	The PO document is not evidence of delivery, but merely authorization for the supplier to supply the goods ordered and, in return, the entity agrees to pay the amounts charged. In some instances the authorization may derive from a formal written contract document and the supply of the goods and services made in terms of that contract, for example, a lease of premises or contract with a cellphone service provider. In these situations a purchase order will not be prepared, but the entity will receive a regular, usually monthly, invoice for charges agreed in the contract for the rentals and other charges, such as electricity and water usage or detailing cellphone charges and calls made.

DOCUMENTS	NATURE OF DOCUMENT
Supplier's delivery note	The supplier will usually have sent its own printed or written *pre-numbered delivery note* with details of the goods delivered and will usually require the customer to sign a printed or electronic copy and return this to the supplier to provide evidence for the supplier that delivery has been made.
Goods received note (GRN)	This is the internal pre-numbered document, prepared manually by goods receiving staff on receipt of the goods ordered, or generated by the computer after the details of the supplier, purchase order number, quantity and description of the goods received have been captured by the goods receiving staff. It is usually this document that provides *evidence of the date of delivery* and receipt of the goods by the entity, i.e. the date on which rights and obligations in the goods are transferred to the entity, and therefore forms the legal basis for recording the purchase and liability and entitling the supplier to claim payment.
	The GRN provides evidence of the *occurrence* of the transaction. The pre-numbering enables the entity to implement sequence controls over goods received to meet the *completeness* assertion for goods and services. The risk lies in goods being received for which the receiving staff fail to prepare a goods received note, or for charges where delivery will not be evidenced in this form.
	Generally payments to suppliers are not made without evidence of delivery, and suppliers will soon complain if they do not receive payment on due date.
Supplier's invoice	This document sets out the billing or charges by the supplier for the goods or services supplied and details the items supplied, the unit prices, the total charged for each line item and in total for all items, and VAT charged on goods supplied, or an indication that the goods are VAT exempt or that the prices are VAT inclusive. The format of an invoice may differ widely, depending on the nature of the goods and services provided, from a simple till slip for a purchase from a supermarket to a complex set of documents including bills of lading, and certified invoices for goods imported, or contract documents, quantity surveyor's reports and an architect's certificate for buildings under construction.

DOCUMENTS	NATURE OF DOCUMENT
Batch header input document	In a batch input system, the documents, purchase order, goods received note, supplier's delivery note and supplier's invoice will be collated and a batch header prepared to list all such invoices captured on a weekly or monthly purchase transactions run.
Monthly VAT returns	These reflect the net of *input and output VAT* collected or paid during the period.

Table 13.5 Common documents for purchases of goods and services

Computerized accounting records

In addition to the above documents that arise from the purchases transactions, the entity will maintain the following computerized accounting records to process expenditure transactions for purchases and payments.

COMPUTER-IZED ACCOUNTING RECORDS	NATURE OF RECORD
Unfilled purchase order file	In an on-line system, a daily or weekly list of unfilled purchase orders may be held in a temporary file and *printed out or accessed on-line* by means of enquiry programs for the buying department and inventory management to monitor deliveries of goods ordered and not yet delivered.
Purchases transaction file	Upon capture of the goods received and the supplier's invoice and processing by the application program, the system will record the transaction as a purchase and update the relevant general ledger purchase or expense account, the accounts payable control account in the general ledger and the supplier's account in the account's payable ledger.

COMPUTER-IZED ACCOUNTING RECORDS	NATURE OF RECORD
Approved suppliers (or vendors) master file	This file contains the comprehensive details of approved suppliers, including the name, *account number*, delivery address, postal address, telephone numbers and contact persons, *credit limits, payment and discount terms*, and frequently a history of purchases made by the entity from the supplier over a period. This master file flags: new suppliers added or deletions of approved suppliers for whatever reason (normally related to unsatisfactory supply services, the closure of the supplier's business, prices that are no longer competitive, or approval of an alternative supplier, or that the entity has discontinued selling the products). Any changes to this file would normally require authorization of the senior buyer or the owner manager in a smaller business. The file contents are sometimes referred to as *standing data* as the details change infrequently.
Accounts payable master file	This file contains the complete record of transactions with each supplier, namely purchases, payments for goods supplied, discount granted and pricing adjustments. It also reflects the balance owing at any point by the supplier/creditor. Details contained in this file form the basis for obtaining an age analysis of the outstanding amount comprising the balance owing to individual suppliers and, of course, for an aged analysis listing of all accounts payable balances at any particular date to agree to the general ledger accounts payable control account and to monitor the average repayment period to suppliers.
General ledger master file	This file contains the detailed accounts recording the purchases of goods and services transactions and balances for each financial accounting period. Accounts affected will be: the *cost of sales and inventory items purchased for resale, various other expense accounts for goods and services supplied to the entity and input VAT.*

COMPUTER-IZED ACCOUNTING RECORDS	NATURE OF RECORD
Inventory master file	This file contains the details of all inventory descriptions and quantities on hand as well as the date of inventory quantities received, returned or sold. This file would be updated during the *purchases processing run* with the products purchased and received from suppliers during the period increasing the balance on hand at the period end. It may well contain a history of purchases for the individual product line items.

Table 13.6 Computerized accounting records for purchases of goods and services

Printouts arising from purchases transactions

In addition to the necessary *documents* the computer system should also produce the following printouts:

PRINTOUTS	NATURE OF PRINTOUT
Monthly list of purchase transactions	A monthly list of *purchase transactions*, from the *purchases transactions file*, which may be analysed by product line, delivery location and whether delivered to the entity's bulk warehouse or particular store. This printout would normally be distributed to the buying department, inventory management and financial management.
Monthly age analysis of accounts payable	Provides a monthly age analysis of accounts payable, as well as a detailed accounts payable listing, reflecting the details of each supplier's account comprising the outstanding balance owing at the date of the listing.
General ledger trial balance	Includes the balances related to the purchases of inventory, cost of sales and other expense or asset accounts affected and accounts payable balances.

PRINTOUTS	NATURE OF PRINTOUT
Key performance indicators	The indicators that management uses to monitor the business and quickly identify potential problem areas may include: gross margins on product lines where purchases have occurred, turnover of inventory balances and slow-moving lines or the number of stock-outs of individual key line items; age analysis of accounts payable balances; percentage discounts received on payments made and average unit costs on key inventory items; any changes to approved suppliers during the period; the number of supplier complaints regarding late payment.
	In addition, this printout would usually show *financial ratios,* such as cost of goods sold: accounts payable; average days outstanding in trade accounts payable; accounts payable as a percent of total assets; current ratio – current assets: current liabilities and quick ratio – current assets (excluding inventory): current liabilities may be useful.
Exception reports	The purchase order details will be matched by the computer system with the subsequent, goods received note, supplier's delivery note and supplier's invoice. Any differences in respect of items delivered, or prices charged, will either result in a rejection of the invoice captured or will be printed out as an exception report for follow up by the buyers or inventory department.
	In processing purchase transactions, application programs will generally be programmed to match all four documents: *purchase order, supplier's delivery note, goods received note* and *invoice.* Where this matching procedure is not performed by the computer system, it is very important that the procedures are performed manually and evidence of the check performed recorded.
	A variety of exception reports could be generated for distribution to the chief buyers and financial management, for review and action, such as:
	• a list of unfilled purchase orders, to be distributed to the buyers and inventory management for follow up with the supplier;
	• a sequence list of goods received notes for which a matching invoice has not yet been processed to accounts payable, to be distributed to the buyers and accounts payable department for follow up and processing; and

PRINTOUTS	NATURE OF PRINTOUT
	• a list of creditors whose payment terms have not been met and discounts lost as a result; gross margins for product lines or categories which do not fall within defined parameters, indicating cut off problems; sales level to major suppliers; and long outstanding accounts payable balances (these may be related to a dispute with the supplier, inefficient processing by the accounts payable clerks, or fraud).

Table 13.7 Common printouts for purchases of goods and services

Senior financial managers and certain staff members, such as buyers, accounts department personnel involved in processing and the payment of suppliers' invoices, may be granted access to the details of accounts payable and inventory files by means of on-line enquiry programs with menu options to enable them to perform the functions for which they are responsible. The enquiry access should not enable any changes to be made to accounts payable or inventory balances without following the normal procedures for processing purchases, or making changes to standing data in approved supplier/inventory master files.

13.2.2.1 The purchases of goods and services functions

There are three distinct functions relative to purchasing activities. These are as follows:

● The ordering of goods and services;
● The receiving of goods and services; and
● The recording of purchases and accounts payable.

Good segregation of duties requires that these functions be performed by different persons.

In order to meet the basic requirement of an effective system of control over credit purchases, the activities under each of the functional areas should be organized and the records prepared in the manner described below.

Ordering of goods and services

Approved suppliers

Management should, after negotiating prices and payment terms, approve a list of suppliers from whom goods may be purchased and services requested. Any alteration or additions to such list should be made only on the authority of senior management, usually the senior buyer. These details should be captured into the supplier master file and provide an important control in monitoring purchase orders placed to ensure the terms of contract agreed with suppliers are applied.

Purchase requisitions

Requisitions for goods or services may originate from those responsible for inventory management or from other departments. Inventory purchases are usually initiated by the buying department. However, other expenditures, for example, administration services and human resource aspects, may be initiated by others. Authorization levels should be specified and are usually linked to the value of purchases and the nature of items being purchased.

Requisitions for routine purchases generally require a lower level of management approval that should be clearly specified, whereas non-routine transactions, for example, purchases of fixed assets, may require more formal approval processes. These might require the approval of the capital expenditure committee, the board of directors, or even shareholder approval.

Requisitions should identify persons originating them. Error reports of rejected requisitions should be referred back to the relevant department for rectification and re-submission.

Purchase orders

The authority to approve purchase orders should be vested in appropriate individuals. In most wholesaler and retail businesses buyers are employed, whose sole responsibility it is to purchase the best products at the keenest prices. The authority to decide on acceptable product quality and prices is delegated to the buyer, subject to the overriding authority of senior management.

The purchase order should contain the name of the supplier and their account number, a description of and quantity of goods ordered, unit prices including discounts and repayment terms, delivery address and the signature (manual or electronic) of the buyer or staff member with authority to place orders.

A regular review of unfilled purchase orders should reduce the risk of stock-out situations. This involves monitoring the unfulfilled orders file and performing sequence checks on orders fulfilled. Appropriate follow up is necessary to ensure the eventual delivery of goods and services or the cancellation of the purchase order should the supplier be unable to deliver.

Use of computer systems – such as e-commerce, electronic data interchange (EDI), and B2B transactions – allows for purchase orders to be automatically generated by the computer system where inventory levels drop below designated levels. Some computerized systems allow suppliers 'read only' access to their customer's records so as to anticipate demand and the likely timing of orders. Such access must be strictly controlled.

In many instances orders may be placed by telephone or by e-mail. It is important, if this is the case, that orders be captured into the system in the normal way so as to exercise control over them.

Receiving of goods and services

On receipt of the goods, staff responsible should check these for type, quality and quantity against purchase orders and delivery notes.

Details of goods received should be captured into the computer system via a terminal in the inventory store which should generate an internal *goods received note* with the same identification number as the original purchase order or a dedicated sequence number with a cross-reference to the relevant purchase order number. Many purchasing systems capturing the details of the receipt of goods, simultaneously updates the pending order master file and records the receipt in the purchase transaction file.

The updating of the purchases transaction file also automatically updates the inventory master file with the quantities of goods received. Where a hardcopy of the order has been sent to the goods receiving department, this is attached to the relevant *supplier's delivery note* and *goods received note*, and forwarded to the accounts department to await the supplier's invoice.

The *goods received note* is an important document for establishing the *occurrence* of transactions and physical *existence* of the inventory received and thus provides justification for raising the liability to accounts payable.

The duties of receiving goods (as described above) and their safe custody should be separated from the duties of ordering goods and checking invoices. All goods received should be inspected, counted and checked to the relevant order and supplier's delivery note for type, quality and quantity. Only once this check has been performed should suppliers' delivery notes be signed and details captured into the computer system to generate the *goods received note* accepting the goods delivered. Damaged or otherwise unacceptable goods should not be accepted and the purchasing department and accounts office should be notified accordingly. The identification of the location of the inventory stored in the warehouse or on the shop shelves can generally be accommodated by computer systems.

Recording of purchases and accounts payable

The receipt of the goods or services creates an obligation of the entity to pay the supplier thereof. Accordingly, the liability must be recorded to accounts payable and charged to purchases, inventory or whichever expense or asset account is affected. Before recording the purchase, the following control activities should be performed:

- An invoice should not be entered in the purchases record unless it has been approved as correct by the person or persons whose duty it is to check the accuracy of the supplier's invoices. Evidence of the check performed should be marked on the invoice by means of a *check stamp*. In order to have a standard way of marking the supplier's invoices as correct for entry, a rubber stamp is commonly used. The 'check stamp' serves the purpose also of indicating that an invoice has been marked as captured, so reducing the risk of duplicate recording.

Example of a Check Stamp

Checked and passed for	Signature/Initial
Quantity, type and quality	
Price	
Additions and extensions	
Account debited – enter account code	
Account credited – enter account code	
Passed for entry	
Passed for payment	
Cheque number ...	

- In an on-line real-time computer system, the recording of invoices into the purchase records occurs as invoices are received and are passed for entry. If a batch input process is used, the invoices are filed under the supplier's name or code number and reconciled to supplier's statements at the end of the month, before being entered onto the relevant batch header sheet for capture into the computer system to produce the purchases transaction file and so updating the general ledger and accounts payable ledger. When suppliers' invoices are received, they should be matched with the appropriate goods received notes and suppliers' delivery notes for description and quantity of goods received, and with the purchase order for prices and terms providing evidence of *completeness, existence and measurement/accuracy* assertions. These matching procedures may be performed manually or be programmed within the computer system and performed during the updating run of the general ledger.

- The date of receipt of goods should be recorded on goods received notes and should be matched to invoices to ensure purchases are recorded in the correct accounting period, providing evidence of the *completeness, occurrence and measurement/accuracy* assertions.

- The clerical accuracy of invoices should be checked to prove the accuracy of its total Rand amount. The invoice, stamped and initialled as correct, is then filed with the relevant goods received note, delivery note and order form attached thereto. This provides evidence of the *measurement / accuracy* and *rights and obligations* assertions.

- Finally, the accounts clerk should establish, by comparison to the purchase order or by enquiry, that invoices have been charged or credited to the correct expense or asset account and to the correct supplier's account. Application software should compare the supplier name and accounts payable account number to the supplier master file to prevent the misallocation of the invoice to the incorrect supplier. Senior accounting staff should review the expense allocation on the 'check stamp' to ensure it appears appropriate.

- All invoices received and disputed should be recorded separately so that at any time the amounts in dispute are known. When the dispute is settled by the return of the goods, the granting of an allowance or in some other way, a note should be made on the record and the invoice and relevant *credit note* entered in the purchases record in the same way that the supplier's invoices are captured. The goods receiving staff should maintain a record of all goods returned to suppliers.

- Refer to chapter 10 regarding computerized application controls over input, processing and output, and to the sample Case 13.1 in this chapter regarding the review and reconciliations to be performed at different stages by different individuals.

- Irrespective of the processing method, whether batch input and batch update or an on-line real-time system, control procedures should be implemented over the purchases transaction runs to update the general ledger and the suppliers' accounts in the accounts payable ledger master file. This involves consideration of the library controls to ensure the correct version of the general ledger master file and accounts payable ledger are used for the processing run. Controls will include also the agreement of run-to-run and/or batch totals and reconciliation of before and after totals, which will provide evidence of the *completeness, existence* and *measurement/ accuracy* assertions.

- Printouts from the purchases update run should be distributed to the appropriate persons to review for reasonability and appropriate investigation of any apparent anomalies and their resolution, where necessary.

13.2.3 Disbursements

13.2.3.1 Control objectives

Payment to a supplier represents the final settlement of a transaction that commenced with the *ordering of goods and services*. The control activities should be designed to ensure the following objectives are met:

- To ensure the *validity* of payments: payments should only be made after appropriate authorization and should only be made to valid suppliers.

- To ensure *accurate* recording of payments: details on cheques should be checked by the cheque signatory to documentation supporting the payment, before the cheque is signed, and discounts due should be deducted from amounts payable; in addition, every payment should be accounted for with a debit to the correct creditor's account and the accounts payable control account and a credit to cash or bank.

- To ensure *completeness* of payments recording: all payments should be recorded in the accounting records; and should be accounted for in the correct accounting period.

In a large retail operation, the entire cash management function is likely to be the responsibility of a central treasury department (discussed in chapter 16), which typically handles both cash receipts (see chapter 12) and the payment of accounts payable to manage the entity's cash flows in the most efficient and effective manner.

13.2.3.2 Common documents and records for payments of accounts payable

The documents commonly encountered in the transactions process relating to payments are set out in Table 13.8 below:

DOCUMENTS	NATURE OF DOCUMENT
Remittance advice	This document may accompany a payment to the supplier. Where the entity pays suppliers on a monthly basis, they will usually prepare a remittance advice explaining how the amount paid has been arrived at. This amounts to a reconciliation of the balance in the entity's accounts payable account, to the balance reflected on the supplier's statement, and will reflect adjustments for (1) invoices charged where goods have not been received, (2) adjustments for price differences, and (3) discount deducted in making the payment, and (4) payments already made, but not reflected on the supplier's statement.
Cheque or EFT transfer advice	This is the document that evidences settlement of the amount owing to the supplier. Cheques may be prepared manually by the accounts department (using blank pre-numbered cheque forms obtained from the entity's bank) or they may be generated by the computer, which automatically pre-numbers the cheque form.
	Signing of cheques may be done manually by the approved cheque signatories, or be applied electronically by the computer in the cheque payment run. EFT transfer advices will generally be a computer-generated acknowledgment from the entity's bank of the detailed transfer instructions authorized and processed.
Bank statements	These are received from the entity's bank and used for checking paid cheques, EFT transfers and bank charges levied (see discussion in chapter 16).

ACCOUNTING RECORDS AND PRINT-OUTS	NATURE OF RECORD
Cash disburse-ment or payments transactions file	This file records all payments by cheque and electronic funds transfer to suppliers/creditors captured into the computer system. The run of the transaction file will update the general ledger master file bank account and accounts payable control account, as well as individual suppliers' accounts in the accounts payable ledger master file.
Cash disburse-ment or payments listing	This printout contains a sequence listing by cheque number of all cheque payments made, and a listing by date of all EFT transfers made. It provides details of the payee, the amount, discounts claimed, account alloca-tions and bank account from which the payment has been drawn. Where the entity operates more than one banking account, separate listings are likely be produced for each bank account. These printouts will be used for preparing regular bank reconciliations to the bank statements.

Table 13.8 Common documents, records and printouts for payment of accounts payable

13.2.3.3 **Payments to accounts payable**

The payments activity may be subdivided into the following three distinct functional areas:

- Control over cheque forms and EFT transfers.
- Drawing and signing of cheques and EFTs.
- Recording of payments.

In order to meet the control objectives, the activities under each of the functional areas should be organized and the records prepared in the following manner.

Control over cheque forms

The Bills of Exchange Amendment Act (Act No 56 of 2000) was recently amended in response to prevalent frauds occurring in respect of cheque payments. Section 72B, 'Prevention of fraud', requires entities that are required by law to have financial statement audits, as well as close corporations, to exercise reasonable care 'in the custody of its cheque forms and the reconciliation of its bank statements'.

Further, Section 77 inserted into the Bills of Exchange Act No Act 34 of 1964 with the Amendment Act No 56 of 2000, now states that: 'it shall not be lawful for any person to obliterate, cancel or, except as authorized by the Act to add to or alter such a crossing'. Banks, accordingly, refuse to accept cheques for depositing, or for cashing, if any changes have been made to details thereon.

Necessary controls are:

- In a large business, which has its cheques specially printed or where computer stationery is used for printing cheques, a register of cheque books and stationery received and issued should be kept. Unused chequebooks or unused computer cheque stationery forms should be locked away and controlled by a senior official.

- All cancelled cheques should be clearly marked 'cancelled' and attached to the relevant cheque counterfoil, or separately filed. Cheques, whether specially printed, obtained from a bank or printed by a computer payments run, should be consecutively numbered. All paid cheques returned by the bank should be filed in numerical order.

Crossing of cheques

Guidance with regard to the meaning of various crossings permitted on the face of cheque drawn is provided in sections 75 to 82 of the Bills of Exchange Act No 34 of 1964 (inserted into Act 34 of 1964 with the Amendment Act No 56 of 2000). Particular aspects are addressed below:

- As a result of the amendments to the Bills of Exchange Act in 2000, and in an attempt to prevent losses from cheque fraud by employees, many businesses have their cheques printed with a crossing of *two parallel lines* with the words *'Not-transferable'* or *'Non-transferable'*, inserted between them. This renders the cheque valid as only between the parties thereto. It will be regarded as being crossed 'generally' unless it also has the words *'Account Payee Only'*. The words of the crossing may not be cancelled at all and any purported cancellation shall be of no effect (Section 75A inserted into Act 34 of 1964 with the Amendment Act in 2000). An important part of a *'Not-transferable'* crossing is that it may be paid only into the account with the same name as that of the payee reflected on the cheque.

- A cheque may also be crossed with two parallel lines with or without the words *'and Company'* or abbreviation thereof, or *'Not negotiable,'* and is regarded as being crossed 'generally'. This means that the cheque may not be cashed and will have to be paid into a banking account.

- Although a not-transferable cheque provides maximum security, it is unfortunately not practicable at the present time to use it for all payments, as some payees may only have savings accounts with a building society which normally requests account holders to sign the back of the cheque endorsing the cheque to the account of the Building Society. The payee cannot endorse a non-transferable cheque over to the building society.

- Cheques issued by banks are usually printed 'to bearer' and have no restrictive crossing on them. In the case of a small business using such cheques, care should be exercised over the physical custody of the chequebooks. Cheques drawn other than for cash required should immediately be crossed restrictively, preferably with the not-negotiable crossing.

- When cash is required from the bank (for example, for wages or petty cash floats), the person who is to collect the cash should be reflected as the payee and the words *'or bearer'* on the cheque should be *crossed out*. In this instance, the bank will request identification from the person cashing the cheque, which protects the entity from persons fraudulently seeking to cash cheques drawn and will also pinpoint accountability on the employee charged with collecting the money.

- The drawing of cash cheques should be avoided by an entity as far as this is possible. Many businesses engage coin security businesses or pay-roll companies to collect and deliver any cash requirements for payroll payouts, till floats, and petty cash requirements.

Drawing and signing of cheques and Electronic Funds Transfers (EFTs)

The drawing and signing of cheques should proceed systematically. The cheques should be drawn for the requisite sums and presented to the person(s) authorized to sign them, together with the appropriate supporting documents (usually statements and invoices) as evidence of the amounts due for payment.

The cheque signatories should examine the documents to satisfy themselves that the amounts shown on the cheques are indeed due to be paid, that any discount due has been taken, and that the names of the payees are correct. The signatories should initial or in some way mark the documents as paid to prevent their being produced again in support of a further cheque in payment of an alleged debt due by the business.

The various computerized systems encountered today may well perform programmed matching checks and then generate and print the relevant cheque or EFT payment automatically. Both forms of settlement will require the signature (manual or electronic) of the authorized cheque signatory for the entity. On processing the payments update, the relevant accounts payable accounts and general ledger bank account will be updated with the amount of the cheque payment drawn – in practice, however, cheques drawn may not yet have been signed or distributed to the supplier/creditor.

Where numerous cheques are drawn for both large and small amounts, the same principle for EFT transfers applies, namely, that all cheques above a certain amount should require the signatures of two senior officials, while cheques for small amounts might require only one signature, which may be that of a more junior member of staff. This procedure saves the directors and other senior executives from having to sign a large number of cheques while, at the same time, control is maintained over cheque signing and issue. As an additional safeguard, the cheques needing only one signature can be overprinted with the maximum amount of the junior staff member's authority – for example, 'not exceeding R10 000'.

Electronic Fund Transfers (EFTs)

Electronic Fund Transfers (EFT) are processed immediately to the bank accounts to which payment is authorized. The entity will usually have dedicated PCs or terminals from which EFT transfers can be made. These terminals may be placed in highly visible areas so that unauthorized persons will be noticed and their presence queried. Access to such terminals will generally be by means of a sign-on password or code, or a card with an electronic pin number encoded which is inserted into the machine by the authorized individual along with his or her own access password.

Prior approval is required for several aspects of the transactions. The making of EFT transfers will require the entity to register on-line access with its bankers. The supplier's details must be loaded by bank staff into the profiles, including the name of the supplier's bankers, the account name in which the creditor's bank account is held, the account number and bank branch code for all creditors who are to be paid by this means. In effect, the standing data for EFT payments is strictly controlled by the bank and loaded by bank staff.

The entity will also need to arrange for Internet access and authorize specified senior persons from its treasury department, usually the financial director, chief accountant or central treasury manager, to have password access to the entity's banking accounts in order to make such transfers. It may be advisable for the entity to restrict any single signatory to authorizing transfers to a maximum amount, say below R10 000, with two 'electronic' signatories required to authorize any single payment higher than that. Clearly the *application controls* around EFT transfers must be as strictly applied as those over computer generated cheque forms, or cheque forms obtained from the company's printers or its bankers.

Another important aspect of controlling EFT transfers is the review by senior financial staff of the printout of all transfers processed in a particular payment run, which provides evidence of the *occurrence* and *measurement/accuracy* of the payment transactions. Printouts may be obtained for individual transfers or, in a business environment, for all EFT transactions processed for a particular batch of payments. In addition, error printouts should be obtained for any rejections or transactions not processed.

Section 95 of the Bills of Exchange Act inserted by Amendment Act No 56 of 2000, recognizes that: '... the signature of the drawer of the instrument may be written or printed thereon by some other person by or under his authority'. Strict controls should be implemented over signed cheques dispatched to suppliers and other creditors to reduce the risk of theft or alteration of details on cheques. All cheques drawn should be accounted for.

Normally this is done by means of regular bank reconciliations to which the cheque and EFT payment listings will be agreed. Care should be taken that the cheque signatories have the responsibility for dispatching cheques to the relevant creditors and that signed cheques are not returned to those who have been responsible for their preparation.

In addition care should be taken to cancel the supporting documents: *remittance advice, supplier statement, invoice, goods received note, delivery note* and *purchase order*, to prevent their re-submission and duplication of payment. This is usually done by stamping the documents *'Paid'* and by writing the cheque number on them as a reference to the payment made. Where the payment is made by EFT, the transaction record of each electronic transfer should be printed out and attached to the supporting vouchers.

Recording of payments

In a computerized accounting system, when the updating processing run is performed, the payments captured in the disbursements or payments transactions file will be used to update the individual accounts payable accounts and the accounts payable control account and bank account in the general ledger.

Persons who draw, sign or handle cheques should not maintain the accounts payable records. Further, cheques returned as paid from the bank should not be available to the individual who maintains the accounts payable records. This separation of duties should prevent cheques being drawn in favour of payees whose names do not correspond with those in the accounts payable record.

Similarly, the accounts payable control account should not be available to the individual who maintains the accounts payable record. This person should submit periodically (usually monthly) the list of balances to a senior official whose duty is to effect agreement between the total of the list of accounts payable and the accounts payable control account. This separation of duties is unlikely to be found in a small owner-managed business.

The procedure ensures that the totals recorded for credit purchases, returns, discounts and payments have been wholly accounted for in the personal accounts of suppliers, although it does not prove that the postings have been made to the correct accounts in the accounts payable ledger. The reconciliation of balances per creditors' statements with balances reflected in the accounts payable records go some way to solving this problem.

13.2.3.4 Petty cash payments

As a general rule disbursements are made by cheque, for convenience and to avoid the risk of theft of cash. There are, however, many small cash payments to be made by any business and for this purpose a cash float is kept.

Keeping and controlling the record

One of the most effective systems of controlling and recording petty cash is the imprest system. Under this system an amount, known as a float, which is considered somewhat more than sufficient for, say, a month's petty cash disbursements is initially drawn by cheque and placed in the petty cash box, a petty cash float account being debited. The balance on this account will remain undisturbed thereafter, unless the float is increased or decreased.

At the close of each month the amount recorded as spent is reimbursed after a scrutiny of the petty cash expenditure record by the responsible person. The petty cash record should be signed to evidence this check. The amount of the float is then reinstated.

The imprest system can be successfully employed for any cash expenditure, for example, a casual wages float. Where the imprest method is not in use, the petty cashier receives round sums from time to time and there is the risk that slackness in control over the petty cash may result, and misappropriations of cash might occur, although it does not necessarily follow.

Control activities applicable to all petty cash expenditure and records

Whichever method is used, the following procedures should be strictly adhered to:

- No cash should be received by the petty cashier except that drawn by cheque to reimburse either wholly or partially the petty cash expenditure incurred.

- The petty cash record may often be maintained manually, for convenience, and should be written up and balanced daily with transactions captured into the general ledger at least once a month, possibly on a batch input basis.

- The person responsible should examine the petty cash record at least once a month. The total spent and the analysis of the expenditure should be scrutinized, the cash on hand should be counted and agreed to the petty cash record, and signed as evidence that this has been done and approved.

- Petty cash vouchers should be properly filed. For much of the petty cash expenditure receipts may not be available. For such items the petty cashier should prepare a petty cash slip (often specially printed), which should be signed by the person requiring the cash and countersigned by some more senior person; alternatively, the entries in the petty cash records may be initialled by the appropriate parties.

- The practice of cashing cheques and making loans against IOUs to staff members should be discouraged as this leads to difficulties in controlling the cash.

Where a substantial cash payment is to be made, one which cannot be accommodated by the petty cash float (for example, casual wages), the exact amount of cash required should be drawn by cheque. If for any reason the whole amount is not paid out, the unpaid cash should be re-deposited in the bank and an appropriate entry made.

13.2.4 Assessing the risk of significant misstatement

As already mentioned, in making a preliminary assessment of significant misstatement the auditor obtains an understanding of the nature of the control activities over purchases of goods and services, and payments. This understanding must be sufficient to plan an effective audit. That is to say, the understanding must enable the auditor to identify the risk of significant misstatement and design, in response to these, appropriate audit tests. A reminder, as discussed in earlier chapters, the risk of significant misstatement involves the auditor in assessing inherent risks (the susceptibility of classes of transactions and balances to material error before considering internal controls) and control risk (the risk that controls will not prevent or detect such material misstatements).

In considering inherent risk in relation to purchases and payments, the auditor should consider, given the nature of the client's business and its circumstances, the possibility of its: accounting for non-business related purchases and expenses; accounting for purchases and expenses at incorrect amounts, or these being allocated to incorrect accounts; and the recording of purchases and payments in the incorrect accounting period.

With regard to control risk, where the auditor considers that the design of the client's controls are such that the risk of significant misstatement for significant classes of transactions and balances arising from the purchases and payments is unlikely, the auditor must perform tests to establish that the controls on which reliance is intended have operated throughout the period. Clearly the appropriateness of the controls will be directly related to their ability to prevent, or detect and correct, misstatements.

Preventative controls are usually implemented at the transaction initiation and recording stage, in contrast to the detection and correction controls exercised after the execution and recording of transactions as part of the monitoring processes of management. For the auditor it might be more efficient to rely on, and test, the detective controls used by management in its monitoring process that cover several assertions, rather than to rely on, and test, the preventative controls focused on individual assertions at the transaction initiation and recording stage.

In a computerized environment, the auditor should consider the effectiveness of the pervasive general controls, as well as the specific application controls applicable to purchases and payments. The more important controls are those over changes to programs and standing data in the suppliers' master file that affect purchases and payments and thus accounts payable, and procedures for handling errors and exceptions reflected in exception reports, including their satisfactory resolution.

In summary, the control over purchases and payments should identify the following:

- Missing goods received notes from a sequence, indicating purchase transactions not recorded.
- Duplicated goods received notes or invoices.
- Supplier invoices, unmatched with orders and goods received notes.
- Supplier name and account code not matched to those in the supplier master file data.
- Arithmetic errors in the processing of suppliers invoices.
- Invalid inventory codes for goods purchased and received.
- Purchases or payments processed in the incorrect accounting period.
- Any attempt to process an electronic funds transfer for a particular supplier to a bank account different to that in the supplier payment profile file.
- Missing cheque numbers in a sequence test.

Circumstances that may justify a low risk assessment of significant misstatement by the auditor are illustrated below:

RISK ASSESSMENT: LOW	RATIONALE
Residual business risk	The process level risk analysis has identified adequate management control activities that would mitigate the chance of significant misstatement in purchases, payments and accounts payable.
Qualifications and competence of the responsible accounting staff	The accountant performs specific cut-off and reconciliation procedures for all major accounts payable and accruals at year-end. The auditor has no reason to doubt the competence of the accountant who has been performing this role for several years and has an in-depth knowledge of the accounts payable suppliers, many of whom are of long standing.
Assumptions on which the estimate is based	The accounts payable amount is based on normal processing of goods received notes and related supplier invoices combined with specific year-end procedures to establish a correct cut-off of goods received. In addition, accruals are provided for other cash disbursements, such as: telephone, municipal rates, electricity and water charges. The accruals estimate is in line with the prior year estimates. The analytical review of purchases and accruals has not identified any significant changes in profiles of purchases or customers that would change the risk profile.

RISK ASSESSMENT: LOW	RATIONALE
Management bias	There is no indication of management bias nor overrides of controls during the period in respect of expensing non-valid company expenses or payments.
Quality of information	The system of recording purchases and accounts payable is well controlled. Invoices are raised based on goods and services received, and payments are made only for valid obligations and recorded when the cheque or EFT is prepared. This should provide an accurate record of accounts payable balances at year-end. The buyer maintains a close relationship with individual suppliers and as such is well informed to make an assessment of any current or imminent problems affecting the estimate of accruals and accounts payable.
Historical accuracy	The prior year accruals and cut-off and reconciliation procedures for all material accounts payable balances were appropriate given occurrences in the current period.

Table 13.9 Assessing the risk of significant misstatement

13.2.5 Testing controls

To comply with SAAS 400, 'Risk assessment and internal control', the auditor should obtain evidence from tests of controls to support a medium to low assessment of control risk. If such evidence is obtained, the auditor may accept a higher level of detection risk and obtain further audit evidence, to a large degree by substantive analytical procedures with reduced reliance on detailed substantive tests of purchase and payment transactions and related balances.

Table 13.10 sets out the risks and controls, computerized and manual, that may be found in a system for processing purchases and payments for goods and services and appropriate tests of controls applicable to these. The reader is referred to chapter 10 for a full discussion of the nature of tests of control that the auditor may perform and how CAATs may be used in their performance.

RISK	PROGRAMMED CONTROLS	MANUAL CONTROLS	TEST OF CONTROLS
Ordering goods and services			
Unauthorized suppliers may be included in the master file of approved suppliers.	Logical access controls allow only authorized persons to effect changes to the approved suppliers master file.	Only senior buying department staff are authorized to add new customer details to the customer master file.	Enquiry from management and inspection of documentation evidencing the performance of these controls.
Purchases may be made from unapproved suppliers.	Computer automatically matches every purchase order (PO) to the supplier master file before processing. Non-matches are printed on an exception report.	Exception reports reviewed and aspects are resolved. Manual overrides are appropriately approved.	Inspect evidence of the review of exception reports and appropriate signatures approving any override.
Purchases may be made by unauthorized persons.	Access controls granted only to authorized staff to process POs and menu levels control authorization limits for individuals.	Formal authorization levels reviewed and amended periodically, buyers entitled to purchase up to specified amounts or to process certain types of expenditures. Manual override to accept order requires approval of chief buyer or senior management.	Enquiry and inspection of documentation of delegated authority and authority for overrides. Inspect orders and confirm that these are within the delegated authority limits.
Goods or services ordered may not be supplied.	Computer automatically pre-numbers all POs issued for later matching to GRN and supplier invoice. Unmatched orders are reflected on a printout.	Long-outstanding orders reflect on the outstanding orders printout are followed up.	Enquiry and inspection of the printout and other documentation evidencing follow up of undelivered orders.
Purchase orders may be for the incorrect items or quantities.	Computer matches product descriptions and inventory codes on orders to inventory master file details. Exception report of orders are produced where the re-order quantities exceed those recorded in the inventory master file, or where the quantity of inventory items on hand exceed re-order levels.	Exception reports are reviewed by the buying department and orders are cancelled or appropriate authority is given to proceed.	Inspect exception reports for adequate resolution of items.
Receiving goods and services			
Goods may be received and not recorded.	Computer generates a pre-numbered GRN when the goods receiving store call up the PO for checking to goods received. Outstanding orders are printed out regularly.	Report of unfilled orders reviewed and followed up by the buying office. Regular reconciliations of statement balances to accounts payable records.	Inspect printout and follow up on unfulfilled orders. Inspect accounts payable reconciliation and re-perform these to obtain evidence of their probity.

RISK	PROGRAMMED CONTROLS	MANUAL CONTROLS	TEST OF CONTROLS
Goods received may not agree with those ordered or may be damaged.	Goods receiving staff capture product description and actual quantities received into goods receiving report (GRN), which matches details to PO and produces an exception report of any non-matching of product description and quantities.	Goods received from suppliers are counted and product description and quantities received are checked to purchase orders. The condition of goods are checked. Exception reports are reviewed and any differences are resolved.	Enquiry into and observation of these checks of physical goods to orders. Inspect printout for evidence of review and follow up.
Recording purchases and accounts payable			
Goods received may not be recorded as a purchase.	Computer prints a list of all outstanding goods receiving notes issued for which there is no matching invoice recorded. In some computer systems the GRN set may generate a pro-forma invoice in a temporary file based on the purchase price agreed on the PO. Amounts transferred when supplier's invoice is actually received.	Accounts department staff follow up on missing invoices.	Enquiry into and inspection of exception reports and other documents for follow up of goods received but not invoiced and recorded as purchases.
Invoices may be recorded for goods or services not received, or their recording may be duplicated.	Computer matches POs, GRNs and Invoices and purchases are only processed to the general ledger if these match; an exception report of unmatched documents or duplicated invoices is produced. In a batch system: the computer compares control totals of GRN amounts and matches them with the corresponding suppliers invoice amounts and prints an exception report of any differences.	Accounts department staff follow up on exception reports of supplier's invoices unmatched to orders and goods received notes or those duplicated.	Enquiry and inspection of the exception report and follow up of invoices received but not matched.
Purchase invoices may be recorded in the incorrect period.	Computer matches the date purchases are recorded against the date on goods received notes and a printout is produced where these dates are in different account periods.	Accounting staff process the necessary entries to ensure appropriate accounting for liabilities in the current accounting period.	Enquiry and inspection of printouts and re-perform cut-off procedures.
Purchases may be recorded at incorrect prices.	Computer matches unit prices on supplier's invoices with those recorded on purchase orders and produces exception reports.	Exception reports are reviewed and problems resolved.	Enquiry and inspection of printouts and evidence of the resolution of differences. Re-perform pricing test by agreeing invoice price to prices on orders.
Invoices may be allocated to the incorrect accounts payable account.	Computer matches account number on PO and GRN with supplier name and account number on invoice and matches these to the accounts payable account details.	Accounts department employees follow up on exception reports of mismatched supplier's names and account numbers.	Enquiry and inspection of exception reports and evidence of the resolution of exceptions. Re-perform tests of expenditure allocation.

RISK	PROGRAMMED CONTROLS	MANUAL CONTROLS	TEST OF CONTROLS
Invoices may not be allocated to individual customer's accounts, or the wrong version of the accounts payable file may be used for updating.	The computer matches the opening balance of accounts payable total plus purchases and payment transactions to the total closing balances of accounts payable and general ledger control account after update run. The accounts payable master file is dated or given a sequence number after each update run and the computer checks the date or version number before each update run.	Reconciliation of run to run totals performed by appropriate accounting staff. Exception report of unallocated purchase invoices reviewed and resubmitted. External file labels and librarian function for indicating which version of the master file is being used.	Inspect printout of run-to-run control total balancing. Enquire into the general controls over IT processing to ensure that the correct version of the accounts payable master file is used.
Errors may be made in recording or processing purchase invoices.	Mathematical accuracy of invoices checked during processing run: inventory stock number, quantities times unit prices and invoice total, plus calculation of discounts receivable.	Monthly reconciliation of accounts payable amounts to suppliers' statements and remittance advices prepared and mailed to suppliers with payment. Enquiries from suppliers dealt with by persons other than those recording the purchase invoices. Total of accounts payable ledger listing reconciled to general ledger accounts payable control account.	Enquiry, inspection and reperformance of reconciliation of the control account.
Goods and services purchased may be recorded in the incorrect general ledger expense or asset accounts.	The computer matches the account code number on the order, goods received note and invoice to the account code number in the general ledger. Weekly or monthly purchase transactions printouts of expense and asset allocations.	Review of transaction printouts for reasonableness.	Enquiry and inspection of printout for evidence of management review. Enquire about corrective action taken for errors identified.
All of the above.		Management reviews actual performance against key performance indicators, for example: • Actual purchases against budgets and monthly trend analysis; • Achieved gross profit percentage; and • Number of days purchases in accounts payable.	Inspect documentation evidencing the adequate identification and resolution of actual performance being out of line with the identified key performance indicators. Enquire as to what management has done to resolve any problems indicated in this regard. Re-perform review and follow-up procedures.

RISK	PROGRAMMED CONTROLS	MANUAL CONTROLS	TEST OF CONTROLS
Recording cheque and EFT payments to suppliers			
Cheques drawn and EFT payments transferred may not be recorded.	Pre-numbered cheques generated by the computer during the cheque payments run. Access controls over blank computerized cheque stationery and programmed access controls for authorizing the cheque run. Cheque payments transactions printout of all cheques drawn for each payments run.	Control over un-issued pre-numbered cheques forms where these are prepared manually. Manual cheque signature plates under control of senior employee. Sequence checks on cheque numbers. Manual reconciliation of total of cheque payments captured to transaction listing of cheque payments made. Bank reconciliation.	Enquire and observation of physical controls and logical access controls. Re-perform sequence checks and bank reconciliations.
EFT payments may be made by unauthorized persons.	EFT payments effected from dedicated terminals in clear view of staff and only designated employees given password and ID access to be able to authorize the payment.	Persons authorizing EFT payments to review printout of EFTs each month (or week or day, depending on volumes) for evidence of unusual and unauthorized payments.	Enquire and observation of physical and logical access controls.
EFT payments may be made to the incorrect supplier bank account.	Strict controls implemented around the bank's loading of supplier banking account details for processing EFTs.	Only senior staff authorized to change or add new supplier bank details in the bank records for purposes of EFTs on settlement. Details to be provided in writing by supplier – kept in confidential files at client entity. Rely on bank security controls for monitoring this.	Enquiry and inspection of documentation for appropriate authorizing signature.
Cheques drawn and EFT payments may not be recorded promptly or allocated to the correct accounts payable account.	Payments processed automatically to the relevant accounts payable or expense account to which they are allocated and to bank on the general ledger update. Run-to-run totals established for each cheque run and reconciliation of control account movements.	Regular bank reconciliations. Monthly reconciliations of statement balances to accounts payable records.	Inspect reconciliations and re-perform these.
Cheques drawn and EFT payments may be made for fictitious or unauthorized purchases.	Computer matching of PO, GRN and Invoice, as well as supplier account number and name to master file of approved suppliers and printout exception reports.	Cheque signatories may sign cheques manually and would then review all supporting documents, including the reconciliation to the suppliers statement and remittance advice before signing the cheque. Management review of accounts payable listing and transaction listing of purchases should detect irregular payments.	Enquiry and observation of the cheque signing procedures. Inspect exception reports for resolution of any problem items.

RISK	PROGRAMMED CONTROLS	MANUAL CONTROLS	TEST OF CONTROLS
Cheques drawn and EFT payments may be duplicated.	Computer matches payment amounts to accounts payable balances and produces a print-out of payment amounts exceeding accounts payable amounts.	Supporting vouchers should be marked as paid to prevent re-submission for payment. Review of printout and resolution of exceptions.	Inspect exception reports for resolution of any payment amounts in excess of balances. Inspect documents for their being marked as paid.
Cheques drawn and EFT payments may be for the wrong amount.	Computer matching of PO, GRN and Invoice, as well as supplier account number and amount per the accounts payable records.	Cheque signatories may sign cheques manually and would then review all supporting documents, including the reconciliation to the suppliers statement and remittance advice before signing the cheque.	Enquiry and observation of cheque signing procedures. Inspect and reperform reconciliations.
Cheques drawn and EFT payments may be altered after signing before being sent to supplier.		Signed cheques should be dispatched to suppliers by someone other than the person preparing the cheques and should not be returned to the cheque preparation clerk after signing. Should also be detected at time of weekly or monthly regular bank reconciliation and review of paid cheques included with the bank statement by the bank.	Enquiry and observation of cheque mailing procedures. Inspect and re-perform bank reconciliations.
All of the above.		**Senior management monitors:** Daily petty cash or *cash payments listing* reflecting total payments allocated to accounts payable and general ledger expense or asset accounts and enquires immediately about odd or unusual amounts or suppliers. Reviews *age analysis* of accounts payable regularly and reconciliation to Accounts Payable Control Account in general ledger. Follows up on odd or unusual balances or unfamiliar suppliers' names. *Key performance indicators* monitored.	Enquiry and inspection of management's documented review procedures and adequate follow up of any unusual aspects. Reperform review and follow-up procedures.

Table 13.10 Risks, controls and tests of controls for purchases and payments transactions

13.3 DETECTION RISK AND SUBSTANTIVE TESTS OF TRANSACTIONS AND BALANCES

13.3.1 Introduction

The preceding discussion should have provided the reader with a sound understanding of the nature of purchases transactions in a business; the control components and typical control activities encountered over purchases and payments; and the assessment of control risk including tests of controls. It remains to consider the substantive audit procedures that the auditor should perform to reduce detection risk to an acceptable level for the balances and classes of transactions from purchases and payments transactions as reflected in the financial statements.

A reminder that SAAS 400 requires that the auditor performs some substantive procedures regardless of the assessed inherent and control risks. The scope of such tests depends on the combined inherent and control risk assessment. The higher the assessed risk of significant misstatement, the more audit evidence is required from the performance of substantive tests of detail to detect possible misstatement in purchases payments and accounts payable, and vice versa.

The main risk of significant misstatement for expenditure transactions is usually one of understatement of expenditure and accounts payable, which results in an overstatement of profits and financial position in the financial statements. Hence, substantive procedures, such as cut-off tests of detail for goods received and paid cheques to obtain evidence that transactions are recorded in the correct period are important. The other major risk of significant misstatement lies in the misallocation or misclassification of goods, services and assets purchased which may be capitalized when they should be expensed, or expensed where they should be capitalized. Both of these errors affect the reported profit in the income statement and the corresponding asset or liability accounts in the balance sheet.

The framework presented in chapter 11, and used in chapter 12, for designing substantive audit procedures to detect any remaining risk of significant misstatement for sales and related balances, can be applied equally to expenditure transactions and balances. Using the framework, Table 13.11 provides examples of substantive procedures that might be used when auditing purchases and other expenses, payments transactions and accounts payable balances.

SUBSTANTIVE TESTS	AUDIT OBJECTIVES				
	C	O/E	M/V	R/O	P/D
1. Obtain and document an understanding of the business:	X	X	X	X	X
Identify significant classes of transactions for purchases of goods and services and accounts payable balances, generally related to core processes.					
• Identify key performance indicators used by management to monitor expenditures and accounts payable relationships with approved suppliers.					
Obtain trial balances or schedules of the significant balances arising from the significant class of transactions (income statement balances, namely purchases and cost of sales, various expense items) and accounts payable balances (balance sheet balances).	X		X		
• Agree opening balances to the previous year's working papers.					
• Review movements in the ledger for unusual items in major expense items, such as purchases, repairs and maintenance, and balance sheet balances such as suppliers' accounts payable and accruals for services provided.					
• Agree closing balances to general ledger.					
2. Substantive analytical procedures:	X	X	X		
Develop a prediction or expectation for accounts payable and expenditure items from knowledge of the business, history of supplier trade terms and industry norms.					
Define a significant difference or threshold for purchases, services and accounts payable, based on ratios and comparisons of the current period's composition of account payable balances and levels of transactions with prior financial periods and budgets.					
Compute the difference between the actual and the expected such as major suppliers reflecting a nil balance and expenditures that are not in line with cyclical trends.					
Investigate significant differences by enquiries of management and staff and exercise judgement to conclude on whether the analytical review is indicating the existence of material errors and design appropriate substantive tests of detail to detect and correct errors.					
Document the basis for the audit conclusion, namely whether the analytical procedures provide sufficient acceptable audit evidence, or whether further audit evidence is required for substantive tests of detail of balances or transactions.					

SUBSTANTIVE TESTS	AUDIT OBJECTIVES				
	C	O/E	M/V	R/O	P/D
3. Tests of detail of transactions:	×	×	×	×	
Select a sample of the main transactions flows at the process level and inspect supporting documents, e.g. select a sample from recorded purchases and cash payments and:					
• Inspect supporting purchase order, goods received notes, supplier delivery notes and supplier invoice and trace to the relevant general ledger expense or asset account and accounts payable account.					
• Where necessary inspect other supporting documents such as contract terms, e.g. rental agreements to determine the monthly rent.					
• For payments, inspect the paid cheque or evidence of EFT payment and the related remittance advice or, if payment is made for each invoice, inspect the related supplier's invoice and trace the payment to the related accounts payable or expenditure account.					
Perform *cut-off tests* of the main transaction flows, e.g. *purchases and cash disbursements* immediately preceding and following the financial year-end.		×	×		
Purchases cut-off:					
• Selecting a sample of recorded purchases and inspecting the related goods receiving documentation to ensure the transactions were recorded in the correct accounting period.					
• Ascertaining the last document numbers at year-end for goods received notes and scrutinizing the sequence reports to detect any higher numbers recorded in the current financial period or missing sequence numbers for transactions omitted or incorrectly allocated to the following accounting period.					
Payments cut-off:					
• Ascertain the last cheque number drawn at the financial year-end and check that later cheques have not been recorded as current period transactions. Trace the payment to subsequent bank statements to ascertain that they have been paid within a reasonable period after the financial year-end.					
• Enquire about cheques drawn, and still on hand at year-end, consider whether these payments should be reversed and recorded in the following period.					

SUBSTANTIVE TESTS	AUDIT OBJECTIVES				
	C	O/E	M/V	R/O	P/D
Search for unrecorded liabilities:	×	×	×		
Ascertain the procedures the client has put in place to identify unrecorded liabilities at year-end and obtain schedules of such items to trace to the relevant transactions recorded as accounts payable.					
Review payment remittances to suppliers and reconciliations to suppliers' statements for major creditors for evidence of invoices omitted and not accrued in the correct accounting period. Enquire about these and determine whether an accrual should be raised in the balance sheet.					
Investigate the exception report of unmatched purchase orders goods received notes and invoices to identify transactions omitted or processed in the incorrect period.					
Review payments recorded subsequent to the year-end to the completion of the audit fieldwork for evidence of expenses incurred prior to year-end.					
Where the audit fieldwork is completed some time after the financial year-end, enquire about any accounts payable still unpaid at that time.					
For construction work in progress inspect architects' certificates or quantity surveyors reports for evidence of unrecorded liabilities.					
Review capital budgets and directors' minutes for evidence of any commitments or contingent liabilities at year-end.					
4. Tests of details of balances:					
Review payment remittances to suppliers, reconciliations to suppliers' statements for evidence of invoices omitted and not accrued in the correct accounting period. Enquire about these and inspect correspondence regarding disputed charges to determine whether an accrual should be raised in the balance sheet.		×	×		
In rare circumstances, the auditor may decide that it is necessary to circularize suppliers to confirm balances owing at year-end. This is most likely to occur when there has been a serious breakdown in controls over purchases from and payments to suppliers, or where records have been destroyed, say in the case of suspected fraud or where accounting records have been lost in a fire or flood.			×		

SUBSTANTIVE TESTS	AUDIT OBJECTIVES				
	C	O/E	M/V	R/O	P/D
5. Presentation and disclosure:					
Determine whether accounts payable have been properly classified and presented in accordance with GAAP and the accounting policies of the entity.				×	×
Review the appropriateness of disclosures relating to related parties and related party transactions.				×	×
Review the disclosures relating to security provided to suppliers or other creditors over assets of the entity.				×	×
Enquire whether all contingent liabilities and commitments of the entity have been properly disclosed.				×	×

Table 13.11 Example of a framework for the content of a substantive audit programme to address specific risks of significant misstatement in purchase transactions and accounts payable balances

13.3.2 Determining the acceptable level of detection risk

To determine the acceptable level of detection risk for accounts payable and the related expenses, or assets, and bank balances, the auditor considers the inherent and control risks of the purchases and payments transactions. As discussed earlier in the chapter, controls over different categories of expenditures may vary and depend on the materiality of such expenditures and management's business risk assessment. Often the most effective controls are found at the higher level in detection controls implemented by management to monitor the business processes. These will include controls such as reconciliations of accounts payable accounts to statements from creditors and receipts and payments printouts or (cash books) to bank statements and the monitoring of actual expenditure against budgets.

The effectiveness of management's monitoring procedures is directly affected by the control components. For example, if the entity has experienced a high turnover of accounting staff responsible for processing purchases and payments to accounts payable, the auditor may find that reconciliations have not been performed for several months and there are thus numerous unresolved queries. In such circumstances, the auditor can not place reliance on controls and thus must perform extended substantive analytical procedures and tests of detail on expenditures, payments and accounts payable balances.

In small to medium sized owner-managed businesses, the general and application control procedures are likely to be far less formal and it will then depend on the auditor's evaluation of the effectiveness of the owner-manager supervisory functions as to whether reliance may be placed on their monitoring procedures over purchases and payments and related balances.

In summary, in order to assess inherent and control risk as medium or low which allows the auditor to accept a higher level of detection risk, the auditor will need to evaluate how effectively and efficiently control procedures are being performed and whether they reduce the risk of significant misstatement (combined inherent and control risk) to an acceptable level. Given that the auditor is able to assess this risk at a low level, allows the acceptance of detection risk at a higher level. This means that the auditor requires less evidence from substantive tests of analytical procedures and tests of detail on expenditure and payment transactions and accounts payable and bank balances. In such circumstances, the auditor may limit the substantive tests to performing analytical review of expenditures and reviewing relatively few reconciliations of statement balances to the accounts payable record balances at the year end. A confirmation of the client's bank account balance should be obtained directly from the bank by the auditor.

The auditor's decision will be based on the audit findings regarding the five internal control components discussed in chapter 9.

13.3.3 Substantive analytical procedures

13.3.3.1 Substantive analytical procedures for purchases of goods and services

As analytical review procedures usually provide evidence in support of more than one audit objective, no attempt is made to link these procedures to the objectives.

- Observe the trend of monthly (or weekly) totals of recorded purchases and compare with those of previous years and budget. Any unexpected fluctuations should be discussed with management and, if necessary, further investigated.

- Compare achieved gross profit with that of previous years and budget. If the entity sells products at differing mark-ups, make the comparison per group of products with similar margins. Any marked differences should be investigated. It must be remembered that achieved gross profit could be distorted by errors in sales, as well as cost of sales, and that cost of sales is affected by errors in recording of purchases.

- Calculate the number of days' credit purchases in accounts payable and compare with prior years. Unexpected changes may be caused by a number of factors including unrecorded purchases, the recording of fictitious purchases or by cut-off problems.

- Certain services and payments for services rendered are made regularly, often monthly – for example, rental and lease payments, telephones and electricity. Scrutinize these and similar accounts to ascertain that all and only monthly charges are recorded.

- Scrutinize recorded purchases for unusual items, for example, particularly large amounts, purchases from unusual suppliers and postings to general ledger inventory account and expense accounts from sources other than purchases records.

Management's risk management monitoring processes would involve management in performing most of the analytical procedures indicated above. As the risk management processes should be documented, the auditor can review such documentation as evidence of the procedures having been performed and management's investigation into, and explanation for, any unusual aspects.

A knowledge of the client's suppliers, negotiated payment terms and purchasing patterns are essential for the auditor to be able to identify potentially erroneous items requiring further investigation.

13.3.3.2 Substantive analytical procedures for cash and bank

Invalid payments, or those made at incorrect rand values, could be detected by a scrutiny of recorded payments and a trend analysis of payments made. When scrutinizing recorded payments, the auditor should look for items that appear to be bigger than usual, possible duplicate payments, or payments made to improbable accounts payable. Again, knowledge of the client's suppliers, negotiated payment terms and purchasing patterns are essential.

13.3.3.3 Substantive analytical procedures for income statement accounts

Audit evidence obtained with regard to balance sheet balances in many instances provide evidence of related income statement accounts. While the identification of core processes facilitates a linkage between income and expenses, as well as to assets and liabilities arising in the related business processes, the assertions for the related balance sheet balances and income statement balances may also be inextricably linked. The following table indicates some of those relationships, which would facilitate a substantive analytical procedures approach in the audit.

As a result of the inter-relationships, a number of highly effective analytical procedures may be performed to obtain evidence regarding income statement balances. These procedures may frequently be linked to the related assertion for the balance sheet balances. CAATs may be used in performing calculations to project expected income statement balances as a result of movements in related balance sheet accounts.

Analytical procedures will include comparisons to prior years or budgets; ratio analysis and comparisons of financial and non-financial information derived from understanding the core processes and related business processes of the entity. Trends may be established from historical information and changes explained by reason of internal and external events that have occurred, changes in accounting policies and changes in management. In some instances, where the income statement balances are not that material, or where their nature is such that the amounts may be determined easily, such as property rental where rents are a fixed monthly amount, the auditor may perform only analytical review procedures in gathering sufficient audit evidence.

BALANCE SHEET ACCOUNT	INCOME STATEMENT ACCOUNT(S)
Equity	Dividends declared/extraordinary items
Loans (interest bearing)	Interest paid
Properties	Rentals received
	Property maintenance expenses
Tangible fixed assets such as plant, equipment, vehicles, computers	Impairment costs/depreciation
	Repairs and maintenance of plant, equipment and vehicles
	Administration and operational expenditures arising from the use of the tangible assets
Intangible assets	Amortization expense
Leased assets capitalized	Lease finance costs
	Impairment costs/depreciation
Investments	Dividends and interest received
	Administration or management fees
	Profits and losses on disposals
Inventory	Cost of sales
Accounts receivable	Sales, net of returns
Provision for irrecoverable balances	Bad debts written off and adjustment for amount provided as irrecoverable balances
Accounts payable	Various expenses, in particular purchases of goods and services
Prepayments and Accruals	Various expenses
Foreign assets or liabilities	Gains or losses on foreign exchange
VAT asset or liability Net Input and Output VAT arising on purchases and sales of goods and services	Input or Output VAT related to Sales and Purchases, but should not be reflected as a separate charge in the income statement, except where penalties are payable
Taxation payable Deferred taxation	Taxation charge or credit for the period Deferred tax adjustment

Table 13.12 Related balance sheet and income statement accounts

In other circumstances, the auditor may have to perform substantive tests of detail. This might be necessary in the following circumstances:

- Where the inherent and control risk of significant misstatement is high. For example, non-routine transactions such as unusual year-end adjustments and unsupported related party transactions.

- Where analytical reviews indicate unexpected trends.

- Where amounts require separate disclosure in the financial statements or are more likely to contain misstatements, such as legal expenses, directors' emoluments, motor and travelling expenses, repairs and maintenance, advertising, taxes, consultancy fees, input and output VAT.

- Where separate analysis is required to support separate disclosure in tax returns.

- Where items require a separate audit report, for example, royalties payable to a foreign licence grantor.

13.3.4 Substantive tests of detail of purchases and disbursements transactions

The audit focus, when auditing the *purchases of goods and services*, is usually to detect:

- understatement of the expenses and related liabilities; and
- misallocations between expenditure and assets.

Audit procedures directed at these two aspects provide assurance regarding the *completeness, occurrence, existence* and *measurement/accuracy* audit objectives.

In the case of the audit of *disbursements*, the main objective is to detect unauthorized or invalid payments made, affecting the *occurrence/validity* audit objectives, or payments made that are misallocated, say, to expenditures rather than accounts payable, or recorded in the incorrect period affecting the *completeness, occurrence* and *measurement/accuracy* audit objectives.

13.3.5 Substantive tests of detail for accounts payable balances

The two main tests of detail that provide the auditor with evidence of *completeness, existence, measurement and valuation* of accounts payable balances are:

- the *review of suppliers' statements*, where these are provided on a regular basis by the supplier; and

- *accounts payable reconciliations* of balances reflected on suppliers' statements, with balances reflected in the accounts payable records as owing at the financial year-end.

Where suppliers do not provide statements, as frequently happens where an entity is importing goods from foreign counties, the auditor should seek other evidence that the rights and obligations in the goods have passed to the client, such as inspection of the indent file with the supporting documents for each import, such as shipping documents, bills of lading, air waybills or rail waybills, freight invoices from clearing agents, evidence of customs' duty paid and insurance premiums covering the shipments.

In other instances, the auditor may deem it necessary to obtain *written confirmation* of amounts owing to creditors, other than the usual suppliers of goods and services. The reader is referred to the discussion in chapter 11 regarding external confirmations.

13.3.6 Substantive tests of detail for cash and bank balances

A proper cut-off of disbursement transactions at year-end is essential to ensure that the bank and cash balances reflect the correct amount in the balance sheet at year-end. The audit of the cash and bank balances are dealt with comprehensively in chapter 17. From the perspective of disbursements, however, the auditor should observe the client procedures for ensuring a correct cut-off is obtained. The auditor will generally re-perform the bank reconciliation as at the year-end date to obtain evidence that all cheques processed through the records, but not presented to the bank at year-end, are reflected as outstanding in the reconciliation. This is best done by identifying outstanding paid cheques from bank statements subsequent to the financial year-end for the period up to completion of audit fieldwork. In addition, the auditor should review the subsequent bank statements and cash payment printouts to detect payments after year-end that relate to liabilities incurred prior to year-end to ensure the correct accruals and accounts payable result.

The auditor may encounter a situation where a large number of outstanding cheques are reflected in the bank reconciliation at year-end. Enquiries should be made to ascertain whether the cheques had been dispatched to suppliers, or whether this is a deliberate attempt by the client to distort the working capital ratios by understating accounts payable and bank balances or overstating bank overdraft amounts. The auditor should consider the materiality of the amounts involved and previous experience of this and may propose that these be reclassified as accounts payable. It may also raise concerns regarding the going-concern ability of the entity.

13.3.6.1 Substantive tests of detail of petty cash records

As petty cash expenditure is usually composed of a large number of small payments, the auditor can best vouch these payments by observing the total of each class of expense month by month, as shown in the analysis of the petty cash expenditure, and by inquiring into the reason for a substantial increase in any month. The auditor should also check any relatively large payments with the vouchers, observing the signatures on the petty cash slips or initials in the petty cash records. When testing the petty cash records with the vouchers, the auditor should not accept a petty cash slip where a document from a third party, such as a receipted statement or invoice, is to be expected as evidence of payment.

Written evidence of approval by the accountant, or assistant, of the periodic expenditure should be seen. The auditor should test the additions and cross-additions of the petty cash record. The auditor should also check the amounts of the cheques drawn to reimburse petty cash, as shown in the petty cash records, with those recorded in the cash records, noting whether the dates coincide.

13.3.7 Enquiries regarding litigation and claims

Where a client is involved in litigation and claims, the auditor may experience difficulty obtaining sufficient appropriate audit evidence as to the adequacy of provisions for liabilities arising or the disclosures of contingent liabilities or contingent assets that might arise. In these circumstances the auditor should seek a confirmation by means of *enquiries* directed to independent attorneys or employee legal advisers *regarding litigation and claims*.

SAAS 502, 'Enquiries regarding litigation and claims', provides guidance for auditors in this situation. SAAS 502 is significantly different from AU 257, 'Enquires of attorneys', which is withdrawn on the issue of SAAS 502. The content of SAAS 502 has been agreed with the Joint Committee of Attorneys and Accountants after due consultation, and sets out the procedure to be followed when attorneys' representation letters are sought.

It must be emphasized that the auditor's enquiries do not relate to every matter handled by an attorney for the client, but relate specifically to *enquiries regarding litigation and claims*. Where open-ended letters of confirmation, without the information required in terms of this statement, are sent to attorneys (refer Appendix to SAAS 502), the attorneys will simply ignore the request.

The principle is stated clearly in paragraph .02, namely that, 'the auditor should obtain sufficient appropriate audit evidence:

- Whether all material litigation and claims have been identified,

- The probability of any material revenue or expense arising from such matters and the estimated amount thereof; and

- The adequacy of the accounting treatment of such matters including their disclosure in the financial statements.'

It is recognized in paragraph .03 that it is the responsibility of management to adopt policies and procedures to identify, evaluate, record and report on the outcome of any material litigation and claims. Since the factors that would be considered in the accounting and reporting are within the direct knowledge and control of management, they are the primary source of information concerning such litigation and claims. However, the auditor should seek corroborating information from other sources.

Audit procedures

The principal audit procedures ordinarily performed by the auditor 'to identify litigation and claims affecting the entity', are set out in paragraph .04 and include the following:

- 'Review and discuss with management the procedures within the entity's internal control structure for identifying and recording litigation and claims and bringing them to the attention of management,
- Review and discuss with management the procedures within the entity's internal control structure for identifying, controlling and recording legal expenses and associated revenues and expenses in appropriate accounts,
- Obtain and discuss with management:
  - A list of litigation and claims, including a description of the matters and an estimate of their likely financial consequences, and
  - An analysis identifying legal expenses,
  - Review relevant documents, for example, correspondence with attorneys, and
- Obtain written representations regarding the completeness of material outstanding litigation and claims from management.'

Further in paragraph .05:

'The auditor's examination ordinarily includes other audit procedures which may be undertaken for different purposes, but which might also disclose litigation and claims. Such procedures include:

- Examining contracts, loan agreements, leases, insurance policies and claims and other correspondence,

- Reading minutes of meetings of the governing body, directors, the audit committee, shareholders and appropriate committees,

- Obtaining information from bank confirmations concerning guarantees,

- Developing a knowledge of the essential characteristics of the entity's business operations, including an understanding of the potential involvement in litigation and claims, and

- Enquiries of management and other employees of the entity.'

These procedures may not necessarily provide the auditor with sufficient appropriate audit evidence regarding the existence of and likely outcome of litigation and claims, or indicate whether the information provided by management is complete. Furthermore, the auditor does not possess the skills necessary to make legal judgements concerning management's assessment of the likely outcome of litigation and claims. In such circumstances, the auditor would seek confirmation from the attorney with whom management has consulted.

Requests for attorneys' representation letters

When material litigation and claims have been identified or when the auditor believes they may exist, the auditor should endeavour to obtain, at the client's cost, written representations from all attorneys with whom management has consulted on material litigation and claims. A written request is sent to attorneys only where the auditor has identified material litigation and claims or believes they may exist, and would not simply be sent as a matter of course (SAAS 502, paragraph .07).

As with any other confirmation request, the written request for the attorney's representation letter, which should be prepared by management and sent by the auditor, should request the attorney to communicate directly with the auditor. The letter would be prepared on the entity's letterhead and would be sent by the auditor to the attorney only when the auditor is satisfied, by virtue of the procedures outlined in paragraphs .04 to .05, that such letter has been properly completed by management. The auditor should be aware that attorneys are under no obligation to respond to a request for confirmation unless the schedule detailing the information required is provided.

The reader is referred to SAAS 502, paragraph .09 for the matters that would ordinarily be covered in a request for an attorney's representation letter. The Appendix to SAAS 502 contains an example of a request for an attorney's representation letter regarding litigation and claims.

Employee legal advisers

The statement introduces for the first time recognition of the role played by legal advisers employed by large corporations and groups who may be involved in handling litigation and claims for the entity and in briefing the independent attorneys or advocates. The documents in the possession of such employee attorneys belong to the entity and as such the auditor of the entity will have a right of access to these documents in terms of section 281 of the Companies Act 1973. The auditor, however, will still lack the skills to interpret the legal implications and thus may require confirmation from such employee attorneys. This is duly provided for in SAAS 502, paragraphs .12 to 1.5, which are set out below:

- 'In circumstances where legal advisors who are employees of the entity, or another entity within the group, have the primary responsibility for litigation and claims and are in the best position to corroborate management's representations, a request for an attorney's representation letter seeking information similar to that sought from an independent attorney should be obtained from such employee legal advisors' (SAAS 502, paragraph .12).

- 'Before relying on the opinion of either an employee legal advisor, or an independent attorney, care must be exercised to ensure that conditions prevail which would make such reliance reasonable. Auditors are advised to refer to the statement of SAAS 620 'Using the Work of an Expert' for guidance on using the work of an expert' (SAAS 502, paragraph .13).

- 'If both employee legal advisors and independent attorneys are involved in advising on the same litigation and claim, the auditor seeks a written representation from the employee legal advisor or independent attorney with the primary responsibility for that matter. However, there may be circumstances where the employee legal advisor has primary responsibility, but the matter has involved substantial participation by an independent attorney, and is of such significance that the auditor considers obtaining a written representation from such attorney that their opinion does not differ materially from that of the employee legal advisor' (SAAS 502, paragraph .14).

- 'In circumstances where both employee legal advisors and independent attorneys have devoted substantial attention to a litigation and claim and primary responsibility rests with the independent attorney, evidence obtained from an employee legal advisor is not an adequate substitute for any information that an independent attorney may refuse to furnish, in which case the procedures outlined in paragraphs .16 to .24 would be followed' (SAAS 502, paragraph .15).

Attorney's response

If the response from the attorney contains a material disagreement with management's original evaluation of a particular matter, the auditor should seek to resolve the disagreement through discussions with management and the attorney, or through alternative audit procedures, unless management subsequently agrees with the attorney's evaluation (SAAS 502, paragraph .16).

Attorney's failure to respond comprehensively or limitations in a response

If a response is not received from the attorney, or the response received is incomplete or indicates a limitation on the attorney's response, the auditor ordinarily requests that management contact the attorney instructing that a complete answer to the original request, or an explanation for the lack of or limitation in a response, be sent directly to the auditor (SAAS 502, paragraph .20).

If, in the judgement of the auditor, the reasons given by the attorney are unacceptable, or if a response is not obtained, the auditor needs to determine whether alternative audit procedures can provide sufficient appropriate audit evidence. Alternative procedures might entail, for example, further enquiries of management, a more detailed review of documents in management's possession concerning litigation and claims or examining accounts rendered by independent attorneys (SAAS 502, paragraph .22).

The auditor also considers any relevant legislation to assist in this regard. For example, section 281 of the Companies Act 1973, entitles the auditor to a right of access at all times to the accounting records and all books and documents of a company, and it also entitles the auditor to require from the directors or officers of the company such information and explanations necessary for the purposes of the audit. Where an attorney refuses to respond in an appropriate manner and the auditor is unable to obtain sufficient appropriate audit evidence by applying alternative procedures, the auditor considers whether there is a scope limitation, which may lead to a qualified opinion or a disclaimer of opinion (SAAS 502, paragraph .23).

Related procedures

The auditor should enquire of management as to new matters referred to an attorney subsequent to the date of the attorney's representation letter and prior to signing the audit report. If any such matters exist which may have a material effect on the financial statements, the auditor requests management to prepare a request for an attorney's representation letter with respect to the matter (SAAS 502, paragraph .25).

If the audit procedures lead to the discovery of matters of a legal nature not previously identified by management, the auditor should consider the impact of each of the matters on the financial statements (SAAS 502, paragraph .26).

13.3.8 Presentation and disclosure

The auditor must ensure that the presentation and disclosure requirements of the identified GAAP framework with which the entity claims to comply and the Companies Act requirements have been met in respect of balances arising from the expenditure transactions of the entity. These will include:

- Accounts payable are properly identified and classified as current liabilities and that debit balances contained in accounts payable balances are reclassified as accounts receivable or, where they involve long-term purchase commitments, these are appropriately disclosed.

- Expenditure items have been included in net income from trading operations and where separate disclosure is required – in the income statement, cash flow statement or notes to the financial statements – that this is provided.

- Appropriate disclosures have been made of any contingent liabilities arising, and of any security provided to creditors over assets of the entity.

- Appropriate disclosures have been made of any related parties and related party transactions affecting accounts payable and expenditures.

- The accounting policies correctly describe those implemented by the entity in so far as they affect accounts payable, expenditures and disbursements.

14

Auditing Production/Inventory Transactions and Balances

Learning objectives

After studying this chapter you should be able to:

1. Describe the nature of manufacturing and inventory management business processes and identify significant classes of transactions and balances.
2. Set audit objectives for manufacturing and inventory transactions and balances.
3. Describe the functions, related control activities and tests of controls to assess control risk at medium or low for the production and inventory business processes.
4. Explain how to determine an acceptable level of detection risk and design substantive audit procedures for manufacturing and inventory transactions and balances.

14.1 NATURE OF PRODUCTION/INVENTORY TRANSACTIONS

14.1.1 Introduction

This chapter discusses specific aspects of production and inventory expenditure where significant classes of transactions and balances arise, which will be the case where a client's business involves the manufacture of inventory and/or purchase of inventory for resale.

The core process of any business will have several business processes occurring. The manufacturing process to produce the finished goods, which the entity will sell to generate its revenue, comprises such a business process. Consequently, the auditor may expect that management will have established controls over what is an important aspect of its business. In a manufacturing company, the production process interfaces with three other business processes, as indicated in Table 14.1 and Figure 14.1.

First interface	The first interface of the production process is with the *purchase of goods and services* (see chapter 13), namely, the controls over the purchases of goods and services, which may include purchases of raw materials, and consumables, and other direct production costs.
Second interface	The second interface is found in the *allocation of direct and indirect labour costs and overheads* to work in progress, which represents the interface between the manufacturing process and the human resources and payroll process (see chapter 15).
Third interface	The third interface occurs on the sale of the manufactured goods (see chapter 12) and follows the *transfer of completed manufactured inventory to finished inventory*, the *pricing* of such inventory for sale and the *management of the finished inventory* until its sale and delivery to customers.

Table 14.1 Interface of the production process with other business processes

Whereas the first and third interfaces involve the entity in transactions with external parties, the second interface comprises an internal processing of transactions and allocation of costs, which increases the risk of error and/or deliberate misstatement by management and employees. In addition, where complex production processes occur together with high volumes of transactions, errors and fraud may happen at different points in the process, all of which could increase the remaining risk of significant misstatement of cost of sales in the income statement and raw materials, work in progress and finished inventory in the balance sheet.

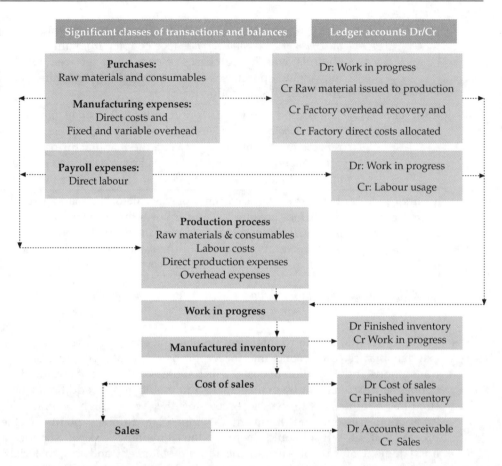

Figure 14.1 Interface of production transactions with other significant classes of transactions

The business processes of different types of businesses have a bearing on the nature of its inventory, as illustrated in the table below:

TYPE OF BUSINESS	THE NATURE OF INVENTORY
The automotive manufacturer or vehicle assembler	An automotive manufacturer may be involved in the manufacture of automotive components, which comprise its *finished products*, for resale. An entity involved in motor assembly will purchase the automotive components and vehicle body parts, which comprise its *raw materials* issued to the assembly line for the assembly of new motor vehicles. The fully assembled vehicle then comprises its *finished inventory*, which will be sold to appointed retail distributors. The business processes involve: first, the management of the manufacturing process or assembly line, including stringent, safety and quality standards, and the transfer of the manufactured product to finished inventory for sale; and secondly, the management of the finished inventory, that is, its storage, marketing and subsequent distribution to retail outlets.
The general manufacturer	A wide variety of manufacturing processes will be encountered appropriate to the goods being produced. Most will involve the issue of raw materials to some form of production process, which results in finished inventory. Once again, the business processes involve the management of the production process, including the maintenance of quality standards, and the management of the finished inventory and its subsequent distribution to customers.
Restaurants and fast food outlets	Will purchase fresh produce and processed foods for preparation of meals supplied to customers. The business processes will involve the management of inventory, much of which will have a short shelf life and require specialized storage facilities, and the maintenance of food health standards. Inventory will include branded food and drink merchandise purchased for resale without any further processing, such as canned or bottled cold drinks or liquor.
Wholesale or retail trading operations	A supermarket or hypermarket and the myriad of traders encountered, including IT consultants (operating as distributors), will ordinarily purchase a wide range of merchandise from manufacturers, wholesale or other retail suppliers, which is then sold. The business process will include product selection and purchasing, inventory management, the provision of customer services, advertising and promotion and maintenance of quality standards.

TYPE OF BUSINESS	THE NATURE OF INVENTORY
Building contractors	Will purchase building materials, for example, brick, sand and cement used in the construction process in accordance with the specifications in a bill of quantities or tender and the building contract, or variation orders of the architect or client. The building contractor will employ trained builders and labourers at the building site during construction, with such direct labour costs and overheads being charged to the construction contract in progress. Subcontractors may be appointed to provide specialized building materials and services at an agreed price, which is paid by the main contractor and similarly allocated to the contract costs. Contract sales and work in progress is likely to comprise significant transactions and balances.
Advertising, financial services and education	Advertising agencies, professional practices, schools and universities, certain public sector entities, banking and financial institutions and insurance companies will merely maintain inventory of consumables such as stationery, teaching materials, and IT requisites for administrative purposes and use in the conduct of their particular businesses, or for meeting service delivery.
Medical service providers	Medical doctors, medical service providers and hospitals (both public and private) will maintain medical supplies for meeting patients' needs, such as drugs and other medical supplies, hospital equipment including bed linen, catering equipment, and food supplies for catering to patients.

Table 14.2 The nature of inventory

As a general rule *inventory* represents a significant class of transactions and balances in every manufacturing or trading operation. It follows that the value placed on inventory and its related cost of sales has a significant effect on the reported profits and financial position. The auditor should therefore be reasonably satisfied that the amount shown for inventory in the financial statements is represented by goods which did, in fact, exist and was owned by the business (meeting the *completeness, existence and rights and obligations* assertions) at the close of the financial period, and that these are fairly valued on a consistent basis (measurement/accuracy and valuation assertions) and in accordance with the entity's stated accounting policies. An overstatement of closing inventory would have the effect of inflating the net profits before tax, or an incorrect determination of the unit cost of manufactured inventory, if below cost. Such an incorrect determination of the unit cost may contribute to the eventual demise of the business if it consistently results in sales prices set below the actual cost of the product. Clearly, any change in inventory balances will directly affect the net profits after tax reflected in the income statement.

14.1.2 **Audit objectives**

As mentioned in preceding chapters, to achieve audit objectives requires the auditor to obtain sufficient appropriate audit evidence regarding significant assertions related to production expenses and inventory to reduce the risk of significant misstatement in the financial statements to appropriately low levels. For manufacturing, or trading operations, it is likely that, because of the significance of transactions and balances, management will implement a well-controlled environment, thus reducing the risk of significant misstatement. Accordingly, the auditor is likely to be able to assess the combined inherent and control risks as medium to low and should the tests of control, which are often focused on detective supervisory controls, provide evidence that such controls operated effectively, the auditor would be justified in performing limited substantive tests. These substantive tests may consist largely of analytical procedures with substantive tests of detail focusing on those specific assertions where the risk of significant misstatement remains.

As many of the transactions in the manufacturing process arise through internal transfers and activities, the risk of the deliberate manipulation of costs is ever present. This may affect the *completeness, occurrence* and *measurement/accuracy* assertions of raw materials issued to production and the calculation of direct payroll expenses and overhead expenses allocated to work in progress – which, in turn, may affect the eventual *measurement/ accuracy* of the manufactured goods transferred to finished inventory and its valuation at period end.

Some businesses may use standard costing in the measurement of their manufactured inventory, requiring some consideration of the balances on standard costing variances, such as price variances, labour variances, overhead variances, etc., at period-end to determine whether the *valuation* of the manufactured goods approximates cost.

It is appropriate firstly to recognize the account balances affected by the production and inventory transactions as shown in Figure 14.1 and set out in Table 14.3 below.

PRODUCTION TRANSACTIONS	ACCOUNT BALANCES DEBITED	ACCOUNT BALANCES CREDITED
Issuance of raw materials and consumables to production	Work in progress	Raw material inventory
Allocation of payroll costs to production	Work in progress	Payroll clearing account

PRODUCTION TRANSACTIONS	ACCOUNT BALANCES DEBITED	ACCOUNT BALANCES CREDITED
Direct manufacturing expenses and overhead expenses allocated	Work in progress	Accounts payable/Cash Disbursements Overhead expenses allocated to manufacturing
Transfer of manufactured goods to finished inventory	Finished inventory	Work in progress
Sale of finished goods	Cost of Sales	Finished inventory

Table 14.3 General ledger account balances affected by production transactions

The auditor's objective is to gather sufficient appropriate audit evidence regarding specific management assertions contained in the income statement and balance sheet balances arising from the manufacturing and inventory transactions. These are related to management's assertions and form the basis of the discussion in this chapter, namely: *existence or occurrence, completeness, measurement, valuation, rights and obligations* and *presentation and disclosure*. The link between the assertions and the corresponding audit objectives for the expenditure transactions and balances are set out in Table 14.4 below.

MANAGEMENT ASSERTION	AUDIT OBJECTIVES
Production transactions	
Completeness	All raw materials issued to production have been recorded. All goods manufactured during the period have been recorded and all movements of manufactured goods to finished goods inventory during the current period are recorded in the correct accounting period.
Occurrence/ validity	Recorded goods manufactured during the period represent raw materials, labour and overhead expenditures that occurred, and none are duplicated.
Measurement/ accuracy	All materials, labour, direct manufacturing costs and overhead expenses allocated to work in progress were calculated in accordance with the GAAP policies adopted by the entity, applied on a consistent basis, and are recorded in the correct accounts.

MANAGEMENT ASSERTION	AUDIT OBJECTIVES
Inventory and cost of sales balances	
Completeness	Cost of goods sold represents the cost of all goods sold during the current period.
	Raw materials, work in progress and finished goods or merchandise inventory represent all inventory items that physically exist at the balance sheet date, none are omitted and none are duplicated.
Existence/ occurrence	Cost of goods sold represents the cost of goods actually sold during the current period.
	Items included in raw materials, work in progress and finished goods or merchandise inventory, physically exist and are on hand at year-end.
Measurement/ accuracy	*Raw material inventory* has been determined through the allocation of purchases of such items in accordance with the accounting policies of the entity applied on a consistent basis.
	Cost of sales has been determined through the allocation of the costs of inventory sold in accordance with the stated accounting policies of the entity applied on a consistent basis.
	Inventory of finished goods has been determined through the allocation of material, labour and overhead manufacturing expenses to manufactured goods, in accordance with the stated accounting policies of the entity, applied on a consistent basis.
Valuation	Inventory of raw materials, work in progress and finished goods are stated at the lower of cost and net realizable value.
Rights and obligations	The entity has valid title to inventory at the balance sheet date and/or the rights of any creditor in respect of inventory factored or pledged at the balance sheet to secure obligations of the entity have been identified.
Presentation and disclosure	Inventory and cost of sales of the entity are correctly disclosed and classified in accordance with the Companies Act 1973 and GAAP policies applied by the entity.
	Appropriate disclosures have been made with regard to inventory factored or pledged to secure liabilities of the business.

Table 14.4 Management assertions and the related audit objectives for production and inventory transactions and balances

14.1.3 Understanding the client's business

In any manufacturing or trading entity, the production and inventory management process is critical to the success of the core process of the business. Consequently, the auditor needs to understand the particular process followed by the client. Such an understanding allows the auditor to appreciate the implications of controls established over sales, purchases and payroll transactions, and in turn to assess the effectiveness of controls over the production process and inventory transactions and balances.

Each type of production process is unique; some are more capital intensive and others more labour intensive. This affects the basis on which overhead costs are allocated to production costs. An understanding and appreciation of the processes enable the auditor to effectively use substantive analytical procedures to identify the risk of significant misstatements. It also enables the auditor to understand the implications of financial and operational ratios for the entity and to relate these meaningfully to the information obtained from the audit of sales and purchases transactions. For example, the percentage that inventory comprises of total assets, the average, high and low inventory turnover periods, the gross margins achieved relative to sales mark-ups applied by the client to different product lines may provide evidence of possible risks of significant misstatement affecting the measurement/accuracy and valuation assertions.

The auditor may find that particular assertions indicate a greater risk of misstatement than others and should adapt the audit procedures accordingly. For example, where inventory items are easily identifiable physically, but allocations of costs are complex, the risk of significant misstatements increases for the *measurement and valuation* assertions. In this case, the auditor may decide to increase the extent of substantive tests of detail performed on this aspect and limit the substantive tests of detail regarding the physical *existence* of the inventory.

The inventory write-downs necessary for particular product lines at year-end affect the *valuation* assertion. The auditor gains the information needed for evaluating the inventory write-downs from the percentage of product rejects in the quality control checks performed at the end of the production run, before transfer of the goods to finished inventory, or from the percentage of returns from customers of defective goods for which credit notes have been passed.

Understanding the client's business enables the auditor to determine an effective and efficient audit strategy. It should alert the auditor to the potential risk of material misstatement in the financial statements arising from external or internal risks that management has not managed effectively or arising from misapplications of GAAP. These may relate to the recognition criteria, measurement and valuation, and may require specific presentation and disclosure in the audited financial statements.

Consideration of materiality

The auditor's assessment of the inherent and control risks is done in the context of the *materiality* of any potential risk of significant misstatement in transactions and balances. For a manufacturing or trading operation, the resultant cost of sales and inventory balances are likely to be significant to the entity. An entity may frequently carry numerous items of inventory, some individually of high cost with lower quantities on hand, and others which may be individually of very low cost, but carried in large quantities. For a manufacturer, revenue and cost of sales are likely to comprise the most significant balances in the income statement and, similarly, inventory is likely to comprise a significant balance in the balance sheet. The reader is referred to the discussion on audit materiality in chapter 5.

A risk of significant misstatement will affect the net income directly and could have the effect of turning a loss into a profit, should management not implement effective control activities to ensure the *completeness, occurrence/ validity and measurement/accuracy* of cost of sales and manufactured inventory. The auditor, in considering the risk of significant misstatement and determining the appropriate audit procedures to be performed, will have regard to both quantitative and qualitative materiality factors. Separate disclosure is required for different categories of inventory in the financial statements, in terms of paragraph 29 of the Fourth Schedule to the Companies Act and AC 108 of GAAP. Since this increases the risk of a significant misstatement influencing the views of users of financial statements, the auditor would accordingly exercise great care to ensure this does not occur.

14.1.4 Analysing production/inventory process level business risks

The variety and complexity of production processes that the auditor may encounter and the nature of the manufactured inventory combined with the high volume of transactions that occur where production is a key process and part of the core process of the entity, increase the risk of significant misstatement from material error or fraud.

The process level business risks within a manufacturing operation will generally relate to the various stages of production and be managed by different departments, such as:

- production planning and design;
- production processing; and
- inventory management.

These are discussed overleaf.

14.1.4.1 Production planning and design

The production planning and design department would be responsible for the scheduling of the production runs. This may be to meet the requirements of individual customers for specific designs involving a job order approach. An example would be the manufacture of wire screening baskets for customers in a variety of different industries, each requiring the use of different raw materials made to different shapes and sizes. The production will involve time for the set up of particular weaving looms in the factory, depending on the type and thickness of wire required, which might vary from fine stainless steel or brass wire to heavy-duty steel wire.

In a process such as the bulk manufacture of potato chips, production runs will be set up for particular flavours, with down-time required between different runs to clean the factory and equipment such as chip fryers and flavouring machines. Different runs may also be needed if different shapes of chips are required. In this instance, the design department will be the chefs employed to develop new brands and styles to appeal to the public taste. If the factory is to operate at maximum capacity, the production planning department will be aware of the time and different machines required for each production run. The production manager will have some flexibility to vary scheduled production runs to meet customer demands for stock-outs in particular ranges. The need for these will be communicated to the production department by the sales department staff.

14.1.4.2 Production processing

This will generally be the responsibility of the factory or production manager and factory employees. A range of different skills may be needed to produce the manufactured goods ordered. The process involves the movement of raw materials and the use of factory or plant and machinery to process the raw material to its finished form (whether these are bales of wire coil or kilos of potatoes, for the two examples above). The set up of the machinery to handle the production, the recording of direct labour time spent, and the allocation of overhead expenditures for each job or process run, all are a part of the production process.

In the first example, the process will include the final cutting and welding of baskets, washing in an acid bath, and final spray-painting if required by the customer, before delivery of the finished products to the customer or into inventory if minimum stock levels are kept to supply this and other customers. In the case of the potato chips, production processing will involve the peeling of the potatoes, dicing to the particular shapes for the production run, bulk frying, flavouring with spices, packaging into variously sized packets, and hermetically sealing of the packets to retain flavour and crispness. The final stage will involve packing and storing as finished inventory (the placing of the sealed packets of chips into storage boxes, and the boxes into warehouses), completing the production stage.

14.1.4.3 Inventory management

The inventory management team will receive the manufactured goods (here, the boxes of potato chips) from the production process. Inventory managers will perform quality checks to ensure the goods meet the customer's or production specifications. The checked and presumably approved inventory will then be stored in warehouses, ready for distribution to customers.

The determination of sale prices would be managed at this stage, possibly by the marketing department, and the sales price master files updated with any changes indicated by production costs or customer orders for goods manufactured to customer specifications.

Where production is tailored to customer order, the task of the inventory management will be to attend to the dispatch of the manufactured goods to the customer. In the case of bulk production runs it would be the task of the dispatch department to fill all outstanding orders for the particular inventory item.

Where the business is a trading operation not involved in manufacturing, the goods received into the finished goods stores would be those purchased from various suppliers. The expenditure process (discussed in chapter 13) for the purchases of goods and services would be followed to this point.

14.1.5 Preliminary assessment of the risk of significant misstatement

The auditor would ascertain the critical success factors and key performance indicators used by management to manage the production and inventory transactions, as these provide pointers to the risk of potential significant misstatements. Where the production process is well controlled, the auditor may assess the risk of significant misstatement as medium or low. This would arise where the auditor obtains an understanding of the types of exception reports received by different levels of management, the various monitoring activities performed, and where there is evidence that prompt and effective action is taken by management to rectify errors and deal with indications of fraud.

The reader is referred to the discussion in chapter 13 of the inherent and control risk likely to be encountered in expenditure transactions. These apply equally to the production/inventory transactions. In addition, the following risks may be encountered due to the existence of the manufacturing environment, as opposed to the purchase of goods and services:

Examples of risks encountered in the manufacturing environment

- The volumes and complexities of the manufacturing transactions increase the risk of errors and fraud.

- The whole basis of costing of manufacturing operations is complex and while allocations of direct expenditures, such as raw materials used and direct labour time, is relatively straightforward, the allocation of overhead expenses may be more complex and different bases of identification and measurement may be applied by different entities in the industry, of which some may be more appropriate than others.

- Changes in staff or computerized accounting systems may lead to situations where allocations of expenditure to manufactured goods are not calculated on a consistent basis from one year to the next.

- The vast diversity of products manufactured may require experts to verify their *quality*, *condition* or *value*. In addition, the methods used to measure the quantities of inventory on hand may vary greatly (for example, measuring stockpiles of coal, grain or sugar in silos, diamonds and other precious and semiprecious stones, timber logs and different wood cuts for a plantation, chemicals and pharmaceutical products). This is not to say that the auditor requires an expert to assist in every inventory count; where the inventory is quite evident, the auditor is as capable of counting and recording the inventory quantities as the client's staff.

- It may be difficult to establish a market value for certain inventory items, which affects the auditor's assessment of the *net realizable value*. This will include inventories where prices are affected by global economic supply and demand factors that fluctuate widely over a period and affect the saleability of the inventory. For example, steel prices fluctuate worldwide, which would have affected the consideration of net realizable value in the earlier example of the production of the steel baskets.

- The entity may sell goods with a warranty and be faced with replacing faulty goods, or may sell its goods on a sale or return basis. Goods exported to other countries carry the risk of damage in transit, which may result in claims from insurers or leave the entity responsible for the replacement of damaged goods.

- Large businesses may store inventory at multiple locations and may transfer goods between different locations, which increases the risk that goods in transit between the two locations may be omitted from both the sending and receiving store, or be duplicated and shown as inventory in both locations at the period end.

- Inventory may be held on a consignment basis. Although physically on the entity's premises, it may not be owned by the entity. Alternatively, the entity's inventory may be placed on consignment with others.

14.1.6 Consideration of internal control components

As discussed in chapter 9, the five internal control components that affect the auditor's assessment of the risk of significant misstatement of expenditure transactions and balances are: the *control environment, risk assessment, information and communication, monitoring* and *control activities*. The internal control components over expenditure and revenue transactions, as discussed in chapters 12 and 13, apply equally to the production/inventory aspects contained in this chapter and are not repeated here. A brief discussion of aspects peculiar to production and inventory transactions follows below.

Due to the extensive controls likely to be implemented in these transactions and the interface with the revenue and expenditure transactions, it is likely that the auditor would seek to assess the combined inherent and control risk as medium to low. If this is the case, the auditor would perform tests of controls upon the key controls identified, followed by substantive analytical procedures with limited substantive tests of detail.

The auditor is likely to focus on management's monitoring activities and the design of detective controls in deciding whether these are appropriate for the objective they are intended to meet before deciding which tests of control to perform, if any.

The auditor gathers an understanding of the internal control components for this core and business level process from inquiries of management and staff, observation of control activities being performed, from knowledge gathered on prior audits and the inspection of documents and procedures manuals. The auditor documents the system in the form of explanatory working papers and the analysis of inputs, processes and outputs.

14.1.6.1 Control environment

As discussed in chapter 9, the control environment includes such factors as integrity, ethical values and organizational culture, competence of employees, management's philosophy and operating style, the manner in which the company assigns authority, the way in which it develops its people, and the direction and attention given by the board of directors.

The following outlines aspects of risk management in a production/inventory environment:

- The first critical aspect affecting integrity and ethical values are the quality control policies and procedures preventing the production of low quality products with defects that are constantly rejected by customers.

- Management needs to display integrity in adopting reasonable accounting policies that do not encourage misallocation of overhead expenditures to work in progress to inflate the cost of finished goods inventory and net income results.

- The human resource policies should allow for the employment of production staff with the appropriate skills and in addition, the company should actively support the training of its staff to develop the required skills. This should minimize the risk of errors occurring and improve the chances of detection and early correction should they arise.

- Management's operating style should convey a responsible and ethical approach to the running of the business. They should be seen to be monitoring the control activities and should avoid attempts at deliberate override of controls. Authority should be delegated in a way that makes production planning and factory management staff accountable for their actions, and the monitoring procedures of management should enforce these processes. If these various factors are not implemented or managed effectively, they will undoubtedly increase the risk of significant misstatement. Management must implement strict controls over inventory management and staff involved in receiving and dispatching goods.

- Accounting staff and costing staff should have the knowledge to understand and apply the costing methods used for the production process in order to correctly record the production expenditures and transfers to inventory and costs of sales entries.

The key to managing the process level business risks for production and inventory lies in establishing the critical success factors and key performance indicators, how these are reported and monitored and what action is taken, by whom, and how frequently, to ensure proper accountability and the management of the risks in the process.

14.1.6.2 Risk assessment

Management's risk assessment processes should identify and evaluate those risks that will impact most directly on the allocation of expenditures to manufactured goods, as well as those that will impact on the quality control processes. In addition, management should implement controls over the transfers of manufactured goods and the receipt of purchased goods and their safe storage in circumstances where inventory will not deteriorate, in order to limit as far as possible the risk of theft or spoilage.

Table 14.5 shows the process level risks the management of a manufacturing operation would need to manage in respect of the manufacture of goods and the movement of manufactured goods to inventory.

PRODUCTION PROCESS LEVEL RISKS	PROCESSING STAGE
Production planning and design	Difficulty in recruiting talented designers and experts in the specific field of manufacture, which may affect the quality of the goods manufactured and supplied.
Production processing	Unexpected down-time of plant and equipment, poor labour productivity or strikes, incorrect materials used, incorrect quantities produced.
Inventory management	Acceptance of goods into inventory that do not meet the quality specifications, resulting in unsaleable inventory which should be written off; the theft of finished inventory by staff; the deterioration of inventory due to unsatisfactory storage conditions; and goods stolen en route to the customer.

Table 14.5 Process level risks in a production/inventory environment

14.1.6.3 Information and communication

The accounting systems for manufacturing operations may be complex and involve control accounts over different cost centres. As the bulk of the production processing transactions are generated internally, the risk of error and manipulation is high. Costing systems will vary according to the nature of the production process, for example, job costing, process costing, assembly lines, standard costing with actual costs and variances to standard recorded. Consequently, the documents and processes followed must be adapted to record the particular manufacturing process and basis used. Typically, the auditor may encounter an integrated database system with the production cycle linked directly to an on-line real-time update of the inventory records from the production transactions that provide information for the invoicing of items to customers.

It is likely that in any production system with high volumes, production planning and scheduling will be computerized and probably interfaced with the computerized accounting systems. This is assumed in the discussion of the control activities.

14.1.6.4 Monitoring

Some of the monitoring activities that management may typically implement in a manufacturing environment may include budgets and performance reviews, consideration of standard cost variances and the use of internal audit to assess the effectiveness of internal control activities to meet the business objectives, monitoring of the accuracy of costing records, and gross margins on individual product lines. External monitoring mechanisms may include feedback from customers, monitoring the number of requests for warranty repairs or product liability claims, as well as returns and complaints received regarding product quality and punctual delivery.

The existence and deterioration of inventory would be monitored by regular inventory counts at all locations where inventory is stored. The use of computers for recording inventory has made it possible for most business to maintain perpetual inventory records. In these instances, management would typically schedule continuous stock counts on a rotational basis for selected items every week, with comparisons to inventory balances and adjustment for shrinkage being made throughout the year. Again, this assumes the use of computerized systems, as well as regular updates to record manufactured goods transferred to finished goods inventory, the receipt of goods purchased from suppliers, and inventory dispatched to customers for sales recorded.

Where the type of inventory is susceptible to theft by staff and customers, management would continuously monitor shrinkage levels and implement a variety of security measures to protect the inventory from theft. Measures may include security cameras over key areas (including continuous monitoring of those storage areas accessible to staff and/or the public), the employment of security staff, and the installation of a fraud 'hot-line' where people may report fraudulent activities observed by them. Again, the establishment of strict personnel policies for employees found guilty of theft and misappropriation of assets is one of the most effective control mechanisms in any production/inventory environment.

14.2 CONTROL ACTIVITIES AND TESTS OF CONTROL FOR PRODUCTION/INVENTORY TRANSACTIONS

14.2.1 Processing production/inventory transactions

Refer to chapter 9 for an extensive discussion of the control activities the auditor could expect to find in an organization and which are made up, in essence, by the policies and procedures established by management to respond to internal and external risks.

To achieve the control objectives, the control activities need to incorporate *internal control principles*, which can be described as being the characteristics or features of the different control activities, that is: segregation of duties; information processing controls (the general controls and application controls); the physical controls over inventory and work in progress; performance reviews and reporting procedures that ensure accountability of individuals for their actions.

The nature of the expenditure transactions will directly affect the form of documents used, the functions that occur, the recording processes followed, and the control activities implemented by management to ensure the input, processing and output for all production and inventory transactions recorded. Where this occurs, management's assertions of *completeness, measurement/accuracy and occurrence/validity* are satisfied.

The process must, additionally, allow for the *balances* arising from the *production and inventory transactions* to support the assertions of management at the period end, namely that of *existence or occurrence, completeness, measurement, valuation, rights and obligations*, and *presentation and disclosure* as indicated in Table 14.4.

Because of the volumes and complexity of the production/manufacturing and inventory transactions, different levels of control activities would usually be performed by different persons in the entity. As the class of transactions is significant, that is, the transaction volumes and amount of individual balances is high, more formal control activities are likely to be implemented by management to manage the business risk exposure.

14.2.1.1 Common documents and records for production/inventory transactions

Documents

The documents commonly encountered in the expenditure transactions process for production/inventory transactions are listed in Table 14.6 and may be in a hard copy (paper) format or captured electronically and printed out at the end of the process.

DOCUMENTS	NATURE OF DOCUMENT
Customer Production Order (CPO)	A document generated for the particular order, where the manufacture is to customer specifications. A CPO: • should be pre-numbered; • may be generated as an on-line computerized *Customer Job Card* to be updated on the way through the process; or • may be a manual document, which is then captured into the computer production system to authorize the commencement of the production process.
Inventory Production Order (IPO) and Inventory or Customer Job Card	A document for the processing of bulk production runs to replenish finished goods inventory, which: • should be pre-numbered; and • generate an on-line computerized *Inventory or Customer Job Card.*

DOCUMENTS	NATURE OF DOCUMENT
Raw materials issues slip	Records raw material issued to the production process.
Customer Job Card (CJC) or *Inventory Job Card (IJC)*	A time card for each job or batch to record machine and human-hours worked on the job or production run. The information could simply be recorded on the *Customer Job Card* (for production to specific customer order) or on the *Inventory Job Card* (for bulk production runs of the same items to replenish manufactured inventory).
Job transfer sheet or *Inventory movement sheet*	A document authorizing the transfer of the work in progress to the next stage of production. • Should be pre-numbered. • May simply be a section of the *job card* or production run batch sheet which is: – signed manually by the particular supervisor approving it for transfer to the next stage of production; or – where production scheduling is computerized, is signed electronically by the factory or production manager • Once signed, the Job Transfer Sheet transfers the accumulated costs and direct labour or machine hours to the next stage of production. • May also record the physical quality control check performed before the goods are accepted into the next stage of production and record rejected items.

Table 14.6 Documents used in production and inventory transactions

Computerized accounting records

In addition to documents which arise from the production and inventory transactions (listed in Table 14.6) and may be manual or computerized, the entity would usually maintain *computerized accounting records* to process these transactions, as shown in Table 14.7.

COMPUTERIZED ACCOUNTING RECORDS	NATURE OF RECORD
Standard cost master file	Where a standard costing system is used, this document provides the basis for the standard costs allocated to each job or production run and allows for the preparation of the *Standard cost variances report*.
COMPUTERIZED INVENTORY MASTER FILES	**NATURE OF RECORD**
Raw material inventory master file	Records the quantities and unit prices of raw materials inventory received, issued to production, and the balance on hand. This master file would typically contain: • a statistical history of usage for individual line items; and • standing data items, such as re-order levels, economic order quantities, suppliers account codes, and last delivery dates and quantities.
Work in progress master file	Accumulates the production costs for each job or production run during the course of the production process and units produced. This master file would typically: • provide the information required to generate the *daily production report*; • update the general ledger for work in progress accounts; • produce the variance reports, where a standard costing system is used; and • transfer, on completion of each job or bulk production run, the accumulated costs and quantities produced to the finished goods inventory master file – and then be used to produce the *Completed production report*.

COMPUTERIZED ACCOUNTING RECORDS	NATURE OF RECORD
Finished goods inventory master file	Records the following: • the quantities of units transferred from work in progress for each completed job or bulk production run and the accumulated costs (or standard costs) which are used to determine the unit costs of inventory items; • quantities of merchandise purchased from suppliers and the unit prices of these, updated from the purchases transactions recording; • quantities of finished goods and merchandise sold and transferred to cost of sales updated from the revenue transactions recording; • finished goods inventory balances on hand; and • the information for production of the *finished goods inventory printout* and updates the general ledger for cost of goods sold. This master file would usually contain: • a statistical history of goods received and sold for individual line items for a specified period; and • standing data items such as re-order levels, economic order quantities and suppliers account codes and last delivery dates and quantities.

Table 14.7 Computerized accounting records for production and inventory transactions

Printouts arising from production and inventory transactions

In addition to the computerized accounting records described in Table 14.7 above, management would need to obtain certain *printouts* from the accounting records relevant to production and inventory transactions. See Table 14.8.

PRINTOUTS	NATURE OF PRINTOUT
Daily production report	This report would typically reflect each job in process and detail the raw materials issued to production and time worked (both machine hours and employee hours), as well as the accumulated costs on individual jobs or production runs. It would be distributed to the production planning, management and accounting staff.
Completed production report	This report would provide information on the total costs of raw materials issued, machine and labour hours worked, as well as the quantity of goods produced for each *bulk production run* or customer *job card*. It would be distributed to the production planning, management and accounting staff.
Report of units rejected	This report would provide details of units rejected on completion of each job or production run. It would be distributed to the production planning and management staff to investigate and remedy problems in order to minimize losses from production defects.
Inventory printouts for: Raw materials; Work in progress; and Finished goods	These reports would be distributed to the stores management staff for periodic inventory counts and for identification of items that need to be manufactured or are below re-ordering levels.
EXCEPTION REPORTS	**NATURE OF REPORT**

It is assumed that the computer program will have various programmed application controls to ensure the *completeness, measurement* and *occurrence* of the transactions. Some will be generated at the initial input stage, with screen formats that reject a transaction with information missing, while others may be programmed to coincide with the processing run and provide printouts and reconciliations of various transactions or errors at the end of the day's production run. Exception reports typically include the following:

Missing or duplicated sequence numbers	For originating pre-numbered documents, namely the Customer orders, Job Cards, Production schedules, and Raw materials issues. This report would identify transactions omitted from the work in progress or duplicated, so as to ensure the *completeness* of the production costing.
Reconciliation of 'Raw material issues slips' to the 'Work in process master file'	Reconciliation from a comparison of the *Raw material issues slips* for the raw materials issued to production each day with those captured into the *Work in progress master file* and printed out on the daily *Production report*.

PRINTOUTS	NATURE OF PRINTOUT
Reconciliation of Employee hours on Job Cards to Payroll time records	Reconciliation from a comparison of the *direct employee hours* worked as recorded on the *time card for each job or batch* or time recorded on the *Job Cards* or *Production schedules* with the *payroll time records* clocked in by individual production employees. Differences would typically be investigated by the production manager and allocated to the relevant variance accounts, if a standard costing system is used.
Comparison of 'Work in progress completed' to its receipt in 'Finished goods inventory'	Comparison of the record of *Work in progress completed* and *transferred to finished goods* to the recording of the *receipt in finished goods inventory*. Any difference between the quantities and total costs transferred out, to those recorded as received in the finished goods inventory, would usually be highlighted in the report for prompt follow up by the production management and inventory management.
Key performance reports	These reports typically reflect ratios, inventory turn-over times, length of production times and level of production costs compared to budgets, number of customer returns and items that were rejected by the production staff or inventory management staff (that is, did not pass quality control checks at the end of the work in progress and before transfer to finished goods inventory).

Table 14.8 Common printouts and exception reports for production and inventory transactions

14.2.1.2 The production and inventory management functions

The control activities are discussed in terms of the three distinct functional areas, which are all assumed to be in a computerized environment:

- *Production planning and design:* The initial design of the items to be manufactured, production planning and control.
- *Production processing:* The issue of raw materials to the production process; the movement of goods through the actual production process as work in progress; and the transfer of manufactured goods to the finished goods inventory.
- *Inventory management:* The receipt and recording of manufactured and purchased inventory; and the storage of manufactured inventory until its dispatch to customers and maintenance of inventory master files.

Production planning and design

Design of the items to be manufactured, production planning and control

This is the start of the production process, which would typically commence with due authorization by the production planning department. The form of authorization would differ from one business to the next, but for normal scheduled production runs implemented on a regular basis, it would probably originate either as an internal pre-numbered *Customer Production Order (CPO)* or an *Inventory Production Order (IPO)*. Both are likely to be based on established trends for the replenishment of finished goods inventory items that have reached 're-order levels' or are 'out of stock', or where sales staff anticipate a future demand for the particular items in excess of existing finished inventory levels.

To ensure an appropriate segregation of duties, the production order should be formally authorized by the Production Planning Department before acceptance by the Production Processing Department or the Factory Manager. The use of computerized software and integrated database applications may automate the whole process so that an electronic signature would authorize the move from one stage of production processing to another, but the authorization may also come in the form of a hard copy CPO or IPO document, which is then captured into the computer system.

Once the production or factory manager has accepted the CPO or IPO, a Customer Job Card (CJC), or Inventory Job Card (IJC) would be generated to capture all the costs involved in the production of the items, such as raw materials used, direct hours worked by production staff and machine hours. As the goods move through the production process, the system should provided for the authorization, electronically or manually, of the person responsible for that particular stage of production, evidencing that the goods being manufactured are transferred to the next stage, until the process is completed.

A *Daily Production Report* of all jobs in process should be produced and copies distributed to the production planning department and the production or factory manager to monitor the progress of all jobs in process and those completed during the day and transferred to finished goods inventory. Management's prompt review of the Daily Production Report should bring to light any unusual charges allocated for raw material, labour and overheads, which should then be queried and rectified where necessary.

Production processing

The issue of raw materials to the production process

The pre-numbered *Raw Materials Issues* slip (RMI) is a request for the raw materials required for the particular customer of inventory production run. It would be prepared either by the production planning department or, more likely, the production department or factory manager. As with the CPO and

IPO, this document could be electronic or a hard copy. All such issues to production must be accounted for as allocated to the particular work in progress Customer Job Card (CJC) or Inventory Job Card (IJC). All raw materials issued to production should be listed on the daily production report and a copy sent to the Raw Materials Stores staff to compare with the *raw material inventory master file records for that day.*

Movement of goods through the actual production process as work in progress

As the job moves through the production process, the time spent on each stage of production, by production employees or in machine time should be captured onto the relevant Job Card (CJC or IJC). This may be done in a variety of ways, either by simply writing the time on the card, or by the employee using the card to 'clock in and out', and similarly clocking in the machine run-time. At the end of each day, the total time recorded on the job cards for the day should be reconciled to the total hours worked by production staff. Any differences should be accounted for, for example, idle time or set-up time. If more hours are recorded on the job card than were actually spent by the employee at work that day, the discrepancy should be queried and corrected by the production manager.

Some production facilities operate 24 hours a day, running in three shifts of eight hours each. This shift work would be recorded on the job card as well. Different senior employees, such as the shift foreman or the person responsible for that stage of the production process would typically be assigned the responsibility of inspecting that each stage of the production process has been properly completed, before the goods may pass to the next stage. As mentioned, this authorization may take the form of an electronic signature, or the manual signature of the person on the hard copy of the relevant Job Card.

Transfer of manufactured goods to finished goods inventory

Once the production process is complete, a quality control inspection would be performed to detect any apparent defects before the produced goods are transferred to the finished goods store. The raw materials, human and machine hours worked, as well as overhead allocations on the completed Job Card should be inspected by the production manager to ensure all production charges are correctly recorded. These should then be compared to the details reflected on the *Completed production report* captured into the computer system. Any differences or variances from standard costs and any unexpected items such as labour overruns should be duly authorized by the production manager, before the goods are physically transferred to and accepted by the *Finished Goods Inventory Stores* staff. The factory or production manager should authorize, by electronic or manual signature, the transfer of the manufactured goods to inventory; the acceptance of the goods into finished inventory should be similarly acknowledged by electronic or manual signature of the *Finished Goods Inventory Stores* staff.

Inventory management

Receipt and recording of manufactured and purchased inventory

The relevant ledger accounts may be updated automatically as cost of work in progress and completed manufactured goods are recorded in the manufacturing process, depending on the computerized system in use. However, the accounting department, possibly with some involvement by the production costing department, has to monitor the production records and ensure that all amounts are recorded in the correct accounts. This would include the recording of:

- direct material costs of raw materials and consumables to work in progress;
- direct payroll costs based on hours worked allocated to the relevant job or production run;
- an overhead allocation for each job or production run, which may be determined in a variety of ways, but is commonly based on labour hours or machine hours worked, depending on the nature of the production process and practices of the entity in prior years;
- the transfer of accumulating costs between production stages or departments in work in progress; and
- the transfer of the final cost of the finished goods manufactured to finished goods inventory.

Where a standard costing system is in use, inventory will be recorded at standard cost and the various standard costing variances must be recorded in the accounting records and monitored by management.

Production entries must be supported by the relevant documents: Raw Material Issues slip, Customer Job Card or Inventory Job Card and machine or labour time recorded on the Job Cards. Evidence of the date and authorization of transfer from one department to the next should be kept until its eventual transfer to the finished goods inventory, when acknowledgement by means of a Goods Transferred Note (GTN) must be recorded. The amounts recorded in the general ledger should be agreed back to the daily production reports, in the case of work in progress, and to the Completed Production Report in the case of manufactured goods transferred to finished goods inventory. Management in the various departments should review the production reports on a regular basis and inquire about charges that appear out of line to expectations. Where standard costs are used, these should also be reviewed regularly to determine whether they approximate cost.

Storage of manufactured inventory and maintenance of inventory master files

Storage and dispatch of manufactured inventory

In any business dealing with raw materials and/or merchandise, all items purchased should be accounted for on receipt into the raw materials store or the merchandise store. All raw materials leaving the store must be accounted for by a charge to production and, similarly, the cost of manufactured goods transferred from work in progress to finished goods should be duly accounted for. Once sold and dispatched to customers, the cost of manufactured inventory or merchandise should be transferred to cost of sales and the relevant customer invoiced, resulting in a charge to accounts receivable or the receipt of cash for cash sales. In real life some loss of physical inventory is likely to occur, whether from theft, breakages, inventory deterioration or other incidents such as floods, fires or malfunctioning of storage equipment (fridges and cold rooms, etc.). It is the responsibility of management to implement effective control activities to safeguard the inventory and minimize losses.

The record of inventory movements maintained can vary considerably. In a large manufacturing and merchandising concern this may take the form of an on-line record of receipts and issues in quantity and value maintained in a computerized integrated database system, such as SAP; in a small owner-managed business only basic records may be maintained, such as simple records of physical quantities moving *in and out* which are kept by means of cards attached to the inventory bins or shelves. In other cases there might be no record of physical movements at all, with the entity merely recording inventory purchases and sales. In the latter situation inventory appearing in the financial statements will be determined by means of a physical count and valuation at the financial year-end. The degree of sophistication of a system depends on the advantages to be derived from it, measured against the cost of its operation and the practicability of operating it in the particular circumstances.

Once manufactured goods are transferred into finished goods, the preparation of a *Goods Transferred Note* (GTN) should update the finished goods inventory record with the manufactured goods physically received. Thereafter, the stores management have the responsibility of ensuring the physical safekeeping of the inventory until such time as it is sold to customers. Physical protection of inventory may include locked stores areas with access restricted to authorized individuals, the presence of security guards and surveillance cameras. Periodic inventory counts will also be performed to agree the physical quantities with the recorded inventory balances and any discrepancies should be investigated and written off if so authorized by a senior employee.

Where the entity operates numerous retail outlets, the finished goods would probably be distributed to the various outlets for sale in accordance with pre-numbered inter-branch or inter-company transfers (IBTs). Refer to the discussion of revenue transactions and controls ordinarily exercised, in chapter 12.

Goods manufactured to specific Customer Orders would be dispatched to those customers as soon as they are received in the Finished Goods Inventory Store. The delivery to the customer would be accompanied in the normal way by a delivery note and sales invoice prepared by the sales staff and sales invoicing system. The finished goods store manager will have the responsibility of monitoring the updating of the finished goods inventory master file for completed manufactured goods received and the subsequent sale of goods to customers or inter-branch transfers.

Where finished goods are purchased from other manufacturers, a *Goods Received Note* (GRN) would be prepared in the normal way for goods purchased and the controls discussed in chapter 13 would apply.

Maintenance of inventory master files

Inventory management must monitor the finished goods inventory levels, existence and valuation on a regular basis, and for the following reasons:

- First, from the perspective of the core process of the business, to ensure 'stock outs' do not occur or are kept to a minimum.
- Second, to monitor slow moving and obsolete or damaged items for scrapping and writing off, or for selling at reduced prices to get them out of inventory while recovering some amounts.
- Third, to monitor deliveries by suppliers and from own manufacture – to consider whether the prices are most competitive and delivery terms are met – as regards quality, prices and delivery lead times.
- Finally, to monitor the existence of inventory, particularly where inventory is susceptible to theft by customers and staff, with regular periodic or continuous inventory counts.

With a computerized inventory record updated on an on-line basis, it is possible to physically count selected items throughout the year; this is known as a *perpetual inventory system*. Such counts should be recorded and compared with the inventory records and any difference accounted for by reference to cut-off of purchases, sales and manufactured goods transferred to finished goods. Management should monitor shrinkage levels continually to ensure security steps are adequate to limit losses as far as possible.

Management may implement a variety of physical and monitoring controls over inventory, depending on the size of the business, sophistication of inventory records and nature of inventory. These may typically include:

- *Perpetual inventory*: This computerized inventory record may take several forms, viz. a loose-leaf ledger, card index or computerized master file. Whatever the form, the inventory accounts provide for a day-to-day record of the inventory movement in quantity and value. An important advantage of the system is that it permits a continuous check to be made by frequent comparisons of the quantities, per count, of some of the inventory or merchandise on hand with those recorded in the relevant inventory accounts, so that all individual inventory accounts are checked over a period of a few months. In these circumstances, any discrepancies are likely to be discovered in a relatively short time and, if they are of a continuing nature, steps can be taken to prevent their recurrence before they reach serious proportions.

- *The issue of goods to sales outlets at selling price:* In some businesses, for example, a departmental store or a concern with a number of shops, or where agents are provided with goods for sale, it may be practicable to charge inventory purchased for a sales centre (a department, a counter or a shop) to an appropriate inventory account at selling price, the relevant sales being credited to the inventory account. The balance on the inventory account should be represented by inventory physically on hand or cash for sales made but not yet recorded. Discrepancies in inventory physically on hand at the time of inventory counts may be due to shortages in goods supplied and charged to a sales centre, pilfering of inventory, misappropriation of cash in the case of cash sales (which are not recorded) or failure to invoice goods in the case of credit sales. It is for the management to scrutinize the inventory accounts regularly and to make such enquiries and take such action as will elicit the cause of the discrepancies. This method may be combined with the perpetual inventory method described above, in which case inventory would be issued from a central store to the sales centres instead of directly charged to the sales centres when purchased.

- *Gross profit as a means of control:* In all businesses, large and small, management can exercise a broad control over inventory by monitoring the percentage of the gross profit to the sales, as shown by the trading account, and comparison with that of previous periods and with the expected percentage based on known mark-ups. Where departmentaliza-tion is feasible, the departments should be so arranged that the goods in each having approximately the same mark-up. This allows for the expected percentage of gross profit to be assessed with a high degree of accuracy, thus making the departmental trading accounts a very effective means of inventory control. If the percentage varies unexpectedly and substantially, enquiries should be made to determine the reason for the variation and action should be taken to rectify the matter promptly. Frequent monitoring of gross margins is desirable and may be possible with the computerized systems implemented by the business. In other circumstances, periodic inventory counts may be performed once or twice each year to allow for the gross margins to be determined.

- *Physical control of inventory:* Management is responsible for the safe-guarding of the assets of the business, including its inventory. Accordingly and in addition to maintaining such records of inventory movement as may be feasible, physical control over inventory movement should be exerted so that all goods invoiced to the business are accounted for by the receipt of the relevant inventory and so that all goods physically issued to production or dispatched to customers or other branches are similarly accounted for.

  There should be only a few specified exits for the movement of goods from the warehouse or store. These should be strictly controlled so that every article or parcel of goods leaving the warehouse or store is matched by a delivery note, a sales invoice or inter-branch transfer, as the case may be. Management at different levels in the entity should monitor the controls over the physical receipt and issue of goods to determine whether the laid-down procedures are being implemented.

- The monitoring of inventory levels is especially important where goods are of a perishable nature or are subject to the vagaries of fashion or technical obsolescence, as inventory may become unsaleable through deterioration or obsolescence. Management should monitor inventory levels so as to match sales demands, identify slow moving goods and prevent out of stock situations. Prompt action should be taken in conjunction with the production, buying and sales departments to ascertain and address the causes, which may be due to a variety of reasons, such as inefficiency in buying, failure to market inventory effectively, uncompetitive prices, failure by suppliers to deliver timeously or poor estimation of market demands.

14.2.2 Assessing the risk of significant misstatement

The auditor should obtain an understanding of the production and inventory management processes of the client in order to identify the risk of significant misstatement and design appropriate substantive tests. Where the auditor believes that the client's controls are such that the risk of significant misstatement for cost of sales, work in progress and inventory is unlikely, the auditor must perform tests of controls to establish that the controls on which reliance is planned have operated throughout the period.

Clearly, the appropriateness of the controls are directly related to their ability to prevent or detect and correct misstatements. As indicated in earlier chapters, preventative controls are usually implemented at the transaction initiation and recording stage, in contrast to the detective controls which are exercised after the execution and recording of transactions as part of management's monitoring procedures. It would be more efficient to test the monitoring controls that cover several assertions, rather than the more focused preventative controls implemented at the input stage.

The auditor's understanding of the controls over the production process and inventory management is obtained from observation of the controls being performed, inquiry of staff, and inspection of documents and printouts, including the prior year audit working papers, evidence of reconciliations of manufacturing costs charged to each job from raw material issues slips, payroll records and calculations of overhead allocations, as well as evidence that exception reports are reviewed and corrective action is promptly taken.

14.2.3 Testing controls

To comply with SAAS 400, 'Risk assessment and internal control', the auditor should obtain evidence from tests of controls to support a medium to low assessment of inherent and control risk (risk of significant misstatement in transactions and balances). If such evidence is obtained, the auditor may accept a higher level of detection risk and obtain audit evidence to a large degree from substantive analytical procedures with reduced reliance on detailed substantive tests of production cost transactions and cost of sales and inventory balances.

Table 14.9 sets out the risks and controls, computerized and manual, that may be found in a system for production and inventory transactions and balances, and provides examples of tests of controls appropriate to these.

RISK	PROGRAMMED CONTROLS	MANUAL CONTROLS	TEST OF CONTROLS
Production planning and initiation			
Production levels inappropriate – either excessive and resulting in unsaleable inventory, or insufficient and resulting in stock outs.	Computerized monitoring of manufactured inventory levels against sales demand levels to indicate re-order levels and economic order quantities for particular inventory items.	Planning and scheduling monitored by the production department and approved by the production manager.	Inspect evidence of authorization of production runs.
Goods not manufactured to customer specifications, resulting in customer refusal to accept the goods, which may then be unsaleable.		Customer approval obtained for designs and specifications before production commences. Planning and scheduling monitored by the production department and approved by the production manager.	Inspect evidence of signed customer approval and production manager approval.
Production processing			
Issue of raw materials to production			
Incorrect materials issued to production. Raw materials out of stock and production delayed. Raw materials issued unallocated or allocated to the incorrect job.	Pre-numbered materials requisitions captured into the system, generate materials issues slips for materials issued to the factory for production. Daily printouts of all material issues to jobs in progress with the related materials requisition number included in the job production reports. Daily printout of unfilled materials requisitions and material issues slips not allocated to particular jobs.	Materials requisitions slips for all job or production runs signed by authorized factory staff. Daily printout of materials issued to jobs in progress reviewed by factory management and agreed to the materials requisitions issued by the factory staff. Factory and production staff monitor unfilled requisitions and follow up on delays in raw material issues. Factory staff signs off job cards from one production stage to the next, indicating that materials recorded for each job are complete and correct.	Inspect evidence of review by factory and production management of job production reports and follow up of misallocated materials and unfilled materials requisitions. In particular, enquire about the effect on work in progress of unallocated material issues slips at the period end.
Unauthorized issues of raw materials, or raw materials stolen.		Physical security over raw materials store, limiting access to authorized persons. Adequate insurance cover obtained. Surveillance cameras over factory or production area, access	By enquiry and observation obtain evidence of controls implemented.

RISK	PROGRAMMED CONTROLS	MANUAL CONTROLS	TEST OF CONTROLS
		security controlled and where production is of very high value or hazardous, very tight security will be in place, e.g. refining of gold bars, cutting of diamonds.	
Movement of goods through production stages			
Direct labour hours not recorded or allocated to the incorrect job. Direct machine hours not recorded or allocated to the incorrect job.	Daily direct labour charged to jobs matched to total labour hours worked per day for each employee's recorded wages time/clocking records. Differences between direct labour hours allocated to jobs and those clocked in each day are printed in an exception report. Machine hours charged to jobs daily are matched to total machine hour capacity and unallocated hours are printed on an exception report of under-recovery of machine hours. Daily production report accumulates hours worked on all jobs and matches that to total hours worked in the factory per day.	Production and factory management review daily production reports and the reconciliation of total hours worked to direct labour hours allocated to jobs. Management review the exception reports and rectify errors in allocation of direct labour hours and machine hours to jobs.	Inspect evidence of management's review of the production reports and the reconciliation of labour hours. Inspect evidence that management review the exception reports of labour differences and inspect evidence of the correction of errors indicated in the exception report.
Jobs in progress do not include all accumulated costs before being moved to the next stage of production.	Movement of jobs through the various stages of production is recorded, but transfer to the next stage requires the electronic signature of the authorized factory staff before being transferred. Access by authorized persons for this purpose is controlled by means of passwords and menus. Costs from the following stage cannot be recorded until the previous stage has been signed off to transfer the job to that following stage. Daily production report records the date and time of transfer of jobs from one stage to the next and identifies the staff member who authorized the transfer. The costs accumulated to the end of each successive stage are similarly reported in the daily production report.	Electronic signature of the authorized persons appears on the relevant section of the hard copy of the job card and the daily production report, signifying that the person has checked that all direct materials, labour and machine hours costs are included correctly and completely before approving the transfer of the job to the next stage. Factory and production management review costs allocated and inquire about any that appear out of line.	For work in-progress at period end, inspect the relevant signatures authorizing the transfer of the job to successive stages. Compare the raw materials, labour hours and machine hours to the job specification for the stages completed, and inspect evidence that the factory and production management monitor and correct any discrepancies.

RISK	PROGRAMMED CONTROLS	MANUAL CONTROLS	TEST OF CONTROLS
Transfer of goods to finished goods store			
Finished goods store personnel fail to record the receipt of the manufactured goods or accept faulty or damaged goods from production.	Movement of completed jobs requires the electronic signature of the factory manager before being transferred to finished goods. Finished goods stores personnel are required to indicate acceptance of the manufactured goods by electronic signature to complete the transfer of the goods from work in progress to finished goods. The computer records the transfer of the quantities and costs of the manufactured goods to the finished goods inventory master file. The computer produces a completed production report for all jobs transferred to finished goods inventory.	Quality control staff inspect the manufactured goods for each production run to ensure they meet quality standards before being passed to the finished goods store personnel. Goods damaged or not meeting quality standards should immediately be withdrawn and destroyed. The job card signed to indicate this check completed satisfactorily. In addition to their electronic signature, finished goods stores personnel may also be required to indicate acceptance of the manufactured goods by means of their signature on the hard copy of the job card indicating acceptance of the completed job/inventory. Factory and production management review the completed production report daily and query/rectify any costs or quantities that are out of line with expectations.	Inspect evidence of the acceptance of the completed jobs into the finished goods store. Inspect evidence of the review by management of costs on the completed production report and follow up by them, of any aspects that appear incorrect. Using CAATs match completed jobs to manufactured inventory accepted into the finished goods store, agreeing quantities and costs transferred.
Finished goods stolen.	Regular printout of finished goods inventory recorded in the inventory master file reflects inventory items in the store.	Physical security over finished goods, such as locked warehouses with limited access for authorized persons only. Surveillance cameras strategically placed in the finished goods store. Continuous inventory counts performed by management and reconciliation of inventory physically on hand to inventory balances per the inventory master file. Cut-off tests performed on finished inventory received, merchandise purchased and sales made.	Enquire about and observe adequacy of security arrangements. Attend and observe continuous or periodic client stock count procedures and reconciliation to recorded inventory balances in the inventory master file. Inspect authorized adjustments put through for inventory shrinkages and cut-off on manufactured goods, merchandise purchases and sales at period end.

RISK	PROGRAMMED CONTROLS	MANUAL CONTROLS	TEST OF CONTROLS
Recording of manufactured inventory and merchandise			
Errors in costs allocated to manufactured inventory include: • Raw materials issued to production; • Direct labour hours and machine hours allocated to the incorrect job or for the incorrect amount.	Daily production report details direct material, labour and machine hours allocated to jobs and matches these to the underlying source documents – raw material issues, hours clocked in for wages records and machine hours worked. Exception reports of unmatched direct costs.	Management review daily production reports and exception reports, and action taken to rectify errors and misallocations during work in progress movement from one stage to the next.	Inspect daily production and exception reports for evidence of management's review and any related action.
Overhead cost allocations made to jobs in progress and completed jobs incorrectly calculated, allocated to the incorrect job, or result in excessive costs carried in inventory that should be expensed.	Computer would usually allocate overhead costs to jobs on the basis of direct labour or direct machine hours or some other basis programmed for the particular production process. Daily production reports should reflect any standard cost variances and overhead allocations to particular jobs.	Management periodically approves overhead recovery rates and the basis of allocation or standard costs to be allocated to jobs in progress. Management reviews and investigates standard cost variances on a regular basis, and considers the net realizable value of manufactured products by reference to market-related sale prices.	Inspect management approvals of standard cost and overhead allocation rates and basis. Enquire as to consistency with accounting policies. Inspect evidence of management review of standard cost variances and net realizable values of manufactured goods.
Costs of production for completed jobs not transferred to finished good inventory.	The daily *Completed production* report reflects costs transferred to finished goods inventory and the signatures of the authorized factory personnel approving the transfer, as well as the authorized finished goods stores personnel accepting the manufactured goods into finished goods inventory.	Factory and production management should review the completed production report daily and query/rectify any costs or quantities that are out of line with expectations.	Using CAATs, match completed jobs to manufactured inventory accepted into the finished goods store, agreeing quantities and costs transferred. Inspect daily completed production reports and evidence of management review.
Storage of inventory and maintenance of inventory master files			
Recorded inventory quantities do not agree with inventory quantities on hand.		Periodic or continuous inventory counts performed and reconciled to inventory master file balances and general ledger inventory control account balance. Cut-off tests performed on finished inventory received, merchandise purchased and sales made.	Inspect evidence of inventory counts and recorded balances. Inspect evidence of authority for any adjustments made to recorded balances.
The total of the inventory master files does not agree with the total of the inventory control account in the general ledger.	Computer matches general ledger and inventory master file in total continuously, prints exception report of unmatched transactions and balances.	Cut-off tests performed on finished inventory received, merchandise purchased and sales made. Reconciliation of inventory master file and general ledger control account performed and adjustments made for inventory shrinkages and errors.	Inspect evidence of management review and authorization of adjustments made on a continuous basis.

RISK	PROGRAMMED CONTROLS	MANUAL CONTROLS	TEST OF CONTROLS
Inventory obsolete, or its condition deteriorated, such that its carrying amount may be in excess of market values.	Printout of inventory sales activity levels for individual line items and extent of current stockholdings based on existing sales demand.	Regular review of obsolete and damaged inventory, decision made to write off such items periodically. Calculation at period end of allowance for inventory write-downs – consistent with accounting policies and past practice for entity. Review of inventory sales activity and last date of sale of individual inventory items and product lines to identify slow moving and unsaleable inventory.	Inspect evidence of management review of inventory obsolescence and calculation of inventory write-downs. Enquire as to competency of persons performing the calculation of the allowance for obsolescence. Ascertain norms for industry and consider whether client assumptions are reasonable. Test programmed controls for determining inventory sales activity levels.
Control environment and control activities not resulting in management being held accountable for inventory movements, measurement or valuation, with consequential high level of potential errors, misstatements in the financial statements and fraud.		**Senior management at appropriate levels monitor:** Levels of production and production costs. Levels of Raw Material and Finished Goods Inventory. Reconciliations of inventory count quantities to inventory master file and levels of inventory shrinkages and theft. The incidence of stock-outs and excessive stock holdings relative to sales demand. Standard cost variances, and overhead allocations appropriate for the entity and those that are norms for the industry. Key performance indicators monitored.	Inspect evidence of the effectiveness of management's monitoring procedures and key performance indicators to prevent, detect and correct errors and fraud related to production and inventory transactions and balances.

Table 14.9 Risks, controls and tests of controls – production and inventory transactions and balances

14.3 DETECTION RISK AND SUBSTANTIVE TESTS OF INVENTORY TRANSACTIONS AND BALANCES

It remains for the auditor to gather substantive evidence regarding the fair presentation of inventory balances for a manufacturer enterprise comprising *raw materials, work in progress and finished goods inventory* and *merchandise inventory* for a wholesaler or retailer enterprise.

14.3.1 Determining the acceptable level of detection risk

A reminder that there is an inverse relationship which exists between the inherent and control risk assessment, and the acceptable level of detection risk required by the auditor. The risks affecting purchased merchandise inventory are discussed in chapter 13, while those affecting management's assertions for manufactured inventory balances are discussed here. These risks pertain primarily to a risk of overstatement of inventories affecting the *existence, occurrence, measurement* and *valuation* assertions for inventories.

The nature of the *measurement and valuation* risks differs for manufactured finished goods and work in progress, compared with purchased merchandise. Where the measurement of purchased merchandise is determined by the supplier's price and any further costs to put the goods into a saleable condition, the measurement of manufactured work in progress and finished goods inventory depends on the more complex manufacturing costs – including raw material used, the allocation of labour costs and fixed and variable overhead expenditures – which may lead to numerous errors in calculation and allocation.

Further, the ascertainment of net realizable values for manufactured inventory may be more difficult to establish and may be dependent upon sales prices that the entity is able to realize, rather than merchandise purchased on the open market where prices are readily ascertainable. Where the entity has slow moving items of manufactured inventory on hand, there may not be any recent sales to indicate the net realizable value. In such circumstances, the auditor may decide that it is prudent to set a lower level of acceptable detection risk for the *measurement* and *valuation* assertions of manufactured items included in finished goods inventory, whilst accepting a higher level of detection risk for those same assertions for items of purchased merchandise included in finished goods inventory.

Another consideration when auditing inventory transactions and balances is the interface with purchases, sales and cost of sales, since evidence gained about an assertion for inventory provides evidence regarding the opposite balance. For example, evidence regarding the completeness and existence of merchandise or raw material inventory, as a result of inventory counts and cut-off tests of goods received, automatically provides assurance with regard to the completeness and occurrence of purchases of raw materials and merchandise for the same period. Similarly, tests of cut-off of sales and delivery notes provide evidence that the cost of goods sold prior to the period end have been excluded from inventory at the period end and are correctly included in cost of sales. Thus these audit procedures simultaneously provide evidence of the *completeness, occurrence and measurement* of sales, cost of sales and finished goods inventory.

The framework discussed, in chapters 11, 12 and 13, for substantive audit procedures to detect any remaining risk of significant misstatement, can be applied to the audit of manufactured inventory, merchandise inventory and cost of sales. The framework presented in Table 14.10 provides examples of the types of substantive procedures that might be used when auditing production and inventory transactions and balances.

SUBSTANTIVE TESTS	AUDIT OBJECTIVES				
	C	O/E	M/V	R/O	P/D
1. Obtain and document an understanding of the business:					
Ascertain the significance of raw materials, manufactured inventory, merchandise and cost of sales to the entity and the related sales and purchases.		×	×		
Identify key performance indicators used by management to monitor production and finished inventory transactions and balances.	×		×		
Ascertain the strategic external and internal business risks affecting the core business of the entity and consider the possible impact on its production and inventory processes.			×	×	
Obtain trial balances or schedules of the significant balances arising from the significant class of transactions (manufacturing expenditures and work in progress, cost of sales, raw material inventory and finished goods inventory):	×		×		
• Agree opening balances to the previous year's working papers					
• Review movements in the general ledger for unusual activity or entries in manufacturing expenses and cost of sales, and balance sheet balances, such as raw material, work in progress and finished goods inventory. Investigate unusual entries.					
• Agree balances in perpetual inventory master files to general ledger control accounts and trial balance.					
2. Substantive analytical procedures:					
Develop a prediction or expectation for production and inventory levels, from sales, cost of sales, gross margins and inventory turnover and expenditure items from knowledge of the business, history of supplier trade terms and industry norms.	×	×	×		
Define a significant difference or threshold for sales, cost of sales and inventory, based on ratios and comparisons of the current period's composition of inventory balances, purchases of inventory and levels of production transactions with prior financial periods and budgets.	×	×	×		
• Compare inventory balances to expectations of turnover.					

SUBSTANTIVE TESTS	AUDIT OBJECTIVES				
	C	O/E	M/V	R/O	P/D
• Compute the difference between the actual and the expected and compare this to key performance indicators used by management.					
• Investigate significant differences by enquiries of management and staff and exercise judgement to conclude on whether the analytical review is indicating the existence of material errors and design appropriate substantive tests of detail to detect and correct errors.					
• Document the basis for the audit conclusion, namely whether the analytical procedures provide sufficient acceptable audit evidence, or whether further audit evidence is required from substantive tests of detail of balances or transactions.					
3. Tests of detail of transactions:					
Select a sample of the main transactions flows through inventory accounts at the process level and inspect supporting documents, e.g. select a sample from recorded inventory purchases, manufactured goods transferred, sales and sales returns and:	×	×	×	×	
• Inspect supporting supplier's documentation, manufacturing cost allocations and completed production reports, sales and sales returns documents.					
• Select a sample of supplier's documentation, manufacturing cost allocations and completed production reports, sales and sales returns documents and trace this to the relevant entries in the general ledger inventory accounts.					
• For items selected, recalculate amounts involved, inspect evidence of authorization and occurrence of transactions.					
Perform cut-off tests of the main transaction flows, e.g. purchases, sales returns, sales and manufactured goods transferred from production immediately preceding and following the financial year-end:	×	×		×	
• Ascertain the last document numbers at year-end for goods received notes and delivery notes and scrutinize the sequence reports to detect any higher numbers recorded in the current financial period or missing sequence numbers for transactions omitted or incorrectly allocated to the following accounting period.					

SUBSTANTIVE TESTS	AUDIT OBJECTIVES				
	C	O/E	M/V	R/O	P/D
4. Tests of details of inventory balances:					
Observe client's physical inventory counts:	×	×	×		
• Agree date and time.					
• Evaluate adequacy of count instructions.					
• Observe procedures followed by client and consider adequacy for ensuring count is complete, accurate.					
• Observe procedures for identifying obsolete and slow moving items, note items for later follow up.					
• Observe client procedures for establishing a correct purchase, manufactured items transferred and sales cut-offs at count date.					
• Observe procedures for ensuring all count slips or tags have been accounted for.					
• Select inventory items for tests counts and retain for later follow through to inventory listing.					
• Ascertain by enquiry that counts have been conducted at all locations at which inventory is held – consider whether audit staff need attend at other locations.					
Ascertain by enquiry whether any inventory on hand is consignment inventory held for the consignee, or whether the client has placed consignment inventory with any distributor who is holding inventory at the count date.				×	
Obtain final inventory listings from count and test for *completeness, existence and measurement*:	×	×	×		
• Trace counts noted at inventory count to final listing.					
• Using CAATs, recalculate extensions and total inventory amounts.					
• Inspect client's count tags or slips for items on final count listings.					
• Agree total of listing to general ledger inventory balances and inspect reconciliations of cut-off items at date of count.					
• Inspect adjustments made for differences and write-offs.					
• Inquire about negative balances in listing and nil balances for main product lines.					
Inspection, computation, enquiry and confirmation of inventory pricing:			×		
• Select a sample of purchased merchandise items and inspect supplier invoices for prices.					
• Select a sample of manufactured goods and inspect the Inventory Job Card and Production records – recalculate the allocation of labour and overhead costs and, where applicable enquire how standard costing variances have been dealt with.					

SUBSTANTIVE TESTS	AUDIT OBJECTIVES				
	C	O/E	M/V	R/O	P/D
• Obtain confirmations regarding inventory held at other locations, or obtain evidence that amounts held are not material, may have sent staff to attend selected counts.					
Inspect contracts for pledge of inventories and consignment agreements.				X	X
Inspection, computation, enquiry and confirmation of the net realizable value of inventory.			X		
• For selected items inspect sales subsequent to year end to ensure prices exceed inventory cost.					
• Select slow-moving, obsolete items and excess holdings and inspect sales invoices – consider client proposed write-downs.					
• Enquire about any general provisions for write-downs, and the consistency with prior years provisions.					
• Consider entity and industry trends and changes planned – potential impact on inventory – any inventory redundancies likely?					
5. Presentation and disclosure:					X
Determine if accounts payable have been properly classified and presented in the draft financial statements in accordance with AC 108 of GAAP, Companies Act requirements and the accounting policies of the entity.					
Review the disclosures relating to security provided to suppliers or other creditors by means of a pledge of inventory.					
Enquire whether all contingent liabilities and purchase commitments of the entity have been properly disclosed.					

Table 14.10 Framework for a substantive audit programme for production and inventory transactions and balances

14.3.2 Substantive analytical procedures

From the discussion earlier in the chapter it is evident that in auditing inventory balances, the auditor may perform a variety of substantive analytical procedures to gain evidence in support of several audit objectives. In performing analytical procedures, the auditor is likely to:

• consider the knowledge of the client and economic and industry circumstances to determine whether inventory balances appear justified and reasonable;

• use CAATs to download inventory master files and general ledger files to calculate financial and operational ratios and compare the results with expectations, for example: gross margins for different product lines – are these as expected, based on the auditor's knowledge regarding mark-ups applied by client? Have inventory turnover rates, or activity levels, changed for significant inventory line items?

- analyse month-by-month movements and analyses on a geographic basis and consider whether these are in line with seasonal variations or economic factors; and

- extract lists of slow moving items in inventory, or items that have not moved for more than six months, items for which there are negative balances.

The auditor should take care not to place over-reliance on averages calculated, since these may hide significant underlying trends. Consequently, analytical procedures should probe individual item or category level relationships, as the potential risk of significant misstatement may not be the same for all items of inventory.

Example

An entity has recently opened fashion stores in another country where it is trying to break into an established retail market.

The risk of overstatement of the carrying value of such inventory may be higher than that for the local inventory holdings, since management may not have judged the potential market correctly and increased provisions for potential write-downs of inventory may be needed for the inventory located in the foreign country. In addition, errors may have arisen in the *measurement* of inventory costs due to the complexities associated with exporting, foreign currency translation and import duties. Consequently, while happy to rely on tests of controls over the inventory held locally, the auditor may decide to direct more extensive substantive tests of detail at the *existence* and *valuation* assertions of the inventory in the foreign country operations.

The auditor would need to ascertain the key performance indicators used by management to control inventory levels and cost of sales and sales, and ascertain what action has been taken with regard to any indicators that indicate potential errors or unexplained differences.

14.3.3 Substantive tests of detail of production transactions

The substantive tests of detail of production and inventory transactions are set out in Table 14.10. Below follows a brief discussion of considerations affecting the substantive tests of detail performed by the auditor, as related to the three main areas of raw materials, that is, work in progress, manufactured goods and merchandise. Bear in mind that tests of detail would be performed on a sample of transactions selected and will not usually involve an audit of every single transaction.

14.3.3.1 Raw materials

The audit of raw materials purchased is discussed in chapter 13. Clearly, audit procedures performed over such purchases already provide evidence of the *completeness* and *measurement* of the amounts to be allocated on the issue of the raw materials to production jobs. Thus the tests of detail of production transactions will relate to determining that all raw materials issued to production are accounted for by a transfer of their cost from the raw materials inventory to the relevant production cost and ultimately to manufactured inventory and cost of sales. Inspection of sequence tests and exception reports of unmatched pre-numbered raw material requisitions and pre-numbered raw material issues slips provide the means for assessing the *completeness* of raw material costs allocated to production runs.

Depending on the nature of the production process, the raw materials would either all be issued at the start of the production process or at different stages of the production process. The client's production records, such as job cards and production reports, usually include information about the variety of processes the auditor may expect to encounter. Determination of the raw material costs to be allocated will depend on the accounting policies of the entity, but where actual costs are allocated these would usually be either the specific costs of the raw materials (if separately identifiable), or the cost of raw materials determined on a first-in-first-out basis.

Where the entity uses a standard costing system, the raw material costs allocated will be based on the approved standard cost with any price or usage variance recorded. Management on an annual basis usually determines standard material costs. Where the raw material inventory itself is valued at standard cost, the auditor must take care to ensure that it approximates actual cost for purposes of allocation to the production jobs and as reflected in the balance sheet at the period end. The *existence, measurement and valuation* of raw material inventory balances at period end is discussed in the section covering substantive tests of balances.

14.3.3.2 Work in progress

Job order and batch production

The aim is for the auditor to be satisfied that materials issued, direct wages and other relevant costs incurred are accounted for in charges to work in progress. The auditor should therefore review the system of controls in these areas and read any exception reports to management regarding errors and deficiencies and steps taken to rectify them. The reader is referred to Table 14.10 for a discussion of the matters to be considered.

The extent of the substantive tests of detail will depend on the auditor's assessment of the effectiveness of the controls and evidence obtained from substantive analytical procedures. The substantive tests of detail will generally be directed to inspections of documents supporting the various cost allocations for a sample of production jobs selected. This will include the inspection of higher level reconciliations and corrective action taken to rectify errors and fraud identified in exception reports or from reconciliation procedures agreeing work in progress to underlying source documents. In particular the auditor should:

- Determine whether the total cost of materials issued in a month (or other period) per the requisition notes is matched by a charge to work-in-progress control account.

- Scrutinize a sample of job records to ascertain whether the direct labour hours allocated to costs have been reconciled to underlying wage records and that factory wages costs are allocated either directly or indirectly to jobs in progress, the auditor should enquire into any marked differences.

- Rates charged to jobs for direct machine hours worked and overhead expenses should be approved by management and applied on a consistent basis to all jobs in progress. The auditor should recalculate the overhead allocations and enquire about the basis of allocation, ensuring that it is consistent with prior years and that the underlying assumptions of management are reasonable.

- Examine a sample of completed job records for goods manufactured to specific customer order and note whether each bears the serial number of an invoice to a customer. The customer invoices for a sample of completed jobs should be inspected to establish that the jobs have indeed been charged out and the costs transferred to cost of sales.

- Scrutinize the work-in-progress control account for jobs cancelled and written off; inspect evidence of authorization for each job written off and be satisfied that there are good reasons for the write-off.

- Finally, the auditor should inspect the transfers from work in progress to finished goods inventory for completed jobs or production runs, ensuring that the accumulated costs have been transferred from work in progress to finished goods inventory.

Continuous process production

In continuous process production the raw materials are fed in at one end and pass through one or more processes, the final product emerging at the other end. The products are usually fairly similar, though they may vary in size and shape. Control over production is usually based on a formula from which can be estimated the output of finished products for a given input of materials, allowing for expected losses in processing.

The auditor should enquire into the controls laid down and test their effectiveness. In particular, two areas should be considered, namely:

- Accounting for the scheduled quantity of completed products from a production run by receipt into finished goods store or charges (per sales invoices) direct to customer(s); and

- Accounting for losses in production beyond the expected, and corrective action taken to minimize them. Reference should be made to any standard text on cost and management accounting for details of the methods employed.

14.3.3.3 Finished goods and merchandise inventory

The auditor should enquire into the system in use, read the reports to management on tests of the system's operation and note any reported deficiencies. These should be followed through to determine whether effective action was taken, or is being taken, to correct the position. The auditor's work should include, where relevant:

- inspection of documents for completed jobs transferred from production to receipt of finished goods into warehouse;

- inspection of suppliers' invoices to receipt of merchandise into warehouse;

- inspection of issues of finished goods, and/or merchandise, to cost of sales and related sales invoices; and

- observation of the operation of security checkpoints at the only exits through which goods issued should pass.

A review by the auditor of any available current trading accounts may complement the audit work discussed in this chapter in providing a sound base on which to assess the *completeness and measurement* of the transactions relating to the production and issue of goods.

14.3.3.4 Testing cut-off of purchase, manufacturing and sales transactions

The purpose and procedures for testing the cut-off of purchases and sales transactions in relation to accounts payable and accounts receivable are discussed in chapters 12 and 13 and will thus not be dealt with further here. The cut-off for manufactured goods, however, must be checked to determine the date of transfer from work in progress to finished inventory and to ensure that inventory amounts are not 'double-counted' and included in both work in progress and finished goods.

The cut-off procedures in each case involve the inspection of the documents providing evidence of the timing/date on which goods were received (purchases of raw materials and merchandise and sales returns), delivered (sales) or transferred from production to finished inventory and received by the finished goods stores (manufactured goods). The auditor would normally select several goods received notes, delivery notes and completed production reports before and after the period end to determine that the transactions were recorded in the correct period. Exception reports of missing sequence numbers of any of these documents should be inspected to determine whether the transactions have indeed been omitted or have been recorded, and if so whether they have been recorded in the correct period. The evidence gathered from the cut-off procedures relates to the *completeness, occurrence and measurement* assertions.

To achieve these audit objectives the auditor should make such enquiries and conduct such tests as to obtain sufficient appropriate audit evidence that proper precautions are taken to guard against errors (unintentional or deliberate) at the financial period end arising from the following risks:

- Omission of stock on hand from inventory;
- Omission of inventory in transit, or in the hands of agents, from the inventory;
- Duplication of the same inventory items;
- Inclusion of inventory, already sold and invoiced but not yet delivered;
- Omission of invoices from the purchase record relating to stock included in the inventory; and
- Pricing and net realizable value errors, especially of items considered obsolete or damaged and those arising from computation errors.

14.3.4 Substantive tests of detail for inventory balances

Table 14.10 sets out a framework of a substantive audit programme to address specific risks of significant misstatement in production and inventory transactions and balances. A further discussion follows here to enable readers to understand the complexity of performing inventory verification and to draw attention to some of the aspects that must be taken care of by the auditor in various circumstances.

The auditor should enquire how management proposes to establish the figure for inventory. Where no continuous inventory records are maintained it is clear that an inventory count, at least annually, is required. Indeed section 284 of the Companies Act specifically requires a company to keep statements of annual stock counts. The audit of inventory quantities is discussed below, as are the audit of work in progress and contract work in progress, which involves special considerations.

14.3.4.1 Where continuous inventory records are not maintained

Planning for a physical inventory count

The establishment of reasonably accurate figures for inventory quantities requires methodical planning prior to the count, which should include the following:

- *Fixing the date:* All employees concerned with the count should be informed, well in advance, of the date of the count, or dates, where the count will occupy several days.

- *Fixing responsibility:* Responsibility for the work should be clearly defined and all staff involved in the count informed to facilitate cooperation. This may be done by dividing the building(s), or portions thereof, in which inventories are stored, into clearly defined areas and assigning each of these to a particular person as supervisor. Counters are then assigned to each supervisor.

- *Control over stationery:* It is imperative to maintain control over the medium used to record the count, whatever the method of recording may be, to ensure accountability for all count forms issued. Thus when inventory count sheets or tags are used these should be pre-numbered and a record made of those issued. The sheets or tags should at the end of the count be checked against the prelisting. Analogous to this control is the numbering of all shelves and/or bins in which inventory may be kept, the prelisting of all such numbers, and accounting for them all on the inventory count sheets at the close of the inventory count.

- *Control over inventory movement:* In law, goods remain the property of the seller until delivery. In practice, however, unopened packages from suppliers for which invoices have not yet been received may be omitted from inventory, and inventory sold, set aside and invoiced may be treated as sales. The effect on profit of the latter is unlikely to be significant so long as the client is consistent in the treatment of such items. The important point is that at or around the financial year-end care should be taken to match goods received into inventory with the recording of the relevant invoices, and vice versa; and similar matching accorded to goods invoiced to customers.

- To this end, a *cut-off* point should be established, to designate the exact point of time up to which goods received are to be included in inventory, and sales made treated as a reduction thereof. After such point goods received from suppliers and goods sold are treated as having been received and issued in the new financial year, the relevant invoices from suppliers and to customers being booked in that year.

- Care must be taken to ensure that a correct cut-off will be obtained at the date of the count for purchases, sales and inter-branch transfers of goods and goods in transit at the year-end. Meticulous recording is required to provide the information for the adjustments. Some undertakings, to avoid difficulties envisaged in this respect, arrange with suppliers to suspend delivery of goods and close their businesses to customers for the inventory count period.

- *Instructions to staff performing the count:* Explicit explanations and instructions in writing should be given to all staff participating in the count and meetings of the appropriate executives and staff should be held to answer employees' queries regarding these instructions. The explanation and instructions should cover the:
  – overall inventory count plan;

- preparation of inventory prior to the count;
- method of counting;
- method of recording the counts;
- responsibility for issuing, collecting and controlling records; and
- the addressee's specific task.

All participants should be fully informed during the planning stages of the procedures to be adopted for the count and each person's part therein, thus providing a framework for an efficient and accurate inventory count. During this period the inventory should be prepared for the count. Care should be taken to identify and separate slow-moving, obsolete and damaged inventory. Good housekeeping, such as neat stacking, like items brought together, aisles kept clear, and other means of facilitating the count should be attended to at this stage.

The inventory count

The actual counting and recording of the inventory should be done under proper supervision and the instructions issued strictly followed.

Provision should be made for the counting, the recording and the checking to be distinct functions. This is usually achieved by having two employees associated with each item counted: A counts, B records; B recounts and A checks the record. Alternatively or additionally, other pairs of employees, testing the counts previously recorded, may do the checking.

The procedure to be followed, where differences arise, with regard to reporting to the supervisor and adjusting the records should be laid down in advance and strictly adhered to.

All counters, recorders and checkers should sign or initial the count sheets (or other record), identifying their functions. The supervisor should scrutinize the record for such signatures or initials and add his or her own.

At the conclusion of the count all count sheets or tags issued – used, unused or spoilt – should be accounted for, first to each supervisor and then to the executive in charge of the whole operation.

The auditor should obtain from the client a copy of the plan of procedures and of written instructions to staff. By a scrutiny of these and discussion with the executive in charge (and, if thought desirable, by attendance at briefing sessions of count personnel), the auditor should be satisfied that the planned control over the count as laid down by management is satisfactory. Prior to this the auditor should have examined the procedure for recording goods received and issued, which would usually be done when conducting the audit of purchases and sales.

The auditor's next step is to ascertain whether the procedures laid down by management are in fact implemented by the staff making the count. The auditor would usually achieve this by attending the inventory count in person.

Observation of the count of inventory

In recording the observation of the client's inventory count procedures, the auditor should proceed in the following manner:

- Obtain (or make) a rough plan of the premises and visit these in the company of an official. During the tour the auditor should observe and note, *inter alia*:
  - areas where high-value items are situated; and
  - inventories which may be troublesome, such as those types that are difficult to count.

- Plan the work to be done during observation, paying particular attention to likely problem areas.

- Arrive at the premises on the day (or first day) of the inventory count prior to its commencement:
  - to observe the issue of count sheets to the respective staff members responsible, and the recording of their serial numbers; and
  - to record the last serial number of the documents issued on receipt and issue of goods into and out of inventory.

- Visit the areas where counting is in progress and observe whether:
  - the count is being done competently, conscientiously and in accordance with instructions;
  - the tags or count sheets are being properly written up;
  - any deterioration of stock overlooked at prior sorting is noted by the counter and recorder; and
  - the procedure of checking the count is proceeding according to instructions.

- Observe the manner in which the inventory count is completed:
  - to ascertain whether instructions in this regard are properly implemented;
  - to witness the return of tags or count sheets to the responsible official; and
  - to note whether all tags or count sheets are accounted for by checking (or testing) the sequence of tags or count sheets returned – used, spoilt and unused – with the record of those issued.

- Settle queries arising from the foregoing with the appropriate supervisor, or with the executive in charge of the whole inventory counting process where necessary.

- Complete the audit working papers on the observations made, noting any weakness in the procedures or failure to implement them. Summarize the conclusions about all aspects of the inventory count.

- Report to management any weaknesses observed in the procedures or implementation thereof which were not eliminated during the count. File a copy in the working papers and ascertain subsequently whether management has taken appropriate action to investigate the matters raised and to rectify them. This may require a recount in particular areas or merely an adjustment of the procedures for subsequent counts.

- It is the practice of some audit firms to make photocopies of the count sheets (or to take hash totals and/or record details of blank lines on the count sheets) to avoid the possibility of these being altered after the count. Further, any alterations to count sheets made at the time of the count should be initialled by counters/supervisors at that time, thus eliminating the possibility of later adjustments going undetected.

Test counts by the auditor

The auditor needs to perform test counts as part of the audit of inventories. This is necessary for the following two reasons:

- in order to ascertain whether the count procedures are properly implemented the auditor should be satisfied not only that the counters have observed the formalities laid down but that they did in fact record the correct inventory quantities;
- having observed the effectiveness of control (laid down and implemented) the auditor should be satisfied that the record of inventory is acceptable for incorporation in the financial statements and to this end he or she should make a test of the entries in the record.

Where test counts are made they should be recorded in sufficient detail to enable the auditor to trace the items to the final inventory sheets. This should be done by listing:

- the tag or count sheet number;
- the location and description of the item;
- the unit used (quantity or weight);
- the quality or grade (which may in some cases be identified by the maker's name); and
- the quantity.

14.3.4.2 Where continuous inventory records are maintained

Inventory records and inventory control

Continuous inventory records (the perpetual inventory) may be kept by a client and, usually, are kept by manufacturing concerns to enable costs of production to be recorded and controlled from day to day and to account for raw materials, work in progress and finished goods at any time. Where such records are kept they are usually in quantity only in the stores, but in both quantity and value in the accounting records.

The quantities recorded on the continuous inventory record as being on hand at any time should be the subject of test counts and comparisons by staff other than store staff, so that all items are subject to check several times in the year. Tests of quantities recorded as received and issued with the relevant received and requisition notes should also be made.

The management should lay down procedures for making such tests, keeping a record of items for which test counts have been made, reporting differences arising, and adjusting differences. If the system is sound, the continuous inventory record can then be relied upon to represent the quantities of inventory at any time and a complete inventory count at the financial year-end is unnecessary. The management should, however, give careful attention to the question of cut-off at the close of the financial year and lay down precise rules for dealing with this matter.

Testing the system

The auditor should proceed as follows:

- Obtain from the management details of procedures laid down for testing the records and a copy of the record of tests made, observations thereon, adjustments required and when made.

- Consider the laid-down procedure and, if necessary, discuss it with the management.

- Scrutinize at least some of the relevant records to be satisfied that adjustments required have been made.

- Test the receipts and issues on a sample of the inventory records with the receipt and requisition notes.

- Note the cut-off point and trace some of the receipts and issues, just before and after cut-off, per the relevant documents, to the entries on the inventory records, to obtain satisfaction that the dates coincide.

- Conduct test counts of items and agree the quantities per the counts with the balances on the relevant inventory records, investigating and clearing any differences.

In some cases, only a few types of materials are involved, such as a few grades of coal dealt in by a coal merchant, and in such cases the record of receipts and issues may be by means of quantity columns in the purchases and sales records. The audit procedure in these circumstances remains broadly as described above, but clearly in a more simplified form. But problems may be encountered in the physical verification of inventory of coal (or similar bulk inventory). A fairly common practice is for the coal dumps to be measured and converted into tons; the auditor, with a little ingenuity, can usually gauge whether the inventory figures are fair approximations of the quantities actually on hand. There may be cases where the measurement of bulk inventories can be done only by experts, and the auditor in such cases would accept a certificate of quantity and value from them.

Where legislation requires detailed inventory records to be kept – for example, the gold book in the case of a manufacturing jeweller, or vehicle register in the case of a new vehicle distributor such as Ford, BMW and VW – the auditor should inspect the records to see that they are properly maintained.

14.3.4.3 Multiple shop inventory control and testing

Another form of continuous stock record is that operated by multiple shops and departmental stores. In these cases the inventory in the central warehouse is closely controlled in the manner described above and the audit procedure is thus similar to that already discussed. Goods issued and on display in the shops (departments or counters), however, are dealt with differently. The usual procedure is for a shop (department or counter) inventory account to be debited at selling price (applying the stipulated mark-up set by management), credited with the sales, the balance at any time representing the inventory selling price in the shop (department or counter).

Management procedures for accounting for and control of such inventories should include requisitions from the main store, control of cash received (or charges to customers) arising from sales, and test counts of inventory in the shops (departments or counters) to establish whether the inventories recorded as being on hand do, in fact, exist. A record of such counts, differences arising, and action taken to rectify differences should be filed.

The auditor should obtain a copy of the procedures adopted by management, consider their efficacy and, if necessary, discuss them with appropriate officials. The auditor should scrutinize a copy of the record of inventory counts and differences and note what action was taken in respect of the latter. The shop (or similar) inventory accounts should be tested with the relevant requisitions and sales records (cash and/or credit). Test counts of inventory in some of the shops (departments or counters) should also be made and compared with the figures shown in the relevant count sheets and inventory accounts at selling price. The auditor should check the reduction of selling price to cost price by the application of the entity's gross profit margins.

14.3.4.4 Work in progress

What has been said above applies to complete, identifiable inventory items. In the case of work in progress, however, it is not always easy to identify the kind and quantity of products in the making and someone from the technical staff of the client may be required to accompany the auditor when making an inspection of incomplete production. Even other means of verifying work in progress may have to be considered.

Work in progress, for audit purposes, may be divided broadly into four classes:

- Job order production;
- Batch production;

- Continuous process production; and
- Uncompleted contracts.

The approach to their verification is discussed accordingly.

Job order production

Authority for and evidence of jobs in progress are usually to be found in the form of job order records which contain, *inter alia*, the description of the job (including quantity), production serial number, date of commencement, the layout of the work to be done, the progress of the job to date and the accumulated costs.

These records are kept in a jobs-in-progress file. When a job is completed the record is matched with the invoice to the customer. The cards remaining in the file represent the work in progress at that date. As work progresses the costs are charged to the relevant jobs and the cost totals to work-in-progress control account. All jobs in respect of work in progress can, therefore, be accounted for by inspecting the serial numbers of jobs commenced and those completed and delivered, and by agreeing the total costs per the records with the balance on the control account.

Work in progress in job order production is usually not too difficult to identify – for example, 50 castings of a particular design for customer, some in the form of rough castings, others represented by moulds into which the metal has been poured.

In such circumstances the auditor should proceed as follows:

- Obtain the records of incomplete jobs.

- Agree the last serial number with the last authority for commencement of a job.

- Agree the total costs in the individual job records with the balance on the work-in-progress control account and work-in-progress schedule total.

- Test individual job records for completed jobs with the relevant invoices to customers and be satisfied that the job descriptions and serial numbers agree.

- Test the records for jobs completed just before and after the financial year-end with the relevant invoices for cut-off.

- Choose a sample of the individual job records for incomplete jobs and, accompanied by an appropriate member of the production staff, inspect the jobs in the factory, identifying as far as is practicable the jobs as described in the records.

- Clear any queries with the production staff member or higher authority if thought necessary.

- Note the serial numbers for jobs inspected and any comments thereon and file in the audit file.

Batch production

This follows much the same lines as for job order production except that the final product may go to a finished goods warehouse instead of directly to a customer. The procedure for delivery to the warehouse, accounting therefor, and cut-off at the close of the financial year is similar to that described above and the auditor should thus conduct the count and related audit work in the manner described for job order production.

Continuous process production

In continuous process production the identity of the articles being produced may emerge only at the end of the process, as for example in bottle manufacture where the molten glass is either in the furnace or being led to the machines where it is injected into the bottle moulds. Inspection of work in progress in these circumstances, if it is to be meaningful, would be limited to the bottles which have emerged from the mould and are awaiting the annealing process.

The auditor would be very much in the hands of the technical staff as to the contents of the furnaces and probably the most he or she could do is to ascertain whether the capacities, shown on the work-in-progress schedule, are consistent with those of previous years and that all furnaces, both alight and empty, are accounted for. In such circumstances other evidence may be had by tracing the work in progress, said to exist at balance sheet date per the production order and work-in-progress schedule, through to the delivery of the completed product to finished goods store or customer as the case may be.

In all cases mentioned above, production control procedures should cover the removal of scrap (which may be of considerable value) to a defined area for reuse or sale and accounting therefor, and the auditor should make sure that such procedures exist and that they are implemented. If it is practicable to do so, the auditor should inspect the scrap and form an opinion of the reasonableness of the quantities shown on the inventory sheets.

14.3.4.5 Auditing net realizable value

Inventory[1]

The accepted basis of valuation is the lower of cost or net realizable value. An alternative in appropriate circumstances is the lower of cost or replacement value. This raises three questions:

- What is cost?
- What is net realizable or replacement value?
- How is the comparison between cost and net realizable or replacement value to be made?

---

[1] AC 108.

These questions are discussed and answered below.

Cost

The elements of cost, which make up the total, depend on the type of inventory under consideration. The types usually to be found in a client's business are merchandise, raw materials, work in progress, finished goods and consumable stores.

Merchandise, raw materials and consumable stores

The cost of these goods is composed of the suppliers' invoice price and the related freight, customs duty and clearing charges (unless the goods are held in bond) and carriage inwards to bring the goods to the place of sale or use. The basis of assessing cost may be:

- the invoice, etc., cost identified with the particular item;
- first-in-first-out, where the cost of earlier consignments is charged against income, leaving the cost of later consignments as that of inventory on hand;
- average cost, where each new consignment at a different price results in averaging the cost of all items on hand; and
- standard cost which is acceptable only if it approximates to one of the accepted bases mentioned above.

Work in progress and finished goods

The cost comprises raw materials, labour, other direct charges and a due proportion of variable overheads. The question of a charge for fixed overheads remains and arguments are given for and against its inclusion. A fair conclusion appears to be that fixed costs are incurred to provide the plant facilities for manufacture and as such are as much a cost of work in progress (and finished goods) as are the others, provided that the cost incurred is, in fact, utilized and not lost through a much lower volume of production than that for which the factory is geared. Fixed overheads should, therefore, be charged to work in progress (and finished goods) at a rate based on the normal production of the factory unless there are good reasons for not doing so.

Net realizable value

Net realizable value is the selling price at the close of the financial year (or the period immediately following during which the goods will be sold) less estimated variable costs of selling. Logically, if there is, say, two months' inventory on hand, the selling price should be that obtainable during the two months following the balance sheet date.

In the case of work in progress the proportionate part of the relevant finished goods price should be taken, the proportion depending on the stage the work in progress has reached. The same may be applied to raw materials if it is practical to do so, otherwise replacement value may be used instead.

Replacement value

Where the lower of cost or net realizable value is taken as the valuation, the effect is to account in the current year for anticipated loss. Where, however, the lowest of cost, net realizable value or replacement value is used, the effect is not only to anticipate a loss but also to bring into the current financial statements the effect of a reduction in the normal mark-up. This latter basis of valuation adopted by some companies in the past is not acceptable.

In the case of raw materials the only practical comparison may be (as already noted above) between cost and replacement value.[2]

Making the comparison

The comparison may theoretically be made:

- item by item; or
- group by group (or department by department); or
- in total.

The first method is unlikely to be used because of the time, labour and expense involved in making the comparisons unless the number of items is few, a situation which is not often encountered.

The most practical and usual method is to compare cost with net realizable value (or replacement value) group by group (and maybe department by department).

Obsolete and damaged inventory will of course be listed and treated separately and not included in the comparison.

In summary, the procedures the auditor should perform to obtain evidence that inventories have been written down to net realizable value where this is less than cost, are as follows:

- Ascertain, by enquiry of management, the procedures followed to identify inventory where net realizable value is less than cost.

- Check that the comparison of cost to net realizable value was done on an item by item, or groups of similar items, basis.

- Test the reasonableness of the calculation of net realizable value by: inspecting selling prices on price lists or sales invoices at, and around, the year-end; establishing the selling prices for similar products sold by competitors; considering any market research findings, in particular that covering the post year-end period.

---

[2] See AC 108, paragraph .27.

- Test the accuracy of the client's calculations of any necessary write-down to net realizable value. In this regard, any selling costs need to be taken into account.

- Where computerized inventory records are maintained, it is often the case that the record contains a cost price field and a sales price field. In these circumstances, a CAAT may be used to interrogate the inventory master file to identify inventory items where sales prices are less than cost and to produce a printout of such items, as well as to calculate the total amount by which costs exceed net realizable value for the entire inventory. This amount should be compared to the client's write down.

- Obtain a management representation letter, covering, *inter alia*, management's assertion that inventories are fairly stated at the lower of cost and net realizable value.

14.3.4.6 Contract work in progress

The cost of an uncompleted long-term contract, that is, work in progress, consists of the costs of materials, labour and services used on the contract together, it may be, with a proportion of the concern's overhead expenses apportioned to the contract on some logical basis as, for example, on the total direct costs of all contracts.

It is the practice of contractors to take credit for estimated profit on incomplete contracts other than those which have recently commenced and on which the expenditure to date is small. The basis of taking profit should be such that due regard is paid to the possibility that circumstances may arise later affecting adversely the final profit when the contract is complete.

The percentage of completion method is perhaps the most common method used. Under this method the costs to complete the contract are estimated, the total cost is compared with the contract price (plus any agreed extras) and the resulting profit apportioned on the basis of work done to date. A portion only (for example, two thirds) of that figure should, and usually is, taken credit for, in recognition of future risks.

Some contractors further reduce the figure by taking account of profit only in so far as progress payments have been received from the contractee.

Another method of profit estimation, used where a contract is almost complete, is to estimate the further costs to be incurred, arrive at total cost and compare that with the contract price. The resulting figure is reduced by an estimate for contingencies and the difference taken to account.

Where the comparisons made (as above) result in an estimated loss, provision should, of course, be made for it.

All that has been said above relating to valuation is subject to the principle that there should be consistency from year to year, and within an inventory classification, in the basis used. If a change in a basis is made it should be disclosed, as should the effect thereof on profit, if significant (see section 14.3.5 of this chapter).

The reader is referred to the South African Institute's Statement AC 109, 'Inventories', on accounting for completed construction contracts and contracts in progress.

14.3.4.7 Rights and obligations

Different rights and obligations may apply to inventory held by any entity and it is appropriate that the auditor enquire about any arrangements affecting the ownership of inventory held at the period end to ensure that the appropriate disclosure is made in the financial statements. In addition to the foregoing, the following audit work should be done in the appropriate circumstances.

Inventory not physically on hand but held under documents of title

Where goods are purchased overseas and are in transit at the close of the period, the auditor should check the entries in the inventory records with the relevant invoices and bills of lading. Where *bills of lading* are held by the entity's bankers, as security for advances, the auditor should obtain certificates from the bankers detailing the quantity and invoice price of the inventory to which the bills of lading give title.

Inventory held in bond

Where goods are in a bonded warehouse pending payment of customs duty on the importation, the warrants in respect of the goods should be examined. The inventory should be checked with the warrants. The invoices for the goods in bond should be debited to purchases and credited to accounts payable. Note that the prices of such goods in the inventory exclude customs duty.

Goods sold on 'sale or return'

If the client's business includes the sale of goods on a 'sale or return' basis, the auditor should be satisfied that the goods sent to customers, but not yet returned or sold, are treated as inventory and not as accounts receivable. The value of such goods should be reduced to cost and included in the inventory at that figure.

Inventory held by agents on consignment or by the client as consignee

Where the business of the client includes the sale of goods through agents, certificates of inventory should be obtained from the consignees. The auditor should be satisfied that the amounts of such inventories exist and are properly valued. It may be practicable for a responsible member of the client's staff to visit the agents (or some of them) to inspect the inventory and to determine that the agents' inventories exist and are appropriately valued. In some cases, where the quantity and value of the inventory carried by agents is considerable (for example, agents for the sale of motor vehicles), it may be considered desirable for the auditor to verify the inventories by personally visiting the agents and making a count of the articles. Where the consignee's place of business is in a remote area and the inventory held is substantial, the inspection of the inventory by a local firm of auditors should be considered. A scrutiny of any accounts sales received by the client from the agents after the close of the financial year and before signing the audit report, would provide further evidence of the existence and value of the inventory stated therein.

High-value identifiable items

In some businesses each article, as opposed to a type of article, is identifiable. For example, a motorcar dealer can and does identify, by engine and chassis serial numbers, each car purchased and sold, so that it is possible for a check to be made at any time not only of the number of cars that should be in inventory but of the identity of each car. The motor dealer is required to maintain a register with these details of all new and used vehicles purchased and sold. Examples of businesses where such detailed records should be kept are dealers in valuable gemstones, highly priced antiques or paintings. SAAS 545, 'Auditing fair value measurement and disclosures' provides guidance on determining the fair values of such inventory items to be reflected as the carrying value in the financial statements.

14.3.5 Presentation and disclosure

14.3.5.1 Classification of inventory

AC 108, 'Inventories', sets out the requirements for financial statement disclosures related to inventories in paragraph .32:

'The financial statements should disclose:

(a) the accounting policies adopted in measuring inventories, including the cost formula used,

(b) the total carrying amount of inventories and the carrying amount in classifications appropriate to the enterprise,

(c) the carrying amount of inventories carried at net realizable value,

(d) the amount of any reversal of any write down which is recognized as income in the period in accordance para .29

(e) the circumstances or events that led to the reversal of a write-down of inventories in accordance with para .29, and

(f) the carrying amount of inventories pledged as security for liabilities.'

And in paragraph .34:

'The financial statements should disclose either:

(a) the cost of inventories recognized as an expense during the period, or

(b) the operating costs, applicable to revenues, recognized as an expense during the period, classified by their nature.'

The Companies Act (1973) further requires in paragraph 29 of the Fourth Schedule that inventory be classified under appropriate subheadings which shall include, where applicable: raw materials (including component parts); finished goods; merchandise; consumable stores (including maintenance spares); work in progress (including standing crops); contracts in progress (which should state whether profits have been taken to account or not, and if so, on what basis). Paragraph .33 of AC 108 also reflects these as common inventory classifications for disclosure purposes. It is, therefore, incumbent on the auditor to satisfy himself of the appropriateness of the inventory classifications as well as that of the total inventory figure subject to the foregoing presenting a fair view of inventory, and provision being made for a reduction in the number of categories where circumstances warrant it.

Difficulty may be experienced in classifying inventory in some circumstances. A manufacturer, for example, may have an inventory of component parts, which may be either sold to customers in their present state, or used in the manufacture of other products. It is clear that if the main purpose of acquiring the components were for use in manufacture, a few isolated sales would not alter their classification as raw materials. Where, however, they are acquired for the dual purpose of use in production or selling, the inventory, if material, should be described for what it is, 'Components – for sale or use in production'. In all cases the prime consideration is the presentation of a fair statement of inventory under classification suitable for the business, which requires, *inter alia*, consistency in classifying the inventory.

Consumable stores, it may be noted, should include all items not acquired for sale in their present state or as part of a manufactured article, used in maintaining and operating the business, examples of which are spares, oil and grease, and stationery.

It is the auditor's task to satisfy himself that the inventory classification disclosed in the financial statements fairly represent the facts and that it is used consistently.

14.3.5.2 Bases of measurement

Paragraph .32 of AC 108 requires the bases and the methods used to determine the value of inventory to be disclosed in the accounting policies of the entity.

'Bases' appears to indicate the manner of comparison of cost with net realizable value or other specified value, while 'methods' relates to the manner in which costs have been computed, examples of which are 'first-in-first-out' and 'average cost'. It may be that the words are synonymous. Whatever the difference, if any, the important point is that the manner of: computing the cost, and comparing it with the net realizable value must be disclosed.

A further matter affecting the cost of work in progress and finished goods is the inclusion or exclusion of fixed overhead and a statement of the treatment of such overhead forms part of the disclosure of bases and methods used.

Some companies hold inventories of spares of considerable value for repairs and maintenance to plant. Replacement of plant with machines of more modern design may make part of the spares obsolete and some provision for this may be required. How this provision is computed clearly affects the consumable stores valuation and the amount of reported profit. Accordingly the method of arriving at such a provision requires disclosure.

In the case of a civil engineering concern or similar business undertaking long-term contracts, an element of profit may be included in the uncompleted contracts valuation and a statement of whether profit has been recognized and, if so, the bases for determining the percentage completion for contracts in progress. Adequate provision should be made for anticipated losses on contracts as soon as it is evident that losses may be incurred.

14.3.5.3 Disclosure

Assuming the classifications of inventory of a company are those listed in paragraph .29, the balance sheet and notes to the financial statements should contain the relevant information to comply with the requirements of the Companies Act, the Fourth Schedule and GAAP AC 108, 'Inventories'.

15

Auditing Human Resources/ Payroll Transactions and Balances

Learning objectives

After studying this chapter you should be able to:

1. Describe the nature of the human resource business processes and identify significant classes of payroll transactions and balances.
2. Set audit objectives for the audit of payroll transactions and balances.
3. Describe the functions, related control activities and tests of controls to assess control risk at medium or low for the payroll business process.
4. Explain how to determine an acceptable level of detection risk for payroll transactions and balances.
5. Design substantive audit procedures for payroll balances and other employee benefits.
6. Explain how the auditor ensures the appropriate presentation and disclosure in the audited financial statements of accounting policies and account balances, related to payroll expenses and post-retirement employee benefits.

15.1 NATURE OF HUMAN RESOURCE/PAYROLL TRANSACTIONS

15.1.1 Introduction

The human resource management of business entities encompasses policies and procedures to recruit, compensate and retain competent personnel who are able to contribute towards the development of entities and thus their sustainability. In large entities a dedicated human resource function is often responsible for handling the recruitment and retrenchment of employees, and for ensuring compliance with the myriad of labour laws and regulations governing employer/employee relationships in South Africa. It also assumes responsibility for sector wage negotiations, handling of disciplinary hearings and the development and offering of skills training programmes for staff.

The payroll preparation function, which may be the responsibility of a separate department or that of the human resources department, involves the recording of time worked by employees, the processing of the weekly and monthly payrolls, allocation of payroll expenses and the payment to weekly and monthly paid employees and payroll deductions accounts payable. Payroll processing is one of the activities of an entity that is sometimes outsourced to a payroll service provider. Payroll transactions affect two significant classes of transactions, namely:

- The payment of salaries and wages as part of disbursement and account payable transactions; and
- The allocation of direct and indirect payroll costs to work in progress in a manufacturing concern.

In a medium to small owner-managed business employing few staff, the human resource aspects may be dealt with by the owner manager and a limited number of staff, possibly only one person, may be responsible for the payroll preparation function. In these circumstances, due to the lack of appropriate segregation of duties, the personal supervision of the owner manager is necessary so as to ensure the completeness, occurrence and measurement of the payroll expenditures.

15.1.2 Recent developments in labour legislation

Businesses in South Africa have been affected by sweeping legislative changes since 1994, to re-mediate historical injustices and support efforts to bring the greater portion of the population into the economic mainstream of the country. Government has attempted to create an environment that actively develops skills and creates reasonable access to employment opportunities in the longer term for persons from designated groups in the population.

Since 1994, there has been wholesale repeal of wage and labour legislation that existed for many decades, and the replacement of these with, *inter alia*, the following important and far-reaching new statutes:

- The Labour Relations Act No 66 of 1995;
- The Basic Conditions of Employment Act No 75 of 1997;
- The Employment Equity Act No 55 of 1998; and
- The Skills Development Act No 97 of 1998 and related Skills Development Levies Act No 9 of 1999.

Failure to comply with the terms and conditions of these Acts carry heavy penalties, which potentially impact costs and provisions in the financial statements. Compliance with the provisions of the various Acts has a direct impact on the employment practices of businesses and has necessitated, for larger organizations, the employment of human resources personnel with knowledge of current labour legislation, the use of legal advisers specializing in labour law, and the appointment of equity employment officers to oversee the development and implementation of equity policies.

It is not the purpose of this text to comment on the legal implications of these Acts, but rather to draw the attention of the reader to those aspects that may require consideration in an audit of financial statements or for which the client may seek a related services engagement to obtain assurance regarding the entity's compliance with legislation. Consequently, a brief overview of key legislation provisions is provided as an introduction to the audit of payroll transactions and balances.

15.1.2.1 The Labour Relations Act No 66 of 1995

The Labour Relations Act gives effect to and regulates the rights conferred by section 27 of the Constitution of South Africa namely, that:

- Every person shall have the right to fair labour practices.
- Workers shall have the right to form and join trade unions and employers shall have the right to form and join employers' organizations.
- Workers and employers shall have the right to organize and bargain collectively.
- Workers shall have the right to strike for the purpose of collective bargaining.
- Employers' recourse to lockouts for purposes of collective bargaining shall not be impaired.

The Act regulates the organizational rights of trade unions and employers to promote collective bargaining at the workplace and at sectoral (industry) levels. It regulates the right of employees to strike and seeks to promote worker participation in decision making through workplace forums. This Act also establishes mechanisms for the resolution of labour disputes through statutory conciliation, mediation and arbitration by the Commission for Conciliation, Mediation and Arbitration (the CCMA) and the establishment of the Labour Court and Labour Appeal Court and appointment of the Registrar of Labour Relations. The Act lays down the powers, area of jurisdiction, rules and proceedings to be followed by the CCMA and the two Labour Courts. It also deals extensively with unfair dismissals and, in schedule 8 of the Act, provides a Code of Good Conduct to be followed in dismissals of employees.

15.1.2.2 The Basic Conditions of Employment Act No 75 of 1997

The Basic Conditions of Employment Act regulates the conditions under which full-time and temporary workers may be employed. Sections of this Act provide, *inter alia*, for:

- Working hours (determined with due regard to health and safety of employees);

- Employees' entitlement to annual, sick, maternity and family responsibility leave;
- Remuneration rates for normal and overtime work;
- Employees' details and wage records to be kept by employers;
- Deductions from employees to be made only with the employee's written permission; and
- Appointments and terminations, including payments on termination and severance pay.

The Act prohibits forced labour and the employment of children under 15 years old, and permits the Minister of Labour to make a sectoral determination for particular industries or geographic areas. The Act contains provisions for the monitoring and inspections by labour inspectors and the protection of employees from discrimination. It establishes also the jurisdiction of the Labour Court and Labour Appeal Court and sets out the offences and penalties under the Act.

15.1.2.3 The Employment Equity Act No 55 of 1998

The purpose of the Employment Equity Act, is set out in section 2 as follows:

'... to achieve equity in the workplace by –

(a) Promoting equal opportunity and fair treatment in employment through the elimination of unfair discrimination; and
(b) Implementing affirmative action measures to redress the disadvantages in employment experienced by designated groups, in order to ensure their equitable representation in all occupational categories and levels in the workforce.'

The Act requires every employer to take steps to promote equal employment opportunities in the workplace by eliminating unfair discrimination in any employment practices, and prohibits unfair discrimination against an employee on one or more grounds, including: race, gender, sex, pregnancy, marital status, family responsibility, ethnic or social origin, colour, sexual orientation, age, disability, religion, HIV status, conscience, belief, political opinion, culture, language and birth. Harassment of an employee is regarded as unfair discrimination. The Act prohibits medical testing of an employee unless permitted by legislation; prohibits psychometric testing and similar assessments of an employee unless the test has been scientifically shown to be valid and reliable, can be applied fairly to employees and is not biased against any employee or group. The CCMA has jurisdiction to resolve disputes.

The Act defines a designated employer (one to whom the affirmative action requirements are applicable) as meaning a person who employs 50 or more persons; or employs less than 50 persons but whose annual turnover exceeds an amount specified by industry ranging from R2 million for the agriculture sector to R25 million for the wholesale trade, commercial agents and allied services sector; the average threshold being set at R10 million; a municipality;

and an organ of state. Designated employers are required to implement affirmative action measures for persons from designated groups who are defined as black people (meaning Africans, Coloureds and Indians), women and persons with disabilities. In terms of the Act, designated employers must:

- Consult with its employees from all groups (section 16);

- Analyse its employment policies, practices, procedures and the working environment to identify barriers adversely affecting persons from designated groups including a profile of its employees within each occupational category and level to determine the degree of under-representation of persons from designated groups in the workplace (section 19);

- Prepare and implement an employment equity plan, which will achieve reasonable progress towards employment equity in that employers' workforce (section 20); and report on this to the Director General (section 21); and

- Designate a senior manager as employment equity officer to monitor and implement an employment equity plan (section 24).

Heavy fines, ranging from R500 000 to R900 000 may be levied for contravention of sections 16, 19, 20, 21, 22 and 23 of the Act. The Act establishes also a Commission for Employment Equity and contains provisions for monitoring by employees and trade union representatives, the enforcement of the provisions by labour inspectors; the appointment of a Director-General with wide powers and responsibility for registering designated employers and monitoring compliance with the Act; provides for legal proceedings to resolve disputes; the protection of employee rights and requires evidence of compliance by any employer concluding contracts with the state.

15.1.2.4 The Skills Development Act No 97 of 1998

The purpose of this Act, as expressed in section 2, is to develop the skills of the South African workforce; increase the investment in education and training; encourage employers to provide employees with an active learning environment and opportunities to acquire new skills, encourage workers to participate in learnership programmes and thereby improve employment prospects particularly for previously disadvantaged persons; ensure the quality of education in the workplace and assist work-seekers and regulate employment services. The Act establishes a National Skills Authority and at section 9 establishes the Sector Education and Training Authority (SETA), which is registered for each different sector of the economy.

The main task of each SETA is to develop a sector skills plan by establishing and registering learnership agreements, approving workplace skills plans, allocating grants to employers and promoting education and training programmes to facilitate the development of skills. The SETAs are authorized to collect and distribute the Skills Development Levies from employers in their sector. The Skills Development Levies Act (1999) currently provides for a levy of 1% of workers' monthly remuneration to be paid by employers to the SETA. The employer may, however, apply for funding from the sector SETA for employee training programmes registered with the SETA.

15.1.3 Audit objectives

Before proceeding to identify the objectives of an audit of the payroll, it is appropriate to recognize first the account balances affected by the payroll transactions as set out in Table 15.1 below:

PAYROLL TRANSACTIONS	ACCOUNT BALANCES DEBITED	ACCOUNT BALANCES CREDITED
Short-term and long-term employee benefits accrued	Gross salaries and wages, commissions, bonuses. Manufacturing wages. Directors' emoluments. Employer contributions to employee benefits such as contributions to pension and retirement plans, medical care, housing, cars and free or subsidized goods or services.	Employees for remuneration accrued. Accounts payable for payroll deductions such as SARS, Pension Service providers, Medical Aid, Trade Unions. Accounts payable for employer contributions toward pensions and medical aid.
Payment to employees and payroll deduction creditors	Employees for remuneration accrued. Payroll deduction accounts payable.	Imprest payroll bank account for payments to employees. General bank account for payments to payroll deduction accounts payable.

Table 15.1 General ledger account balances affected by payroll transactions

The auditor needs to gather sufficient appropriate audit evidence regarding specific assertions contained in the income statement and balance sheet balances arising from payroll transactions. In so doing, the auditor should bear in mind the relevant GAAP and Companies Act sections affecting the *recognition, measurement, valuation* and *presentation and disclosure* of employee benefits. The requirements of the JSE Securities Exchange Listing Requirements affecting specific disclosures, for example, details of individual directors' emoluments, must also be considered where the reporting entity is a listed company.

The link between management's assertions in financial statements and the corresponding auditing objectives for payroll transactions and related balances are set out in Table 15.2 below:

MANAGEMENT ASSERTION	AUDIT OBJECTIVES
Payroll transactions	
Completeness	Recorded payroll expenses include all such amounts due for personnel services during the period.
Occurrence/ validity	Recorded payroll expenditures relate to authorized compensation for services rendered during the period by valid employees of the entity, and none are duplicated.
Measurement/ accuracy	All payroll expenses are correctly calculated in accordance with the terms of appointments of staff and remuneration policies adopted by the entity; and are recorded in the correct accounts in accordance with GAAP policies applied on a consistent basis.
Payroll balances	
Completeness	Payroll expenses represent all expenditures incurred for employee benefits earned by them during the period. Payroll liabilities at period end represent all amounts owed at the balance sheet date.
Existence/ occurrence	Payroll expenses represent all expenditures actually incurred for remuneration and benefits earned by valid employees during the period. Payroll liabilities at period end represent amounts properly owed to employees and payroll deduction accounts payable at the balance sheet date.
Measurement/ accuracy	Payroll expenses and payroll accounts payable have been correctly calculated and are recorded in terms of contractual arrangements and laws, regulations applicable to the entity. The recognition and measurement of employee benefits is in accordance with GAAP.

MANAGEMENT ASSERTION	AUDIT OBJECTIVES
Valuation	Where applicable, the fair value measurements of post-retirement benefits for employees have been determined and recognized in accordance with GAAP.
Rights and obligations	Payroll liabilities reflect the actual and constructive obligations of the entity at period end.
Presentation and disclosure	Current payroll expenditures, and accrued payroll liabilities are correctly disclosed and classified in accordance with the Companies Act 1973 and GAAP.

Post-retirement benefits are appropriately disclosed and classified in accordance with GAAP. |

Table 15.2 Management assertions and the related audit objectives for payroll transactions and balances

15.1.4 Understanding the client's business

In planning the audit of the entity's payroll transactions and balances, the auditor needs to understand the significance of employee costs to the entity. In a continuing engagement, the auditor will have gathered knowledge of the client's payroll expenditures from prior audits and this knowledge would need to be updated during the current audit. In order to decide upon the most effective and efficient audit strategy, the auditor's knowledge needs to be sufficient to understand:

● The relative significance of human resource policies and practices and their impact on the payroll expenditures and liabilities of an entity (including procedures to ensure compliance with laws and regulations);

● The nature and complexity of compensation paid, whether hourly, weekly or monthly, and different control activities implemented, including key performance indicators used by management to monitor payroll expenditures and liabilities;

● The dependence of an entity on computerized software packages for payroll processing and maintenance of employee records, and whether this is handled in-house or outsourced to a payroll service provider; and

● The nature of executive compensation packages that may provide an incentive for management and senior employees to misstate financial results, such as substantial share options and bonuses dependent on profit targets being met.

Consideration of materiality

Payroll expenditures in service industries – such as professional firms, educational institutions, the hospitality industry, financial institutions, hospitals, public sector entities, such as municipalities providing services to the communities – are likely to be a significant amount because these are very labour intensive.

Entities involved in high technology industries, such as electronics and computer software development, the design and production of sophisticated medical equipment, and portfolio asset managers in financial institutions, are dependent on the skills and talent of their employees. Consequently, they may devise complex compensation packages to recruit, and retain, the best available personnel. In such an entity, payroll expenditures are likely to be significant notwithstanding there being relatively few employees. Such circumstances may also give rise to expenditures on premiums paid for 'keyman' insurance policies to manage the risk of the loss of skills that could threaten an entity's continuance or profitability.

In manufacturing operations, the significance of payroll expenditure is dependent on the extent to which the production processes are labour intensive. Clients involved in the construction industry are likely to employ both skilled and unskilled labour and the mix of these categories will directly affect the amount of direct and indirect labour costs incurred.

The auditor will seldom be concerned regarding the *completeness* assertion affecting payroll expenditures, as employees will soon complain if they are not paid amounts due to them. What is less likely to be detected, however, is whether or not the entity has paid over timeously, and correctly, all payroll deductions made to the relevant payroll deduction creditors, being SARS for PAYE, retirement funding plans or medical care funds. This may pose a risk of significant misstatement affecting the verification of payroll liabilities at period end as penalties may be levied against the employer should deductions have not been appropriately paid over.

15.1.5 Analysing human resource process level business risks

In analysing the process level business risks for human resources, the auditor should consider the critical success factors and key performance indicators that management has identified. For example, a professional accounting practice, an entity involved in sophisticated technology services or manufacture of sophisticated equipment, or an entity involved in fashion design, will regard as its critical success factors the ability to recruit and retain highly skilled and talented employees in their particular fields.

Should the recruitment practices, or remuneration policies, fail to attract the appropriate quality of skills, or to retain employees with such skills, the ability of the entity to continue successfully is at risk. Management may well have identified key positions and the requisite number and qualifications of personnel to fill these, and will require regular reports to indicate the extent to which these key positions remain vacant.

Another example of human resources process level business risks affecting the critical success factors of many entities, particularly in Southern African countries, is the incidence of HIV/Aids amongst the workforce. Key performance indicators used by senior management may be the number of employees who have voluntarily undergone medical tests to ascertain their HIV status and the percentage, identified as HIV positive, who are participating in medical care programmes established by the entity. Another key performance indicator may be the increase or reduction of the number of labour hours lost each month through sick leave or death and what portion of these appear to be attributable to staff participating in medical care programmes of the entity, versus those not participating, and whether the cause of illness or death appears to be HIV related, as opposed to other illnesses and accidents.

The impact of these matters on the entity may be extensive, causing reduced production capacity and leading to an increase in unproductive costs and reduction in revenues. Management would seek in the longer term to bring the health threat under control to reduce the loss of skilled personnel and lost labour hours through illness and incapacity.

15.1.6 Preliminary assessment of the risk of significant misstatement

Payrolls comprise monthly paid employees on fixed salaries that are reviewed annually, as well as weekly paid employees whose remuneration is based on hours worked and hourly pay rates, where hours worked may fluctuate. In the case of salaried staff, the auditor may be able to obtain a high level of assurance regarding the *completeness, occurrence and measurement* of monthly salary transactions and balances merely from the performance of substantive analytical procedures by way of a weekly or monthly trend analysis of the expenditure and confirmation of period-end balances owing.

In auditing the weekly wages payroll, the auditor may seek to assess control risk as medium to low, by testing specific controls over the *existence* of employees and *occurrence and measurement* of time recording and processing of the weekly wages payroll, in order to accept a higher level of detection risk to justify performing substantive analytical reviews and reducing the extent of substantive tests of detail on the wages expenditure.

Whilst it is true that payroll expenses may have a high inherent risk of fraud due to wages being drawn for non-existent employees and then misappropriated; it is also true that, with the extensive regulation surrounding employee benefits and where the volume and amount of payroll transactions and balances comprise a significant class of transactions, entities will usually implement extensive preventative and detective control activities over payroll processes. Thus, the risk of a significant misstatement remaining is reduced.

In such circumstances, the auditor should ascertain the appropriateness of the design of controls over payroll expenditure to support the medium to low assessment of significant risk remaining. Controls of particular importance, on which the auditor might wish to rely, are the high level detective controls exercised by management in their monitoring procedures.

15.1.7 Consideration of internal control components

15.1.7.1 Control environment

The control environment, as indicated in chapter 9, includes such aspects as *integrity, ethical values and organizational culture, competence of employees, management's philosophy and operating style*, the manner in which the company assigns authority and the way in which it develops its people, and the attention given to control aspects by the board of directors.

The first critical aspect affecting *integrity and ethical values* are the human resource policies and procedures that ensure the recruitment and retention of competent employees. People are critical to an entity's ability to function, and consequently, responsibility for the human resources function is normally assigned to an executive director, or possibly the CEO of the entity to whom the human resources manager will report.

At the executive level, the King II Report (2002, page 64) recommends that the process for recruitment and appointments of directors be transparent and that:

> 'The board of directors should establish a nomination committee comprised of non-executive directors with a majority of independent non-executive directors to recruit and recommend suitable persons for the appointment to the board of directors.
>
> Directors should be given a formal orientation programme to familiarize incoming directors with the company's operations, senior management and its business environment and to induct them in their fiduciary responsibilities and duties.
>
> New directors with no or limited board experience should receive development and education to inform them of their duties, responsibilities, powers and potential liabilities.'

In addition, the King II Report (2002, page 59) recommends that the 'board of directors should establish an independent remuneration committee comprising only independent non-executive directors with authority for determining the remuneration of senior management and executive directors. CEOs may be members of such a committee or invited to provide input, but must be absent from any discussion relating to their own packages'. The executive directors would normally appoint such a remuneration committee to determine and review salary levels and compensation packages.

With regard to other employees in the organization, executive directors together with human resource personnel would generally handle sector negotiations between management and trade unions, or other employee bodies, for wage determinations on a periodic basis.

Management's operating style should convey a responsible and ethical approach to the running of the business. They should be seen to be monitoring the control activities and should avoid attempts to deliberately override controls. Delegation of authority should be done in such a way as to make human resources and payroll staff accountable for their actions and the monitoring procedures of management should enforce these processes. If these various factors are not implemented or managed effectively they will undoubtedly increase the risk of significant misstatement.

The human resource policies should cater for the employment of human resource and payroll personnel who are knowledgeable about labour laws and regulations and tax laws affecting payroll, and in addition, a company should actively support the training of its staff to develop skills needed. This should minimize the risk of errors and fraud and improve the chances of detection and early correction should they arise.

A sound control environment will provide for accountability in managing the human resources and payroll process level business risks. This will then be monitored by establishing the critical success factors and key performance indicators, how these are reported, and monitored, and what action is taken, by whom, and how frequently, to ensure proper accountability and the management of the risks of fraud and error in the process.

15.1.7.2 Risk assessment

Management's risk assessment processes related to payroll transactions and balances should identify and evaluate the risks of errors and fraud in processing the payroll so as to limit these. Management's risk assessment should address potential errors and fraud that might occur in authorization processes for the hiring and firing of staff. The risk assessment should also consider the risk of incorrect recognition and measurement of employee benefits. Accounting staff should be suitably qualified to deal correctly with the GAAP requirements relating to the accounting for employee benefits. Management should be seen to implement effective, appropriate controls over aspects where the risks are most significant so as to ensure the completeness, occurrence and accuracy of time recording and the processing and payment of payroll expenditures. The auditor needs to obtain an understanding of the processes followed by management in order to evaluate the effectiveness of control activities implemented by them.

15.1.7.3 Information and communication

The auditor needs to understand the input, processing and output processes, including the design and operation of preventative and detective controls, implemented by the organization for recording its payroll and maintaining employee and payroll records. In most instances, the payroll recording will be computerized and comprise employee master files with standing data, such as rates of pay and deductions, and transaction files of weekly and monthly payrolls that are processed and updated to the general ledger master file in an update run. As payroll transactions are all generated internally, the inherent risk of error and fraud is high.

The auditor must consider whether the division of responsibilities between the human resources staff and payroll staff is likely to limit the risk of fraud and error. Where the employee standing data master file is maintained on-line, access to it should be restricted to senior human resource staff, whereas the employee master file containing cumulative pay data would be maintained by the payroll staff and updated after every weekly wage or monthly salary payroll run. Consequently, many payroll systems will involve a batch input and computerized processing system rather than an on-line real-time update system. Another feature of computerized payroll systems is that payment of amounts due to employees, other than for cash pay-outs of weekly wages, will invariably be paid with EFT payments credited directly to the employees' banking accounts, usually by means of an electronic tape sent to the entity's bank on a monthly or weekly basis. Strict controls must be implemented over the loading of new employees' banking account details for purposes of the EFT payments and should, as with the recording of employee hiring and firing, be restricted to the human resource staff rather than the payroll staff.

The auditor may encounter situations where the payroll processing function is outsourced and in such circumstances needs to understand the terms of the service level agreement with the outsource provider. The auditor should also obtain an understanding of the division of responsibilities between the functions performed by the client entity and those performed by the outsource provider. It may be necessary to review controls at the outsource provider or to obtain a report from the outsource provider's auditor of the effectiveness of controls implemented. The service level agreement, and practical outsource arrangements, should provide for the employer to control any changes to standing data master file records. The reader is referred to the discussion on this aspect in chapter 9.

15.1.7.4 Monitoring

Monitoring activities will include a review by senior management of key performance indicators for human resources and payroll related matters, as discussed earlier in this chapter. Aspects to review include: reports of staff turnover (which may be analysed at departmental levels); the reconciliation of gross payroll totals and any changes to pay rates; the review of reconciliations of payroll deduction accounts payable; reports by internal audit of the effectiveness of controls over payroll processes and reports to the board of directors by the audit committee or board remuneration committee regarding executive remuneration packages. Feedback would usually be sought from employees and employee organizations regarding human resource policies and procedures, and periodic remuneration negotiations.

15.2 CONTROL ACTIVITIES AND TESTS OF CONTROL OF PAYROLL TRANSACTIONS

15.2.1 Processing payroll transactions

This section discusses first the typical documents and records that may be encountered and thereafter the functions and control activities that may typically occur for payroll transactions.

15.2.1.1 Common documents and records for payroll transactions

Documents

Documents may be in a hard copy format or with computerized systems details may be captured electronically and only printed out at the end of the payroll preparation process. The documents and records to be maintained by an employer in South Africa are set out in sections 29 to 35 of the Basic Conditions of Employment Act (1997). The documents set out below are those that provide input for capturing and processing employee standing data and current payroll data necessary for the preparation for each payroll and the resultant output and do not include all possible documents and correspondence that may be contained in an employee's file by either the human resource or payroll department.

DOCUMENTS	NATURE OF DOCUMENT
Pre-numbered employee change form	This document should be initiated by the human resources department. It contains the employee's personal details used for recording the standing data on hiring of an employee and any change thereafter, affecting the employee's status for payroll purposes. This information is captured as standing data in the *employee standing data* master file. The employee change form should be signed by the person/s authorized to approve hiring, firing and changes to standing data, such as rates of pay and deductions.
Employee personnel file	Should contain all communications relating to the employee's employment, including the letter of appointment, rates of pay and any increases, deductions authorized by the employee, leave record, employee evaluations, employee non-cash benefits, such as share options granted, loans and advances, disciplinary hearing details and outcomes. It is usual practice for each employee to be allocated an employee number for identification in the computerized standing data and payroll records.

DOCUMENTS	NATURE OF DOCUMENT
Clock Card or Employee ID Smart Card	This records the times of arrival at and departure from work by the employee. In a manual clocking system the *Clock Card* should be placed on a rack at the entrance to the place of work near the clocking-in machine, which records the time of arrival and departure when the card is inserted into it. In a computerized environment the clock card is usually replaced by an *Employee ID Smart Card* that is used to gain access to the premises by swiping it through a card reader that activates the opening of the barrier guarding access; at the end of the day the card is swiped through the card reader to record the time of departure. The system electronically records the time spent by the employee at work and calculates hours worked for the payroll week.
Job Time Ticket	In a manufacturing environment the time worked by manufacturing employees on individual jobs or production runs are recorded on the *Job Time Ticket* and captured into the relevant payroll run for purposes of allocating the labour costs from the weekly or monthly payroll to work in progress for the particular job or production run.
Employee Pay Slip	This document, which reflects the information contained on the payroll printout, is printed and given to each employee as his/her record of remuneration.
Payroll cheque or EFT transfer advice	Where the employee is paid by cheque, this would be printed out by the system, inserted in an envelope together with the *Employee Pay Slip* and given to the employee. If payment is made by EFT this fact would be printed on the employee's pay slip, indicating the Bank and Account number into which it has been deposited.
Pay packet	Where the employee is paid in cash, usually for weekly paid employees who might not have banking accounts, the net pay due per the *payroll printout* is inserted into a pay envelope, either by payroll staff or a cash security company appointed to perform this task. The filled *Pay Packet* which includes the *Employee Pay Slip* is given to the employee at the wage pay-out.

DOCUMENTS	NATURE OF DOCUMENT
IRP 5 or IT 3 Tax Certificate	These are pre-numbered tax certificates reflecting an employee's gross earnings and allowable tax deductions such as pension or retirement fund contributions and medical aid contributions and PAYE or SITE deducted and paid to SARS by the employer during the year.
Payroll Imprest Banking Account Bank Statements	These are received from the bank in respect of the *Payroll Imprest Banking Account*. These details are highly confidential and accordingly this account will be reconciled to the payroll by senior payroll staff and the monthly bank reconciliation reviewed by the Human Resource manager.
Various returns to Payroll Deduction Accounts Payable	These would comprise the standard monthly returns to SARS for PAYE and SITE tax deductions from employees, employee and company contributions to Pension, Retirement and Medical Aid Funds, employee contributions to Trade Unions and any other deductions authorized by the employee for payment to third parties. The returns would be accompanied by a cheque in payment of the amount due or an 'EFT transfer advice' if payment is made by EFT. Depending on the entity, payments to payroll creditors may be made from the *Payroll Imprest Banking Account* or the general banking account of the entity.

Table 15.3 Common documents for payroll transactions

Records

Assuming a computerized accounting environment, the following records and printouts pertain to the payroll function.

COMPUTERIZED ACCOUNTING RECORDS	NATURE OF RECORD
Employee standing data master file	Contains the employee's personal and appointment data used by the computer program to calculate the weekly or monthly payroll and *Employee Pay Slip*. It typically contains the following information: • Particulars of engagement and termination of service; • Authorized rate of pay and any changes thereto; • Authorized deductions for retirement fund, medical aid and any other such contributions; • Authorized holidays and sick leave; • Name and address of the employee; • Identity number; and • Income tax reference number and tax status.
Employee earnings master file	Contains the cumulative earnings history of each employee. The record allows for the accumulation of earnings on a tax year basis in order to produce the annual IRP 5 or IT 3 Tax Certificate of earnings for the employee to submit with his/her annual tax return to SARS.
Payroll payments transactions file	Records all payroll payments to employees by cheque or EFT from the *Payroll Imprest Banking Account*.
Unclaimed wages register	This is often a manual record of pay packets not paid out at the weekly wages pay-out. It should be kept by a designated senior payroll staff member until collected by the relevant employee. If not collected within a reasonable period of time, monies should be re-deposited in the Payroll Imprest Banking Account.

Table 15.4 Computerized accounting records for payroll transactions

Printouts

Report printouts relevant to payroll transactions include the following:

PRINTOUTS	NATURE OF PRINTOUT
Payroll printout	Produced for each weekly or fortnightly wages run, or monthly for salaries. It contains the full *current pay period details* such as: Employee name and number, pay status, gross earnings, analysed by nature, all deductions and net pay amount due or paid. It contains also the *year to date cumulative pay information* for the relevant tax year, which may not necessarily coincide with the entity's financial period end. The printout is confidential and is usually retained in the payroll department.
Payroll cost distribution summary	Produced for each payroll run and analyses the cost centre to which the employees' gross pay and company contributions to payroll deduction accounts payable is to be allocated in the general ledger. Depending on the computer system, the relevant general ledger payroll expense accounts and wages or salary clearing account may have been updated as part of the payroll update run or, if not, is captured into the general ledger as a batch input from the *Payroll cost distribution summary*.
Payroll payments transactions printout	Details all cheque and EFT payments made for the particular period. The printout is usually retained by the payroll department for subsequent comparison with, and reconciliation to, the relevant *bank statements* received for the *Payroll Imprest Banking Account*.
EXCEPTION REPORTS	
Payroll computer programs will usually have various programmed application controls to ensure the *completeness, measurement* and *occurrence* of the payroll transactions, some at the initial input stage with screen formats that reject a transaction if the information related to it does not conform with established criteria. Other controls may be programmed and performed during the payroll processing run. These generate payroll transaction printouts and exception reports reflecting changes in standing data, errors for correction and re-submission, reconciliations of various payroll transactions at the end of the payroll run and key performance indicators. (See overleaf.)	

PRINTOUTS	NATURE OF PRINTOUT
Payroll exception reports	These reflect a variety of information, arising from programmed checks performed during the running of the payroll transactions:
	• Employees' names and code numbers omitted from the payroll or duplicated on the payroll.
	• Employees whose hours worked exceed maximum hours specified.
	• Unallocated labour costs.
	• Printout of all changes to the *employee standing data master file* made during the month for review and approval of the human resources manager or director.
	• Reconciliation of total employees on the current payroll, being the number of employees on the previous payroll plus new employees engaged in the current period, less employees dismissed or who resigned in the current period.
	• Pay rates which are out of line with the employee category.
	• Analysis of equity targets and achievements in the current workforce.
	• A printout of key performance ratios prepared for management.

Table 15.5 Common printouts for payroll transactions

15.2.1.2 Payroll transactions functions

The processing of payroll transactions involves the following four functions:

- Initiating payroll transactions:
  - hiring of new employees and termination of employment; and
  - changes in employee standing data.
- Recording time worked or services provided.
- Preparation and recording of payroll transactions.
- Paying the payroll:
  - payments to employees; and
  - returns and payments to outside payroll deduction creditors.

Initiating payroll transactions

Hiring of new employees

Manipulation of the wages record is probably one of the easiest ways of concealing substantial misappropriations of cash and therefore the most commonly resorted to. It is imperative, therefore, particularly in the case of large businesses employing a substantial number of workers, that persons other than the payroll processing staff are authorized to hire new employees and handle the discharge, retrenchment or retirement of existing employees. A formal interview process will generally be followed prior to appointments, regard being had to the Basic Conditions of Employment Act (1997) and the Employment Equity Act (1998). The appointment would be formally advised to the employee by means of a letter from the Human Resources director or manager setting out the terms of employment. A copy of the letter signed by the employee acknowledging receipt and accepting the terms and conditions should be kept in the employee's personnel file – this constitutes the formal agreement between the entity and the employee.

In the case of appointments of directors, the requirements of the Companies Act and the company's Articles of Association must be observed. A director's appointment will normally be minuted by the shareholders, usually at the Annual General Meeting, and the appropriate returns will be lodged with the Registrar of Companies. Refer the earlier discussion regarding the recommendations of the King II Report (2002) for the selection and appointment of directors. Directors may of course resign at any time. The company may enter into employment contracts with executive directors to secure a longer term involvement with the entity and provide for employee benefits.

Usually this authority for approving appointments should be given to the human resource manager or director or in the case of a small business the owner manager, whose authority also should be required for capturing new employee details into the employee standing data master file. The control will be exercised by restricting access to the employee standing data master file to the human resources manager.

New additions should be captured at the PC or terminal in the human resources division and will require password access to that particular payroll menu to capture new employee details. A printout of the standing data should be obtained on a regular basis and checked to employee details in their personnel files. These controls will reduce the risk of fictitious employees added to the payroll and provides controls over the *existence, occurrence* and *rights and obligations* assertions.

Termination of employment

The discharge of employees may occur for several reasons and will normally, as with the hiring of employees, be handled by the human resources division, or the owner in a small owner-managed business. Employees may be dismissed for breach of the employment contract or behaviour or actions such as being implicated in fraud, which gives rise to disciplinary action taken against them in terms of the Basic Conditions of Employment Act. Employees may simply reach retirement age or take advantage of early retirement packages offered by an entity. Employees may be retrenched as a result of cutbacks in the number of employees or restructuring arrangements at an entity. The discharge will give rise to a liability on the part of the employer for settlement of wages, leave pay and any other benefits the employee is entitled to in terms of the employment contract that have accrued to date of discharge. Settlement packages will be negotiated between the employer and employees on retrenchment. These are generally based on the period the employee had been employed at the entity. Employees retiring may be entitled to post-retirement benefits and the entity may have responsibilities, for example, to continue contributions to a medical fund for the former employee or to pay a monthly pension amount. Employees may have contributed to an outside pension or retirement scheme during their employment and future pension or retirement annuity payments will be made to them from this source, including lump sum payments that may become payable to them on retirement. Controls similar to those required for the hiring of new employees should be put in place to ensure the *completeness, occurrence* and *measurement* of amounts paid to employees on termination of their services.

Changes in employee standing data

Any changes to employee status, including promotions, change in marital status, number of dependants, changes to pay rates and deductions authorized by the employee should be supported by copies of relevant documentation in the employee's personnel file. A *pre-numbered employee change form* with the changes to be captured into the *employee standing data master file* should be prepared.

A formal process should be established by the entity to authorize pay rate changes for different categories of staff. As discussed earlier, the remuneration packages of directors and senior managers should be approved by a separate remuneration committee, comprised of non-executive directors and independent non-executive directors, appointed by the board of directors. Approval should be in writing and signed by the chairman of that committee. Approval of changes to other employees' pay rates would usually be given by the board of directors or the human resources director with written advice to individual employees signed by the human resources director.

In small businesses, approval of pay increases or other changes in the employee's appointment would usually be given by the owner/manager. In large entities with one or more employee organizations recognized by management, the approval of pay changes for such employees is usually negotiated between management and the relevant employee trade union in a bargaining council.

There must be a clear segregation of duties between those approving pay rate changes, those recording the changes in the employee standing data master file and payroll staff preparing and processing the payroll. A printout of the employee standing data master file should be obtained after pay rate changes are approved, and captured, and should be checked by the human resources manager or director to ensure all changes approved have been correctly recorded. The person performing this comparison should sign the printout as evidence that the changes have been captured correctly. Any errors found should, of course, be corrected.

Recording time worked or services provided

Time worked by hourly paid 'wage' employees is usually recorded in one of two ways, either manually on time sheets, or registers, or mechanically by using a clocking device. Most businesses employing a large labour force whose members are paid for hours worked use the latter method. The clocking device contains a mechanism which prints the time on a clock card when the card is inserted into it. The clock should be located at the entrance to the premises so that employees can 'clock in' and 'out' by inserting a clock card bearing their name and employee number into the clock as they arrive and leave. A supervisor should be on hand to observe employees clocking in and out to ensure that only one clock card is franked by each individual.

In a computerized environment the clock card would be replaced by an *Employee ID Smart Card* that would be used to gain access to the premises by swiping it through a card reader that activates the opening of the door or barrier at the entrance. Similarly, at the end of the day the card is swiped through the card reader to record the time of departure. The system electronically records the time spent by each employee at work in a temporary file pending the weekly transfer of total hours worked at the end of the week to the payroll department. The supervisor responsible for hourly paid staff should review the total hours recorded by each employee in the department each week before transferring the file to the payroll department for processing. Evidence of this review could be provided electronically or by means of a printout signed by the supervisor and sent to the payroll department. This provides evidence of the *existence, occurrence* and *measurement* assertions.

To allow sufficient time to calculate wages payable, and to fill wage packets for payment on a Friday, many businesses have Wednesday as their weekly cut-off date of the wages week. Where this is the case and clock cards are used, each Thursday a fresh clock card is used and the number of hours worked is calculated from the previous week's clock card. The calculation of hours worked should be checked by a separate individual who should initial each clock card as evidence of having checked it. If overtime has been worked, a relevant foreman should approve the total number of hours worked by initialling clock cards.

Monthly paid salaried staff do not normally clock in and out, but may be required to sign an attendance register, or at least to complete a leave application form when they are not present at the business premises or are out on business of the entity. Their monthly gross pay amount is normally fixed and thus not calculated on an hourly rate by the payroll system. For this reason, the weekly wages payroll and monthly salary payroll are usually run separately.

Preparation and recording of payroll transactions

Where clock cards are used, after the total number of hours worked have been calculated, checked and any overtime approved, payroll staff should capture into the payroll batch file the hours worked, as reflected on clock cards. The total number of hours reflected on all the clock cards should be calculated and compared to the total numbers of hours as recorded in the batch file after input. If time-keeping is computerized, the payroll run should only commence once the printout of time worked has been reviewed and authorized. In a manufacturing entity, the hours worked by each employee should be captured on a *Job Time Ticket*, which should also be transferred simultaneously to the payroll department by the supervisor once a printout of the times recorded has been reviewed and approved by the supervisor. The payroll department should compare the totals of hours worked per the time records and those charged to work in progress to ensure that all hours worked are accounted for before processing the week's payroll.

Once the hours worked by each hourly paid employee are captured, whether electronically or by manual input by the payroll department, the weekly payroll program is run. Wage rates, allowances and the relevant deductions from wages are obtained from the employee standing data master file. The *payroll printout*, individual *employee pay slips* and *pay packets*, *payroll cost distribution summary* and *exception report* should be printed out as the output from the payroll run and distributed to the payroll department. In addition, the payroll run should update the general ledger with the payroll costs and payroll deduction accounts payable.

A senior manager should review the payroll printout and payroll cost distribution summary before the payroll cheque is drawn for the net payroll amount to be paid out. In a manufacturing company, the factory or production manager would usually be the person to approve the amount to be drawn in respect of wages by signing the printout. The review should be of the employees' gross and net pay, and hours worked to identify any odd or unusual amounts or errors and to consider the reasonableness of the payroll cost distribution summary allocating the payroll costs to the various jobs worked on during the week.

In the case of the monthly salary payroll, the payroll department should first check that new additions or dismissals have been approved by the human resource manager and enquire about any other changes that have been made to the *employee standing data master file*. Then, the monthly payroll program should be run to generate the monthly *payroll printout* and *employee pay slips*. This payroll should be reviewed and approved by the human resources director, or financial director, before EFT payments are made and employee pay slips distributed to salaried staff.

For both the wages and salaries payroll program run, the gross pay, deductions and net pay is calculated for each employee and then totalled for all employees. A payroll cost distribution summary will similarly be prepared for both wages and salaried staff, although the latter will generally be an allocation to different departmental cost centres, rather than being allocated to work in progress. The payroll program run should update the general ledger expense accounts and payroll liabilities in accordance with the payroll cost distribution summary, a copy of which should be sent to the payroll department for review and filing in the payroll department. A copy of the payroll cost distribution summary would be sent to the accounts department for processing.

Paying the payroll

Payments to employees

Net wages due are to be paid in cash in South African currency, by cheque, or by way of direct deposit to a bank account designated by the employee (section 31 of the Basic Conditions of Employment Act 1997).

If the entity maintains a separate payroll imprest banking account, the total amount to be paid out for the weekly or monthly payroll should be transferred from the general banking account to the imprest banking account in time to meet the EFTs, cash drawn to pay wages, or cheques drawn to pay salaried employees and payroll accounts payable.

The payroll program will normally provide the breakdown of the cash to be drawn to fill the pay packets of the staff. To avoid exposing payroll or other staff to risk of heists, arrangements are usually made for a coin security service provider to collect the cheque for cashing at the bank and to then fill the pay packets which are brought to the entity in time for the pay-out. If the collection of cash and filling of pay packets is done by the entity's own personnel, this should be done by staff who have taken no part in preparing the time records and payroll and, if the work has been done properly, there should be neither shortage, nor surplus, of cash when the last envelope has been filled.

At the pay-out, a pay packet containing the cash and the employee's pay slip is handed to each employee, who should sign the payroll as evidence that his or her pay has been collected (section 33 of the Basic Conditions of Employment Act).

The pay-out should be performed from a secure pay-point by the person responsible in the presence of the foreman or factory manager who identifies the employee and also acts as witness that the wage envelopes have been properly distributed. The items not marked as paid represent unclaimed wages and should be clearly marked 'unclaimed'. The person distributing wages and the authorized witness should ascertain that the relevant envelopes for the unclaimed items are on hand and should sign the wages record as evidence that:

- Envelopes relating to the items marked 'paid' have been distributed;
- Each worker who is paid is identified, which is either done by:
  - identification by the appropriate foreman who is present when wages are paid; or
  - identification by employee ID cards, or smart cards, which will frequently contain a head and shoulders photo of the relevant employee. At the pay-out, the paymaster will identify the employee from the ID card and will compare the details on the employees ID with the details in the wages sheets.
- The envelopes for items marked 'unclaimed' were in the hands of the disbursing clerk at the close of the wage pay-out.

Unclaimed wages should be locked away in a safe on return to the payroll department until collected by the absent employees. If not collected within a reasonable period of time, the amount should be re-deposited in the payroll imprest bank account and the amount drawn out when the employee finally claims it.

It is unusual for salaried employees to be paid in cash, so payments will ordinarily be by way of EFT payments to bank accounts designated by the employee or by way of a cheque printed out during the payroll program run.

Returns and payments to payroll deduction creditors

One or more persons in the payroll department should be designated with responsibility for handling the returns and payment to the various deduction accounts payable: SARS for PAYE and SITE returns; medical aid funds for medical aid contributions by the employee and employer; and pension and retirement funds for pension and retirement contributions by employee and employer; Skills Development Levy payments, Unemployment Insurance Fund (UIF) payments and payments to other third parties for deductions authorized by the employee.

The maintenance of the returns and regular communication with the relevant services providers about changes in the employee's status and the addition of new employees, and withdrawal of others, take a considerable amount of work which should be monitored, particularly where the entity has a large number of employees. The terms and conditions of many retirement and medical plans are complicated requiring the responsible payroll staff member to be well informed.

In addition to the monthly PAYE and SITE tax returns, the employer has to prepare the annual IRP 5 and IT 3 Tax certificates of gross remuneration, and reconcile the total amounts deducted from employees during the year for PAYE and SITE with the total paid across to SARS. The payroll staff handling the PAYE and SITE deductions need to be reasonably well informed regarding the taxes payable to SARS and the tax deductions to be made, particularly in respect of lump sum payments made to staff on resignation or dismissal. In such circumstances, it may be necessary for a tax directive to be obtained from SARS as to the amount of tax to be deducted from the lump sum payment portion of the termination benefits due to the employee.

15.2.2 Assessing the risk of significant misstatement

The main risks of significant misstatement of payroll transactions and balances are due to:

- Fictitious (dummy) employees included on the payroll.

- Unauthorized changes to gross pay rates by an individual with access to alter the employee standing data master file.

- Employees paid for hours not worked.

- Errors in the processing of the payroll as a result of data captured incorrectly, or invalid data, or data lost during the processing of weekly wages or monthly salary payroll runs. This may result in incorrect amounts shown as due to individual employees, or incorrect allocations to different general ledger cost centres, including the allocation of direct labour costs to work in progress.

- Payroll deductions may be incorrect, or not authorized by the employee, resulting in incorrect returns and payments to deduction accounts payable.

- EFTs made to incorrect bank accounts.

- Payroll payments made to the wrong employee. This is more of a problem in certain industries than others, for example, in the construction industry where casual labour may be hired by the site foreman.

- Unclaimed wages misappropriated if left unclaimed for long periods.

- Incorrect amounts paid to payroll deduction accounts payable.

The auditor gathers an understanding of the payroll processes in the usual way: by enquiry, inspection of documents, observation of control activities performed and evidence of monitoring procedures performed by management, payroll staff and human resources staff.

If the payroll expenditure is significant, extensive controls will be put in place by management over payroll functions such that the auditor will usually be able to assess the risk of significant misstatement of payroll transactions and balances as low to medium. The remaining risk of misstatement usually applies to the first three potential errors or fraud aspects outlined above, affecting the *existence, occurrence* and *measurement* assertions. The auditor will usually seek to gain assurance, by means of tests of controls, that the controls over these three aspects are properly designed and operated throughout the period.

Testing controls

Where payroll expenditure is significant, entities will usually introduce programmed input validation controls into the computer system. These include alpha-numeric checks on codes, range checks on hours worked, hourly rates of pay and amounts of deductions relative to gross payments. To establish the effectiveness of such controls, the auditor may seek the client's permission to run test data through the payroll system to test whether the various programmed controls detect deliberately introduced errors.

Alternatively, the auditor may select a sample of payroll transactions and inspect evidence of the control activities implemented over the processing of the transactions selected to ensure that specific controls on which the auditor wishes to rely have operated throughout the period. Whatever the emphasis, the auditor's procedures should include the examination of authorized signatures on various printouts and reconciliations reviewed and approved by senior management, and other evidence of key performance indicators monitored by management.

Table 15.6 below sets out the risk considerations, the computerized and manual controls that may be found in payroll systems and provides examples of tests of controls that the auditor may perform to test the effective operation of such controls. Should the auditor decide to perform tests of controls, it is likely that these would involve enquiry and observation of selected preventative controls and re-performance of the higher level detective controls, whether programmed or manual.

RISK	PROGRAMMED CONTROLS	MANUAL CONTROLS	TEST OF CONTROLS
Payroll hiring, terminations and changes to standing data			
Fictitious employees (dummy workers) may be added to the payroll, or where employment is terminated, may remain.	Logical access controls allow only authorized personnel to add new employees and record terminations in the employee master file. Printouts are produced of all changes to standing data on the employee master file.	Persons with authority to hire and terminate employment should have no other payroll functions. Human resources department personnel authorize hiring of new employees and terminations following formal hiring or termination procedures. Only authorized human resource staff can initiate a pre-numbered employee change form which is required before changes are captured to the employee master file. Printouts of all changes to employee standing data are reviewed by senior management to ensure that only authorized changes are made. Unclaimed wages are strictly controlled (see below).	By enquiry and observation determine that the persons with authority to hire employees and terminate employment perform no other payroll functions. Inspect employee change forms and letters of employment and termination signed by the person with authority and contained in the employee personnel files. Inspect evidence of management's review of the printout of new hiring and terminations. Inspect the first payroll after the period of termination as reflected on the printout to confirm that such employees are not reflected thereon. Attend a wages pay-out and observe the distribution of

RISK	PROGRAMMED CONTROLS	MANUAL CONTROLS	TEST OF CONTROLS
			wages to employees, record any unclaimed wages and trace these to corresponding employee personnel files and evidence of subsequent payment. Obtain a printout of all employees recorded in the employee master file and conduct a head count of staff, inspecting at the same time the employee's staff card.
Unauthorized changes may be made to gross pay rates, employee status and deductions in the standing data in the employee master file.	Logical access controls allow only authorized senior personnel to make changes to standing data on employee master files. Printouts are produced of all changes to standing data on the employee master file.	Only authorized human resource staff may amend employee standing data by making changes to rates of pay and other deductions and these are recorded on change forms signed by those with authority. Such changes are communicated to all affected employees. Printouts of all changes to employee standing data reviewed by senior management to ensure only authorized changes are made.	Inspect employee change forms signed by persons with authority. Inspect evidence of management's review of the printout of changes to standing data. Select a sample of standing data changes reflected on printouts and inspect the relevant supporting documentation in the employee's personnel files for evidence of the appropriate authority for changes in status, gross rates of pay and deductions.
Recording time worked or services provided			
Errors or fraud in recording the hours worked.	Use of employee smart cards for access to the business premises automatically updates the wage records for time worked. Programmed controls match total time worked by employees to hours allocated to jobs in production, other cost centres, or idle time. Weekly and monthly payroll printout of wages and salaries with allocation to relevant cost centres or work in progress.	Supervision of employees clocking in and out to ensure that employees do not clock in for anyone other than themselves. Weekly clock cards reviewed and signed by production management, or foreman, to authorize normal and overtime hours worked. If the total number of hours worked are calculated manually from information on clock cards, independent checks of the calculation of hours are checked before time worked is captured into the system. If the time-recording function is computerized, the printout of hours worked is reviewed and authorized.	Observe the clocking-in-and-out procedures to ascertain that this activity is being supervized, negating the possibility of one employee clocking others in. Inspect a selection of clock cards or printouts of time worked for evidence of approval of normal and overtime hours worked and check of the accuracy of the calculation of hours worked.

RISK	PROGRAMMED CONTROLS	MANUAL CONTROLS	TEST OF CONTROLS
Preparation and recording of payroll			
Errors may arise through data being captured incorrectly or lost during the processing of weekly wages or monthly salaries. Payroll deductions may be incorrect or not authorized by employees.	Programmed limit and reasonableness checks of hours worked, as well as input validation checks of employee name and code numbers. Programmed calculations of weekly and monthly payrolls from hours-worked records and standing data for gross pay rates, and deductions and the analysis of cost allocations, and automatic production of the payroll printouts and individual pay slips for employees. Exception reports printed for employees' names or code numbers duplicated or omitted from the payroll; hours worked in excess of norms; and gross pay rates that exceed parameters per category of employee and missing data such as unallocated costs.	Payroll staff review payroll printouts and agree control totals. Review of exception reports and steps taken to promptly rectify errors. Review of the reconciliation of payroll changes for employee numbers – previous month, or week, plus new employees, less terminations, and check changes to standing employee data processed during the period. Employees check their pay slips, and may query any incorrect amounts. Exception reports are reviewed, any errors corrected and the reports resubmitted.	Select several weekly and monthly payroll printouts and inspect the signatures thereon of those responsible for checking the accuracy of preparation and their authorization for payment. Inspect evidence of the checking of the reconciliation of hiring and terminations for monthly paid staff to total employees on the payroll. Enquire as to any instances of employee queries and their resolution. Inspect exception reports for evidence of review and follow up.
Recording payroll transactions			
Payroll transactions may be allocated to incorrect general ledger accounts or may not be recorded at all.	Programmed controls over payroll processing that automatically update the relevant general ledger accounts. Exception reports of amounts not allocated to general ledger accounts but recorded in suspense accounts pending correction and re-submission.	Monitoring by payroll staff initially checking the weekly and monthly payroll and exceptions reports to detect and correct errors and omissions. Reconciliations prepared of payroll suspense accounts and returns to deduction accounts payable.	Inspect evidence of monitoring of exception reports, preparation and checking of reconciliations and error correction. Inspect evidence of preparation and checking of payroll reconciliations.

RISK	PROGRAMMED CONTROLS	MANUAL CONTROLS	TEST OF CONTROLS
Payroll pay-out			
Payment may be made to the incorrect persons or EFTs made to incorrect employee bank accounts.	Logical access controls over recording of employee bank accounts for EFT transfers and changes to employee bank details, or payment details. Printout of all employee net pay amounts made by EFT from the imprest payroll banking account. Payroll cheques printed as part of the payroll run for employees paid by cheque from the imprest payroll banking account. Printout of the makeup of cash required for payroll pay-out in cash, usually to weekly paid employees. Payroll payments transactions printout of all cheque and EFT payments made to employee bank accounts, weekly or monthly.	Employees identified prior to pay envelopes being handed to them, either by their producing employee cards or being identified by foremen. Review of changes to employee standing data affecting bank account details to ensure these are supported by authorization of the employee and confirmation by the bank of employee bank details accepted for EFTs. EFTs approved by the bank signatories before being transferred. Cheque drawn for transfer of gross payroll to payroll banking account checked by signatories to payroll before signing and cheque number recorded on payroll, agreed to subsequent payroll imprest account bank deposit stamped deposit slip. Cheque drawn for weekly payroll given to coin security service provider for cashing and filling of pay packets for pay-out. Filled pay packets compared to weekly payroll printout to ensure complete and accurate prior to pay-out. Payroll payments printout compared to payroll imprest bank account and monthly bank reconciliation prepared by payroll staff and reviewed by senior accounting staff or human resources department manager.	Attendance at wage pay-outs to observe the application of controls over the payment of wages to employees. Inspect the signatures on the payroll printout of the persons (usually two) responsible for paying out the wages. Inspect evidence of monthly bank reconciliation performed on the payroll imprest bank account and review by senior management. Inspect evidence of authorization of EFTs to employee bank accounts and evidence of review of changes to bank details in standing data in employee master file.

RISK	PROGRAMMED CONTROLS	MANUAL CONTROLS	TEST OF CONTROLS
Unclaimed wages may be as a result of fictitious employees added to the payroll. Unclaimed wages may be misappropriated.		Pay packets not collected at pay-out, noted on payroll by the person paying out and department supervisor attending the pay-out. Unclaimed wages recorded in an unclaimed wages register and pay packets held in safe for a short period to allow employee to collect on return to work. Unclaimed wages re-banked if not collected within a reasonable period. Employees sign unclaimed wages register when collecting pay.	By enquiry and observation confirm separation of duties. Observe the recording of unclaimed wages on the payroll at the conclusion of the pay-out, delivery of packets to the cashier and the recording of details of such packets in the unclaimed wages register. Ascertain that the unclaimed wages are for genuine employees who were not able to claim their wages by inquiring immediately into the reasons for such unclaimed wages. This enquiry is important, as it may reveal wages drawn for fictitious employees. Inspect evidence that employees collecting unclaimed wages are identified before payment is made to them and that they sign the unclaimed wages register to confirm receipt of wages.
Payroll deductions may not all be paid over to payroll deduction accounts payable or are not timeously paid.	Printout of IRP 5 and IT 3 Certificates payroll run generated at Tax year-end extracted from cumulative payroll records for individual employees.	Different payroll staff allocated responsibility for particular deduction accounts payable returns and payments. Reconciliation of amounts deducted per payroll records plus employer contributions, where applicable, matched to current returns submitted to deduction accounts payable. Payment to deduction accounts payable made and recorded in relevant general ledger accounts. Annual preparation of IRP 5 and IT 3 tax certificates prepared by payroll staff may be done manually or a computerized printout obtained. In each situation, total tax deductions per the certificates must be agreed to total PAYE and SITE payments to SARS during the period. Management review the matching, investigate and correct any differences. Reconciliations of deduction accounts payable performed or reviewed by payroll management or senior accounting staff, on a regular basis and queries monitored.	Inspect evidence of returns submitted regularly and reconciliation to payroll deduction analysis and ledger accounts. Inspect evidence of review by senior management of reconciliations and returns submitted and matching to payments and refunds on payroll or general bank statements.

RISK	PROGRAMMED CONTROLS	MANUAL CONTROLS	TEST OF CONTROLS
Payroll monitoring			
All of the above.		**Senior management at appropriate levels monitor:** Monthly reconciliation of employee movements in hiring and terminations to total employee numbers. Changes to standing data in the employee master file. Allocations of gross payroll amounts to relevant cost centres. Payroll reconciliations to imprest banking account reconciliations. Employee complaints of incorrect payments. Key performance indicators monitored, including meeting of equity targets if applicable.	Inspect evidence of the effectiveness of management's monitoring procedures and key performance indicators to prevent, detect and correct errors and fraud related to payroll transactions and balances.

Table 15.6 Risks, controls and tests of controls – payroll transactions and balances

Outsourcing of payroll processing

Companies often outsource the payroll processing function. In such circumstances, different risks will arise requiring the implementation of further control activities. The auditor will thus need to understand and assess the appropriateness of the design and effectiveness of implementation of computerized and manual controls, not only by the client, but also by the outsource provider to ensure the *completeness, occurrence* and *measurement* of payroll transactions. Depending on the complexity and volumes involved, this review may be performed by the audit firm's IT experts, or by obtaining a report on internal controls at the outsource provider. The reader is referred to the discussion in chapter 9 regarding the risks, controls and audit procedures to be followed.

Amongst the more important of these are:

- If the client has entered into a service level agreement, this should set out the responsibilities of the entity and the outsource provider; the rights of access to the records of the outsource provider, or process by which the client and auditor may gain assurance regarding the effectiveness of the general and application controls implemented by the outsource provider.

- The client should retain the responsibility for making changes to the standing data regarding hiring and terminations, changes in gross pay rates, deductions and employee banking details.

- Where the time records sent to the outsource provider are by way of clock cards which are then captured by staff of the outsource provider, sufficient information must be kept by the client's payroll staff to check that all such clock cards have been processed, none lost in transit, and none duplicated. If sent electronically, checks of the adequacy of communication controls are necessary.

- The client establishes reconciliation and monitoring controls to ensure that all transactions for each payroll run are recorded and that the input provided to the outsource provider agrees to the printouts received back on completion of the payroll run. The audit procedures set out in Table 15.6 would be modified to test the reconciliation and monitoring controls of the client that ensure the *completeness, measurement* and *occurrence* of the transactions appearing in each week's, or month's, payroll.

- The client will also usually retain responsibility for the returns to deduction accounts payable, but may arrange for the outsource provider to process the EFT payments, and to handle the weekly pay-out of wages. Responsibility for unclaimed wages usually remain with the client.

15.3 DETECTION RISK AND SUBSTANTIVE TESTS OF PAYROLL BALANCES

15.3.1 Introduction

Substantive tests of payroll balances are normally performed towards the period end. The complexity of the recognition, measurement, and presentation and disclosures required in terms of GAAP, AC 116, 'Employee benefits', in respect of payroll accruals and provisions, requires the auditor to exercise caution and assign more senior audit staff to perform the period-end verification procedures for payroll liabilities and expenditure balances. The audit of the payroll imprest banking account is dealt with in chapter 17 when considering the audit of cash and bank.

15.3.2 Determining the acceptable level of detection risk

As already indicated, the main risk of significant misstatement in payroll transactions and related balances is one of overstatement of the expenses that arise from the risk of wages drawn for fictitious employees, payments for hours not actually worked, or payments at unauthorized pay rates (*existence* and *occurrence* assertions).

Due to the highly regulated environment, the sensitive and confidential nature of payroll activities and the risk of heavy penalties for non-compliance with laws and regulations, management will invariably implement stringent detective controls over the entity's payroll systems that will in most instances be effective and lead to the early detection, and correction, of fraud and error. Consequently, the auditor will frequently assess the risk of significant misstatement for payroll transactions and balances, after testing the appropriate application of key controls, as low. This would justify an audit strategy to gather most of the substantive audit evidence needed from analytical procedures, with limited substantive tests of detail on transactions and balances.

Any remaining risk of significant misstatement is addressed by focusing the substantive tests of detail on the verification of the *measurement and valuation*, and *rights and obligations* of payroll accruals and liabilities at period end, and the *presentation and disclosure* of present and post-retirement employee benefits required in terms of GAAP – AC 116, 'Employee benefits', and the Companies Act and JSE Securities Exchange Listing Requirements relating to the disclosure of directors' emoluments and benefits.

15.3.3 Substantive analytical procedures

As indicated above, the auditor usually applies substantive analytical audit procedures to gather much of the evidence required for the audit of human resources and payroll transactions and balances. Substantive analytical procedures are useful in identifying potential areas of significant misstatement from fraud or error, or in confirming fair presentation of payroll expenditures.

Analytical procedures include comparisons to prior years or budgets; ratio analysis, comparisons of financial and non-financial information, derived from understanding the core processes and related business processes of the entity. Trends may be established from historical information and changes explained by reason of internal and external events that have occurred during the period, such as business expansion or retrenchments, and wage agreements reached with trade unions for employees in different industry sectors, changes in accounting policies and changes in management.

Where the audit is a continuing engagement, the auditor would have a record of analyses prepared in prior years on which to base initial expectations for the current period's analyses. These expectations need to be modified, for the current period, for known changes in the business or economic circumstances. In this regard, the following factors might affect changes in payroll amounts:

● Changes in the mix of different categories of employees and average or range of pay levels for different categories.

● Changes in employee numbers and the stability of these given that there may be seasonal variations.

● Any increases given or bonuses paid at particular times of the year due to overtime worked as the result of the seasonal nature of an entity's business or production deadlines.

- Retrenchments or discontinuation of particular operations or, in contrast, increases in personnel in circumstances where the business is expanding and/or pursuing acquisitions of other entities.

- Where the entity has obtained major contracts and is operating at full capacity, or has lost major customers or suppliers and is functioning at much lower levels of capacity.

- Whether the entity operates on a shift basis or merely a '9-to-5' basis, five days a week, with overtime worked when necessary.

The use of generalized audit software programs (CAATs) enables the auditor to sort payroll expenses and payroll liabilities data in a variety of ways for meaningful analyses, for example:

- By *cost centres* such as Accounting, IT, Technical, Production, Manufacturing and Marketing; by skilled versus unskilled labour or other suitable *categories of labour*; by *geographic locations*; and by *senior management, directors and other staff*.

- A comparison of average pay rates by category of employee to detect a potential overstatement of wages. The analysis may further cover the various aspects of Gross Pay and deductions for: PAYE and SITE, Employee Contributions to Pension Funds, Retirement Funds, Medical Funds, other payroll accounts payable; and Company Contributions to such funds.

- Analyses of payroll transactions prepared on a monthly basis for salaried staff, and a weekly basis for wages staff, and reconciliations made with prior periods.

Other analytical procedures may include the following:

- Explanations obtained from management as to the occurrence of standard cost labour variances and their implications for the valuation of manufactured inventory.

- Analytical procedures on payroll deduction accounts payable, and company and employee contributions paid, as these are usually based on either a percentage of gross pay or fixed contribution.

- Analyses of the payroll printouts and payroll cost distribution summaries could highlight unusual trends for further investigation.

- Where the weekly wages amount is predictable, the auditor may obtain a significant amount of audit assurance from the analytical review trend analysis technique.

A scrutiny of selected weekly or monthly payrolls might be considered necessary where payroll amounts are not predictable within reasonable levels of accuracy to detect large or unusual items for further investigation. Such items might include:

- amounts out of line with the norm;
- excessive hours worked; and
- none or minimal payroll deductions.

The auditor should obtain explanations from management for unexpected variations and corroborate such explanations by inspection of the underlying documents or employee payroll or personnel records.

Where the weekly and monthly payroll amounts are significant, it would necessitate the preparation of reconciliations by payroll staff of the week on week and month on month changes in gross pay for review by management. The auditor may check the propriety of a selection of these by:

- tracing hiring, terminations and rates of pay changes reflected on reconciliations to the employee personnel records;
- checking the arithmetical accuracy of the reconciliations; and
- agreeing gross amounts to relevant payrolls.

15.3.4 Substantive tests of detail of payroll transactions

The substantive tests of detail of transactions and balances, presented in Table 13.11 for the audit of expenditures and accounts payable in chapter 13, apply equally to payroll expenditure and related balances, except that the auditor will normally not obtain confirmation of balances owing to accounts payable or have recourse to statements of amounts due, as the information on which the accruals are raised are generated by the entity's internal payroll function and advised to the payroll deduction accounts payable. Consequently, other than for a discussion of the audit procedures that would be performed during attendance at a wages pay-out, a detailed framework for substantive audit procedures of payroll transactions and balances is not presented in this chapter. A more detailed discussion of the implications for substantive tests of detail for balances flowing from the application of AC 116, 'Employee benefits', is however presented.

Attendance at a wages pay-out

Auditors usually attend a payroll pay-out to observe controls over the payment of wages to employees, which provides evidence related to the *existence and occurrence* audit objectives.

The audit procedures followed in attending and observing a wages pay-out and the nature of the audit evidence obtained are as follows:

- Select a number of employees recorded on the payroll and ascertain that the relevant employee details thereon are agreed to those recorded in the employee standing data master file.

- Inspect evidence that authorized clock cards or employee ID smart cards exist for employees selected. A scrutiny of Unemployment Insurance Fund cards, PAYE and SITE returns, where applicable, provides further evidence of the existence of such employees.

- Re-perform the calculation of hours worked per clock cards selected for testing, and trace details of name and hours worked to the relevant payroll.

- When attending a wages pay-out, the auditor should arrive after the cheque for wages for the week has been drawn and/or the filled employee pay packets have been received from the coin security company and should:
  - Check the total number of pay packets into which wages have been placed to the week's payroll printout;
  - Count the money in a few packets and agree the amount to the pay slips and the payroll printout;
  - Assign members of the auditing staff to all pay-out points and travel with the client's staff distributing wages and the pay packets to each pay-out point;
  - Observe identification of and payment to employees of pay packets;
  - Observe the recording of unclaimed wages on the payroll printouts and delivery of packets to the cashier and the recording details of such packets in the unclaimed wages register;
  - Ascertain by enquiry that the unclaimed wages are for genuine employees who were not able to claim their wages. This enquiry is important, as it may reveal wages drawn for fictitious employees; and
  - Inspect the signatures on the payroll printout of the persons (usually two) responsible for paying out the wages.

15.3.5 Substantive tests of detail for payroll balances and other employee benefits

The revised AC 116, 'Employee benefits', published in April 2001 applies to financial statement periods commencing on or after 1 January 2001. The statement provides for the recognition and *measurement, presentation and disclosure* of a variety of employee benefits that an entity may provide to its employees. Whilst this text does not comprehensively address accounting principles, in auditing the human resources and payroll transactions and balances, the auditor audits the financial statements prepared in accordance with a recognized accounting framework, namely AC 116, and accordingly, must have an understanding of the requirements of the statement.

Given the complexity of AC 116 , the auditor would need to be satisfied that clients have complied with the specific requirements of the statement in accounting for payroll expenditure and accruals and have made appropriate disclosures for each of the categories of employee benefits dealt with therein. Definitions and selected principles set out in the statement are presented below so as to illustrate the implications thereof for the auditor.

Employee benefits are defined in paragraph .08 of AC 116 as:

'All forms of consideration given by an enterprise for service rendered by employees.'

Five categories of compensation are identified, being:

- Short-term employee benefits;
- Post-employment benefits;
- Other long-term employee benefits;
- Termination benefits; and
- Equity compensation benefits.

Table 15.7 below sets out examples of the types of employee benefits included in each category. The different categories have different characteristics, which may give rise to different risks and their effect on the nature, timing and extent of audit procedures necessary, including the possible need for the use of an actuary to provide actuarial valuations of the entity's future liabilities and commitments for post-retirement benefits.

DEFINITIONS (AC 116, PARA .08)	EXAMPLES OF EMPLOYEE BENEFITS
Short-term employee benefits: Employee benefits (other then termination benefits and equity compensation benefits), which fall due wholly within twelve months after the end of the period in which employees render the service.	Wages, salaries, social security compensation, paid annual leave and paid sick leave, profit sharing, and bonuses, and non-monetary benefits (such as medical care, housing, cars and free or subsidized goods or services for current employees (AC 116, para .05).
Post-employment benefits: Employee benefits (other then termination benefits and equity compensation benefits), which are payable after the completion of employment.	Pensions, other retirement benefits, post-employment life insurance, and post-employment medical care (AC 116, para .05).
Other long-term employee benefits: Employee benefits (other than post-employment benefits, termination benefits and equity compensation benefits), which do not fall due wholly within twelve months after the end of the period in which the employees render the related service.	Long service leave or sabbatical leave, jubilee or other long service benefits, long-term disability benefits, and profit sharing bonuses and deferred compensation paid 12 months or more after the period-end in which it is earned (AC 116, para .05).

DEFINITIONS (AC 116, PARA .08)	EXAMPLES OF EMPLOYEE BENEFITS
Termination benefits: Benefits payable as a result of either: (a) An enterprise's decision to terminate an employee's employment before the normal retirement date, or (b) An employee's decision to accept voluntary redundancy in exchange for those benefits.	Termination benefits are typically lump sum payments but may also include: (a) Enhancement of retirement benefits or other post-employment benefits; or (b) Salary until the end of a specified notice period where the employee renders no further service providing economic benefits to the enterprise (AC 116, para .136).
Equity compensation benefits: Employee benefits under which either: (a) Employees are entitled to receive equity financial instruments issued by the enterprise (or its parent); or (b) Where the amount of the enterprise's obligations to employees depends on the future price of equity financial instruments issued by the enterprise.	Shares, share options and other equity instruments at less than the fair value at which those instruments would be issued to a third party; and Cash payments, the amount of which will depend on the future market price of the reporting enterprise's shares, referred to as phantom share schemes. (AC 116, para .145). The employee's rights will depend on the nature and terms including vesting provisions of the equity compensation plan (AC 116, para .148).

Table 15.7 AC 116: Definitions and examples of employee benefits

15.3.5.1 Short-term employee benefits

The preceding discussion of audit procedures of payroll transactions and related balances has focused primarily on the audit of the short-term employee benefits category, although reference has been made to company contributions and employee deductions for contributions to pension, retirement and medical funds. To the extent that audit evidence is obtained from substantive analytical procedures and substantive tests of details of payroll transactions, the remaining substantive audit procedures for verifying the *completeness, existence, measurement, rights and obligations* and *valuation* assertions for payroll accruals, arising from short-term employee benefits which are dealt with in AC 116, paragraphs .11 to .24, are similar to those discussed in chapter 13 for other accruals and provisions.

Substantive tests of detail for short-term employee benefits

Tests of control and substantive analytical procedures performed over short-term employee benefits are discussed earlier in this chapter. The auditor would ordinarily obtain a schedule of payroll accruals from the client, which may include: accruals for weekly wages to the period end, PAYE and SITE deducted and payable to SARS, current and arrear contributions due to retirement benefit funds and medical funds, bonuses based on profits for the period, leave pay to which employees are entitled and commissions on sales to the period end. While most accruals will result from the normal weekly or monthly payroll processing, others such as bonuses and commissions based on profits or turnover and leave pay accruals may only be calculated at the period end. The auditor would ordinarily perform the following substantive tests of detail for short-term employee benefits:

- Review the schedules of accruals prepared by the client, in order to ascertain the basis on which all material accruals have been calculated, and consider whether the basis is in accordance with AC 116 and the accounting policies adopted by the entity applied on a consistent basis.

- In a continuing audit, the basis of calculation of accruals may be determined by inspection of the schedule of payroll accruals contained in the prior year's audit working papers. The basis used in the current year should be consistent with that used previously.

- Inspect the terms of agreements or letters of appointment of employees to verify the basis of the employee *rights* giving rise to the entity's *obligations*.

- Depending on the materiality of the accruals and the auditor's assessment of the risk of significant misstatement, the auditor may decide that sufficient audit evidence may be obtained from performing substantive analytical procedures on individual accruals, or may select a sample of items from the detailed schedules, for substantive tests of detail. For example:
  - Inspecting individual employee's leave records, to verify the days' leave accrued at period end, as well as the employee's gross pay rates as reflected on the schedule.
  - Considering the underlying assumptions of management in calculating the amounts accrued and thereafter re-performing the computations to verify the total amount provided for leave pay.

- The auditor would also consider the reasonableness of the underlying assumptions used in the calculation of the other payroll accruals, for example, amounts due to SARS for PAYE and SITE, and to retirement and medical funds for employee deductions and company contributions due. A review of the annual reconciliation of PAYE and SITE deductions to the total tax deductions reflected on IRP 5 certificates issued to employees provides evidence of the discharge of the employer's responsibilities for the collection and payment of employee taxes to SARS.

● A review of subsequent payments and returns to accounts payable provides further evidence to support the payroll accruals for short-term employee benefits.

15.3.5.2 Post-employment benefits

Post-employment benefits include retirement benefits such as pensions, premiums to be paid for life insurance and contributions to medical funds or medical expenses in providing post-retirement medical care. Where the employer carries the liability, it is necessary for the quantum to be actuarially calculated for purposes of the recognition and disclosure of post-retirement benefit obligations in the annual financial statements. The auditor will ordinarily enquire from management who is responsible for the continuing payments, the retired employee, or the employer entity and to corroborate the response by inspection of the relevant employee contract and retirement or medical benefit contracts. A wide variety of retirement plans are encountered and the auditor will need to establish the exact nature of the plans to which the client and employees contribute. These may include multi-employer plans, state plans for public sector entities, and insured benefits, as well as entity pension and retirement plans. Ultimately a distinction is drawn in AC 116 between *defined contribution plans* and *defined benefit plans* depending on the economic substance of the plan as derived from its principal terms and conditions (AC 116, paragraph .26). A brief discussion of this distinction follows so as to explain the possible impact on the auditor's assessment of the risk of significant misstatement.

Defined contribution plans

Defined contribution plans are defined in AC 116, paragraph .08, as:

> 'post-employment benefit plans under which an enterprise pays fixed contributions into a separate entity (a fund) and will have no legal or constructive obligation to pay further contributions if the fund does not hold sufficient assets to pay all employee benefits relating to employee service in the current and prior periods.'

Under defined contribution plans 'the enterprise's legal or constructive obligation is limited to the amount it agrees to contribute to the fund. Thus, the post-employment benefits of an employee are determined by the contributions of the employee and the employer paid by an enterprise to a post-employment benefit fund, or to an insurance fund, together with investment returns arising from the contributions. In consequence, actuarial risk (that benefits will be less than expected) and investment risk (that assets invested will be insufficient to meet expected benefits) fall on the employee' (AC 116, paragraph .26(a) and (b)).

An enterprise should disclose the total amount recognized as an expense for defined contribution plans. Where required by AC 126, 'Related Party disclosures', information about contributions made to defined contribution plans for key management personnel are to be disclosed (AC 116, paragraph .48).

Defined benefit plans

Defined benefit plans are defined in AC 116 paragraph .08 as 'post-employment benefit plans other than defined contribution plans.'

The risk of significant misstatement arises particularly in the *measurement, valuation and disclosure* assertions for post-employment benefits of *defined benefit plans*, which may include, pension, retirement annuity plans and medical care plans.

Accounting for defined benefit plans is complex, because actuarial assumptions are required to measure the obligation and the expense, and there is a possibility of actuarial gains or losses that should be recognized. Moreover, the obligations are measured on a discounted basis using the Projected Unit Credit Method in order to determine the present value of benefits generated by each year of service rendered by the employee and current service cost, because the benefits may be settled many years after employees rendered the related service (AC 116, paragraph .51).

In essence, the enterprise is guaranteeing a certain level of benefit for the employee in the future and is responsible for making good any shortfall. Consequently, the enterprise is underwriting both the actuarial and investment risks associated with the plan. As a result the expense recognized for the financial period comprises the current service cost and actuarial gains and losses recognized, plus interest on the present value of the obligation. In addition, the enterprise has to determine at the balance sheet date the fair value of plan assets out of which the defined benefit obligations are to be settled in order to reflect the net total defined benefit obligation (AC 116, paragraphs .49 and .55 to .57).

Guidance is provided as to the actuarial assumptions to be made which are described as 'an enterprise's best estimates of the variables' that should be *'unbiased and mutually compatible'*. The actuarial assumptions comprise firstly, *demographic assumptions* about the future characteristics of current and former employees (and their dependants) who are eligible for benefits, such as: mortality during and after employment, rates of employee turnover, proportion of plan members with dependants eligible for benefits, and claim rates under medical plans. Secondly, financial assumptions such as the discount rate, future salary and benefit levels, in the case of medical benefits, future medical costs, including the cost of administering claims and benefit payments, and the expected rate of return on plan assets AC 116, paragraph .51). Actuarial assumptions are regarded as being mutually compatible if they reflect the economic relationships between factors such as inflation, rates of salary increase, return on plan assets and discount rates (AC 116, paragraphs .73 to .76).

Where a post-employment plan is a defined benefit plan, the enterprise should account for the defined benefit obligation, plan assets and costs associated with the plan or plans and should disclose the detailed information required in terms of AC 116 paragraph .121. The auditor will need to obtain sufficient appropriate audit evidence to support the actuarial assumptions made and the calculation of the present values of defined benefit plans and plan assets, the actuarial gains or losses and returns on plan assets, in order to determine whether the recognition and disclosures properly reflect the obligations and expenses of the entity.

It will be appreciated that where an entity has a large number of current and past employees, the measurement, valuation and disclosure of post-retirement liabilities in the financial statements could be significant, amounting in some instances to tens, if not hundreds of millions of Rand. The sensitivity of the principal demographic and financial actuarial assumptions to change, directly affects the amount of the valuation, which increases the risk of significant misstatement.

The auditor should follow the guidance provided in SAAS 620, 'Using the work of an expert', in obtaining sufficient appropriate audit evidence that the work of the actuary is adequate for the purposes of the audit. In this regard, the auditor would consider:

• the competence and objectivity of the actuary;

• the scope of the work – which is, in essence, specified in AC 116; and

• the results from the performance of the actuary's work. This will include a review of the actuarial valuations received, the consideration of the demographic and financial assumptions made and whether they appear reasonable in the circumstances of the client.

If the auditor is not satisfied, any concerns must be discussed with the client and the actuary and resolved. Consideration may be given to applying additional procedures, which may include engaging another actuary or modifying the audit report.

Previously, recognition of post-retirement liabilities and commitments were directed primarily at pension and retirement plans and recognition was not generally provided for post-retirement medical care plans. With the advent of the revised AC 116 in 2001, the impact of requirements for the recognition and disclosure of the economic realities and liabilities which were previously treated as 'off balance-sheet' liabilities, has prompted moves by many employers during the past five years, to shift the risk to their employees by persuading or requiring their past and current employees to change from defined benefit plans to defined contribution plans.

The statement provides guidance in AC 116 paragraphs .30 to .43, with regard to difficulties affecting recognition, measurement and disclosures for contributions to multi-employer plans, state plans and insurance plans that are in effect defined benefit plans, but where the information required for determining measurement, valuation and disclosures may not be possible to ascertain.

The recognition by the employer of an asset resulting from the over-funding of the defined benefit obligation, giving rise to actuarially determined pension plan surpluses is problematic with regard to who is entitled to ownership of such surpluses, the employer, the employee or the pension plan fund. The recent amendments to the Pension Funds Act, contained in the Second Amendment Bill of 2001, contain proposals regarding the right of the fund, its members and the employer to use actuarial surpluses in such funds, which may entitle the employer to refunds under certain circumstances.

Transitional provisions

AC 116, in paragraphs .155 to .157, sets out the transitional provisions for the determination by an enterprise of its transitional liability for defined benefit plans where an enterprise adopts this statement for the first time.

Substantive tests of detail for post-retirement benefits

The auditor would ordinarily perform the following substantive tests of detail for post-retirement benefits:

- Assign senior audit staff with the appropriate expertise to audit the liabilities, expenses and disclosures relating to post-retirement employee benefits.

- Ascertain at the planning stage, by enquiry and inspections of plan contract documents, the exact nature of the rights and obligations of all post-retirement benefits, both defined contribution plans and defined benefit plans. In particular, the auditor will attempt to identify any potential liability or commitment of the enterprise to contribute to any shortfall that might arise in plan assets to meet obligations for defined benefit plans. Notes of the nature of these commitments should be documented in the audit working papers and any changes updated each year. The auditor should clarify the nature of the entity's rights and obligations, by inspection of the fund rules and discussions with management.

- Plan timeously, with the client, for actuarial valuations to be obtained, where necessary, to support the estimates used for the recognition and *measurement, presentation and disclosure* of post-retirement benefits in the financial statements, in accordance with the bases specified in AC 116.

- Finally, the auditor would inspect the presentation and disclosures in the financial statements regarding defined contribution plans and defined benefit plans to be satisfied that these are in accordance with the actuarial valuations and are not materially misstated.

15.3.5.3 Other long-term employee benefits

The measurement of other long-term benefits is not subject to the same level of uncertainty as the measurement of post-retirement benefits. The amount to be recognized as a liability and an expense is set out in AC 116, paragraphs .129 to .130.

Substantive tests of detail for other long-term employee benefits

The audit procedures set out above for post-retirement benefits would apply equally to the audit of other long-term benefits where such amounts are material to the financial statements.

15.3.5.4 Termination benefits

Termination benefits differ from the previous benefits since the event that gives rise to them is the termination, rather than the service, of the employee. Consequently, termination benefits should be recognized as an expense in the year of termination of service.

'The enterprise should recognize the liability and expense when, *and only when*, the enterprise has a present obligation (legal or constructive) to either:

- Terminate the employment of an employee or group of employees before the normal retirement date, or provide termination benefits as a result of an offer made in order to encourage voluntary redundancy'. (AC 116, paragraph .134)

'An enterprise has a present obligation (legal or constructive) when, *and only when*, the enterprise:

- Has a detailed formal plan for the termination identifying at least the business or part of the business concerned, the principal locations, the location, function and approximate number of employees who will be compensated for terminating their services, the expenditures and when the plan will be implemented; and has raised a valid expectation in those affected that it will carry out the plan.' (AC 116, paragraph .135)

The enterprise is required to disclose an indication of the uncertainties about the amount and timing of payments required to settle provisions. One such uncertainty is the number of employees who will accept a voluntary offer of termination benefits. The enterprise is required, in terms of AC 130 paragraph .49, to disclose the major assumptions concerning future events, where necessary, to provide adequate information.

Where the nature, and amount of termination benefits is of such a size, nature or incidence that it is relevant to explain the performance of the enterprise, it may require separate disclosure (AC 116, paragraphs .142 to .143).

The auditor should bear in mind that the Basic Conditions of Employment Act contains provisions relating to payments to be made on termination which the client should observe in the termination settlements, failing which, penalties may become payable or litigation may arise.

Payments to directors for compensation for loss of office, or as consideration for, or in connection with a director's retirement from office, or loss of office in connection with a section 313 Scheme of Arrangement, or in terms of any takeover offer or scheme which constitutes an affected transaction in terms of section 440, may not be made by any company unless full disclosure has been made to the members and the making of the payment or grant of the benefit for the specific transaction has been approved by special resolution (Companies Act section 227(1)(a) – (c)). Any payment made or benefit granted contrary to these provisions will be regarded as paid in trust to the director for the company and where such payment relates to a takeover, arrangement shall be regarded as held in trust for any persons who have sold their shares as a result of the takeover offer concerned.

Substantive tests of detail for termination benefits

As with the preceding types of employee benefits, the auditor would obtain a schedule from the client setting out the termination benefits accrued and recognized in the income statement. The auditor would ordinarily perform the following substantive tests of detail for termination benefits:

- Enquiring into, and inspection of, the client's formal termination plans, evidence of the employees' acceptance of the termination packages offered and the subsequent payments to employees.

- In the case of termination packages for voluntary redundancy, the auditor would seek confirmation of the number of employees who have indicated they intend accepting the termination packages offered, to determine that the financial statement accruals and disclosures are not materially misstated.

- Re-perform the computation of the benefits payable or paid to individual employees based on their years of service and the basis of compensation offered by the enterprise and accepted by the employees.

- Inspect the shareholders minutes reflecting the special resolution approving such payments and re-perform the computation of the amounts payable to the director/s for the specific terms approved.

- Ascertain that payments to directors for compensation for loss of office are separately disclosed in the financial statements.

- A further consideration that might arise where employees services are terminated is whether the entity is a going concern and still able to pay its other creditors in the ordinary course of business, after paying its employees the agreed termination packages, or whether the entity is insolvent and about to be placed into liquidation, when such payments may amount to an undue preference granted, albeit to preferred creditors, and which could be set aside later by the liquidator. The auditor may need to seek legal advice or advice from an insolvency practitioner in such circumstances.

● Consideration of other contingent liabilities or commitments arising from terminations that would require disclosure in terms of AC 130, and disclosure of related parties in terms of AC 126.

● Inspect the disclosures in the financial statements to ensure these are in accordance with AC 116, 130 or 126 and the Companies Act.

15.3.5.5 Equity compensation benefits

Equity compensation benefits include benefits in forms such as:

● shares, share options, and other equity instruments, issued to employees at less than the fair value at which those instruments would have been issued to a third party; and

● cash payments, the amount of which depends on the future market price of the reporting enterprise's shares (AC 116, paragraph .145).

AC 116 does not require recognition of equity compensation benefits as an expense in the period they are granted, but does require comprehensive disclosure of these in the financial statements. Accordingly, the benefit is only recorded as an expense in the period that it is actually paid. There is some debate whether employee share or stock options should be expensed, rather than the present treatment generally applied, which is to recognize share options as equity only when exercised, by means of a Debit to Bank and Credit to Equity, without any recognition of an expense in the income statement. It seems that present accounting standards do not accommodate the economic realities of the benefits derived by employees from holding share options. There is also some debate around whether the benefit should be determined and measured at the grant date, the vesting date or the exercise date, as employees are not legally obligated to perform future services for the entity when they receive equity stock options and the entity usually has the right to cancel options not exercised when the employee leaves the employ of the entity.[1]

Detailed disclosures are required in the financial statements with regard to equity compensation plans, which are specified in AC 116 paragraphs .148 and .149.

---

[1] Mozes H., *The FASB's Conceptual Framework and Political Support: The Lesson from Employee Stock Options*, ABACUS, Vol 34, No 2, 1998 (pages 141–161).

In terms of section 223 of the Companies Act, employee share options plans granted to directors require the approval of the shareholders by way of a special resolution. In terms of section 38 (2)(b) and (c) of the Companies Act, a company may:

- 'In accordance with any scheme for the time in force, provide money for the subscription for, or purchase of, shares of the company or its holding company by trustees, to be held by or for the benefit of employees of the company, including any director holding a salaried employment or office in the company; or

- The making by a company of loans to employees to persons other than directors, bona fide in the employment of the company with a view to enabling those persons to purchase or subscribe for shares of the company or holding company to be held by themselves as owners.'

As the directors' power to allot shares is restricted in terms of section 221 of the Companies Act, any such employee share or share option schemes require the approval of the shareholders by means of a specific authority granted for the particular scheme. Usually this will include the specific allocation of shares to the trustees for the purpose of the scheme. The terms of the scheme will be set out in the agreement and the trustees will have to abide by the conditions in granting such shares or share options to employees and employee directors. The Companies Act requires disclosure of the full details to be made in the notes to the financial statements.

The King II Report (2002, at pages 27, 58 and 62) with regard to the suggested allocation of share options to non-executive directors advises directors to:

- 'Apply a vesting period to avoid short term decision taking and to consider the impact of such options on the independence of the non-executive director;

- Any re-pricing of share options proposed should require shareholder approval and details of the share options of any executive and non-executive director who stands to benefit should be provided to shareowners and subject to approval individually for each director.

- If share options are to be issued at a discount to the ruling price, shareowners should vote separately on this clause in the trust deed establishing the share scheme at inception.'

Substantive tests of detail for equity compensation plans

As with the other types of employee benefits already mentioned, the auditor should obtain a schedule from the client setting out the equity compensation benefits to support the disclosures required in terms of paragraphs 148 and 149 of AC 116. The auditor would ordinarily perform the following substantive tests of detail for equity compensation plans:

- In a continuing audit, details of the accounting policies, opening balances and details of share and share option schemes and agreements for the payment of cash bonuses based on equity movements should be agreed to the prior year's audit working papers.

- As these equity compensation schemes are invariably placed into trusts, the auditor needs to have access to the trust deed and trust records to inspect movements by way of shares and/or share options issued to employees, sold or lapsed and cancelled in terms of the share scheme.

- Inspect shareholders' minutes for any new shares or share options allocated for this purpose and agree the terms of the equity compensation plans to the relevant trust deed.

- Inspect movements on loans granted to employees by the trust and re-payments made by employees in respect of capital and recalculate the interest charges for amounts owing. Enquire whether the interest benefit has been included in the employees' gross income for purposes of the IRP 5 Tax Certificate issued by the reporting enterprise.

- Inspect the supporting documentation, such as that of brokers or STRATE, bought and sold notes for shares purchased or sold by employees exercising their rights during the period, as well as the tax paid to SARS in respect of the taxable benefit arising on the profit on disposal by the employee of any shares or options exercised. Similarly trace the benefit realized to the employees, IRP 5 tax certificate, or accumulated short-term employee benefits.

- Review and re-perform the computation of amounts reflected on the clients' schedule for the calculation of the fair value measurement of the entity's own financial instruments at the beginning and end of the period and in respect of equity issued by the entity or equity compensation plans during the period. Obtain confirmation of the discount rate applied to determine the fair values of the instruments.

- Obtain confirmation from employees entitled to participate in equity compensation plans in respect of amounts owing by them at period end, as well as repayment terms and interest rates charged, on loans granted for the purchase of shares or share options to the company or trust set up to administer the share or share option schemes.

- Inspect the presentation and disclosures in the financial statements to be satisfied that these conform to the requirements of AC 116.

15.3.6 Presentation and disclosure

The presentation and disclosure requirements contained in AC 116 are comprehensive, as are the requirements for the recognition and measurement of employee benefits. The auditor will need to be satisfied that there is adherence to the disclosure requirements of AC 116 and other relevant AC statements, as well as requirements of the Companies Act, and JSE Listing Requirements for public listed companies, or any other Act regulating the particular entity that might affect its financial statement disclosures. Due to the comprehensive nature of these disclosures, they are not represented here.

16

Auditing Investing and Financing Transactions and Balances

Learning objectives

After studying this chapter you should be able to:

1. Describe the nature of the investing and financing business processes and identify significant classes of transactions and balances related thereto.
2. Set audit objectives for the audit of *investing* and *financing* transactions and related balances.
3. Describe the functions and control activities for *investing* and *financing* transactions and balances.
4. Explain how the assessment of the risk of significant misstatement by the auditor determines an acceptable level of detection risk for *investing* and *financing* transactions and balances.
5. Design substantive audit procedures to respond appropriately to the risk of significant misstatement for *investing* and *financing* transactions and balances.
6. Discuss the factors to be considered when auditing fair value measurements for balances arising from *investing* and *financing* activities.

16.1 OVERVIEW OF INVESTING AND FINANCING ACTIVITIES

The preceding chapters have dealt with the significant classes of revenue and expenditure transactions arising from the core business processes of business entities. This chapter focuses on the nature and audit of capital resources from *investing* and *financing* activities of the entity, while chapter 17 deals with *investment* activities and the audit of the entity's *cash and bank* transactions and balances.

The capital *investing* and *financing* activities provide the infrastructure for the business to accomplish its strategic business objectives and implement its core business processes. Management will acquire and employ a variety of capital resources to generate income and grow the business and will finance these capital resources from equity or borrowings. In many entities, the amount invested in long-term assets will be significant, requiring substantial external funding. In some instances, the management of certain categories of an entity's assets may itself constitute a core process. Business continuity risks may arise where the entity is unable to generate expected returns from assets employed, or where it is unable to support the cost of long-term financing, or is unable to repay long-term borrowings when due.

In order to evaluate the risk of significant misstatement and determine appropriate audit responses, the auditor needs to understand the following aspects of the entity's *investing* and *financing* activities:

- The nature and significance of tangible and intangible assets used in the business operations.
- The nature and incidence of additions and disposals of assets that have occurred during the financial period.
- How the assets acquired have been funded.
- Management's expected returns on assets acquired.
- Management's strategic plans for growing the assets of the business and how management proposes funding future acquisitions, including capital commitments arising from further capital expenditures approved, and whether or not already contracted for at the period end.

16.1.1 Investing activities

Investing activities comprise the acquisition, disposal and management of tangible assets. Such tangible assets include land and buildings, plant and machinery, motor vehicles, furniture and equipment, computer hardware, software and communication networks. GAAP AC 123 'Property, plant and equipment', and GAAP AC 135 'Investment property' address these aspects. An entity may incur further expenditure on existing assets when upgrading them so as to increase their income-earning capacity.

Investing activities include also the acquisition, disposal and management of intangible assets such as goodwill, research and development expenditure, patents and trademarks (including brands and franchises), scientific and technical know-how, intellectual property rights such as copyright, and mining and mineral rights and licences. GAAP AC 129, 'Intangible assets', discusses the appropriate treatment of these.

Entities must adopt accounting policies for depreciating, or systematically expensing, the cost of its long-term assets over the expected useful lives of these, which results in a recognition of the current depreciation charge in the income statement, and a balance of accumulated depreciation reducing the carrying value of assets in the balance sheet. The basis for measuring and recognizing depreciation must comply with GAAP AC 123, 'Property, plant and equipment', and these should be applied on a consistent basis.

Management must consider whether impairment losses have arisen for any of the entity's tangible assets by determining the asset's recoverable amount, which is the greater of an asset's 'value in use' and its 'net selling price' (AC 128 paragraph .06). An impairment loss is defined as 'the amount by which the carrying amount of an asset exceeds its recoverable amount'. Impairment losses charged against assets reduce their carrying values as reflected in the balance sheet. The term 'value in use' is defined in GAAP AC 128, 'Impairment of assets', which gives guidance also on how it should be measured and recognized. The basis that should be used for amortization of intangible assets capitalized is dealt with in GAAP AC 129, 'Intangible assets'.

Although the amount invested in tangible and intangible assets for an established business may be significant, long-term assets are generally fairly stable, often with few acquisitions and disposals during any one accounting period. Consequently, the auditor may assess the risk of significant misstatement of such transactions and balances as low. The audit approach to investing activities in such circumstances comprises substantive analytical procedures for calculating the current depreciation expense, impairment losses and amortization for all assets with substantive tests of detail that focus on obtaining audit evidence to support the *completeness, occurrence* and *measurement* of additions, and disposals, and recognition of gains and losses on disposal of assets, and the *completeness, existence, measurement, valuation* and *rights and obligations* of significant asset and repairs and maintenance balances at period end. The rationale behind this approach is that because there are often few investing transactions in number, which constitute a substantial proportion of the movement in asset account balances for the period, obtaining substantive evidence for relatively few purchases or sales transactions would cover a substantial monetary amount of the movement in fixed assets accounts for the period.

16.1.2 Financing activities

Financing activities are the means by which the entity obtains its funding. This may be in the form of funds obtained from the issue of shares or borrowings. Financing activities also include finance leases and operating leases entered into for the specific acquisition, or use of, capital assets.

Financing transactions give rise to receipts from new share issues, or loans and payments for the repurchase and cancellation of shares of the company, now allowed by the 1999 Companies Act, as long as certain requirements are met. The reader is referred to sections 85 to 90 of the Act. Payments also arise in meeting debt repayment obligations.

The auditor should obtain an understanding of the entity's financing arrangements and the different *rights* and *obligations* arising from them. These might include the following for loans:

- Security granted to a lender in the form of:
  - mortgage bonds registered over fixed property;
  - ownership rights retained by lessors over fixed assets acquired under finance leases; and
  - notarial bonds passed by an entity over movable assets, such as inventory, to secure loans provided by a lender.
- Amounts owing by accounts receivable pledged to a discount finance house against advances provided to the entity on discounting its book of accounts receivable.
- Guarantees provided by a holding company to a third party lender for loans granted to its subsidiary companies.

Interest rates, finance charges and repayment terms will differ depending on the terms of the loan. The rights and obligations of both parties will be contained in the relevant loan contract documents. Certain classes of shares may carry preferential rights to dividends, details of which will be contained in the Articles of Association and governed by the Companies Act. The related expenditure transactions and balances include cash outflows for:

- Dividends declared;
- Interest charges;
- Finance charges on leases;
- Lease rentals for operating leases;
- Foreign exchange gains and losses might arise where borrowings are obtained from a foreign source;
- Hedge gains and losses may also arise, where management enters hedge transactions for certain assets and liabilities. The requirements for recognition and measurement of such transactions are contained in GAAP AC 133, 'Financial instruments: recognition and measurement'.

The volume of transactions from purchases or disposals of assets during a financial period are usually not significant other than in circumstances where the investing and financing activities comprise core business processes, or in the event of major capital expansion initiatives or the discontinuance of operations. Whilst few in number, such transactions often involve significant monetary amounts.

Financing activities, whether by way of equity, long-term or short-term borrowings and leasing of key resources acquired, are usually directly linked to the investment in capital resources as part of an entity's core business activities. Consequently, obtaining evidence about one aspect provides evidence of the other. For example, confirmation from a lessor regarding amounts owing for a finance lease provides evidence of the *existence, measurement, valuation* and *rights and obligations* of the lease liability, while simultaneously providing evidence of the *existence, measurement* and *rights and obligations* of the particular capitalized asset leased.

The auditor would usually assess the risk of significant misstatement for these transactions as low because, whilst the amounts raised from a share issue or loan obtained may be significant, the incidence of these is likely to be few, if any, in any financial period, and further because funds obtained will generally be used for the acquisition of new assets. On the other hand, short-term financing, such as bank overdraft facilities, will be ongoing and linked to the daily treasury management of cash and bank transactions. The high volume of cash and bank transactions is likely to lead to an assessment of the risk of significant misstatement as high, unless the auditor can obtain evidence that management's controls and monitoring procedures over cash and bank are effective.

The nature of investing and financing transactions are such that they generally involve a high level of formal authorization, usually minuted at meetings of the board of directors or shareholders that provide authorization of specific transactions or the delegation of authority to senior management. Certain transactions are further regulated by statute, such as share issues. Consequently, where regular and significant investing and financing transactions occur but management has strict controls in place and effective monitoring processes and key performance indicators, the auditor may assess the risk of significant misstatement from investing and financing activities as medium to low and follow a test of controls approach. The auditor will then set a higher level of detection risk and obtain much of the audit evidence required for the entity's investing and financing activities from substantive analytical procedures with limited substantive tests of detail performed.

By obtaining an understanding of the critical success factors and key performance indicators used by management to monitor the relationships between the resources acquired, the financing of these and the effect on the income statement of the related income and expenditure transactions and balances flowing from them, the auditor is able to perform meaningful substantive analytical procedures. The results of the substantive analytical procedures would identify the risk of significant misstatement remaining, and enable the auditor to focus the substantive tests of detail effectively to detect and correct material errors and fraud related to specific audit objectives of: *completeness, occurrence/validity, measurement/accuracy* of transactions during the period, and the *existence/occurrence, valuation, rights and obligations* and *presentation and disclosure* of significant balances at period end.

When auditing the asset and liability balances and transactions discussed in this chapter and in applying a risk based top-down audit approach, the auditor must bear in mind his or her statutory responsibilities, as contained in section 20(1)(e) of the Public Accountants' and Auditors' Act, *inter-alia*: 'to obtain evidence of the *existence* of *all assets and liabilities* shown in such financial statements'. Similarly, in section 300(e) of the Companies Act, 'to examine or satisfy him/herself as to the *existence of any securities* of the company', and in section 300(l) of the Companies Act, 'to comply with any applicable sections of the Public Accountants' and Auditors' Act'.

16.2 NATURE OF INVESTING TRANSACTIONS AND BALANCES

16.2.1 Introduction

As already discussed, the investing activities of the entity relate to the purchase or leasing, and sale, of land and buildings, factory plant and equipment, computer hardware and software, office furniture and equipment and motor vehicles. Such tangible assets are not acquired for the purpose of resale, but are intended for use by the entity in its core business processes, whether manufacturing, trading, the provision of services or for rental to others. Investing activities may also relate to the acquisition or development of intangible assets, such as purchased goodwill, or research and development expenditure for new product development and registration of patents and trademarks.

Tangible and intangible assets held on a long-term basis by an entity tend to be fairly stable from one period to the next and, accordingly, the verification of such assets by the auditor in a continuing engagement may be directed to the *completeness, occurrence* and *measurement* of purchases and disposals of the assets during the period and to establishing the *existence and valuation, ownership and rights and obligations,* as well as the *presentation and disclosures* of balances at the period end, in accordance with the relevant GAAP statements that apply, such as: AC 123 'Property, Plant and Equipment', and AC 129 'Intangible Assets', and AC 128 'Impairment of Assets'.

Where land and buildings are held by the owner or lessee under a finance lease, to earn rentals, or for capital appreciation and sale in the ordinary course of business, or are held for sale in the ordinary course of business (for example, land which comprises inventory in the hands of a property developer), such land and buildings are regarded as investment properties and would be accounted for in accordance with GAAP AC 135, 'Investment Property'. Properties that do not meet the criteria of an investment property, such as those used in the production or supply of goods and services or for administrative purposes, are accounted for in terms of AC 123. For convenience, the audit procedures contained in this chapter relating to land and buildings deal with both investment properties and owner occupied properties rather than being dealt with under investment activities in chapter 17.

The risk of significant misstatement for long-term assets lie in the *occurrence* and *measurement* criteria applied to individual transactions entered into and recorded, in the nature of *ownership and rights and obligations* over particular assets, as well as in the determination of the carrying values, *valuation,* at period end. Documents of title differ from one form of asset to another and it is important therefore for the auditor to recognize, where applicable, what documentation provides reliable audit evidence of existence and rights and obligations. These aspects are discussed later in this chapter.

The auditor should obtain evidence of charges against income that relate to assets such as the *measurement* of depreciation in respect of tangible assets, the amortization of intangible assets, and the recognition of impairment losses on assets required to reduce the carrying value of an asset to its recoverable amount or its value in use, determined in accordance with GAAP.

16.2.2 Audit objectives

Before proceeding to identify the objectives of an audit of investing transactions and balances, it is appropriate first to recognize the account balances affected by such activities, as set out in Table 16.1 below:

INVESTING TRANSACTIONS	ACCOUNT BALANCES DEBITED	ACCOUNT BALANCES CREDITED
Purchase of assets; Capitalization of assets acquired under a finance lease; Capitalization of leasehold property expenses.	Land and buildings; Plant and equipment; Shop fittings; Motor vehicles; Office equipment (including computer hardware and software).	Accounts payable; Long-term loans; Lease accounts payable (for capitalized finance leases) Bank.
Disposals of assets capitalized.	Accounts receivable or Bank; Accumulated depreciation; Revaluation reserve; Loss on disposal.	Land and buildings; Plant and equipment; Motor vehicles; Office equipment; Profit on disposal.
Purchase or development of intangible assets.	Goodwill; Patents or trademarks; Research; Development.	Accounts payable; Bank.
Revaluations of fixed assets.	Land and buildings; Plant and equipment.	Revaluation reserve (NDR).

INVESTING TRANSACTIONS	ACCOUNT BALANCES DEBITED	ACCOUNT BALANCES CREDITED
Depreciation or Amortization.	Depreciation expense; Amortization of intangibles.	Accumulated depreciation; Accumulated amortization.
Impairment losses of assets and reversal of impairment loss.	Impairment loss; Accumulated depreciation.	Accumulated depreciation; Impairment loss reversed.
Maintenance of capital assets.	Repairs and maintenance.	Accounts payable or Bank.

Table 16.1 General ledger account balances typically affected by capital investing transactions

Whilst there are a number of different accounts affected by different investing activities, only the purchase and sale of assets and maintenance expenditures involve transactions with third parties. The other transactions involve transfers between balance sheet and income statement accounts. The internal transfers arise from the application of accounting policies and exercise of judgement regarding the carrying values of assets, determined in accordance with various GAAP statements. Such estimates could give rise to a risk of significant misstatement affecting the *valuation* assertion.

The auditor needs to gather sufficient appropriate audit evidence regarding specific assertions contained in the income statement and balance sheet balances arising from investing transactions. The audit objectives specific to the investing transactions and balances are set out in Table 16.2. The auditor should identify those assertions most likely to lead to a risk of significant misstatement for different assets to focus the audit procedures accordingly.

MANAGEMENT ASSERTION	AUDIT OBJECTIVES
Purchases and sales of tangible and intangible assets	
Completeness	Recorded acquisitions and disposals of tangible and intangible assets include all such transactions that occurred during the period.
	Recorded proceeds from disposals include all disposals of assets that occurred during the period.
	All recorded expenditures on repairs and maintenance occurred during the period.

MANAGEMENT ASSERTION	AUDIT OBJECTIVES
Occurrence/ validity	Recorded acquisitions and disposals of tangible and intangible assets actually occurred during the period, were properly authorized and none are duplicated.
	The proceeds from all disposals that occurred during the period are recorded and were received during the period.
	Recorded repairs and maintenance expenditures represent transactions that actually occurred during the period and none are duplicated.
Measurement/ accuracy	Acquisitions and disposals of tangible and intangible assets, proceeds from disposals, and repairs and maintenance expenditures have been recognized and measured in accordance with the GAAP policies applied by the entity on a consistent basis.
Investment in tangible and intangible assets	
Completeness	Tangible and intangible asset balances at balance sheet date include the effect of all investing transactions during the period.
Existence	Recorded tangible assets exist and represent productive assets in use at balance sheet date.
Measurement/ accuracy	Tangible assets are stated at cost or revaluation.
	Accumulated depreciation at balance sheet date represents the allocation of the cost of tangible assets and any impairment losses in accordance with GAAP and the accounting policies of the entity applied on a consistent basis.
	Intangible assets are stated at cost less amounts amortized to balance sheet date.
Valuation	Tangible assets are stated at cost or revaluation less accumulated depreciation and less any write down for impairment of the tangible assets to reduce them to their carrying value at balance sheet date. Intangible assets are stated at cost less amounts amortized to balance sheet date.
Rights and obligations	The entity owns, or has the rights to, all recorded tangible assets at balance sheet date. The rights of any lender or lessor in respect of property mortgaged, leasehold improvements or assets capitalized under a finance lease to secure obligations of the entity, have been correctly identified.

MANAGEMENT ASSERTION	AUDIT OBJECTIVES
Presentation and disclosure	Disclosures of the cost or revaluation, carrying values, depreciation methods, and useful lives of major classes of tangible assets are appropriately disclosed. Appropriate disclosures have been made of assets mortgaged, capitalized leased assets and assets pledged as security for obligations of the entity.

Table 16.2 Management assertions and the related audit objectives for investing

16.2.3 Understanding the client's business

The auditor's understanding of the entity's core business processes enable development of expectations regarding the nature of tangible and intangible assets held by the entity, and how these are used to support its core business processes, which differ widely from one business to another, and from one industry to another, as indicated in earlier chapters. The history of ratios extracted by management for calculation of key performance indicators, such as percentage returns on assets invested, and those ratios obtained by the auditor from substantive analytical procedures related to fixed assets and financing provide an indication of percentages that such assets normally comprise and their relationship to financing activities. These relationships enable the auditor to identify unusual trends for discussion with the entity's management and staff so as to obtain explanations therefore.

Materiality

Fixed assets usually comprise a material part of the assets of most manufacturing and retailing businesses. Businesses in the service industry, such as profession consultancies, may require little investment in fixed assets to support their business activities. Other than for movable assets, such as motor vehicles or PCs, which are susceptible to theft, the material misstatement related to the *existence* assertion may be regarded as a low risk. Misallocations of expenditures between capital and expenditure on the other hand may give rise to a risk of significant misstatement and accordingly be assessed by the auditor as medium to high. Where few purchases and disposals of fixed assets occur during the year, this low incidence of transactions reduces the risk of error.

16.2.4 Analysing process level business risks

Where additions and disposals of fixed assets occur infrequently, which is often the case, the investing activities would be dealt with as one of the business level processes of the main core business processes of the entity. The process level business risks and controls to mitigate these are similar to those discussed in chapter 13, in which expenditure transactions and related balances were addressed. The auditor should obtain an understanding of the specific authorization requirements to be followed for acquisitions and disposals of long-term assets. These generally require the specific approval of top management, such as approval by the board of directors, and in certain circumstances may by statute require approval by shareholders, such as section 228 of the Companies Act, where the company disposes of the greater portion of the assets of the business. In a smaller business, authorization will generally be given by the owner manager.

Agreements for the acquisition, or leasing, of assets may be incorporated in comprehensive legal contracts setting out the rights and obligations of both parties. In large companies, the board of directors may set up a separate capital expenditure committee responsible for considering and prioritizing capital expenditure requests, the obtaining of tenders, negotiation of contracts, both for the acquisition of particular assets and borrowings to finance the acquisitions, and for presenting capital expenditure proposals to the board of directors for approval. The directors should monitor the implementation of capital expenditures approved.

In such circumstances, the auditor obtains the necessary audit evidence required mainly from substantive analytical procedures applied to the calculation of depreciation, impairment provisions and amortization, with substantive tests of detail procedures focused on the audit of fixed asset additions and disposals occurring during the period. As it is usually the case that these are few in number but significant in monetary amount, the gathering of audit evidence related to a relatively small number of transactions may cover a significant monetary amount of the total balance.

Consider the case of a *major retail trading operation* with several hundred supermarket stores located throughout South Africa. Whilst trading is the core business process, the volume of property transactions and their significance to income statement and balance sheet balances usually would result in *property management* forming a second core process. The auditor's understanding of the business process analysis may indicate a number of control activities over the *property management process* that appear to be applied effectively, and which, if tested and found to be effective, may enable the auditor to assess the risk of significant misstatement affecting these transactions and balances as medium to low. If the results of the tests of controls provide evidence of their effective operation, this evidence, when combined with audit evidence from substantive analytical procedures, justifies a reduction in the extent of substantive tests of detail to be performed.

16.2.5 Assessing the risk of significant misstatement

The auditor should consider the risk of significant misstatement affecting investing transactions and be alert to those that could occur in the particular client's business. The reader is referred to Table 11.2 and the discussion in chapter 11 in evaluating the overall risk of significant misstatement. The *inherent risks* likely to be encountered that are specific to investing transactions and balances include:

- *Management bias and incentive to misstate capital expenditure*, whether to achieve budgets, increase performance bonuses, inflate profits for reporting in the financial statements, to secure additional funding from banks, or to attract a potential purchaser for the business or to influence the share price on the local securities exchange.

- The *nature and complexity of the assets acquired* may lead to errors in recognition and *measurement*, such as incorrect account allocation. For example, maintenance costs capitalized when they should be expensed. Property development, such as the building and equipping of a new factory, could take several months and involves numerous costs, some to be capitalized and others to be expensed.

- The *valuation of intangible assets*, such as goodwill and brands, for which appropriate amortization rates may be difficult to establish.

- Difficulties in determining the *useful lives* of assets, or their *value in use* or *fair market values*, affect the measurement of depreciation, estimated impairment losses and the eventual carrying value of the assets in the balance sheet.

- The risk of *management override of controls* may give rise to *unauthorized acquisitions of assets* or to acquisitions in which management has a personal 'undisclosed' interest and derives undue benefit. For example, property purchased by a company from a director at a price that is well above market values and where the director has voted on the resolution at the board meeting where the decision to acquire the property was taken.

- The *risk of fraud and theft* of assets may be high for certain types of fixed assets, for example, theft of motor vehicles, personal computers and laptops or construction equipment, where security controls are ineffective or the entity carries inadequate insurance cover. This may affect the *existence* of assets reflected in the asset register.

- Evidence of *ownership* of assets and *rights and obligations* may be difficult to obtain if assets are leased under a finance lease, are mortgaged, or are part of a sale and leaseback arrangement. Terms of contracts entered into may be unclear, leading to incorrect disclosures in the financial statements.

- Where investing transactions are non-routine, this may lead to *errors in the recording* of such transactions by staff unsure of how to allocate the relevant acquisition or to adjust for the profit or loss on disposal of fixed assets.

- Proceeds on disposal of fixed assets may be overlooked and/or allocated to sundry revenue accounts with the result that the adjusting entries to record the disposal and the profit or loss on disposal of such assets may not be processed. The omission may be detected only as a result of a physical count of the assets and comparison to the details in the fixed asset register.

Before performing the tests of controls and substantive test procedures the auditor makes a preliminary assessment of the *risk of significant misstatement for the investing transactions and balances* in the financial statements. The auditor considers each of the following factors and documents his or her overall assessment as *high, medium or low, after assessing the effect of each factor*:

● The *historical accuracy/measurement*, that is, the previous experience of the auditor with the entity in respect of the investing transaction cycle, account balances and/or the different assertions.

● The *underlying assumptions used*, for example, whether depreciation rates are based on GAAP or industry specific rates for the particular class of assets; difficulty in estimating useful lives of assets or provisions for impairment losses, or accounting for capitalized finance leases and finance charges; and deferred tax implications of timing differences between wear and tear for tax purposes and depreciation and impairment losses expensed.

● The *qualifications and competence of the personnel* involved in accounting and recording and the *complexity of the estimating process* for the class of transactions or balances involved for the particular assertions affected.

● Any evidence of *management bias* and incentive to misstate, whether due to personal benefits to be derived, market pressures and expectations, and budget pressures from management or group companies.

The auditor should seek corroborating information by way of enquiries, inspection of documents or observation of control procedures performed, to support the preliminary assessment of the *risk of significant misstatement*, identifying the effect on the financial statements for particular account balances and designing appropriate audit procedures to detect and correct any risk of significant misstatement remaining.

16.2.6 Determining the acceptable level of detection risk

For the reasons discussed earlier in this chapter, the auditor's tests of the investing transactions and balances will usually include a greater proportion of substantive analytical procedures and substantive tests of detail, other than circumstances where the fixed assets form a core business process, necessitating an assessment of the risk of significant misstatement and possible tests of controls being performed. The engagement circumstances also must be taken into account.

16.2.6.1 First time audit

In the *first audit* of any client, the auditor needs to comply with the requirements of SAAS 510, 'The audit of opening balances', and must obtain sufficient appropriate audit evidence regarding the opening balances of fixed assets, capitalized leased assets, accumulated depreciation, provisions for impairment losses, and amortization of intangible assets. Necessary considerations are:

- 'The opening balances do not contain misstatements that materially affect the current period's financial statements;

- The prior period's closing balances have been correctly brought forward to the current period or, when appropriate, have been restated; and

- Appropriate accounting policies are consistently applied, or changes in accounting policies have been properly accounted for and adequately disclosed' (SAAS 510 paragraph .02). This includes the revaluation of any assets and treatment of the related revaluation reserves.

The audit evidence required to establish that the opening balances for assets do not contain material misstatements, relates to the *existence, measurement, valuation, rights and obligations* assertions for the different classes of fixed assets reflected in the opening balances. Factors that affect the auditor's determination of the acceptable level of detection risk in a first audit will include:

- Whether or not the opening balances have previously been audited by another auditor:
  - If previously audited, the current auditor may be able to obtain sufficient appropriate audit evidence by reviewing the predecessor auditor's audit working papers and considering the professional competence and independence of the predecessor auditor.
  - If not previously audited, the current auditor will have to perform far more substantive tests of detail to establish the existence and the appropriateness of the carrying values attributed to the opening balance of fixed assets.

- Whether the entity's fixed asset register details are in agreement with the total of the opening balances in the general ledger.

- Whether or not there is any indication that there are significant misstatements in the opening balances.

Where sufficient appropriate audit evidence regarding the various assertions for the opening balances of fixed assets cannot be obtained, the auditor may perform a substantive roll backward, taking account of the current period's closing balance, additions, disposals, depreciation, impairment losses and amortization charges, to establish the correctness of the opening balances by deduction.

16.2.6.2 Continuing audit engagement

In a *continuing audit engagement*, the work on the opening balances involves agreeing the amount of cost and accumulated depreciation and provisions for impairment losses and revaluation reserves to these items in the prior year's audit working papers and audited financial statements.

Thereafter, the auditor should consider the assessed risk of significant misstatement affecting the *completeness, occurrence and measurement* assertions in order to determine the substantive tests of detail needed to audit the current period's additions and disposals of assets to achieve an acceptable level of detection risk.

The audit of the current year's depreciation and impairment losses requires the auditor to consider:

- the assumptions of management regarding the expected useful lives of the assets, and their fair value measurement, being the asset's value in use or its realizable value on sale; and hence

- whether the depreciation rates applied, the impairment losses provided for, and the calculation of depreciation and impairment losses or amortization of assets during the period of the audit provide sufficient appropriate audit evidence of the *valuation* assertion to achieve an acceptable level of detection risk.

16.2.7 Substantive analytical procedures

As described in earlier chapters, substantive analytical procedures include comparisons of current information to prior years or budgets; ratio analysis, comparisons of financial and non-financial information derived from understanding the core processes and related business processes of the entity. Trends in *investing activities* may be established from historical information and changes explained by reason of internal and external events that have occurred, such as business expansion or discontinued operations or changes in accounting policies and management.

Where the audit is a continuing engagement, the auditor would have a record of past analyses of the entity's investing activities prepared in prior years on which to base initial expectations for the current period's analyses. These expectations are then modified for the purposes of the current audit for known changes in the business or economic circumstances.

The relevance of financial ratios for fixed assets differs widely and is dependent on the type of business and industry. As fixed assets are normally determined on historical cost, standard financial ratios may be meaningless. For example, the cost of plant purchased 30 years ago that is fully depreciated, yet is still being used in the manufacturing process, bears no relation to its replacement value or to the turnover generated from its use, as turnover and replacement value reflects current market values. Consequently, management should develop and use key performance indicators appropriate to the particular business enterprise, for example:

- A manufacturing operation with considerable investment in plant and equipment may try to measure the extent of utilization of the existing plant, or the productive output from the plant, where new plant and equipment is acquired, compared to budgets and projections at the time the plant was acquired.

- A hotel business may monitor room occupancy rates as an indication of the utilization of its investment in fixed assets.

- A company that holds investment properties may measure its returns on the basis of rentals from properties let versus unoccupied properties, or on rentals per square metre for different properties or those located in different areas.

- The geographic location of the business will affect the expected returns, for example, a fair return on assets (EBIT – based on net earnings before interest and tax) based on revenue of a manufacturing business may be 15% in South Africa (inflation around 12% in 2002), 100% in Zimbabwe (inflation at 140% in 2002), and 5% in Australia (inflation around 3% in 2002). The differential is driven by the economic situation in each country and the inflation rates experienced, as well as industry norms.

Thus, where applicable, the auditor should ascertain global benchmarks for the industry and compare these to the key performance indicators used by management to assess the performance of their entity.

In many instances entities will make use of computerized fixed asset registers and the application software will be programmed to calculate the depreciation expense and tax wear and tear allowances for every asset in accordance with rates contained in the standing data for each category of asset. Provided the initial take on information for each asset – such as: asset description, cost, date of acquisition, category of asset, expected useful life and any special tax allowances and wear and tear rates – has been correctly captured into the register, the auditor can effectively use CAATs to test the programmed calculations and thereafter may stratify these into different categories of assets and recalculate the overall depreciation expense and the wear and tear tax allowance for the period.

Chapter 11 identified five steps to be followed in using substantive analytical procedures in order for any analytical reviews to be effective in throwing into relief significant departures from the prediction or expectation, or confirming that recorded amounts are in line with these. When substantive analytical procedures are applied to the fixed asset transactions and balances comprising the financial statements these are:

Develop a prediction or expectation

This would relate to expectations for total or average fixed assets and any expected increases or changes in the composition of different classes of fixed assets and fixed asset utilization for the particular entity, industry norms or global norms. The auditor would exercise great care in accepting audit evidence from substantive analytical procedures in the case of repair and

maintenance expenditures due to the risk of misstatement from misallocations between the fixed asset accounts and repair and maintenance
expenditure accounts and, accordingly, should perform additional substantive tests of detail to verify the measurement of additions. Where
management has an incentive to understate profits, for example, to reduce
tax liability, it may expense acquisitions that should be capitalized, and
where management has an incentive to overstate profits, it may capitalize
items that should be expensed, or fail to provide adequately for impairment
losses.

Compute the difference between the actual and the expected

This would involve the re-performance of various ratios, including key
performance indicators used by management to monitor the business. These
results are compared to prior periods, to budgets or strategic returns set by
management, and to a history of such ratios maintained by the client or
auditor. Calculation of key performance indicators used by management and
enquiry about corrective action taken where problems are indicated provide
evidence of the effectiveness of management's monitoring procedures. Using
a property management core business process, the key performance
indicators used may include:

- Footfalls per store;
- Conversion rate of customers entering to customers purchasing;
- Capital budget overruns;
- Sales per square metre of store area; and
- Other relationships that are relevant to the particular assets and their use
  (these would be developed by management and be ascertained by the
  auditor).

Investigate significant differences and exercise judgement

The auditor would analyse ratios relative to expectations formulated above.
Any unexpected fluctuations should be discussed with management and
where necessary investigated further.

Define a significant difference or threshold to conclude

The auditor would ascertain whether the ratios and benchmarks used by
management as key performance indicators indicate any risk of significant
misstatements and consider the implications of trends identified affecting the
profitability, cash flows and sustainability of the business. Consider the
effectiveness of management's monitoring procedures to detect and correct
significant misstatements for the various assertions.

Document the basis for conclusion

The auditor would conclude on whether or not the audit evidence gathered
supports the assertions/audit objectives.

16.2.8 **Substantive tests of detail of transactions**

The auditor's substantive tests of detail applied in the audit of investing transactions focus on obtaining evidence of the *completeness, occurrence, existence and measurement* of fixed asset additions, disposals, depreciation, and profits and losses on disposals. At period end the focus is on gathering audit evidence relating to the *existence, valuation, ownership, rights and obligations* and the *presentation* and *disclosure* of the various account balances, to reflect the appropriate carrying values of fixed assets and capital commitments, determined in accordance with GAAP.

A framework for possible substantive tests of fixed asset transactions and related balances is set out in Table 16.3.

SUBSTANTIVE TESTS FOR EACH CATEGORY OF ASSETS	AUDIT OBJECTIVES				
	C	O/E	M/V	R/O	P/D
1. Obtain and document an understanding of the business:	X	X	X	X	X
Identify significant classes of assets for the entity:					
– Identify strategic plans of management with regard to investing activities and changes in fixed assets; – Identify critical success factors and key performance indicators used by management; – Identify economic and industry circumstances affecting the client; – Identify industry norms for measurement and valuation of assets and accounting policies applied by the client.					
Obtain trial balances or schedules of the balances of fixed assets costs and accumulated depreciation, provisions for impairment of assets, amortization and revaluation reserves:	X		X		
– Agree opening balances for fixed assets and accumulated depreciation to the previous year's working papers; – Review movements of fixed asset and repairs and maintenance accounts in the general ledger for unusual entries and investigate these; – Obtain a schedule of fixed asset additions, disposals and retirements, depreciation, impairment losses and profits and losses on disposal, to support the carrying values reflected in the general ledger, financial statements and register of fixed assets; – Cast schedules, general ledger and fixed assets register and agree total of fixed assets register to the fixed assets schedule and closing balances in the relevant fixed assets, accumulated depreciation, provision for impairment and amortization accounts in the general ledger.					

SUBSTANTIVE TESTS FOR EACH CATEGORY OF ASSETS	AUDIT OBJECTIVES				
	C	O/E	M/V	R/O	P/D
2. Substantive analytical procedures:	×	×	×		
Develop a prediction or expectation based on the auditor's knowledge of the business activities and strategic business risks and the industry.					
Define a significant difference or threshold – based on materiality at account balance level.					
Calculate various relevant fixed asset ratios and key performance indicators used by management.					
Compute the difference between the actual and the expected, compare to prior periods, to budget and to a history of such ratios maintained.					
Investigate significant differences and exercise judgement to conclude on implications and trends.					
Document the basis for the audit conclusion.					
3. Tests of detail of transactions:	×	×	×	×	×
Select all material transactions recorded and inspect supporting documents for approval (such as minutes, invoices, documents of title), and agreements such as leases, mortgage bonds and pledges of assets used to secure liabilities for: – Purchases of fixed assets; – Disposals and retirements of fixed assets and sundry revenue received for proceeds from disposals; – Maintenance and expenditure transactions; – Research and development costs for internally generated intangible assets.					
Review minutes and capital expenditure authorizations for indications of capital commitments.		×	×		×
Inquire about significant events affecting fixed assets whether during the period or subsequent to period end (e.g. assets damaged by fire or theft, discontinued operations, major new developments, or acquisitions of other businesses).		×	×		×
4. Tests of details of balances: Physically inspect assets reflected in the fixed asset registers; look for evidence of impaired condition and indications of assets disposed of, but still recorded, and new assets acquired.		×	×		
Inspect documents of title and contracts for assets such as property, vehicles, capitalized leased assets and assets partially completed at period end and included in capital work in progress.		×	×	×	×
Recalculate depreciation and impairment losses for period and assess consistency and appropriateness of depreciation rates applied and estimated useful lives and residual values of assets.				×	×
Recalculate profits and losses on disposals and retirement of assets.				×	×

SUBSTANTIVE TESTS FOR EACH CATEGORY OF ASSETS	AUDIT OBJECTIVES				
	C	O/E	M/V	R/O	P/D
4. continued					
Review minutes and capital expenditure authorizations for indications of capital commitments approved and contracted for.		×	×	×	×
Inquire about significant current and/or subsequent events, e.g. assets damaged by fire or theft, discontinued operations that may affect the *measurement and/ or valuation* of fixed assets.		×			×
5. Presentation and disclosure:					
Determine that the *presentation and disclosure* of asset cost, accumulated depreciation and provisions for impairment or amortization, revaluations and carrying values of assets and related depreciation, gains and losses accord with GAAP and are properly identified and classified in the financial statements.					×
					×
Determine whether the financial statement notes reflect the *rights and obligations* of the entity with regard to assets mortgaged, pledged or leased to secure liabilities of the entity, or others, and capital commitments approved and contracted for.					×

Table 16.3 Framework for the content of a substantive audit programme for investing transactions and balances

Substantive tests of detail of transactions relate to the audit of transactions between the client entity and third parties, to gather audit evidence regarding the *completeness, occurrence and measurement* of each class of transaction, namely:

- Fixed asset additions;
- Disposals of fixed assets; and
- Repairs and maintenance.

Given the variety and diversity of capital expenditure encountered in different businesses and industries, when auditing each of the three aspects mentioned above, the auditor should take care to recognize what constitutes sufficient appropriate audit evidence in the particular circumstances, and should exercise professional scepticism in accepting explanations from management or employees, remaining alert to the possibility of error or fraud that may lead to significant misstatement in the financial statements. Matters which the auditor should consider when auditing each of the classes of transactions, are discussed briefly below.

16.2.8.1 Fixed asset additions

Authorization of fixed asset additions

All fixed asset additions should be supported by the appropriate authorization. Depending on the size of the entity and the nature and materiality of the cost of the asset being acquired, this may take the form of formal written proposals from a capital expenditure committee (charged with the responsibility for overseeing all capital expenditures) submitted to the board of directors for approval. Such proposals will usually be supported by quotes obtained from different suppliers, or where more complex projects are proposed, may involve input and presentations to the board of directors from various professionals, for example, from architects and quantity surveyors in a proposed property development project; from IT consultants where proposals for significant changes are proposed to the entity's IT systems; from technical advisers such as engineers, chemists and environmental experts for new factory plant and equipment acquisitions being negotiated.

The decision of the board of directors should be minuted at the directors' meeting, which approval will invariably include authorization for specific directors to sign the relevant contracts flowing from the capital commitment approved. Such contracts may include those for the acquisition of the assets, maintenance and warranties provided by the supplier, installation contracts for plant and equipment or computer systems, building contracts, mortgage bonds over property, lease agreements and guarantees to mention but a few.

Capital acquisition proposals put to the board of directors will invariably include an indication of the source of financing to be used for funding the acquisition of the assets, particularly where the amounts are significant and will require additional funding to be obtained beyond the existing resources of the entity. The directors will have regard to the borrowing powers granted to them in terms of the articles of association of the company and the capacity of the entity to service the capital repayments and interest or dividends. The financing aspects are dealt with later in this chapter.

In very large organizations, the board of directors may well have established different levels of authorization for capital acquisitions for different amounts and categories of assets, allowing for the delegation of responsibility to department management. For example, a branch manager may have authority to authorize individual asset purchases of certain categories of assets up to say R10 000, but will be required to submit capital expenditure requests or proposals to the board of directors for approval for individual transactions in excess of R10 000. Alternatively, the organization may approve capital budgets for different departments or core business processes that the responsible management has the authority to spend on acquisitions of fixed assets.

In a smaller or owner-managed business, the authorization process will be far less formal and may simply involve administration, accounting or technical staff obtaining a few quotes from possible suppliers for consideration by the owner manager who then considers his or her options and decides what to purchase, from which supplier, negotiates the terms and conditions, and signs the purchase order as evidence of approval. Where such a business is conducted as a company, it is possible that few directors' meetings will be held during the year, and the board approval of fixed asset additions during the period may be by means of approval of the list of all fixed asset additions and disposals during the period minuted at the directors' meeting at which the annual financial statements are approved. There is an increased risk, in such circumstances, that fixed asset additions may be misallocated to expenditure accounts, that costs incurred may be omitted in error or that personal capital expenditures of the owner manager are recorded as capital expenditures of the business. Where the business is conducted in the form of a partnership or a trust, the authorization required for expenditure on assets will be from the partners or the trustees respectively.

An aspect that the auditor needs to be alert to is the possibility that directors may fail to disclose their interest in contracts for the acquisition of assets and such non-disclosure and acquisition may be prejudicial to the entity, or the directors involved may gain an undue benefit or enrichment from the transaction or may have gone so far as to defraud the company.

Once approved, most capital expenditures follow the usual issue of a purchase order, evidence of the receipt of the assets, which may be the delivery note from the supplier signed by the person receiving the items, the receipt of the invoice from the supplier and paid cheque or printout of the EFT payment to the supplier. The reader is referred to chapter 13 for a detailed discussion of the nature and audit of expenditure transactions and balances.

In other instances, the acquisition of fixed assets will require a formal, signed contract and formal statutory procedures and documentation to evidence the receipt of the goods and ownership by the entity. In auditing fixed asset additions, the auditor should inspect the relevant supporting documentation described to establish the *completeness, occurrence and measurement* of the items. Care should be taken to ensure that all related costs of delivery, customs duty if imported, and installation costs are allocated appropriately to capital or relevant expenditure accounts in the general ledger.

Assets acquired under a lease

Where the fixed assets have been acquired under a capital lease, the auditor should ascertain whether the lease is a *finance lease*, which is defined in AC 105, 'Leases', in paragraph .04 as:

'A lease that transfers substantially all the risks and rewards incident to ownership of an asset';

or an *operational lease*, which is defined in AC 105, 'Leases', in paragraphs .04 and .07 as:

'A lease other than a finance lease, i.e. it does not transfer substantially all the risks and rewards incident to ownership'.

The determination of the lease as a finance lease or operational lease will determine the correct accounting treatment to be followed, namely, either to capitalize the cost of the assets and to raise the lease creditor as a liability at the fair value at inception of the lease (AC 105 paragraph .14); with lease payments being apportioned between the finance charges and the reduction of the outstanding liability. The finance charges should be expensed over the lease period. The finance lease gives rise to a depreciation expense for the asset on a basis consistent with that applied to the relevant category of asset.

In the case of an operating lease, lease rentals are recognized in the income statement on a straight line basis spread over the lease term (AC 105 paragraph .27) with a note in the financial statements as to the future commitment for lease payments on operating leases and the periods in which such payments will fall due in terms of AC 105 paragraph .29.

Inspection of the purchase documents and lease agreement, combined with evidence of delivery of the asset and inspection of the documents of title (see Table 16.4) provides evidence of the *occurrence and existence* of the assets. Inspection of the lease contract provides evidence of the *rights and obligations* of the parties, including ownership rights in the asset and provides the basis for *valuation* of the assets acquired. Table 16.4 sets out the documents that may provide evidence of title to land and buildings, and motor vehicles.

Commitments for capital expenditure

In terms of paragraph 36 of the Fourth Schedule to the Companies Act and GAAP AC 123, any commitments in respect of contracts for capital expenditure should be stated as a note to the balance sheet, distinguishing between capital expenditure authorized, but not yet contracted for, and that already contracted for, and the source from which funds to meet such expenditure will be obtained.

The auditor should obtain evidence regarding the *completeness, valuation* and *rights and obligations* for capital commitments of an entity, both approved and contracted for, and those approved but not contracted for, at period end, and the source of funding to meet such commitments, by inspection of the relevant directors' board minutes or capital expenditure committee's minutes approving the expenditures, and any signed contracts for the supply of the assets and provision of funding. In the case of a sole trader or partnership, the auditor should enquire from the owner or partners.

A scrutiny of the purchase orders for a few months immediately prior to the period end may disclose orders for machinery or other fixed assets, which are outstanding at the close of the year. Again, if the audit is not completed until a considerable time after the close of the financial year, a scrutiny of the records of purchases of fixed assets for the subsequent period may supply information as to commitments in respect of the relevant contracts, which had been concluded prior to the period end.

16.2.8.2 Disposals of fixed assets

Proceeds from disposals of fixed assets usually take the form of cash receipts or trade-in values offset against the purchase prices of new assets purchased to replace the assets disposed of, such as motor vehicle trade-ins. They may also take the form of claim payouts from insurers for assets stolen or damaged in an accident or fire or other *casus fortuitous* or 'act of god', such as an earthquake or tornado. Insurance policies may, however, exclude claims and losses arising from terrorist acts such as bombings, leading to the destruction of property or lives. In such instances, the entity may be left with a claim against the government.

As disposals and scrapping of fixed assets are unlikely to form the core business of the entity, or to occur frequently, even in a large organization, the control procedures are likely to be less formal. Consequently, there is a risk that proceeds on disposal may be overlooked and the carrying values of the assets disposed of may still be reflected in the balance sheet as fixed assets at period end, and the resultant profit or loss on disposal not being recognized in the income statement. Where the carrying value of assets is significant, this gives rise to a potential *risk of significant misstatement*, related to the *completeness, existence and valuation* assertions for fixed assets.

Where disposals arise from discontinued operations of the business or a disposal of a part of the business, it is possible that formal authorizations and minuting of the transactions, as well as signed contracts, would be available for the auditor to inspect in order to obtain evidence of the correct allocation of the proceeds. Where operations are discontinued, there is a risk that proceeds on disposal of assets may not be recorded.

The auditor would generally perform a number of substantive tests of detail related to the *completeness, occurrence, measurement* and *valuation* of disposals and scrappings of fixed assets, *inter alia*:

- Enquire from management as to assets disposed of, scrapped or damaged and the subject of insurance claims.

- Where insurance claims arise from the destruction of significant assets, for example, where a store and its entire contents are destroyed by fire, the insurance claim may be complex, with a part being in respect of fixed assets, a part attributable to inventory and records destroyed, and a part attributable to claims for loss of profits for the period during which the business is unable to operate. The auditor should inspect the relevant claims documentation, or may be requested to audit the insurance claim itself as a related service engagement, to determine that the claim proceeds have been allocated to the correct accounts, are correctly reflected in the general ledger and financial statements, and the related assets destroyed in the fire have been removed from the general ledger and net recovery or loss is recognized in the income statement in the correct accounting period.

- Inspect correspondence with insurers regarding claims lodged and the related settlements for assets stolen, or damaged. Where claims are pending at the period end, it may be necessary to obtain a confirmation from the insurers of the amount of the settlement anticipated or approved subsequent to period end, for accrual in the current financial statements at period end.

- Review sundry receipts recorded in the cash receipts record and inspect documents supporting receipts recorded in sundry revenue accounts in the general ledger. Where receipts are in respect of disposals of fixed assets, inspect the related recognition of depreciation recoupments or losses on disposal in the income statement and the removal of the assets cost and accumulated depreciation on disposal from the general ledger accounts and fixed asset register.

- Where a part of the business operations have been discontinued, enquire from management about the disposals of fixed assets and inspect the receipt of proceeds from disposal.

- Inspect the fixed assets register for evidence that assets disposed of or scrapped have been closed off and reflect nil balances as carrying values.

Fixed assets recorded in the fixed asset register that are selected by the auditor for physical inspection but cannot be found may reveal errors related to the overstatement of assets affecting the *existence* assertion or disposals or scrappings not yet accounted for.

16.2.8.3 Repairs and maintenance of assets

The purpose of the auditor's review of repairs and maintenance accounts is to determine the reasonableness of the *measurement* of transactions allocated to these accounts to detect possible misallocation of items that should be capitalized to fixed assets rather than expensed as repairs and maintenance. Entries that appear unusual or which do not appear to be consistent with accounting policies applied by the client, should be selected for substantive tests of detail, such as the inspection of the underlying source documents to ascertain the exact nature of the expenditures to determine whether the accounting treatment is correct. Where material items appear to be misallocated, these should be discussed with management and appropriate adjustments made.

The auditor should not lose sight of the possibility that management may have capitalized as assets, costs that should have been expensed to repairs and maintenance accounts, affecting the *measurement, existence* and *valuation* assertions. This may occur where management has an incentive to misstate profits, either to boost the share market price or to increase their share of management bonuses where these are based on profits, or where the nature of the expenditure capitalized may be complex and the correct split difficult to determine. In such circumstances, management, either unknowingly or intentionally, may spread the cost of capital items over a period instead of recognizing the full expense immediately. Examples are:

- Misallocations may typically arise in high technology entities, such as Internet service providers, webmasters or dot.com entities and those conducting business by means of e-commerce transactions, and entities involved in the telecommunications field.

- Where extensive repairs to buildings include additions, increasing the capacity of the building, the auditor should inspect the contract terms and discuss with the architects or quantity surveyors what portion of the building additions create new capacity and what portion relates merely to repairs of existing facilities to establish that the allocation is according to the facts and acceptable GAAP accounting practices, for an incorrect allocation of a substantial amount will inflate or reduce the recorded profit.

These misallocations may arise where the distinction between expenditure incurred in providing the infrastructure as opposed to expenditure incurred directly in the production of income is difficult to measure. Accounting staff recording the entries may not be sufficiently aware of the technical criteria determining the appropriate allocation between capital and revenue to query the allocations. Such misallocations have been used as a means for companies to deliberately defer expenditures that should be expensed and by this means to smooth income or inflate profits excessively.

16.2.9 Substantive tests of detail of balances

The auditor's substantive tests of detail of fixed asset balances are performed to obtain sufficient appropriate audit evidence regarding the *completeness* and *existence* of assets reflected in the financial statements, whether their carrying values of assets have been properly determined in accordance with GAAP, providing evidence of the *valuation* assertion, and the nature of ownership and *rights and obligations* over the assets to ensure they are properly *presented and disclosed* in the financial statements. Some important considerations for the auditor when performing substantive tests of detail of fixed asset balances are discussed below.

16.2.9.1 Existence of assets

The *existence* of tangible fixed assets will be established, by the auditor, by means of a physical inspection of tangible assets such as land and buildings, factory plant and equipment, office furniture and equipment, IT equipment (although not all components may be possible to view physically, such as telecommunication networks) and motor vehicles. In order to detect potential misstatement, the auditor should select a sample of items from the fixed asset register, including material new additions to inspect, and in so doing obtain evidence of the existence of assets. A sample of assets on hand should also be selected and traced to the relevant entries in the fixed asset register, to detect assets not recorded. The physical inspection and discussion with client staff would give the auditor some idea of the condition of various assets physically inspected and whether or not they are being used by the entity, which provides evidence to support the *valuation* assertion and management's estimates of provisions for impairment losses, particularly for any items no longer utilized. Physical inspection of assets does not, however, provide evidence of ownership, or particular rights and obligations, attaching to assets.

16.2.9.2 Rights and obligations relating to assets

Audit evidence regarding the *rights and obligations* related to particular assets or categories of assets are obtained from an inspection of the underlying documents of title and contracts, and confirmation from the third parties involved.

There are several different statutes governing evidence of ownership of freehold and leasehold property, which prescribe the manner in which ownership is to be registered. The more important of these are:

- the Deeds Registries Act No 47 of 1937, as amended, regulating the registration of freehold and leasehold property. A property may not be registered in terms of the Deed Registries Act No 47 of 1937, unless it has first been surveyed and registered with the Deeds office, the statutory requirements for which are contained in the Land Survey Act No 8 of 1997;

- the Sectional Titles Act No 95 of 1986, as amended, which governs ownership of property in a sectional title scheme such as a Townhouse complex; and

- the Share Blocks Control Act No 59 of 1980, which regulates property held by way of shares in a share block company.

The Deeds Registries Act permits a search by a member of the public of title deeds and records held at the relevant Deeds Office on the payment of a statutory search fee. When appropriate, auditors should make use of this facility to confirm the details of property holdings, especially where the client owns several properties, such as an investment property company. While many entities, and their auditors, may retain a photocopy of property title deeds, the auditor should take care to ensure that, before relying on the authenticity of the document, it is established as being the *original title deed*, stamped by the Deeds Office, and has not been mortgaged or alienated in any way. Any intended reliance by an auditor on a photocopy of a title deed as evidence of title to a property that the client claims is owned, could be sadly misplaced as the property may have been sold, mortgaged, had servitudes passed over it or portions appropriated by the State, and these will not necessarily be reflected on the photocopy carefully placed in the audit file or retained by the client. The type and nature of documents encountered that provide evidence of property purchases and title are discussed in Table 16.4. Appendix 3 contains a Specimen Deed of Transfer for freehold property.

Several statutes have been passed, or amended, in recent years to address land redistribution and transformation within South Africa, which fall under the Department of Land Affairs. These include:

- the Upgrading of Land Tenure Rights Act No 112 of 1991;
- the Land Titles Adjustment Act No 111 of 1993 as amended;
- the Provision of Land and Assistance Act No 126 of 1993;
- the Restitution of Land Rights Act No 22 of 1994;
- the Development Facilitation Act No 67 of 1995;
- the Land Administration Act No 2 of 1995;
- the Land Reform (Labour Tenants) Act No 3 of 1996;
- the Communal Property Associations Act No 28 of 1996;
- the Interim Protection of Informal Land Rights Act No 31 of 1996;
- the Extension of Security of Tenure Act of 1997; the Distribution and Transfer of Certain State Land Act of 1997; and
- the Transformation of Certain Rural Areas Act No 94 of 1998.

Discussion of these statutes is beyond the scope of this text. Readers interested in particular statutes may download copies from the government web site at http://pwv.gov.za/legislation_policies/acts.htm.

Properties owned by entities being audited may be affected by any of these statutes, and to the extent that they affect the rights and obligations of the entity over the said property, could affect the carrying values in the balance sheet and disclosures in the notes to the financial statements. In such circumstances, the auditor must obtain an understanding of the relevant statutory implications.

Where buildings are being constructed on the property of an entity at period end, the auditor should examine the construction contract, and the documents mentioned in Table 16.4, to determine the stage of completion and costs to be included in building work in progress at period end. Rights and obligations of a lessor and lessee are set out in a lease agreement that gives the lessee the right to use property, plant and equipment or motor vehicles for a specified period. In terms of GAAP AC 105, where the lease constitutes a finance lease, the assets that are leased are capitalized and the fair value of future lease rentals is raised as a liability at the inception of the lease.

Registration of ownership of motor vehicles is governed by the Road Traffic Act 1989. The auditor should be aware that although leased motor vehicles may be registered in the name of the lessee, and the annual vehicle licence issued in the name of the lessee, who has the responsibility to run and maintain the vehicle, the lessor retains ownership of the said vehicle which may, or may not, pass to the lessee at the end of the lease on payment of an agreed consideration. Consequently, the auditor should refer to the lease agreement to ascertain the exact terms of *ownership* of capitalized leased assets that will affect their *presentation and disclosure* in the financial statements.

Rights to intangible assets, such as licences granted to manufacture certain products; software licences to use multiple copies of software systems in businesses; use of copyright; mineral rights granted to mining entities; and franchise arrangements such as MacDonalds, Wimpy, etc., are usually contained in a written agreement between the entity and the relevant third party. The agreements usually provide for the payment of royalties, licence fees, or commission, to the grantor of the rights. In the case of a franchise agreement, conditions may be imposed on the franschisee related to the layout and design of restaurants and a requirement to purchase all franchise branded products directly from the franchisor who in turn, may centralize its buying operations and establish a product distribution network to its franchisees.

The auditor should request written confirmation of the terms of agreements and balances owing at the period end. Where agreements are entered into with related parties, such as other group companies, confirmation may be obtained by agreement of inter-group balances and transactions. The auditor will need to follow the guidance in SAAS 550, 'Related parties', to obtain evidence regarding the identification of related parties and related party transactions in order to ensure the appropriate disclosures are made in the financial statements. Written management representations should be obtained with regard to the *completeness, measurement and presentation and disclosures* of related party transactions.

An important part of performing substantive tests of detail of balances is that the auditor recognizes what constitutes appropriate and relevant documentary evidence. Examples of the key documents that the auditor needs to examine when auditing fixed property or motor vehicles are set out in Table 16.4 below.

DOCUMENTS	NATURE OF DOCUMENT
Purchase/ownership of fixed property	
Offer to purchase	Every purchase and sale of land in South Africa is initiated by a formal, written 'Offer to purchase' given by a willing buyer to a willing seller. On signing the offer to purchase, the seller agrees to sell the property and any improvements described therein to the buyer. The seller also warrants therein that he, she or the entity has legal title to the property and the legal capacity to sell the property.
	Where the property is owned by a legal entity, or the buyer is a legal entity, the signature of the authorized official (e.g. a director of a company) being the representative seller or buyer, the Deeds Office will require evidence that said director is authorized to act. This will require copies of minutes of the relevant directors' meeting authorizing the specific sale or purchase of property.

DOCUMENTS	NATURE OF DOCUMENT
Deed of Transfer	The formal document that gives title to a property owner named therein of the property described therein. Once the offer for a purchase of land is accepted, a formal registration process is followed by attorneys, registered as conveyancers, who draw the various legal documents for signing by all parties to the agreement and then lodge these, together with the existing Deed of Transfer for registration of the change of ownership in the Deeds Office. (Refer to Appendix 3 for a Specimen Deed of Transfer.) The buyer is required to provide evidence of his or her identity and legal capacity to contract. Different attorneys may act for the buyer and the seller, but frequently to expedite a transaction, the same attorney is appointed to act for both parties.
Mortgage Bond	A formal written agreement between a lender and a borrower, providing the lender with security over fixed property described in the mortgage bond contract. The mortgage bond sets out the terms of the loan, repayment of which is secured by the passing of the mortgage bond. This document has to be lodged with the Deeds Office and the rights of the bondholder are endorsed on the *Deed of Transfer* until such time as the loan is fully repaid and the mortgage bond is cancelled in terms of sections 50 to 62 of the Deeds Registries Act, 1937. Cancellation of a mortgage bond can only be done by means of written permission of the bondholder and is similarly formally recorded in the Deeds Office by cancellation of the original mortgage bond endorsement on the *Deed of Transfer*. Both the preparation of the mortgage bond agreement and cancellation of an existing mortgage bond require the formal drawing of legal documents prepared by the attorney conveyancer handling the transaction or acting for the lender. Where a property is mortgaged, the lender will generally retain possession of the original *Deed of Transfer* for so long as monies are owed to the lender. A copy will usually be given to the property owner. Once the debt is fully repaid, the owner may request the lender to cancel the mortgage bond and regain possession of the *Deed of Transfer*, or may simply leave the *Deed of Transfer* with the bondholder for safekeeping.

DOCUMENTS	NATURE OF DOCUMENT
	If the mortgage bond is not cancelled, the owner may obtain a *re-advance* of the original loan and the security of the lender will effectively continue to be covered by the original mortgage bond agreement. Obviously should the amount of the new advance exceed that originally given, a further endorsement will have to be made, failing which, the security of the lender will be limited to the amount originally recorded. (Refer to Appendix 4 for a Specimen Mortgage Bond over Freehold Property.)
Buildings under construction	
Architects Certificate	This document is issued to the property owner, or property developer, authorizing interim and final payments to the main building contractor for a building under construction.
	Depending on the type of building contract, the percentage completion reflected on the *Architects Certificate* may be based on reports of bills of measured quantities prepared by the appointed quantity surveyor, or based on a cost plus basis monitored by the architect, or on the estimated stage of completion determined by the architect according to the progress on the construction plan.
	The *Architects Certificate* reflects retention amounts withheld from payment until the completion of the contract that will not be due for release until a specified date. The building costs will generally be capitalized by the entity for which the building is being constructed. Where the building is incomplete at period end, it will be carried as *construction work in progress* and will only be capitalized to *buildings* once the building is brought into use.
Joint Building Contracts Committee (JBCC) 2000 Series Documentation	Accepted by the Building Federation, architects, quantity surveyors and engineers. It comprises a series of documents, forms and certificates containing standard terms and conditions for all aspects of a building contract between the owner or developer and the main contractor and nominated subcontractors, including tenders, guarantees, engineering conditions, payment certificates, etc.

DOCUMENTS	NATURE OF DOCUMENT
	A complete set of documentation for any building contract includes details of what is being built and where, on what basis (i.e. bill of quantities, fixed price contract, cost plus contract and the price agreed plus any escalation clauses), and who the parties to the contract are (i.e the main contractor and the names of nominated subcontractors appointed). The rights and obligations of the parties for any defects or non-compliance with contract terms are set out, including penalties payable for late completion, insurance arrangements and retentions to be withheld.
Purchase/ownership of motor vehicles	
RS1 /RC 1 Certificate of Registration	The RC 1 Certificate of Registration in respect of Motor Vehicle is the formal document of title evidencing ownership of a vehicle by the registered owner issued in terms of section 14 of the Road Traffic Act, 1989.
	Where the purchase of the vehicle is financed by means of a hire purchase agreement or is leased in circumstances where the lessee will become the eventual owner of the vehicle, the RC 1 form will reflect the purchaser as the registered owner.
	The instalment-sale or lease agreement will, however, vest ownership in the lender or lessor until such time as the debt is repaid in full and the lender or lessor will physically retain the original RC 1 Form until that time. The purchaser will, however, enjoy full use of the vehicle unless or until he or she defaults in payment to the lender or lessor, in which case the latter will be entitled to take legal steps to physically recover the vehicle to offset the debt owed.
	In the case of a *new vehicle* purchased from an authorized vehicle distributor, the authorized vehicle distributor, the seller, will lodge the documents for the first registration of the vehicle, in the name of the purchaser, on behalf of the buyer. The RC 1 Certificate of Registration document issued by the licensing authority is then given to the purchaser on delivery of the vehicle.

DOCUMENTS	NATURE OF DOCUMENT
MVL 1 Motor Vehicle Licence and Licence Disc	These provide evidence that the registered owner reflected on the RC 1 Certificate of Registration in respect of Motor Vehicle has paid the annual licence duty on the vehicle to the local vehicle licensing authority.
CRW Certification of Roadworthiness	When purchasing a second-hand motor vehicle, the purchaser is obliged to obtain a certificate of roadworthiness for the vehicle before the licensing authority will consider an application to register the vehicle into the name of the new owner.
RLV Application for Registration and Licensing of Motor Vehicle	This form is completed and submitted to the local licensing authority to apply for the registration of a second-hand vehicle into the name of the new owner who has bought the vehicle. The buyer will have to provide his or her identify document and the NCO form signed by the seller before the licensing authority will register the vehicle to the new owner.

Table 16.4 Documents typically encountered when auditing assets

16.2.9.3 Valuation of assets

The carrying values of fixed assets are calculated by deducting the entity's accounting estimates of *accumulated depreciation* (AC 123), and *provisions for impairment losses* (AC 128) for tangible assets, and *accumulated amortization* (AC 129) for intangible assets, from the cost, or re-valued amounts, of such assets (*valuation* assertion). The carrying values are reflected in the financial statements and are determined in accordance with the requirements of the relevant accounting framework, as indicated above, for South African GAAP statements, and the Companies Act. Consequently, the auditor's substantive tests of detail of balances related to the *valuation* assertion should be designed to obtain sufficient appropriate audit evidence of the following accounting estimates at the period end:

- Revaluation of assets;
- Accumulated depreciation;
- Amortization of intangible assets; and
- Provision for impairment losses.

The auditor must consider the guidance contained in SAAS 540 'Audit of accounting estimates', and SAAS 545 'Auditing fair value measurements and disclosures', when auditing these balances. Particular aspects that the auditor should consider when obtaining sufficient appropriate audit evidence for each of these balances, as well as important aspects of SAAS 540 and 545, are dealt with overleaf.

Revaluation of assets

Where assets are re-valued, the auditor must obtain evidence of the fair value measurement of such assets. For example, where the revaluation is performed by a registered or sworn valuator, the auditor would inspect the report setting out the basis of the valuation. As with other circumstances where the auditor uses work performed by an expert, the auditor should consider the guidance in SAAS 620, 'Using the work of an expert', and consider the independence, standing and competence of the valuator, the scope of the engagement, the reasonableness of the underlying assumptions made and whether the basis of the revaluation is in line with industry norms.

Most commonly, revaluations will be performed for land and buildings, but may on occasion be applied to the revaluation of plant and equipment. The reader is referred to GAAP AC 123, which deals with the accounting treatment for *measurement*, and *presentation and disclosure* requirements arising from revaluations of assets. Where depreciable assets are re-valued, depreciation is calculated on the re-valued amount of such assets and the auditor should consider this in checking the calculation of the depreciation charge and accumulated depreciation balance for such assets for the period.

Accumulated depreciation

The auditor will generally obtain a *Fixed Assets Summary* schedule from the client, prepared from the accounting records and fixed asset register, and setting out: the opening balances of cost, plus additions less disposals, and the resultant closing cost balances; the current depreciation charge and accumulated depreciation amount at the start and end of the period and net carrying values for each category of assets for the entity at the start and end of the period.

The recognition and measurement of depreciation of assets, subsequent to acquisition, are provided for in paragraphs .53 to .56 of GAAP AC 123. In auditing the depreciation charge for the period, the auditor should obtain evidence regarding the rates and basis of calculation of depreciation ordinarily applied by the entity. This may be ascertained from the prior year audit working papers and from the accounting policies and notes disclosed in the published financial statements of the previous year. By enquiry and the checking of calculations, the auditor should ascertain that the rates and basis of calculation applied previously have been applied on a consistent basis in the current year. Use may be made of CAATs to perform these calculations.

The auditor needs also to obtain evidence of the estimated useful lives of the assets to determine the reasonableness of the depreciation method and accumulated depreciation for each category of assets, which is dealt with in GAAP AC 123, paragraphs .53 to .56. This area poses a potential risk of material misstatement as certain assets may continue in use long after their original cost has been fully expensed, such as plant and equipment in a factory installed, say, 20 or 30 years earlier that is still being used to manufacture the entity's products.

Other assets may become obsolete after a relatively short period due to technology changes, and yet are reflected at a carrying value in the financial statements when in fact they have no further useful life and will need to be replaced, or upgraded on a regular basis. The auditor will have to consider the past history of the client, nature of the business and impact on different categories of assets, in estimating the useful lives and the reasonableness of the depreciation provisions at period end. Evidence will be obtained by enquiry of the client and inspection of the profits and losses realized on assets disposed of or retired. Significant losses on the disposal of assets would indicate that depreciation provisions have not been sufficient. Significant profits on disposal, on the other hand, would indicate that depreciation provided annually has been excessive.

The auditor needs to establish the rates used to calculate wear and tear allowances on assets for taxation purposes. This evidence would be used in auditing the calculation of the entity's normal tax liability. Where wear and tear and depreciation rates differ, this gives rise to a timing difference which affects the calculation of deferred tax. As with the audit of depreciation, the auditor should obtain evidence of the wear and tear rates and basis of calculation for each category of assets and establish that these have been applied consistently in the client's calculations for the current period.

Amortization of intangible assets

The *carrying amount* of an intangible asset is defined, in paragraph .08 of GAAP AC 129, as 'the amount at which the asset is recognized in the balance sheet after deducting any accumulated amortization and accumulated impairment losses'.

The *amortization period* is defined in paragraph .08 of GAAP AC 129, 'Intangible assets', as: 'the systematic allocation of the depreciable amount of an intangible asset over its useful life'; and in paragraph .80 of GAAP AC 129: 'there is a rebuttal presumption the useful life of an intangible asset will not exceed 20 years from the date when the asset is available for use'. If the control over the future economic benefits from an intangible asset is achieved through legal rights that have been granted for a finite period, the useful life of the intangible asset should not exceed the period of the legal rights, unless these are renewable and the renewal is virtually certain (GAAP 129 paragraph .86).

The *amortization method* used should reflect the pattern in which the asset's economic benefits are consumed by the enterprise. If that pattern cannot be determined reliably, the straight-line method should be used and the charge for each period recognized as an expense in the income statement (GAAP 129, paragraph .89). AC 129 provides guidance on a variety of methods that can be used to allocate the depreciable amount of an intangible asset on a systematic basis, and the principle set out in the preceding sentence should be followed. The auditor would inspect evidence of the rights attaching to the intangible assets and management's projections regarding the economic benefits to determine the reasonableness of the amortization method and period applied.

Impairment of assets

Management must assess at the balance sheet date whether there is an indication that an asset may be impaired; the estimated impairment loss should be provided for and recognized immediately in accordance with the relevant financial reporting framework applied by the entity. *Impairment loss* is defined, in paragraph .08 of AC 128, 'Impairment of assets', as the 'amount by which the carrying amount of the asset exceeds its recoverable amount'. *Recoverable amount* is then defined as 'the higher of an asset's net selling price or its value in use', and *value in use* is defined as 'the present value of the estimated future cash flows expected to arise from the continuing use of an asset and from its disposal at the end of its useful life'.

In such circumstances, the entity must estimate the recoverable amount of the asset. Where potential impairment losses are material, a risk of significant misstatement in the carrying value of assets may arise should the impairment losses not be provided for. Consequently, the auditor would enquire about and obtain evidence of factors, such as those indicated in AC 128 paragraph .10, to determine whether an impairment of assets has occurred, namely:

- 'Market value has declined significantly;
- Changes have occurred in technological, market, economic or legal environments in which the entity operates;
- Market interest rates or returns on investments have increased affecting the discount rate used in calculating the asset's value in use, decreasing its recoverability;
- The carrying amount of the net assets is more than its market capitalization;
- Assets are physically damaged or obsolete;
- Planned discontinued operations or restructuring of the entity may lead to early retirements or disposals of assets;
- Economic performance of the asset is worse than expected;
- Any other aspects indicating impairment.'

It may happen that assets are badly damaged in the course of a particular event, such as a fire or flood, or that changes in legislation adversely affect the values of assets of the entity, for example, changes affecting a decline in property values. In such instances, impairment losses should be provided for in accordance with GAAP AC 128. Guidance is provided in AC 128 for estimating the net selling price, the value in use of the asset, the measurement of future cash flows and discount rates to be applied, and for the recognition of impairment losses as an expense in the income statement. AC 128 deals separately with impairment losses arising for cash-generating units and also recognizes that impairment losses may reverse in subsequent periods.

The auditor should ascertain the underlying assumptions of management and re-perform the calculation of the impairment losses to obtain evidence that the estimates of value in use, selling price and discount rates used for calculating future cash flows are appropriate for the particular situation of the entity and are recognized in the financial statements in accordance with AC 128.

16.2.9.4 Auditing accounting estimates

The audit of the balances of accumulated depreciation, accumulated amortization and impairment losses amount to the audit of *accounting estimates*, since any change will result in a change in the carrying values of the related asset in the financial statements affecting the *valuation* assertion. The auditor should follow the guidance in paragraph .10 of SAAS 540, 'Audit of accounting estimates', where the basic principles to be applied in the audit of accounting estimates are stated as:

- 'Review and test the process used by management to develop the estimate,

- Use an independent estimate for comparison with management, and

- Review subsequent events, which confirm the estimate made.'

The steps involved in reviewing and testing the process used by management are set out in paragraph .11 of SAAS 540, with explanatory guidance contained in paragraphs .12 to .21:

- 'Evaluate the data and consider the underlying assumptions on which the estimate is based,

- Test the calculations involved in the estimate,

- Compare, where possible, estimates made for prior periods with the actual results of those periods, and

- Consider management's approval process.'

The auditor should make a final assessment of the reasonableness of the estimate, based on his or her understanding of the business and whether or not the estimate is consistent with other audit evidence obtained during the audit (SAAS 540, paragraph .24). Because of the uncertainties inherent in accounting estimates, evaluating differences or errors may be more difficult than in other areas, which increases the risk of significant misstatement. Where the auditor identifies material differences in the calculation of *accumulated depreciation, provisions for impairment losses and accumulated amortization balances* and the client refuses to revise the estimates, the auditor should consider the difference a misstatement to be considered along with all other misstatements in assessing whether a risk of significant misstatement remains in the financial statements (SAAS 540, paragraph .27).

16.2.9.5 Auditing fair value measurements

Comprehensive guidance regarding the procedures to be applied by the auditor in auditing fair value measurements are contained in SAAS 545, 'Auditing fair value measurements and disclosures'. The guidance provided is in line with the principles contained in SAAS 540 and applies to the audit of the fair value measurement of assets and liabilities where this is required by the relevant accounting framework, such as the requirements contained in AC 123, AC 128 and AC 129. SAAS 545 sets out the following principles:

- The auditor should obtain sufficient appropriate audit evidence that fair value measurements and disclosures are in accordance with the entity's identified financial reporting framework. (paragraph .03)

- The auditor should obtain an understanding of the entity's process for determining fair value measurements and disclosures and of the relevant control procedures sufficient to develop an effective audit approach. (paragraph .10)

- Paragraph 12 contains the following examples of factors the auditor should consider to understand the process:

  - 'Relevant control procedures over the process used to determine fair value measurements.

  - The expertise and experience of those persons determining the fair value measurements.

  - The role that information technology has in the process.

  - The types of accounts or transactions requiring fair value measurements or disclosures (for example, whether the accounts arise from the recording of routine and recurring transactions or whether they arise from non-routine or unusual transactions).

  - The extent to which the entity's process relies on a service organization to provide fair value measurements or the data that supports the measurement. When an entity uses a service organization, the auditor complies with the requirements of the International Standard on Auditing (ISA) on Audit Considerations Relating to Entities Using Service Organizations. (Readers are referred to chapter 9 for a discussion of the SAICA Audit and Accounting Guide: 'Reports on the processing of transactions by service organizations – Guidance for auditors'.)

  - The extent to which the entity uses the work of experts in determining fair value measurements and disclosures (see paragraphs .29 – .32).

  - The significant management assumptions used in determining fair value, documents supporting management's assumptions and the methods used to develop and apply management assumptions and to monitor changes in those assumptions.

- The integrity of change controls and security procedures for valuation models and relevant information systems, including approval processes.

- The controls over the consistency, timeliness and reliability of the data used in valuation models.'

- After obtaining an understanding of the entity's process for determining fair value measurements and disclosures, the auditor should assess inherent and control risk related to the fair value measurements and disclosures in the financial statements to determine the nature, timing and extent of the audit procedures (paragraph .14), examples of which are:

  - The auditor should evaluate whether the fair value measurements and disclosures in the financial statements are in accordance with the entity's financial reporting framework. (paragraph .17)

  - The auditor should obtain evidence about management's intent to carry out specific courses of action, and consider its ability to do so, where relevant to the fair value measurements and disclosures under the entity's financial reporting framework. (paragraph .22)

  - Where alternative methods for measuring fair value are available under the entity's financial reporting framework, or where the method of measurement is not prescribed, the auditor should evaluate whether the method of measurement is appropriate in the circumstances under the entity's financial reporting framework (paragraph .24), and the entity's method for its fair value measurements is applied consistently (paragraph .27).

  - The auditor should determine the need to use the work of an expert. (paragraph .29)

  - Based on the assessment of inherent and control risk, the auditor should test the entity's fair value measurements and disclosures. (paragraph .33)

  - Where applicable, the auditor should evaluate whether the significant assumptions used by management in measuring fair values, taken individually and as a whole, provide a reasonable basis for the fair value measurements and disclosures in the entity's financial statements. (paragraph .39)

  - The auditor should test the data used to develop the fair value measurements and disclosures and evaluate whether the fair value measurements have been properly determined from such data and management's assumptions. (paragraph .50)

- The auditor should consider the effect of subsequent events on the fair value measurements and disclosures in the financial statements. (paragraph .53)

- In making a final assessment of whether the fair value measurements and disclosures in the financial statements are in accordance with the entity's financial reporting framework, the auditor should evaluate the sufficiency and appropriateness of the audit evidence obtained, as well as the consistency of that evidence with other evidence obtained and evaluated during the audit. (paragraph .61)

- The auditor should obtain written representations from management regarding the reasonableness of significant assumptions, including whether these appropriately reflect management's intent and ability to carry out specific courses of action on behalf of the entity where relevant to the fair value measurements or disclosures. (paragraph .63)

16.2.9.6 Additional considerations when auditing fixed assets

The audit of certain categories of assets is complex due to the nature of the assets and statutory requirements, or lack thereof, or client circumstances – such as may be encountered in a multinational situation or with electronic communication transactions, affecting the *rights and obligations* of different parties, particularly where evidence of ownership or title is dependent on various conditions being met. This may give rise to a risk of significant misstatement in the financial statements affecting:

- *measurement*, where costs are misallocated;
- *rights and obligations*, such as ownership, due to these not being clearly understood or disclosed; or
- *valuation*, involving complex calculations of fair values where the underlying assumptions, models or data may be incorrect.

While attention has been given earlier, in this and other chapters, to different categories of fixed assets, the discussion below illustrates the complexities in auditing land and buildings and provides the reader with some idea of the breadth of inquiry that may be needed to fully understand the nature of the particular asset and in order to gather sufficient appropriate audit evidence regarding the *existence, measurement, valuation* and *rights and obligations* assertions. In the event of an audit of any asset where rights and obligations are contained in legislative requirements, it is advisable that the auditor familiarize him or herself with the specific legislation. Further, where the auditor encounters complex situations arising from accounting framework requirements, affecting *presentation and disclosures* in financial statements, it may be necessary for the auditor to adapt the planned substantive tests of detail accordingly.

16.2.9.7 Property held under freehold title

Property held under freehold title was discussed earlier in this chapter and will not be addressed further here, other than to refer the reader to the Appendices 3 and 4 containing the following specimen documents: a deed of transfer for freehold property and mortgage bond documents.

16.2.9.8 Property held under sectional title

The Sectional Titles Act of 1986 provides for the division of a building into sections and the granting of real rights to the sections and appropriate interest in the common property of the building and the land on which it stands. In order to audit such an asset, some understanding of the procedure of division and the consequent establishment of a body corporate of which the sectional title-holders are members, is desirable. The procedure, briefly, is as follows:

- The property owner (the developer) prepares a scheme of division and applies to the local authority for approval.

- Having obtained approval, the developer applies to the Registrar of Deeds, in whose registry the land is registered, for registration of the sectional plan.

- When satisfied that the relevant provisions of the Act have been met, the Registrar registers the sectional plan and opens a sectional title register in respect of the land and buildings shown on the plan. At the same time the Registrar closes the entry in the land register relating to the developer's title deed and refers therein to the relevant sectional title register.

- When the developer sells a section (or sections), there comes into being automatically a body corporate of which the sectional title-holders, including the developer if some sections are unsold, are members.

- Each sectional title-holder has a quota (laid down in the plan) representing a proportionate interest in the section (for example, a flat) and in the common property.

- The body corporate is administered by trustees (appointed by the members) who, *inter alia*, levy on the members charges for the maintenance of the property. Members are jointly (but not severally) liable for the debts of the body corporate.

A sectional title-holder thus has a:

- Real right to a section (and proportionate common property); and
- Responsibility to contribute to the upkeep of the property.

The evidence of ownership takes the form of a certificate of registered sectional title signed and sealed by the Registrar. Should the section owner sell his or her section, transfer is recorded by endorsement on the certificate. The sectional title may be mortgaged and reference to the mortgage will appear on the certificate.

16.2.9.9 Property held under share block schemes

An alternative to the acquisition of a section of a property by sectional title is to acquire shares in a share block company owning a property, which (by agreement between the developer and company) confers on the owner of that share block company the use and occupation of a particular section of the property and the obligation to undertake responsibility for the proportionate share of any liability of the share block company and to contribute by way of a levy to any expense necessary for the reasonable maintenance of the property.

The basic difference between sectional title and share block schemes is that under the former the purchaser acquires a real right to the section (for example, an apartment), whereas under the latter all that is acquired are the shares plus a personal right statutorily granted by the share block company to use and occupy the section.

The Share Block Control Act of 1980 provides, *inter alia*, that certain matters specific to share block operations be included in the memorandum and articles of a share block company and that every such company include as part of its name the words 'Share Block'.

The procedure for operating a share block scheme is, broadly, along the following lines:

- The developer (the owner of the shares in the property company) divides the issued share capital into blocks of shares; the blocks may be of similar or different size.

- The developer enters into a use and occupation agreement with the company in respect of each property section.

- The developer sells the shares in the share block company and at the same time cedes to each purchaser (new share owner) the rights in the relevant use and occupation agreement.

- The purchaser agrees to pay the levy for the upkeep of the building, the amount being in proportion to the number of shares acquired.

- Where the property company (share block company) has borrowed (usually on mortgage of the property) to finance the acquisition of the property, a portion of the loan is allocated to each share owner. On the sale of any shares in the share block company, the purchaser (new share owner) agrees to contribute to the interest on and repayment of the loan according to the allocation.

A careful analysis of the rights and obligations of various parties arising from the effect of the terms of the Share Block Control Act of 1980, reveals that the share block company is divested of the beneficial ownership of the property, often comprising blocks of flats or a townhouse development, since the company is obliged to enter a right of use agreement with the share owner, leaving the company with the bare dominium rights only. In addition, as the share owner is required to assume the responsibility for any liability of the share block company, the company has no liability to repay or any means of generating income from its bare dominium asset, which is invariably leased out by the share owner who is then the recipient of rental income. In addition, the share owner has a responsibility to pay a levy into a levy trust fund to meet necessary maintenance expenditure for the property, once again indicating the share block company does not have any responsibility for this expenditure.

The effect of this is that several thousands of share block companies in South Africa have been used as a means of banks providing structured finance deals to property owning clients who wished to move property assets 'off balance sheet'. It is argued that share block companies therefore comprise special purpose entities to which the requirements of GAAP AC 412, 'Consolidations – special purpose entities', apply, since the share owner controls the voting rights, assets and operating policies of the entity.

If this principle is recognized, AC 412 requires the share owner to bring the carrying values of the share block company assets and liabilities onto its own (that is, the bank's) balance sheet. From the share owner's perspective, the value of the right of use of the property asset is the present value of the future lease rentals to be earned from letting of the property to the occupier of units to the share owner, the liability for repayment of any loan granted for the purchase or development of the property and payment of a levy to meet any expenditure necessary for the maintenance of the property.

From the perspective of the share block company, there is a strong argument that the property asset is fully impaired since the company has no beneficial right of use of the asset, which vests in the share owner, and the share block company is unable to generate any future economic benefits from the asset. Consequently, the property should be reflected in its balance sheet at a nominal value of R1 and any liability which vests in the share owner should similarly be reflected at R1, as the share block company is not responsible for its repayment. This is illustrated in Figure 16.1.

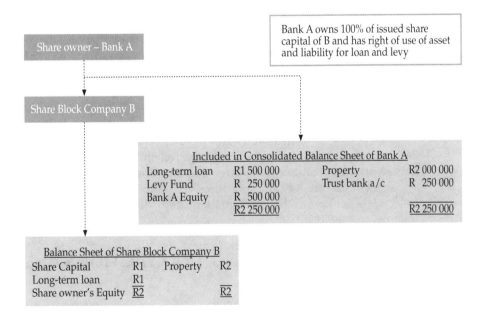

Figure 16.1 Share block company and share owner relationship

16.2.10 Presentation and disclosure

It is evident from the earlier discussions that the financial statement presentation and disclosures for tangible and intangible assets required by the accounting frameworks and by statute are extensive. South African GAAP statements applicable to presentation and disclosure requirements are those indicated earlier, namely AC 105, AC 123, AC 128, AC 129 and AC 135. In addition, the Fourth Schedule and other sections of the Companies Act have further specific disclosure requirements for fixed assets affecting the balance sheet, income statement, cash flow statement, notes to the financial statements, and directors' report.

The disclosure requirements include the cost of the assets, accumulated depreciation, amortization, provisions for impairment losses and capitalized leased assets which are reflected in total in the balance sheet with details in the notes to the financial statements. The depreciation charge, amortization amount and impairment losses recognized for the current year, as well as profits and losses on disposals of fixed assets and revaluations of assets during the period are disclosed in the notes to the financial statements and the relevant asset and reserve balances in the balance sheet. Acquisitions and proceeds on disposals of assets are disclosed in the cash flow statement. Capital commitments for capital expenditures approved and contracted for, distinguished from those approved but not contracted for, are shown in the notes to the financial statements. Disclosures affecting deferred taxation appear in the balance sheet, income statement and notes to the financial statements.

In addition, details of any fixed assets pledged as security for any liability of the entity or to secure a liability of another party must be disclosed, such as property mortgaged to a bondholder, and capitalized leased assets securing the related liability to the lessor must be disclosed. The accounting policies related to the valuation and treatment of fixed assets must be stated in the notes to the financial statements.

The auditor should inspect the presentation and disclosures in the financial statements related to the fixed asset balances and consider the appropriateness of these in accordance with the requirements of the relevant accounting framework, any statutory requirements and audit evidence gathered from the substantive analytical procedures and substantive tests of detail that collectively support the presentation and disclosures in the financial statements.

16.3 NATURE OF FINANCING TRANSACTIONS AND BALANCES

16.3.1 Introduction

Financing activities are the means by which the entity obtains its funding for its business operations and capital investment. Funding is obtained from two main external sources, namely, owners' equity or capital, and short-term and long-term borrowings, and generated internally in the form of retained profits.

16.3.1.1 Owner's equity

Equity transactions and balances arise from the receipt of cash, or other assets, received from the issue of shares less any payments made for share buy-backs, which shares are then to be cancelled and treated once again as authorized, un-issued share capital. Equity transactions may also involve payments to preference shareholders on redemption of redeemable preference shares and creation of a capital redemption reserve fund; and share capitalization issues in lieu of dividends declared. Subsidiary companies may purchase up to 10% of the issued shares of their holding company to hold as treasury shares.

The related income statement transactions and balances will be in respect of dividends declared and paid and STC tax payable thereon.

16.3.1.2 Borrowings

Borrowing transactions may be entered into with shareholders, outside third parties or inter-group treasury operations. The transactions and balances will arise from cash inflows from long-term or short-term borrowings received and the subsequent repayment of the capital sum and interest charged. Borrowings may be unsecured or secured by a mortgage bond over fixed property of the entity or a pledge of movable assets or guarantees. Borrowings may also take the form of secured or unsecured debentures issued.

Short-term borrowings will usually take the form of bank overdraft facilities, which similarly, may be secured or unsecured, or through group treasury cash management activities. Financing activities may include finance leases and operating leases for specific capital assets acquired or leased.

The related income statement transactions and balances will be in respect of interest payments and finance charges. Where borrowings are from a foreign source this may give rise to foreign exchange gains or losses.

The financing transactions and balances interface with chapter 13 on expenditure transactions and balances when cash is disbursed for interest and dividend payments, buy-backs of shares, redemption of redeemable preference shares and repayments of borrowings.

16.3.2 Audit objectives

Before proceeding to identify the objectives of an audit of investing transactions and balances, it is appropriate first to recognize the account balances affected by such activities, as set out in Table 16.5 below:

FINANCING TRANSACTIONS	ACCOUNT BALANCES DEBITED	ACCOUNT BALANCES CREDITED
Company		
Issue of shares	Bank (or other assets)	Share capital or Stated capital: Ordinary (different classes) or Preference share capital, Share premium
Retained income	Various income and expenditure accounts to arrive at the *Net Income after tax and dividends* transferred to retained income	Retained income
Dividends declared and paid	Dividends declared	Shareholders for dividends
	Shareholders for dividends	Bank
Share buy-backs	Share capital (cancelled)	Bank
Redemption of preference shares	Preference shareholders	Bank
	Share premium account	Capital redemption reserve fund
	Retained income	
Sole trader, partnership, and close corporation		
Capital contributed	Bank or other assets	Capital contributed
Drawings	Drawings	Bank
Capital contributed	Bank or other assets	Members' contributions
Profit distributions	Undrawn profits	Bank

FINANCING TRANSACTIONS	ACCOUNT BALANCES DEBITED	ACCOUNT BALANCES CREDITED
All entities		
Loans/Borrowings received	Bank	Lender
Debentures issued	Bank	Debenture-holders
Loans, debentures repaid	Lender, Debenture-holder	Bank
Interest paid	Interest expense	Bank
Leased assets acquired	Capitalized lease assets	Lease creditor
Finance charges	Finance charges expense	Lease creditor
Payments to lease creditor	Lease creditor	Bank
Interest paid	Interest expense	Bank

Table 16.5 General ledger account balances typically affected by financing activities

The transactions and balances arising from financing activities affect very few general ledger accounts. Entries to these accounts arise from transactions that are regulated by statute, in the case of share issues and debentures, or by terms contained in detailed contracts, such as long-term loans and leases. Dividends declared require specific authorization by either the board of directors or the shareholders, in terms of the Companies Act and the entity's Articles of Association. Interest rates and repayment terms for borrowings are contained in the relevant agreements with the lenders.

Consequently, the risk of significant misstatement for financing transactions and balances will usually be assessed as low.

The audit objectives specific to the financing transactions and balances are set out in Table 16.6. The auditor should identify those assertions most likely to lead to a risk of significant misstatement for equity and reserves, and long-term borrowings to focus the audit procedures accordingly.

MANAGEMENT ASSERTION	AUDIT OBJECTIVES
Financing by way of equity and borrowings – transactions	
Completeness	Recorded issues and repayments of equity; borrowings received and repayments made; and finance leases entered into include all such transactions that occurred during the period.
	Recorded dividends declared, interest expense and finance charges recognized include all such transactions that occurred during the period.
Occurrence/ validity	Recorded issues and repayments of equity; borrowings received and repayments recorded; and finance leases entered into actually occurred during the period, all are properly authorized and none are duplicated.
	Recorded dividends, interest and finance charges transactions and balances are properly authorized, actually occurred and represent the effects of equity and borrowings transactions and balances that occurred during the period.
Measurement/ accuracy	Recorded issues and repayments of equity; borrowings received and repayments recorded; finance leases entered into; and the related dividends, interest and finance charges have been recognized and measured in accordance with GAAP applied by the entity on a consistent basis.
Financing by way of equity and borrowings – period end balances	
Completeness	Shareholders' equity and reserves represent all the interests of owners that exist at balance sheet date.
	Long-term loan balances and finance lease accounts payable at balance sheet date represent all payables owed to long-term lenders and lessors for finance leases at balance sheet date.
Existence	Shareholders equity and reserve balances represent the interests of owners that exist at balance sheet date determined in accordance with the GAAP applied by the entity on a consistent basis.
	Recorded long-term loan balances and accounts payable to lessors represent debts that exist at balance sheet date.

MANAGEMENT ASSERTION	AUDIT OBJECTIVES
Measurement/ accuracy	Shareholders' equity balances represent amounts received from shareholders net of repayments of capital.
	Balances on retained income and other reserves represent the accumulated results of transactions and events of the entity to the balance sheet date, allocated in accordance with GAAP applied by the entity on a consistent basis.
	Recorded long-term loan balances and amounts owing to lessors for finance leases reflect the accumulated borrowings and finance lease transactions determined in accordance with GAAP applied by the entity on a consistent basis.
Valuation	Shareholders' equity and reserves reflect the accumulated results of the entity's transactions valued in accordance with GAAP applied by the entity on a consistent basis.
	Long-term loan balances represent the accumulated results of advances, repayments and financing transactions; and accounts payable to finance lessors represent the present value of future lease payments determined in accordance with GAAP applied by the entity on a consistent basis.
Rights and obligations	Recorded shareholders equity and reserves balances represent the claims of owners on the net assets of the entity at balance sheet date.
	The recorded long-term debts, and accounts payable to lessor for finance leases, are obligations of the entity at the balance sheet date.
	Securities provided for long-term debts and finance leases and entity assets mortgaged or pledged are identified and represent obligations of the entity at the balance sheet date.

MANAGEMENT ASSERTION	AUDIT OBJECTIVES
Presentation and disclosure	Shareholders equity and reserves and long-term debt obligations are correctly identified and classified in the financial statements in accordance with GAAP and the Companies Act.
	All details of shares authorized and issued, including different classes, and whether of par value or no par value, the number and details of shares held by directors, share options granted and exercised, details of employee share schemes, and dividends declared are adequately disclosed in the financial statements in accordance with GAAP and the Companies Act.
	Details of retained income and other reserves and movements on these during the period are correctly identified and classified in the financial statements in accordance with GAAP and the Companies Act.
	All terms of long-term debts, debentures and accounts payable to lessors for finance leases, including interest rates, repayment periods, security provided and the identification of assets mortgaged or pledged are adequately disclosed in the financial statements in accordance with GAAP and the Companies Act.

Table 16.6 Management assertions and the related audit objectives for financing

16.3.3 Understanding the client's business

The auditor should obtain an understanding of the strategic business objectives of management in order to consider the implications for the financing activities and core business processes. Management has many options for obtaining the necessary level and source of funding to finance its strategic business objectives. These may range from a small owner-managed company, where the share capital is a nominal amount and the financing is provided primarily from long-term loans by the shareholders or a bank, with overdraft facilities arranged to fund the entity's working capital requirements; to a large listed public company where significant long-term funding is obtained from public share issues and long-term borrowings from banks, other financial institutions and shareholders.

In addition, management may choose to finance its investing activities by means of finance leases or operating leases as opposed to outright purchases of items, or may enter into sale and leaseback arrangements for selected categories of assets to free up cash for other purposes. As most entity's have only a few equity and long-term loan transactions occurring during any accounting period, unless the entity itself is a money-lending institution such as a bank or financial institution where the obtaining and making of loans would constitute a core business activity, a risk of significant misstatement in the financial statements arising from financing transactions is unlikely, for most entities. Consequently, the auditor will usually assess the risk of significant misstatement for financing transactions and balances as low.

16.3.3.1 Electronic share trading – STRATE

STRATE introduced electronic settlement to the South Africa and Namibia securities exchanges by creating the South African market infrastructure and implementing sophisticated software programs for trading in securities of companies listed on the JSE Securities Exchange and Namibia Securities Exchange. The establishment of STRATE led to the introduction of section 91A in the Companies Act in 1998, which made statutory provision for 'uncertificated securities' or dematerialized scrip, to replace the existing printed share certificates (scrip) used by listed companies. The section sets out the requirements for dematerialization of listed companies' scrip and allows for the introduction of electronic trading in securities of listed companies.

The detailed register of shareholders of companies listed on the JSE Securities Exchange who have dematerialized their scrip is held in electronic form as *sub-registers* by central securities depository participants (CSDPs), currently seven CSDPs are registered with STRATE, the sole central securities depository (CSD). With the exception of Computershare, the other registered CSDPs are all Banking institutions.

Shareholders who dematerialize their share certificates relinquish their original printed share certificates to the CSDP, which then records their dematerialized scrip holding in the relevant company's electronic sub-registers and records subsequent dealings in the dematerialized scrip. A monthly statement is provided to the shareholder of the details of companies scrip held in dematerialized form and registered in their name in the CSDP *sub-register* (this is akin to the monthly bank statement that a customer would receive from his or her banker on accounts held at the bank).

Each company secretary receives a monthly statement from the CSDPs of all members holding dematerialized scrip and the scrip transfers on each sub-register during the month. Such printouts may be requested on a more frequent basis as share movements are often monitored closely by the board of directors. In order to obtain evidence of the disclosures with regard to the shareholdings of directors and others disclosed in the annual report, the auditor would obtain and inspect the printouts of shareholdings obtained from the CSDPs as at the balance sheet date and several days' movements for a few days before and after the period end to detect any unusual movements in share dealings.

The CSDP is required in terms of section 91A(3)(b) to record all such details of members in a sub-register as required under sections 105 and 133 of the

Companies Act and, further, in terms of section 91A(3)(c) to warrant the correctness of all information in the sub-registers for each company. The conversion of listed companies shares on the JSE Securities Exchange to dematerialized scrip has been phased in over the past three years and by April 2002 approximately 74% of the total number of shares listed on the JSE Securities Exchange had been dematerialized. It is anticipated that the strict controls around the dematerialization of scrip will reduce the risk of tainted scrip in the market in future.

The CSDPs agree their aggregate holdings on a daily basis with the total shares in issue according to the company's records and with the CSD and the JSE Securities Exchange, which both maintain an electronic record of the daily share trades and total shares held by each CSDP's *sub-register* and the aggregate shares in issue for all listed companies. The relationship between the CSD and the CSDPs may be likened to that between the Reserve Bank and the Commercial Banks in the country. Transfer of ownership in dematerialized scrip shall be 'effected by the debiting and crediting respectively, of the account in the sub-registers from which the transfer is effected, to the account in the sub-register to which the transfer is to be made' – section 91A(4)(a). The changes to the JSE Securities Exchange and section 91A(7)(b)(iv) of the Companies Act require a shareholder in a listed company to dematerialize their shares before the transfer of such shares can be processed by a CSDP. A monthly statement of dematerialized shares held in their *sub-register* is to be sent by the CSDP to each shareholder. Unlisted securities of a public company may also be dematerialized and the scrip record will then be maintained by the CSDPs in a *sub-register* for the company.

Strict controls are set up and maintained by STRATE and the JSE Securities Exchange over central securities depository participants (CSDPs) and brokers. The JSE Securities Exchange has on-line electronic access to all brokers by means of the Broker Dealer Accounting (BDA) system and is thus able to monitor all share dealings in companies listed on the exchange.

Section 140A of the Companies Act, which requires nominees to disclose the names of the beneficial owners of shares registered in the nominees' name on a quarterly basis, applies equally to nominees registering dematerialized scrip with the any CSDP sub-register. Accordingly, section 91A(3)(b) does not permit a CSDP to register any shares in the sub-register maintained by it, in its name as a nominee, since the CSDP would have access to the name of the beneficial owner and should thus record this immediately on transfer. In practice, each CSDP obtains the names of the beneficial shareholders from each underlying nominee, whether broker or bank, on a monthly basis and records this information in the relevant sub-register and provides the details to the company secretary. Figure 16.2 demonstrates the relationship between the CSD, the CSDP and shareholders.

Dividends declared by a listed company are distributed by CSDP to all the shareholders registered in their sub-register on the *last day to trade (LTD)* for the dividend declared. The company secretary or company transfer secretary, if appointed, remains responsible for the distribution of dividends declared, maintenance of the unclaimed dividends account and regular reconciliation of dividend cheques or EFT transfers to the company's dividend bank account statement.

Register of members for a private company

In the case of a private company, the register of members is to be maintained by the company secretary. A private company may, with the written consent of all the shareholders, appoint its auditors as the *company secretary* to perform the statutory services. Mention of the appointment must be made in the audit report on the annual financial statements. A private company in its Articles of Association restricts the right to transfer shares requiring the consent of all members and consequently changes occur infrequently. With a limited number of shareholders, dividend declarations are usually approved at the annual general meeting of shareholders.

16.3.3.2 Share buy-backs and payments to shareholders

The introduction in 1999 of sections 85 to 90 in the South African Companies Act introduced significant changes to the handling of equity and affected the distributable nature of a company's reserves. These changes not only enabled a company to repurchase its own shares (section 85), which are then to be cancelled and restored to the status of authorized shares, but also permitted subsidiary companies to acquire shares in their holding company 'up to a maximum of 10% in the aggregate number of issued shares' which may then be held as *treasury shares* entitling the subsidiary to receive dividends declared by the holding company (section 89), although no voting rights attach to the shares.

The introduction of section 90(1) provides for a company to make any payments, in any form, to its shareholders arising out of their shareholding, provided the company is authorized by its articles of association and subject to solvency requirements being met after such payments are made. The solvency requirements set out in section 90(2) are:

- That the company is able to meet its debts in the ordinary course of business after the payment; and
- That the consolidated assets of the company, fairly valued, after the payment are not less than the consolidated liabilities of the company.

Should the solvency requirements not be met, following payments made to its shareholders, the shareholder will become liable to the company for any payment received in contravention of the section.

In terms of section 90(3), payments to shareholders allowed include any direct or indirect payment or transfer of money or other property to a shareholder by virtue of their shareholding, but excludes a buy-back of shares under section 85, the redemption of redeemable preference shares under section 98, any acquisition of shares in terms of an order of court (in a restructuring), or the issue of capitalization shares in the company.

		Register for ABSA Shares
CSD	**STRATE - records aggregate shares of ABSA held by each CSDP:**	
	CSDP 1	100 000 000
	CSDP 2	100 000 000
	CSDP 3	20 000 000
	CSDP 3	12 000 000
	CSDP 4	8 000 000
	Total ABSA shares in issue	**240 000 000**

(Agreed daily to company total in issue)
Note: that it is not then possible for the auditor to confirm with the **CSD** who owns which shares as the underlying information is maintained by the **CSDP** and may in fact be sub-held by a nominee.

CSDP 4	Mr Jones	20 000
	Mr Smith	18 000
	Mr Fox	22 000
	Company XYZ	**2 000**
	Other shareholders ...	7 678 000
	Nominee – Investec Unit Trusts	140 000
	Nominee – ABC Securities	**120 000**
	Total ABSA shares in CSDP 4 sub-register	**8 000 000**

The auditors of **Company XYZ** would therefore confirm the shareholding with **CSDP 4** at the company's financial year end.
Who is the **beneficial shareholder** of Investec Unit Trusts' portfolio? As the shares in a unit trust would be subdivided into less than one share and one shareholder for each share held cannot be identified, the unit trust is considered to be the beneficial shareholder.
In the case of a stockbroker nominee **ABC Securities**, the beneficial shareholders would be contained in the broker's records as follows:

Nominee ABC Securities	Mr Pierce	20,000
	Mr Rock	10,000
	Mr Strydom	10,000
	Company PQR	80,000
	Total scrip held by ABC Securities as a nominee	**120,000**

The auditors of PQR would then confirm with the **broker** that **Company PQR** holds the ABSA shares.
Note that nominee companies contained below this level require the specific approval of the Financial Services Board and this is only likely to be given to asset managers (LISPs), pension funds, long-term and short-term insurers.

S91A requires the following to disclose their beneficial shareholdings:

1. CSDP

2. Nominee companies

Figure 16.2 Relationship between the CSD, the CSDP and shareholders

16.3.3.3 **Materiality**

Although new share issues or long-term loans may occur infrequently, the amount of equity and loan balances at period end may be significant, as might the obligations arising from them, being the effect of financing costs on the net income of an entity and the effect of dividends declared on retained earnings, these affecting the auditor's assessment of quantitative materiality. In addition, the extent of detailed presentation and disclosure requirements both for equity and borrowings make these balances and rights and obligations significant, affecting the auditor's assessment of qualitative materiality.

Unless financing activities are a core business process, as would apply to the audit of one of the CSDPs, share issues require the authorization of the shareholders and long-term loan transactions require the authorization of the board of directors. The directors will be involved in the subsequent implementation and recording of the transactions. As a result, the auditor will invariably adopt an audit approach involving substantive analytical procedures and limited substantive tests of detail of balances, and will generally not perform detailed tests of controls.

16.3.4 **Analysing process level business risks**

Where new share issues and share buy-backs or redemptions and negotiation of loans or issue of debentures occur infrequently, the financing activities would be dealt with as part of the resource management process of the entity. The process level business risks and controls in respect of equity would of course be specific to the issue and dealing in the shares of the company and declaration of dividends, and in respect of long-term borrowings, would be specific to contractual arrangements entered into by directors within their borrowing powers. Authorization of share issues and debentures are regulated by statute, and for South African listed companies, the JSE Securities Exchange listing requirements. These similarly require the specific approval of top management, such as approval by the board of directors, and in the case of new share issues, approval by the shareholders.

Where the company issues debentures, the terms and conditions are regulated by sections 116 to 132 of the Companies Act, the terms of the debenture trust deed and the Articles of Association of the company. A trustee may be appointed to administer the debenture issue and to hold the security for the debenture holders, and this person may not be a director or officer of the company. As with shares and long-term loans, debenture issues, repayments and interest payments are provided for in the debenture trust deed, with specific transactions approved by the board of directors.

Agreements for the acquisition or leasing of assets are usually incorporated in comprehensive legal contracts setting out the rights and obligations of both parties, rather than a simple purchase order and goods received note generated as discussed in chapter 13. In large companies, the Capital

Expenditure Committee of the board of directors may handle the negotiation of contracts for borrowings to finance its capital acquisitions which contracts are then approved by the board of directors.

In such circumstances, the auditor may decide to obtain the audit evidence required from substantive analytical procedures applied to the calculation of interest payable and dividends declared with limited substantive tests of detail focused on the audit of new share or debenture issues, share buy-backs, redemptions of redeemable preference shares or debentures, and advances and capital repayments of loans received during the period, and confirmation of balances owed and rights and obligations at the period end.

Examples of the key documents and records encountered when auditing share and debenture issues and loan agreements are set out in Table 16.7.

DOCUMENTS	NATURE OF DOCUMENT
Shares and debentures	
Minutes of share-holders and directors	Provide the approval for the relevant share issue or debenture issue, the buy-back of shares and re-demption of debentures. The Companies Act and Articles of Association set out the level of authoriza-tion required. Minutes also provide approval for dividends de-clared.
Debenture Trust Deed	Sets out the terms of the debenture issue and the rights and obligations of debenture-holders, the debenture trustee and the entity.
Prospectus	Document prepared for every public offer of shares or debentures containing details required by the Companies Act sections 142–169 and Schedule 3 to the Companies Act.
Share certificate or debenture certificate	Document issued by a company to its shareholder evidencing title to the number and type of shares mentioned therein. Scrip relinquished by a member on conversion to dematerialized scrip.
CSDP Statement	Statement issued monthly by the CSDP to share-holders reflecting all the dematerialized scrip regis-tered in their name in the particular company in the relevant CSDP sub-register.

DOCUMENTS	NATURE OF DOCUMENT
CSDP Printout of sub-register	Printout of the *sub-ledger* maintained for each listed company by a CSDP reflecting the member details and total shares held by the CSDP at a particular date, as well as all movements in the scrip for the period of the report. Report sent to the company or transfer secretary and the company directors.
Long-term borrowings and leases	
Loan or Lease Contract	Contract setting out the terms of the loan, or lease, including the amount of the loan, repayment terms, and interest rate or amount payable and security, if any provided. Approval of the loan terms is usually recorded in a directors' minute.
Mortgage bond	Agreement signed over property of the company to secure repayment of the loan.
Cash receipts and deposits	Remittance diary and bank deposit slips or EFT advices.
Cheque payments or EFT	Cheque or EFT payments are made for share buy-backs, and loan repayments, interest and dividends paid and STC on dividends.
Journal voucher	Several entries are made by journal entry, e.g. the accrual of interest or dividends declared, and recording of finance lease liabilities to the lessors at their carrying values. The journal voucher with relevant documents attached reflect the calculations made and reasons for the entries.

Table 16.7 Documents typically encountered when auditing financing activities

16.3.5 Assessing the risk of significant misstatement

The auditor should consider the risk of significant misstatement affecting financing transactions and, based on the understanding obtained of the client's business, be alert to those that could occur in the particular client's business. Given the highly regulated environment and strict controls exercised by the directors over financing activities, unless the auditor has concerns regarding management integrity, the risk of material misstatement will usually be assessed as low for these transactions and balances.

One aspect may, however, be problematic for the auditor and that is the comprehensive disclosure requirements in terms of GAAP and the Companies Act, required for both equity and borrowings, which may present a potential *risk of significant misstatement* for the *completeness, valuation, presentation* and *disclosure* assertions. While the account balances are unlikely to be misstated, there is a risk that information concerning rights and obligations may be omitted or misstated, for example, where assets are pledged or guarantees given by one company in a group situation to secure liabilities of another group company. There are several instances where such arrangements have resulted in the liquidation of the companies, not only those incurring the liabilities but also those providing the guarantees that are called in by the lender. The auditor must be alert to this possibility, particularly when indications of going-concern problems arise in a group.

Where the entity is a large public company operating in global markets, whose shares are listed on both local and foreign stock exchanges, the complexity of the laws and regulations in other legal jurisdictions may affect the auditor's assessment of the risk of significant misstatement, for example, when issuing new shares. In these circumstances, borrowings may be obtained from foreign lenders and this may give rise to foreign exchange gains and losses being recognized in the income statement. In this case, the *risk of significant misstatement* for financing transactions and balances may be assessed as medium to high, with a risk of *completeness* and *valuation* and a risk of unrecorded liabilities and contingent liabilities.

Before performing the substantive test procedures, the auditor will make a preliminary assessment of the *risk of significant misstatement for the equity, loans interest and dividend transactions and balances* in the financial statements. The auditor would consider each of the factors and document the overall assessment as *high, medium or low*. This will then influence the auditor's decision to follow a mainly substantive approach by way of substantive analytical procedures and substantive tests of detail of balances. The reader is reminded that the preliminary *risk of significant misstatement* would be assessed for the various factors discussed earlier in this chapter, under 16.2.5, which are not reproduced here.

The auditor seeks corroborating information by way of enquiries, inspection of documents or observation of control procedures performed, to support the preliminary assessment of the *risk of significant misstatement* identifying the effect on the financial statements for particular account balances and designing appropriate audit procedures to detect and correct any risk of significant misstatement remaining.

16.3.6 Determining the acceptable level of detection risk

For the reasons discussed earlier in this chapter, the auditor's assessment of the risk of significant misstatement of shareholder's equity and long-term borrowings transactions and balances is likely to be assessed as low, other than in circumstances where the financing activities form a core business process, when reliance on the system might be sought which requires that tests of controls be performed. Consequently, a higher level of detection risk will be acceptable and the audit procedures will comprise primarily substantive analytical procedures and limited substantive tests of detail. The engagement circumstances must also be taken into account where these introduce particular risks, not usually present when auditing financing transactions and balances.

It will clearly be inefficient for the auditor to attempt to follow a test of controls approach with a limited number of financing transactions, which is usually the case. Where, however, a primarily substantive audit approach is taken, the auditor needs to document the control activities over the financing activities to identify any risk of misstatement that might arise, to ensure the substantive audit procedures performed are the appropriate response to the risk of misstatement identified.

16.3.7 Substantive analytical procedures

Substantive analytical procedures include comparisons to prior years or budgets, ratio analysis, comparisons of financial and non-financial information based on the auditor's understanding of the core processes and related business processes of the entity. Trends may be established from historical information and changes explained by reason of internal and external events that have occurred, such as business expansion or discontinued operations or changes in accounting policies and management. Where the audit is a continuing engagement, the auditor is likely to have a record of analyses prepared in prior years on which to base initial expectations for the current period's analyses. These expectations could then be modified in the current audit for known changes in the business or economic circumstances.

In chapter 11 five steps to be followed in using substantive analytical procedures were identified in order for any analytical reviews to be effective in throwing into relief significant departures from the prediction or expectation, or in confirming recorded amounts if in line with these. When substantive analytical procedures are applied to the equity and borrowings transactions and balances, these are:

- *Develop a prediction or expectation.* The ratios that are used for these transactions and balances will fall broadly into the category of capital performance and financial management. It will be evident from the earlier discussions that a great diversity will be found in the type and mix of equity and loan funding that a business obtains to meet its strategic business objectives. Consequently, the capital performance and financial management ratios may not be comparable on an industry basis. The comparison over time of an entity's business performance is thus a preferable technique.

- *Compute the difference between the actual and the expected.* Computing the difference involves the performance of various ratios, including key performance indicators used by management to monitor the business, as discussed above. These are compared to prior periods, to budgets or strategic returns set by management and to a history of such ratios maintained by the client or auditor. Enquiry regarding the key performance indicators used by management and the calculation of these, and enquiry about corrective action taken where problems are indicated, provides evidence of the effectiveness of management's controls. Ratios that management may typically use and which are generally available may include:

Capital performance:
- Return on shareholders/owners equity;
- Growth of shareholders interest/equity;
- Preference share capital cover;
- Headline earnings to equity;
- Earnings per share (EPS); earnings yield (EY); and Price/Earnings ratio (P/E Ratio); Dividend yield (DY);
- Earnings before tax to capital employed (EBT);
- Retained earnings to earnings after tax (EAT);
- Dividends declared to shareholder's interest/capital;
- Economic value added (EVA) to capital employed;

Financial management:
- Loan capital cover;
- Lease capital cover;
- Average interest rate (before and after tax);
- Rate of interest and dividends to 'Gross capital';
- Interest paid to earnings before and after tax;
- Outside funding to capital employed;
- Retained earnings to capital employed; and
- Financial leverage.

- *Investigate significant differences and exercise judgement.* The auditor should analyse ratios that are appropriate to the expectations of the audit team formulated above. Any unexpected fluctuations should be discussed with management and, where necessary, investigated further.

- *Define a significant difference or threshold to conclude.* The auditor ascertains by enquiry whether or not the ratios and benchmarks used by management as key performance indicators indicate any risk of significant misstatements and considers the implications of trends identified affecting the profitability, cash flows and sustainability of the business and the effectiveness of management's monitoring procedures.

- *Document the basis for the audit conclusion.* The auditor must conclude on whether the audit evidence gathered supports the assertions/audit objectives that the auditor was trying to substantiate.

16.3.8 Substantive tests of detail of transactions and balances

Substantive tests of detail performed in the audit of the financing transactions will focus on obtaining evidence of the *completeness, occurrence and measurement and rights and obligations* arising from equity and long-term borrowings. At period end the focus will be on gathering audit evidence relating to the *existence, valuation, rights and obligations*, and the *presentation and disclosure assertions to reflect the carrying values of equity and long-term loans in accordance with GAAP.*

16.3.8.1 Substantive tests of detail of long-term loans, leases and debentures

Substantive tests of detail of transactions

Where new agreements have been entered into for long-term loans, or debentures have been issued during the current period, the auditor inspects the relevant contracts and related authorizations, and the bank deposit for the receipt of the cash or journal entries for other assets received.

The auditor may also select a sample of repayments made during the period to the lender or debenture holders to inspect the relevant paid cheque or evidence of EFT transfer made to the lender. Repayments may be made on a monthly, quarterly, semi-annual or annual basis. Where payments are made on a monthly basis, the client may have signed a bank stop order or debit order in favour of the lender and the auditor would then inspect the bank statements of the entity for evidence of such payments made.

Substantive tests of detail of balances

Generally long-term loans and debentures are evidenced by written contracts providing for the interest payable and repayment terms, which have been approved by the board of directors. Where such loans are secured, this will usually be by way of a mortgage bond registered over property of the company, or notarial bonds registered over movables of the company. In such circumstances, the risk of material misstatement in the account balances is low and the substantive audit procedures, as suggested in the framework for substantive tests of detail set out in Table 16.8, will primarily involve obtaining an external confirmation of each loan balance and its terms, and the performance of substantive analytical procedures to calculate the reasonableness of the related interest expense in the income statement and any accrual or prepayment of interest at the period end.

Guidance is provided in SAAS 505, 'External confirmations', which indicates the auditor should arrange with the client to request the lender to send to the auditor directly, a certificate of the amount outstanding in respect of the loan and accrued interest, if any, and by agreeing the figures on the certificate with the amount(s) shown in respect of the relevant item(s) in the balance sheet. If the loan is secured, as is usually the case, the certificate should also contain particulars of the security.

The confirmation details should agree with the particulars as to security on the relevant loan account in the general ledger and with the statement relating to security in the notes to the financial statement and the balance sheet. Where there are several loans, a list of these should be obtained from the management and checked. The total of the list should agree with the relevant figure in the balance sheet.

A debenture is in essence a loan. If the debentures have been issued to only one person or to a few, the verification of the outstanding balance and the security (if any) follows exactly the same procedures as for a loan. If there are several debenture holders, the security for the debentures is normally held by trustees for the debenture holders, in which case the auditor should obtain a certificate giving particulars of the security from the trustees. In both cases, the auditor should check the list of balances extracted from the register of debenture holders and agree the total with the liability for debentures reflected in the balance sheet. Where debentures have been redeemed during the year under audit, the auditor should inspect the relevant cancelled debentures for evidence of the *completeness, occurrence and measurement* of the redemption. Enquiry of management or the debenture trustee and inspection of the debenture trust deed would reveal whether any conversion rights attach to the debentures and whether these have been exercised during the period. The recording of the relevant transfers to equity and issue of shares would be examined.

As in previous chapters, a framework for possible substantive tests of long-term loans, leases and debentures transactions and balances is set out in Table 16.8.

SUBSTANTIVE TESTS	AUDIT OBJECTIVES				
	C	O/E	M/V	R/O	P/D
1. Obtain and document an understanding of the business:	×	×	×	×	×
Identify significant classes of assets for the entity: • Identify strategic plans of management with regard to financing activities; • Identify critical success factors and key performance indicators used by management; • Identify economic and industry circumstances affecting the client; • Identify industry norms for using debt and equity financing and the impact of financing costs on earnings generated.					
Obtain trial balances or schedules of the balances of long-term loans, finance leases and debentures and • Agree opening balances for long-term loans and debentures to the previous year's working papers; • Review movements on loan and interest accounts in the general ledger for unusual entries and investigate these; • Obtain a schedule of long-term loans to support the carrying values reflected in the general ledger and financial statements at period end; • Cast schedules and general ledger and agree balances to relevant ledger accounts.	×		×		

SUBSTANTIVE TESTS	AUDIT OBJECTIVES				
	C	O/E	M/V	R/O	P/D
2. Substantive analytical procedures:	×	×	×		
Develop a prediction or expectation based on the auditor's knowledge of the business activities and strategic business risks and the industry.					
Define a significant difference or threshold – based on materiality at account balance level.					
Calculate various relevant financial management ratios and key performance indicators used by management.					
Compute the difference between the actual and the expected, compare to prior periods, to budget and to a history of such ratios maintained.					
Investigate significant differences and exercise judgement to conclude on implications and trends.					
Document the basis for the conclusion.					
3. Tests of detail of transactions:					
Inspect supporting documents for approval such as minutes, invoices, agreements such as leases, mortgage bonds and pledges of assets used to secure liabilities for all loan advances.	×	×	×	×	×
Inspect bank deposits for cash received and paid cheques or EFT transfers for repayments of the principal sum and interest or finance charges and the recording in the general ledger.	×	×	×		×
Recalculate interest expense recorded and recognized in the income statement.	×	×	×		×
4. Tests of details of balances:					
Inspect authorizations and contracts for leases and long-term loans.		×	×		
Review minutes and capital expenditure authorizations for indications of capital commitments approved and contracted for.		×	×	×	×
Obtain an external confirmation from all long-term lenders and debenture trustees of the balance at period end, terms of the loans, security held and repayment terms.			×	×	×
5. Presentation and disclosure:					
Determine if the *presentation and disclosure* of long-term loans, leases, interest expense accords with GAAP and are properly identified and classified in the financial statements.					×
Determine whether the financial statement notes reflect the *rights and obligations* of the entity with regard to long-term loans and contingent liabilities.					×

Table 16.8 Framework for the content of a substantive audit programme for long-term loans, leases and debentures

16.3.8.2 Substantive tests of detail of leases and instalment sales

Substantive tests of detail of transactions

Buildings, plant, vehicles, etc., may be leased instead of being the subject of an outright purchase. Such a lease is known as a finance lease. It may be looked upon as an alternative to raising a loan to obtain the funds with which to pay for the asset and repaying the loan with interest over the period of the asset's useful life. This is in contrast to an operating lease, which merely gives the lessee the use of the asset for an agreed time in return for a periodic rental, which is recognized in the income statement when paid.

The acquisition of an asset through finance lease or instalment sales agreement is a means of spreading the financial burden over a period of time, instead of having to find the funds immediately to pay for the asset. GAAP AC 105, 'Leases', provides guidance as to the recognition, *measurement, valuation* and *presentation and disclosure* requirements for finance leases and operating leases.

Where there are several leases (finance and operating), the details of each should be entered in a register of leases,[1] distinguishing between the two types and also between the main categories of assets leased. The auditor should inspect the relevant contracts and authorization for each new lease transaction entered into during the period. The auditor determines by an examination of relevant terms in the lease contracts, relevant minutes of meetings and by discussion with management which are finance leases, and which are operating leases. The auditor may perform substantive analytical procedures to calculate reasonableness of the total rental recorded for the period for operating leases and may select a sample of rental payments for substantive tests of detail.

The entries in the general ledger relating to lease repayments, interest and finance charges, should be inspected to ensure the correct recognition and *measurement* has occurred for all leases entered into:

- Where assets acquired under finance leases have been capitalized, the obligation of the lessee to the lessor is accounted for in terms of AC 105 paragraph .14, at the fair value of the leased property or, if lower, at the present value of the minimum lease payments.

- For operating leases, the entity records the rental payments as they occur, usually on a monthly basis, but is required to disclose the lease commitments and periods of operating leases in the notes to the financial statements.

The auditor should examine the lease, determine the amount (or estimated amount) of the cost, and trace it through the register of leases (if any) to the relevant asset account. The audit of depreciation and profit and loss on

---

[1] GAAP AC 105 recommends that a register be maintained.

disposals, and the verification of the asset(s) held under finance leases are dealt with in the preceding section of this chapter.

Substantive tests of detail of balances

Lessors for *finance leases* will ordinarily send a monthly statement to the entity setting out the details of assets leased, and repayment terms. The auditor may select a sample of these statements to inspect as evidence of the *existence, measurement and valuation* of the recorded leases. They do not provide evidence, however, of the completeness of lease liabilities reflected and, accordingly, where lease liabilities are material, the auditor would usually also request an external confirmation from all lessors to whom monthly payments are being made for evidence of the total amounts owed and details of all lease contracts with the lessor.

Instalment sales agreements should be examined by the auditor to ascertain the total amount payable for the assets acquired, and its division into cost and interest charges, the former being debited to the asset account and the latter written off on some equitable basis over the period of the agreement. The substantive analytical procedures and tests of detail of depreciation and inspection of the asset are as set out above. The auditor should confirm that such assets, divided into appropriate categories, are described in the financial statements as 'held under instalment sales agreements'.

16.3.8.3 Contingent liabilities

The nature of and, if practicable, the amount of each contingent liability should be stated by way of note to the balance sheet, if not provided for in the financial statements. This requirement is specifically provided for in the case of limited companies.[2] As, however, the balance sheet of any business cannot be said to fairly present the state of affairs unless contingent liabilities are shown, the requirement applies to the balance sheets of all businesses.

Examples of contingent liabilities are:

- Debts of third parties guaranteed by the client; and
- Litigation and claims against the client, in process or pending.

The auditor should be satisfied that the amount shown for each contingent liability, of which the auditor is aware, is reasonable, but should realize that the amount is an accounting estimate, so by its very nature will be imprecise. The auditor will refer to such evidence as may be available. In some instances an exact figure is obtainable; in others, the auditor may be largely dependent on the opinion of the management. This will usually be the case where there is a legal action in process or pending against the company. Where the amount of a contingent liability cannot be calculated on any reasonable basis, it is better that no amount be stated, rather than a sum which is arrived at by mere guesswork.

---

[2] Paragraph 35 in schedule 4 of the Companies Act.

The auditor should follow the guidance in SAAS 560, 'Subsequent events', for the audit procedures to be followed to obtain audit evidence regarding contingent liabilities identified at the period end. If, after the close of the financial year under review but before the audit is completed, an actual liability has been incurred in respect of what, in the light of the information available at the financial year-end, was a contingent liability, due provision should be made for the liability in the financial statements at the year-end and the item omitted from the note in respect of contingent liabilities. An example of this is a legal action against the client in process or pending at the financial year-end in respect of which judgement has been given before the audit has been completed.

The auditor should, by an intelligent scrutiny of the accounting records (and in particular any attorneys' accounts) both before and after the year-end, by a comparison with the previous year's balance sheet and by discussing the matter with the management, be reasonably satisfied that all contingent liabilities have been the subject of a note to the balance sheet.

Where the contingent liability arises through litigation and claims, the auditor would follow the guidance provided in SAAS 502, 'Enquiries regarding litigation and claims', to obtain external confirmation from the attorneys regarding litigation and claims. The reader is referred to chapter 13 where the audit procedures required are discussed in detail.

Further information may be obtained in the case of a limited company by scrutinizing the minutes, which may disclose relevant particulars, for example, any guarantees which the company may have given during the year. The auditor should obtain external confirmations from the entity's bankers regarding guarantees provided (see chapter 17).

16.3.8.4 Substantive tests of detail of shareholders equity and reserves

As issues of shares and share buy-backs occur infrequently, balances on share capital remain fairly static and consequently audit procedures may be performed at or after the period end. Movements on reserves, such as retained income, generally occur at the period end and can only be audited once the financial statements are in the process of being finalized. Movements on other reserves – for example, on revaluation of assets – will arise through specific events or transactions and will also occur infrequently, so will similarly be audited at the completion stage of the audit. Although transactions themselves may be highly regulated, such as a new issue of shares, the recording of the entries to equity accounts affected are non-routine, which increases the risk of error and significant misstatement in their recording. The auditor must be alert to this.

Entries to the reserves are affected by the recognition, *measurement* and *valuation* requirements of the relevant GAAP AC statements, or arise by virtue of statutory requirements or terms contained in the Articles of

Association of the entity. Consequently the risk of significant misstatement for equity balances and disclosures arises through possible misapplication of GAAP accounting policies affecting *existence, measurement, valuation* and *presentation and disclosure* assertions. The risk of significant misstatement is more likely to affect reserves than equity balances.

As in previous chapters, a framework for possible substantive tests of shareholders equity and reserves, transactions and balances is set out in Table 16.9.

SUBSTANTIVE TESTS	AUDIT OBJECTIVES				
	C	O/E	M/V	R/O	P/D
1. Obtain and document an understanding of the business: Identify significant classes of assets for the entity: – Identify strategic plans of management with regard to financing activities; – Identify critical success factors and key performance indicators used by management; – Identify economic and industry circumstances affecting the client's ability to attract further equity financing and to pay dividends; – Identify industry norms for using equity financing.	×	×	×	×	×
Obtain trial balances or schedules of the balances of share capital and reserves and: – Agree opening balances for share capital and reserves to the previous year's working papers; – Review movements on shareholder equity accounts in the general ledger for unusual entries and investigate these; – Obtain a schedule of shareholders equity and reserves to support the balances reflected in the general ledger and financial statements at period end; – Cast schedules and general ledger and agree balances to relevant ledger accounts.	×		×		
2. Substantive analytical procedures: Develop a prediction or expectation based on the auditor's knowledge of the business activities and strategic business risks and the industry. Define a significant difference or threshold – based on materiality at account balance level. Calculate various relevant capital ratios and key performance indicators used by management. Compute the difference between the actual and the expected, compare to prior periods, to budget and to a history of such ratios maintained. Investigate significant differences and exercise judgement to conclude on implications and trends. Document the basis for the audit conclusion.	×	×	×		

SUBSTANTIVE TESTS	AUDIT OBJECTIVES				
	C	O/E	M/V	R/O	P/D
3. Tests of detail of transactions:					
Inspect supporting documents for approval of new share issues, share buy-backs and repayments of redeemable preference shares transactions.	X	X	X	X	X
Inspect minutes and dividend advice notes for dividends declared and paid cheques or EFT transfers in payment of the dividends or capitalization issues recorded.	X	X	X	X	X
Review changes in retained earnings and inspect supporting items for net income from trading.	X	X	X	X	X
4. Tests of details of balances:					
Inspect company memorandum and articles of association for authorized and issued share capital and different classes.		X	X		
Review shareholders minutes for new issues authorized and employee share options approved.		X	X	X	X
Inspect members share register or obtain printout of share registers from transfer secretaries and confirm analysis of shareholdings for purposes of the annual report of listed companies.			X	X	X
Obtain confirmation from directors of all shares and share options held and whether these are beneficially owned or merely as a nominee.			X	X	X
5. Presentation and disclosure:					
Determine that the *presentation and disclosure* of shareholders equity accords with GAAP and are properly identified and classified in the financial statements.					X
Determine whether the financial statement notes reflect the details of equity and reserves of the entity in accordance with GAAP and the Companies Act.					X

Table 16.9 Framework for a substantive audit programme for shareholders equity

Sole trader or partnership capital

Further capital contributions may arise on the introduction of new partners or an agreement among existing partners to contribute further capital. The evidence for such contributions should be found in the partnership agreement, original or amended. The auditor should read the agreement and be satisfied that the terms have been implemented by the partnership's receipt of the relevant cash and / or other assets and credit to the appropriate partners' capital accounts.

Substantive tests of detail of transactions

The auditor should inspect the supporting documentation for changes to share capital accounts that occurred during the period. In all instances, the auditor will consider the relevant Companies Act and Articles of Association requirements that regulate share issues.

A new issue of shares

The auditor should inspect the minutes of shareholders, receipt and bank deposits of cash from the share applicants, the allocation of shares, whether by way of share certificates for unlisted companies or dematerialized scrip issues for listed companies. The auditor should obtain printouts from the CSDP providing evidence that the new share issues have been recorded in the CSDP's sub-register of members. For listed companies, the auditor will enquire about the market price at the time of the issue to consider the reasonableness of the issue price. The reader is referred to the earlier discussion around STRATE and electronic members' registers.

Where the shares have been issued as part settlement of an acquisition of an investment in another entity or business, the auditor enquires about the nature and agreed value of the assets thus acquired to obtain audit evidence that the assets and shares are correctly recorded in the general ledger. In such circumstances, the auditor should also inspect the purchase agreement and make inquiries about any warranties and onerous conditions that may apply that may affect the *presentation and disclosure* in the financial statements.

Where the shares are issued to members of a private company, the auditor obtains evidence from inspection of the shareholders minutes and share registers that the existing shareholders have agreed to the new share issue and to the admission of the new shareholder as a member of the company.

Buy-backs of shares

The auditor should inspect the relevant directors' or shareholders' minutes approving the buy-back, and for listed companies the relevant brokers note for the shares repurchased, and paid cheque or EFT transfer in settlement of the purchase price. The auditor will inspect evidence that the shares bought back have been cancelled and restored to authorized share capital, by inspection of the members' register. The appropriate disclosures are to be made in the financial statements.

Redemptions of redeemable preference shares

Where redeemable preference shares are redeemed during the period, the auditor should inspect evidence that this has occurred in accordance with the relevant clause in the articles of association and evidence of the payment made to the preference shareholder. Care should be taken that any repayment has been made in accordance with section 98 of the Companies Act and that any premium payable on redemption has been provided for from retained income or out of the share premium account and that the transfer to the capital redemption reserve fund is recorded from retained income, should the issue not be funded from a fresh issue of ordinary shares.

Dividends declared

In many cases the articles provide that the company in general meeting may declare dividends and that the directors may pay interim dividends. Table A (articles 84 and 85) and Table B (articles 83 and 84) so provide. In such circumstances the usual procedure is for the directors to pay an interim dividend (if it is justified by the profits) and to propose, in their report, a final dividend, which may be declared at the annual general meeting.

On the other hand, the articles may give the directors an unrestricted power to pay dividends, in which case there will be no question of proposing a dividend for the year under audit but of declaring it either prior to the year-end or at a later date when the draft financial statements have been prepared and the profit is known.

The auditor should calculate the total amount of dividend by reference to the issued or paid-up share capital, the articles and the relevant minute of meeting. The other substantive audit procedures follow the same lines as for the audit of debenture interest payments. The auditor should check the amount of the liability for dividend by reference to the issued or paid-up share capital, the articles and the relevant minutes of meeting. The dividend may be based on the issued share capital or the paid-up share capital. The former applies if the articles are silent on the point.[3] Although shares may no longer be allotted or issued unless the full issue price for such shares has been paid to and received by the company (see section 92 of the Companies Act), it is still permissible for a company which had at 1 January 1974 partly paid shares as its issued capital (or part thereof) to retain the unpaid portion for as long as it wishes. The auditor should consult the articles (or the permanent audit notes) to ascertain the basis, which is applicable.

In the case of larger companies and public listed companies with many shareholders, a company secretary will be appointed and several CSDPs will maintain separate sub-registers of members and be responsible for distributing dividends declared to members registered on the last day to trade (LDT). The auditor would obtain a printout of the shareholdings prepared from the members' register, showing details of each shareholding on the last day to trade (LDT) and the amount of dividend payable. The procedures for control over the dividend calculation and payment are, *mutatis mutandis*, the same as those for debenture interest.

The auditor should enquire about the liability of the entity for payment of Secondary Tax for Companies (STC) payable on dividends declared and for any withholding tax payable on dividends declared to foreign residents. The relevant tax returns and paid cheque or EFT would be inspected and calculations of the amount payable performed.

---

[3] Most articles of association provide specifically for this. Article 87 of Table A and article 86 of Table B so provide.

Where the declaration of the dividend occurs prior to the period end but payment is due to be made only after the period end, the accrual of shareholders for dividend declared should be reflected as a current liability in the financial statements. Where a final dividend requires the approval of the shareholders at the annual general meeting, the amount should not be disclosed as a provision because at the period end there is no contractual obligation to pay the dividend.

Substantive tests of detail of balances

Share capital

Where no change has occurred in the issued share capital of the entity during the period, the auditor will merely agree the balances to the prior year balance brought forward and the disclosures in the financial statements for the prior year.

For public and listed companies, additional disclosures are required in the financial statements regarding the persons holding shares in the company, the number of shares held, percentage holding and whether such shares are beneficially owned or held as a nominee for another party. The reader's attention is drawn to the requirements of section 140A of the Companies Act that now requires disclosure of the beneficial owner of all nominee shareholdings. In addition, shareholdings of directors are to be disclosed in the financial statements. Accordingly, the auditor should obtain printouts from the CSDPs of the sub-registers for listed company shares and agree the totals to the total shares in issue, after which the auditor should inspect the member's register as at the period end and use this to assess the accuracy of management's analysis of the members for purposes of the financial statement disclosures. This review will also provide the auditor with a means of identifying possible related parties requiring disclosure in the published financial statements.

Reserves

The question of the auditor's duty with regard to reserves depends partly on the form of the business of the client. The position of sole traders and partnerships by comparison with a limited company is considered below.

Sole traders and partnerships

In the case of sole traders or partnerships the question of the need for, or the desirability of, making a reserve is entirely one for the owners or partners to decide. They may consult the auditor in the matter but the latter, qua auditor, has no duty other than to ascertain that appropriate authority has been given for any reserve that may be created. The signatures of the owner or partners on the copy of the financial statements retained by the auditor, is sufficient evidence of this.

Limited companies

The Companies Act 1973, Fourth Schedule paragraph 4, defines 'distributable' and 'non-distributable' reserves as follows:

> *'Distributable reserve* means any amount which has been transferred to reserves and which may be distributed by way of dividend; and
>
> *Non-distributable reserve* shall be construed accordingly;'

Non-distributable reserves

The only non-distributable reserve arising from the Act is the capital redemption reserve fund[4]. There may also be cases where the articles provide that certain profits shall not be available for dividend, for example, profit on the sale of immovable property. Consequently, the auditor will inspect the Articles of Association to ascertain whether any restriction is placed on the distribution of particular reserves.

It may be that a reserve is non-distributable because of the decision of the directors. In such a case, the reserve classified as non-distributable in the balance sheet at one date may appear as distributable at a later date because of changed circumstances.

Where the creation of reserves are required by the Companies Act, by the articles, or by particular GAAP statements, the auditor should determine whether the proper amount has been credited to the reserve and whether the reserve is properly described in the balance sheet.

Distributable reserves

Distributable reserves are usually at the discretion of the directors.[5] The question of the necessity for or adequacy of reserves is a matter for the management. The auditor's only duty in this regard would appear to be to ascertain that all transfers to or from reserves which have been authorized by the board, and only those, have been properly recorded in the records and that the appropriate reserves have been properly described in the balance sheet. The evidence of the authorizations should appear in the board minutes.

The transfer of the net income for the period after tax would be compared to the published financial statements. Any other direct entries, such as dividends declared, have already been discussed above. The adequacy of the client's provisions for taxation or deferred taxation would be reviewed. Where necessary, this review would be performed by experts in the tax department of the auditing practice.

---

[4] Sections 98(1)(b) and 98(4) of the Companies Act 1973.

[5] Most articles of association provide specifically for this. Article 87 of Table A and article 86 of Table B so provide. This topic is treated at length in J T Pretorius et al., *Hahlo's Company Law through the Cases*. See also H S Cilliers & M L Benade, *Corporate Law*.

Should there be any changes in accounting policies giving rise to a prior year adjustment, the auditor would need to inspect the underlying data and recalculate the amounts and inspect the disclosures in the financial statements to determine whether they are adequate. Other balances in the income statement would have been considered during the audit of the various income and expenditure transactions and balances affected by the core business processes and sub-processes, discussed in detail in chapters 12 to 17.

16.3.9 Presentation and disclosure

It is evident from the discussion in the preceding pages that the financial statement presentation and disclosures for shareholders equity, reserves, long-term loans, debentures, and required by statute are extensive while disclosures for leases are affected by requirements of South African GAAP AC 105.

In addition, Schedule 4 and other specific sections of the Companies Act have further specific disclosure requirements for share capital, reserves, long-term loans, debentures and leases affecting the balance sheet, income statement, cash flow statement, notes to the financial statements, and directors' report.

The auditor should inspect the presentation and disclosures in the financial statements related to the equity, loan funds and lease balances and consider the appropriateness of these in accordance with the requirements of the relevant accounting framework, any statutory requirements, and audit evidence gathered from the substantive analytical procedures and substantive tests of detail that collectively support the *disclosures* and *presentation* in the financial statements.

17

Auditing Investment and Cash Transactions and Balances

Learning objectives

After studying this chapter you should be able to:

1. Describe the nature of the *investment* and *cash* business processes and identify significant classes of transactions and balances.
2. Set audit objectives for the audit of *investment* and *cash* transactions and balances.
3. Describe the functions, related control activities and assessment of the risk of significant misstatement for *investment* and *cash* transactions and balances.
4. Explain how to determine an acceptable level of detection risk for *investment* and *cash* transactions and balances.
5. Design substantive audit procedures to respond appropriately to the risk of significant misstatement for *investment* and *cash* transactions and balances.
6. Discuss the factors to be considered when auditing fair value measurements for balances arising from *investment* and *cash* activities.

17.1 OVERVIEW OF INVESTMENT AND CASH TRANSACTIONS

The preceding chapters 12 to 15 cover the significant classes of revenue and expenditure transactions, and chapter 16 the nature and audit of capital resources from *investing* and *financing* activities. The discussion turns now, in chapter 17, to *investment activities* and the audit of *cash and bank* transactions and balances, in effect the means by which the entity accomplishes its strategic business objectives and implements its core business processes. In some instances, investments and the management of cash and bank may themselves constitute a core process, as discussed later in the chapter.

In the section on *investments*, a broad distinction is drawn between *equity and debt investments* and *derivative financial instruments*, since the nature and risk of significant misstatement for these categories of financial assets, and therefore the audit implications, differ in important respects.

17.1.1 Equity and debt investments

Equity and debt investments may be acquired in private or public companies and held for the long-term purpose of gaining a strategic advantage. For example, securing key supply or distribution lines by investing in a subsidiary, associate or joint venture, with the purpose of enhancing the operating activities of a group of companies. Other investments may comprise the short-term investment of surplus cash resources in listed equity instruments, or debt investments such as term deposits at banks, to generate investment income in the form of interest, dividends or realize capital profits from trading in those equity instruments, and with the purpose of supplementing the entity's usual operating income. For many entities, investment transactions may occur infrequently and investment balances and income may be insignificant. In these circumstances, the auditor may obtain sufficient audit evidence from substantive tests of detail over purchases and sales of investments and balances at year-end.

In other entities – such as: investment dealers; financial institutions; pension, provident and retirement annuity funds; life insurers and unit trusts – equity and debt investments comprise a core business process. Accordingly, purchases and sales of investments, investment holdings and related income from such holdings form a significant class of transactions, giving rise to material balance sheet and income statement balances. In such circumstances, management is likely to implement extensive formal control activities, risk management processes, and key performance indicators over investment transactions.

17.1.2 Derivative financial instruments

A comprehensive discussion of the audit of derivatives is beyond the scope of this book, but a brief discussion of the principles follows in the investments section of the chapter.

Activity in *derivative financial instruments* range from those whose primary objective is to reduce or eliminate risk (hedging) to those whose primary objective is to maximise profits (speculating). All other things being equal, risk increases, as the maximization of profits becomes the focus of derivative activity. Derivative financial instruments are becoming more complex, and more commonplace, which has required an expansion of accounting principles in as far as providing fair value and other information in the financial statement presentations and disclosures.

Values of derivatives may be volatile. Large and sudden decreases in value may increase the risk that a loss to an entity using derivatives may exceed the amount, if any, recorded on the balance sheet. The use of derivative financial instruments is under intense scrutiny, following major losses experienced by multinational investment analysts, such as JP Morgan and Proctor & Gamble, and collapses of several major banking operations such as Barings Bank plc.

> 'Because of the complexity of derivative activities, management, and the auditor, may not fully understand the risks of using derivatives. For many entities, the use of derivatives for hedging transactions and balances has reduced exposures to changes in exchange rates, interest rates and commodity prices, as well as other risks. On the other hand, the inherent characteristics of derivative activities and derivative financial instruments also may result in increased business risk in some entities, in turn increasing audit risk and presenting new challenges to the auditor.'[1]

An important aspect of the short-term and long-term business strategies of management is to optimize the returns on the business resources affecting the sustainability of the business, which relates directly to movements in the investing, investment, and cash and bank activities. The volume of transactions for new investments is unlikely to be significant, whereas the management of cash and bank transactions will be ongoing and linked to all transactions of the business. The resultant asset, liability and equity balances and related income and expenditure balances are likely to be significant to the financial statements.

The nature of investment transactions is such that each transaction would usually require authorization by a high level of management, frequently the board of directors. Consequently, unless the investment activities comprise the core business of the entity, the auditor is unlikely to follow a test of controls approach and would opt, instead, for substantive analytical procedures and substantive tests of detail to reduce detection risk to acceptable levels.

In order to evaluate the risk of significant misstatement and determine appropriate audit responses for investment and derivative activities, the auditor would need an understanding of the following aspects:

- The nature and significance of direct and indirect equity and debt investments by the entity in other entities.

- Whether these interests relate to listed or unlisted equity investments, or to fixed interest bearing loans advanced or guarantees provided.

- The nature and extent of the control exercised by the entity over the investee, which determine whether the investee is a subsidiary, an associate, joint venture or special purpose entity.

- The nature of derivative financial instruments, the extent to which they are used, as well as how management determines the fair value measurement of its derivative financial instruments.

---

[1] SAAPS 1012, 'Auditing derivative financial instruments', paragraphs .02, .03, .20.

- The control activities and key performance indicators management uses to manage the foreign currency risk, interest rate risk, liquidity risk and credit risk inherent in its equity and debt investments and derivative financial instruments.

- The nature of related income and expenditure flows, gains and losses on derivative financial instruments, and the *rights and obligations* of the entity in respect of such investment income and expenditures, including the identification of related parties and related party transactions, and their disclosure in the financial statements.

17.1.3 Cash and bank

Cash and bank transactions occur daily in all business entities. Although the cash and bank balances may not be individually significant, annually the volume of such cash and payments transactions and bank deposits represent a significant class of transactions for any business, however large or small. Cash and bank transactions interface with all other classes of transactions, as discussed in the relevant cash receiving and disbursement sections of chapters 12 to 16. Cash and bank transactions carry a high risk of fraud and theft, making this an area of activity over which management invariably implements strict controls. This chapter discusses the controls over the entity's cash management processes and the implications for both tests of controls and substantive audit procedures in auditing cash and bank balances.

Many large businesses maintain treasury departments and use a variety of financial instruments in their cash management process, which in itself may constitute a core business process. In smaller businesses and owner-managed businesses, the controls over cash and bank may vest in the owner or one or two employees, which points to inadequate segregation of duties and, therefore, increased risk. In evaluating the risk of significant misstatement, and in determining the appropriate audit responses for cash and bank activities, the auditor needs to understand the following aspects:

- The significance of cash and bank transactions and balances, the nature of cash *inflows* and *outflows*, and the controls implemented by management over these.

- The impact of the entity's revenue and expenditure transactions, acquisition and disposal of tangible and intangible assets, financing and investment activities on the cash and bank transactions and balances of the business.

17.1.4 Financial instruments

Since an audit of financial statements is conducted in accordance with an accepted accounting framework, it is necessary for the auditor to be aware of the principles underlying the accounting recognition, measurement, valuation and presentation requirements to fully assess the risk of significant misstatement and whether management's controls are sufficient to prevent, detect and correct errors and fraud. Equity and debt investments, derivative financial instruments and cash and bank balances are all classified as financial instruments in terms of GAAP AC 133, 'Financial Instruments: recognition and measurement'.

The reader is referred to AC 133 'Financial Instruments: recognition and measurement', and AC 125 'Financial Instruments: disclosure and presentation', for the full requirements. The following important terms, necessary to an understanding of this chapter, are defined in AC 133, firstly in paragraph .09:

- 'A *financial instrument* is any contract that gives rise to both a financial asset of one enterprise and a financial liability or equity instrument of another enterprise.

- A *financial asset* is any asset that is:
  (a) cash,
  (b) a contractual right to receive cash or another financial asset from another enterprise,
  (c) a contractual right to exchange financial instruments with another enterprise under conditions that are potentially favourable, or
  (d) an equity instrument of another enterprise.

- A *financial liability* is any liability that is a contractual obligation:
  (a) to deliver cash or another financial asset to another enterprise, or
  (b) to exchange financial instruments with another enterprise under conditions that are potentially unfavourable.

- An *equity instrument* is any contract that evidences a residual interest in the assets of an enterprise after deducting all of its liabilities.

- *Fair value* is the amount for which an asset could be exchanged, or a liability settled, between knowledgeable, willing parties in an arm's length transaction.'

Additional relevant definitions are provided in AC 133, paragraph .11, as follows:

- 'A *derivative instrument* is a financial instrument:
  (a) whose value changes in response to the change in a specified interest rate, security price, commodity price, foreign exchange rate, index of prices or rates, a credit rating or credit index, or similar variable (sometimes called the 'underlying'),
  (b) that requires no initial net investment or little initial net investment relative to other types of contracts that have a similar response to changes in market conditions, and
  (c) that is settled at a future date (or which may lapse, for example options not exercised, in which case there is no settlement).'

Four categories of financial assets that determine the basis of measurement and valuation of a financial asset or liability are defined in paragraph .11 of AC 133 as follows:

- 'A *financial asset or liability held for trading* is one that was acquired or incurred principally for the purpose of generating a profit from short-term fluctuations in price or dealers margin. A financial asset should be classified as held for trading if, regardless of why it was acquired, it is part of a portfolio for which there is evidence of a recent pattern of short-term profit taking. *Derivative financial assets and derivative financial liabilities are always deemed 'held-for-trading'*, unless they are designated as effective hedging instruments.

- *Held-to-maturity investments* are financial assets with fixed or determinable payments and fixed maturity that an enterprise has the positive intent and ability to hold to maturity, excluding loans and receivables originated by the enterprise (see below).

- *Loans and receivables originated by the enterprise* are financial assets created by the enterprise by providing money, goods, or services directly to a debtor, but not including those originated with the intent to be sold immediately or in the short term, which should be classified as held for trading. Loans and receivables originated by the enterprise are classified separately under this statement and are not included in held-to-maturity investments.

- *Available-for-sale financial assets* are those financial assets that are not:
  (a) loans and receivables originated by the enterprise;
  (b) held to maturity investments; or
  (c) financial assets held for trading.'

Other GAAP statements deal with specific types of investments, such as:

- AC 132 'Consolidated financial statements and accounting for investments in *subsidiaries*';
- AC 110 'Accounting for investments in *associates*';
- AC 131 'Business combinations';
- AC 119 'Financial reporting of interests in *joint ventures*'; and
- AC 412 'Consolidation – *special purpose entities*'.

The nature and extent of investment in an equity instrument of another entity, and the degree of control exercised will determine which particular GAAP statement applies. And as indicated, the type of investment, whether equity, debt or derivatives, has a direct effect on the audit procedures that the auditor performs to gather sufficient appropriate audit evidence regarding the recognition and *measurement* of investment transactions, *existence* and *valuation* of asset or liability balances, and in determining whether the client has complied with particular laws and regulations.

In auditing the asset and liability balances and transactions, and in applying a risk-based top-down audit approach, the auditor must not lose sight of statutory responsibilities, as contained in section 20(1)(e) of the Public Accountants' and Auditors' Act, *inter alia*: 'to obtain evidence of the *existence of all assets and liabilities* shown on such financial statements'. Similarly, according to section 300(e) of the Companies Act, the auditor has to examine or gain satisfaction 'as to the *existence of any securities* of the company' and, in section 300(l), comply with any applicable sections of the Public Accountants' and Auditors' Act.

17.2 NATURE OF INVESTMENT ACTIVITIES

17.2.1 Introduction

To determine the relative significance of the investments to the total assets and activities of the entity, the auditor needs to ascertain the nature and purpose of the entity's acquisition, disposal and holding of equity and other investments, as well as how these fit in with the strategic business objectives. In some circumstances, the investments may be incidental to the main operations of the business, in others they may comprise the core business and generate most of the entity's income – for example, a holding company in a group situation with equity investments in several major operating subsidiaries.

17.2.2 Understanding the client's business

The auditor needs to understand the entity's core business processes in order to recognize the nature and significance of investments and derivatives held by the entity, including rights and obligations attaching to those that are critical for the success of the business, and the key performance indicators used by management to evaluate the return on the investments.

17.2.2.1 Equity and debt investments

Where the entity holds *equity investments*, these may comprise *shares in private or public companies* held as *subsidiaries*, where the investor controls the investee, or as an associate if the investor is able to exercise significant influence over the investee. A company is defined in section 3 of the Companies Act as being a subsidiary of another company if:

'(i) 'That other company is a member of it and –

(aa) holds a majority of the voting rights* in it; or

(bb) has the right to appoint or remove directors holding a majority of the voting rights at meetings of the board; or

(cc) has the sole control of a majority of the voting rights in it, whether pursuant to an agreement with other members or otherwise; or

(ii) it is a subsidiary of any company which is a subsidiary of that other company; or

(iii) subsidiaries of that other company or that other company and its subsidiaries together hold the majority of the rights referred to in (i) (aa), (bb) or (cc).'

(* Refers to voting rights as a registered beneficial holder of equity shares.)

An *associate* is defined in paragraph .02 of AC 110, 'Accounting for investments in associates', as an enterprise in which the investor has significant influence and is neither a subsidiary nor a joint venture of the investor. The investor is presumed to have significant influence if it holds 20% or more the voting power and participates in the financial and operating policy decisions of the investee. This is generally demonstrated by representation on the board of directors, participation in the policy-making processes, material transactions between the investor and the investee, interchange of managerial personnel and provision of essential technical information.

The type of investment affects the nature and source of audit evidence the auditor will be able to obtain to support the fair value of the investment at period end and the related income received. The market value of a listed investment is readily available from the daily share price listings, whilst the fair value of an unlisted investment may be determined by the directors and be based on the present value of future returns expected – based, in turn, on the financial statements and adjusted for a variety of factors, particularly where there is an indication of potential impairment in the net asset value or, on the other hand, an increase in goodwill.

The entity may also enter a joint venture with one or more parties, according to which the contracting parties exercise joint control over an operation, asset or entity. The contract should provide for shared control so that neither party can act unilaterally.

Investments may take the form of fixed interest, long-term or short-term debt investment (or loans) advanced to equity investees or others. Such loans may be secured by means of a mortgage bond over fixed property of the loan debtor, or notarial bond over movables of the loan debtor, or by guarantees provided by the debtor or other third parties, or the loans may be unsecured. The nature of these securities is discussed in chapter 16 and the same principles apply here, except that the entity making the loan will be the holder of the security. Investments may also be fixed interest investments, examples of which are stocks and bonds issued by governments, municipalities or other public authorities.

An entity's equity and debt investments interface with two other significant classes of transactions and to this extent they comprise sub-business processes of the core business processes. The interfaces occur as follows:

- Firstly, purchases of equity investments or advances of loans interface with expenditure transactions and balances, including cash disbursements (see chapter 13).

- Secondly, sales of equity investments, repayments received from borrowers and income received from investments in the form of interest and dividends or profit and loss on disposal of equity investments, interface with revenue transactions and balances including cash deposits (see chapter 12).

Although a number of the controls ordinarily present for these classes of transactions and balances will apply to the investments, certain additional controls specific to the acquisition and disposal of equity investments are likely to be implemented by management, to ensure the *completeness, occurrence* and *measurement* of investment transactions, and the *existence* and *valuation* of *balances*. These are discussed later in the chapter.

An important aspect in respect of equity and debt investments, is management's intention with regard to each investment. The auditor will have to consider, in order to determine the appropriate basis of initial measurement and carrying value at period end, whether the investments are *held-for-trading* and *available-for-sale*, or *held-to-maturity*. Equity investments are valued at fair value at period end, while debt investments are carried at amortized cost, namely original debt less principal repayments received and amortization.

The fair value of listed investments is determined by reference to exchange-quoted equity share prices at the close of business on the balance sheet date.[2] Where there are no recent trades at period end in a particular listed share, a fair value is determined by the JSE Securities Exchange on an auction basis, in which a 'bid price' is established for investments in such shares. The auditor would enquire about the 'bid price' to ascertain the fair market value for such an investment at period end.

Unlisted investments are carried at fair value determined by utilization of an accepted valuation technique. The auditor needs to: examine the most recent set of audited financial statements available, evaluate the reasonableness of management's assumptions in arriving at their valuation of unlisted equity and debt investments, enquire about the basis of the calculation and reliability of the underlying data, the prior history of the investment and returns achieved, and any circumstances indicating that the investment is impaired, for example, investments in foreign countries where the entities are unable to remit funds to its South African shareholder. Where unlisted investments are accumulating material losses, the auditor of a holding company needs to consider the intent and ability of that company to continue supporting the investment, as well as its strategic importance to the group of companies in evaluating its fair value.

Exchange traded funds are carried at fair value, determined with reference to the JSE Securities Exchange quoted prices or indices at the close of business on the balance sheet date. Commodity prices for trades in commodities and futures may similarly be established from the same sources as those for published prices of listed shares.

17.2.2.2 Derivative financial instruments

As indicated earlier, derivative financial instruments are only recognized once the entity has become a party to the contractual provisions of the derivative instrument and it meets the conditions contained therein.

---

[2] *McGregor's Securities Exchange Digest*, published by Carla Soares twice yearly (in May and September); JSE Securities Exchange details are published daily in the business section of *The Star* and *Cape Times* newspapers, and weekly in the *Financial Mail*.

Derivative instruments include forward exchange contracts, futures contracts, options, swaps, caps and floors. The entity may acquire futures contracts or options from an established exchange, such as SAFEX, Agricultural Futures Exchange, London Metal Exchange and International Commodities Exchange. Such deals are known as an exchange traded or standard instrument, to mention a few. The prices may be based on various Indices available, including the All Share Index (ALSI), the Top 40 Index, and Quoted Commodities Indices.

Forward exchange contracts, options, swaps, caps and floors may be obtained from financial institutions and are known as custom made instruments or 'over the counter trades'. Derivatives may be used as hedging instruments in the form of a fair value hedge or a cash flow hedge. In terms of AC 133, all derivatives not classified as hedging instruments are regarded as held-for-trade derivatives and are deemed to be speculative instruments.

Derivative assets and liabilities, which are traded in an organized financial market, may be re-measured at the current quoted market bid price for assets held or liabilities to be issued, or at the offer price for assets to be acquired or liabilities held at the balance sheet date. Most entities, however, use the mid-price to mark their positions to market at close of business to determine the fair values at period end. AC 133 provides for the recognition and measurement of gains and losses, in the income statement or in equity, arising from changes in the subsequent fair value measurement of financial instruments that are not hedged, and for fair value hedging instruments and cash flow hedging instruments.

Due to the complexity of derivative financial instruments and liability exposures for the entity in entering such contracts, many companies will not enter into such contracts, or will enter only a few hedging or forward cover transactions during the financial period. An entity trading in derivative contracts will often outsource the deals to experts to handle. In the case of banks or other financial institutions, however, trade in derivative instruments form a part of the core business with millions of deals taking place around the world daily. In the latter instance, strict controls would be implemented by management, with well-trained risk managers and dealers working in the front and back offices, transacting and monitoring the derivative transactions and managing the high risk exposure on a daily basis. Uncovered risk positions may result in huge losses, such as those which led to the liquidation of Barings Bank plc several years ago, following a period of inadequate control over the deals of a 'rogue trader' employed in one of the bank's offices in the Far East.

Detection of the potential risk of significant misstatement requires an auditor of *derivative financial instruments* to be well aware of the *completeness, measurement, valuation, rights and obligations,* and *disclosure* implications for the different types of transactions, as required by the relevant GAAP statements. From an audit perspective, the major risk areas relate to establishing the *completeness* of all derivative transactions, the *valuation* and *financial presentation and disclosure* of assets and liabilities at period end and related profits and losses in the income statement.

To this extent, where a client entity has numerous derivative transactions, the auditor would be well advised to involve an expert in complex financial instruments, whether from the audit firm or external, to assist with the audit of the particular transactions and balances reflected in the financial statements at period end. As discussed in chapter 9, the auditor will have regard to the guidance in SAAS 620 in using the work of an expert in this context, and to the SAICA Audit and Accounting Guide: 'Reports on the processing of transactions by service organizations – Guidance for auditors'. These apply where the entity has outsourced its derivative trades to derivative consultants and the auditor needs to obtain confirmation regarding the effectiveness of the outsource provider's controls over the entity's deals and assets and liabilities and risk exposures at period end.

The auditor is likely to encounter a complex variety of financial instruments and circumstances, and it is appropriate, therefore, to recognize not only the balance sheet and income statement balances, but how these will differ, depending on the type of equity or debt investment or derivative financial instrument held. Examples of the balance sheet and income sheet balances are set out in Table 17.1.

INVESTMENT TRANSACTIONS	DEBIT BALANCES	CREDIT BALANCES
Investment in subsidiaries AC 132		
Income Statement		
Dividends received		✕
Interest received		✕
Management fees		✕
Balance Sheet		
Investment in subsidiary Breyt (Pty) Ltd	✕	
Loan to subsidiary Breyt Ltd (Pty) Ltd	✕	
Investment in associates – equity method AC 110		
Income Statement		
Income of associates		✕
Goodwill amortization	✕	
Profit on sale of investments		✕
Loss on sale of investments	✕	

INVESTMENT TRANSACTIONS	DEBIT BALANCES	CREDIT BALANCES
Balance Sheet		
Investment in associate Jay Ltd (Unlisted shares)	✕	
Loan to associate Jay Ltd	✕	
Financial instruments – Assets and Liabilities AC 133 and AC 125		
Income Statement		
Dividends received		✕
Interest received		✕
Fair value gains		✕
Fair value losses	✕	
De-recognition losses	✕	
Balance Sheet		
Mark-to-market reserve		✕
Loan from AB Bank Ltd		✕
Investment in debentures of AVI Ltd	✕	
Equity investment in SAB Ltd (Listed shares)	✕	
Loan to KNA (Pty) Ltd	✕	
Trade debtors	✕	
Trade creditors		✕
Derivative financial instruments AC 133 and AC 125		
Income Statement		
Hedge gains		✕
Hedge losses	✕	
Foreign exchange differences	✕	
Balance Sheet		
Mark-to-market reserve		✕
Derivative asset: Options	✕	
Derivative asset: Forward exchange contracts	✕	
Derivative asset: Cash flow hedges	✕	
Derivative liability: Forward exchange contracts		✕
Derivative liability: Cash flow hedges		✕

Table 17.1 Balance sheet and income statement balances arising from equity investments and derivative transactions[3]

---

[3] Adapted from WJJ Botha, *Overview of selected GAAP Audit Items in South Africa*, Lynnwoodridge 2002, at pages 53, 149, 155 and 164.

17.2.3 **Audit objectives**

The audit objectives specific to long-term and short-term investment transactions and balances are set out in Table 17.2. The auditor will identify those assertions most likely to lead to a risk of significant misstatement for long-term and short-term investments to focus the audit procedures accordingly. The table illustrates the link between management assertions and audit objectives.

MANAGEMENT ASSERTION	AUDIT OBJECTIVES
Transactions in investments held for trading and available for sale	
Completeness	All acquisitions and disposals of investments occurring during the period are recorded. All proceeds from disposals of investments that occurred during the period are recorded. All investment income, realized profits and losses on disposal and unrealized holding gains and losses arising from investment transactions and events are recorded.
Occurrence/ validity	All recorded acquisitions and disposals of investments actually occurred during the period and are properly authorized. The proceeds from all disposals during the period are recorded and were received during the period. Investment income, realized profits and losses on disposal, and unrealized holding gains and losses arising from investment transactions and events recorded represent transactions that actually occurred during the period.
Measurement/ accuracy	Investment income, realized profits and losses on disposal, and unrealized holding gains and losses arising from investment transactions and events recorded have been recognized and measured in accordance with the GAAP policies applied by the entity, and are recorded in the correct accounts in the general ledger.

MANAGEMENT ASSERTION	AUDIT OBJECTIVES
Balances for investments held for trading and available for sale	
Completeness	All short-term and long-term investments at balance sheet date are included in the balance sheet investment accounts.
	All investment income, realized profits and losses on disposal and unrealized holding gains and losses arising from investment transactions and events are included in the financial statements.
Existence	Recorded tangible assets exist and represent productive assets in use at balance sheet date.
Measurement/ accuracy	Investments are reported on the balance sheet at fair value, cost or amortized cost, or the equity accounted amount appropriate to the type of investment and in accordance with GAAP and the accounting policies of the entity applied on a consistent basis.
	Investment income and realized and unrealized profits and losses are recorded in accordance with GAAP and the accounting policies of the entity applied on a consistent basis.
Valuation	Investments are reported on the balance sheet at fair value, cost or amortized cost, or the equity accounted amount appropriate to the type of investment and in accordance with GAAP and the accounting policies of the entity applied on a consistent basis.
	Investment income and realized and unrealized profits and losses are recorded in accordance with GAAP and the accounting policies of the entity applied on a consistent basis.
Rights and obligations	The entity owns or has the rights to all recorded investments at balance sheet date.
	The rights of the entity in respect of property mortgaged, to secure loans granted by the entity have been identified.

MANAGEMENT ASSERTION	AUDIT OBJECTIVES
Presentation and disclosure	Investment balances are properly identified and disclosed in the financial statements in accordance with GAAP.
	Appropriate disclosures with regard to the basis for valuing the various types of investments held, details of investments pledged to secure liabilities of the entity and securities held for debt investments, and related parties and related party transactions in accordance with GAAP and the Companies Act.

Table 17.2 Management assertions and the related audit objectives for investments

When applied to *derivative financial instruments* the assertions can be categorized as follows:

MANAGEMENT ASSERTION	AUDIT OBJECTIVES
Derivative financial instruments	
Completeness	There are no unrecorded assets, liabilities, transactions or events, or undisclosed items. For example, all of the entity's derivatives are reported in the financial statements through measurement or disclosure.
	All off balance sheet activity is correctly measured and recorded.
Occurrence/ validity	A transaction or event took place that pertains to the entity during the period. For example, the transaction that gave rise to the derivative occurred within the financial reporting period.
Existence	An asset or liability exists at a given date. For example, the derivatives reported in the financial statements through measurement or disclosure, exist at the date of the balance sheet.

MANAGEMENT ASSERTION	AUDIT OBJECTIVES
Measurement/ accuracy	A transaction or event is recorded at the proper amount and revenue or expense is allocated to the proper period. For example, the amounts associated with the derivatives reported in the financial statements through measurement or disclosure were determined in accordance with the financial reporting framework, and the revenues or expenses associated with the derivatives reported in the financial statements were allocated to the correct financial reporting periods.
Valuation	An asset or liability is recorded at an appropriate carrying value. For example, the values of the derivatives reported in the financial statements through measurement or disclosure were determined in accordance with the financial reporting framework.
Rights and obligations	An asset or a liability pertains to the entity at a given date. For example, an entity has the rights and obligations associated with the derivatives reported in the financial statements.
Presentation and disclosure	An item is disclosed, classified and described in accordance with the applicable financial reporting framework. For example, the classification, description and disclosure of derivatives in the financial statements are in accordance with the financial reporting framework.

Table 17.3 Management assertions and the related audit objectives for derivative financial instruments[4]

Materiality

Whether investments and investment income, and derivative financial instruments traded, are material to the business depends entirely on the nature of the business and the strategic objectives of management. Where a company is primarily an operating entity, such as a manufacturer or trading operation, investments are likely to be short-term investments of surplus cash and the revenues are unlikely to be significant in the income statement, although the amount invested on any particular day may be significant. Where the entity is a holding company in a group situation or a share dealer,

---

[4] SAAPS 1012, 'Auditing derivative financial instruments', paragraph .22.

however, both investments and investment income could be significant to the financial statements and the net income for the period.

The larger the entity and more complex its operations, the more likely it is to enter into derivative financial instruments, whether to hedge certain positions or to trade speculatively. It must be recognized that speculative trading in derivatives is high risk; entities could incur significant losses if management is not fully aware of the risks or fails to control derivatives dealings.

17.2.4 Analysing process level business risks

17.2.4.1 Equity and debt investments

Where additions and disposals of equity and debt investments occur infrequently, the investing activities would be dealt with as one of the business level processes of the main core business processes of the entity. The process level business risks and controls would be similar to those discussed in chapters 12 and 13, dealing with income and expenditure transactions and balances. Authorization of non-routine acquisitions and disposals of investments generally requires the specific approval of top management, such as the board of directors, and would generally be preceded by careful consideration of the strategic objectives. In the case of the acquisition of equity investments, this may include the performance of a due diligence review of the target entity.

Where the entity operates as a share dealer holding significant portfolios of equity and other investments, both long-term and short-term, controls over the acquisition and disposal of equity and debt investments would be formalized. For example, the directors usually appoint asset managers with particular instructions as to criteria, limits and risk profiles to be followed in making investment acquisition and disposal decisions. Formal control procedures would usually be implemented and applied to every transaction. In a smaller business, the owner manager usually authorizes the purchases and sales of investments. The principles discussed in chapters 12 and 13 apply also to acquisitions and disposals of equity investments in listed companies. The share dealer transacts through a registered share broker, who issues the relevant brokers bought or sold notes to the entity. Settlement of amounts owing by or to the entity, will be made to the relevant broker, who then forwards the settlement to the Central Security Depository Participant (CSDP) who has, in their particular sub-register, the demater-ialized scrip that has been bought or sold.

Prior to investments being acquired or disposed of in private companies or unlisted public companies careful consideration should be given by the directors to determine whether the acquisition fits their strategic business objectives. If it does, and following the appropriate consultations, the directors would negotiate a fair value for the purchase or sale. Where appropriate, a due diligence review report may be obtained to identify any 'deal breakers' that may prevent the acquisition, and to identify any aspects that could affect the purchase consideration or any warranties provided by the seller.

In instances where investments occur infrequently, the auditor would obtain an understanding of the formal authorization process followed for purchases and disposals and for determining the fair values of investments at period end. The remaining audit evidence would be obtained from substantive analytical procedures applied to the calculation of investment income and substantive audit procedures, which would focus on the audit of additions and disposals of investments during the period and the calculation of the fair values of investments at period end, held for trading and available for sale.

A further important aspect are the procedures in place to ensure that all income earned from the investments is properly accounted for, and received. This will involve procedures for monitoring the receipt of dividends declared by listed companies, and those from unlisted and private companies, and the monitoring of interest received from debt investments.

17.2.4.2 Derivative financial investments

Management is responsible for the design and implementation of a system of internal control to: monitor risk and financial control; provide reasonable assurance that the entity's use of derivatives is within its risk management policies; ensure the entity's compliance with applicable laws and regulations, as well as the integrity of the entity's accounting and financial reporting systems and thus the reliability of management's financial reporting of derivative activities.

SAAPS 1012, 'Auditing derivative financial instruments', provides guidance in paragraphs .35 to .38 regarding the business processes that management needs to implement to control and monitor the entity's trading in derivative financial instruments. The auditor considers management's overall attitude toward and awareness of derivative activities as a part of obtaining an understanding of the control environment, including any changes to it. It is the role of those charged with governance to determine an appropriate attitude towards the risks. It is management's role to monitor and manage the entity's exposures to those risks. The auditor should obtain an understanding of management's assessment of risks for derivatives transactions and controls implemented to mitigate these.

To effectively monitor and manage its exposure to risk, an entity implements a structure that:

- is appropriate and consistent with the entity's attitude toward risk as determined by those charged with governance;
- specifies the approval levels for the authorization of different types of instruments and transactions that may be entered into and for what purposes. The permitted instruments and approval levels should reflect the expertise of those involved in derivative activities;

- sets appropriate limits for the maximum allowable exposure to each type of risk (including approved counterparties). Levels of allowable exposure may vary depending on the type of risk, or counterparty;
- provides for the independent and timely monitoring of the financial risks and control procedures; and
- provides for the independent and timely reporting of exposures, risks and the results of derivative activities in managing risk.

Management should establish suitable guidelines to ensure that derivative activities fulfil the entity's needs. In setting suitable guidelines, management should include clear rules on the extent to which those responsible for derivative activities are permitted to participate in the derivative markets. Once this has been done, management can implement suitable systems to manage and control those risks. Three elements of the control environment deserve special mention for their potential effect on controls over derivative activities, namely: direction from management; segregation of duties; and whether or not the general control environment has been extended to those responsible for derivative activities. A discussion of each element follows below.

Direction from management

Management is responsible for providing direction, through clearly stated policies, for the purchase, sale and holding of derivatives. These policies should commence with a clear statement regarding the management objectives with regard to risk management activities and include an analysis of the investment and hedging alternatives available to meet those objectives. Policies and procedures should then be developed that consider and address:

- The level of the entity's management expertise;
- Sophistication of the entity's internal control and monitoring systems;
- The entity's asset/liability structure;
- The entity's capacity to maintain liquidity and absorb losses of capital;
- The types of derivative financial instruments that management believes will meet its objectives; and
- Uses of derivative financial instruments that management believes will meet its objectives, for example, whether derivatives may be used for speculative or hedging purposes.

An entity's policies for the purchase, sale and holding of derivatives should be appropriate and consistent with its attitude toward risk and the expertise of those involved in derivative activities.

Segregation of duties and the assignment of personnel

Derivative activities may be categorized into three functions:

- Committing the entity to the transaction (dealing);
- Initiating cash payments and accepting cash receipts (settlements); and

- Recording of all transactions correctly in the accounting records, including the valuation of derivatives.

Segregation of duties should exist among these three functions. Where an entity is too small to achieve proper segregation of duties, management should take a more active role in monitoring derivative activities.

Some entities have established a fourth function, risk control, which is responsible for reporting on and monitoring derivative activities. Key responsibilities in this area may include:

- Setting and monitoring risk management policy;
- Designing risk limit structures;
- Developing disaster scenarios and subjecting open position portfolios to sensitivity analysis, including reviews of unusual movements in positions; and
- Reviewing and analysing new derivative instrument products.

In entities that have not established a separate risk control function, reporting on and monitoring derivative activities may be a component of the accounting function's responsibility or management's overall responsibility.

Whether or not the general control environment has been extended to those responsible for derivative activities

An entity may have a control culture that is generally focused on maintaining a high level of internal control. Because of the complexity of some treasury or derivative activities, this culture may not pervade the group responsible for derivative activities. Alternatively, because of the risks associated with derivative activities, management may enforce a stricter control environment than it does elsewhere in the entity.

Some entities may operate an incentive compensation system for those involved in derivative transactions. In such situations, the auditor needs to consider the extent to which proper guidelines, limits and controls have been established to ascertain whether the system could result in transactions that are inconsistent with the overall objectives of the entity's risk management strategy.

When an entity uses electronic commerce for derivative transactions, it should address the security and control considerations relevant to the use of an electronic network.

17.2.5 Preliminary assessment of the risk of significant misstatement

The auditor should consider the combined effect of the risk of significant misstatement affecting equity and debt investment transactions and be alert to those that could occur in the particular client entity. The reader is referred to Table 11.2 and the discussion in chapter 11 relating to the assessment of the overall risk of significant misstatement. The *inherent risks* likely to be encountered that are specific to investing transactions and balances include:

- *Management bias and incentive to misstate investments or derivatives* whether to achieve budgets, increase performance bonuses, inflate profits for reporting in the financial statements, to secure additional funding from banks, or to attract a potential purchaser for the business or mislead shareholders affecting the share price on the local Securities Exchange.

- The *nature and complexity of the assets acquired* may lead to errors in recognition and *measurement*, such as incorrect account allocation. Although most entities may hold few investments and have infrequent purchases and sales of investments, the non-routine nature of the transactions may lead to errors in accounting for the investments in accordance with GAAP. Where accounting staff are unaware of the complexity of the measurement or valuation requirements for different types of investments, these errors may not be detected easily by management.

- The *fair values* for investments held could be difficult to measure, particularly where material investments are held in unlisted entities or where such investments are held in other countries with varying economic circumstances and fair rates of return. This becomes particularly important when considering amortization and provisions for impairment losses.

- Difficulties in determining the *fair market values* of a held-for-trading or held-to-maturity asset may affect the eventual carrying value of the investments and derivatives assets and liabilities in the balance sheet.

- The risk of *management override of controls* may give rise to *unauthorized acquisitions of investments* or acquisitions in which management has a personal, 'undisclosed' interest, from which undue benefit is likely to be derived. An example would be investments purchased from a director who had voted at the board meeting where the decision to purchase was taken. Another example would be directors who are risk averse and overextend the entity with continuing support for loss-making investments.

- The *risk of fraud and theft* of equity securities may be high where security controls are insufficient, affecting the *existence* of investments. The advent of dematerialized scrip reduces the risk.

- Evidence of *ownership* of assets and *rights and obligations* may be difficult to obtain. Unclear terms of contracts may lead to incorrect disclosures in the financial statements. Equity acquisitions may be complex, such as those involving multinational companies in a group and entities dealing in large volumes in derivative financial instruments.

- Where a limited number of transactions occur annually, this may lead to *errors in the recording* of fixed assets transactions by accounting staff unsure of the allocation of the relevant acquisition or, upon disposal, the adjustment for any profit or loss.

- *Disposals of investments may not be recorded.* Persons responsible for recording the disposals may not be aware that investments have been sold and this may only be detected on a physical inspection of the scrip at period end. Again, dematerialization of scrip and the receipt of monthly returns from CSDP reduces the risk. (Refer to the discussion in chapter 16.)

By now it will be clear that the risk of significant misstatement depends on the nature of the investments and the use to which they are put, and that there will be significant variations in the types of investments encountered at different businesses.

Before performing the tests of controls and substantive test procedures, the auditor would make a preliminary assessment of the *risk of significant misstatement for the investing transactions and balances* in the financial statements. The auditor would consider each of the following factors and document the overall assessment as *high, medium* or *low*. This then influences the auditor's decision to follow a test of controls approach or a mainly substantive approach by way of analytical procedures and specific substantive tests of detail of transactions and balances. The reader is reminded that the risk would be assessed for the following factors and the reasons for each factor documented:

- *Residual business risk*: What, if any, risks remain after consideration of the strategic and business process-level risks, in this instance the key financial risks, namely market risk, basis risk, credit risk, settlement risk, solvency risk and legal risk of the financial instruments and management's procedures to manage and control these risks?[5]

- *Quality of the information available:* Is it internal or external, corroborated, factual or based on estimates? As the fair values involve estimation, depending on the types of investments, this may or may not present a significant risk.

- *Historical accuracy/measurement:* What was the auditor's previous experience with the entity in respect of the investment transactions and account balances and/or any particular assertions?

- *Underlying assumptions used:* For example, the estimate of fair value, the volatility of interest rates and foreign exchange rates, the market performance for that category of shares and type of derivative, to mention a few.

---

[5] The reader is referred to SAAPS 1012 for a full discussion of the inherent and control risks and appropriate controls that management would implement over derivative financial instruments, as well as a comprehensive 'Appendix' setting out definitions of the various terms encountered.

- *Qualifications and competence of the personnel involved*: Does the level of accounting and recording match the *complexity of the estimating process* for the class of transactions or balances involved for the particular assertions affected?

- *Evidence of management bias* and incentive to misstate: Are there personal benefits to be derived, market pressures and expectations, and budget pressures from management or group companies?

The auditor would seek corroborating information, by making enquiries, inspecting documents or observing the performance of control procedures, to support the preliminary assessment of the *risk of significant misstatement*. Upon identifying the effect on the financial statements for particular account balances, the auditor would design appropriate audit procedures to detect and correct any risk of significant misstatement remaining.

The complexity of derivative financial instruments traded should not be underestimated, nor the potential for containing a significant risk of misstatement. In addition to more conventional derivative instruments, the auditor may encounter embedded derivatives in contracts that are difficult to identify, credit derivatives to hedge credit exposures of the entity, and inflation linked bonds to hedge exposure to inflationary increases. The complexity of the mathematical calculations affecting fair value measurements and the accounting requirements for such derivative instruments become extremely difficult for the auditor to understand and where the derivative trades comprise a significant class of transactions for the entity, the auditor needs to involve an expert in derivatives to audit the transactions and balances.

17.2.6 Control activities and tests of control

The auditor needs to understand the controls implemented by management over the purchase and sale of equity investments and the resultant income flows. Are the equity investment transactions handled by suitable individuals within the entity? Are these persons of integrity who have the requisite skills and knowledge, understand the risks and can record the accounting entries in accordance with GAAP? Are they capable of implementing the required monitoring procedures effectively and briefing the board of directors adequately when making buy and sell decisions? Are they capable of preparing the relevant fair value accounting estimates and processing the adjustments at period end and for specific transactions and events? Does management have proper risk assessment processes in place to monitor performance of the entity's investments?

Each of the categories of control activities, as set out in chapters 9 and 10, applies to investments. These control aspects are discussed later in the chapter.

Documents that will be encountered in the audit of investments are set out in Table 17.4 overleaf.

DOCUMENTS	NATURE OF DOCUMENT
Broker's bought note or Broker's bought advice	Document evidencing the purchase of equity investments listed on a securities exchange. Contains details of the number of shares purchased, the investee company, the *share bought price*, transaction costs, date of purchase, settlement date, and total due by the entity on settlement. This document provides the primary evidence of the occurrence of the equity purchase transaction.
Broker's sold note or Broker's sold advice	Document evidencing the sale of equity investments listed on a securities exchange. Contains details of the number of shares sold by the entity, the investee company whose shares have been sold, the *share sold price*, transaction costs, date of sale, settlement date, and total due to the entity on settlement. This document provides the primary evidence of the occurrence of the equity sale transaction.
Share certificate (scrip)	Evidences prima facie ownership by the shareholder (entity) recorded thereon as the registered owner of the number of shares in the investee company. Also reflects the type of shares, i.e. ordinary, preference and class, e.g. Class A, Class B, N shares, Founders shares etc., where the investee entity has different classes of ordinary shares in issue.
Statement of dematerialized shares owned by the investor as recorded in the sub-register maintained by the appointed CSDP	Monthly statement of dematerialized shareholdings of the investor recorded in the electronic sub-register of members maintained by the appointed central securities depository (CSDP). Refer to the discussion in chapter 16 of STRATE and the dematerialization of shares of companies listed on the JSE Securities Exchange.
Broker's or banker's statement of securities held in safe custody	*Broker's monthly statement* of securities held in safe custody by the brokers on behalf of the entity.
Dividend advice	Sent to all shareholders, indicating the shareholder, the dividend number, amount in cents per share and in total for the entity's holding on the last day to trade. The relevant date of declaration, last day to trade and payment due date are reflected on the dividend advice.

DOCUMENTS	NATURE OF DOCUMENT

Deal initiation record for derivative contracts	Clearly identify the nature and purpose of individual transactions, and the rights and obligations arising under each derivative contract. In addition to the basic financial information, such as a notional amount, these records should include:
	
	• the identity of the dealer;
	• the identity of the person recording the transaction, if that person is not the dealer;
	• the date and time of the transaction;
	• the nature and purpose of the transaction, including whether or not it is intended to hedge an underlying commercial exposure; and
	• information on compliance with accounting requirements related to hedging, if applicable, such as:
	  – designation as a hedge, including the type of hedge;
	  – identification of the criteria used for assessing effectiveness of the hedge; and
	  – identification of the hedged item in a hedging relationship.

Counter party confirmation	The acknowledgement of the acceptance of the derivative transaction entered into, which is sent directly to the entity entering the derivative transaction and not to the dealer placing the deal.
Brokers statements for derivative transactions	Reflect the derivative deals arranged for the entity and should be matched to the counter party confirmations received by the entity.
Contract documents evidencing derivative contracts for futures, options, swaps, etc.	These documents may take various forms, depending on the nature of the derivative entered into, the terms arranged, and the parties involved.

COMPUTERIZED ACCOUNTING RECORDS AND PRINTOUTS	NATURE OF RECORD
Cash receipts and cash payments transactions printout	The normal monthly cash receipts and payments printout reflecting receipts from the sale of investments and receipt of investment income and payments for purchases of investments. These entries provide the source for recording the initial transaction at cost.
	Where a separate bank account is maintained for investment activities, all such transactions should be recorded therein. Only likely where the entity is a share dealer or broker or unit trust entity with numerous transactions recorded daily.
Investment master file and general ledger	Records full details of all investments held by the entity, including investment income earned/received.
	The investments account in the general ledger records the initial purchase and subsequent carrying values of the entity's equity investments.
Investment journal	May be maintained by the entity to record all *non-cash investment transactions*, such as mark-to-market adjustments at period end to reflect investments at their fair values in accordance with GAAP, and the recording of gains and losses on disposal of investments.
Derivative database records or register or subsidiary ledger	Transaction records may be maintained in a database, register or subsidiary ledger, depending on the sophistication and frequency of transactions.
	These records should be reconciled on a regular basis to *counterparty confirmations* and related banking transactions and bank statements. Where significant numbers of transactions occur, these reconciliations may be done on a daily basis to monitor the risk exposure of the entity.

Table 17.4 Common documents and records for equity and derivative transactions

17.2.6.1 Purchase and sale of equity and debt investments

Control activities

Where the client holds many investments with large numbers of purchase and sale transactions, effective procedures should be implemented to control:

- purchase and sale transactions;
- the movement of scrip or recording of dematerialized securities; and
- the resulting cash received and paid.

Where numerous investments are held, an *investment master file* should be kept to which detailed information regarding each investment is captured or uploaded from the investment purchase and sales input documents, the total purchase costs being allocated to the investment account in the general ledger. Where a limited number of investments are held, the entity may simply maintain a record of investment details on a computerized spreadsheet.

The internal control activities over equity investment purchases and sales should include the following:

Initiation and settlement of investment transactions

- Authorization by senior management for all investment purchase and sale transactions. The greater the number of transactions, the more formal the authorization procedures must be.

- *Sales* supported by broker's sold note, or contract and directors' minutes approving sales of unlisted investments, details agreed by senior staff to receipt and banking of cash. This function should be separated from the approval and recording of the investment sale. Care should be taken to ensure the correct calculation of gains and losses realized on disposal of the investments.

- *Purchases* of listed investments should be supported by brokers' bought notes. Purchases of unlisted investments would be supported by the relevant contract and both would have directors' minutes (or other authorization) approving purchases of equity investments. Details agreed by senior staff to these documents prior to settlement of the purchase price. Cheque payments or EFT transfers or the exchange of other assets for equity investments purchased should be made on settlement date. This function should be separated from the approval and recording of the investment purchase.

Receipt and storage of securities

- Receipt of scrip and safeguarding of securities should be stored with the entity's broker or in a locked safe deposit box with the entity's bankers. With the dematerialization of scrip for companies listed on the JSE Securities Exchange, the scrip record will be kept by the CSDPs in their electronic sub-register and the investor entity should receive a monthly statement of all such scrip registered in its name, in much the same manner as it receives a monthly bank statement from its bankers.

- Where investments are held in scrip that has not been dematerialized, access to scrip and securities held at the client's premises should be strictly controlled and physically segregated from other investment purchase and sale duties. The auditor should be alert to the risk that scrip is not authentic and has simply been 'produced' by management using a PC and word processing packages. Where the auditor suspects that this has occurred, external confirmation should be obtained from the company secretary of the investee entity as to the registered shareholding of the investor entity.

Receipt of income from investments

- Receipt of dividend and interest cheques through the mail should be recorded and traced to bank deposit slips. There should be appropriate identification and correct allocation of EFT payments received for dividend and investment income. Where numerous investments are held and traded, the entity may maintain a separate banking account to which all investment income should be deposited. Where the entity's broker holds its listed scrip in safe custody, dividends receipts may be received and deposited directly to the entity's bank account by the broker.

- Regular reconciliations of the relevant bank account/s should be prepared.

- Dividend receipts should be recorded in the investment ledger, including the dividend number, and dividend dates: date of declaration, last day to trade and payment date. This should be updated and reviewed regularly by senior staff to ensure the *completeness* of dividend income received and recorded.

- Interest income would generally be in accordance with the debt investment contract and payment arrangements would be scheduled. Senior staff should similarly ensure the correct calculation and depositing of such payments received. Where monthly repayments are made, these may be done by debit order or EFT, which should be identified and recorded monthly. Care should be taken to ensure the correct cut-off and allocation of interest receipts in the financial period.

Monitoring processes

- Periodic review by management involving:
  - Periodic counts of scrip on hand or inspection of monthly statement for dematerialized listed securities held by the CSDP for the investor entity and comparison with investment ledger balances at that date, which provides evidence of *existence* of securities.
  - Inspection of all purchase and sale transactions for evidence of proper authorization where a limited number of transactions occur, and on a test basis where the entity is a share dealer with numerous transactions, which provides evidence of completeness and *occurrence* of securities.
  - Inspection of broker's bought and sold notes supporting all purchase and sale transactions (or other documents where unlisted securities are purchased or subscribed for) where a limited number of transactions

occur, and on a test basis where the entity is a share dealer with numerous transactions, and agree these to recorded details in the investment master file and general ledger, which provides evidence of *completeness, occurrence* and *measurement* of securities.

- Reconciliation of cash received/cheques paid with relevant authorized purchase and sale transactions and income receipts.

• Assess investment performance and reporting involving:

- Establishing key performance indicators and monitoring actual performance against these on a regular basis to detect poor performance or returns.
- Monitoring of holdings and returns to budgets and classification of investments to predetermined strategic plans.

The evidence of such review should be the initials or signature of senior management in the relevant records and reports tabled at management meetings. Evidence of follow up and resolution of discrepancies should also be documented.

17.2.6.2 Internal controls over derivative financial instruments

SAAPS 1012, 'Auditing derivative financial instruments', provides guidance in paragraphs .40 to .48 on control objectives and procedures that should be implemented to ensure effective control over derivatives. Control objectives over derivatives include the following:

• *Authorized execution.* Derivative transactions are executed in accordance with the entity's approved policies.

• *Complete and accurate information.* Information relating to derivatives, including fair value information, is recorded on a timely basis, is complete and accurate when entered into the accounting system, and is properly classified, described and disclosed.

• *Prevention or detection of errors.* Misstatements in the processing of accounting information for derivatives are prevented or detected on a timely basis.

• *Ongoing monitoring.* Activities involving derivatives are monitored on an ongoing basis to recognize and measure events affecting related financial statement assertions.

• *Valuation.* Changes in the value of derivatives are appropriately accounted for and disclosed to the right people from both an operational and a control viewpoint. Valuation may be a part of ongoing monitoring activities.

Internal controls include adequate segregation of duties, preparation of reconciliations, and risk management monitoring procedures.

The level of sophistication of an entity's internal controls over derivatives vary according to:

- the complexity of the derivative and the related inherent risk – more complex derivative activities will require more sophisticated systems;

- the risk exposure of derivative transactions in relation to the capital employed by the entity; and

- the volume of transactions – entities that have significant volumes of derivative transactions require sophisticated accounting systems and internal control.

In larger entities, where derivative transactions might be significant, it is likely that sophisticated computer information systems keep track of derivative activities. Such computer systems may generate automatic postings to clearing accounts to monitor cash movements. Proper controls over processing will help to ensure that derivative activities are correctly reflected in the entity's records. Computer systems may be designed to produce exception reports to alert management to situations where derivatives have not been used within authorized limits, or where transactions undertaken were not within the limits established for the chosen counterparties.

Derivatives, by their very nature, can involve the transfer of sizable amounts of money to and from the entity. Often, these transfers take place at maturity. In many instances, a bank is only provided with appropriate payment instructions or receipt notifications. Some entities may use electronic fund transfer (EFT) systems. Such systems may involve complex password and verification controls, standard payment templates and cash pooling/ sweeping facilities. The statement of SAAS on 'Auditing in a Computer Information Systems Environment' requires the auditor to consider how computer information systems (CIS) environments affect the audit and to obtain an understanding of the significance and complexity of the CIS activities and the availability of data for use in the audit. The auditor should obtain an understanding of the methods used to transfer funds, in order to make a preliminary assessment of risk of misstatement.

Regular reconciliations are an important aspect of controlling derivative activities. They should be performed on a regular basis to ensure that the financial records are properly controlled, all entries are promptly made and dealers have adequate and accurate position information before formally committing the entity to a legally binding transaction. Reconciliations should be reviewed and checked by persons independent of their preparation. The following are the more significant reconciliations required for derivative activities:

- Reconciliation of dealers' records to internal records used for the ongoing monitoring of derivative positions and profit and losses shown in the accounting records;

THE PRINCIPLES AND PRACTICE OF AUDITING

- Reconciliation of subsidiary ledger balances to control accounts in the general ledger;

- Reconciliation of all clearing and bank accounts and broker statements to ensure all outstanding items are promptly identified and cleared; and

- Reconciliation of the entity's accounting records to records maintained by service organizations, where applicable.

An entity's deal initiation records should clearly identify the nature and purpose of individual transactions, and the rights and obligations arising under each derivative contract. In addition to the basic financial information, such as a notional amount, these records should include:

- The identity of the dealer.

- The identity of the person recording the transaction, if that person is not the dealer.

- The date and time of the transaction.

- The nature and purpose of the transaction, including whether or not it is intended to hedge an underlying commercial exposure.

- Information on compliance with accounting requirements related to hedging, if applicable, such as:
  - designation as a hedge, including the type of hedge;
  - identification of the criteria used for assessing effectiveness of the hedge; and
  - identification of the hedged item in a hedging relationship.

Transaction records for derivatives may be maintained in a database, register or subsidiary ledger, which are then checked for accuracy with independent confirmations received from the counterparties to the transactions. Often, the transaction records will be used to provide accounting information, including information for disclosures in the financial statements, together with other information to manage risks, such as exposure reports against policy limits. Therefore, it is essential to have appropriate controls over input, processing and maintenance of the transaction records, whether they are in a database, a register or a subsidiary ledger.

The most important control over the completeness of the recording of derivative transactions is the independent matching of counterparty confirmations against the entity's own records. Counterparties should be requested to supply confirmations and address these to management of the entity who are independent of the dealers, to guard against dealers suppressing confirmations and 'hiding' transactions, and all details should be checked off against the entity's records. Persons responsible should resolve any exceptions contained in the confirmations, and investigate any confirmation that is not received.

17.2.6.3 Tests of controls for derivatives

Where the auditor's preliminary assessment of control risk is medium to low, and where the auditor wishes to place reliance on controls, tests of controls must be performed to obtain evidence that controls operated thoughout the period. If an entity undertakes only a limited number of derivative transactions, or where the magnitude of these instruments is insignificant to the entity's total operations, the auditor may adopt a substantive approach to gather sufficient audit evidence, sometimes in combination with tests of control, to justify limited substantive tests of detail.

Items should be selected for detailed testing from those recorded in the accounting records so as to gather evidence in relation to the *existence, occurrence/validity* and *measurement* assertions and others selected from other sources, for example, counterparty confirmations and trader tickets, so as to gather evidence in relation to the completeness assertion.

Should the auditor's planned approach involve reliance on the systems of control, examples of tests of controls include the following:

- Reading minutes of meetings of those charged with investment responsibilities for the entity, which might be an Asset/Liability Risk Management Committee, for evidence of that committee's authority for and review of derivative activities, including the effectiveness of hedging activities.

- Comparing derivative transactions, including those that have been settled, for their compliance with the entity's policies. For example, the auditor might:
  - Test that transactions have been executed in accordance with specified authorizations;
  - Test that pre-acquisition sensitivity analyses required by the investment policy are being performed;
  - Test transactions to determine that the entity obtained the required approvals for the transactions and used only authorized brokers or counterparties;
  - Enquiry of management to establish that derivatives and related transactions are being monitored and reported upon on a timely basis and read any supporting documentation;
  - Re-perform calculations of recorded purchases of derivatives, including their classification and prices, and the entries used to record related amounts;
  - Inspect the reconciliations for evidence of their review and that reconciling differences are investigated and resolved on a timely basis. Organizations that have a large number of derivative transactions may require reconciliations and reviews of these on a daily basis;
  - Inspect the entity's third-party confirmations and evidence of management's resolution of difference between these and recorded amounts.

17.2.7 Determining the acceptable level of detection risk

17.2.7.1 Determining the acceptable level of detection risk for equity and debt investments

In determining an acceptable level of detection risk, the auditor considers the significance of investment transactions and balances, as well as the assessment of the effectiveness of the controls implemented by management. Should investment transactions be insignificant, or are significant but subject to effective controls, the acceptable level of detection risk may be determined as medium to high. As indicated earlier in this chapter, in many instances, investment transactions are few and after obtaining an understanding of the systems of control, the auditor will perform substantive tests of detail to provide evidence of the existence and carrying value of investments at the period end and to determine that the related income balances appear complete and properly measured.

Where, however, the entity is a share dealer, the auditor usually seeks audit reliance from the client's systems and accordingly would test the effectiveness of controls before determining the extent of audit evidence still required from substantive analytical procedures and substantive tests of detail.

17.2.7.2 Determining the acceptable level of detection risk for derivative financial instruments

If the volume and amount of derivative transactions are significant to an entity's activities, and due to the complexity of accounting for derivatives, effective controls would usually be implemented by management to reduce the risk of material misstatement. The auditor, in assessing the risk of significant misstatement, would consider the following:

- Whether or not policies and procedures over derivative activities are sufficient to achieve management's objectives.

- The extent to which management has informed personnel of laid-down procedures and monitored adherence to them.

- The procedures in place to record accurately information concerning derivative transactions.

Where trading in derivatives is significant and apparently well controlled, and tests of control have provided evidence of the effective operation of such controls, the auditor can determine an acceptable detection risk at a medium to high level. This is true also where trading in derivatives is insignificant and controls appear adequate.

17.2.8 Substantive analytical procedures

The effectiveness of substantive analytical procedures depend on the nature and significance of the entity's equity and debt investment transactions and balances. Where there are few purchases and sales of investment transactions during the period, appropriate sufficient audit evidence can efficiently be obtained in respect of these from substantive tests of detail. If investing transactions are significant, however, substantive analytical procedures may be directed towards the interrelationships between the investments and investment income in the current period and compared with previous periods and budgets.

Where different types of investments are maintained, such as various categories of listed investments, bonds, and loans, the entity may have policies as to the mix of investments to be maintained and management may be monitoring these with key performance indicators. The auditor may recalculate the relevant ratios to test the effectiveness of management's key performance indicators. The auditor would enquire about action taken by management where the key performance indicators were not in line with expectations. Any discrepancies or unexpected trends should be discussed with management as these may indicate potential material errors or fraud.

The complexity and diversity of derivative financial instruments and deals are such that substantive analytical procedures are seldom very effective as a consequence of the difficulty of predicting the outcomes against which to measure recorded amounts due to often significant fluctuations and trends. Again, substantive tests of detail to verify the completeness and valuation of derivatives at period end is the usual approach adopted by auditors.

17.2.9 Substantive tests of detail of transactions

17.2.9.1 Audit of investments purchased

As indicated in the previous section, where investing transactions are few, which is usually the case for retailing or manufacturing entities, the audit approach to them is usually substantive tests of details based. Where the number of investment transactions is substantial, however, the auditor would expect to find control activities as described above. The auditor should assess the extent of reliance to be placed on the system of internal control. The auditor should confirm from initials or signatures of the reviewing management that reviews have been conducted fairly frequently and call for a copy of any report made by the reviewer relating to weaknesses or breakdowns in the system and enquire into the action taken to rectify the matter.

Investment purchases transactions will be the subject of journal adjustments input into the system or recorded through the relevant settlement cheque or EFT payment.

The relevant broker's bought note or contract should be inspected and details agreed to the relevant entries captured to determine that the information is recorded correctly, providing evidence of the *occurrence* and *measurement* of the transaction.

The information captured into the investment master file or register and general ledger should include:

- The name of the company or other institution whose shares, etc., have been purchased.

- The description of the investment – for example, preference shares, ordinary shares, or debentures.

- The number of shares or debentures acquired.

- From whom purchased.

- The cost of the investment. Cost includes the various transaction expenses incurred in acquiring the investment in addition to the share purchase price. Cost may include accrued income to date of acquisition.

- The date of purchase. Apart from the fact that the date of purchase should be properly recorded, it is the basis of ascertaining what income should have been received on the investment and also the basis of any apportionment of income on the investment between capital and revenue. The date of purchase for dematerialized scrip is the date of recording of the purchase or sale in the CSDP sub-register.

The authority for the purchase should be inspected. Where the investment has been purchased through a securities exchange the evidence of purchase is a broker's note. The brokerage, stamp duty and marketable securities tax are usually treated as part of the cost of the investment. The auditor should ascertain, however, that where several investments have been purchased there is consistency in the treatment of brokerage, stamp duty and marketable securities tax.

Investments (for example, shares) may, however, be purchased by private arrangement, in which case the auditor should examine the appropriate evidence of the purchase, which may be, *inter alia*, correspondence between the parties or a formal contract of sale.

Where shares or debentures acquired are part of a new issue, the relevant evidence is the prospectus and the letter of allotment (if available), which between them show the amount payable on application and allotment, the number of shares or debentures allotted and the date of allotment.

Similar forms of advice are available where government or municipal stocks are acquired as part of a new issue. In some cases, the company or other institution making the issue may require the letter of allotment to be returned to it when it issues the share certificates, etc. In such a case the auditor may obtain a letter of confirmation from the company, or other institution, setting out the details of the allotment.

Where the investment is in the form of interest-bearing securities (debentures or government and municipal stocks) and these have been purchased between the due dates of interest, the apportionment of the interest, subsequently received, between capital and revenue should be checked. Good accounting practice requires the apportionment of the interest to be made.

The proper treatment of dividends on shares purchased, cum dividend, in the period between a declaration of a dividend and the closing of the share register for dividend purposes is not so clear. It would appear that the declared dividend, when received, might be treated as reducing the cost of the shares. The argument in favour of this treatment is that the cost of the investment is inflated by the dividend to be received. On the other hand, as shares purchased, even before any dividend is declared, are acquired for the purpose of earning income in the shape of dividends, it is extremely difficult to choose, on any logical basis, a date of purchase which would be the deciding factor in treating a dividend subsequently received as capital recoupment and, therefore, there are good grounds for treating all dividends as income, even those received on shares purchased after a declaration. Probably all that the auditor can do in these cases is to see that there has been consistency in the treatment of dividends.

17.2.9.2 Audit of investments sold

Where there are many sales transactions, the opening paragraph on the audit of investments purchased (see 17.2.9.1) applies to sales of investments also. As in the case of investments purchased, for the sale of investments each transaction will be the subject of a journal adjustment input into the system or captured through the relevant settlement cheque or EFT payment.

The information captured into the investment master file or register and general ledger should include:

- The name of the company or other institution whose shares etc., have been sold.
- The description of the investment sold.
- The number of shares or debentures sold.
- To whom sold.
- The amount realized on the sale.
- The date of the sale.

The authority for the sale should be inspected. What has been said above regarding the acquisition of investments through a stock exchange or by private arrangement and the questions of the expenses of acquisition and the apportionment between capital and revenue applies equally to the sale of investments.

The profit or loss on the sale of the investment, which represents the difference between the amounts realized and the carrying amount, should also be the subject of a journal adjustment, which the auditor should check.

- Where part only of an investment is sold, for example, one thousand shares out of a holding of five thousand in a particular company, which has been acquired in small lots from time to time, the profit or loss on sale is partially dependent on the method of arriving at the recorded value of the shares sold.

- Where shares held have been valued at mark-to-market at period end, the auditor will need to ascertain whether the fair market gain or loss has been recognized in the income statement or carried in equity. If carried in equity, the portion attributable to the equity shares sold would be recognized in the income statement on disposal.

- The auditor would take care to ensure that the basis used to determine the profit or loss on disposal is calculated in accordance with GAAP AC 133.

- Where a provision for impairment loss has been made, because market value has fallen below cost, the provision may have been arrived at by comparing cost with market value for each lot of shares acquired or for the total holding. The recorded value of the shares sold is arrived at by deciding:
    - the cost of the shares sold; and
    - the appropriate amount (if any) of the provisions for loss on these shares, which is deducted from the cost of the shares.

17.2.9.3 Income from investments

Income from holding shares in companies accrues from dividends declared by such companies. Having audited and been satisfied about the existence and ownership of investment held at the previous year-end, and having obtained evidence of purchases and sales of investments during the current year, the auditor is well positioned to establish that dividends, declared by companies in whom shares are held, are received and accounted for.

Where there are many investments, a schedule of them should be obtained from the entity and checked with the ledger accounts, and other relevant evidence. The income, recorded as received, applicable to each investment should be stated in the schedule to facilitate the audit work in respect of income from investments.

The dividends, which are due to be received, may be ascertained as follows:

- *From the published financial statements* of the company whose shares are held. Where these statements, which have been received by the client, cover the whole period under audit, the necessary information is available from them, except in the case of a final dividend recommended, the date of payment of which is not obtainable from these statements. If the financial statements for the requisite period are not available, other means of proving the correctness of the recorded investment income must be found.

- *From dividend statements, or dividend notifications.* Many companies issue dividend statements, which are attached to the dividend cheques; a few others issue dividend notifications in advance of payment. In such cases, the statement or notification is adequate evidence of the amounts of the relevant dividends and, if the statements or notifications bear serial numbers of the dividends, there is also evidence that all dividends have been accounted for. If the dividends are not numbered, recourse will have to be had to other evidence to prove that all dividends paid have been recorded as received, for example, the published reports of company dividends.

- *From published newspaper reports* of company dividends declarations or official stock exchange reports or reports of reputable financial publications.[6] The auditor may obtain from these publications the requisite information relating to dividends declared, but apply only to shares that are quoted on the stock exchange.

- *By direct enquiry from the company whose shares are held.* Where the shares held are not quoted, the information obtainable from published reports of company dividends is not applicable and, in the absence of the requisite published financial statements or dividend statements or notifications (bearing serial numbers), the only means of obtaining evidence as to the correctness of the dividends recorded as received is direct enquiry by the auditor from the relevant company.

17.2.9.4 Framework for substantive tests of details of transactions and balances

Following the above discussions of control activities and nature of investments, and as in previous chapters, a framework for substantive tests of detail for equity and debt investments is set out in Table 17.5 below:

SUBSTANTIVE TESTS FOR EQUITY AND DEBT INVESTMENTS	AUDIT OBJECTIVES				
	C	O/E	M/V	R/O	P/D
1. Obtain and document an understanding of the business: Identify the significance of investments to the entity: – Identify plans of management with regard to strategic investments of surplus cash. – Identify critical success factors and key performance indicators used by management. – Identify economic and industry circumstances affecting the entity.	×	×	×	×	×

---

[6] *McGregor's JSE Securities Exchange Digest*, published by Carla Soares twice yearly (in May and September); securities exchange details are published daily in the 'Business Report' section of *The Star* and *Cape Times* newspapers, and weekly in the *Financial Mail*.

SUBSTANTIVE TESTS FOR EQUITY AND DEBT INVESTMENTS	AUDIT OBJECTIVES				
	C	O/E	M/V	R/O	P/D
Obtain trial balances or schedules of the balances of investments and investment income:	X		X		
– Agree opening balances for investments to the previous year's working papers. – Review movements on investment and investment income accounts in the general ledger for unusual entries and investigate these. – Obtain a schedule of investments at period end to support the carrying values reflected in the general ledger and financial statements. – Cast schedules and general ledger accounts and agree balances to relevant ledger accounts and investment master file or register printout.					
2. Substantive analytical procedures:	X	X	X		
Develop a prediction or expectation based on the auditor's knowledge of the business investment activities and strategic business risks.					
Define a significant difference or threshold – based on materiality at account balance level and calculate various relevant financial management ratios and key performance indicators used by management to monitor investments.					
Compute the difference between the actual and the expected, compare to prior periods, to budget and to a history of such ratios maintained.					
Investigate significant differences and exercise judgement to conclude on implications and trends.					
Document the basis for the audit conclusion.					
3. Tests of detail of transactions:					
Inspect supporting documents for approval of purchases and sales of investments, and investment income such as:	X	X	X	X	X
– Directors' minutes, brokers' bought and sold notes, purchase and sale contracts (unlisted investments). – Loan contracts and interest rates. – Mortgage bonds and other securities used to secure all loan advances (as an asset). – Sets of financial statements of companies in which shares are held, securities exchange reports, and dividend notices as evidence of dividends declared.					
Inspect bank deposits for cash received and paid cheques or EFTs for purchases of shares and repayments of the principal sum of loans and interest or finance charges.	X	X	X		X
Recalculate interest expense recorded and recognized in the income statement.	X	X	X		X
Compare supporting documents for movements to investment register or investment master file printout.	X	X	X		X

SUBSTANTIVE TESTS FOR EQUITY AND DEBT INVESTMENTS	AUDIT OBJECTIVES				
	C	O/E	M/V	R/O	P/D
4. Tests of details of balances:					
Count scrip on hand at entity or that held in safe custody by others (if possible).		×		×	×
Obtain a confirmation of securities (scrip) held by third parties as security for liabilities.				×	×
Inspect statement from CSDP for dematerialized scrip held and obtain a confirmation from the CSDP of the entire scrip holding at balance sheet date.		×		×	×
Obtain an external confirmation from all loan debtors (debt investments), including inter-company loan balances of the balance owing at period end and repayment terms.			×	×	×
Review loan investments for default in payments and inspect security held, consider the adequacy of any provisions for bad debts and sufficiency of the value of the security.			×		×
Determine the classification of investments in accordance with GAAP, namely held-to-maturity, held-for-trading and available-for-sale securities according to the nature of the investments held and management's documented intent and ability to hold debt investments to maturity.		×	×	×	×
Obtain written representations from management regarding their intent and confirming the classifications of investments.		×	×	×	×
Recalculate the fair values of investments at period end (refer SAAS 545):			×		×
– In accordance with market rates quoted at balance sheet date.					
– Fair values from brokers, dealers and other experts for unlisted investments.					
– Consider the reasonableness of the underlying assumptions of management.					
– Obtain confirmation of present value, discount and interest rates used.					
– Assess the reasonableness of non-standard valuation models used.					
– Consider the consistency of the fair value estimates with previous years.					
– Inspect adjusting entries to record investments at mark-to-market and amortized carrying values.					
5. Presentation and disclosure:					
Determine whether the *presentation and disclosure* of equity and debt investments accord with GAAP and are properly identified and classified in the financial statements.					×
Determine whether the financial statement notes reflect the *rights and obligations* of the entity with regard to the valuation bases for investments, realized and unrealized gains and losses, and related party disclosures.					×

Table 17.5 Framework for a substantive audit programme for equity and debt investments

Where trades in derivative financial instruments comprise a significant class of transactions, the auditor will usually seek to obtain audit assurance in relation to recording of these from the systems of control and thus would accordingly need to perform tests of controls, to obtain information of their effective operation. Examples of the tests of controls that might be performed were dealt with earlier. As discussed earlier, because of the diversity of derivatives, and their fluctuation of values, it is difficult to estimate a prediction of the likely position against which to measure actual performance. Accordingly, substantive analytical procedures are unlikely to be effective. Where the tests of controls provide evidence of satisfactory operation of controls, the auditor will perform limited substantive tests of detail of transactions and balances for derivative instruments. Substantive tests would need to be extended if tests of controls yield unsatisfactory results. Examples of substantive tests are set out in Table 17.6.

SUBSTANTIVE TESTS FOR DERIVATIVE INSTRUMENTS	AUDIT OBJECTIVES				
	C	O/E	M/V	R/O	P/D
1. Obtain and document an understanding of the business:					
Identify the significance of derivatives to the entity:	×	×	×	×	×
– Identify plans of management with regard to the use of derivatives. – Identify critical success factors and key performance indicators used by management. – Identify economic and industry circumstances affecting the entity.					
Obtain trial balances or schedules of the balances of derivative assets and liabilities and related gains and losses:	×	×	×		
– Agree opening balances for derivative assets and liabilities to the previous year's working papers. – Review movements on derivative assets and liabilities and gains and losses on derivatives accounts in the general ledger for entries of significant amounts and investigate these. – Obtain a schedule of derivative assets and liabilities at period end to support the carrying values reflected in the general ledger and financial statements. – Cast schedules and general ledger accounts and agree balances to relevant ledger accounts and derivatives master file or register or subsidiary ledger printout.					

SUBSTANTIVE TESTS FOR DERIVATIVE INSTRUMENTS	AUDIT OBJECTIVES				
	C	O/E	M/V	R/O	P/D
2. Tests of detail of transactions:					
Inspect supporting documents for approval of purchases and sales of derivatives investments, and related income such as:	✕	✕	✕	✕	✕
– Inspecting minutes of the meetings of those charged with making derivatives acquisition and settlement transactions. – Reviewing brokers' statements for the occurrence of derivative transactions and positions held. – Reviewing counterparty confirmations received but not matched to transaction records. – Reviewing unresolved reconciliation items. – Inspecting agreements, such as loan or equity agreements or sales contracts, for embedded derivatives. (The accounting treatment of such embedded derivatives may differ among financial reporting frameworks.) – Inspecting documentation for activity subsequent to the end of the reporting period.					
Inspect bank deposits for cash received and paid cheques or EFTs for payments related to derivatives.	✕	✕	✕		✕
Inspect reconciliations of deals to registers and bank statements, and differences recorded as gains and losses due to market movements and deal terms.	✕	✕	✕		✕
Compare to supporting documents for movements to derivative register, master file or subsidiary ledger printouts.	✕	✕	✕		✕
3. Tests of details of balances:					
Perform cut-off tests of deal blotters and unsettled trades from back office records and compare these to the relevant general ledger balances.	✕		✕		
Obtain external confirmation from the holder of, or counterparty to, the derivative to provide details of all derivatives and transactions with the entity. In sending confirmation requests, the auditor determines which part of the counterparty's organization is responding, and whether the respondent is responding on behalf of all aspects of its operations.	✕	✕		✕	✕
Send zero-balance confirmations to potential holders or counterparties to derivatives, to test the completeness of derivatives recorded in the financial records.	✕	✕	✕		✕
Review brokers' statements for the existence of derivative transactions and positions held.	✕	✕	✕		
Review counterparty confirmations received but not matched to transaction records.	✕				
Review unresolved reconciliation items.	✕				
Inspect agreements, such as loan or equity agreements or sales contracts, for embedded derivatives. (The accounting treatment of such embedded derivatives may differ among financial reporting frameworks.)	✕			✕	

SUBSTANTIVE TESTS FOR DERIVATIVE INSTRUMENTS	AUDIT OBJECTIVES				
	C	O/E	M/V	R/O	P/D
Inspect documentation for activity subsequent to the end of the reporting period.	×				
Enquiry of management and observation of the procedures in the back office and front office or dealing rooms to ensuring correct cut-off and recording of transactions around the year-end.	×	×			
Inspect the underlying agreements and other forms of supporting documentation, including confirmations received by an entity, in paper or electronic form, for amounts reported.		×	×	×	×
Inspect supporting documentation for subsequent realization or settlement after the end of the reporting period.		×	×	×	×
Substantive procedures to obtain evidence about the *occurrence, measurement and valuation* of derivative financial instruments may include:		×	×		
– Inspection of documentation of the purchase price. – Confirm with the holder of or counterparty to the derivative. – Review the creditworthiness of counterparties to the derivative transaction. – Obtain evidence corroborating the fair value of derivatives measured or disclosed at fair value. – Recalculate gains and losses recorded and fair value adjustments recognized in the income statement.					
Recalculate the fair values of investments at period end (refer SAAS 545):			×	×	×
– In accordance with market rates quoted at balance sheet date or fair values from brokers, dealers and other experts for unlisted investments. – Consider the reasonableness of the underlying assumptions of management. – Obtain confirmation of present value, discount and interest rates used. – Assess the reasonableness of non-standard valuation models used, especially where the entity is generating its own yield curves. This may require input from an expert in quantitative financial techniques. – Where management is calculating the values by means of spreadsheet modeling and macros, consider whether these have all the functions necessary to correctly calculate the values for the variety of derivatives and factors required for valuation models. – Consider the consistency of the fair value estimates with previous years. – Inspect adjusting entries to record investments at mark-to-market and amortized carrying values.					
Determine the classification of derivatives in accordance with GAAP, namely held-to-maturity, held-for-trading and available-for-sale securities according to the nature of the investments held and management's documented intent and ability to hold debt investments to maturity.			×	×	×

SUBSTANTIVE TESTS FOR DERIVATIVE INSTRUMENTS	AUDIT OBJECTIVES				
	C	O/E	M/V	R/O	P/D
Obtain written representations from management responsible for derivative activities within the entity regarding their intent and confirm the classifications of investments. This may include representations about:		×	×	×	×
– Management's objectives with respect to derivative financial instruments, for example, whether derivatives are used for hedging or speculative purposes. – The financial statement assertions concerning derivative financial instruments, for example: – the records reflect all derivative transactions; – all embedded derivative instruments have been identified; and – the assumptions and methodologies used in the derivative valuation models are reasonable.					
– Whether all transactions have been conducted at arm's length and at fair market value. – The terms of derivative transactions. – Whether there are any side agreements associated with any derivative instruments. – Whether the entity has entered into any written options. – Whether the entity complies with the documentation requirements of the financial reporting framework for derivatives in respect of specified hedges.					
4. Presentation and disclosure: Determine whether the presentation and disclosure of derivative instruments accord with GAAP and are properly identified and classified in the financial statements.					×
Determine whether the financial statement notes reflect the *rights and obligations* of the entity with regard to the valuation bases for derivative assets, and liabilities realized, and unrealized gains and losses, and related party disclosures.					×

Table 17.6 Framework for a substantive audit programme for derivative instruments

17.2.10 Substantive tests of detail for balances

17.2.10.1 Existence of equity investments

The auditor should obtain from the client a list of equity investments and should check the list against the information in the accounting records relating to each investment, that is to say, the name, the description, the number of shares (or the nominal value of stock) and their carrying value.

Where the entity has many investments and dealings therein are frequent, some form of investment ledger or register should be maintained by it. The schedule of investments should be checked with the investment ledger, or register, and the total of the schedule agreed with the balance of the investments account in the general ledger.

The auditor should then verify the existence of unlisted and listed investments, and those where the scrip has not yet been dematerialized, in the following manner.

- Examine each share certificate and note whether the name of the company, the description and number of shares agree with the details given on the list.

- Observe whether the shares are in the entity's name or, if not, whether a blank transfer deed duly dated and signed by the transferor whose name appears on the certificate is attached thereto. Alternatively, in lieu of a share certificate and blank transfer deed, there may be a certified transfer deed.

- If the shares have been purchased only recently and the certificate has been deposited with the company for registration of transfer, a transfer office receipt from the company should be available as evidence. The same applies where a part of the holding represented by one share certificate has been sold and a new certificate, for the lesser number of shares, has not yet been received. However, it is not the practice of all companies to demand the surrender of the transfer office receipts and therefore it is more evidential to obtain direct confirmation from the appropriate company.

- Where the investments are in the form of bearer shares, no transfer deed is necessary, the property in the shares passing by mere delivery of the share certificates. Such share certificates will have attached to them dividend coupons, which are exchanged for dividends paid by the company whose shares are held. By seeing that a dividend has been received for the last coupon removed, the auditor should be satisfied that all dividend coupons, which should be attached to the share certificate, are in fact there.

For dematerialized shares, the auditor will inspect the monthly statement of dematerialized shareholdings of the investor recorded in the electronic sub-ledger of members maintained by the appointed central securities depository (CSDP). The reader is referred to the discussion in chapter 16 of STRATE and dematerialization of shares of companies listed on the JSE Securities Exchange. The auditor may also obtain a confirmation from the CSDP regarding dematerialized scrip held in the name of the entity at the period end.

Where the number of investments is considerable, as in the case of a bank or investment trust company, the auditor may, if satisfied with the control exercised over investments, seal the packages of like investments with a seal and note on the package attesting to the contents thereof. At subsequent audits the auditor may accept the packages with unbroken seals as evidence of the investments described on each package. In such circumstances, a test should be made of the contents of the packages in such a manner that, by breaking the seals of several, checking the contents and resealing each year, over a few years all packages will have been opened and the share certificates contained therein checked.

When making the count of the share certificates said to be in the entity's possession, the auditor should obtain possession of all such scrip at one time to prevent the possibility of the same scrip being produced twice as alleged evidence of two holdings. Again, especially if it is the entity's practice to carry substantial cash balances, the auditor should perform a cash count when in control of all scrip, otherwise it is possible for management, bent on fraud, to pledge or sell shares in order to obtain the requisite cash and, immediately after the cash count, to repay the loan or repurchase the shares.

If share certificates have been deposited with a bank or the broker or similar institution for safe custody, the auditor should, with the consent of the client, obtain direct from the custodian a detailed certificate to the effect that it holds the relevant scrip for safe custody. If the certificates are held for safe custody by a bank or other recognized institution, a certificate should be obtained[7] which shows in detail the shares and/or debentures and states that they are held for the entity. If the certificates are in the hands of other third parties, for example, stockbroker or attorney, the auditor cannot regard this as proper security and should insist that either the entity obtains possession of the certificates or that they are placed in the custody of a bank or similar institution.

17.2.10.2 Existence of debt investment – loans advanced

The terms of a loan advanced are usually contained in a written contract with the borrower. The auditor would normally note the following details in the audit working papers:

- Name of the lender, which should be the entity's name.

- Name of the borrower, the debtor.

- Principal amount of the loan.

- Rate of interest; and basis of calculation of interest (for example, calculated daily, or monthly, or half-yearly); terms of payment of interest (for example, payable monthly, or quarterly, and whether payable in advance or in arrear).

- Terms of repayment of the loan (for example, whether wholly repayable on a specified date or repayable in instalments on specified dates).

The auditor should compare the loan account with the loan agreement, noting whether interest has been received timeously and, where repayment of the loan is to be made in instalments, whether all instalments due have been received timeously.

The auditor should request the client to arrange for the borrower to confirm directly to the auditor, the amount of the loan outstanding at the date of the balance sheet as well as the interest and repayment terms.

---

[7] Refer SAAPS 1100, 'Bank Confirmations'.

The entity may have stipulated in the agreement that the loan must be repaid in instalments of fixed amounts at fixed dates without giving the borrower the option to repay the loan, either wholly or partially, at an earlier date. In such a case, the auditor can calculate from the loan agreement how much should have been received by way of repayment and thus the balance of the loan outstanding at the date of the balance sheet. It is, however, open to the entity to waive, at any time, the foregoing condition and accept larger (or smaller) sums than those stipulated by way of repayment, so that even in this case a certificate from the borrower as to the amount of the loan outstanding at the date of the balance sheet is desirable.

17.2.10.3 Security for debt investment – loans advanced

As a general rule a loan is secured in some way. The security may be in the form of:

- a pledge of shares or debentures;
- a pledge of corporeal movable property; or
- a mortgage of immovable property.

In the last instance, the evidence of the loan agreement and the security are contained in the same document, known as a mortgage bond, which is registered in the Deeds Office by means of endorsement on the title deeds. The reader is referred to the discussion in chapter 16 regarding mortgage bonds and other securities.

Pledge of shares or debentures for debt instruments and for obligations of the entity

Where shares or debentures have been pledged by a borrower to the entity as security for a loan granted, the accounting records should contain a note of the security. The auditor should call for the relevant certificates to which there should be attached blank transfer deeds signed by the persons whose names appear on the certificates, unless the shares or debentures have been transferred to the name of the entity. Alternatively, there may be certified transfer deeds. An alternative to the use of blank transfer deeds (or certified transfers) is for the borrower to give to the entity an irrevocable power of attorney to transfer the shares, should it become necessary to do so. This method is often adopted where the loan is likely to be outstanding for several years, as the terms of the Stamp Duties Act require that transfers be registered within six months of the dates of the relevant transfer deeds, otherwise a penalty is imposed if transfer subsequently takes place. In such a case, the auditor should inspect the power of attorney as well as the relevant share certificates. The certificate from the borrower should detail the scrip pledged to the entity. The auditor should see that the note on the loan account regarding the security agrees with these details.

When performing a scrip count, the auditor should take control of all share certificates and/or debentures, whether held as security for debt investments or held by the entity as beneficial owner. The information regarding the latter is obtained from the relevant investment accounts. This procedure should be followed to eliminate the possibility of the same share certificates and/or debentures being fraudulently produced twice, once as evidence of the security and once as evidence of ownership.

Where equity investments owned by the entity have been pledged as security for obligations of the entity, the loan account and possibly also the relevant investment account should contain a note of the number and description of the shares pledged. The client should request the lender to send a certificate, showing details of the shares held, directly to the auditor. (The certificate should also include a statement to the effect that the share certificates are held as security. Although this is not necessary to provide evidence of the entity's ownership of the shares, it is required for the purpose of the note on the balance sheet regarding security for the loan.) Where the lender is a bank or other recognized financial institution, the certificate may be accepted without further evidence that the share certificates are in fact in its possession. If, however, the lender does not fall into this category, the auditor should, with the consent of the client, also call upon the lender and inspect the relevant share certificates, or if, because of considerations of distance, it is not practical to do so, appoint a reliable agent (for example, another accountant situated near the lender's address) to make the inspection.

Where dematerialized shares or unit trusts owned by the entity have been pledged as security for obligations of the entity, confirmation should be obtained from the CSDP or Unit Trust Fund that the pledge has been marked in the CSDP sub-register or the Unit Trust Fund account as being 'held for security' in favour of a third party.

Pledge of corporeal movable property

No effective pledge of movable property can be made unless:

- the property is in the entity's possession; or
- the property is in the possession of an independent third party, who declares that it is held for the audit client.

In the first case, the auditor should see the deed of pledge and note that the articles stated therein are in the entity's possession at the date of the balance sheet. In the second case, a certificate should be obtained from the third party, listing the movable property held and stating that these are held for the entity. An auditor should accept such a certificate only if it comes from a person whose normal business is to hold such articles, for example, a storage company.

The movable property constituting the security should be insured for at least the amount of the loan and accrued interest. The auditor should inspect the policy, which may cover the respective rights of both the entity and the borrower. If, however, the policy is in the name of the borrower only, it should have been ceded to the entity and the cession registered with the insurance company. The auditor should ascertain, by reference to the endorsement on the policy, whether this has been done, and should request a confirmation from the insurer that the endorsement is still registered in favour of the lender.

Mortgage of immovable property

A mortgage of immovable property is only effective if it is registered against the borrower's property with the Registrar of Deeds.

The auditor should read the mortgage bond and note, in addition to the items listed for the verification of loans, that:

* the property mortgaged is in respect of the relevant loan; and
* the deed bears the seal of the Registrar of Deeds.

An effective mortgage does not require the title deeds to be in hands of the mortgagee. The important point is that the mortgage has been registered in the appropriate Deeds Registry (refer the discussion in chapter 16). Nevertheless, there may also be a clause in the bond giving the mortgagee custody of the title deeds, and, if there is, the auditor should ascertain, either by inspection of the deeds or by confirmation from a proper custodian such as a bank, that the deeds are in their possession but are held in safe custody for the audit client.

Where buildings constitute a substantial part of the security, the auditor should ascertain whether the property is insured for at least the amount of the loan and accrued interest. The protection of the client's rights relating to insurance cover, discussed above, applies equally.

The policy should contain a clause to guard the mortgagee against the avoidance of liability by the insurer resulting from breach of the conditions by the insured (the mortgagor) unknown to the mortgagee. For example, there may be a condition that inflammable materials not be stored in the building. If, in contravention of the condition, the insured did store such materials in the building and the latter was then destroyed, the insurer would be under no obligation to compensate for the loss incurred and the value of the mortgagee's security would have been greatly reduced. It is therefore the practice of insurance companies to insert, if required, a clause in the policy to cover the mortgagee against the foregoing contingency. This is known as the 'Mortgagee Clause'.

17.2.10.4 Valuation of security for loan

If it is apparent that the borrower is financially sound, the auditor need not normally pursue the question of the valuation of the security (if any). There may, however, be indications that the borrower is in financial difficulties, as for example, where the interest or instalments of the capital sum have not been received, or received timeously by the entity, in which case consideration of the present value of the security (if any) is required. Such consideration is also required, no matter what the borrower's financial position may be, where the loan is stated on the balance sheet as 'secured', for the balance sheet cannot be said to fairly present the position unless the value of the security is sufficient to cover the loan.

The question of the valuation of shares or debentures (which may have been pledged as security) has been discussed at length earlier in this chapter. In the case of movables pledged as security, the circumstances may be such that it is obvious, even to a layman, that the value of the pledged article is far in excess of the loan – for example, an expensive video machine of recent manufacture pledged as security for a loan of R5 000. Again, information may be readily available as to the approximate present worth of movables, for example, the price-lists of second-hand cars issued to the motor trade. Where the circumstances differ from those indicated above, the auditor may have difficulty in assessing the value of the articles and a sworn appraisement of them may be considered necessary.

Where the security is a mortgage of land, it may be evident that the security exceeds substantially the amount of the loan (for example, the mortgage of a property valued at R400 000 as security for a loan of R250 000). Where, however, this is not so, an assessment of the value by a competent official or a sworn appraisement of the value of the immovable property may be considered necessary.

Where the borrower's ability to pay is not in doubt, or the balance of the loan is fully secured, the loan should be stated in the balance sheet at its full value. If, however, there is evidence of the borrower's probable inability to pay and the loan is either unsecured, or the security does not appear to be sufficient to cover the loan, provision should be made for the impairment loss. Interest accrued on the loan is normally taken into account (as a current asset), but if the client makes a practice of taking account of interest only when it falls due, this is also acceptable.

17.2.10.5 Classification of investments

AC 125, 'Financial instruments disclosure and presentation', requires investments to be classified for purposes of disclosure in the financial statements as follows:

- *Held-for-trading and available for sale investments*:
  - *Marketable securities* are carried at fair value, which is calculated by reference to securities exchange quoted selling prices at the close of business on the balance sheet date.
  - *Unlisted investments* are carried at fair value, which is determined by utilization of an accepted valuation technique.

* *Held-to-maturity securities*, such as loans, are carried at amortized cost using the effective interest rate method.

AC 133 provides for the disclosures regarding gains and losses arising from changes in the fair value of financial instruments to be included in net profit or loss, or under certain circumstances to be carried in equity until the underlying asset is realized.

The question of management's intent with regard to the different investments has to be ascertained and corroborated. The auditor will enquire of management regarding their intent, and consider the past history of the client, as well as strategic objectives of management affecting future plans that may lead to a change in intent. The auditor should obtain written representations from management with regard to their intent where investment transactions or balances are significant.

17.2.10.6 Auditing fair value of investments

Where investments are carried at fair value, the auditor must obtain evidence to support the fair value determined. In the case of listed investments, the market values are published in various financial journals, for example, the JSE Securities Exchange publishes a table of share prices and indices in the business section of various newspapers, which reflects the day's close, day's high and day's low prices for all companies listed on the JSE Securities Exchange. These values may also be obtained from the official lists of the securities exchange or through a stockbroker.

For unlisted equity investments or debt investments, the entity may determine fair value by adoption of particular valuation models, or by a valuation performed by a third party. In such circumstances, the auditor may consider it necessary to use an expert to confirm the fair values so determined.

Finally, management should consider whether there has been any impairment in the value of equity or debt investments, below its fair value, which appears to be other than temporary. Provision should be made to account for such losses anticipated. In such circumstances, the auditor will need to consider the basis of management's assumptions to determine whether the impairment condition exists and obtain evidence to support management's assumptions regarding their estimate of the impaired value. Factors that would be considered are:

* A loan debtor's inability to pay the outstanding debt balance.

* Adverse economic conditions in the geographical area where the investment is held that are not expected to reverse in the foreseeable future.

* An unlisted equity investment incurring ongoing losses and has reduced dividend payments, or is unable to remit dividend to its holding company,

due to exchange or other restrictions in the legal jurisdiction in which it operates.

17.2.11 Presentation and disclosure

The recognition and measurement requirements affecting financial instruments – including equity and debt investments and derivative financial instruments – are complex, and the presentation and disclosure requirements are extensive.

The auditor assesses whether the presentation and disclosure of derivatives conforms with the financial reporting framework. This may affect:

- the classification of balances appearing on the balance sheet;

- the recognition of realized and unrealized gains and losses from hedging and changes in fair value measurements in the income statement;

- the original cash flows from transactions; and

- comprehensive notes to the financial statements dealing with the different classifications of investments and financial instruments.

The auditor's conclusion as to whether derivatives are presented in conformity with the financial reporting framework is based on the auditor's judgment as to whether:

- the accounting practices selected and applied are in conformity with the financial reporting framework;

- the accounting practices are appropriate in the circumstances;

- the financial statements, including the related notes, provide information on matters that may affect their use, understanding, and interpretation;

- disclosure is adequate to ensure that the entity is in full compliance with the current disclosure requirements of the financial reporting framework under which the financial statements are being reported;

- the information presented in the financial statements is classified and summarized in a reasonable manner, that is, neither too detailed nor too condensed; and

- the financial statements reflect the underlying transactions and events in a manner that presents the financial position, results of operations, and cash flows stated within a range of acceptable limits, that is, limits that are reasonable and practicable to attain in financial statements.

In addition, where investments are held to secure strategic business objectives, the investment relationships may give rise to related parties and related party transactions as defined in AC 126, 'Related parties', which will also require specific disclosures to be made in the notes to the financial statements.

Consequently, great care must be exercised by the auditor to ensure that the disclosures comply with the numerous and complex GAAP statements. Where necessary, the auditor should involve audit staff with expertise in the treatment of financial instruments to ensure that the balances are indeed complete, fairly valued and properly presented.

17.3 NATURE OF CASH ACTIVITIES

17.3.1 Introduction

Cash and bank activities may be likened to the life blood of the business. Ultimately, all transactions are reduced to flowing through cash and bank whether they arise from capital or revenue receipts deposited, or assets acquired or expenses disbursed. Provided a healthy positive cash inflow is maintained, on balance the business will survive and flourish; if that should become an unhealthy negative cash outflow with few signs of reversing, the entity will soon find itself in financial difficulty, raising doubts about its going-concern ability.

17.3.1.1 Cash balances

Cash balances comprise the following:

- *Cash* comprises *physical banknotes and coins or currency*;

- *Petty cash imprest floats* are maintained in the form of banknotes and coins for payment of sundry cash expenses, which are reimbursed on a regular basis; each petty cash float is managed by a designated employee in the business to maintain accountability for the monies and expenses. The amount of the float will depend on the business needs for cash payments and may be a few hundred or several thousand Rand. The term *imprest float* denotes that the reimbursement will be for the amount of the expenses to restore the float to its original level. For example, a float of R1 000: if the cashier has spent R875, leaving a balance on hand of R125, the float will be reimbursed by an amount of R875 to restore it to its original R1 000;

- A similar principle is followed for the establishment of *Till floats* in a trading operation, where the cashier is required to have sufficient change to give to customers and will be given a fixed float for this purpose. When cashing up the day's takings, the amount of the float will be set aside and stored in the safe until the cashier's next shift, that is, the float amount will not be banked with the day's takings from that till;

- *Unbanked receipts* from cash sale customers and accounts receivable awaiting deposit into the bank account of the entity, which could comprise *notes and coins, cheques and credit card payment vouchers*;

- *Travellers' cheques* that may be cashed almost anywhere and exchanged by the holder for their face currency or the local currency of the country.

17.3.1.2 **Bank balances**

Bank balances refer to the variety of accounts that may be maintained by the entity at one or more banks for the deposit of monies received and withdrawals of amounts for the payment of expenses and liabilities, using negotiable instruments such as cheques, bank transfers, electronic fund transfers in and out and between accounts of the entity. The opening of a bank account is a formal agreement giving rise to rights and obligations between the bank and its clients, *inter alia*, that the bank agrees that all amounts deposited in such accounts will be available to the client on demand, or in accordance with the terms of the deposit or overdraft facilities granted to the entity. The entity undertakes in return to abide by the terms of the Bills of Exchange Act and the conditions of the bank in operating its accounts honestly and with integrity, that is, money laundering operations by the business are unacceptable.

Bank accounts commonly opened by a business with its bankers will include:

- A *Current Account*, commonly referred to as a *cheque account* for general deposits and payments of the business, which may at times reflect a balance and at other times an overdraft position, where overdraft facilities have been granted by the bank. Reconciliations of amounts reflected on bank statements and account balances per the records are prepared on a regular basis.

- Where the business has a number of branches around the country, branch bank accounts may be opened at local branches of the bank and an electronic cash management facility with on-line banking may be provided by the bank to link branch accounts around the country on a continuous basis, allowing for the offset of overdrafts and balances to limit bank interest charges to the net overdraft position of the business entity on a daily basis. This system also allows for the rapid transfer of monies between different branch accounts. Many large businesses maintain a central *treasury department* at the head office to manage the resultant significant cash flows to the best advantage of the business.

- An *Imprest Bank Account* used as a clearing account for payment of particular expenses where confidentiality of transactions is important, such as a *Payroll Imprest Bank Account*, a *Dividend Imprest Bank Account* opened for each dividend declared by a public listed company. The gross payroll, plus company contributions for payroll accounts payable, is deposited into the account that is then used to effect transfers to individual employees' bank accounts and to the various payroll accounts payable. Once all employees and payroll accounts payable have been paid, the account balance should reduce to a nil balance. Payroll department staff or the company Transfer Secretaries would perform the reconciliations of these respective bank accounts to the relevant bank statements in order to maintain the confidentiality of payments to individual employees or to shareholders for dividends.

- *Short and long-term* interest bearing *investment or deposit accounts* for the investment of short-term cash surpluses.

- *Credit card, debit card or garage card* accounts may be opened by an individual, or by businesses, for individual employees that provides the holder with card access to charge expenses to the account within authorized limits; these are then billed to the customer and are due to be settled on a monthly basis from the designated current account operated at the bank.

- A separate *Trust banking account* will be opened by businesses where client or other trust monies are received to be held pending payment to other third parties. Such accounts will generally be opened by attorneys, estate agents, stockbrokers, registered accountants and auditors, and trustees, all of whom may handle monies of clients whether for the settlement of litigation claims, transfer of property purchased, settlement for shares purchased or funds managed for trust beneficiaries, such as those from a deceased estate. An important aspect of a trust banking account is that the monies therein do not form part of the insolvent estate of the person or entity if declared insolvent, since the monies therein belong to other parties and must be dealt with according to the specific mandate for which they are held.

- Businesses that operate on a multinational basis may operate accounts in several countries in order to meet foreign expenses and liabilities in those other countries, referred to as *offshore* accounts. Such accounts opened by a South African resident will generally be subject to Reserve Bank exchange control approval of monies being transferred in and out of South Africa.

17.3.1.3 Relationship between cash and bank and the transactions and balances of the business

As indicated above, cash and bank interface with all the significant classes of transactions and balances discussed in chapters 12 to 17. These include revenue transactions, expenditure transactions including production expenses, payroll transactions, investing activities, financing activities, and investment activities. Earlier chapters dealt with aspects related to the nature and controls over the receipt and deposit of cash, and the disbursement of expenses and settlement of liabilities.

17.3.2 Audit objectives

As the specific controls and tests of controls over cash receipts and disbursements were dealt with extensively in earlier chapters, this chapter focuses only on the overall cash management controls and the substantive audit procedures that the auditor should perform to audit cash and bank balances. The reader is referred to Table 12.3 in chapter 12 and Table 13.3 in chapter 13 for the audit objectives related to cash and bank arising from revenue transactions and expenditure transactions, which are not repeated here.

The audit objectives specific to cash and bank balances are set out in Table 17.7 below. The auditor will identify those assertions most likely to lead to a risk of significant misstatement for cash and bank to focus the audit procedures accordingly.

MANAGEMENT ASSERTION	AUDIT OBJECTIVES
Cash and bank balances	
Completeness	Recorded cash balances include the effects of all cash and bank transactions that have occurred during the period.
	All inter-bank transfers have been recorded in the correct accounting period and none have been omitted.
Existence	Recorded cash and bank balances exist at balance sheet date and recorded bank overdrafts are obligations of the entity at the balance sheet date.
Measurement/ accuracy	The aggregate cash and bank balances are reported on the balance sheet at cost determined in accordance with GAAP and the accounting policies of the entity applied on a consistent basis.
Valuation	The aggregate cash and bank balances are reported on the balance sheet at cost, determined in accordance with GAAP and the accounting policies of the entity applied on a consistent basis, and are realizable at the amounts stated thereon.
Rights and obligations	The entity has legal rights to all cash and bank balances reflected in the balance sheet at balance sheet date.
	Overdraft balances and other loans owing by the entity at balance sheet date have been identified and are owed by the entity.
	Security provided over assets of the entity to secure loans granted to the entity by its bankers has been identified.

MANAGEMENT ASSERTION	AUDIT OBJECTIVES
Presentation and disclosure	Cash and bank balances are properly identified and classified in the financial statements and, where offset is permitted, this has been done in accordance with GAAP.
	Overdraft balances and other loans owing by the entity at balance sheet date have been identified and are properly disclosed in accordance with GAAP.
	Appropriate disclosures have been made with regard to the overdraft and loan facilities granted to the company and pledges or mortgages of assets of the entity to secure liabilities of the entity or its group companies in accordance with GAAP and the Companies Act.

Table 17.7 Management assertions and the related audit objectives for cash and bank

17.3.3 Understanding the client's business

The auditor needs to consider several important aspects when obtaining an understanding of the business relative to cash and bank transactions and balances. The first of these is the recognition that cash and bank, by virtue of the volume of transactions that occur over a financial year, probably constitutes the most significant class of transactions of the entity, giving rise to a risk of error and fraud. Secondly, that cash and bank is highly susceptible to fraud and theft by employees, often in collusion with third parties affecting the *completeness, occurrence and existence* assertions.

To mitigate risks related to cash and bank balances, management will usually implement stringent control policies and procedures for cash handling and recording, including preventative and detective controls appropriate to the nature of the business. Most important are the control procedures that allow for segregation of duties between different functions; restriction of access to cash and bank to those employees who need to have access; daily cashing up procedures where appropriate; strict control over mail opening and depositing of receipts from accounts receivable where large volumes of receipts are received through the mail; regular reconciliation of recorded balances to bank statements and strict control procedures over processing of payments.

Management's policies and procedures with regard to the hiring of employees should be such that only persons who have the necessary skills and competence, and who have a proven record of integrity, should be appointed to handle and control cash and bank activities. In particular, these should include procedures for screening of employees to ascertain that they have not previously been discharged from employment elsewhere or have a criminal record for fraud and theft. Other preventative control measures take the form of physical security, such as security guards, surveillance cameras over tills and monitoring of public customer areas, the use of drop safes and security companies to transport cash deposits to the bank and collect payroll cash for wage payouts. In addition, the entity should carry adequate cash insurance to at least allow for a recovery of losses should these arise.

In contrast to the complexities affecting valuation and recognition of investments, particularly derivatives, the *measurement, valuation* and *rights and obligations* relating to cash and bank balances are relatively simple as the cash receipts and payment transactions are factual and do not involve estimates or fair value measurements.

17.3.4 Analysing process level business risks

Earlier chapters discussed the process level business risks and related control activities associated with cash receipts and payments. In particular, the reader is reminded of the five essential aspects discussed in detail in chapter 9 that should be considered in so far as they relate to the management of risks inherent in the management of cash and bank to enable an effective internal control system, namely: the control environment, risk assessment, information and communication, control activities and monitoring processes.

As cash and bank involve mainly routine transactions, they lend themselves to formal control procedures, many of which may be computerized, reducing to a large extent the potential risk of errors and allowing for the early detection and correction of errors and fraud. As indicated in earlier chapters, the auditor should communicate timeously to management any control weaknesses identified relative to cash and bank as these are subject to a high risk of fraud and theft.

17.3.5 Preliminary assessment of the risk of significant misstatement

The reader is referred to Tables 12.7 and 13.8 in chapters 12 and 13 for an indication of the control considerations, typical control procedures, both programmed and manual, and tests of control that an auditor may choose to perform in order to assess the risk of significant misstatement from cash and bank transactions, and balances.

Because of the lack of staff numbers in a small owner-managed business, good segregation of duties over cash and bank aspects may not be possible, which increases the risk of fraud and theft. In such circumstances, the owner manager should carry the responsibility for performing, or at least reviewing, the bank reconciliations and retain the responsibility for signing of all cheques after reviewing appropriate supporting documentation. Careful and regular monitoring of cash sales levels and outstanding accounts receivable balances should enable the owner manager to detect irregularities occurring.

What is true for any business, however, is that should the controls be slack and management's monitoring processes ineffective or performed spasmodically, employees and others will quickly spot the opportunities and take advantage of them. In such an environment, the auditor will be likely to assess the risk of significant misstatement as medium to high and may not be able to identify effective detective controls. In these circumstances, the auditor may not be able to place reliance on controls and will accordingly have to extend the substantive tests of detail of cash and bank transactions and balances. More extensive substantive analytical procedures may also be performed, linking cash movements to related revenue and expenditure transactions areas, budgets and cash flow projections.

17.3.6 Control activities and tests of control

The reader is referred to chapters 12 and 13 which discuss the types of source documents encountered in cash and bank transactions, and control activities over cash receipting and depositing, and cash disbursements.

To sum up, in any business where effective controls are implemented over the routine cash and bank transactions, the auditor would generally identify controls, usually the detective controls such as reconciliations and monitoring controls, to test, in order to support an assessment of control risk as low. Substantive analytical procedures then will be directed at management's key performance indicators and monitoring processes over cash flow and accountability procedures for cash and banking, with limited substantive tests of detail focused on gathering evidence relating to the *existence and completeness* of cash and bank balances at the period end and the *completeness* and *occurrence* of cash and bank transactions during the period of the audit.

Circumstances may be identified in the consideration of the control environment that gives rise to concern, such as: concerns over management integrity; breakdowns in internal controls during the period; known or suspected attempts by staff at theft and fraud during the period; a rapid turnover of staff responsible for handling or recording cash and bank; or an evident lack of skills and competence by employees responsible for cash and bank transactions – these increase the risk of significant misstatement in the financial statements and the auditor would extend the substantive tests of detail to be performed accordingly.

17.3.7 Determining the acceptable level of detection risk

The assessment of the risk of significant misstatement and level of reliance to be placed on controls over cash and bank directly affect the level of detection risk set by the auditor and the determination of the nature and extent of audit evidence required from substantive analytical procedures and substantive tests of detail.

Clearly evidence of the *existence* and *completeness* of cash and bank at period end is a critical area directly affecting the financial statements. This will involve the auditor in:

- the performance of physical cash counts at all locations where significant cash balances are held;

- the re-performance of reconciliations of bank accounts to bank statements at period end to ensure a proper cut-off of cash and bank transactions is achieved; and

- the obtaining of bank confirmations directly from the entity's bankers for all bank accounts held.

In addition, the scheduling of inter-bank transfers for all bank accounts operated by the entity, where a cash management system operates, is important to detect any transfers between bank accounts of the entity which have been recorded in one account but not in the other account, resulting in an incorrect *cut-off* being achieved and consequent errors in bank balances reflected in the financial statements. For example, where a transfer of R500 000 is made from the Port Elizabeth branch bank account on 31 October to the Head Office bank account in Johannesburg, which is recorded as a deposit on the Head Office bank account and bank statement only on 4 November. The bank balance in the balance sheet at 31 October would be understated by R500 000 unless the receipt was detected and brought into the Head Office bank balance as at 31 October and reflected on its bank reconciliation as an outstanding item at that date. Comparison and agreement of the equal and opposite balances on inter-company account balances or inter-branch and head office accounts will assist in the detection and correction of such discrepancies.

17.3.8 Substantive analytical procedures

Cash and bank balances are volatile, being sensitive to the operating, investing, financing and investment policies and procedures implemented by management to achieve the strategic business objectives. As a result, not much reliance is usually placed on substantive analytical procedures by auditors. That said, management will undoubtedly regard the establishment and monitoring of key performance indicators over cash and bank as critical to ensuring the sustainability of the business. In addition, management will usually have restrictions on borrowing limits imposed by the Articles of Association or in terms of a Debenture Trust Deed, or will need to monitor the utilization of bank overdraft facilities granted by its bankers. In the case of foreign-held companies, the Reserve Bank may impose restrictions on the percentage of local borrowing limits to foreign capital and borrowings provided by the foreign holding company.

Even a small business will devise a means for monitoring its cash flows, however rudimentary the process may be. The availability of computerized cash management systems and computerized bank reconciliation software provides the possibility for management to track the cash and bank movements on a daily basis.

The reader is referred to earlier chapters for explanations of the principles to be followed in performing effective substantive analytical procedures. A few useful ratios[8] that could be used to monitor cash and bank are set out below:

- Acid test ratio indicating liquidity: Cash and debtors/current liabilities;

- Overdraft used to overdraft limits × 100. As this fluctuates continuously, it is advisable to use the average overdraft used over the past 6 to 12 months;

- Debtors to creditors and overdraft: Debtors/Creditors + Overdraft;

- Net funds to overdraft: (Debtors + Cash) less Creditors/Bank overdraft = times covered;

- Overdraft to working capital: Bank overdrafts/Working Capital × 100, link to Net Trading Funds/Overdraft to provide both liquidity and solvency margins;

- Cash flow (based on the cash flow statement for the current period) to sales: Cash Flow/Sales × 100;

- Cash Flow to overdraft and creditors: Cash Flow/Bank Overdraft and Creditors × 100;

- Cash Flow to Current Liabilities: Cash Flow/Current Liabilities × 100; and

- Cash Flow to Total Debt: Cash Flow/Total Debt × 100.

These ratios provide an indication of the solvency and liquidity of the business and give early indications of overtrading that could lead to insolvency. Management would select those most suited to its situation to establish norms over time and monitor movements in these to identify movements that are not in line with expectations.

17.3.9 Substantive tests of detail of transactions

Substantive tests of detail for cash and bank transactions were dealt with in chapters 12, 13 and 15. Substantive tests of detail on the year-end cash and bank balances are influenced by the auditor's reliance on the systems of control and substantive evidence gathered on transactions involving cash and bank.

17.3.9.1 Framework for substantive tests of details of balances

A framework for substantive tests of detail for cash and bank balances is set out in Table 17.8.

---

[8] Bentley R, *Financial Ratios for Management*, 1994, Bentley, Stockwell, Anderson and Partners.

SUBSTANTIVE TESTS FOR CASH AND BANK BALANCES	AUDIT OBJECTIVES				
	C	O/E	M/V	R/O	P/D
1. Obtain and document an understanding of the business:	X	X	X	X	X
Identify the significance of cash and bank transactions and balances to the entity:					
– Identify plans of management with regard to the investment of surplus cash. – Identify critical success factors and key performance indicators used by management to monitor cash and bank. – Identify economic and industry circumstances affecting the entity's cash flows.					
Obtain trial balances or schedules of all cash and bank balances and bank overdrafts:	X		X		
– Agree opening balances for cash and bank to the previous year's working papers. – Review movements in cash and bank accounts in the general ledger for entries unusual in amount or source and investigate these – this may be done using CAATs. – Obtain a schedule of cash and bank at period end to support the amounts reflected in the general ledger and financial statements. – Cast schedules and general ledger and agree balances to relevant general ledger accounts.					
2. Substantive analytical procedures:	X	X	X		
Develop a prediction or expectation based on the auditor's knowledge of the business investment activities and strategic business risks.					
Define a significant difference or threshold based on materiality at account balance level and calculate various relevant financial management ratios and key performance indicators used by management to monitor cash and bank.					
Compute the difference between the actual and the expected, compare to prior periods, to budget and to a history of such ratios maintained.					
Investigate significant differences and exercise judgement to conclude on implications and trends.					
Document the basis for the audit conclusion.					

SUBSTANTIVE TESTS FOR CASH AND BANK BALANCES	AUDIT OBJECTIVES				
	C	O/E	M/V	R/O	P/D
3. Tests of detail of transactions:					
Perform cash cut-off tests for receipts and payments (refer chapters 12 and 13 for details):	×	×	×		
– Inspect that receipts from cash sales and accounts receivable received on the last day of the financial year are recorded as cash on hand or in transit at period end, ensure receipts from the subsequent period are excluded.					
– Inspect daily cash summaries, mail registers of cash and cheques received and bank stamped deposit slips for a few days before and after period end to determine that a proper cut-off is achieved.					
– Record the last cheque numbers drawn on all accounts run by the entity and inspect the cheque numbers recorded in the cash payments record during the last month of the period and those recorded subsequent to period end to determine that a correct cut-off of payments has been achieved.					
– Inspect dates on cheques issued prior to year-end and inquire as to whether these have been dispatched to the payees, or are kept back and reflected in the bank reconciliation as outstanding cheques to prevent them from being disclosed in current liabilities as accounts payable.					
– Inspect exception reports generated by the entity's accounting system for missing sequence numbers of cheques recorded prior to period end and inquire about these.					
– Obtain copies of EFTs made and received for a few days before and after period end and determine whether they have been recorded in the correct accounting period.					
Obtain a schedule of inter-bank account transfers between the entity's various bank accounts for the last month before and subsequent to period end and inspect the entries recorded in the general ledger and reflected on the bank statements prior to and subsequent to period end to determine that they are recorded in the correct period. Care should be taken to ensure that both the receipt and disbursement are recorded in the same accounting period.	×	×	×		
Re-perform the bank reconciliations for all bank accounts included in cash and bank on the balance sheet comparing the account records to the bank statement received from the bank and inquire into long outstanding uncleared items.	×	×	×	×	

SUBSTANTIVE TESTS FOR CASH AND BANK BALANCES	AUDIT OBJECTIVES				
	C	O/E	M/V	R/O	P/D
4. Tests of details of balances:					
Count cash on hand at entity and, as indicated above, inspect the recording of the cash, in the cash receipts or cash disbursements records, in the correct accounting period.	×	×	×	×	
Obtain a confirmation directly from the bank (ref SAAPS 1100) with details of:	×	×	×	×	×
– all bank balances held for the entity; – bank overdraft facilities granted to the entity; – accounts closed and opened during the period; – securities held and the reasons for this; – contingent liabilities for bills receivable discounted, not yet due; – forward exchange contracts entered into on behalf of the client; – derivative positions; – authorized signatories; and – cash management system operated with the bank, if any.					
Inspect subsequent bank statements for evidence:	×	×	×	×	
– that outstanding items have been cleared; – of deposits or payments relating to the previous accounting period that are not yet recorded as accounts receivable or accruals at period end; and – of attempts at window-dressing bank balances.					
Where there is a concern that fraud may have occurred, the auditor may need to review bank reconciliations for several months and where necessary re-perform several months' bank reconciliations.	×	×	×	×	
5. Presentation and disclosure:					
Determine whether the *presentation and disclosure* of cash and bank accord with GAAP and are properly identified and classified as current assets in the financial statements.					×
Determine that bank overdrafts are classified as current liabilities in the financial statements.					×
Where overdrafts have been set off against bank balances, enquire whether a right of set-off exists and determine that the correct classification is achieved.					×
Inspect directors' minutes, agreements, debenture deeds and bank confirmations to determine that the financial statement notes correctly reflect the *rights and obligations* of the entity with regard to overdraft and loan facilities, guarantees provided for other group companies and any restrictions on bank balances, such as Trust Accounts.					×

Table 17.8 Framework for a substantive audit programme for cash and bank balances

17.3.9.2 **Checking bank deposits and withdrawals**

The auditor should be satisfied that:

- all money recorded in the cash record as having been deposited has in fact been deposited in the bank timeously;
- all sums recorded in the cash record as having been withdrawn from the bank are correct; and
- the bank balance at the close of the period under review, as recorded in the general ledger bank account/s, are correct.

It should be apparent that the above points are interdependent, so that if any two are proved correct the third (at least in total) must be correct. This fact may allow the auditor to reduce the amount of detailed checking and still be satisfied that the records in respect of bank transactions are in order. The substantive audit procedures relating to the bank balances are dealt with in section 17.3.10, substantive tests of detail of account balances.

Bank deposits

The reader is referred to chapter 12 for a detailed discussion of bank deposits. The auditor should check the entries in the cash records reflecting deposits with the deposits recorded on the bank statement. When checking the entries, the auditor should note that the deposits have been made timeously by ascertaining that the dates of the deposits in the bank statement agree with the relevant dates in the cash summary printouts.

It should be appreciated that a delay between making the entry for the reduction of cash on hand in the cash records and the deposit of the money in the bank could provide an unscrupulous cashier with a loan and, if such a delay occurred for many deposits, there could be a more or less continuous (though illegal) loan by the business to the cashier. It is important, therefore, that the foregoing checks or tests relating to timeous depositing should be made.

Bank withdrawals

The reader is referred to chapter 13 for a detailed discussion of bank withdrawals. The entries of payments in the cash record should agree with withdrawals indicated on the bank statement and the auditor must be satisfied that this is so. The dates of these entries differ, however, as a cheque is not normally presented for payment until several days after the date of its issue.

Many businesses have their cheques specially printed, while others use the cheques provided by the banks. All cheques, whether specially printed or issued by a bank, contain in print: the name of the account holder, the account number of the account holder, and the serial numbers in unbroken sequence. The fact that cheques are pre-numbered in an unbroken sequence allows the auditor to check such sequence to obtain satisfaction that all cheques have been accounted for in the cash record. Most computerized accounting systems provide for the printing of computerized cheques. The risk that has to be managed in such cases is the adequacy of controls over cheque signing equipment and stationery. A computerized environment has been assumed throughout the text, but the auditor could nonetheless encounter situations where manual cheques are used and the principles still apply.

If the auditor has checked the numerical sequence of cheques, a test only of the cheque payment entries in the cash record with the relevant entries in the bank statement is sufficient. Indeed, where cheque payment entries have been vouched with the paid cheques, it would appear to be unnecessary to make any such test except for those entries which are not represented by paid cheques, such as bank charges, bank overdraft interest, and cheques (previously deposited) returned by the bank unpaid. The entries for bank charges and overdraft interest must in any case be vouched and the best evidence for such expenditure would be the relevant entries in the bank statement.

It should be clearly understood that the limited test, described above, is based on the improbability of an employee being able to steal an employer's cheque, other than out of the current cheque book. In the latter case, the sequence of the serial numbers would be broken. Of course, there is always the possibility that, in the case of specially printed cheques, cheques may be fraudulently removed from the unused cheque books in store, if security in that respect is lax, and it is for the auditor to be satisfied that unused cheque books are properly safeguarded and accounted for before he or she can rely on a test of cheque payments only. Given the high incidence of cheque fraud, this risk must be taken seriously where manual cheque forms are used.

Where entries appear in the bank statement for cheques credited by the bank but later returned as not being in order, the auditor should check the relevant entries in the cash record with the bank statement. If it is the practice of the cashier not to make entries in the cash record for such cheques, which have been re-deposited, the auditor should ascertain whether the debits in the bank statement in respect of such cheques are matched by subsequent credits for re-deposits. If many entries appear for cheques deposited and subsequently returned by the bank, the auditor should make inquiries and obtain satisfactory explanations.

The reader is referred to the extensive discussion in chapter 13 regarding the use of cheques and the stringent regulations introduced by the latest amendments to the Bills of Exchange Act in this regard.

17.3.10 Substantive tests of detail for balances

The revenue/receipt transactions are completed when amounts received from accounts receivable, cash sales or miscellaneous income are deposited in the bank. Control features to ensure that all amounts received are banked, and the audit procedures to test that the system was adhered to and amounts received correctly accounted for, are explained in chapter 12. It remains for the auditor to obtain evidence that the cash and bank balances recorded in the accounting records are correct. It follows that if there is satisfactory internal control and audit tests of transactions have proved accurate recording of cash receipts and payments (see chapters 12 and 13), the cash and bank balances will be correctly reflected.

Conversely, the satisfactory verification of cash and bank balances confirms that cash receipts and payments transactions were correctly recorded during the period under audit.

To confirm the cash and bank balances requires not only a cash count and an examination of the bank statement and certificate but also a check of the addition of the records, the totals of which result in the foregoing balances. The audit work required may be classified as follows:

- Audit of cash balances;
- Checking bank deposits and withdrawals;
- Checking the bank reconciliation; and
- Checking of the additions of the cash records.

17.3.10.1 Audit of cash balances

When the auditor plans to perform a cash count it should be done immediately after notice to the cashier, so that no time elapses between giving notice and making the count, otherwise the cashier may have an opportunity of putting further money into the cash box to make up the required sum. If an auditor is of the opinion that it is necessary to perform a cash count at the close of business on the last day of the financial year, before being able to report on the balance sheet at that date, and makes a practice of doing so, a defaulting cashier, being aware that a count will be made on a specific day, will make every attempt to beg, borrow or steal the cash required to make up a deficiency on that day.

In such cases, the auditor should supplement the year-end count with other counts during the year, without giving prior notice of intention to do so. This practice not only provides evidence of the cashier's honesty, but also shows whether the work is being performed conscientiously from day to day. The best hours of the day to carry out a count are either in the morning before the mail has been opened or in the evening immediately after the close of business. At these times there is less likelihood of a cashier having available the entity's money, which has not been recorded in the cash records, to make up a deficit of the cash on hand. Also, if the cash is counted while the bank is open, it is impossible to know at what time transactions recorded in the bank statements for that day took place and the balance in the bank at the time of the cash count can never, therefore, be established with certainty. Where the entity employs internal auditors, they may perform periodic surprise cash counts. The external auditor may review the counts and reports of the internal auditor in order to determine whether the work of the internal auditors may be used for purposes of the external audit.

The auditor should proceed to verify the *existence* and *measurement* of the cash balance(s) in the following manner:

- Obtain possession of:
  - the cash;
  - the cash records;
  - all documents pertaining to the receipt of cash (examples of which are forms of cash sale slips and receipts and daily cash summaries) in current use by the cashier;
  - vouchers for cash payments for the day of the cash count and a few days preceding it.

- Retain possession of the items listed above until the following has been done:
  - The cash has been counted and listed.
  - The last sequence numbers of the cash sale slips, receipts and other relevant documents, the originals of which have been issued, have been noted.
  - The cash payments recorded for the day of the cash count and a few days preceding it have been vouched or, if the payments have not yet been recorded, the relevant vouchers have been listed.

- Count the cash on hand and record how much is composed, respectively, of notes and coins. List the amounts of any cheques on hand and the names of the drawers. List the amounts and particulars of any postal orders and any other forms of money on hand. If there are any IOUs, record the relevant particulars. The foregoing should be done in the presence of the cashier, who should be requested to sign the summary of cash on hand as evidence of agreement that it is correct and that all the money has been returned.

- Check the entries in the cash record for the receipt of cash for the day of the cash count and a few days preceding it. Ascertain that all items up to the last consecutive number of each of the documents pertaining to the receipt of cash, already noted, have been recorded in the cash record or, if some have not been recorded, that these are taken into account when reconciling the recorded cash balance with the amount of the count.

- Vouch the cash payments recorded for the day of the count and a few days preceding it to ascertain whether all recorded payments have in fact been made at the date of the count. It is possible for a cashier to make one or more cash payment entries immediately prior to the cash count, without having paid these sums. In this way the recorded cash balance may be manipulated to make it equal to the amount of cash on hand, and immediately after the count the cashier could make the relevant payments.

- Check the additions and the cross-additions of the cash receipts records and cash summary sheets up to the time of the cash count.

- Ascertain whether forms of money other than actual cash (for example, cheques, money orders) included in the cash count are identified with the relevant entries in the cash record, to ensure that the cashier has not included a cheque, for which a receipt has not yet been issued, to make up a deficiency in the cash.

- Ascertain whether forms of money other than actual cash included in the count are deposited soon after the date of the count.

- Obtain (preferably directly from the bank) a bank statement as at the date of the cash count. Reconcile the bank balance shown in the cash record with the balance appearing on the bank statement. This should be done to rule out the possibility of the cashier manipulating the cash and bank balances to conceal a deficiency. An example of this would be to enter in the cash record an amount deposited, but not to make the deposit until after the time of the cash count, thus utilizing the money to make up a deficiency in the cash balance.

- Subsequently scrutinize the bank statement for the period immediately following the deposit of the forms of money mentioned above to ascertain whether all cheques included therein have been paid, or, if not, whether any unpaid cheque is genuine.

Where IOUs, or other written evidence of borrowing, constitute part of the cash on hand, the auditor should raise the matter with an appropriate member of the management and obtain a signature on the statement of cash counted as authority for the sums borrowed and as evidence of the genuineness of the IOUs. The auditor should make every effort to dissuade the management from allowing the practice to continue, as it tends to reduce the efficiency of the control over cash. Further, it cannot be said in such a case that the cash records reflect the facts, for IOUs are evidence of loans, not cash in hand, and should be shown accordingly in the balance sheet.

17.3.10.2 The bank reconciliation

The bank balance in the cash records does not usually agree exactly with the balance shown in the relevant bank statement, chiefly because some of the cheques recorded in the cash record as having been drawn are presented to the bank for payment until after the balancing date. The auditor should expect, therefore, to find that cheques drawn during the last few days of the financial year are outstanding. The auditor should not only be satisfied that all outstanding cheques listed in the bank reconciliation were in fact outstanding at the relevant date, but that there were no further outstanding cheques which have been omitted from the reconciliation to conceal a shortage in the bank balance, as shown by the bank statement. Any such cheque would usually be fairly current, for otherwise the statement of the creditor to whom it was allegedly sent, and who had not received and deposited it, would reflect the difference.

The serial numbers and amounts of outstanding cheques may be ascertained in several ways:

- The first is for the auditor to note the entries in the cash record and in the previous bank reconciliation statement for cheques drawn, which have not been marked as checked onto the bank statement in the current period. It will be appreciated that if the information as to outstanding cheques is to be obtained in this manner, the cash record entries for cheques drawn must be checked with the bank statement. If, therefore, a test only of bank withdrawals is made in such a case, this test should cover the last month of the financial period.

- A second way is to scrutinize the bank statement for the first month or two following the close of the financial period under review and to note all entries for cheques paid which have serial numbers applicable to cheques drawn in the previous period.

- A third method is based on the date stamp of the paying bank, which appears on paid cheques returned to the entity. If, when vouching cheque payments, paid cheques are used as part of the requisite evidence, the auditor may obtain the information as to outstanding cheques by noting the serial numbers and amounts of cheques containing bank-stamp dates subsequent to the end of the financial period under audit. Any cheques appearing as outstanding in the previous bank reconciliation statement should of course also be examined.

Where any cheques have been outstanding for a considerable time, the auditor should ascertain the reason for the delay in presenting these cheques for payment. It may be that a cheque has been lost or inadvertently destroyed. If this is the position, the auditor should ascertain whether another cheque has been issued in its place and, if so, check the adjusting entry to reverse the entry for the issue of the original cheque. In such a case, the bank should have been instructed to stop payment of the original cheque and confirmation from the bank should be inspected. There may be circumstances which make it clear that the fault for the loss lies with the payee, in which case a letter of indemnity in respect of the contingent liability may have been received from the payee. Where cheques have been issued in place of those lost or destroyed, the auditor should ascertain whether letters of indemnity have been received and, if so, inspect these. The auditor should be alert to the possibility that a high incidence of long outstanding, uncleared items in a bank reconciliation may indicate fraud by employees. Where this is encountered, the auditor should extend the audit to review other bank reconciliations during the financial period to identify unusual items and should obtain explanations from management for these.

Where amounts are banked on the day following their receipt, a deposit shown in the cash record as having been made on the last day of the financial year will not actually have been made until the following business day and therefore will appear in the bank statement for the following month. This will cause a difference between the bank balance as shown in the cash record and that shown in the bank statement at the year-end. The amount of such a deposit is, in fact, cash on hand and should be included in a cash count made at the close of the financial period, if indeed a cash count is deemed necessary.

Having regard to the preceding comments, the following is the routine to be observed in checking the bank reconciliation:

- Obtain a Bank Confirmation Certificate[9] directly from the bank. Care should be taken that the certificate is sent by the bank directly to the auditor, as bank certificates sent to the entity to pass on to the auditor may be altered by the cashier or accountant.

- Check the balance as shown on the bank certificate with that shown on the bank statement and also with that shown in the reconciliation.

- Check the bank balance as shown in the cash record with the relevant figure in the bank reconciliation.

- Ascertain whether all sheets of the bank statement are accounted for by checking the amounts carried forward from one sheet to the next.

- Check the reconciliation for the serial numbers and amounts of outstanding cheques.

- Check the reconciliation for the amount of any outstanding deposit.

- Be satisfied from a scrutiny of subsequent bank statements that all cheques outstanding at the close of the period under audit were accounted for in the reconciliation statement. It is not enough to trace the cheques shown as outstanding in the reconciliation statement to subsequent bank statements, for this would not disclose an outstanding cheque which has been deliberately omitted from the reconciliation statement to conceal a shortage of cash.

17.3.10.3 Cash records additions and balances

In a computerized accounting system, individual receipt and payment transactions would normally be recorded to the relevant general ledger accounts, and the situation described below, relating to a manual cash book environment, would not arise. However, it is entirely possible that a small to medium-sized business may still maintain a manual cashbook for capturing summarized details into a computerized ledger, in which case, in the view of the authors, the discussion below will be of use to readers.

The additions of the bank columns of the cash record should be checked to prove the arithmetical accuracy of the bank balance as reflected therein and, where the cash record contains cash columns, the additions of these should

---

[9] The Appendix to SAAPS 1100, 'Bank confirmations', provides an example of a standardized format of bank certificate.

also be checked to prove the arithmetical accuracy of the recorded cash balance.

Where the credit side of the cash record contains analysis columns, they are usually divided broadly into columns for personal account items, for nominal account items and for sundry items. Each entry in the bank column (or cash column, if any) should be accounted for in one of the analysis columns, so that the sum of the totals of all the analysis columns should equal the total of the bank column (or cash and bank columns). Accordingly, the cross-additions should be checked.

As the items in the 'sundries' column are posted individually, it follows that the addition of this column should be checked, to determine whether the total of the amounts posted to the general ledger equals the amount recorded in the bank column (or cash and bank columns, if cash columns are used).

In checking the additions and cross-additions as outlined above and finding them to be correct, it follows that the sum of the totals of all the analysis columns must be correct, but it does not prove that there has not been a transposition between one analysis column and another (or some other compensating error). If such a transposition is between one nominal account column and another, it neither affects the balancing of the trial balance nor the amount of profit. It merely means that one expense account is understated and another overstated and, as a general rule, the auditor is concerned with the net effect and not with the detailed composition of the profit. However, if such a transposition is between a personal account column (accounts payable) and that for a nominal account, both the relevant control account and the profit will be affected. It may be said, therefore, that the auditor should check the additions of either the personal account columns or those of the nominal account columns, whichever may be less onerous, for if the one group of columns is proved correct, the total of the other group must be correct.

Whether or not the additions of the nominal account columns should also be checked depends on the attitude of the auditor. The auditor may consider that one of the main tests is the comparison of income and expense accounts with those of previous years and that reliance cannot be placed on the figures shown in the accounts unless checks are made of the additions of the nominal account columns in the cash record from which much of the information is derived.

What has been said above regarding the credit side of the cash record does not necessarily apply to the debit side, however. If it is the practice of a business to enter receipts initially in the appropriate analysis columns and then to extend the periodic total (usually daily) into the bank or cash column, depending on the ruling of the cash record, it is not a matter of proving that all that has been entered in the bank (or cash) column is accounted for in the analysis columns, but the reverse. It is possible for a cashier to understate the amount of an entry in the bank (or cash) column and then to undercut one of the analysis columns, so that the total of the analysis columns appears to equal the total of the bank (or cash) column, although the latter column total (and the actual deposits) is less than it should be. Accordingly, where the cash record is written up in this way (which must always be the case where the cash records have no cash columns), the additions of all analysis columns on the debit side, as well as the cross-additions, should be checked.

The additions of the discount columns should also be checked to prove that the total of all items of discount debited or credited to the personal accounts have been accounted for in the relevant nominal and control accounts.

The auditor should check the carry forward of the bank balance (and cash balance, if any) to the commencement of the next period.

17.3.10.4 Fixed deposits and term deposits

The auditor should call for the fixed deposit receipt and note that it is in the name of the entity. The auditor should check that the interest recorded as accrued on the deposit is correct, either by checking the calculation. In addition, the auditor requests the client to obtain a bank confirmation, to be sent directly to the auditor, by the relevant bank or building society, confirming the capital amount, investment period and interest earned and accrued at period end for all the fixed deposits or term deposits held by the bank for the entity.

Where the client places surplus funds into term or notice deposits at the bank, such accounts would similarly need to be reconciled and period end balances confirmed with the bankers. Under normal circumstances, the entity would receive a monthly bank statement for all term deposit accounts reflecting the deposits, withdrawals and interest credited.

17.3.10.5 Detection of lapping or kiting

An aspect that remains is the issue of the detection of misappropriation of cash by staff responsible for the maintenance of cash and bank records. Such misappropriations usually arise where there is a lack of segregation of duties, so the employee may have the opportunity of misappropriating cash, and having access to the accounting record, can alter account balances to conceal the theft.

Lapping is usually associated with the misappropriation of receipts in cash, whether from cash sales or receipts from accounts receivable. The employee will remove an amount of cash, say R500, and will substitute a cheque for R500 received from debtor A through the mail to deposit, destroying all evidence relating to the mail receipt and recording the cheque as the cash sale amount stolen. Some days later, the employee may pass a journal entry to credit the debtor's account balance with R500, transferring the amount to debtor B's account, often one that is inactive and won't arouse suspicion. As far as debtor A is concerned, the debt is discharged and the cheque has been paid to the supplier's bank account, so no query will be raised.

Another way of misappropriating monies, referred to as kiting, is where the employee removes the cash, say R1 000, and reflects this as an outstanding deposit on the bank reconciliation. The employee then later draws a cheque to record 'fictitious' expenses for the amount of R1 000. The company cheque is then deposited by the employee in the company bank account and used to clear the outstanding receipt in the bank reconciliation. The total shortage at this stage would be R1 500.

Audit procedures to detect lapping or kiting would be performed when the review of controls over cash and bank revealed the lack of segregation of duties and the auditor had reason to be concerned that circumstances of fraud may exist.

Procedures that would detect such practices include:

- Positive confirmation of accounts receivable performed on a surprise basis at an interim date.

- Surprise cash counts and simultaneous preparation of the bank reconciliations of all bank accounts at an interim period, and detailed comparison of source documents for transactions in that month or period.

- Compare details of daily cash summaries, entries in cash receipt and cash payment records and mail register details with the details of the corresponding bank-stamped deposit slips, in particular, the mix of cash and cheques comprising the deposit and actual dates of receipt by comparison with the bank deposit dates to detect delays in the recording.

- Where the entity's own cheques are deposited in its banking account and reflected as sales, due enquiry should be made as to the reasons for such entries and the relevant expenditure documents should be examined.

17.3.11 Presentation and disclosure

The auditor should inspect the financial statements to determine whether the *presentation and disclosure* of cash and bank accord with GAAP and are properly identified and classified as current assets in the financial statements or, if the balances are bank overdrafts, that these are classified as current liabilities in the financial statements.

In a situation where the entity maintains several bank accounts for different branches or even at different banks, and where bank overdrafts in one account have been set off against bank balances in another account, the auditor must enquire whether a right of set-off exists and determine that the correct classification is achieved. Where the overdraft and balance are in accounts held at different banks, it is unlikely that a right of set-off applies and the gross amounts of each should be classified separately as current assets and current liabilities.

18

The Auditor's Report on Annual Financial Statements

Learning objectives

After studying this chapter you should be able to:

1. Outline the legal prerequisites to audit reporting on financial statements.
2. Describe the basic elements of audit reports on financial statements.
3. Describe the circumstances or matters that could lead to a modification of the audit report that do not affect the audit opinion and how these impact on the report.
4. Describe the circumstances or matters that do affect the audit opinion and how these impact on the report.

18.1 INTRODUCTION

The issue of the audit report is the final stage in the audit of annual financial statements. The auditor of a company is required in terms of section 282 of the Companies Act to report to its members. Details of the matters to be dealt with in the report are set out in section 301 of the Companies Act. The Public Accountants' and Auditors' Act 80 of 1991, in section 20(1), spells out the prerequisites for an unqualified report by an auditor on any financial statements. The requirements of this section are echoed in section 300 of the Companies Act.

Before discussing the detailed form and content of the auditor's report it is as well to remember that the services provided by the professional accountant and auditor cover a wide range and may be conducted both locally and internationally. These services commonly include audits, other assurance engagements, accounting and secretarial services, management consulting services, computer specialist consultations, investment, tax and estate planning advice, mergers, takeovers and public listing of companies, litigation support services, and acting as accounting officer to a close corporation. Some of these activities will require the professional accountant to issue and sign some written report, certificate, statement or document to indicate clearly and concisely the extent of responsibilities assumed, procedures undertaken and the level of assurance users may obtain from the report expressed. It is obvious that any report produced must have some general or specific purpose. The purpose of the document will normally dictate the persons to whom it is addressed.

Three main categories of assurance reports normally issued by registered accountants and auditors have been identified. These are:

- reports issued in connection with the independent audit of the financial statements of any entity, generally referred to as 'The Auditor's Report on Annual Financial Statements';[1]
- reports on special purpose audit engagements;[2] and
- reports on engagements to review financial statements.[3]

The content and presentation requirements for the auditor's standard report on annual financial statements in compliance with the reporting standards are discussed in this chapter, as are the circumstances giving rise to a modification of the standard audit report on financial statements.

The requirements for the other two categories of reports are discussed in the following chapter.

18.2 REPORTING STANDARDS

SAAS 700, 'The auditor's report on financial statements', sets out standards and provides guidance on the form and content of the independent auditor's report on financial statements. Standards and basic principles related thereto are set out in the body of the standard, while appendices to it give numerous examples of the form of audit report that might be appropriate in certain stated circumstances. As the circumstances used for each illustrative report are only briefly stated there is a caution that the examples given should not be used when there is only a superficial relationship between such circumstances and the particular circumstances faced by the auditor.

18.3 PREREQUISITES FOR REPORTING

18.3.1 Legal requirements

A professional accountant may not, without an appropriate qualification, certify or express an opinion in a report to the effect that any account, financial statement (including any annexure thereto), or other document relating to the business or financial affairs of the undertaking presents fairly,

---

[1] SAAS 700.
[2] SAAS 800.
[3] SAAS 910.

or gives a true and fair view of, or reflects correctly the matters dealt with therein[4] unless:

'(a) [the auditor] has carried out the work free of any restrictions whatsoever;

(b) he has obtained all information, vouchers and other documents which in his opinion were necessary for the proper performance of his duties; and

(c) he is satisfied, as far as is reasonably practicable, having regard to the nature of the undertaking in question and of the audit carried out by him, as to the fairness or the truth or the correctness, as the case may be, of such financial statement or annexure'.

This means that both reports on audited financial statements and other special purpose audit reports fall within the ambit of the Public Accountants' and Auditors' Act. The South African Institute of Chartered Accountants has issued a number of Statements and Exposure Drafts over the years in an attempt to attain uniformity in audit reports presented, to identify particular categories of reports and to identify clearly the degree of responsibility of auditors and the level of assurance which may be obtained by users.[5]

18.3.2 General considerations

Before signing the audit report, the audit partner responsible must be satisfied that the audit was conducted with the degree of care and diligence required by South African auditing standards. On completion of the audit, the partner in charge should review the working papers to determine whether or not all work decided upon at the planning stage and subsequently has been done, and whether all questions raised at the various review stages in the audit have been settled satisfactorily. This is commonly referred to as the final or partner review and is a crucial stage of the audit process which will determine the content of the audit report to be issued.

18.4 CONTENT AND PRESENTATION OF THE AUDITOR'S REPORT ON ANNUAL FINANCIAL STATEMENTS

SAAS 700, in appendix II, presents the following as an illustrative example of an audit report for companies without subsidiaries where there has been full compliance with statements of GAAP.

---

[4] Public Accountants' and Auditors' Act 80 of 1991, sections 20(1) and 20(2).
[5] The Auditing Standards Board of the PAAB is now responsible for establishing auditing standards.

'REPORT OF THE INDEPENDENT AUDITOR TO THE MEMBERS OF ...

We have audited the annual financial statements of ... set out on pages ... to ... for the year ended .... These financial statements are the responsibility of the company's directors. Our responsibility is to express an opinion on these financial statements based on our audit.

Scope
We conducted our audit in accordance with statements of South African Auditing Standards. Those standards require that we plan and perform the audit to obtain reasonable assurance that the financial statements are free of material misstatement. An audit includes:

- examining, on a test basis, evidence supporting the amounts and disclosures in the financial statements;

- assessing the accounting principles used and significant estimates made by management; and

- evaluating the overall financial statement presentation.

We believe that our audit provides a reasonable basis for our opinion.

Audit opinion
In our opinion, the financial statements fairly present, in all material respects, the financial position of the company at ... and of the results of its operations and cash flows for the year then ended in accordance with South African Statements of Generally Accepted Accounting Practice, and in the manner required by the Companies Act in South Africa.

Name *Registered Accountants and Auditors*

Chartered Accountants (SA)

Address

Date.'

18.5 BASIC ELEMENTS OF AUDIT REPORTS

The standard unqualified or unmodified audit report contains five basic elements:

- heading;
- opening or introductory paragraph;
- scope paragraph;
- opinion paragraph; and
- identity of the auditor and the date of the report.

18.5.1 **Heading**

This aspect titles the report and identifies the addressee.

Use of the words 'Report of the independent auditor' in the title is important for it distinguishes the report from others that might have been generated by persons within the employ of the entity (for example, management or internal auditors) and which might be seen to lack credibility due to a perceived lack of objectivity.

The auditor's report should be appropriately addressed as required by the circumstances of the engagement. This depends on whether the audited financial statements are required by law or by specific arrangement with the client. Where the client is regulated by law, the specific legislation will normally cover the relationship. For example, in the case of a company, the annual financial statements should be addressed to the members (Companies Act section 282). Where the client is not regulated by law, the engagement letter will set out the reporting relationship.

18.5.2 **Opening or introductory paragraph**

This paragraph identifies the financial statements that have been audited and usually includes a reference to the pages on which these are set out. This is necessary because the annual report issued by a company often includes other information which has not been subjected to audit, for example, the chairman's statement, financial summaries and highlights, and employment data. The paragraph also includes a statement of the respective responsibilities of the entity's management and that of the auditor, this being as follows:[6]

> The 'financial statements are the responsibility of the entity's management'; and

> 'the responsibility of the auditor ... is to express an opinion on the financial statements based on the audit'.

The need for this responsibility statement has arisen as a result of many misunderstandings on the part of both management and users of financial statements as to the respective roles of management and the auditor and their responsibility for information contained in the financial statements.

18.5.3 **Scope paragraph**

It is important both to the auditor and to the reader that the report conveys the scope of the examination. It is important to the auditor because it may be a defence against allegations of negligence concerning the extent of work done. It is important to the users of audit reports because they are informed of the extent of assurance that may be obtained from the report. South African auditors have traditionally considered that, as they have a right to conduct an unrestricted audit in the case of any undertaking governed by

---

[6] SAAS 700, paragraph .09.

statute (most common among these being audits of companies), no explicit statement of the scope of the audit need be included. This changed in 1990 when the revised statement on audit reports was issued and required that an implicit statement of the scope of the audit be set out in the audit report.

With regard to the content of the scope paragraph, SAAS 700[7] states as follows:

> 'The auditor's report should include a section headed "Scope" which describes the scope of the audit by stating that the audit was conducted in accordance with statements of SAAS.'

Further, the report should:

> '... include a statement that the audit was planned and performed to obtain reasonable assurance about whether the financial statements are free of material misstatements',

and should describe the audit as including:

- 'examining, on a test basis, evidence to support the amounts and disclosures in the financial statements;

- assessing the accounting principles used in the preparation of the financial statements;

- assessing the significant estimates made by management in the preparation of the financial statements; and

- evaluating the overall financial statement presentation'.

The scope paragraph should be concluded with 'a statement by the auditor that the audit provides a reasonable basis for the opinion'.[8]

18.5.4 Opinion paragraph

The auditor's report[9]

> '... should clearly indicate the financial reporting framework used to prepare the financial statements (including identifying the country of origin) and state the auditor's opinion that the financial statements fairly present, in all material respects, the entity's financial position, and the results of its operations and cash flows in accordance with that financial reporting framework and, where appropriate, whether the financial statements comply with statutory requirements'.

As discussed in chapter 3 (section 3.2.4), two financial reporting frameworks are recognized in South Africa. One is based on Statements of Generally Accepted Accounting Practice issued by the Accounting Practices Board; the other is based on generally accepted accounting practices, which is uncodified, but has evolved and is accepted as a result of its general usage

---

[7] SAAS 700, paragraphs .12, .13, .14.
[8] SAAS 700, paragraph .15.
[9] SAAS 700, paragraph .17.

over time by a number of companies. The framework based on Statements of GAAP is commonly referred to as big GAAP and that based on practice are referred to as little gaap. The usage of little gaap is allowed by AC 101, 'Presentation of Financial Statements', but only in rare circumstances, and is referred to in appendix II to SAAS 700 as a 'fair presentation override'.

The Companies Act sets out the statutory requirements that must be met by financial statements of limited companies.

An unqualified opinion should be expressed when the auditor concludes that the financial statements are fairly presented, in all material respects. Where this is the case, the opinion paragraph should be headed 'Audit Opinion'. Where the auditor concludes that there are matters that affect the opinion, the auditor should qualify or disclaimer the audit opinion. In these circumstances the opinion paragraph should be headed 'Qualified Audit Opinion', or 'Adverse Audit Opinion', or 'Disclaimer of Audit Opinion'. These aspects are discussed in the next section.

18.5.5 Identity of the auditor and the date of the report

This section requires the auditor to 'date the report as of the completion date of the audit'[10], to 'name a specific location, which is ordinarily the location where the auditor maintains the office that has responsibility for the audit'[11], and to sign 'in the name of the audit firm, or personal name of the auditor'[12] should the auditor be a sole practitioner.

18.6 MODIFIED AUDIT REPORTS

The standard audit report might need to be modified to take account of prevailing circumstances or matters that have been identified by the auditor. These fall into two categories, namely:

- circumstances or matters that do not affect the auditor's opinion; and
- those that do affect the opinion, which is thus referred to as a qualified opinion or a disclaimer of opinion.

18.6.1 Matters that do not affect the opinion

Modification of the standard unqualified audit report as set out in section 18.4 of this chapter may be necessitated by a number of different circumstances. These are as follows:

- drawing attention to matters set out in the financial statement;
- reporting significant uncertainties;
- highlighting a matter regarding a going-concern problem;

---

[10] SAAS 700, paragraph .22.
[11] SAAS 700, paragraph .24.
[12] SAAS 700, paragraph .25.

- reporting on additional statutory responsibilities; and
- drawing attention to unaudited information in a document containing the audited financial statements; and
- drawing attention to the fact that the financial statements have not been drawn up in accordance with South African Statements of GAAP.

The form of modification usually consists of adding an additional paragraph to the audit report, termed an emphasis of matter paragraph, which should be placed below the opinion paragraph in the report. The emphasis paragraph should begin with the words, 'Without qualifying our opinion above, we draw attention to …'.

18.6.1.1 Drawing attention to matters in the financial statements

There may be occasions when the auditor may wish to draw attention to certain important matters disclosed in the financial statements to ensure these are not overlooked. Such emphasis of matter should be restricted to the matters that have been adequately disclosed in the financial statements.[13]

18.6.1.2 Reporting significant uncertainties

Significant uncertainties arise in circumstances where it is not possible for the auditor to reach an objective conclusion about the possible outcome of events which have not yet taken place, with the result that the effect of these on the financial statements cannot be determined with substantial accuracy. It should be noted that if the outcome of future actions or events are under the direct control of management to the entity these would be outside the definition of an uncertainty.[14]

The uncertainty hinges on the outcome of the circumstances themselves rather than on any limitations imposed by the entity which prevent the auditor from performing audit procedures to gather sufficient evidence to form a view on the outcome of the matter. Examples are the pending outcome of major litigation proceedings and the financial outcome of long-term construction contracts in progress, particularly at their earlier stages.

SAAS 700 at paragraph .36 states:

> 'The addition of a paragraph emphasising a … significant uncertainty is ordinarily adequate to meet the auditor's reporting responsibilities regarding such matters.'

In extreme cases, for example, where there are multiple uncertainties affecting the financial statements, a disclaimer of opinion might be preferable to an emphasis of matter paragraph.

---

[13] See example report SAAS 700, paragraph .30, and appendix II paragraph .15.
[14] See example report SAAS 700, paragraph .14.

18.6.1.3 Highlighting a matter regarding a going-concern problem

Where the going-concern ability of an entity is dependent on the as yet unknown successful outcome of some matter (or matters) – for example, negotiations with long-term financiers to extend loan repayment terms and the successful outcome of a rights issue of shares – the matter should be treated by way of an emphasis of matter paragraph in the audit report.[15] However, this would only be the case if the auditor is satisfied that adequate disclosure of the matter(s) has been given in the financial statements and that the successful outcome would result in the entity being a going concern.

18.6.1.4 Reporting on additional statutory responsibilities

For entities regulated by statute, the auditor may be required to provide specific statutory information in the audit report. For example, if, in the case of a private company, with the consent of all shareholders, the auditor has provided secretarial or bookkeeping services, this fact must be stated in the report.[16] Further, in terms of section 297 of the Companies Act, if inadequate disclosure of directors' emoluments as required by the section has been given, the auditor must provide the necessary disclosure.

For entities regulated by statute, the auditor may also be required to report on non-compliance by the entity with any statutory requirements. Examples are the failure of a company to maintain certain registers (directors' and officers' interest in contracts, and a fixed asset register), or failure to hold an annual general meeting as required by the Companies Act. The auditor is required to report on non-compliance irrespective of the fact that such non-compliance is unlikely to distort fair presentation of the financial statements.

18.6.1.5 Drawing attention to unaudited information in a document containing audited financial statements

Under this heading there are two possibilities, the first being unaudited supplementary schedules (such as a detailed income statement, taxation schedules and supplementary current cost income statements). In these circumstances, the auditor should add an additional paragraph to the audit report referring to the supplementary schedules and disclaiming an opinion on them. This may be worded as follows:[17]

> 'The supplementary schedules set out on pages ... to ..., do not form part of the annual financial statements and are presented as additional information. We have not audited these schedules and accordingly we do not express an opinion on them.'

The second possibility is where, as is often the case, other information besides the audited financial statements is included in the group report. Should the auditor conclude that aspects of that other information are

---

[15] See example report SAAS 570, appendix II, paragraph .02.
[16] See example report SAAS 700, paragraph .11.
[17] SAAS 700, appendix II, paragraph .10.

misstated and the client refuses to alter such other information, the auditor should include an emphasis of matter paragraph describing the misstatement.

18.6.1.6 Drawing attention to the fact that the financial statements have not been drawn up in accordance with South African Statements of GAAP

As already mentioned, there are two acceptable accounting frameworks for the preparation of financial statements in South Africa. Should the client opt to deviate from compliance with South African Statements of GAAP (big GAAP) and use instead generally accepted accounting practice (little gaap) as the bases for preparing financial statements in the interest of better achieving fair presentation, the auditor needs to:

- 'consider whether or not the decision to deviate from the requirements of statements of GAAP is justified; and

- establish that adequate disclosure has been given in the financial statements of the deviation, the reasons therefore and the effect on the financial statements of such deviation.'

Given that the auditor is satisfied with the above two matters, the emphasis of matter paragraph in the audit report should draw attention to the deviation and the note in the financial statements setting out the deviation, the reason therefore and its financial effect.

18.6.2 Matters that do affect the opinion

Experience and professional judgement are required of the auditor when evaluating audit evidence gathered and concluding on the fair presentation of the financial statements. The auditor should consider the sufficiency of the evidence gathered in support of management's assertions underlying the financial statements. The auditor must also evaluate the differences between the amounts included in the financial statements and amounts supported by audit evidence gathered by the application of substantive audit procedures. These differences are referred to as misstatements and arise from misstatements of fact, the misapplication of accounting practices, or unreasonable accounting estimates.

The auditor should be mindful of the fact that the risk of material misstatement is generally greater when amounts include accounting estimates rather than factual data. The difference between the estimated amounts recorded and the amount supported by audit evidence should be considered as misstatements. While the audit differences arising from accounting estimates may be individually insignificant, it might well be that they exhibit a trend that might indicate management's desire to achieve a desired level of disclosed earnings. If some evidence of management bias becomes apparent, the auditor should reconsider the estimates taken as a whole. In these circumstances, management's representations should be treated with professional scepticism and it might well be necessary to perform other substantive procedures to gather and consider evidence from sources independent of management to arrive at a final conclusion.

When evaluating the effect of misstatements, the auditor should consider unadjusted misstatements of prior accounting periods where these misstatements also affect the financial information under review. These prior period misstatements should be aggregated with misstatements identified during the current audit when deciding whether or not the financial statements are materially misstated.

As the identified aggregate of uncorrected misstatements approaches the materiality level set by the auditor, consideration needs be given to the risk that unidentified misstatements, if added to those identified, might exceed materiality. In the circumstances, the auditor should consider reducing audit risk by performing additional procedures so as to project more accurately the likely total error.

Thus far the emphasis has been on the quantitative aspect of materiality and the need for the auditor to quantify planning materiality in order to appropriately plan the nature, timing and extent of audit procedures so as to detect, if any, material misstatement in financial statements. At the conclusion stage of the audit, however, when considering likely misstatements or omissions in the financial statements and how these impact on overall fair presentation, the auditor needs also to consider the qualitative aspects of materiality. Qualitative aspects of materiality relate to the nature of items rather than solely their monetary effect on the financial statements. Misstatements or omissions in financial statements may thus be viewed by the auditor as being quantitatively immaterial, but because of their nature to be qualitatively material.

Examples of circumstances that might be considered as quantitatively immaterial but qualitatively so are:

- inappropriate description of accounting policies used in the preparation of financial statements;

- failure to disclose breaches of statutes, regulations or other known irregularities, the financial consequences of which are not quantitatively material; and

- misstatements which are quantitatively immaterial but if corrected would result in reported profits reflected as losses, or would reflect a contravention of loan agreement covenants. For example, loans might require to be immediately repaid where current liabilities exceed a particular proportion of current assets.

Should the auditor conclude, based on the evidence gathered, that the financial statements are materially misstated, management should be requested to make appropriate adjustments. Should management refuse to do so, a qualification of audit opinion is necessary. Should misstatements not materially affect the fair presentation of financial statements, however, the auditor need merely bring to management's attention the misstatements that have been identified.

18.6.2.1 Forms of qualification

Based on the audit evidence gathered and the auditor's judgement, the auditor may conclude that modification of the audit opinion is necessary. A qualified audit opinion results from two categories of circumstances, namely:

- limitation on the scope of the auditor's work; or
- disagreement with management regarding the acceptability of the accounting policies used and/or their application or the adequacy of disclosures in the financial statements.

The form of qualification which should be used in the particular circumstances, is set out in the following matrix:

CIRCUMSTANCES	MATERIAL BUT NOT PERVASIVE	MATERIAL AND PERVASIVE AND/OR FUNDAMENTAL
SCOPE LIMITATION	QUALIFIED OPINION	DISCLAIMER OF OPINION
DISAGREEMENT	QUALIFIED OPINION	ADVERSE OPINION

Material but not pervasive

In deciding on whether or not a qualification is needed, the auditor must consider the materiality of the matter in the context of the financial statement disclosures. In general terms, the matter should be regarded as material if knowledge of it could influence the economic decisions of users taken on the basis of the financial statements. Materiality may be considered in the context of the financial statements as a whole, or in the context of individual elements, such as the balance sheet, income statement, cash flow statement or individual items in the financial statements.

A qualified opinion should only be given where the aggregate of uncorrected misstatements is material to fair presentation of the financial statements.

Material and pervasive and/or fundamental

Having decided that a qualification is necessary on the grounds of material uncorrected misstatement or the possibility of such, the auditor needs to consider whether or not such misstatement is pervasive and/or fundamental to fair presentation of the financial statements – this because the form of qualification changes where the effect of misstatement on the financial statements is more than material to fair presentation. If this is the case as a result of a scope limitation, a disclaimer of opinion is required; if it is as a result of disagreement, an adverse opinion should be expressed.

SAAS 700 does not define the term 'pervasive and/or fundamental', and it does not give guidance on interpreting when uncorrected misstatement, or possible misstatement, might be considered to be both material and pervasive and/or fundamental. This having been said, two example reports given in appendix II of SAAS 700 confuse the issue. Reports .22 and .29 are example reports in circumstances of disagreement being considered to be material and pervasive and/or fundamental, leading to an adverse opinion. In the opinion of the authors the circumstances given would not be considered material and pervasive and/or fundamental to the financial statements. Example report .22 is as a result of goodwill no longer being justified at the balance sheet amount, and example .29 the use of an inappropriate accounting policy being a failure to value inventory at the lower of cost or net realizable value.

The authors' view is based on the dictionary definition of 'pervasive', namely: '(adjective) able to pervade, and pervade (verb) to spread or be present throughout, to permeate'. An overstatement of goodwill in the first instance, and a possible overstatement of inventory in the second, leading to overstatement of one asset in the balance sheet in both instances, and a possible overstatement of operating profits in the second, are not pervasive according to the definition of the word.

Statement AU 321, which was replaced by SAAS 700, used the word 'fundamental' as opposed to 'pervasive and/or fundamental', provided the following guidance on when to disclaim an opinion or give an adverse opinion:

* A scope limitation becomes material and fundamental when its potential impact on the financial statements is so great that the financial statements as a whole could be misleading.

* A disagreement becomes material and pervasive when its impact on the financial statements is so great that fair presentation as a whole has been undermined or the financial statements have been rendered meaningless or misleading.

This guidance should assist auditors in deciding which form of modified report is appropriate so as to conform with the requirements of SAAS 700.

18.6.2.2 Scope limitations[18]

A scope limitation arises if the auditor is unable to obtain all the information and explanations considered necessary for the purpose of the audit. The imposition of a scope limitation by the client in the case of a statutory audit is unacceptable. However, conditions may exist which prevent the auditor applying normal auditing procedures, for example, the destruction of the accounting records as the result of a fire, or difficulty in verifying that all donations received by a welfare organization have been recorded. In these

---

[18] SAAS 700, paragraphs .42 and .43.

circumstances, alternative procedures to those normally used should be considered in an attempt to obtain sufficient evidence.

For example, the auditor might not have attended the client's year-end inventory count, possibly because at that time the auditor had not as yet been appointed. In the circumstances, appropriate alternative audit procedures to obtain evidence of inventory quantities on hand at the year end might be to conduct test counts subsequent to the year end, and after appointment, and reconciling this count with the year end quantities by way of checking movements of inventory out (sales) and those coming in (purchases). This approach is only likely to provide satisfactory evidence of quantities at the year end if reliance can be placed on the systems of control over movements of inventory and the accurate recording thereof in the accounting records.

In the case of non-statutory engagements or engagements to provide related services, the auditor may accept a limitation of scope. Limitations are usually imposed by the client and agreed to by the auditor; for example, the auditor is requested to audit and report on cash aspects of the business only, or at the client's request conducts certain specified audit procedures. These situations give rise to different categories of reports and may apply, *inter alia*, in the audit of partnerships, close corporations, and engagements to audit specific elements of the financial statements, report on information prepared in accordance with specific contract terms or report on profit forecasts. Reports flowing from these categories of engagements are dealt with in the next chapter.

Effect on the audit report

Where a scope limitation results in the auditor being unable to carry out the audit in accordance with generally accepted auditing standards, the audit report should be qualified by a qualification paragraph immediately preceding the opinion paragraph, setting out clearly the nature of the circumstances giving rise to the conditions which prevented the application of normal auditing procedures, and quantifying, if this is possible, the potential impact on the financial statements.

In this event the auditor will have to exercise professional judgement to determine the appropriate form of qualification to be expressed in the audit report. If the scope restriction has a material impact on the financial statements, the audit report might be modified as follows.

'REPORT OF THE INDEPENDENT AUDITORS TO THE MEMBERS OF ...

Qualification
The company did not carry out a physical inventory of its raw material inventory stated in the financial statements at R... The company's records did not permit the application of adequate alternative auditing procedures regarding this inventory. Consequently, we did not obtain all the

information and explanations we considered necessary to satisfy ourselves as to the existence and valuation of raw material inventory.

Qualified audit opinion
In our opinion, except for the effect on the financial statements of the matter referred to in the preceding paragraph, the financial statements fairly present, in all material respects, the financial position of the company at ... and the results of its operations and cash flows for the year then ended in accordance with South African Statements of Generally Accepted Accounting Practice, and in the manner required by the Companies Act in South Africa.'

Example: *Standard auditor's report qualified: Scope limitation:* no count of raw material (considered to be material, but not fundamental). Appendix II to SAAS 700, paragraph .18.

On the other hand, if the scope restriction is regarded as being so significant that the financial statements might be rendered completely misleading, the auditor should include a qualification paragraph setting out clearly the circumstances and implications of the scope restriction and issue a disclaimer opinion paragraph. This is to conform with the requirement of SAAS 700 paragraph .39, which reads as follows:

'A disclaimer of opinion should be expressed when the possible effect of a limitation of scope is so material and pervasive and/or fundamental that the auditor has not been able to obtain sufficient appropriate audit evidence and accordingly is unable to express an opinion on the financial statements.'

In this situation an appropriate audit report might read as follows:

'REPORT OF THE INDEPENDENT AUDITOR TO THE MEMBERS OF ...

Qualification
As stated note ... to the financial statements, a fire at the company's computer centre destroyed many of the accounting records. In these circumstances, we were unable to carry out all the auditing procedures, or to obtain all the information and explanations we considered necessary, or to satisfy ourselves that proper accounting records have been kept.

Disclaimer of audit opinion
Because of the significance of the matters discussed in the preceding paragraph, we do not express an opinion on the financial statements.'

Example: *Limitation of scope – disclaimer:* accounting breakdown (considered to be pervasive and/or fundamental). Appendix II to SAAS 700, paragraph .24.

18.6.2.3 **Disagreements**

The auditor and management may disagree on the presentation of information in the financial statements.

Nature of disagreement

A disagreement may arise as the result of:

- a departure from the requirements of a statement of GAAP where big GAAP is the adopted and disclosed accounting framework;[19]
- the adoption of little gaap as the basis of preparation of financial statement which in the opinion of the auditor is not appropriate to the circumstances of the entity;[20]
- the adoption of little gaap as the basis of preparation of financial statement with which the auditor concurs, but where appropriate disclosure of departure from statements of GAAP is not given in the financial statements;[21]
- disagreement as to facts or amounts included in the financial statements;
- disagreement as to the manner and extent of disclosure of facts or amounts in the financial statements; and
- failure to comply with relevant legislation or other requirements resulting in fair presentation not being achieved.

Effect on audit report

In the event of any disagreement having a material impact on the financial statements, the auditor will have to qualify the audit opinion. A qualification paragraph which clearly and concisely describes the circumstances and implications on the financial statements of the disagreement should precede the qualified opinion paragraph. In these circumstances the audit report might read as follows:

'Qualification

As stated in note X to the financial statements, the company has not recognized a deferred tax liability. In accordance with the South African Statement on Income Taxes, AC 102, a deferred tax liability should be recognized for all taxable temporary differences, unless otherwise stated in that Statement. Had this been done, a liability for deferred tax would have been stated in the balance sheet at R... and the accumulated profits would have been reduced accordingly. Net profit and earnings per share would have been reduced by R... and ... cents per share, respectively.

---

[19] See example report SAAS 700, appendix II paragraphs .19 and .20.
[20] See example report SAAS 700, appendix II paragraphs .28 and .29.
[21] See example report SAAS 700, appendix II paragraph .27.

Qualified audit opinion
In our opinion, except for the effect on the financial statements of the matter referred to in the preceding paragraph, the financial statements fairly present, in all material respects, the financial position of the company at ... and the results of its operations and cash flows for the year then ended in accordance with South African Statements of Generally Accepted Accounting Practice, and in the manner required by the Companies Act in South Africa.'

Example: *Disagreement – inappropriate policy* (considered to be material, but not pervasive). Appendix II to SAAS 700, paragraph .19.

On the other hand, if the disagreement is regarded as being pervasive and / or fundamental, that is to say, so significant that the financial statements are completely misleading, the auditor should add a qualification paragraph which clearly explains the circumstances and implications for the financial statements and give an adverse opinion. The standard wording of an adverse opinion reads as follows:

'Adverse audit opinion
In our opinion, because of the effect on the financial statements of the matter referred to in the preceding paragraph, the financial statements do not fairly present, in all material respects, the financial position of the company and the group at ... and of the results of their operations and cash flows for the year then ended in accordance with South African Statements of Generally Accepted Accounting Practice, and in the manner required by the Companies Act in South Africa.'

Example: *Opinion paragraph: Disagreement:* adverse opinion. Appendix II to SAAS 700, paragraph .22.

18.6.2.4 Procedures to be followed prior to the issue of a qualified opinion

The auditor must have a sound reason for qualifying the audit opinion. In the case of a scope limitation, the auditor should attempt to carry out reasonable alternative procedures to obtain sufficient evidence to support an unqualified opinion. In both scope limitations and disagreements, the auditor should discuss the matter with management to give management the opportunity to provide further evidence which may obviate the need for qualification. Where there is material disagreement, management should be requested to adjust the financial statements. Adequate adjustment would remove the need for a qualified opinion.

In the particular circumstances, if the auditor still considers that modification of the audit opinion is necessary, careful consideration is required as to what type of qualified opinion should be expressed. This decision will be determined by whether the potential impact of the matter on the financial statements is material, or material and pervasive and/or fundamental.

18.6.2.5 **Dating the report**

'The auditor should date the report as of the completion date of the audit. Since the auditor's responsibility is to report on the financial statements as prepared and presented by management, the auditor should not date the report earlier than the date on which the financial statements are signed and approved by management.'[22]

If the auditor were to delay the dating for some time after completing the audit, some further fact or circumstance may have arisen in the intervening period which ought to have been taken into consideration in deciding whether the financial statements subject to audit were fairly presented. The auditor is, of course, reporting on the financial statements of the client and, accordingly, the report should not be dated prior to the date of their approval by the directors or management.

The Companies Act (section 298) requires the financial statements to be approved by the directors and signed on their behalf, but no provision is made in this section for the financial statements to be dated. Again, section 299 requires a directors' report but says nothing about dating it. However, the Fourth Schedule [paragraph 60(2)] requires the directors to deal with any material fact or circumstance between the balance sheet date and the date of their report. It follows that, as the auditor has a responsibility to report on the directors' report [sections 286(2) and 300(j)], the date of the auditor's report should not be earlier than the date of approval shown on the directors' report.

The Public Accountants' and Auditors' Act [section 20(4)] requires an accountant or auditor to issue the report within a period of four months after the date on which the assignment was completed. The Companies Act (section 179) requires a company to hold its annual general meeting, at which its audited financial statements must be tabled, not more than nine months after its financial year-end unless an extension of time, usually not more than three months later, has been granted.

18.7 OTHER REPORTING RESPONSIBILITIES

There are several specific circumstances which may affect the content of the auditor's report on annual financial statements. Those most commonly encountered and the implications for the auditor, both in terms of specific additional procedures which may have to be carried out and their impact on the wording of the audit report, are discussed below.

---

[22] SAAS 700, paragraphs .22 and .23.

18.7.1 Other information in documents containing audited financial statements

18.7.1.1 Circumstances

Entities often publish other information in the same document as their audited financial statements, or publish such information in a separate document which is issued with and intended to be read with the audited financial statements. Typical examples for public companies include management's reports on the entity's internal control systems and its going-concern ability as required by King II (see chapter 21), management's operational reports, the chairman's statement, employee reporting information, the financial ratios, and highlights. In the case of small private companies, various detailed schedules in support of the client's tax return are frequently bound in with the audited annual financial statements. In the absence of a request by the client, the auditor does not express an opinion on such other information and accordingly has no responsibility to perform audit procedures on such other information.[23]

18.7.1.2 Impact on auditing procedures

Where other information is published with the audited financial statements, the auditor must be given timeous access to the information prior to publication so that it may be reviewed to determine that it is not materially inconsistent with the audited financial statements, nor contains a possible misstatement of fact. In the event of an inconsistency, the auditor should determine whether the audited financial statements or the other information requires revision and should advise the client accordingly.

If a revision to the audited financial statements is required and the client refuses to make such revision, the auditor will have to consider which form of modification of the audit opinion is appropriate. If the revision is necessary to the other information and the client refuses, the auditor should consider including an emphasis of matter paragraph in the report, describing the inconsistency, or else withholding the report on the financial statements.

If there is a possible misstatement of fact, it must be discussed with the client. If the auditor concludes that there exists a misstatement of fact which could affect the judgement of a reader relying on the information and which the client refuses to correct, the auditor should consider reporting the matter as a material irregularity in terms of section 20(5) of the Public Accountants' and Auditors' Act and whether or not legal advice is necessary to assist in resolving the matter.

18.7.1.3 Effect on audit report

If the auditor is prepared to accept responsibility for reporting on supplementary schedules or information such as that referred to above,

---

[23] SAAS 720, 'Other Information in Documents Containing Audited Financial Statements'.

this falls into the category of additional work and should be subjected to normal auditing procedures to enable the auditor to express an opinion on them. The audit report should clearly include a reference to these schedules or information.

If, however, the auditor is not prepared to accept responsibility for supplementary information, there are two possible courses available, viz.:

- to persuade the client not to attach the schedules or include the additional information in the document with the annual financial statements; or
- to include in the audit report a paragraph, following after the opinion paragraph, which states that no opinion is expressed on the schedules or additional information. This could be worded as follows:

> **Supplementary information**
> 'The supplementary schedules set out on pages ... to ... do not form part of the annual financial statements and are presented as additional information. We have not audited these schedules and accordingly we do not express an opinion on them.'
>
> Example: *Standard unqualified auditor's report for a company without subsidiaries where unaudited supplementary schedules are bound in with the financial statements.* Appendix II to SAAS 700, paragraph .10.

18.7.2 Events discovered after the issue of the audit report

18.7.2.1 Circumstances

The auditor has a responsibility to review clients' records to identify any material events which might have occurred between the date of the balance sheet and the date on which the financial statements are approved for issue,[24] to identify items which require adjustment or disclosure in the financial statements. However, the auditor has no responsibility, after the date of the audit report, to perform further procedures to identify such subsequent events. There have been occasions in the past (and there are likely to be similar occasions in the future) where an auditor became aware of additional facts affecting the financial statements, which existed but were not known at the time. If faced with this situation, the auditor should investigate the facts completely to ascertain whether or not the financial statements previously reported on are materially misstated. The auditor will need to discuss the matter with management and consider, in the particular circumstances, what action is necessary.

18.7.2.2 Action to be taken by the auditor

Should there be a delay between the dating of the audit report and the issuing of the financial statements, management has the responsibility to

---

[24] AC 107; SAAS 560, 'Subsequent Events'.

inform the auditor of facts that may materially affect the financial statements. If the financial statements are amended to take account of a subsequent event, the auditor should issue a new report which should be dated on its date of issue. In these circumstances, the usual enquiries and procedures aimed at identifying subsequent events should be performed to cover the period from the date of the first to the date of the subsequent report. When management does not amend the financial statements in circumstances where the auditor believes amendment is necessary, the auditor should withdraw the initial audit report and express a qualified or an adverse opinion in the revised audit report.

If the financial statements have already been issued, management may decide to recall the original financial statements. The auditor will have to carry out appropriate auditing procedures required to report on the revised financial statements. This audit report should have a new date and indicate the reason for the revision in an emphasis of matter paragraph. The auditor would also need to review the adequacy of the procedures adopted by management to withdraw the originally issued financial statements.

If management refuses to revise the financial statements or to take adequate steps to inform users of the defect, the auditor should notify management of the proposed action to prevent further reliance on the report. This might include a public announcement in the press and/or the auditor exercising the right to be heard at the annual general meeting. The auditor should seriously consider taking legal opinion on the wording of any public announcement.

If the auditor concludes that the financial statements previously issued are materially misstated and that the audit opinion given thereon was therefore incorrect, the auditor should take action to ensure that all users are advised that the audit report has been withdrawn and thus cannot be relied upon.

Where the financial statements for the subsequent financial year are due to be circulated within a short period, it may be impracticable to issue revised statements or to inform shareholders or third parties. In this case a clear statement of the facts will have to accompany the financial statements for the subsequent year.

18.7.3 Going-concern issues

18.7.3.1 Introduction

In terms of AC 101, 'Presentation of Financial Statements', financial statements should be prepared on a going-concern basis unless management either intends to liquidate the enterprise or to cease trading, or has no realistic alternative but to do so. AC 101 paragraph .24 requires management, when preparing financial statements, to make an assessment of an enterprise's ability to continue as a going concern. Should management conclude that an enterprise is a going concern, but there are material uncertainties related to events or conditions that may cast significant doubt upon the enterprise's ability to continue as a going concern, those uncertainties should be disclosed.

The auditor's responsibility is to consider the appropriateness of management's use of the going-concern assumption in the preparation of the financial statements, and to consider whether there are material uncertainties about the entity's ability to continue as a going concern that need to be disclosed in the financial statements (SAAS 570, paragraph .07). If the auditor concludes that the going-concern basis has been inappropriately applied or there are material uncertainties faced, modification of the audit report is necessary.

18.7.3.2 Effect on the audit report

Appendix II to SAAS 570, 'Going Concern', gives three examples of auditors' reports where consideration is given to a going-concern problem. They cover the range of possibilities, namely:

- adequate disclosure in the financial statements of the going-concern problem and the uncertainties related thereto, leading to an unqualified audit opinion with an emphasis of matter paragraph;
- inadequate disclosure of the going-concern problem and related uncertainties, leading to disagreement and a qualified audit opinion; and
- disagreement where the effect of the going-concern problem on the financial statements is material and pervasive and/or fundamental leading to an adverse opinion.

Much has been written about the self-fulfilling prophecy of 'going-concern' related qualifications of audit reports, the argument being that should the auditor qualify where uncertainties exist, this will surely lead to the appointment of a judicial manager or liquidator. Reported research by R J Taffler and M Tseung (*The Accountant's Magazine*, July 1984) revealed that this is not necessarily the case, in that out of a group of 86 public companies which were liquidated, only 24% had a going-concern qualification in their last financial statements prior to failing. A more disturbing finding was that only 20% of companies whose financial statements carried a going-concern qualification were subsequently declared bankrupt.

The auditor should not refrain from issuing a modified report on the grounds that this may lead to the demise of the entity.

18.7.4 The audit report when a material irregularity exists

18.7.4.1 Nature of circumstances

The auditor may have reported a material irregularity to the company in terms of Section 20(5) under the Public Accountants' and Auditors' Act which, at the date of the audit report on the financial statements, has not been resolved. Section 20(1)(g) of the Act places a further statutory duty on the auditor, namely that an unqualified report may not be issued, unless, *inter alia*, 'any material irregularity which had been reported to the person in charge of that undertaking had been adjusted to his satisfaction'.

It appears that section 20(1)(g) must be read in conjunction with section 20(5)(b). To satisfy the auditor that the material irregularity has been resolved, management must, within 30 days, satisfy the auditor:

- 'that no such irregularity has taken place or is taking place; or

- that adequate steps have been taken for the recovery of any such loss caused; or

- that adequate steps have been taken for the prevention of any such loss likely to be caused.'

If management fails to satisfy the auditor within 30 days, the auditor is required to report the matter to the Public Accountants' and Auditors' Board, which will take appropriate action depending on the circumstances of each case. This may include reporting the matter, amongst others, to the Attorney-General or any other officer in the public service.

It is not clear whether the auditor's duty to qualify the audit report on the financial statements comes to an end immediately after a material irregularity has been adjusted in one of the three ways mentioned above or has been reported to the Board. If the report to the Board does not bring the auditor's duty concerning material irregularities to an end and is not interpreted as satisfying the requirement of being 'adjusted to his satisfaction', then the onus will be on the auditor to be kept informed on a regular basis as to the ultimate outcome of the material irregularity, as the qualification to the audit report will have to be perpetuated until the matter has 'been adjusted to the auditor's satisfaction'. The authors believe that once the material irregularity has been reported to the Board, the obligation to qualify the report in terms of section 20(1)(g) is removed.

18.7.4.2 Effect on audit report

The form of qualification which should be expressed in the audit report will depend on the auditor's assessment of the nature and materiality of the irregularity in relation to the financial statements being reported on, as well as whether the matter constitutes an uncertainty about or disagreement with disclosure in the financial statements. Depending on the situation, any one of the qualifications envisaged in this chapter could be relevant. It may also be that this responsibility could be discharged by adding an information paragraph, following after the opinion paragraph, as an 'emphasis of matter'. This is because, in the particular circumstances, it might be that the material irregularity and its ultimate resolution might not distort fair presentation of the financial statements.

18.7.5 Corresponding figures

18.7.5.1 Background

Corresponding figures are amounts and other disclosures for the preceding period which are included as part of the current period financial statements, and which are intended to be read in relation to the amounts and other disclosures relating to the current period (referred to as 'current period figures'). These corresponding figures are not presented as complete financial statements capable of standing alone, but are an integral part of the current period financial statements, intended to be read only in relation to the current period figures.[25]

The South African audit reporting framework does not require the auditor to report on the corresponding figures which are required by the South African financial reporting framework. Notwithstanding this fact, SAAS 710, 'Comparatives', requires that 'the auditor should obtain sufficient appropriate audit evidence that the corresponding figures meet the requirements of the financial framework'.[26] This requires that the auditor do no more than ensure that the accounting policies used for the corresponding figures are the same as used for the current period financial statements and that the corresponding figure amounts agree with the previous period financial statements. In the event of a change in accounting policies between the current and the prior period, the auditor would need to be satisfied that appropriate adjustment and disclosures have been made in terms of statement AC 103.

While performing the current audit, the auditor may become aware of the possibility of material misstatement in the prior period financial statements. In these circumstances the auditor should perform additional procedures to confirm whether or not this is so.

18.7.5.2 Effect on the audit report

The auditor's report ordinarily makes no reference to the corresponding figures presented in the financial statements, because the auditor's opinion is on the current period financial statements.

There are, however, two possible circumstances where the auditor needs make specific reference to corresponding figures in the audit report. These are:

'When the auditor's report on the prior period, as previously issued, included a qualified opinion, disclaimer of opinion, or adverse opinion and the matter which gave rise to the modification is:

* unresolved, and results in a modification of the auditor's report regarding the current period figures, the auditor's report should also be modified regarding the corresponding figures; or

---

[25] SAAS 710, paragraph .03.
[26] SAAS 710, paragraph .06.

• unresolved, but does not result in a modification of the auditor's report on the current period figures, the auditor's report should be modified regarding the corresponding figures.'[27]

Appendix II to SAAS 710 gives example reports which are appropriate to each of these situations. The qualification and opinion paragraphs of these are stated as follows.

Where the prior period matter is unresolved and it affects the current financial statements

> **'Qualification**
> As discussed in note ... to the financial statements, no depreciation has been provided in the financial statements, which practice, in our opinion, is not in accordance with AC 123, 'Plant, Property and Equipment'. This is the result of a decision taken by management at the start of the preceding financial year and caused us to qualify our audit opinion on the financial statements relating to that year. Based on the straight-line method of depreciation and annual rates of 5% for the building and 20% for the equipment, the loss for the year should be increased by R... in 20X1 and R... in 20X0, the fixed assets should be reduced by accumulated depreciation of R... in 20X1 and R... in 20X0, and the accumulated loss should be increased by R... in 20X1 and R... in 20X0.
>
> **Qualified audit opinion**
> In our opinion, except for the effect of not providing for depreciation as referred to in the preceding paragraph, the financial statements fairly present, in all material respects, the financial position of the company at ..., and of the results of its operations and cash flows for the year then ended in accordance with South African Statements of Generally Accepted Accounting Practice and in the manner required by the Companies Act in South Africa.'

Where the prior period matter is unresolved, but there is no impact on the current financial statements

> **'Qualification**
> Because we were appointed auditors of the company during 19X0, we were not able to observe the counting of the physical inventories at the beginning of that period or satisfy ourselves concerning those inventory quantities by alternative means. Since opening inventories enter into the determination of the results of operations, we were unable to determine whether adjustments to the results of operations and opening retained earnings might be necessary for 20X1. Our audit report on the financial statements for the period ended 31 December 20X0 was modified accordingly.

---

[27] SAAS 710, paragraph .12.

Qualified audit opinion
In our opinion, except for the effect on the corresponding figures for 20X0 of the adjustments, if any, to the results of operations for the period ended 20X0, we might have determined to be necessary had we been able to observe beginning inventory quantities as at 1 January 20X0, the financial statements fairly present, in all material respects, the financial position of the company at 31 December 20X1 and of the results of its operations and cash flows for the year then ended in accordance with South African Statements of Generally Accepted Accounting Practice and in the manner required by the Companies Act in South Africa'.

Should the auditor have issued an unmodified audit opinion on the prior period financial statements but, during the current audit, becomes aware of material misstatement therein, the auditor should consider the guidance in SAAS 560, 'Subsequent Events', and:

- if the prior period's financial statements have been revised and reissued with a new auditor's report, the auditor should be satisfied that the corresponding figures agree with the revised financial statements, or
- if the prior period's financial statements have not been revised and reissued, and the corresponding figures have not been properly restated and / or appropriate disclosures have not been made, the auditor should issue a modified report on the current period's financial statements modified with respect to the corresponding figures included therein'.[28]

If the prior period's financial statements have not been reissued, but the corresponding figures in the current year's financial statements have been appropriately adjusted and / or appropriate disclosure given, 'the auditor may include an emphasis of matter paragraph describing the circumstances and referring to the appropriate disclosures'.[29]

When an auditor is reporting on an entity's financial statements for the first time, no reference should be made to the fact that the corresponding figures were audited by another auditor. If, however, the prior period financial statements were not audited, the auditor should make reference in the report to the fact that the corresponding figures are unaudited.[30] This, however, would not justify the auditor failing to perform appropriate procedures regarding opening balances of the current period. Should the newly appointed auditor identify 'that corresponding figures are materially misstated, the auditor should request management to revise the corresponding figures or, if management refuses to do so, appropriately modify the report'.[31]

---

[28] SAAS 710, paragraph .15.
[29] SAAS 710, paragraph .16.
[30] SAAS 710, paragraphs .17 and .18.
[31] SAAS 710, paragraph .19.

18.7.6 Communication with those charged with corporate governance

During the course of an audit facts or circumstances may come to the attention of the auditor; these should be reported to those charged with corporate governance so as to assist them in better fulfilling their corporate governance responsibilities. Those charged with corporate governance include the board of directors, senior management and the audit committee or others. In deciding on whom to report to, the auditor would need to consider the corporate governance structure of the company. If the company has an audit committee, corporate governance issues of audit significance would ordinarily be reported to it.

SAAS 730, 'Communication of Audit Matters with those charged with Governance', identifies at paragraph 12 matters that should be ordinarily communicated, as follows:

- 'the selection of, or changes in, significant accounting policies and practices that have, or could have, a material effect on the entity's financial statements,

- the potential effect on the financial statements of any significant risks and exposures, such as pending litigation, that are required to be disclosed in the financial statements,

- audit adjustments whether or not recorded by the entity that have, or could have, a significant effect on the entity's financial statements,

- material uncertainties related to events and conditions that may cast significant doubt on the entity's ability to continue as a going concern,

- disagreements with management about matters that, individually or in aggregate, could be significant to the entity's financial statements or the auditor's report. These communications include consideration of whether the matter has, or has not, been resolved and the significance of the matter,

- expected modifications to the auditor's report,

- other matters, warranting attention by those charged with governance, such as material weaknesses in internal control, questions regarding management integrity, and fraud involving management, and

- any other matters agreed upon in the terms of the audit engagement.'

The auditor should clearly indicate in making such communication that an audit of financial statements is not designed to identify all matters of governance interest and that the communication covers only those matters that have come to the auditor's attention during the conduct of the audit.

Whilst the communication of the matters described above would usually happen during the completion phase of the audit, it might be appropriate for the auditor to report certain matters at an earlier date, that is closer to the time they were identified.

19

Other Engagements and Reporting Issues

Learning objectives

After studying this chapter you should be able to:

1. Describe the principles and procedures relating to special purpose audit engagements.
2. Describe the principles and procedures relating to review engagements.
3. Describe the principles and procedures relating to engagements to perform agreed upon procedures.
4. Outline the auditor's considerations where asked to change the terms of engagement or report in a prescribed form.
5. Describe the principles relating to the preparation, presentation, review and the reporting accountant's report on profit forecasts.
6. Describe, in relation to prospectuses, the responsibilities of the directors and the auditor.
7. Describe the principles and procedures relevant to compilation engagements.
8. Explain the circumstances giving rise to material irregularities as set out in the Public Accountants' and Auditors' Act.
9. Describe the procedures the auditor should follow on encountering a material irregularity.

19.1 INTRODUCTION

In addition to reporting on audited annual financial statements, the auditor may be requested to undertake other assurance engagements which will require the issue of a report expressing an opinion on information other than financial statements prepared in accordance with generally accepted accounting practice. These are termed 'special purpose audit engagements'. The auditor may also be engaged to review financial statements or profit forecasts. As indicated in chapter 2, engagements to audit financial

763

statements, special purpose engagements and review engagements are referred to as assurance engagements. Alternatively, an auditor may be engaged to do the following:

- perform procedures agreed upon by the clients, others and the auditor;
- comply with the statutory requirements of the Companies Act regarding the auditor's duties towards prospectuses issued by clients in the circumstances of a share issue to the general public;
- collect, classify and summarize a client's financial information, termed a compilation engagement.

These engagements are referred to as related services to distinguish them from assurance engagements. This chapter first discusses standards and requirements applicable to special purpose and review engagements and then the various categories of related service engagements.

Section 20(5) of the Public Accountants' and Auditors' Act lays on the auditor the duty to report material irregularities. Material irregularities and the auditor's responsibilities in respect of them are also discussed.

19.2 SPECIAL PURPOSE AUDIT ENGAGEMENTS

19.2.1 Introduction

Special purpose audit engagements are those in which an auditor is requested to report by expressing an opinion on information other than financial statements prepared in accordance with generally accepted accounting practice. SAAS 800, which establishes standards and provides guidance on such engagements, identifies four categories of information that might be the subject of the audit. These are:

- financial statements prepared in accordance with a comprehensive basis of accounting other than generally accepted accounting practice;
- specified amounts, elements of accounts, or items in a financial statement (referred to as components of financial statements);
- compliance with contractual agreements; and
- summarized financial statements.

Aspects relevant to these categories are discussed in section 19.2.4 of this chapter.

19.2.2 Scope and level of assurance

A report expressing an opinion gives the same level of assurance as an unqualified opinion on annual financial statements. Such an engagement may be performed in conjunction with the audit or as a separate engagement. Accordingly, the scope of the auditor's examination must be unrestricted and the procedures performed must be in accordance with generally accepted auditing standards. The auditor should use professional judgement in determining the auditing procedures necessary to obtain sufficient evidence to support the audit assurance expressed in the opinion. The nature and extent of such procedures would obviously depend on the nature of the information being reported on.

To the extent that information being reported on is dependent on the operation of internal control procedures, the auditor will have to be satisfied as to the reliability of those procedures. An example of this would be where royalties payable are based on quantities of items manufactured under licence. The accuracy of the quantities used in the royalty calculation may be dependent on the completeness and accuracy of the information being recorded in the costing records of the manufacturer. If this is the case, the auditor will have to be satisfied that the operation of internal controls will ensure the complete and accurate recording of all items manufactured under licence. Where such reports have been given in previous years, it is important to ensure that the basis applied in the current year is consistent with that previously applied.

19.2.3 Reporting considerations

The following is an example of the appropriate form of report:

'REPORT OF THE INDEPENDENT AUDITOR TO...

We have audited the accompanying schedule of ... profit participation for the year ended 31 December 20X1 as set out on pages ... to .... This schedule is the responsibility of the company's directors. Our responsibility is to express an opinion on the schedule based on our audit. This report is furnished solely for your information and should be used by your company only for the stated purpose.

Scope
We conducted our audit in accordance with statements of South African Auditing Standards. Those standards require that we plan and perform the audit to obtain reasonable assurance that the schedule is free of material misstatement. An audit includes:

- examining, on a test basis, evidence supporting the amounts and disclosures in the schedule;

- assessing the accounting principles used and significant estimates made by management; and

- evaluating the overall presentation of the schedule.

We believe our audit provides a reasonable basis for our opinion.

Audit opinion

In our opinion, the accompanying schedule of . . .'s directors' profit participation fairly presents in all material respects . . .'s directors' participation
in the profits of the company for the year ended 31 December 20X1, in
accordance with the provisions of the employment agreement between the
directors and the company dated 1 June 20X1.

Name

Registered Accountant and Auditor

Chartered Accountant (SA)

Date

Address'[1]

The form and content of the report is the same as for audit reports on
financial statements, with the following potential differences:

- the report will usually be addressed to persons other than the members of
  the company;
- the information reported on (other than financial statements drawn up on
  other than a generally accepted accounting practice basis) will usually be
  set out on a schedule or schedules;
- the auditor may wish to indicate in the report the purpose for which the
  report is prepared and any restrictions on its distribution and use;
- the criterion against which fair presentation is measured may not be
  generally accepted accounting practice and the Companies Act. Accordingly the report should express an opinion as to whether or not the
  information is presented fairly in accordance with the disclosed basis of
  accounting or provisions of an agreement, where appropriate.

Where, in the auditor's opinion, the information is not fairly presented,
guidance given in SAAS 700 should be followed concerning the appropriate
form of qualification and issue an adverse or qualified opinion, or disclaim
an opinion.

19.2.4 Guidance specific to the different categories of special purpose reporting engagements

19.2.4.1 Reports on financial statements prepared in accordance with gaap

Examples of other comprehensive reporting frameworks include a cash or
income tax basis of accounting.

---

[1] SAAS 800, Appendix I, paragraph .05.

'The auditor's report on financial statements prepared in accordance with any other comprehensive basis of accounting should include a statement that indicates the basis of accounting used, or should refer to the note to the financial statements giving that information.'[2]

If the financial statements prepared on any other comprehensive basis are not suitably titled, or the basis of accounting is not adequately disclosed, the auditor should issue an appropriately modified report.'[3]

19.2.4.2 Reports on components of financial statements

When reporting on a component of financial statements, the auditor should relate the measurement of materiality to the individual component being reported on, rather than to the financial statements as a whole. As the component is a smaller base than the financial statements against which to quantify materiality, the auditor's examination will be more extensive than would be the case where the component is audited as part of the audit of financial statements.

'In determining the scope of the engagement, the auditor should consider those financial statement items that are interrelated, and that could materially affect the information on which the audit opinion is to be expressed.'[4]

Accordingly, if engaged to report on inventories it might be necessary to examine also sales and accounts receivable, as well as purchases and accounts payable.

Where an adverse opinion or disclaimer of an opinion on the financial statements as a whole has been given, the auditor may be approached to report on components of such financial statements. The auditor should only accept such engagements 'if the components are not so extensive as to constitute a major portion of the financial statements'.[5]

19.2.4.3 Reports on compliance with contractual agreements

Engagements to express an opinion as to an entity's compliance with contractual agreements should be undertaken only when the overall aspects of compliance relate to accounting and financial matters within the scope of the auditor's professional competence.[6] If there are only certain matters forming part of the engagement that are outside the auditor's expertise, the engagement may be accepted and an expert's work utilized where necessary. Examples of contractual agreements are debenture trust deeds or mortgage bond and other loan agreements. These often have covenants that need to be complied with, such as interest payments, maintenance of predetermined

---

[2] SAAS 800, paragraph .10.
[3] SAAS 800, paragraph .11.
[4] SAAS 800, paragraph .13.
[5] SAAS 800, paragraph .17.
[6] SAAS 800, paragraph .19.

ratios and restrictions on dividend payments. The report should state whether, in the auditor's opinion, the entity has complied with the particular provisions of the agreement.[7]

19.2.4.4 Reports on summarized financial statements

The auditor should not accept an engagement to report on summarized financial statements unless such auditor has audited the financial statements on which the summaries are based.

'The auditor's report on summarized financial statements should include the following basic elements, ordinarily in the following layout:

• Title.

• Addressee, appropriately addressed as required by the circumstances of the engagement.

• An identification of the audited financial statements from which the summarized financial statements were derived.

• A reference to the date of the audit report on the unabridged financial statements and the type of opinion given in that report.

• An opinion as to whether the information in the summarized financial statements is consistent with the audited financial statements from which it was derived. When the auditor has issued a modified opinion on the unabridged financial statements, yet is satisfied with the presentation of the summarized financial statements, the report should state that, although consistent with the unabridged financial statements, the summarized financial statements were derived from financial statements on which a modified auditor's report was issued.

• A statement, or reference to the note within the summarized financial statements, that indicates that, for a better understanding of an entity's financial performance and position and of the scope of the audit performed, the summarized financial statements should be read in conjunction with the unabridged financial statements and the auditor's report thereon.'[8]

19.3 REVIEW ENGAGEMENTS

19.3.1 Introduction

The framework for South African standards on auditing and related services, as set out in SAAS 120, refers to review engagements as follows:

'In a review engagement, the auditor expresses a moderate level of assurance that the information subject to review is free of material misstatement. This is expressed in the form of negative assurance.'[9]

---

[7] SAAS 800, paragraph .20.
[8] SAAS 800, paragraph .25.
[9] SAAS 120, paragraph .14.

SAAS 910, 'Engagements to Review Financial Statements', issued in November 2001, establishes standards and provides guidance on the auditor's responsibilities when engaged to review financial statements and on the appropriate form of report to be given.

The standard sets out the objective of a review engagement as follows:

'The objective of a review of financial statements is to enable an auditor to state whether or not, on the basis of procedures which do not provide all the evidence that would be required in an audit, anything has come to the auditor's attention that causes the auditor to believe that the financial statements are not prepared, in all material respects, in accordance with an identified financial reporting framework and / or statutory requirements (negative assurance).[10]

SAAS 910 sets out principles and guidance on procedures that are necessary when auditors are engaged to review financial statements. The procedures to be performed are less extensive than those leading to a report expressing an audit opinion. A report expressing negative assurance thus provides a lower level of assurance than a report expressing an audit opinion. It is obvious that if the auditor does no or very little work, it is unlikely that matters which indicate that information is misstated will be detected. SAAS 910, accordingly, identifies in the body of the statement three broad categories of necessary procedures and sets out in appendix III to it, illustrative detailed procedures that may be performed so as to ensure compliance by the auditor with the standard.

19.3.2 Scope of a review

The three broad categories of necessary procedures are:

- knowledge of the business;
- enquiries of management and others; and
- analytical review procedures.

These are briefly discussed below.

19.3.2.1 Knowledge of the business

The auditor should obtain or, if the current auditor, update a knowledge of the entity's business and the industry within it operates. This knowledge should encompass the following:

- core and related business processes;
- business risks identified by management and how these are managed by the internal controls adopted; and
- the entity's adopted accounting framework and the adequacy of the controls over the entity's financial information systems to ensure the validity, accuracy and completeness of the accounting processes.

---

[10] SAAS 910, paragraph .03.

19.3.2.2 Enquiries to management

Such enquiries should cover at least the following:

- whether or not all transactions have been recorded;
- whether or not the financial statements have been prepared in accordance with the entity's disclosed accounting framework;
- any changes in the entity's business activities and the accounting therefore; and
- any events subsequent to the date of the preparation of the financial statements being reviewed that might need to be taken into consideration.

19.3.2.3 Analytical review procedures

Such procedures should be performed to identify relationships and individual items that appear unusual. These procedures should include the following:

- comparing the current financial statements being reviewed with prior period financial statements; and
- the comparison of the financial statements disclosures with anticipated results as set out in forecasts and budgets.

In summary, the essential differences in the necessary procedures when performing a review as opposed to an audit engagement are as follows:

- With regards to the systems of internal control, the auditor merely needs to obtain (or if the current auditor, update) a knowledge of the entity's accounting systems to be satisfied that there is no reason to believe that the information produced by it is unreliable. In an audit engagement the auditor needs to perform tests of controls to obtain evidence that the internal controls operated as designed throughout the audit period.

- Responses to inquiries from management and employees of the entity need not be corroborated by seeking other evidence, provided the responses seem plausible. Review procedures will thus ordinarily not include the physical inspection of assets, confirmation of information from others, the inspection of documentation in support of recorded transactions and checks of the clerical accuracy of accounting computations.

- Review engagements justify the auditor relying sorely on analytical review procedures, whereas audit engagements require a combination of the performance of substantive tests of detail and analytical review procedures depending on the circumstances of the audit client and the auditor's judgement.

If the auditor, based on the knowledge of the business, enquiries and analytical review procedures, has reason to believe that the financial statements being reviewed may be materially misstated, the auditor should carry out additional procedures to be able to express negative assurance or to confirm that a modified report is required.

Apart from the specific categories of necessary procedures mentioned above, the auditor should do the following when performing review engagements:

- comply with the Accounting Profession's Codes of Professional Conduct;
- plan and perform the review with an attitude of professional scepticism, recognizing that circumstances may exist which cause the financial statements being reviewed to be materially misstated;
- agree with the client the terms of engagement which should be set out in an engagement letter;
- when using work performed by another auditor or an expert, be satisfied that such work is adequate;
- document matters providing support for the review report and the auditor's compliance with the standard.

19.3.3 Reporting considerations

The report should state that an audit has not been performed, that the procedures undertaken provide less assurance than an audit, and that an audit opinion is not expressed.

Where the auditor has no significant uncertainty or disagreement regarding the presentation of the information being reported on, a statement should be made that nothing came to the auditor's attention which would give the auditor reason to believe that the information required modification.

Appendix IV of SAAS 910 sets out the form of an unqualified review report as follows:

'REVIEW REPORT TO ...

We have reviewed the accompanying balance sheet of ... at ..., and the related statements of income and cash flows for the year then ended. These financial statements are the responsibility of the company's management. Our responsibility is to issue a report on these financial statements based on our review.

Scope
We conducted our review in accordance with the statement of South African Auditing Standards applicable to review engagements. This standard requires that we plan and perform the review to obtain moderate assurance that the financial statements are free of material misstatement. A review is limited primarily to enquiries of company personnel and analytical procedures applied to financial data and thus provides less assurance than an audit. We have not performed an audit and, accordingly, we do not express an audit opinion.

Review opinion
Based on our review, nothing has come to our attention that causes us to believe that the accompanying financial statements are not fairly

presented, in all material respects, in accordance with South African Statements of Generally Accepted Accounting Practice [and/or relevant statutory requirements].

Name

Registered Accountants and Auditors

Chartered Accountants (SA)

Address

Date'

However, where there are significant reservations, the nature of any uncertainty or misstatement and, if known, the effects thereof, should be clearly disclosed.

Appendix V of SAAS 910 sets out an example for the qualification of a review report for a departure from South African Statements of Generally Accepted Accounting Practice. The qualification and review paragraphs of the example report read as follows:

'Qualification
Management has informed us that inventory has been stated at its cost which is in excess of its net realizable value. Management's computation, which we have reviewed, shows that inventory, if valued at the lower of cost and net realizable value as required by the South African Statement of Generally Accepted Accounting Practice on Inventories, would have been decreased by R..., and net income and shareholders' equity would have been decreased by R....

Qualified review
Based on our review, except for the effects of the overstatement of inventory described in the previous paragraph, nothing has come to our attention that causes us to believe that the accompanying financial statements are not fairly presented, in all material respects, in accordance with South African Statements of Generally Accepted Accounting Practice [and/or relevant statutory requirements].'

19.4 PROFIT FORECASTS

In August 1989, the South African Institute of Chartered Accountants issued an *Audit and Accounting Guide on Profit Forecasts*. The Guide summarizes the important principles involved in preparing, presenting, reviewing and reporting on profit forecasts that are of practical use to persons engaged in that type of work.

A profit forecast is defined as 'an estimate of future financial results of an entity that is made to the best of the responsible party's knowledge and belief, and is based on certain assumptions reflecting conditions expected to exist and the courses of action the entity expects to take'.[11]

It is important to distinguish between profit forecasts and profit targets or other projections which are an essential part of an entity's strategic planning. Profit forecasts reflect the level of profitability that the directors honestly expect will be achieved, whereas profit targets usually represent management's profit goal.

There are no statutory, stock exchange or other requirements that necessitate the presentation of a profit forecast. They are often prepared in practice, however, to inform present and prospective shareholders or lenders of the trading prospects of a company which is seeking to raise further share capital, acquire a listing on the JSE Securities Exchange or obtain loan finance. Where a profit forecast is presented in a prospectus, which involves a company listed or one seeking a listing on the JSE Securities Exchange, the listing requirements stipulate that the forecast should be reported on by a reporting accountant. The report may be provided by any registered accountant and auditor. In practice, however, it is usually provided by the company's auditor.

Profit forecasts presented in other documents such as interim or annual financial statements are not required to be reported on by an auditor. Where the auditor is reporting on annual financial statements, and a profit forecast is included in such documents, the auditor is required merely to read the forecast and consider whether or not the forecast contradicts and so could raise doubts about information contained in the audited financial statements.

A chartered accountant can be involved in profit forecasts in three different roles, namely:

- in the capacity as a director;
- as an adviser to assist directors in the preparation of profit forecasts; and
- as the reporting accountant.

19.4.1 The role of directors and advisers

The directors of a company are solely responsible for profit forecasts and for the assumptions underlying them. Accordingly, the directors are responsible for ensuring that forecasts represent their best estimates of the results that they honestly believe can and will be achieved.

When assistance from advisers and/or employees is required to compile a forecast, the directors should adequately brief the people involved about the assumptions they are to use in preparing the detailed workings. As the responsibility for forecasts cannot be delegated, it is considered good practice that the board of directors formally approve forecasts on their completion.

---

[11] SAICA Auditing and Accounting Guide on Profit Forecasts, paragraph .02.

19.4.2 The role of the reporting accountant

The reporting accountant's report provides users of a forecast with some assurance that it has been properly compiled and presented. As forecasts are dependent on subjective judgements it is not possible for the reporting accountant to express any assurance concerning the accuracy of the profit forecast. Indeed, Disciplinary Rule 2.1.11 of the Public Accountants' and Auditors' Board prohibits registered accountants and auditors from allowing their names to be used in connection with any estimates of earnings contingent upon future transactions in a manner which may lead to the belief that they vouch for the accuracy of such estimates. A reporting accountant can, however, reasonably accept responsibility for examining the accounting bases and calculations. The reporting accountant may also express an opinion that the assumptions provide a reasonable basis for the preparation of the profit forecast, and that the forecast has been properly compiled from the underlying assumptions and information, and is presented on a basis consistent with the accounting policies normally adopted.

When approached to report on a profit forecast, a chartered accountant should consider the following matters before accepting the engagement:

- The degree of sophistication of the company's forecasting procedures, including the reliability of any previous forecasts or budgets prepared by management. If the procedures are unsophisticated and the history of achieved accuracy is poor, the engagement should, for obvious reasons, be declined.

- The nature of the entity's business activities might be such that it is almost impossible to forecast, with any degree of certainty, the future profitability of the entity. This is particularly true of companies about to pursue new business ventures of a speculative nature, such as, for example, film making. In such circumstances an auditor should decline the engagement or, alternatively, the directors should be forewarned that the report will probably be qualified due to the uncertainties inherent in the business.

- The period covered by the forecast. The uncertainties underlying forecasts increase markedly the further forward in time the forecasts are projected. The Guide, accordingly, recommends that a reporting accountant should not normally undertake to report on a forecast for more than the current financial year. Where, however, a significant part of the current financial year has elapsed, the forecast for the following financial period may be reported upon.

- The date by which the report is required should allow the reporting accountant sufficient time to carry out the work deemed necessary. If unable to agree with the prospective client on what is considered to be reasonable, the engagement should be declined.

To avoid any misunderstanding at a later stage, the engaged reporting accountant should confirm the responsibilities assumed and terms of the engagement in an engagement letter. The letter should also state that the engagement will be carried out free of restrictions on the scope of the work. The engagement letter should be sent as soon as possible after the terms of the engagement have been settled and should be acknowledged by the directors.

19.4.3 Profit forecast preparation

There are a number of important principles underlying the preparation of forecasts. These include:

● As the preparation of forecasts involves the exercise of judgement about future events, compilers thereof should exercise good faith. This involves the exercise of due care when developing appropriate assumptions. Undue optimism or pessimism should be avoided and in no circumstances should the forecast be prepared in such a way as to arrive at a predetermined result.

● Skills in addition to those normally required for the preparation of historical financial information are usually needed. For example, information or opinions may be required from personnel with competence in marketing, engineering and other technical areas. In addition, expertise in financial modelling and forecasting techniques may be required.

● Information used may come from sources within and outside the entity. As different sources provide varying degrees of reliability, the process used to develop the forecast should identify the best information available. The cost of acquiring the information, however, should be commensurate with the anticipated benefits to be derived from its use.

● It is important to identify all significant matters upon which an entity's future results are expected to depend. For the purpose of the Guide these matters are referred to as key factors. Some examples are interest rates for a company with substantial loan finance; currency exchange rates for companies dealing extensively in foreign markets; and labour relations for manufacturing and mining companies utilizing extensive manual labour in their production and mining processes respectively. Key factors vary by entity and by industry, and constitute the areas in which assumptions will have to be made. For example, if manufacturing labour is identified as a key factor, assumptions will need to be developed for labour requirements, labour rates of pay and any loss of productive time due to labour disputes or unrest. The reasonableness of the assumptions affect directly the quality of the forecast. They should not be vague generalities therefore, but rather supportable specific judgements of future economic, commercial and financial circumstances that are likely to affect the future profitability of the company.

● Changes in certain assumed conditions can result in relatively large variations in forecast results, while changes in others may have little effect on forecast results. For example, the profits would be more markedly affected by a variation in turnover of a company selling relatively fewer items at higher mark-ups than another with high volumes at low profit margins. Attention should be paid to those assumptions that are particularly sensitive and have a high probability of variation.

- The compilers of profit forecasts should adequately document the work done in developing the forecast. Documentation provides the discipline necessary for developing reliable forecasts; it facilitates the examination of a reporting accountant; and it can serve as evidence in the event of a dispute.

19.4.4 Presentation of profit forecasts

Profit forecasts are usually presented in monetary terms. When no particular figure is mentioned, certain forms of words may constitute a profit forecast. Examples mentioned in the Guide are 'profits will be somewhat higher than last year' and 'the profits of the second half of the year are expected to be similar to those earned in the first half-year'. The Guide includes within the definition of profit forecasts 'a form of words which puts a floor under, or a ceiling on, expected performance, or contains the data necessary to ascertain an approximate figure for future profits by an arithmetical process'. Profit forecasts are often presented together with historical financial information. It is important, therefore, that profit forecasts are clearly identified as such to preclude users from confusing them with historical financial statements.

The disclosure of significant assumptions made is essential to a user's understanding of the uncertainties associated with profit forecasts. Assumptions stated should relate only to matters which, if they did not occur, would have significant effect upon the forecast. Assumptions, therefore, need only be stated where uncertainty attaches to future happenings. The Guide cites the example of a company exporting products to illustrate the principle. If the volume of export sales can be estimated with reasonable accuracy, the sales volume need not be stated as an assumption. On the other hand, if major uncertainty relates to export sales revenue as a result of anticipated fluctuations in exchange rates, exchange rates used in the forecast should be stated as an assumption. In certain circumstances, it may be necessary to disclose the rationale for assumptions to assist users in forming a judgement as to the reasonableness of the forecast and the main uncertainties underlying it.

When disclosing assumptions, vague generalities such as 'it is expected that the company will continue to increase its market share' should be avoided. Wherever possible, assumptions should be stated in specific and definite terms – for example, 'the demand for products in the industry in which the company is operating will continue at present levels and the company will increase its market share by 10% over current levels'.

19.4.5 **The reporting accountant's examination**

When engaged to report on a profit forecast, a registered accountant and auditor should be mindful of the fact that the environment will normally be different to that when carrying out an audit of annual financial statements. If the forecast is presented in connection with a listing on the JSE or to raise further equity or loan finance, management might be tempted to forecast in overly optimistic terms. On the other hand, the forecast might be prepared in the emotional climate of a struggle for control of an entity and thus be presented in unduly pessimistic terms.

In carrying out the examination, the main matters to which the reporting accountant will direct attention are as follows:

- the nature and background of the company's business;
- the accounting policies normally used;
- the assumptions on which the forecast is based;
- the procedures followed for preparing the forecast; and
- if part of the forecast period has expired, the reasonableness of actual results included in the forecast.

An appendix to the South African Institute's Guide on forecasts lists detailed procedures that may be used in each area and should assist greatly those engaged to report on profit forecasts. The appendix warns that the list is to be viewed neither as a complete summary of all possible procedures nor as an outline of minimum procedures, but rather as an aid to the development and selection of possible procedures that may be used.

The suggested procedures are divided into four categories:

- procedures to determine the scope of the examination;
- procedures to evaluate the assumptions;
- procedures to review the preparation and presentation of the profit forecast; and
- procedures to consider the validity of historic data included in profit forecasts.

The scope of the examination is directly affected by:

- the nature of the company's business;
- the processes involved in preparing the forecast;
- the competence of persons involved in preparing the forecast;
- the adequacy of the documentation underlying the preparation of the forecast; and
- the level of accuracy achieved in the past.

In considering the processes involved in preparing the forecasts, the reporting accountant should consider the methods employed to:

- identify key factors;
- collect information used as a basis for assumptions made;

- translate assumptions into forecast amounts; and
- review and approve the forecast.

When evaluating the assumptions, the reporting accountant needs to consider whether or not all key factors have been identified and whether the assumptions made regarding these factors are appropriate, based on all the evidence available. To this end, the reporting accountant should:

- obtain knowledge of the client's business and the industry within which it operates and, in the light of this knowledge, consider the completeness and validity of the assumptions made;
- consider whether assumptions have been made regarding factors that are known to have influenced prior period results;
- consider whether assumptions have been made for factors known to have been considered in other forecasts of similar entities;
- consider the assumptions in the light of any public statements, strategic plans and budgets, and the minutes of meetings of directors for any contradictions.

For key assumptions, the reporting accountant should ascertain the adequacy of internal and external sources of information used in formulating the assumptions and should evaluate whether or not the information was correctly considered in formulating the assumptions. If information is taken from internal sources it might be necessary to examine the supporting information. Where appropriate, external sources of information might be directly confirmed.

The review of the preparation and presentation of a profit forecast should involve:

- testing the mathematical accuracy of the computations made in translating the assumptions into the forecast amounts;
- evaluating the appropriateness of mathematical equations, statistical techniques or modelling procedures used;
- recomputing the aggregation of amounts and tracing aggregated amounts to the profit forecast;
- testing that assumptions made were actually used in preparing the forecast;
- checking that the effect of assumptions is reflected on all amounts. For example, if a manufacturing company is forecasting a dramatic increase in revenue due to increases in levels of production and sales, the effect on likely increases in production costs would need to be taken into account; and
- determining that the presentation of the profit forecast is in accordance with that recommended in the Institute's Guide.

If part of the forecast period has expired, the reporting accountant should:

- determine the adequacy of the accounting system as a means of generating reliable information;

- determine the reasonability of accounting estimates, such as provisions for stock obsolescence and doubtful debts, in relation to the reporting accountant's knowledge of the business and to discussions with management;
- consider whether the accounting policies are appropriate and consistently applied;
- test the historic information to the accounting records;
- perform analytical review procedures such as trend and ratio analysis techniques on the information, to test its plausibility.

19.4.6 Applicability of generally accepted audit standards

The Guide sets out the following matters as being applicable to the auditor when carrying out an examination of profit forecasts.

- The examination should be performed by a person or persons with adequate technical training and proficiency in examining profit forecasts.
- In all matters relating to the task, the reporting accountant should maintain an independent mental attitude.
- Due professional care should be exercised in the performance of the examination and the preparation of the report.
- The work should be adequately planned and assistants, if any, should be properly briefed and supervised.
- The reporting accountant should obtain an understanding of the process by which the entity develops its profit forecasts as a basis for determining the scope of the review.
- Sufficient evidence should be obtained to afford a reasonable basis for the reporting accountant's report.

Adequate working papers should be prepared to demonstrate that the six aspects mentioned above have been complied with.

19.4.7 The reporting accountant's report

To emphasize that the report on the forecast is given by an independent reporting accountant, the word 'independent' should be incorporated in the heading of the reporting accountant's report. The report will usually be addressed to the directors and should be dated on the date of completion of the examination. This date should coincide with the date on which the directors formally approve the forecast for issue.

The report should set out the following:

- The scope of the examination. As this should be in accordance with the guidance contained in the Institute's Guide, a statement to that effect should appear in the report;
- That the directors are solely responsible for the profit forecast;
- That no opinion is expressed on whether or not the forecast will be realized;
- An expression of opinion as to whether or not:

- the assumptions provide a reasonable basis for the preparation of the profit forecast;
- the forecast has been properly compiled on the basis of the assumptions; and
- the forecast is presented on a basis consistent with the accounting policies normally adopted by the entity.

The opinion should be qualified if the reporting accountant believes that material assumptions are either invalid, unfounded or misleading, or if an assumption or other information of importance has been omitted. Qualification is also necessary if the reporting accountant is unable to obtain satisfaction regarding the plausibility of the forecast or the reasonability of the form of words used.

Where the reporting accountant is reporting on a profit forecast that is to be included in a prospectus, the requirements of the Companies Act place the obligation on the reporting accountant to give consent in writing to the issue of the document which includes the report, with explicit reference to the form and context in which it is included. To fulfil this requirement, the reporting accountant should be satisfied that it is appropriate, and not misleading, for the report on the profit forecast to appear in the form and context in which it is included.

Appendix IV, 'Profit Forecasts', of the Auditing and Accounting Guide sets out an illustrative example of an unqualified reporting accountant's report on a profit forecast as follows:

'INDEPENDENT ACCOUNTANT'S REPORT ON PROFIT FORECAST PREPARED FOR THE PURPOSE OF ...

To the directors of ...
We have examined the profit forecast for the months/year ended ... set out on pages ... to ... of this circular. The forecast was compiled by you and you are solely responsible therefore. (The forecast includes unaudited results for the period ending ....)

Our examination was carried out in accordance with the guidelines laid down by The South African Institute of Chartered Accountants. In carrying out our examination we have analysed the accounting policies and have checked the calculations used in the profit forecast, and we have confirmed that the underlying information used in the forecast has been presented on a basis consistent with the accounting policies normally adopted by the entity. We consider that our procedures were appropriate in the circumstances to enable us to express our opinion presented below.

In our opinion:
● the assumptions provide a reasonable basis for the preparation of the profit forecast

- the forecast has been properly compiled on the basis of the assumptions

- the forecast is presented on a basis consistent with the accounting policies normally adopted by the entity.

Since the forecast is based on assumptions concerning future events, actual results may vary from the forecast which has been presented, and the variations may be material. Accordingly, we express no opinion on whether or not the forecast will be achieved.

Note:
Where the reporting accountant has not conducted an examination in accordance with this Guide, the scope of the examination should be set out in the report.

The words in parenthesis may be left out where the forecast does not include actual unaudited figures.'

19.4.8 Appendices

The following are set out in appendices to the Guide:

- illustrative examples of matters that should be included in an engagement letter;
- recommended procedures for an examination of a profit forecast as already mentioned;
- an illustrative example of presentation of assumptions;
- an example of a reporting accountant's unqualified report on a profit forecast;
- specimen reporting accountant's letter of consent to issue a circular containing the reporting accountant's report;
- an illustrative example of a management representation letter; and
- a checklist of the reporting accountant's working papers for an examination of profit forecasts.

19.5 ENGAGEMENTS TO PERFORM AGREED-UPON PROCEDURES

19.5.1 Introduction

With regard to the objective of an agreed-upon procedures engagement, SAAS 920 states as follows:

'The objective of an agreed-upon procedures engagement is for the auditor to carry out procedures of an audit nature, to which the auditor and the entity and any appropriate third party have agreed, and to report on factual findings.'[12]

---

[12] SAAS 920, paragraph .04.

19.5.2 Scope and level of assurance

'As the auditor simply provides a report of the factual findings of agreed-upon procedures, no assurance is expressed. Instead, users of the report assess for themselves the procedures and findings reported by the auditor and draw their own conclusions from the auditor's work.'[13]

The auditor should agree upon the following matters:

- 'nature of the engagement including the fact that the procedures performed will not constitute an audit or a review and that accordingly no assurance will be expressed;

- stated purpose for the engagement;

- identification of the financial information to which the agreed-upon procedures will be applied;

- nature, timing and extent of the specific procedures to be applied;

- anticipated form of the report of factual findings; and

- limitations on distribution of the report of factual findings. When such limitation would be in conflict with the legal requirements, if any, the auditor would not accept the engagement.'[14]

An engagement letter provides a record of the scope of the procedures, the extent of the auditor's responsibilities and the form of report to be issued. Appendix I to SAAS 920 sets out an example of such a letter.

The extent to which the auditing standards apply is a matter of professional judgement, taking into account the nature and circumstances of the engagement. The auditor should comply with the planning standard. In particular, the auditor should consider whether or not the nature of the engagement is such that its satisfactory completion is dependent on having a knowledge of the client's business and the industry within which it operates. Where appropriate, the auditor should obtain this knowledge if it is not already possessed.

The internal control standard applies only to the extent that a review of the accounting system and related internal controls forms part of the procedures agreed upon.

The audit evidence standard, which requires that sufficient evidence to support the content of the report is obtained, will always apply. The auditor should report only actual findings. To report findings without having performed the work is fraud.

Finally, the auditor should document in working papers the terms of engagement, evidence that the relevant standards were adhered to and evidence to support the report of factual findings.

---

[13] SAAS 920, paragraph .05.
[14] SAAS 920, paragraph .09.

19.5.3 **Reporting considerations**

In engagements leading to reports on factual findings, the audit assurance conveyed in the report varies according to the nature and extent of the procedures agreed upon and the auditor's findings. It is important, therefore, that the procedures agreed upon and the auditor's findings are stated in the report in sufficient detail to provide a reasonable basis for a reader of the report to assess the level of assurance given to the information.

'The report of factual findings should contain:

- a title;
- an addressee, ordinarily the client who engaged the auditor to perform the agreed-upon procedures;
- identification of specific financial or non-financial information to which the agreed-upon procedures have been applied;
- a statement that the procedures performed were those agreed upon with the recipient;
- a statement that the engagement was performed in accordance with statements of SAAS applicable to agreed-upon procedures engagements;
- a statement (when applicable) that the auditor is not independent of the entity;
- identification of the purpose for which the agreed-upon procedures were performed;
- a statement that the responsibility for determining the adequacy or otherwise of the procedures agreed to be performed by the auditor is that of the recipient;
- a listing of the specific procedures performed;
- a description of the auditor's factual findings, including sufficient details of errors and exceptions found;
- a statement that the procedures performed do not constitute either an audit or a review and, as such, no assurance is expressed;
- a statement that had the auditor performed additional procedures, an audit or a review, other matters might have come to light that would have been reported;
- a statement that the report is restricted to those parties that have agreed to the procedures to be performed;
- a statement (when applicable) that the report relates only to the elements, accounts, items or financial and non-financial information specified and that it does not extend to the entity's financial statements taken as a whole;
- the date of the report;
- the auditor's address; and
- the auditor's signature.'[15]

---

[15] SAAS 920, paragraph .18.

An example of a report of factual findings in connection with accounts payable appears below.

'REPORT OF THE INDEPENDENT AUDITOR TO ... ON ... FACTUAL FINDINGS

Scope

We have performed the procedures agreed with you and described below with respect to the accounts payable of ... as at (date), set forth in accompanying schedules which we have initialled for identification purposes [not shown in this example]. Our engagement was undertaken in accordance with the statement of South African Auditing Standards applicable to agreed-upon procedures engagements. The responsibility for determining the adequacy or otherwise of the procedures agreed to be performed is that of [those who engaged the auditors]. Our procedures were performed solely to assist you in evaluating the validity of the accounts payable. The procedures are summarized as follows:

1. We obtained and checked the addition of the trial balance of accounts payable as at (date); prepared by ..., and we compared the total to the balance in the related general ledger account.

2. We compared the attached list [not shown in this example] of major suppliers and the amounts owing at (date) to the related names and amounts in the trial balance.

3. We obtained suppliers' statements or requested suppliers to confirm balances owing at (date).

4. We compared such statements or confirmations to the amounts referred to in 2. For amounts which did not agree, we obtained reconciliations from .... For reconciliations obtained, we identified and listed outstanding invoices, credit notes and outstanding cheques, each of which was greater than R.... We located and examined such invoices and credit notes subsequently received and cheques subsequently paid, and we ascertained that they should in fact have been listed as outstanding on the reconciliations.

Findings

We report our findings below:

(a) With respect to item 1 we found the addition to be correct and the total amount to be in agreement.

(b) With respect to item 2 we found the amounts compared to be in agreement.

(c) With respect to item 3 we found there were suppliers' statements for all such suppliers.

> (d) With respect to item 4 we found the amounts agreed, or with respect to amounts which did not agree, we found ... had prepared reconciliations and that the credit notes, invoices and outstanding cheques of R... were appropriately listed as reconciling items with the following exceptions:
>
> [Detail the exceptions]
>
> Because the above procedures do not constitute either an audit or a review made in accordance with statements of South African Auditing Standards, we do not express any assurance on the accounts payable as at (date).
>
> Had we performed additional procedures or had we performed an audit or review of the financial statements in accordance with statements of South African Auditing Standards, other matters might have come to our attention that would have been reported to you.
>
> Our report is solely for the purpose set out in the first paragraph of this report and for your information, and is not to be used for any other purpose nor to be distributed to any other parties. This report relates only to the accounts and items specified above, and does not extend to any financial statements of ..., taken as a whole.'[16]

19.6 GENERAL MATTERS RELATING TO OTHER REPORTING ENGAGEMENTS

19.6.1 Change in engagement[17]

An auditor may accept an engagement to report on an element of financial statements when a qualified opinion, or an opinion has been disclaimed, on the financial statements as a whole. However, the auditor should consider carefully the effect of the uncertainty or disagreement on the element being reported on.

An auditor should not agree to report on certain elements of financial statements instead of reporting on the financial statements as a whole in order to avoid qualifying or disclaiming an opinion on such financial statements.

When engaged to issue a certain category of special report, the auditor should not issue a different category of report to avoid a qualification of such report.

An auditor may be requested by the client to change from one category of special reporting engagement to another before completing the engagement. A change in circumstances affecting the client's requirements or a

---

[16] SAAS 920, Appendix II, example paragraph .03.
[17] SAAS 210, paragraph .18.

THE PRINCIPLES AND PRACTICE OF AUDITING

misunderstanding by the client of the nature of the engagement and form of report are ordinarily reasonable justification to change the engagement. If, however, the change results in an imposition of a restriction on the auditor's scope of examination, or is done deliberately to avoid a qualification in the auditor's report, it would in all probability not be acceptable. In this circumstance, the auditor should withdraw from the engagement unless there is a responsibility remaining to report to those to whom it was originally intended.

19.6.2 Reports on prescribed forms [18]

Auditors are sometimes required to submit a special report on a prescribed form to government authorities and others. Prescribed forms may omit essential wording or may require the auditor to give assurance which cannot be provided (for example, where the auditor is required to certify the correctness of information). In these circumstances, the auditor should make changes to the form, or, rather, attach an appropriately reworded report to it. It may also be appropriate to dispatch a letter setting out the auditor's reservations regarding the prescribed form.

An example of this is the introduction of regulation 27 to the Deposit-Taking Institutions Act 94 of 1990, which requires the auditor to express an opinion on the following returns: Dl 100, 200, 300, 310, 410, 420, 510 and 600, furnished to the Registrar in respect of the balance sheet and income statement at the year-end date. The auditor is further required to review and report annually on the following returns: Dl 110, 120, 130, 140, 210, 400, 500, 520 and 700, furnished to the Registrar.

19.7 PROSPECTUSES

The Companies Act prohibits the offering of shares for subscription,[19] or sale,[20] to the public unless accompanied by a prospectus complying with the requirements of the Act and registered in the Companies Registration Office. Section 148 requires that every prospectus issued shall state at least the matters specified, and set out the reports referred to, in Parts I and II of Schedule 3 to the Act. It requires further that the prospectus shall contain a fair presentation of the state of the affairs of the company, the shares of which are being offered. If a renounceable rights issue of shares in an unlisted company is being made, reduced disclosure, as set out in Part III of Schedule 3, is required.[21] As this form of issue is unusual, the abridged form of prospectus is not discussed here.

Some of the more important disclosure requirements, as required by Part I of Schedule 3, are details of the directors and management; history, state of

---

[18] SAAS 800, paragraphs .06 and .07.
[19] Section 145.
[20] Section 146.
[21] Section 148(1)(b)

affairs and prospects of the company; profits or losses and dividends paid over the past five years; the purpose of the offer; details of share capital and loans; property to be acquired out of the proceeds; and the particulars of the offer. The fair presentation of the contents of the prospectus as set out in Part I of Schedule 3 is entirely the responsibility of the directors.

Part II of Schedule 3 stipulates the reports to be set out in the prospectus. Apart from a report by the directors as to any material changes in assets and liabilities since the last reporting date to the date of the prospectus,[22] the reports required are the auditor's responsibility.

19.7.1 The auditor's report to the prospectus

In the case of a company with no subsidiaries, Part II of Schedule 3, paragraph 25, requires a report by the auditor of the company with respect to:

- profits or losses of the company in respect of the five financial years immediately preceding the issue of the prospectus;
- the dividend rate(s) (or the fact that no dividends were declared) in respect of each of the preceding five financial years, specifying the class in respect of which dividends were paid or withheld; and
- the assets and liabilities of the company as at the date of the most recent annual financial statements of the company.

If annual financial statements have been made out for a lesser period than five years (for example, because the company was incorporated less than five years ago), the profit or loss and dividend information should be given for such lesser period.[23] Further, if no annual financial statements have been prepared in respect of any part of the period of five years ending on a date three months before the issue of the prospectus, that fact should be stated.[24]

In the case of a company with subsidiaries, Part II of Schedule 3, paragraph 25, requires that, in regard to profit and losses, the auditor's report should deal separately with the company's profit and loss and, in addition, deal:

- as a whole with the company's share of the combined profits or losses of all subsidiaries; or
- individually with the company's share of the profits and losses of each subsidiary; or
- as a whole with the consolidated profits and losses of the company and all its subsidiaries.

If a subsidiary incurred losses, the amount of such losses must be stated and the manner in which provision was made therefore.

---

[22] Schedule 3, paragraph .31.
[23] Schedule 3, paragraph .29.
[24] Schedule 3, paragraph .25(1)(b).

In regard to assets and liabilities, Part II of Schedule 3, paragraph 25, requires 'that the auditor's report should deal separately with the company's ... assets and liabilities and, in addition, deal either:

• as a whole with the combined assets and liabilities of all subsidiaries; or
• as a whole with the consolidated assets and liabilities of all subsidiaries.

Irrespective of which method of disclosure is used, an indication must be given of the assets and liabilities of subsidiaries.

In terms of Part II Schedule 3, paragraph 25(4), the auditor must be satisfied, as far as reasonably practicable, that as stated in the report:

'(a) the debtors and creditors do not include any accounts other than trade accounts;

(b) the provisions for doubtful debts are adequate;

(c) adequate provision has been made for obsolete, damaged or defective goods and for supplies purchased at prices in excess of current market prices;

(d) intercompany profits in the group have been eliminated;

(e) there have been no material changes in the assets and liabilities of the company and of any subsidiary since the date of the last annual financial statements'.

Paragraph 30 of Schedule 3 envisages that the auditor will make adjustments to the already audited and reported figures when preparing the five-year profit history report and the statement of assets and liabilities at the last balance sheet date. This is because the auditor is required to make adjustments and indicate that they have been made, or that any adjustments be indicated by way of a note.

The JSE Securities Exchange regulations[25] and listing requirements extend the disclosure requirements when adjustments are made to previously reported figures. These further requirements are as follows:

• if the effect of the adjustments is to convert a previously reported loss in any one year into a profit, details are to be disclosed;
• where adjustments are made to assets and liabilities, the reasons for the adjustments must be stated.

The objective of the auditor's reports on the profit history and assets and liabilities of a company offering shares to the public is to provide a prospective investor with useful information in order to make an investment decision. The historically achieved levels of profitability serve as a guide for projecting future performance potential, while the statement of assets and liabilities reflects the financial strength of the undertaking. Given that the prospective investor will attempt to assess future performance by consider-

---

25 'Listing requirements', paragraphs 9.8.1, 9.8.2 and 9.8.3.

ing past results, it is logical that results previously reported should be adjusted where the circumstances of the company have, or will, change. In essence, in making adjustments, the auditor should seek to disclose what profits would have been, given the current circumstances and financial position of the business entity.

When deciding whether or not to make adjustments, the auditor needs to make a professional judgement. This is done by the auditor using knowledge of the business to identify significant changes in the circumstances of the entity over the five-year reporting period and to interpret the financial effect of these on previously reported amounts.

Some examples of circumstances that would ordinarily require the consideration of adjustment include the following:

- changes in accounting policies;
- fundamental accounting errors;
- non-'arm's length' transactions at other-than-normal commercial values;
- accounting estimates made which in hindsight proved incorrect;
- changes in financial structure and concomitant costs of finance; and
- fundamental changes in business operations.

An important principle to bear in mind when considering possible adjustments is not to create a subjective account of what might have happened had different management business decisions been taken. To illustrate by way of two examples: adjustments should not be made to reverse losses on business ventures, notwithstanding that similar ventures are unlikely to be entered into again, nor foreign exchange losses as a result of management's decision not to cover forward the risk of exchange rate movements.

In August 1996 the South African Institute of Chartered Accountants issued Exposure Draft 105, 'Report on Financial Information to be included in a Prospectus'. The exposure draft states that the report of financial information contained in a prospectus should indicate that it is the responsibility of the directors of the issuer.[26] For this recommendation to become acceptable, an amendment to paragraph 25 of Part II of Schedule 3 would be necessary. The paragraph currently requires of the auditor to report the information.

Two months short of four years later, Exposure Draft 140, 'Report on Historical Financial Information to be included in a Prospectus or JSE Circular' (which is based on, and replaced ED 105), was issued in June 2000. At the time of writing (August 2002), paragraph 25 of Part II of Schedule 3 still remains unamended. With regard to adjustments made to previously reported historical financial information ED 140 has this to say:

> 'A statement of adjustments should be disclosed, detailing the amounts and reasons for the adjustments, in respect of any adjustments made to previously

---

[26] ED SAAS 105, paragraph .27

reported historical financial information in preparing the report of historical financial information. This should be provided in the form of a reconciliation between the previously reported historical financial information and adjusted historical financial information included in the report of historical financial information. If no adjustments are made there should be disclosure of that fact.

Adjustments should only be made to give effect to:

(a) retrospective application of changes in accounting policies; and

(b) retrospective correction of fundamental errors.

Thus adjustments are not made to the information contained in the report of historical financial information for:

(a) events which have not yet occurred (other than for proposed changes in accounting policies), for example, interest savings likely to result from utilizing the proceeds of the share issue to reduce interest-bearing borrowings;

(b) changes in estimates;

(c) correction of errors that are not fundamental; and

(d) non-arm's length transactions.'

Should this be accepted, of the six examples of circumstances that might be adjusted for (given above), only the first two would require adjustment.

In anticipation of an amendment to Schedule 3, which would make it the responsibility of the directors to report on the financial information contained in a prospectus, the question arises as to the level of assurance to be provided by the auditor on such information. This matter was considered by the Auditing Standards Committee of SAICA which, in June 2000, issued Exposure Draft 139. Paragraph .12 of ED 139 sets out the reporting accountant's responsibility as follows:

'The reporting accountant should provide the following opinion on the components of the report of historical financial information:

(a) An audit opinion on financial information and adjustments relating to the financial year preceding the issue of the prospectus or JSE circular.

(b) Either an audit or a review opinion on financial information and adjustments relating to the financial years prior to the financial year preceding the issue of the prospectus or JSE circular.

(c) A review opinion on interim financial information and adjustments thereto.

Separate reports should be provided for the issuer and each business undertaking acquired or to be acquired.

Where the historical financial information is audited, the objective of the engagement is to enable the reporting accountant to express an opinion that the historical financial information, in all material respects, fairly presents the financial position of the entity at specific dates, and the results of its operations and cash flows for the periods ended on those dates, in accordance with statutory and regulatory requirements.

Where the historical financial information is reviewed, the objective of the review is to enable the reporting accountant to state that, on the basis of procedures that do not provide all the evidence that would be required for an audit, nothing has come to the reporting accountant's attention that causes the reporting accountant to believe that the historical financial information is not prepared, in all material respects, in accordance with statutory and regulatory requirements.'

19.8 COMPILATION ENGAGEMENTS

SAAS 930, 'Engagements to Compile Financial Information', establishes standards and provides guidance on the accountant's professional responsibilities when an engagement to compile financial information is undertaken, and the form and content of the report the accountant issues in connection with such a compilation. The statement applies to such work carried out by chartered accountants registered with the Public Accountants' and Auditors' Board, as well as those who are not. However, it does not apply to chartered accountants acting in the capacity of employee or treasurer of an entity.

The objective of a compilation engagement is for an accountant to use accounting expertise, as opposed to auditing expertise, to collect, classify and summarize financial information. While a compilation engagement could include the preparation of annual financial statements, the engagement could include other information such as, for example, monthly management accounts, branch financial statements or tax returns with supporting schedules.

Other than the independence principle which is essential for a client / auditor relationship, the accountant should comply with the 'Code of Professional Conduct' issued by the South African Institute of Chartered Accountants. However, where the accountant is not independent, a statement to that effect should be made in the accountant's report.

19.8.1 Terms of engagement and procedures

The accountant should ensure that the client clearly understands the terms of the engagement. The client should understand the following:[27]

- the nature of the engagement, including the fact that neither an audit nor a review will be carried out and that, accordingly, no assurance will be expressed;
- the fact that the engagement cannot be relied upon to disclose errors, illegal acts or other irregularities, for example, fraud for defalcations that may exist;

---

[27] SAAS 930, paragraph .07.

- the nature of the information to be supplied by the client;
- the fact that management is responsible for the accuracy and complete-ness of the information supplied to the accountant to ensure the completeness and accuracy of the compiled financial information;
- the basis of accounting on which the financial information is to be compiled and the fact that this, and any known departures from it, will be disclosed;
- the intended use and distribution of the information, once compiled;
- the form of report to be rendered regarding the financial information compiled, when the accountant's name is to be associated therewith; and
- the requirements of section 275 of the Companies Act, 1973.

The client should receive an engagement letter encompassing the terms of the engagement. Appendix 1 to SAAS 930 contains an illustrative example of such an engagement letter.

The accountant should plan the work so that an effective engagement will be performed. This entails the accountant obtaining a general knowledge of the business and operations of the entity, as well as the accounting principles and practices of the industry in which the entity operates. This knowledge should be sufficient for the accountant to understand the nature of the entity's business transactions and the accounting basis on which the financial information is to be prepared. The accountant ordinarily obtains knowledge of these matters through experience with the entity or inquiry of the entity's personnel.

There is no requirement to do the following:

- make any inquiries of management to assess the reliability and completeness of the information provided;
- assess internal controls;
- verify any matters; or
- verify any explanations.

However, if the accountant becomes aware that information supplied by management is incorrect, incomplete, or otherwise unsatisfactory, the accountant should consider performing the above procedures and request management to provide additional information. If management refuses to provide additional information, the accountant should withdraw from the engagement, informing the client of the reasons for the withdrawal.[28]

Once the information has been compiled, the accountant should read it and consider whether it appears to be appropriate in form and free from obvious material misstatements. In particular, the accountant should be satisfied that adequate disclosure has been made of the financial reporting framework utilized.

---

[28] SAAS 930, paragraph .15.

If the accountant becomes aware of material misstatements, for example, any known departures from the identified financial reporting framework, the accountant should try to agree appropriate amendments with management. If such amendments are not agreed upon and the financial information is considered to be misleading, the accountant should withdraw from the engagement, informing the client of the reasons for the withdrawal.

19.8.2 Reporting

SAAS 930 requires that the accountant prepares a report on the financial information that has been compiled. This should contain the following:[29]

- a title;
- the addressee;
- a statement that the engagement was performed in accordance with the statement of South African Auditing Standards applicable to compilation engagements;
- when relevant, a statement that the accountant is not independent in appearance of the entity;
- identification of the financial information noting that it is based on information provided by management;
- a statement that management is responsible for the financial information compiled by the accountant;
- a statement that neither an audit nor a review has been carried out and that accordingly no assurance is expressed on the financial information;
- a paragraph, when considered necessary, drawing attention to the disclosure of material departures from the identified financial reporting framework;
- the date of the report;
- the accountant's address;
- the accountant's signature.

Further, such financial information compiled should contain a reference such as 'Unaudited', 'Compiled without Audit or Review', or 'Refer to Compilation Report' on each page of the financial information or on the front of the complete set of financial statements.

Appendix II of SAAS 930 sets out the form of an example of a report on an engagement to compile financial statements as follows:

'COMPILATION REPORT TO ...

On the basis of information provided by management we have compiled, in accordance with the statement of South African Auditing Standards applicable to compilation engagements, the balance sheet of ... at December 31, 20X1, and the related income statement and cash flow

---

[29] SAAS 930, paragraph .18.

statement for the year then ended, as set out on pages ... to ....
Management is responsible for these financial statements. We have not
audited or reviewed these financial statements, and accordingly express
no assurance thereon.(*)

Accountant CA(SA)

Date

Address

*It may also be appropriate for the accountant to refer to the special
purpose for which, or party for whom the information has been prepared.
Alternatively, or in addition, the accountant may add some form of
caution designated to ensure that it is not used for purposes other than
those intended.'

19.9 OTHER REPORTING ISSUES

19.9.1 Reporting a material irregularity

In the discussion on the auditor's responsibilities in chapter 3, attention
was drawn to section 20(5) of the Public Accountants' and Auditors' Act
1991 concerning the added responsibility in South Africa for the auditor to
report on material irregularities. It is not easy to decide what acts or
omissions constitute a material irregularity. This problem has existed ever
since this responsibility was imposed on the auditing profession in 1951.
The problem is still unresolved, although a number of efforts have been
made to resolve it.

Some doubt still exists in the minds of registered accountants and auditors as
to whether or not, when losses are suffered by undertakings as a result of
fraud, theft or defalcation, report should be made of it by the auditors of such
undertakings.

In August 1982, the PAAB issued Circular B1/1982, which was subsequently
revised and reissued, in an attempt to clarify for auditors their responsibility
to report a material irregularity arising from fraud or the carrying on of a
company's business recklessly or with intent to defraud, by a director or
other person, which circumstances are regarded as a criminal offence under
section 424 of the Companies Act 1973.

Circular B1/1982 (paragraph 3) points out that an auditor's duty to report on
material irregularities arises exclusively from section 26(3), now section
20(5), of the Public Accountants' and Auditors' Act 1991. No such duty flows
from the provisions of section 424 or any other penal provision; they do not
add to the duty in section 20(5).

Paragraph 4 states:

'The mere fact of an entity trading in circumstances where its liabilities exceed its assets, is not regarded by the Board as an "irregularity" as contemplated in s 20(5). But there is of course no doubt that this fact creates a situation which is particularly susceptible to the taking place of certain material irregularities. These irregularities can take the form of fraud or recklessness in the carrying on of business in those circumstances.

Common-law fraud can be committed by any client and its officers and employees, whether or not the client is a company. Whereas s 424 of the Companies Act 1973 and its provisions relating to "intent to defraud" and "recklessly" are only significant where the Companies Act is applicable to the client.'

The circular further states in paragraphs 5 and 6 that there can be no doubt that common-law fraud is an 'irregularity', as is the situation where directors and others are carrying on the business of a company with 'intent to defraud', or are 'reckless' in their conduct of a company's business. If there is clear proof of gross negligence, each of these constitutes a statutory offence in terms of section 424 of the Companies Act 1973.

But it is only if it is material, and has caused or is likely to cause financial loss, that the auditor has a duty to act. Paragraph 7 of the circular stresses that the auditor's primary concern is the danger of financial loss to the company, its members or creditors. Other than complying with section 20(5), it is not the auditor's function to ensure that criminal prosecutions are instituted against directors.

Circular B2/87, issued by the Board, amplifies Circular B1/1982 and clarifies the position where clients are trading while their liabilities exceed their assets and the auditor issues a report in terms of section 20(5). The circular explains the procedures of the Board in referring such reports to the Attorney-General for further investigation. An auditor is advised to submit an affidavit in support of the report to the Board and to seek legal advice in drawing up such affidavit. It also deals with the action to be taken by practitioners where such reports are followed up by the Commercial Branch of the South African Police Services who may wish to gain access to documents in the possession of the auditor in the course of their investigation.

Accordingly, the auditor will have to use the legal opinions obtained by the Board and other literature to decide whether an 'irregularity' falls within the ambit of section 20(5). In the process of reaching this decision, the auditor will have to consider whether the act or omission:

- is material;
- is irregular;
- is taking place 'in the conduct of the affairs' of the undertaking;
- has caused, or is likely to cause, financial loss to:
  - the undertaking; or
  - any of its members; or
  - creditors.

19.9.1.1 Is it material?

The reader is referred to chapter 5 where this nebulous concept is discussed at some length. In the context of section 20(5) it is important to establish whether 'material' refers to the irregularity or the financial loss. Most writers agree that the 'materiality' refers to the irregularity.

19.9.1.2 Is it irregular?

Naudé,[30] who was involved in the drafting of section 26(3) of the Public Accountants' and Auditors' Act 1951, classifies irregularities into three categories:

* common-law or statutory offences;
* breach of trust; and
* negligence.

In the first category the following are included: fraud, forgery, theft, bribery, and statutory offences. The second category covers a breach of fiduciary duties and includes the exceeding of delegated powers. The relationship between partners is one of trust and a breach of this trust would constitute an irregularity. In the case of negligence on the part of a director or partner, the company or the other partners will have a right to recover damages where the director or partner did not exercise the care and skill required by law.

19.9.1.3 Is it taking place 'in the conduct of the affairs' of the undertaking?

An important question to answer is whether the auditor's duty to report extends to irregular acts of all employees or only to irregularities perpetrated by management. Naudé, who disagrees with Hunt,[31] contends that this duty extends only to acts of management, and supports his opinion by referring to the Afrikaans text in his argument that 'management can itself adequately protect the undertaking in relation to mere servants who act irregularly'. Although Naudé does not mention it specifically in his opinion, it may be helpful to refer to the definition of a 'manager' in section 1 of the Companies Act, as he states that the 'material irregularity must have taken place on a managerial level'. In relation to a company, a manager is defined as '... any person who is a principal executive officer of the company for the time being, by whatever name he may be designated and whether or not he is a director'.

19.9.1.4 Has it caused, or is it likely to cause, financial loss?

Several questions need answering:

* How strong must a probability be to become a likelihood, and how is the auditor to read the future?

---

[30] S J Naudé – Legal opinion given to the PAAB, 2 December 1981.
[31] P M A Hunt, 'Material irregularities – Watchdog or Witchdoctor?' *The SA Chartered Accountant*, December 1963, page 186.

- What is the timescale on which the auditor must operate to determine the likelihood of the loss?
- What should the auditor's attitude be in cases where the 'material irregularity' causes profits?

In the first case, the usual answer is that the auditor must use professional judgement. The problem in the second question is that, although there is no financial loss at present, an exposure of the irregularity may lead directly to a loss. In relation to the last question, Naudé states that '... in the absence of loss or the likelihood thereof, even the most serious irregularity is not reportable under the section'.

This raises the vexed question arising from a situation where a substantial consideration (in money or in kind) is made to some third party, in order to procure a substantial contract. As a result of this 'bribe' the undertaking earns substantial profits. However, in the event of the bribe coming to light in the future, it is likely that losses could be suffered as a result of the cancellation of the contract and prosecution of the guilty party. In this situation in the short term, can it be argued that because the undertaking is earning profits as a result of the bribe, this is not a material irregularity, as is suggested by Naudé? The authors are of the opinion that such payments are material irregularities as the four necessary criteria are all present.

19.9.1.5 Summary

In deciding whether or not there is an obligation to report on material irregularities in terms of section 20(5), the registered accountant or auditor should in the first place determine whether the relationship with the client is that of auditor or accountant. Only an auditor has the obligation to report. All the following conditions must apply before it becomes necessary to report on a 'material irregularity':

- It must be irregular.
- The irregularity must be 'material'.
- It must be perpetrated by management.
- It must be in the 'conduct of affairs' of the undertaking.
- It must have caused, or be likely to cause, financial loss.

The auditor must have reason to believe that a material irregularity has taken place or is taking place – but need not necessarily discover it while conducting the audit.

The reader is referred to the Audit and Accounting Guide, *Trading while Factually Insolvent*, issued by the South African Institute of Chartered Accountants in July 1999. It is of interest to note that the vast majority of material irregularities reported to the Board involves undertakings trading under insolvent circumstances.

19.9.2 **The reporting responsibility**

In addition to what is discussed above, section 20(1)(g) places a further statutory duty on the auditor, namely, that an auditor to any undertaking may not issue an unqualified opinion unless, *inter alia*, any material irregularity which had been reported to the person in charge of that undertaking had at the date of the report been adjusted to the satisfaction of the auditor. There are, therefore, three stages in reporting on a material irregularity.

- On discovering a material irregularity, the auditor reports the particulars to the person in charge of the undertaking.

- Unless the material irregularity has 'been adjusted to his satisfaction' within 30 days, the auditor must furnish the Board with copies of the report and other documents.

- The auditor must qualify the report on the financial statements in terms of section 20(1)(g), unless the material irregularity has at the date of the report been adjusted to the auditor's satisfaction.

It appears that section 20(1)(g) must be read in conjunction with section 20(5)(b). To avoid the material irregularity being reported to the Board, the onus is placed on the person in charge of the undertaking to satisfy the auditor:

- that no such irregularity has taken place or is taking place; or
- that adequate steps have been taken for the recovery of any such loss caused; or
- that adequate steps have been taken for the prevention of any such loss likely to be caused.

On having received a written report from the auditor that a material irregularity has taken place or is taking place, the person in charge of the undertaking is given 30 days in which to provide evidence to prove the contrary. It is obvious that it will depend on the nature of the irregularity whether the person in charge will be able to satisfy the auditor that the irregularity has not taken place or is not taking place. It is not possible, for example, to undo theft or forgery. Other irregularities, stemming, for example, from the failure to comply with certain statutory requirements, can be rectified.

Where it is not possible for the person in charge to correct an omission, or the nature of the irregularity is such that it is not possible to undo it, it is still possible to prevent the auditor from having to report the matter to the Board by recovering the financial loss from the culprit or some other source. In cases where the auditor has reason to report a material irregularity because of the likelihood of its causing a loss, the person in charge of the undertaking may then take steps to prevent the loss from being incurred. Failing this, the auditor has a duty to report the matter to the Board.

A question which often arises is whether the auditor should report an irregularity to the person in charge of the undertaking in circumstances where the undertaking is adequately covered by insurance against the loss incurred as a result of the irregularity. For example, where cash stolen by a manager is fully recoverable in terms of a fidelity policy, Naudé rightly points out that although the loss may be recoverable, the loss was in fact incurred. Where the loss is recoverable, this fact will be considered by the auditor after having reported the irregularity to the person in charge of the undertaking.

In cases where nothing has been or can be done to satisfy the auditor, the material irregularity must be reported to the Board. It is not clear whether the auditor's duty comes to an end immediately after the matter has either been adjusted in one of the three ways indicated above or has been reported to the Board. If the report to the Board does not bring the auditor's duty concerning 'material irregularities' to an end and is not interpreted as satisfying the 'been adjusted to the auditor's satisfaction' requirement, then the onus will be on the auditor to be kept informed on a regular basis as to the ultimate outcome of the 'material irregularity'. The qualification of the audit report will have to be perpetuated until the matter has 'been adjusted to the auditor's satisfaction'. The authors believe that once the 'material irregularity' has been reported to the Board the obligation to qualify the report in terms of section 20(1)(g) is removed. The reasons for this opinion are the following:

It is doubtful whether the spirit of the Act had in mind that 'a material irregularity' once reported to the Board, should be noted in a qualification of the audit report on the financial statements until the relevant statutory body or the Attorney-General or the Board has decided on what action should be taken.

If an auditor has reported a material irregularity and the Board has decided not to take any action, does this mean that the auditor should be satisfied, or is a conviction required before the auditor is satisfied in terms of the matter 'being adjusted'? Surely not the latter.

Where an auditor has reason to believe that in the conduct of the affairs of a company a material irregularity has taken place or is taking place, the auditor may not be removed from office until the provisions of section 20(5) have been complied with. If the interpretation is that a report to the Board does not satisfy the auditor in terms of the matter being adjusted, the incoming auditor will have to qualify the audit report in respect of a material irregularity discovered by the outgoing auditor. If an irregularity took place some years earlier, can it reasonably be expected of the incoming auditor to reinvestigate the whole case again to be satisfied that it did take place? Surely not.

Although Naudé does not deal with this problem directly in his legal opinion, he expresses the opinion that section 20(5) is specifically aimed at protecting the undertaking (whatever the legal form), its members and its creditors against financial loss flowing from material irregularities in the conduct of the affairs of the undertaking. It is logical to conclude that the most the auditor can attempt to see to is that the financial loss is made good or that, through the offices of the Board, the appropriate authority (for example, the Attorney-General) is informed so that appropriate legal action, where considered justifiable, can be taken. This view has support in Circular B2/87 of the Board. However, if this is the correct interpretation, then it appears that the auditor will have to qualify the audit opinion only if the audit report on the financial statements is issued during the 30-day period and the matter has not been adjusted to his or her satisfaction.

A further question which arises is what form the qualification, if any, should take in terms of SAAS 700. The reader is referred to the discussion of this issue in the previous chapter. Each particular case will have to be considered in relation to the fairness of the financial statements as a whole. A study of the details of the reported material irregularities shows that virtually any one of the types of qualifications as set out in SAAS 700 could have applied in the various circumstances as reported.

20

Group Financial Statements and Audit

Learning objectives

After studying this chapter you should be able to:
1. Describe the auditor's approach to the audit of group financial statements with particular emphasis on the following:
    – Audit planning;
    – Reliance on other auditors; and
    – Reporting requirements.

20.1 THE NATURE OF A GROUP AUDIT

20.1.1 Companies Act requirements

The Companies Act requires a holding company to prepare consolidated annual financial statements which deal with the affairs of the company and its subsidiaries and are presented to members at the annual general meeting of the company.[1] The responsibility for the preparation of the group financial statements lies with the directors.[2] It is the duty of the holding company auditor to examine the group annual financial statements and to report on them.[3] If the directors decide that group financial statements need not be prepared or that certain subsidiaries should not be dealt with in the group financial statements, the auditor must report on such decision.[4] Approval of the Registrar of Companies is needed and the auditor's report on the decision should accompany the application.[5]

---

[1] Section 288(1).
[2] Section 288(3).
[3] Section 301(1).
[4] Section 294.
[5] Sections 290 and 291.

20.1.2 **What constitutes a group?**

While the Companies Act refers to holding and subsidiary relationships, different combinations of company group structures exist. These include:[6]

- 'a company with subsidiary companies and/or associates;
- a close corporation or other legal business entity with subsidiaries and/or associates;
- a company or other legal business entity with branches or divisions'.

The group structure may be determined by different types of economic activity which may be similar to, or quite different from, the business conducted by the holding company. For example, an investment holding company may hold shares in a number of subsidiary companies engaged in such diverse fields as manufacture, construction, finance, travel and tourism, marketing, food distribution, and retail operations. Alternatively, individual companies in the conduct of their business may be divided into branches or divisions on a geographic or activity centre basis to facilitate the management of the business. For example, banks and building societies may have hundreds of branches spread countrywide, all of which are part of the same company and provide similar financial services to their many customers.

20.2 GROUP AUDIT PLANNING

20.2.1 **Scope of the group audit**

The independent auditor who has the responsibility of reporting on the group financial statements is generally referred to as the principal auditor. As the report of the principal auditor on the group financial statements is a statutory requirement, the scope of the auditor's examination may not be restricted.

- A scope limitation may arise from a problem within a particular component of the group which has the effect of preventing the auditor of that component from obtaining all the audit evidence regarded as necessary and leads to a qualification of the audit report due to the consequent uncertainty.

  The nature of such a scope limitation and its relative importance to the overall results of the group must be considered by the principal auditor to determine whether the qualification in the audit report of the component should be carried through to the audit report on the group.

- A scope limitation may also arise where the auditor of a component has issued an unqualified report on the financial statements of the component, but the principal auditor has reason to believe that the audit of that component has not been carried out in accordance with South African

---

[6] SAAS 600.

auditing standards and thus that the other auditor's report cannot be relied upon.

This may cause doubt about the reliability of information to be incorporated in the group financial statements. In order to resolve any doubts, the principal auditor may consider it necessary to obtain further explanations from the management of the component, review the other auditor's audit working papers (by arrangement with the management of that component), or examine the accounting records of that component. If the principal auditor is not granted access to this additional information, this constitutes a scope limitation. The potential effect of this on the group financial statements will have to be assessed and the audit report drafted accordingly.

20.2.2 **The planning process**

The principles set out in SAAS 300 regarding the main elements of the planning process apply equally to any planning undertaken by the principal auditor in a group audit situation, namely to:

- obtain an understanding of the business and complexity of the group;
- determine the materiality of the financial information of the individual component(s) relative to the group financial statements;
- consider the audit risk which may affect the group financial statements; and
- formulate an audit approach which is appropriate for the group structure.

When planning, the principal auditor has to determine what information is required to support the audit opinion on the group financial statements, and how that information will be obtained. It is important that the principal auditor should communicate with the other auditors during the planning stage, to advise them that reliance is intended on their work and their audit reports, to make them aware of the group reporting requirements and to discuss any potential problem areas.[7] In this regard the management of components of the group would need to authorize their auditors to communicate with the principal auditor.

In formulating the audit approach, the principal auditor must consider the structure of the group and the results of any procedures performed which indicate that further evidence is required for a component audited by another independent auditor.

20.2.3 **Knowledge of the business**

The auditor must gather sufficient information about the business conducted by the entity to be able to assess the audit risks and plan the audit approach in accordance with generally accepted auditing standards. The principal auditor of a group has to consider a number of additional factors, such as:

---

[7] SAAS 600, paragraph .09.

- The number and nature of the different components of the group, that is, are there branches, divisions, subsidiaries, associates or other operating units?

- Are there any foreign components? If so, are these audited by other auditors?

- The significance of the assets and liabilities controlled by each component and their contribution to the results of the group.

- The relative importance of each component to the group results. Are any results out of line with expectations?

- Problems identified in prior audits of any of the components or the holding company which could lead to errors or misstatements in the current group financial statements and which therefore require closer scrutiny.

- The nature and extent of related-party transactions between components of the group.

- The locations and significance of computerized information systems.

- The extent to which centralized controls are exercised from head office.

- The extent to which information systems and controls are standardized within the group, which would facilitate selection and testing during the audit.

- The extent of reliance which can be placed on information generated by the group for analytical review purposes.

- The extent of coverage by internal auditors and the possible effect on audit procedures of the external auditor.

- The extent to which components are audited by other independent auditors, and who they are.

20.2.4 Materiality considerations for a group audit

Auditors use various methods for determining quantitative materiality. Elements of financial statements such as assets, income or revenue are commonly used and quantitative materiality may be based, for example, on 1% – 2% of total assets or 0.5% – 1% of the turnover of the group. In choosing such elements, the auditor must endeavour to choose the elements which are most indicative of size and provide the most stable indicators from one accounting period to the next.[8]

Readers are referred to chapter 5, which sets out the issues to be considered in assessing materiality for audit purposes at the planning stage, during the audit and at the completion stage. Although these principles still apply in a group audit situation, consideration should also be given to the items overleaf.

---

[8] SAAS 320.

Where the group comprises a company with several branches or divisions

Planning materiality should be set for the company as a whole. Accordingly, audit samples drawn for testing transactions or for verification procedures at individual branches or divisions should be based on materiality for the company.

The reason for not quantifying materiality at branch or division level is because the principal auditor is reporting on the financial statements of the company as a whole and not on each individual branch or division. It follows that if a particular branch's figures are immaterial in relation to the company as a whole, limited audit procedures can be applied as it is unlikely that an error, if overlooked, would materially affect the company's financial statements.

Where other firms of auditors are contracted to perform audit work at any of the branches, the principal auditor should advise the branch auditor(s) of the materiality amount to be used. If the branch auditor identifies items below quantitative materiality which are regarded as material from a qualitative point of view, these should be brought to the attention of the principal auditor. It is important that all identified misstatements be reported to the principal auditor so that they may be aggregated with all other misstatements to assess their combined affect on the financial statements as a whole.

Where the group comprises a holding company with subsidiaries

In this situation the principal auditor is reporting on the consolidated financial statements of the group. Accordingly, an assessment of the final materiality amount relative to the combined results of the group is required in order to detect errors or irregularities which could lead to material misstatement in the consolidated financial statements. This amount will generally be higher than that set at the planning stage of the audit of the individual companies in the group.

The principal auditor may not specify what amount the auditors of the individual companies in the group should regard as material in relation to their audits of those companies. This is so because the independent auditors of the subsidiary companies within the group have the responsibility of reporting on the financial statements of those companies.

The principal auditor, in the course of obtaining information for purposes of the consolidation of the group financial statements, will usually request the auditors of other components to disclose any unadjusted misstatements or material matters which may require disclosure or adjustment in the consolidated financial statements based on the group materiality amount set by the principal auditor.

20.2.5 Assessing audit risk for the group

The principal auditor, in reporting on the consolidated financial statements of the group, is required to assess the risk that material errors or misstatements may occur in the group financial statements. The principal auditor considers whether or not the subsidiary's auditor has appropriately assessed inherent and control risks and has done sufficient audit work to reduce detection risk to acceptable levels.

Errors or misstatements may occur as the result of:

● errors or misstatements in the financial statements of subsidiaries, the incorrect details of which will be incorporated into the consolidated financial statements of the group; or
● errors made in passing *pro forma* journal entries when preparing the consolidated financial statements.

If the principal auditor is also the auditor of all subsidiary companies within the group, there is little risk of error in their financial statements not being reduced to acceptable levels. Where subsidiary companies which are significant in size in relation to the group have been audited by other auditors, the principal auditor may not unquestioningly accept an unqualified audit report as being sufficient evidence to reduce the risk of error or misstatement to acceptable levels. Enquiries should be made regarding the competence and independence of the other auditors and the audit procedures they have performed. This aspect is discussed later in this chapter.

To reduce the risk of errors being made by the client when preparing the consolidated financial statements, the auditor needs to consider the following:

● the competence of the client's staff responsible for preparing the consolidated financial statements;

● the system or mechanism used to ensure that the correct information needed to pass appropriate *pro forma* journal entries is available. Examples of such information are group intercompany transactions and profit elements thereof, indebtedness between group companies at the year-end and the sale by subsidiaries of assets which were assigned values different to book values at the date of acquisition of the subsidiaries by the holding company. The use of standardized consolidation packs or working papers is a means often used to ensure that the necessary information is gathered from subsidiary companies in a disciplined manner. It is usual that the auditor of the subsidiary attests to the fair presentation of the information set out in the consolidation pack;

● the adequacy of the consolidation working papers supporting the consolidated financial statements. These should contain at least the following information for each subsidiary:
   – the asset, liability, revenue and expense as disclosed in the audited

financial statements and how these have been grouped and classified for disclosure in the consolidated financial statements;

- adjustments required to convert the subsidiary company book values to those values assigned at the date of acquisition, if these differ;
- adjustments to any profits or losses arising from the disposal of assets by subsidiaries where such assets were assigned different values at acquisition;
- adjustments required, if deemed necessary, to achieve uniformity of the application of accounting policies across the group companies where subsidiary companies have used policies which differ;
- adjustments required to eliminate intergroup profits, intercompany indebtedness and other intergroup transactions;
- computation of goodwill or premium on acquisition, being the difference between the cost of the shares in the subsidiary and the holding company's share of net asset value as adjusted at the time of acquisition;
- amortization of any goodwill arising on acquisition of shares in subsidiary companies;
- adjustments required in respect of any dividends paid by subsidiaries out of pre-acquisition profits; and
- computation of the minority interest.

The auditor needs to verify the appropriateness of the consolidation *pro forma* journal entries and check the arithmetical accuracy of all calculations.

Where goodwill arises on consolidation, the auditor needs to consider carefully whether or not there has been a permanent diminution in value of goodwill since acquisition. Evidence of this would be changes in business conditions leading to reduced profitability or even losses being incurred.

There are three potential risks arising where there are foreign subsidiaries within the group. These are:

- The accounting framework used to prepare the financial statements might be different to that used by the holding company and its South African subsidiaries.
- Reliance might be placed on the work of a foreign auditor whose audit may not conform to or be performed to lesser standards than South African Auditing Standards.
- Misstatements might arise on the translation of foreign currency for the preparation of the group report in the local currency.

Should a different accounting framework have been used, adjustments are required to achieve uniformity such that the group financial statements are prepared in accordance with one framework. The auditor would need to be satisfied that any differences in accounting policies used have been identified and that appropriate adjustments have been made for consolidation purposes.

Should there be concerns regarding the auditing standards applicable to the foreign auditor, special instructions regarding any additional audit work required by South African Auditing Standards would need to be given to the foreign auditor. This the South African auditor would do via management of the holding company.

The auditor would need to check that the appropriate rate of exchange was used to translate the foreign currency and that the calculations are correct.

20.2.6 Formulating an audit approach or strategy for the group audit

A group audit provides opportunities for the principal auditor to rationalize the audit approach.

Group comprising a component with branches and/or divisions

The principal auditor can achieve savings of audit time and fees in the case of the audit of a component with branches or divisions where the systems are centralized, by standardizing audit programmes and possibly going so far as to determine the sample sizes and to select the samples which are to be tested at the branches by branch auditors.

Where individual branches are not material, visits to these branches could be done on a rotation basis thus limiting the auditing procedures during other periods to analytical reviews of branch returns of assets, liabilities and income to head office. In the case of decentralized systems, the inherent and control risks of each branch will have to be individually assessed and the audit programmes for each adapted accordingly.

Where accounting systems are computerized, the possibility of using CAATs at the head office should be considered, in order to test application controls for compliance, produce analytical reviews of information contained in computerized records, or select samples for further detailed substantive testing. This can lead to a reduction in the extent of audit procedures which need to be conducted at the individual branches.

Group comprising a holding company with subsidiaries

The principal auditor's prime responsibility is to report on the group financial statements. In determining the audit approach, analytical review procedures should be carried out at the planning stage to identify key components of the group and any potential problem areas.

The principal auditor, together with management, is responsible for preparing instructions that set out the group consolidation accounting, auditing and reporting requirements – this including the design of a consolidation pack for completion by all group companies to facilitate the gathering of information required for consolidation purposes and, also, in setting and ensuring adherence to year-end timetables and maintaining liaison with group auditors either directly or through the management of the components audited by them.

The principal auditor will review the completed consolidation returns and, where necessary, arrange for and conduct a review of audit working papers of other group auditors. If it appears that the report of the subsidiary company auditors cannot be relied upon, it may be necessary for the principal auditor, with the consent of the management of subsidiary companies, to extend the analytical review of the accounting records of group components to ensure that sufficient audit evidence has been obtained to support the unqualified audit report on the consolidated financial statements. Where components are audited by other auditors and the results are significant to the group, the principal auditor must either obtain completed audit questionnaires to assess the audit approach and evidence gathered by those auditors or review their audit working papers.

20.3 RELIANCE ON OTHER AUDITORS

20.3.1 Responsibilities of the principal auditor

The structure of the group has important implications for the principal auditor. In reporting on the fairness of the group financial statements, sufficient evidence has to be obtained to support the audit opinion. This requirement includes determining whether amounts included in the group financial statements relating to components are acceptable and can be relied upon. SAAS 600 states:

> 'The principal auditor should perform procedures to obtain sufficient appropriate audit evidence that the work of the other auditor is adequate for the principal auditor's purposes, in the context of the specific assignment'.[9]

20.3.2 Assessing the reliance that may be placed on the other auditor

Before the principal auditor can rely on work performed by another auditor, reasonable assurance has to be obtained that the work performed is adequate. To obtain this assurance, the principal auditor has to be satisfied as to the competence and independence of other auditors of components, as well as their audit approach, evidence gathered and documentation. Procedures which the principal auditor could carry out in this regard are:

- Inquire of professional organizations, bankers and other auditors concerning their assessment of the professional competence and integrity of the other auditor. If the other auditor firm is known to the principal auditor, these enquiries would probably not be necessary. If there is doubt about the professional qualifications, competence or integrity of the other

---

[9] SAAS 600, 'Using the Work of Another Auditor', paragraph .08.

auditor, available alternatives should be considered, as well as the possible effect on the audit opinion.

- Obtain written representations from the other auditor confirming compliance with independence requirements.

- Advise the other auditor of the accounting, auditing and reporting requirements and obtain written representation as to compliance with these.

- Perform such procedures as are necessary to obtain reasonable assurance that the work undertaken by the other auditor is adequate for the purpose of the group audit. This could include discussions with the other auditor regarding audit procedures applied, a review of the other auditor's audit working papers and the completion of a group audit questionnaire dealing with that auditor's audit procedures and findings.

- Discuss with the other auditor and the management of the component, the audit findings or other material matters affecting the financial statements.

- If supplementary tests are deemed necessary, these should be performed either by the principal or other auditor.

20.3.3 Rights of access of the principal auditor

To determine whether reliance on information from components included in the group financial statements is justified, the auditor needs access to information about the audit of each component in the group. While this will be relatively easy for those group companies and branches audited by the same firm, this may be more difficult when reliance is necessary on the work of other independent auditors with respect to financial information of one or more components included in the group financial statements.

The principal auditor's right of access to information is determined by legislation governing the holding company and its component and by any agreement between the principal auditor and the owners of the component. Where the entity is governed by the Companies Act, the rights of access of the principal auditor are set out in section 281, which recognizes the following circumstances:

- Where the component is a branch, division or other part of the entity, the principal auditor has full right of access to all accounting records and to any information and explanations considered necessary for the performance of the principal auditor's duties.[10]

- Where the component is a subsidiary, the principal auditor has the right of access to all current and former financial statements and has the right to receive from the directors of the holding company or subsidiary full information and explanations as regards the financial statements and the

---

[10] Section 281(a).

accounting records which the auditor considers necessary, but the auditor does not have the right of access to the accounting records, books or other documents.[11]

Although the principal auditor has restricted access in the case of subsidiaries audited by other auditors, this can be, and usually is, extended by agreement with management. Arrangements are often made for the principal auditor to obtain explanations directly from the other auditors and to review their audit working papers where this is considered necessary.

Where the component is a trust, partnership, a joint venture or an associate company, the auditor is only entitled to information that is made available to all shareholders, members and owners of the component or that may be made available to the auditor in terms of any agreement between the owners such as that referred to in the previous paragraph.

20.3.4 Determining the principal auditor's responsibilities

The principal auditor's responsibilities vary according to the nature of the entity and its components.

- Where the component is part of the same legal entity, such as a branch or division, the principal auditor is responsible for the audit and the content of the audit report of the entity as a whole, including those components which are audited by other auditors.

  In this situation the principal auditor will generally instruct the other independent branch auditor to conduct specific procedures or tests and will also advise the branch auditor of the planning materiality amount to be used. If the company has a centralized accounting system, the principal auditor may also select the samples which the branch auditor is to examine during the course of the audit work. If during the course of an audit at the branch, the branch auditor considers additional work is necessary or, for example, that the materiality amount should be varied, this should be discussed with the principal auditor before finalizing the report on the branch.

  The principal auditor will also communicate directly with branch auditors regarding any matters relevant to the assignment. These may include timetables, the format in which branch information is to be communicated to the head office and any important facts concerning the branch which may need to be known by the branch auditor.

- Where the component is a separate legal entity, such as a subsidiary company, the principal auditor is responsible for the audit and audit report of the group, which includes the information relating to the component audited by the other auditor. SAAS 600, paragraph .07, indicates that 'when planning to use the work of another auditor, the principal auditor should consider the professional competence of the other auditor in the context of the specific assignment'.

---

[11] Section 281(b).

20.4 REPORTING REQUIREMENTS

The Companies Act imposes a duty on the holding company auditor to examine the group annual financial statements and to deal with them in the audit report.[12] If the directors decide that no group financial statements need be prepared or that certain subsidiaries need not be dealt with in the group financial statements and the Registrar of Companies has given his approval,[13] it is the responsibility of the auditor to report on any such decision of the directors.[14]

The principal auditor reports on the group financial information as a whole. When expressing an unqualified opinion, the principal auditor should not normally refer to the work or findings of the other auditor(s) as this may be misconstrued as a qualification of the principal auditor's opinion.

If, however, any other auditors have qualified or disclaimed their opinion on a component, the principal auditor will need to consider the nature and significance, in relation to the group financial statements, to determine whether or not a qualification or disclaimer of the principal auditor's opinion is warranted.[15]

Where the principal auditor concludes that the work of the other auditor cannot be used and it has not been possible to carry out sufficient additional procedures to remove any uncertainty which may be material to fair presentation, the audit opinion on the group financial statements should be qualified or disclaimed.[16] Clearly the results of that component must be material to the group results before such a qualification or disclaimer is issued. Readers are referred to chapter 18 on audit reports for the appropriate wording of an unqualified and a qualified audit report on annual financial statements.

---

[12] Section 301(1).
[13] Sections 290 and 291.
[14] Section 294.
[15] SAAS 600, paragraph .19.
[16] SAAS 600, paragraph .18.

21

Corporate Governance

Learning objectives

After studying this chapter you should be able to:

1. Describe the principles and requirements set out in the 'King Report on Corporate Governance in South Africa – 2002', covering the following matters:
   - Boards and directors;
   - Risk management;
   - Internal audit;
   - Integrated sustainability reporting;
   - Accounting and auditing; and
   - Compliance and enforcement.
2. Outline the guidance given in the South African Institute of Chartered Accountants' guides on Corporate Governance.

21.1 INTRODUCTION

The King Committee on Corporate Governance, formed as a result of initiatives by The Institute of Directors in South Africa, reported its recommendations in 1994 – often referred to as the King I Report or the King Report 1994. Using the guidelines of Britain's Cadbury Report, the King Committee addressed the following issues:

- declining ethical business standards;
- the role and responsibilities of executive and non-executive directors;
- the duties and responsibilities of auditors; and
- management's disclosure responsibilities to the company's stakeholders.

In 1995 the Regulations of the JSE Securities Exchange South Africa were amended to require listed companies to disclose compliance (or, where applicable, non-compliance, giving reasons) with the Code of Corporate Practices and Conduct for accounting periods commencing after 30 June 1995. In March 2002 the King Committee on Corporate Governance issued its second report, often referred to as the King II or King 2002. Four guiding principles were established for the purposes of the review leading to the report. These are set out in the report at paragraph .29 as follows:

813

'... to review the King Report 1994 and to assess its currency against developments, locally and internationally, since its publication on 29 November 1994;

to review and clarify the earlier proposal in the King Report 1994 for an "inclusive approach" for the sustainable success of companies;

to recognise the increasing importance placed on non-financial issues world-wide, and to consider and to recommend reporting on issues associated with social and ethical accounting, auditing and reporting ("SEAAR") and safety, health and environment ("SHE"); and

to recommend how compliance with a new Code of Corporate Governance for South Africa can be measured and based on outcomes, that is, how the success of companies can be measured through the "balanced scorecard" approach for reporting.'

The content of the report covers the following:

An executive summary which sets out

- an introduction and background to the report;
- a summary of the content of the code of corporate practices and conduct; and
- recommendations that require statutory amendments and other actions.

The King Report on Corporate Governance in South Africa 2002, which contains six sections:

- Boards and Directors;
- Risk Management;
- Internal Audit;
- Integrated Sustainability Reporting;
- Accounting and Auditing; and
- Compliance and Enforcement.

Fourteen Appendices which, *inter alia*, give details of the members of the committee, the terms of reference for the task teams, guidance on how aspects raised in the report might be implemented, and selected bibliography and useful websites on corporate governance. In addition, many of the observations and recommendations contained in the King Report 1994 remain current and have thus been repeated for the purpose of completeness in King 2002.

The following represents a summary of the introductory and background information to the Report and the main recommendations of the King 2002 Report on Corporate Governance and its Code of Corporate Practices and Conduct. Readers are cautioned that the authors, in presenting an overview of King 2002, have identified, in their opinion, the more important aspects covered and, for the sake of brevity, these have been summarized. Readers wishing a complete report should contact The Institute of Directors in Southern Africa, P O Box 908, Parklands 2121, South Africa. Telephone 011 – 643 8086, Fax 011 – 484 1416.

21.2 KING REPORT 2002 – INTRODUCTION AND BACK-GROUND

King 1994 went beyond the financial and regulatory aspects of corporate governance by emphasizing the need for companies to recognize that they cannot act independently from the society and environment in which they operate. It advocated an integrated approach to good governance in the interest of a wide range of stakeholders having regard for the fundamental principles of good financial, social, ethical and environmental practice. Following this integrated approach (termed an inclusive approach in King 2002), the board of directors of companies have to consider not only the regulatory aspects, but also industry and market standards, industry reputation, the investigative media, and the attitudes of customers, suppliers, consumers, employees, investors, and communities (local, national and international), ethical pressure groups, public opinion, public confidence and political opinion.[1]

The inclusive approach recognizes that, besides the shareholders, other stakeholders such as the community in which the company operates, its employees, its customers and its suppliers need to be considered when developing the strategy of a company. The approach thus requires that the board identifies stakeholders relevant to the company's business and that it defines the purpose of the company and the values by which the company will conduct its daily business. These aspects would need to be considered by the board when developing strategies to achieve the company's goals and these should be communicated to all stakeholders.

Further, the board has a duty to monitor that its agreed-upon strategies are implemented by management.

In considering a company's economic performance reference is sometimes made to the bottom line, meaning the profit earned as reflected, usually, as the last item in the Income Statement. King 2002 refers to the move from the single to the triple bottom line, which embraces the economic, environmental and social aspects of a company's activities. The economic aspect involves the financial aspects as well as the non-financial ones relevant to the company's business. The environmental aspects include the effect on the environment of the product or services produced by the company. The social aspects embrace values, ethics and the reciprocal relationships with all stakeholders.

King 2002 identifies seven characteristics of good corporate governance as follows:[2]

'**Discipline**
Corporate discipline is a commitment by a company's senior management to adhere to behaviour that is universally recognized and accepted to be correct

---

[1] King Report on Corporate Governance for South Africa 2002 (King 2002 Report).
[2] King 2002, paragraphs .18.1 to .18.7.

and proper. This encompasses a company's awareness of, and commitment to, the underlying principles of good governance, particularly at senior management level.

Transparency

Transparency is the ease with which an outsider is able to make meaningful analysis of a company's actions, its economic fundamentals and the non-financial aspects pertinent to that business. This is a measure of how good management is at making necessary information available in a candid, accurate and timely manner – not only the audit data but also general reports and press releases. It reflects whether or not investors obtain a true picture of what is happening inside the company.

Independence

Independence is the extent to which mechanisms have been put in place to minimise or avoid potential conflicts of interest that may exist, such as dominance by a strong chief executive or large shareowner. These mechanisms range from the composition of the board, to appointments to committees of the board, and external parties such as the auditors. The decisions made, and internal processes established, should be objective and not allow for undue influence.

Accountability

Individuals or groups in a company, who make decisions and take actions on specific issues, need to be accountable for their decisions and actions. Mechanisms must exist and be effective to allow for accountability. These provide investors with the means to query and assess the actions of the board and its committees.

Responsibility

With regard to management, responsibility pertains to behaviour that allows for corrective action and for penalising mismanagement. Responsible management would, when necessary, put in place what it would take to set the company on the right path. While the board is accountable to the company, it must act responsively to and with responsibility towards all stakeholders of the company.

Fairness

The systems that exist within the company must be balanced in taking into account all those that have an interest in the company and its future. The rights of various groups have to be acknowledged and respected. For example, minority shareowner interests must receive equal consideration to those of the dominant shareowner(s).

Social responsibility

A well-managed company will be aware of, and respond to, social issues, placing a high priority on ethical standards. A good corporate citizen is increasingly seen as one that is non-discriminatory, non-exploitative, and responsible with regard to environmental and human rights issues. A company is likely to experience indirect economic benefits such as improved productivity and corporate reputation by taking those factors into consideration.'

Corporate governance is essentially about leadership. King 2002 identifies four areas of leadership as follows:[3]

- 'leadership for efficiency in order for companies to compete effectively in the global economy, and thereby create jobs;

- leadership for probity because investors require confidence and assurance that the management of a company will behave honestly and with integrity in regard to their shareowners and others;

- leadership with responsibility as companies are increasingly called upon to address legitimate social concerns relating to their activities; and

- leadership that is both transparent and accountable because otherwise business leaders cannot be trusted and this will lead to the decline of companies and the ultimate demise of a country's economy.'

King 2002, at paragraph .35, summarizes the board's responsibilities as follows:

'The responsibilities of a board under the inclusive approach in the 21st century will be to define the purpose of the company and the values by which the company will perform its daily existence and to identify the stakeholders relevant to the business of the company. The board must then develop a strategy combining all three factors and ensure that management implements this strategy. The board's duty then is to monitor that implementation. The board must also deal with the well-known financial aspects. The key risk areas and the key performance indicators must be identified, as well as how those risks are to be managed. In regard to the obligation to report as a going concern, the directors need to ensure that the facts and assumptions they rely on in coming to that conclusion are recorded. The board needs regularly to monitor the human capital aspects of the company in regard to succession, morale, training, remuneration, etc. In addition, the board must ensure that there is effective communication of its strategic plans and ethical code, both internally and externally. The board must see to it that there are adequate internal controls and that the management information systems can cope with the strategic direction in which the company is headed. There must be a "licence to operate" check in language understandable to all those to whom it is communicated.'[4]

The following represents a summary of the main recommendations of the King 2002 Report on Corporate Governance and its Code of Corporate Practices and Conduct.

---

[3] King 2002, paragraph .39.
[4] King 2002, paragraph .35.

21.3 THE CODE OF CORPORATE PRACTICES AND CONDUCT

21.3.1 Introduction

The Code and recommendations are directed at the following business enterprises:

- all companies listed on the main board of the JSE Securities Exchange South Africa;
- banks, financial and insurance entities as defined in the various legislation regulating the South African financial services sector;
- public sector enterprises and agencies that fall under the Public Finance Management Act and the Local Government: Municipal Finance Management Bill (still to be promulgated) including any department of State or administration in the national, provincial or local sphere of government.

All companies should, however, be encouraged to adopt the Code.

21.3.2 Board and directors

The board of directors is ultimately accountable and responsible for the affairs of the company and its performance. This includes the responsibility for ensuring that the company complies with all relevant laws, regulations, and codes of business conduct. The delegation of authority to others does not mitigate or dissipate such duties and responsibilities.

When deciding on whether or not authority be delegated to others the board should define levels of materiality and should retain authority to itself for deciding on material matters. Where authority has been delegated to management, this should be set out in writing and the board should monitor management's implementation of the board's plans and strategies.

The board must give strategic direction to the company, and must retain full and effective control over the company's affairs. To this end, the board should identify key risks areas and key performance indicators of the company's business and introduce controls to manage these risks. These aspects should be regularly reviewed and monitored, with particular attention being given to technology and systems.

The directors should have unrestricted access to all company information, records, documents and property. They should also have access to the advice and services of the company secretary and be entitled to seek independent professional advice about the company's affairs at the company's expense.

King 2002 introduces an important recommendation in suggesting that the board of directors should have a charter setting out its responsibilities and that this charter should be disclosed in the company's annual report. At a minimum, the charter should confirm the board's responsibility for the adoption of strategic plans, monitoring of operational performance and management, the determination of policy and processes to ensure the integrity of the company's risk management and internal controls, communication of policy, and director selection, orientation and evaluation.

21.3.3 Board composition

The board should comprise a balance of executive and non-executive directors, preferably with a majority of non-executive directors who are independent of the company. Executive directors are individuals who are involved in the day-to-day management of a company and hold salaried positions of employment. Non-executive directors who are independent of a company are those who do not derive any benefits from the company other than their fees.

The board should ensure that the mix of directors is such that no one individual or group of individuals can dominate the board's decision taking. Non-executive directors should be individuals of calibre and credibility who can bring an independent judgement to bear on issues of strategy, performance, resources, transformation, diversity and employment equity, standards of conduct and evaluation of performance.

The selection and appointment of directors should be matters for the board as a whole to decide. If assisted by a nomination committee, the composition of such a committee should consist of non-executive directors.

The board should establish a formal orientation programme to inform incoming directors of the company's business environment, operations and management. Appointees who have no prior experience as directors should receive assistance to inform them of their duties, responsibilities, powers and potential liability.

The board should regularly review its required mix of skills and experience and other qualities such as its demographics and diversity in order to assess its effectiveness.

21.3.4 Chairperson and chief executive officer

The chairperson should preferably be a non-executive director of the company and should not also be the chief executive officer. Appraisal of the performance of the chairperson and chief executive officer should be conducted at least on an annual basis. The results of such appraisals should be considered by the Remuneration Committee in deciding on appropriate remuneration packages.

21.3.5 Remuneration

Levels of remuneration should be sufficient to attract, retain and motivate executives. Directors' remuneration, including that of non-executive directors, should be the subject of recommendations to the board of a Remuneration Committee. Its membership should comprise persons who are competent to determine the appropriate remuneration of senior executives, with the majority of its members (including the chair) being non-executive directors.

Performance-related elements of remuneration are encouraged, rewarding achievement rather than status.

There should be a separate full and clear disclosure of the total of executive and non-executive directors' earnings on an individual basis. Separate figures should be given for salary, fees, benefits, share options and bonuses.

21.3.6 Board meetings

To carry out its functions the board must meet regularly. How regularly or at what intervals must be determined by each board, having regard to its company's own circumstances. A board should, however, meet at least once a quarter. The annual report should disclose the number of meetings held and the details of attendance of each director.

Non-executive directors should have access to management and be furnished with all available information so as to be able to make a meaningful contribution to the board's deliberations.

21.3.7 Dealing in securities

A listed company should communicate to its directors, officers and selected employees that they are prohibited from dealing in the company's securities for a designated period preceding the announcement of its financial results.

21.3.8 Company secretary

The company secretary, through the board, has an important role to play in good corporate governance. Accordingly, the board should empower the company secretary to enable such a person to properly fulfil his or her duties. Apart from statutory duties, the company secretary should do the following:

- provide the board and individual directors with guidance as to proper discharge of their duties;
- play an important role in the induction of new or inexperienced directors;
- assist in determining the annual board plan and administration of other issues of a strategic nature at the board level;
- provide a central source of guidance and advice to the board, management and employees on matters of good governance.

21.4 RISK MANAGEMENT

The board is responsible for risk management and for forming an opinion on the effectiveness of the process. Management is accountable to the board for the designing, implementing and monitoring of the process of risk management and for integrating it into the daily activities of the company.

Use should be made of generally recognized risk management and internal control models and frameworks in order to provide reasonable assurance regarding the achievement of organizational objectives with respect to:[5]

- 'effectiveness and efficiency of operations;
- safeguarding of the company's assets (including information);
- compliance with applicable laws, regulations and supervisory requirements;
- supporting business sustainability under normal as well as adverse operating conditions;
- reliability of reporting; and
- behaving responsibly towards all stakeholders.'

The board is responsible for ensuring that a systematic documented assessment of the processes and outcomes surrounding key risks is undertaken at least annually, for the purpose of its making a public statement on risk management. The risk assessment should address the company's exposure to at least the following:[6]

- 'physical and operational risks;
- human resource risks;
- technology risks;
- business continuity and disaster recovery;
- credit and market risks; and
- compliance risks.'

The reader is referred to chapter 9 of this text where risk management and internal controls are discussed at length.

21.5 INTERNAL AUDIT

Companies should have an effective internal audit function that has the respect and cooperation of the board and management. Where there is no such function, reasons therefore must be disclosed in the annual report, as well as how in the particular circumstances assurance is obtained regarding the effectiveness of internal controls.

Internal audit should report at a level which allows it to meet its responsibilities. This would usually be to the audit committee.

The appointment or dismissal of the head of internal audit should be with the concurrence of the audit committee.

An effective internal audit function should provide:[7]

- 'assurance that the management processes are adequate to identify and monitor significant risks;

---

[5] King 2002, paragraph .3.1.4.
[6] King 2002, paragraph .3.1.5.
[7] King 2002, paragraph .4.2.2.

- confirmation of the effective operation of the established internal control systems;

- credible processes for feedback on risk management and assurance; and

- objective confirmation that the board receives the right quality of assurance and information from management and that this information is reliable.'

The audit committee should approve the internal audit work plan. This plan should be based on risk assessment as well as issues raised by the audit committee or board and senior management. The internal audit function's assessment of risks should confirm that of the board's own assessment.

Internal audit should liaise and cooperate with other internal providers of assurance and with the external auditors to ensure proper attention to financial, operational and compliance controls and to minimize the duplication of effort.

21.6 INTEGRATED SUSTAINABILITY REPORTING

Every company should report at least annually on the nature and extent of its social transformation, ethical, safety, health and environmental management policies, and practices.

King 2002 identifies three levels of reporting as follows:[8]

- 'First level would be disclosures relating to acceptance and adoption of business principles and/or codes of practice that can be verified by reference to documents, board minutes or established policies and standards.

- Second level should address the implementation of practices in keeping with accepted principles involving a review of steps taken to encourage adherence to these principles evidenced by board directors, designated policies and communiqués, supported by appropriate non-financial accounting mechanisms.

- Third level should involve investigation and demonstration of changes and benefits that have resulted from the adoption and implementation of stated business principles and/or codes of practice.'

Matters requiring specific consideration include:[9]

- 'Description of practices reflecting a committed effort to reducing workplace accidents, fatalities, and occupational health and safety incidents against stated measurement targets and objectives and a suitable explanation where appropriate. This would cover the nature and extent of the strategy, plan and policies adopted to address and manage the potential impact of HIV/AIDS on the company's activities.

---

[8] King 2002, paragraph .5.1.2.
[9] King 2002, paragraph .5.1.4.

- Reporting on environmental corporate governance must reflect current South African law by the application of the "Best Practicable Environmental Option" standard (defined as that option that has most benefit, or causes the least damage to the environment at a cost acceptable to society).

- Policies defining social investment prioritization and spending and the extent of initiatives to support black economic empowerment, in particular with regard to procurement practices and investment strategies.

- Disclosure of human capital development in areas such as the number of staff, with a particular focus on progress against equity targets, achievement of corporate training and development initiatives, age, employee development and financial investment committed. This should also address issues that create the conditions and opportunities for previously disadvantaged individuals, in particular women, to have an equal opportunity to reach executive levels in the company and to realize their full potential. It should include progress made in this regard, and mechanisms to positively reinforce the richness of diversity and the added value and contribution from this diversity.'

21.7 ORGANIZATIONAL INTEGRITY/CODE OF ETHICS

Every company should demonstrate its commitment to organizational integrity by setting out its standards in a code of ethics.

Companies should demonstrate their commitment to their codes of ethics by:[10]

- 'creating systems and procedures to introduce, monitor and enforce its ethical code;

- assigning high level individuals to oversee compliance to the ethical code;

- assessing the integrity of new appointees in the selection and promotion procedures;

- exercising due care in delegating discretionary authority;

- communicating with, and training, all employees regarding enterprise values, standards and compliance procedures;

- providing, monitoring and auditing safe systems for reporting of unethical or risky behaviour;

- enforcing appropriate discipline with consistency; and

- responding to offences and preventing reoccurrence.'

Disclosure should be made by the directors of adherence to the company's code against the above criteria.

---

[10] King 2002, paragraph .5.2.2.

21.8 ACCOUNTING, AUDITING AND THE AUDIT COMMITTEE

21.8.1 Accounting and auditing

The audit committee should recommend the appointment of external auditors for the consideration of the board and acceptance by the shareholders.

Consultation between internal and external auditors is necessary to ensure efficient audit processes and in so doing minimizing the duplication of effort. This can be done by holding meetings and the exchange of working papers, letters and reports.

The audit committee should set principles for recommending the use of the accounting firm of the external auditors for non-audit services. The notes to the annual financial statements should disclose the nature of such services rendered, together with amounts paid for such services.

21.8.2 Audit committee

The board should appoint an audit committee that consists of a majority of independent non-executive directors, one of whom should be chairperson. The chairperson should not also be chairperson of the board. The majority of its members should also be financially literate. The board should consider whether or not the chief executive officer should function as a member of the audit committee or attend meetings only on invitation.

The audit committee should have written terms of reference that deal with membership, authority and duties. The annual report should state whether the committee has satisfied its responsibilities in compliance with its terms of reference. Members of the committee should also be disclosed in the annual report and the chairperson should attend the annual general meeting to answer questions about its work.

21.9 RELATIONS WITH STAKEHOLDERS

Companies should enter into dialogue with institutional investors based on constructive engagement and an understanding of objectives. Institutional investors should evaluate a company's corporate governance arrangements, particularly those relating to board structure and composition.

Institutional investors in particular should attend the annual general meeting of companies in which they hold shares.

Each item of special business included in the notice of the annual general meeting should be accompanied by a full explanation of the effects of the proposed resolution. The chairperson should allow sufficient time for discussion of important matters.

Important decisions taken at meetings should be disseminated so that shareholders who were not present are informed or have ready access to such information.

21.10 COMMUNICATION

It is the board's duty to present a balanced and understandable assessment of the company's position in reporting to stakeholders. The quality of the information must be based on the guidelines of openness and substance over form. Reporting should address material matters of significant interest and concern to all stakeholders.

Reports and communications must be made in the context that society now demands greater transparency and accountability from corporations regarding their non-financial affairs, including, for example, their employment policies and environmental issues.

Reports should present a balance between the positive and negative aspects of the activities of the company.

The directors' report should include statements that:

- the financial statements are their responsibility and that they fairly present the state of affairs of the company;
- the auditor is responsible for reporting on the financial statements;
- adequate accounting records and an effective system of internal controls have been maintained;
- appropriate accounting policies supported by reasonable and prudent judgements and estimates have been used in the preparation of the financial statements;
- applicable accounting standards have been adhered to or, if there has been any departure in the interests of fair presentation, this departure has not only been disclosed and explained but also quantified;
- there is no reason to believe the business will not be a going concern in the year ahead or an explanation if it is believed otherwise;
- the Code of Corporate Practices and Conduct has been adhered to or, if not, in what respects it has not been adhered to.

21.11 GUIDANCE ON THE CODE OF CORPORATE PRACTICES AND CONDUCT

The Code of Corporate Practices and Conduct, contained in the King Report on Corporate Governance, sets out certain requirements which affect both directors and auditors of companies. The South African Institute of Chartered Accountants has published a series of guides on corporate governance which should assist directors in meeting the requirements of the Code. These are:

- *Guidance for Directors: Reporting on Internal Control;*
- *Stakeholder Communication in the Annual Report;*
- *Guidance for Directors: Going Concern and Financial Reporting;* and
- *Guidance for Directors: The Role of Internal Audit.*

A summary of the contents of these guides follows.

21.11.1 Guidance for Directors: Reporting on Internal Control

The Code of Corporate Practices and Conduct requires directors to report in their company's annual report on 'the maintenance of adequate accounting records and an effective system of internal control'. Further, a statement must be made that to the best of the directors' knowledge there has been no major breakdown during the year in the operation of the system of internal control or, if indeed a breakdown has occurred, full details must be given with comment on the remedial action taken or being taken. Where a company is a holding company, the Guide suggests that directors should report on the systems of internal control in all material subsidiaries. The same applies to directors of companies holding material investments in associate companies or material joint ventures.

The Guide defines internal control as follows:

'Internal control is broadly defined as a process, effected by a company's board of directors, management and other personnel, designed to provide reasonable assurance regarding the achievement of objectives in the categories of:

1. economy, efficiency and effectiveness of operations,
2. internal financial controls; and
3. compliance with applicable laws and regulations.'

Operational controls are aimed at the business objectives of achieving predetermined profitability goals, while internal financial controls provide reasonable assurance of the safeguarding of assets against unauthorized use or disposition, and the maintenance of proper accounting records and the reliability of financial information used within the business or for publication.

In principle, the definition of internal financial controls excludes efficiency, value for money, and legal and regulatory compliance issues.

Controls to ensure compliance with laws and regulations are quite obviously those controls instituted to provide assurance that the operations of a business entity are within the law.

Because of the inherent limitations of internal controls, when reporting on these, directors should not give the impression that nothing can go wrong. Such limitations include the following:

- management's usual requirement that the cost of internal control does not exceed the expected benefit to be derived;

- the tendency for internal controls to be directed at routine transactions rather than non-routine transactions;
- the potential for human error due to carelessness, distraction, mistakes of judgement and the misunderstanding of instructions;
- the possibility of circumvention of internal controls through the collusion of a member of management or of an employee with parties outside or inside the company;
- the possibility that a person responsible for exercising an internal control could abuse that responsibility, for example, a member of management overriding an internal control; and
- the possibility that procedures may become inadequate due to changes in conditions and, therefore, compliance with procedures may deteriorate.

The Guide defines the roles of three parties, namely directors, external auditors and internal auditors, in relation to the implementation and monitoring of an internal control system as discussed below.

Role of the directors

The board of directors is ultimately responsible for all aspects of the system of internal control used in the company or group, and for monitoring its effectiveness. The detailed design, implementation and operation of adequate internal controls will normally be delegated to management by the board of directors.

Role of the external auditors

The implementation and monitoring of an internal control system is not the responsibility of the external auditor.

External auditors traditionally look at the system to determine the reliance which they can place on the accuracy of the information processed through the system and contained in the annual financial statements. In the audit of financial statements, the auditor is only concerned with those policies and procedures within the accounting and internal financial controls that are relevant to the financial statement assertions. The understanding of relevant aspects of the accounting and internal financial controls, together with the inherent and control risk assessments and other considerations, will enable the auditor to:

- identify the types of potential material misstatements that could occur in the financial statements;
- consider the factors that affect the risk of material misstatements; and
- design appropriate audit procedures.

Role of the internal auditors

The internal auditors, like the external auditors, are not ultimately responsible for the system of internal control. However, internal auditors play an important role in evaluating the effectiveness of the system of internal control, and contribute to its ongoing effectiveness. Because of its organizational position and authority in a company, an internal audit function often plays a significant monitoring role.

Typical tasks for internal audit include:

* reviews of the design and operation of the accounting system and related internal financial controls;
* examination of the financial and operating information systems;
* reviews of the economy, efficiency and effectiveness of operations and of the functioning of non-financial controls;
* reviews of the implementation of corporate policies, plans and procedures; and
* special investigations.

The directors' report on internal control

The SAICA guide identifies and makes recommendations on two controversial matters, namely:

* which internal controls must be reported on, and
* what the internal control report must address.

Addressing the first issue, the Guide raises the question as to whether the directors' reporting responsibility extends to all internal controls or only internal financial controls. The UK Cadbury report on corporate governance and the local King Report give no guidance on this matter. The UK working group responsible for compiling guidance on the recommendations of the Cadbury Report concluded that it would be sufficient for directors to report only on the internal financial controls. The SAICA guide follows this line of thinking but goes further in that it states:

> 'In South Africa, directors should at a minimum report on the internal financial controls. However, directors are encouraged to report on all internal controls, as directors' responsibilities are not limited to internal financial controls. If the scope of the directors' statement is restricted to internal financial controls, the fact should be stated clearly.'

With regard to the second issue, the Guide suggests that the requirement to report on the effectiveness of internal control may be interpreted in two ways, namely:

* that directors should express an opinion on the effectiveness of the internal control systems, or
* that directors should report on the process followed in reviewing the system of internal control.

The Guide concludes that directors should as a minimum report on the process followed in assessing the effectiveness of the internal financial controls. However, it encourages directors to express an opinion on the effectiveness of all internal controls or internal financial controls.

The Guide outlines the process to review the effectiveness of internal control as follows.

- Decide on whether all or only internal financial controls are to be assessed.
- Develop an action plan, including assignment of responsibilities and timing of procedures. The action plan should include the following:
  - identify and record the key risks;
  - identify controls in place over these risks;
  - design tests of controls and assign responsibility for these; and
  - review external and internal auditor's reports on internal control and confirm that key recommendations are implemented.
- Execute the plan.
- Evaluate and conclude on findings.
- Prepare an appropriate report.

The Guide provides the following guidance on the reporting of major breakdowns in the system of internal control.

> 'A major breakdown is defined as those weaknesses in the system of internal control identified during the year that resulted in material losses, contingencies or uncertainties, which have been disclosed in the financial statements or the auditor's report. Major breakdowns in the system of internal control that have been corrected during the year and have not resulted in material losses, contingencies or uncertainties, which had to be disclosed in the financial statements or the auditor's report, need not be reported by the directors.'

In instances where a major breakdown has occurred during the year, the directors should provide full details of what happened and what remedial action was or is being taken.

With regard to the content of the directors' report the Guide suggests that, at a minimum, it should contain the following:

- acknowledgement by the directors that they are responsible for the company's system of internal control;
- explanation that such a system can provide only reasonable, not absolute, assurance against material misstatement or loss;
- description of the key procedures that the directors have established to provide effective internal financial control;
- confirmation that the directors have reviewed the system of internal control; and
- information about major breakdowns in the system of internal control identified during the year under review and resulting in material losses, contingencies or uncertainties which have been disclosed in the financial statements or the auditor's report, as well as remedial actions taken on discovery of the material breakdowns.

As already mentioned, directors are encouraged to express an opinion on the effectiveness of the system of internal control. If this is done, it is considered sufficient if directors report on the basis of negative assurance. Such a statement would read:

'Nothing has come to the attention of the directors to indicate that any material breakdown in the functioning of internal controls has occurred during the period under review.'

The directors' statement should cover the period of the financial statements, but it should also take account of material developments between the balance sheet date and the date upon which the financial statements are signed.

As regards the positioning of the report on internal controls, the Guide draws attention to the fact that the Code itself states that the directors should report on the system of internal control in the annual report, while in the body of the King 2002 Report it is suggested that it should be included in the financial statements. This distinction is important from the external auditor's point of view, for if it is positioned in the annual report but not as part of the annual financial statements, the auditor does not express an opinion on it. If it does form part of the annual financial statements, however, the auditor would need to obtain appropriate evidence to support any assurance provided regarding the directors' statement on internal control.

The Guide concludes that directors should position the statement where it is most appropriate in the context of the specific company. It does suggest that directors should discuss with the external auditor the form and words they contemplate using in their statement, the nature of the related supporting documentation as well as the position of the statement.

21.11.2 Stakeholder Communication in the Annual Report

The King 2002 Report on Corporate Governance identified the annual report as being a vital link in communication between the company and its stakeholders. In its Code of Corporate Practices and Conduct, the King Committee recommended that the board of directors should present in the annual report a balanced and understandable assessment of the enterprise's overall financial and operational position. The quality of such information should be based on guidelines of openness and substance over form, and should cover material matters of significant interest and concern to all stakeholders. While the Companies Act Schedule 4 requires a directors' report to deal with all matters material for an appreciation of the state of affairs of an enterprise, such reports typically provide a general review of the business and operations which are usually not sufficiently comprehensive to satisfy the needs of all stakeholders.

The *Guide on Stakeholder Communication in the Annual Report* provides a framework within which directors can discuss and interpret the business of the enterprise so as to give users of financial statements a more expansive foundation on which to base their decisions. In general terms, the communication should cover the following:

- the main business features of the entity;
- any risks and uncertainties it faces;
- the entity's financial structure; ard

- factors relevant to an assessment of the entity's future prospects.

It is suggested that the communication should be a discussion of trends and changes and not merely an extraction of increases, decreases and percentages. Profit forecasts and other future projections should be considered in general terms as opposed to specific and accurate amounts.

The essential qualities of the communication are that it should:

- be clear, succinct and readily understood by the average stakeholder;
- be objective, unbiased and balanced, dealing fairly with both positive and negative aspects;
- deal with comments made in previous communications not borne out by events, as well as those that were, for example, sales/margin trends, expansion, new products, and refinancing;
- follow a 'top-down' structure, discussing the individual aspects of the business in the context of the business as a whole, rather than in isolation;
- contain an analytical qualitative discussion rather than numeric analysis, although it should be supported by figures where necessary;
- indicate how any ratios and numeric information which it contains relate to the financial statements;
- be forward looking, as well as a review of historic events; and
- be prompt, relevant, open, transparent (with substance ruling over legal form), and fairly set out the position.

Detailed guidance on the recommended coverage of the communication is set out under the following headings:

- Operating results for the period of the financial statements.
- Risks and uncertainties faced by the entity.
- Investment for the future, both capital and revenue.
- Shareholders' returns.
- Accounting policies.
- Areas of judgement.
- Capital structure.
- Treasury.
- Cash from operating activities and other sources.
- Current liquidity position.
- Fair value of the balance sheet.
- Employment issues.
- Environmental issues, and
- Social responsibility.

An overview of the detailed guidance as to what aspects should be covered under each heading follows.

Operating results

- All aspects of the income statement to the level of operating profit/loss before taxation.

- Overall business activities and those of significant segments and divisions, and their contributions towards the enterprise's performance.
- Changes in the industry within which the business operates, and the impact of such changes on the results. Changes could include:
  - market conditions;
  - new products/services introduced;
  - market share or position;
  - turnover and margins;
  - discontinued and discontinuing activities; and
  - acquisitions, including comment on the realization of expectations.
- Any other special factors affecting results, for example, trends not expected to continue in the future, or significant restructuring.

Risks and uncertainties

- The main factors and influences that may affect future results, whether or not these were significant during the period under review.
- The principal risks and uncertainties in the main lines of operation.
- The approach of the enterprise to managing such risks and uncertainties.
- A qualitative assessment of the impact (actual and/or potential) of such risks and uncertainties.
- How the enterprise sees itself reacting in the broad environment of customer demands and expectations.

Risk factors include such things as skill and expertise shortages; expiry of patents, licences, franchises; dependence on major suppliers or customers; and foreign suppliers/markets and exchange rate fluctuations.

Investment for the future

- Significant activities and expectations during the current financial period intended to enhance future profitability, such as advertising or other promotional activities, training programmes and maintenance activities. Capital expenditure is normally a significant part of investment activities. The discussion should typically include:
  - the current level of capital expenditure;
  - planned future capital expenditure (committed expenditure, authorized but not committed expenditure, and intended expenditure);
  - lead times in capital projects;
  - major projects in progress;
  - likely benefits expected;
  - sources of funds to meet the capital commitments; and
  - merger and takeover negotiations, where not confidential.

Such discussion should focus on the business as a whole, as well as major business segments and geographical areas. It should also emphasize the impact of such expenditures on future earnings, with an estimated quantification of the impact, if practicable.

Shareholder returns

An explanation to stakeholders is required of the relationship between operating results and shareholders' earnings and dividend payments, the relationship between the financial statements and the overall value of the enterprise, and how value to shareholders has been enhanced. There should be a commentary directed specifically at the shareholders, including:

- the overall return to shareholders in the form of:
  - dividends;
  - movements in shareholder funds; and
  - contributions from other specific gains/losses reported as part of total shareholder funds, for example, revaluations;
- the relationship between profit and dividends (in total and per share);
- the enterprise's dividend policy;
- other measures of earnings per share (EPS) that are more indicative of future trends, especially where the traditional EPS figure is too volatile and is not a good predictor of future EPS;
- the return on assets; and
- the return on equity.

Accounting policies

Directors should consider the accounting policies adopted or to be adopted by the enterprise, and should discuss the following:

- the reasons for changes in accounting policies and the impact of the changes;
- a commentary on accounting standard developments and their impact, both current and future;
- where the enterprise has delayed implementation of a new accounting standard.

Areas of judgement

Directors should highlight areas of judgement to which the financial statements may be particularly sensitive, such as valuations, depreciation rates on assets subject to rapid obsolescence, recognition of profit on long-term contracts, and development costs to be carried forward. Significant estimates and assumptions used to determine material asset and liability amounts should be discussed.

Capital structure

The directors should discuss the enterprise's current capital structure, explaining the purpose and impact of financing transactions entered into during the period under review, as well as future transactions that may alter the current structure. The discussion should typically cover the following:

- objectives and policies;
- maturity profile of debt;
- types of capital instruments used;
- interest rate structure (fixed, floating, capped);
- a commentary on key ratios, such as interest cover or the debt/equity ratio;
- analysis of changes in interest expense for the period between rate changes and changes in borrowing levels;
- intended foreign stock exchange listings, or any raising of debt on international markets; and
- qualitative and quantitative information about the risks associated with off-balance-sheet financing arrangements.

Treasury

The discussion should typically cover the following factors:

- control and reporting arrangements;
- currencies of borrowings of cash or cash equivalents;
- the nature and extent of the use of financial instruments in hedging;
- potential impact of future currency movements on profit levels, for example, forward exchange cover on future sales;
- information about the management of exchange risk.

Cash from operating activities and other sources

The cash generated, or used, in operations, and other cash inflows or outflows during the period under review should be discussed. In particular, instances where cash flows from certain segments are not in line with the profits from such segments – for example, because of capital expenditure in that segment – should be highlighted.

Current liquidity

The annual report should comment on the liquidity of the enterprise and should address all aspects of liquidity, including the following:

- objectives and policy;
- year-end liquidity position;
- level of borrowings as at year end;
- seasonality of borrowing requirements;
- the peak level of borrowings during the period;
- the maturity profile of outstanding borrowings;
- the maturity profile of committed borrowing facilities;
- access to borrowing facilities;
- negotiations with lenders that have imposed covenants;
- measures taken and remedies proposed where covenants have been breached.

Fair value of the balance sheet

Most financial statements are prepared using the historical cost-based accounting model, but stakeholders view fair-value information as useful for particular types of assets and liabilities and in certain types of industries. For a greater appreciation of the position of the enterprise, directors should therefore comment on:

- strengths and resources not reflected, or partly reflected, on the balance sheet, such as intangibles, trademarks, and brands;
- the current value of such items and any changes therein; and
- the fair value or replacement cost of significant items reflected on the balance sheet.

Employment

The stakeholder would be interested in a discussion of employment issues in the annual report, such as:

- staffing levels;
- skills levels;
- new jobs created;
- retrenchment policy and occurrences during the period;
- affirmative action policy;
- unionization;
- wage negotiations in progress;
- training programmes and other investments in staff proficiency;
- productivity levels; and
- employee benefits, such as retirement benefits, medical benefits, housing, family education and staff loans.

Environmental issues

The enterprise should see itself as a resident in the broad community and should act in a spirit of social consciousness and awareness. It should be sensitive to the needs of the local communities. With this in mind, the annual report should contain a full and separate commentary of relevance to the community at large which should address, where applicable, matters such as:

- environment protection policies and goals;
- compliance with consumer protection standards and consequences of violation;
- compliance with environmental laws and regulations and consequences of violation;
- existing and planned pollution control;
- protection and restoration costs; and
- potential liability and any current or pending investigations or proceedings by regulators.

Social responsibility

The enterprise should forge its links with all stakeholders and should address matters of concern and interest to them. Society now expects greater accountability with regard to non-financial matters. The King Report recognizes this expectation, and recommends that management comment on how it has fulfilled its broader social responsibilities. Stakeholders at large would be interested in information on:

- activities and programmes (completed, in progress, or intended) aimed at upliftment and improvement of social structures; and
- large donations made or intended.

Communication with stakeholders is the responsibility of the directors. As the King Report recommends such communication be part of the non-statutory section of the annual report, external auditors are required merely to read the information to ensure that the views expressed and information presented are neither misleading nor contradict the information presented in the statutory annual financial statements. Accordingly, external auditors do not report on such information.

21.11.3 Guidance for Directors: Going Concern and Financial Reporting

This document provides guidance to directors on the requirement in the King Report on Corporate Governance for them to report, in their company's annual report, that there is no reason to believe that the business will not be a going concern in the year ahead, or to provide an explanation for believing otherwise.

In terms of section 299 of the Companies Act, directors are required to report on all matters material to an appreciation of the state of affairs, business and profit or loss of the company or of the company and its subsidiaries. This imposes an obligation on directors to report on any doubts they may have as to the ability of the company and/or the group to continue as a going concern.

The reporting provided in response to the Act, however, generally only addressed the subject of going concern where there was doubt as to an entity's ability to continue as a going concern.

The Code of Corporate Practices and Conduct (the 'Code'), contained in the King Report on Corporate Governance, requires specific reporting on going concern. The requirements of the Code do not alter the basic responsibilities of directors, but have the effect of formalizing the reporting function.

21.11.3.1 Technical aspects relevant to going concern

In order to adequately report on whether or not an entity will be a going concern in the foreseeable future, it is important for the directors to be aware of certain technical aspects relevant to the matter. These are the definition of 'going concern'; the period to which reporting on going concern applies; and the use of the going-concern basis, discussed below.

Definition of going concern

AC 000, 'Framework for the Preparation and Presentation of Financial Statements', contains the following definition relating to going concern:

> 'The financial statements are normally prepared on the assumption that an enterprise is a going concern and will continue in operation for the foreseeable future. Hence, it is assumed that the enterprise has neither the intention nor the need to liquidate or curtail materially the scale of its operations; if such an intention or need exists, the financial statements may have to be prepared on a different basis and, if so, the basis used is disclosed.'

Period to which reporting on going concern applies

AC 000 uses the term 'foreseeable future' in the context of going concern without explaining the meaning of the term. It may therefore be argued that directors should take account of all information of which they are aware at the time of reporting, and that any minimum period after which there should be a sudden change in the approach adopted is artificial and arbitrary. As a practical matter, however, forecasts and budgets often only extend a year ahead and, as such, it may be difficult for the directors to apply their minds meaningfully to periods beyond the next year.

The King Code requires directors to report that they have no reason to believe that the business will not be a going concern in the year ahead. As such, the directors' statement on going concern, provided in terms of the Code, should refer to a year from the date of the end of the financial period to which the financial statements relate.

Use of the going-concern basis

As the going-concern basis is an underlying accounting assumption, the directors usually prepare financial statements on a going-concern basis. Use of the alternative 'break-up' basis is unusual and often impractical.

Thus, although the directors may have identified factors that cast doubt on the validity of the assumption that the company will continue in operational existence for the year ahead, such doubts may not necessarily make the use of an appropriate alternative basis preferable as it may be less useful or may be impractical to apply. Where such doubts exist and the going-concern basis is applied, appropriate additional disclosure should be made.

Doubt as to the ability of a company to continue as a going concern does not necessarily mean that the company will become insolvent. The solvency of a company is determined by a comparison of its assets and liabilities, and by its ability to meet its liabilities as they fall due. Nevertheless, there may be a perception that disclosure of the directors' doubts regarding the company's ability to continue as a going concern may adversely affect the public's view of the company and may precipitate the end of its operational existence. Where directors are unable to state that the going-concern basis is appropriate, they should consider taking professional advice. Concern that the reporting of doubts about the company's ability to continue as a going concern might precipitate its demise would not justify directors failing to report such doubts where they exist.

21.11.3.2 Procedures to assess going-concern potential

There are many factors that could have an impact on the ability of a company to continue in operational existence in each year to follow. Some of these factors are within the control of the directors; others are not and they usually vary by industry as well as by company. The guide identifies seven main general matters that should be considered by directors. These are:

- Forecasts and budgets.
- Borrowing requirements.
- Liability management.
- Contingent liabilities.
- Projects and markets.
- Financial risk management.
- Other potential solvency warning signals.

An appendix to the guide sets out, under these seven headings, a list of detailed procedures, the performance of which should be helpful to directors in determining the appropriateness of the going-concern basis in preparing annual financial statements. A synopsis of these procedures follows.

Forecasts and budgets

Directors should prepare monthly cash flow forecasts and budgets covering, at a minimum, the period to the next balance sheet date. These should be supported by a detailed listing of key assumptions which underlie the forecasts. These assumptions should be confirmed as being realistic. Key assumptions include such matters as:

- sales levels;
- gross margins, both operating and capital;
- anticipated expenditure; and
- timing of cash flows in and out.

Consideration of the source and accuracy of data used to generate forecasts and budgets, as well as the accuracy of past budgets, should provide a guide as to the likely accuracy of current budgets.

Borrowing requirements

Available facilities should be compared to the projected cash flow positions as shown in the forecasts. Negotiations for further facilities to cover any likely deficits would be necessary. Performance of a sensitivity analysis using worst estimates of key assumptions in cash flow forecast might be necessary to establish the adequacy of current borrowing facilities and potential further facilities.

Interest arrears and any breach of covenants on existing borrowing need to be considered in the light of the possible withdrawal of facilities should this be the case.

Liability management

This should involve a scheduling of all known liabilities and their future repayment dates to ensure that these commitments are included in the projection of cash outflows. Where cash flow projections show outflows unmatched by inflows, consideration needs to be given as to how the necessary funds may be raised.

Any marked deterioration in the gearing ratio and interest cover ratio may indicate poor liability management.

Contingent liabilities

Consideration needs to be given to the company's exposure to any contingent liabilities, such as:

- legal proceedings;
- guarantees and warranties;
- uninsured product liabilities; and
- any retentions.

The potential effect of these on cash outflows should be taken into account.

Products and markets

Directors should consider the position of the company's products in its markets, its share of such markets, and how these have changed over time and are likely to change in the foreseeable future. In projecting future markets and sales, attention needs to be given to the quality of the company's products as against those of its competitors and any likely technical obsolescence of products. Other aspects to consider are the company's marketing strategies, including advertising, and for companies in industries where obsolescence of products is the norm, such as electronics and computer-related products, their commitment to research and development of new products.

Financial risk management

Directors should identify financial risks to which the company is exposed, the potential impact of the risks under differing scenarios and how these risks are managed. Particular aspects to consider are adverse movements in interest and foreign exchange rates, as well as any fixed price or fixed rate contracts.

Other potential solvency factors

The guide lists 30 other factors directors should consider when determining the appropriateness of the going-concern assumption. Some of the more important are:

- recurring operating losses;
- dividends being paid out of retained rather than current earnings;
- an increase in accounts receivable and inventory levels in relation to turnover;
- work stoppages or other labour difficulties;
- loss of key management or staff;
- loss of key patents or franchise;
- frequent customer complaints;
- high level of related-party transactions; and
- inadequate insurance cover.

21.11.3.3 Assessment of factors

When the directors have performed all the individual procedures they consider appropriate, they should consider the range of potential outcomes for the company and the probability of each of these outcomes, in order to determine the probable commercial outcomes. Factors that mitigate risks, for example, alternative sources of funds, should be specifically considered in this context. The directors should also be aware of the implications, arising from interaction between the various factors.

When evaluating the likely commercial outcomes and the effects of these on the validity of the going-concern assumption, the directors should consider the financial adaptability of the company. This is the ability of the company to alter the amounts and timing of cash flows to respond to unexpected needs and opportunities and, as such, may mitigate some of the negative factors.

In assessing the financial adaptability of a company, the directors should consider the ability of the company to:

- dispose of assets, or to postpone the replacement of assets without significantly affecting cash flows;
- lease rather than purchase assets;
- obtain new sources of finance;
- renew or extend loans;

- restructure debts;
- raise additional share capital;
- obtain financial support from other group companies; and
- continue business by making limited reductions in the level of operations or by making use of alternative resources.

21.11.3.4 Content of the directors' statement

There are three possibilities, namely:

- Going-concern assumption is appropriate.
- Going-concern basis used despite doubts as to the validity of the going-concern assumption.
- Going-concern basis is not appropriate.

Where, as a result of the procedures they have performed, the directors are of the opinion that the going-concern assumption is appropriate, they should make a statement to that effect.

It should be noted that, in many cases, the additional work required in support of the going-concern statement should be relatively minor, as the nature of the work should primarily involve the compilation and formal documentation of existing work and evidence.

Suggested examples of the disclosure where the going-concern assumption is appropriate are as follows:

'After making all necessary enquiries the directors have no reason to believe that the company will not be a going concern in the period to the date of the next financial statements. For this reason they continue to adopt the going-concern basis in preparing the annual financial statements.'

or

'After making all necessary enquiries the directors believe that the company will be a going concern in the foreseeable future. For this reason they continue to adopt the going-concern basis in preparing the financial statements.'

Where there are factors that, in the event of an unfavourable outcome, could cast doubt on the appropriateness of the going-concern assumption, but the directors nonetheless use the going-concern basis, this fact should be stated. In making their statement on going concern, the directors should explain the circumstances and the factors giving rise to the problem(s) (including any external factors outside their control), and explain how they intend to address and resolve the problem(s). The quantified financial effect of the problem(s) should be disclosed where practicable. It should be noted that a statement of this nature will not limit the liability of the directors, nor will it operate as a substitute for the proper discharge of their responsibilities.

The following is an example of the disclosure for a company where there is a breach of loan covenants and related negotiations with the providers of finance have not been completed:

'The company is in breach of certain loan covenants at its balance sheet date and, as such, the company's bankers could recall their loans at any time. The directors continue to be involved in negotiations with the company's bankers and, as yet, no demands for repayments have been received. The negotiations are at an early stage and, although the directors are optimistic about the outcome, it is as yet too early to make predictions with any certainty.

In the light of the actions to raise additional capital described elsewhere in the annual report, the directors consider it appropriate to adopt the going-concern basis in preparing the annual financial statements.'

Where, as a result of the procedures they have performed, the directors are of the opinion that the company will not be a going concern in the year ahead, they should explore the feasibility of preparing the financial statements using a basis other than the going-concern basis. Alternatively, the directors should amplify the financial statements prepared on the going-concern basis by providing an indication or an estimate of the financial effect of applying an alternative basis.

There is no example in the SAICA guide of a directors' statement where the going-concern basis is not appropriate. The reason given for this is that the wording will depend on the basis on which the financial statements are prepared, the disclosure provided in regard to this basis and any legal advice obtained in relation to the wording of the directors' statement.

21.11.3.5 Disclosure of the statement on going concern in the annual report

The directors' statement on going concern should be disclosed in one of the following locations in the annual report:

- as part of the directors' report, providing the statement does not include commentary, elements of which cannot be objectively verified;
- as part of a statement on corporate governance; or
- as part of the 'directors' approval' or 'directors' responsibility' statement. This is a statement by the directors approving the annual financial statements and has, in many cases, been expanded to include the elements of the reporting required by the Code.

It should be noted that the disclosure locations suggested above, with the exception of the directors' report, are separate from the annual financial statements and are, therefore, not subject to audit. The directors' statement on going concern will, however, be subject to review by the company's auditors, irrespective of where it is located in the annual report.

The directors of a parent company preparing group financial statements should make their statement regarding going concern in respect of both the parent company and the group as a whole. Where material, the statement in relation to the group should identify any doubts as to the ability of any of the subsidiaries to continue as a going concern.

Although directors cannot be expected to consider going concern as fully for interim reporting as they would for final reporting purposes, they should undertake a review of their previous work. They should consider the position at the previous year end and determine whether or not any of the significant factors identified at that time have changed to such an extent as to affect the appropriateness of the going-concern assumption at the interim stage. Unless there has been a significant change in circumstances since the date of approval of the last annual financial statements, the directors are not required to make an explicit statement on going concern in their interim report.

21.11.4 Guidance for Directors: The Role of Internal Audit

The Code of Corporate Practices and Conduct suggests that companies have an effective internal audit function. Should such function not exist, a disclosure and reasons should be set out in the annual report. The Guide on the role of internal auditors covers the following more important aspects:

- the objective and role of internal audit;
- the characteristics of an effective internal audit function, these being:
- independence
- professional proficiency
- scope and performance of work
- the relationship between internal and external auditors.

These aspects are discussed below.

21.11.4.1 The objective and role of internal audit

The objective of internal audit is to assist the board and management to discharge their responsibilities. In so doing, the internal audit function provides those charged with corporate governance with independent analyses, appraisals, recommendations and information concerning activities reviewed.

Internal audit adds value to good corporate governance in the following ways:[11]

- 'Contributing to an organization's performance by assisting management in improving the economy, efficiency and effectiveness of their operational units.

- Assisting the board and management in identifying internal control weaknesses and inefficiencies.

- Improving the quality of the management process by assisting management in improving performance management skills, enabling members of management to improve performance in their operational units. These skills include:

---

[11] 'Guidance to Directors: The Role of Internal Audit', paragraph .31.

- setting objectives for their units,
- identifying risks,
- assessing the probability of risks occurring and their seriousness should they occur,
- designing appropriate internal controls to reduce the probability of risk occurrence and/or limit the seriousness should it occur,
- assessing the quality of their internal controls, and
- assessing actual performance.

• Assisting management in solving problems by performing consulting assignments. However, the performance of these assignments should not result in the internal audit plan being neglected or the internal audit function's independence being questioned.

• Enhancing the prevention and detection of fraud. The internal audit function is responsible for assisting management in the deterrence of fraud by examining and evaluating the adequacy and effectiveness of internal controls, commensurate with the extent of the potential exposure / risk in the organization's operations.'

The purpose, authority and responsibility of the internal audit function should be documented. This should be approved by the board and management. The document or charter should:[12]

• 'establish the function's position within the organization,

• authorize access to records, personnel and physical properties relevant to the performance of internal audits, and

• define the scope of the internal audit activities.'

21.11.4.2 Characteristics of an effective internal audit function

These are identified as independence, professional proficiency, scope and performance of work and management of the internal audit function.

Independence

The internal audit function should be independent of operational activities it audits. Its organizational status and to whom it reports enhance the internal audit function's objectivity and effectiveness. The internal audit function may be outsourced. This decision should be based on commercial considerations regarding the required quality service at a competitive cost.

Professional proficiency

The audit function should be performed by capable personnel or be supervised by them. In this regard, the employment of technically competent individuals, providing necessary training to those less experienced and providing appropriate direction and supervision are important.

---

[12] 'Guidance to Directors: The Role of Internal Audit', paragraph .11.

Scope and performance of work

The Guide identifies areas in which the internal audit function can assist the board and management to identify and manage risks. These encompass the following:[13]

- 'Reviewing the reliability and integrity of financial and operating information, and the means used to identify, measure, classify and report such information.
- Reviewing the systems established to ensure compliance with those policies, plans, procedures, laws and regulations that could have a significant impact on operations and reports, and determining whether or not the organization is in compliance.
- Reviewing the means of safeguarding assets and, where appropriate, verifying the existence of such assets.
- Appraising the economic and efficient management of the organization's financial, human and other resources, and the effective conduct of its operations.
- Reviewing operations or programmes to ascertain whether or not results are consistent with established objectives and goals, and whether or not the operations are being carried out as planned.'

To be effective in assisting the board and management in their identification and management of risks, the internal audit function should be appropriately managed to ensure that:[14]

- 'the audit coverage of risk areas in the organization is planned,
- policies and procedures to guide the audit staff are implemented,
- the quality of work is of an appropriate level,
- staff performance is monitored and managed, and
- the function is effective in fulfilling its responsibilities.'

21.11.4.3 The relationship between the internal and external auditors

Communication and cooperation between internal and external auditors should maximize optional audit coverage. The Guide suggests that the relationship can be summarized as follows:[15]

- 'The head of internal audit should regularly evaluate the level of coordination between the internal and statutory auditors.
- A sufficient number of meetings between the internal and statutory auditors should be held to ensure appropriate coordination of audit work, minimize duplicate audit efforts, ensure that audit activities are efficient and timely, and ensure that the scope of the planned audit work is appropriate. It is proposed that, based on the joint audit coverage planning meeting, an internal and statutory audit planning memorandum is compiled for submission to the audit committee.'

---

[13] 'Guidance to Directors: The Role of Internal Audit', paragraph .22.
[14] 'Guidance to Directors: The Role of Internal Audit', paragraph .29.
[15] 'Guidance to Directors: The Role of Internal Audit', paragraph .43.

22

Auditing in the Public Sector

Learning objectives

After studying this chapter you should be able to:
1. Describe how public sector audits differ from audits of annual financial statements of limited companies.
2. Outline the auditor's mandate for a performance audit in the public sector, the conduct of such an audit and the report thereon.

22.1 INTRODUCTION

The Auditor-General Act, No. 12 of 1995, and the Audit Arrangements Act, 1992, provide for the appointment, functions, administration and powers of the Office of the Auditor-General. A public sector audit is usually performed by the Office of the Auditor-General or, if not performed by the Auditor-General, by a person registered as an accountant and auditor in public practice with the Public Accountants' and Auditors' Board (hereafter referred to as the private sector auditor). Section 58 of the Public Finance Management Act No. 1 of 1999 allows for the appointment by a public entity of a private sector auditor if its audit is not performed by the Auditor-General. Should this be the case, the entity must consult with the Auditor-General on the appointment of the private sector auditor. The private sector auditor in this case reports to the executive authority responsible for the public entity concerned, who in turn reports to Parliament or the respective legislative body concerned.

The Reporting by Public Entities Act, 1992, required for the first time that a public entity as defined under regulations to that Act, establish, *inter alia*, an audit committee, conduct internal audits, submit directors' reports to Parliament and undergo an annual external audit. It also, in effect, required performance audits of these entities. To promote more effective external reporting, the entities were required to prepare financial statements in accordance with generally accepted accounting practice and the Fourth Schedule to the Companies Act, 1973. The Public Finance Management Act, approved in March 1999, repealed the Reporting by Public Entities Act with effect from April 2000. The requirements of having an audit committee conduct internal audits, submit reports to Parliament and undergo an annual external audit, remain as before. Obviously realizing, however, that compliance by all categories of public entity with Codified Generally Accepted Accounting Practice and the Fourth Schedule to the Companies Act, might not adequately promote the objective of transparency in and effective management of revenue, expenditure, assets and liabilities, the Legislature delegated power in the Act to the Finance Minister to establish an Accounting Standards Board.[1] In terms of section 89 of the Public Finance Management Act, the functions of the Accounting Standards Board involve the following:

- setting of generally recognized accounting practice for the annual financial statements of departments, public entities, constitutional institutions and municipalities and boards, commissions, companies, corporations, funds or other entities under the ownership control of a municipality;
- preparing and publishing directives and guidelines concerning the Standards set by it;
- recommending to the Minister effective dates of implementation of these Standards for the different categories of institutions to which these Standards apply; and
- performing any functions incidental in advancing financial reporting in the public sector.

In setting standards, the Board takes into account all relevant factors, including best accounting practices, both locally and internationally, and the capacity of the relevant institutions to comply with these.

As private sector auditors often perform public sector audits, South African Audit Standards contain a Public Sector Perspective which is set out towards the end of each Standard. This perspective addresses additional matters or differences that are applicable to auditing in the public sector. The South African Institute of Chartered Accountants has issued two Public Sector Auditing Guidelines to provide guidance on public sector audits. These are entitled:

- 'Auditing in the Public Sector'; and
- 'Performance Auditing'.

A brief outline of the contents of each follows.

22.2 AUDITING IN THE PUBLIC SECTOR

The stated purpose of the guideline is to provide the private sector auditor with an introduction to the differences between public sector and private sector auditing standards.

---

[1] Public Finance Management Act, No. 1 of 1999, section 87.

In carrying out the audit of a public sector entity, the audit is generally performed in a similar manner to a private sector audit, with the exception of the requirement for a performance audit. The thrust of the document is aimed at work performed on behalf of the Auditor-General. The International Organization of Supreme Audit Institutions (INTOSAI) has developed and issued a set of auditing standards known as the INTOSAI Auditing Standards. The Office of the Auditor-General in South Africa has adopted these standards as the South African Generally Accepted Government Auditing Standards (GAGAS). Public sector audits performed on behalf of the Office of the Auditor-General should be performed in accordance with GAGAS. Because private sector auditors have training and knowledge primarily in the application of SAAS, and not in the INTOSAI Auditing Standards, the Office of the Auditor-General lays down guidelines for persons conducting audits on its behalf, to explain formally the activities of the Auditor-General and also to set out procedures regulating working methods. Any areas of uncertainty can be clarified with the Office of the Auditor-General.

A public sector entity employs resources to achieve a variety of social and economic goals, and while audited financial statements provide an accounting of its financial operations, these statements by themselves may not adequately report performance. The governing body of such an entity is typically interested in information relating to:

- compliance with legislative and related authorities;
- accounting for the safeguarding of assets;
- adequacy of management control systems;
- integrity of information;
- the economical and efficient management of resources; and
- the effective performance of the entity's functions.

Persons performing the audits of public sector entities are typically required to report to the governing bodies on shortcomings in respect of these matters. Management, however, may not be required to make public representations on all of these matters. In such circumstances, auditors provide their own assessments to the governing bodies on the matters, rather than attesting to the credibility of representations by management. This kind of reporting is made public, and is a unique feature of auditing such entities.

22.2.1 The public sector audit

Where a public entity is not audited by the Auditor-General, the entity appoints the private sector auditor as its auditor. The terms of such an engagement must be agreed upon and set out in an engagement letter. Where the Auditor-General is the auditor of a public entity, the Auditor-General may approach a private sector auditor to perform audit work on its behalf. In such a case, the audited entity is not in a client relationship with the auditor. The powers and duties of the Auditor-General's office are laid down in legislation, and the auditor has to discharge the statutory mandate freely and impartially in forming audit opinions, conclusions and recommendations, and owing no responsibility to the management of the audited entity for the scope or the nature of the audits undertaken.

The audit and reporting requirements specified in audit mandates establish the audit objectives. Audit objectives are the principal basis for determining appropriate auditing standards. When audit objectives are the same, the same standards should apply regardless of the nature of the entity being audited, whether in the public or private sector, because users of the audit reports are entitled to a uniform quality of assurance and would not be well served by the application of alternative standards to the same type of audit.

Mandates for private sector auditors performing audits on behalf of the Auditor-General vary in accordance with the expressed concerns of the Legislature or other governing bodies and directives issued by the Office of the Auditor-General. Most require private sector auditors to examine the financial statements and report to the Office of the Auditor-General or the Executive Authority responsible for the public entity. Some directives may also require private sector auditors to examine a variety of other matters and report to the Office of the Auditor-General or the relevant Executive Authority.

Audits of public sector entities are generally known as *comprehensive audits*. Comprehensive auditing falls into the following two categories:

- regularity auditing; and
- performance auditing.

22.2.1.1 Regularity auditing

Traditional or regularity auditing relates mainly to the keeping of proper accounting records, due collection of revenue, authorized expenditure backed by evidence, effective checks and balances within systems of control and compliance with regulations.

22.2.1.2 Performance auditing

Because a public sector entity makes use of public funds in order to achieve public objectives, it is important to ensure control of public funds by the Legislature, and public accountability in the financial affairs of public sector entities.

Performance auditing encompasses an independent and objective review of financial and operational performance to determine whether or not the control measures which have been introduced ensure that available resources are utilized economically, efficiently and effectively.

It should be noted that a regularity audit may be entirely satisfactory, yet a performance audit of the same entity could well reveal unsatisfactory aspects. The criteria being different, such a result would not necessarily be inconsistent.

The audit of a private sector entity typically includes aspects of regularity auditing, but does not necessarily include a performance audit.

22.2.2 The auditor's report

The reporting procedures of the Office of the Auditor-General are laid down in legislation. The reporting procedures are consequently more comprehensive than is normally the case in a private sector audit. Within thirty days after finalization of the audit, a report must be directed to the Office of the Auditor-General and must be accompanied by copies of queries issued during the audit and the replies thereto. The report is addressed to the Office of the Auditor-General who in turn reports to Parliament or the respective legislative body concerned and the entity. The report should, however, follow the principles for auditors' reports, which are laid down in South African Auditing Standards.

22.3 PERFORMANCE AUDITING

The guideline recommends standards for private sector auditors engaged in performance auditing in the public sector. These standards relate to the professional qualities of auditors, the conduct of their audit examination and the content of their audit reports.

The standards are intended to apply to audits carried out for the purpose of examining and reporting on matters related to the adequacy of management systems, controls and practices, including those intended to control and safeguard assets, to ensure due regard to economy, efficiency and effectiveness.

22.3.1 The audit mandate

Because of the need for accountability of public funds, attention needs to be focused on the measures instituted by public sector entities to ensure that resources are utilized economically, efficiently and effectively so that value for money may be obtained and the stated objectives of the entity may be attained. Performance auditing refers to an independent evaluation of the arrangements to promote and achieve economy, efficiency and effectiveness.

The Public Finance Management Act, No. 1 of 1999, in effect requires performance audits to be carried out in all public entities as defined in the Act. In terms of the Auditor-General Act, No. 12 of 1995, the public sector auditor is to be satisfied that reasonable management measures have been taken to ensure that resources are acquired economically and utilized economically, efficiently and effectively.

These three terms are defined as follows:

- *Economy* refers to the acquisition of the appropriate quality and quantity of financial, human and physical resources at the appropriate time and place, and at the lowest possible cost.

- *Efficiency* refers to the use of financial, human and physical resources so that output is maximized for any given set of resource inputs, or input is minimized for any given quantity and quality of output provided.
- *Effectiveness* refers to the extent of achievement of the objectives or other intended effects of programmes, operations, activities or processes.

Performance audits may be carried out with respect to an entity or only a portion of an entity, such as a programme, management control system or organizational unit. The terms of the private sector auditor's mandate, whether embodied in legislation or established by contract, specify the audit and reporting requirements. The private sector auditor may be required to examine all or only some of these matters.

The reporting requirements of performance auditing mandates also vary. Many performance auditing mandates, such as those relating to government departments, may require the private sector auditor to report deficiencies observed. However, other auditing mandates may require the private sector auditor to express an opinion, such as whether or not there is reasonable assurance, based on specific criteria, that there are no significant deficiencies in the system and procedures examined.

In carrying out performance auditing work in the public sector, it is not the private sector auditor's function to question policy objectives, unless specifically requested to do so in terms of the mandate. The private sector auditor will, however, examine the accuracy and completeness of the information on which, or arrangements by which, policy decisions are reached, and will consider the effects of policy and the way in which objectives are achieved.

The private sector auditor may also attest to written assertions prepared by management to demonstrate management's due regard for economy, efficiency and/or effectiveness in discharging its responsibilities.

A clear mandate should be obtained prior to commencing the performance audit. This mandate should generally include reference to:

- the objectives of the performance audit;
- the scope of the performance audit, including areas selected for review and applicable standards;
- the legislation or regulations to which the entity should adhere;
- the fees to be charged and the basis on which such fees are to be computed, rendered and paid; and
- the manner, nature, expected form and timing of eventual reports, and to whom they should be addressed.

22.3.2 The application of auditing standards

22.3.2.1 Training and proficiency

The person or persons carrying out the examination should have, or collectively have, adequate technical training and proficiency to fulfil the requirements of the particular audit.

Knowledge in many fields may be required to carry out specific performance auditing engagements. The audit may focus on any of the entity's management systems, controls and practices and/or its operating performance or programme effectiveness. Depending on the matters subject to audit, knowledge of and proficiency in fields such as engineering, statistical analysis, human resource management and economics, among others, may be required to make appropriate analyses and competent assessments.

The private sector auditor is not expected to possess the expertise of specialists on the audit team, but must have a level of knowledge sufficient to define the objectives and terms of reference governing the work assigned to it. When using specialists on the audit team, the private sector auditor should obtain reasonable assurance concerning the specialists' competence in their fields.

22.3.2.2 Assurance engagement procedures

South African Auditing Standards regarding the requirements to

- adequately plan the assignment;
- supervise staff; and
- gather sufficient evidence in support of the audit report

apply equally to performance auditing.

An additional aspect to be taken into account is the requirement that criteria be established for the evaluation of matters which are being subjected to audit. These criteria should be identified and their suitability assessed in the particular circumstances. Such criteria are reasonable and attainable standards of performance and control against which the adequacy of systems and procedures and the extent of economy, efficiency and effectiveness of operations can be assessed.

There is no body of generally accepted criteria for all aspects of performance auditing. Criteria may be developed from various sources, including:

- legislation or policy statements;
- standards of best practice developed by professions or associations;
- statistics or practices developed within the entity or among similar entities; and
- criteria identified in similar performance audits.

Criteria identified from these sources may require interpretation and modification to ensure their relevance to the entity under audit.

Where management has developed criteria for assessing systems, procedures and operations, the private sector auditor would use those criteria if, in the auditor's opinion, the criteria are suitable. If the private sector auditor believes that criteria proposed by management are not suitable in the circumstances, the private sector auditor should attempt to resolve the differences in opinion. If differences cannot be resolved, the private sector auditor should consider the alternative courses of action available.

In no circumstances should the private sector auditor perform the audit and report on the basis of criteria that are believed to be unsuitable.

In formulating an opinion, the private sector auditor may find it necessary to rely on evidence that is persuasive rather than conclusive. Thus, the private sector auditor normally seeks corroborating evidence from different sources or of a different nature in making assessments and forming conclusions.

22.3.2.3 The reporting standards

The overall structure of the report will also vary according to circumstances, but the report should normally contain certain basic features, including:

- the mandate and objectives of the performance audit;
- the scope, including any limitations on the work carried out in comparison with the original mandate;
- any limitations to the work carried out arising out of restricted access to client staff or information;
- the scope of the work carried out in relation to any planned coverage as part of a series of cyclical examinations;
- a statement that it is management's responsibility to institute proper arrangements for securing value for money from the use of resources, and to ensure that the use is economical, efficient and effective;
- a statement that the performance audit was performed in accordance with the standards recommended in the guideline and accordingly included such tests and other procedures as the auditor considered necessary in the circumstances;
- identifying the criteria; and
- describing the findings that form the basis for the private sector auditor's conclusions.

Performance audit reports may also incorporate the private sector auditor's recommendations, as well as management's responses with respect to the matters reported. When making recommendations, the private sector auditor should ensure that responsibility for implementing corrective action does not, and is not seen to, rest with the private sector auditor.

APPENDICES

APPENDIX 1

South African Auditing Standards as at November 2002

SAAS	TITLE	DATE ISSUED
000	Preface to statements of South African Auditing Standards	May 2000
INTRODUCTORY MATTERS (100 – 199)		
100	Assurance engagements (SAAES)	Dec 2000
110	Glossary of terms	Jun 1999
120	Framework for South African Standards on auditing and related services	Nov 1995
RESPONSIBILITIES (200 – 299)		
200	The objective and general principles governing an audit of financial statements	July 1996
210	Terms of audit engagements	Nov 1995
220	Quality control for audit work	July 1996
230	Documentation	July 1996
240	The auditor's responsibility to consider fraud and error in an audit of financial statements	July 2001
250	Consideration of laws and regulations in an audit of financial statements	Apr 1997
2501	The consideration of environmental matters in the audit of financial statements	Jun 1999
PLANNING (300 – 399)		
300	Planning	July 1996
310	Knowledge of the business	Nov 1995
320	Audit materiality	July 1996
INTERNAL CONTROL (400 – 499)		
400	Risk assessments and internal control	July 1996
401	Auditing in a computer information environment	Apr 1998
AUDIT EVIDENCE (500 – 599)		
500	Audit evidence	Jan 1997
502	Enquiries regarding litigation and claims	Oct 2002

SAAS	TITLE	DATE ISSUED
505	External confirmations	Dec 2000
510	Initial engagements - opening balances	Nov 1995
520	Analytical procedures	Jan 1997
530	Audit sampling and other selective testing procedures	Apr 1998
540	Audit of accounting estimates	Jan 1997
545	Auditing fair value measurements and disclosures	Oct 2002
550	Related parties	Aug 1997
560	Subsequent events	Jan 1998
570	Going concern	Feb 2000
580	Management representations	Apr 1997
USING THE WORK OF OTHERS (600 - 699)		
600	Using the work of another auditor	Jan 1997
610	Considering the work of internal audit	Nov 1995
620	Using the work of an expert	Mar 1998
AUDIT CONCLUSIONS AND REPORTING (700 - 799)		
700	The auditor's report on financial statements	Nov 1997
	Appendix revised	May 2000
710	Comparatives	Nov 1997
720	Other information in documents containing audited financial statements	Nov 1997
730	Communication with those charged with governance	Feb 2000
SPECIALIZED AREAS (800 - 899)		
800	The auditor's report on special purpose engagements	Nov 1997
RELATED SERVICES (900 - 999)		
910	Engagements to review financial statements	Nov 2001
920	Engagements to perform agreed-upon procedures	Jan 1998
930	Engagements to compile financial information	July 1996

South African Auditing Practice Statements

SAAPS	TITLE	DATE ISSUED
1000	Inter-bank confirmation procedures	July 2001
1001	IT Environments – Stand-alone personal computers	Nov 2001
1002	IT Environments – On-line computer systems	Nov 2001
1003	IT Environments – database systems	Nov 2001
1005	The special considerations in the audit of small entities	Feb 2000
1009	Computer assisted audit techniques	Nov 2001
1012	Auditing derivative financial statements	July 2001
1013	Electronic commerce – effect on the audit of financial statements	Nov 2001
1100	Bank confirmations	Dec 2000

SAICA Audit and Accounting Guides

Profit forecasts	Aug 1989
Trading whilst factually insolvent	July 1999
Data warehousing	May 2000
Reports on the processing of transactions by service organizations - Guidance for auditors	June 2002

Exposure drafts

SAAS ED	Audit Risk: Amendment to SAAS 200, Objective and principles governing an audit of financial statements	Oct 2002
SAAS ED	Understanding the entity and its environment and assessing the risks of material misstatement	Oct 2002
SAAS ED	The auditor's procedures in response to assessed risks	Oct 2002
SAAS ED	Audit evidence	Oct 2002
SAAPS ED	Reporting on compliance with International Reporting Standards	Oct 2002

APPENDIX 2

The Public Accountants' and Auditors' Amendment Act 42 of 1982:

Liability to Third Parties and Other Aspects[1]

In essence the PAA Amendment Act 42 of 1982[2] does three things. Firstly, and most importantly, it codifies the law relating to the liability of an accountant or auditor to third parties for negligent misstatements. Secondly, it changes s 26(3A)[3] of the PAA Act, mainly to exclude the possibility of liability on the ground of breach of statutory duty where the auditor fails to report. And, thirdly, it re-enacts the exclusion of no-fault liability of an accountant or auditor to either his client or a third party.

Liability *to the client company* for professional negligence is based on breach of contract or delict, and involves fundamentally the same principles as the liability of other professions to their clients. The Amendment Act effects no change here.

Common-law liability of accountants and auditors *to third parties* for negligent misstatements has in recent years developed in other legal systems with almost breathtaking rapidity. Differences and certain approaches gave cause for concern. In this country there is, since 1979, no shadow of doubt about such a liability; however, in view of the approach taken in the leading case, it is extremely difficult to predict with any degree of confidence the circumstances that will give rise to this liability.

Hence the main purpose of the codification was to obtain certainty as to the basic requirements for liability. As any other Act, these provisions have to be interpreted. This certainly is for the benefit of third parties as well as members of the accountancy profession. Certain problems that had emerged in other systems were also excluded in the statutory dispensation.

---

[1] Naudé S (1980), 'Auditor's Liability to Third Parties', *The South African Chartered Accountant*, March 1980.

[2] The Public Accountants' and Auditors' Amendment Act No 42 of 1982 has since been repealed and replaced with the current Public Accountants' and Auditors' Act No 80 of 1991. Further amendments have been: Amendments Acts No's: 70 of 1993, No 23 of 1995, No 88 of 1996, No 5 of 1997 and No 47 of 1997. The principles dealt with by Naude in this article (see note 1), however, are still relevant.

[3] References to section 26 referred to in the article are now codified in section 20 of the Public Accountants' and Auditors' Act No. 80 of 1991, as amended. Specific section references mentioned in the article have changed as follows: section 26(3), *now section 20(5)*; section 26(3A), *now section 20(6)*; section 26(5), *now section 20(9)*; section 26(6), *now section 20(10)*; section 26(7), *now section 20(11)*; and section 26(8), *now section 20(12)*.

1 The Amendment Act in General

Important amendments to s 26 of the Public Accountants' and Auditors' Act 51 of 1951 (the 'PAA Act') were effected by the Public Accountants' and Auditors' Amendment Act 42 of 1982 (the 'Amendment Act'), which was promulgated on 24 March 1982.

For convenience the amended text of subsections (3A) to (8) of s 26 is given in the Annexure hereto.

The Amendment Act deals mainly with aspects of professional liability: it clarifies certain uncertainties, eliminates certain dangers of unreasonable exposure to liability, for instance for breach of a statutory duty, and excludes no-fault liability. It did not create any new liability. Judicial developments of great significance for the professional liability of members of the accountancy profession to third parties have taken place in this country and elsewhere in recent years.

2 Matters Affected – An Overview

The provisions of the Amendment Act affect three important aspects of accountants' or auditors' legal position.

2.1 Codification of liability to third parties (s 26(5)(b)-(8))

By far the most important effect of the Amendment Act is that it codifies the law relating to the professional liability of accountants and auditors to *third parties* (that is, persons other than the client) for *negligent* misstatements.

In view of their importance, these provisions will be dealt with separately in 3 below.

2.2 Auditor's duty to report under s 26(3A)

The basic statutory duty to report on 'material irregularities' is of course contained in s 26(3). In 1975 s 26(3A) was inserted. This new subsection prescribed the duties of an auditor in regard to 'material irregularities' in the conduct of his client's affairs where the client had been sequestrated or liquidated. Section 26(3A) was then changed by the Amendment Act, in two respects.

2.2.1 Request by liquidator (s 26(3A)(aA))

At the request of the trustee or liquidator, the auditor concerned must inform him whether a report on material irregularities is required, and if so, the auditor must forthwith despatch that report.

The duty to report already existed under s 26(3A)(a). The new provisions do strengthen the position of the trustee or liquidator; but they clearly do not add anything of substance to the duties of the auditor. It is obviously still for the auditor, and not the trustee or liquidator, to decide whether circumstances require the report to be made.

2.2.2 Exclusion of liability for breach of statutory duty (s 26(3A)(b))

A potentially dangerous exposure to liability lurked in the provisions of s 26(3A). Those provisions could quite convincingly be interpreted as impliedly providing for the personal liability of the auditor who had failed to perform his reporting duty, on the ground of breach of statutory duty. This interpretation was strongly supported by the fact that liability for breach of the statutory reporting duty under s 26(3) was expressly and conspicuously excluded in s 26(3)(e); however, a similar exclusion was equally conspicuously absent from the closely related s 26(3A).

For policy reasons this exposure to liability (to the client or its members or creditors) purely on the ground of the breach of the statutory duty in s 26(3A) was unacceptable. That is why the Amendment Act inserted a reference to s 26(3)(e) in s 26(3A)(b). This makes it perfectly clear that s 26(3A) (like s 26(3)) confers no right of action against an auditor upon any person, which that person would not otherwise have.

2.3 Exclusion of no-fault liability (s 26(5)(a))

The somewhat curiously worded original s 26(5) prohibited the institution of an action against an accountant or auditor for professional conduct, unless it was proved that he had acted 'maliciously or negligently'. Section 8(2) of the Companies Act contains a similar provision.

The real significance of these provisions is that they exclude any possible inference that an accountant or auditor could incur professional liability without proof of fault ('malice or negligence').

In the amended s 26 this exclusion was re-enacted in the differently worded s 26(5)(a), which in effect provides that an accountant or auditor shall incur no liability to the client or a third party unless it is proved that he has acted 'maliciously or pursuant to a negligent performance of his duties'. The concepts of 'malice' or 'negligence', used in the alternative, were retained because they had appeared in the original s 26(5) and are still used in s 8(2) of the Companies Act.

3 LIABILITY TO THIRD PARTIES

3.1 Codification in s 26(5)(b)-(8), and diminishing significance of common law

For the reasons given in para 5 below, the law governing the professional liability of accountants and auditors to 'third parties' for negligent misstatements was codified in the [then] new s 26(5)(b)-(8) of the PAA Act. This new dispensation took effect on 24 March 1982.

The common law continues to apply where the cause of action arose prior to the commencement of the Amendment Act, but it is clearly of diminishing significance.

3.2 Distinction between liability to client and to third party

The codification must of course be seen against the background of the fundamental distinction between an accountants's or auditor's liability to the *client* (who for the purpose of the discussion is assumed to be a company) and to *a third party*, respectively. Different principles apply.

3.3 Liability to client company: a summary

The professional relationship of an auditor is of course with the client company, and not with its members, creditors or any other third party. This relationship is typically contractual. The scope of the work to be done by the auditor under this contract may differ from case to case – subject of course to the statutory duties attracted by the agreement, for example s 26 of the PAA Act, and s 269–83, 294 and 300–301 of the Companies Act. The duties undertaken to be performed may arise from or be affected by the company's memorandum or articles of association, with which the auditor has to familiarize himself.

Whether the contract is oral or in writing, the law implies as a term thereof the duty to perform the work undertaken with reasonable care and skill; the auditor has to bring to bear on the work the skill, care and caution which a reasonably competent, careful and cautious auditor would use.

It follows that the *client company* has an action for damages based on *breach of contract* if the auditor negligently (i.e. without reasonable care and skill) causes it loss in the execution of his duties.

Such an auditor also incurs an Aquilian (i.e. delictual) liability to the client, and the company therefore has the *choice* of couching its action in *delict*.

A few statutory provisions have relevance for professional liability to the client. Section 8(2) of the Companies Act and the [then] new s 26(5)(a) of the PAA Act in effect exclude the possibility of no-fault liability, whether for breach of statutory duty or of contract. In terms of s 247 of the Companies Act the articles or a contract with the company may not exempt the auditor from or indemnify him/her against liability to the company. However, under s 248 the Court may under certain circumstances relieve the auditor from such liability. It seems, though, that an auditor is not an 'officer' for the purpose of the summary remedy in s 423 of the Companies Act.

Fundamentally the principles governing an auditor's liability to the client for professional negligence are the same as those applying to all professional persons. This is why the new codification was carefully designed not to disturb the existing professional relationship between an accountant or auditor and the client.

3.4 Common-law liability to third parties prior to 24 March 1982

Persons other than the client company typically have no contractual relationship with the auditor relevant to his performance of duties for the particular client. Such a third party may be a member of the client company, and may even quite conceivably be another client of the same auditor. Every person other than the client concerned is a third party.

In the absence of a contract, which is typical, a third party who has suffered loss as a result of reliance on negligently made misstatements by accountants or auditors has to couch action for damages in delict.

The extreme uncertainty for many years in almost all modern legal systems about the requirements for, and even the existence of, delictual liability for mere financial loss caused by honest but negligent misrepresentations, is too well known for repetition. At the root of this uncertainty was a fear of 'indeterminate' liability. What merits emphasis is that rapid judicial developments over the last decade, and particularly in very recent years, have completely destroyed any complacent belief that the accountancy profession's exposure in this regard is academic.

This new reality is clearly reflected in cases against auditors in several Commonwealth countries, e.g. *Diamond Manufacturing Co Ltd v Hamilton* [1969] NZLR 609 (CA); *Scott Group Ltd v McFarlane* [1978] 1 NZLR 533 (CA), and *Haig v Bamford* 72 DLR (3d) 68 (1976) (Supreme Court of Canada). These developments are set out in some detail in *The South African Chartered Accountant* 1980 from 102 and 157, and in *Modern Business Law* 1979 at 121–137. In the recent English case of *Jeb Fasteners Ltd v Marks, Bloom & Co* [1981] 3 All ER 289 (QBD) Woolf J said that –

> 'the appropriate test for establishing whether a duty of care exists appears in this case to be whether the defendants [a firm of accountants] knew or reasonably should have foreseen at the time the accounts were audited that a person might rely on those accounts for the purpose of deciding whether or not to take over the company and therefore could suffer loss if the accounts were inaccurate . . . First of all, they must have relied on the accounts and, second, they must have done so in circumstances where the auditors either knew that they would or ought to have known that they might' (at 296 H–I).

> '"Everything has now changed", a leading English company lawyer commented, "with a rapidity which has left tort lawyers breathless" (*The Company Lawyer* vol 3 at 26). Woolf J's judgment was upheld by the Court of Appeal in July 1982 (still unreported), and also influenced a Scottish decision in March 1982 in the Court of Sessions (*Twomax Ltd and Goode v Dickson*, still unreported) where a firm of accountants was held liable to three investors who had purchased shares on the strength of accounts which had been negligently audited (*The Company Lawyer* vol 3 at 174). English writers refer to "the trend for open-ended auditors' liability".'

In South Africa any semblance of doubt about availability of an Aquilian action for negligent misstatement – and hence about the delictual liability of an accountant or auditor to third parties – was destroyed by the Appeal

Court in *Administrateur, Natal v Trust Bank van Afrika Bpk* 1979 (3) SA 824 (A). Apart from other requirements such as fault and causation, there has to be wrongfulness. Wrongfulness depends on whether the defendant had a legal duty not to make a misstatement to the plaintiff. In the absence of such a legal duty (which is not the traditional English concept of a 'duty of care') there can be no wrongfulness. The important question as to when such a legal duty arises depends on the particular circumstances of the case and on policy considerations.

This important case leaves no doubt as to the existence of liability for accountants and auditors. However, it is impossible to confidently make any significant inference as to the circumstances in which members of the profession will incur this liability in regard to duties performed every day.

3.5 The codification on 24 March 1982

3.5.1 Reasons

Several reasons contributed to a request for codification and the positive official reaction.

- There was an urgent need for certainty on the basic requirements for liability to third parties. The Trust Bank case left the profession with absolute certainty about liability, but with serious uncertainty as to the circumstances where it will occur. Foreign cases were instructive, but they evidenced clear differences in approach, and views or dicta in some judgments gave cause for concern. Moreover, the 'duty not to make a misstatement' referred to in Trust Bank was not identical to the 'duty of care' on which those cases were based. For the profession the effect of the uncertainty was serious. By the nature of their duties members of the accountancy profession have a unique and constant exposure to this liability, with potentially enormous consequences. Uncertainty induced questionable settlements in order to avoid the cost and embarrassment of establishing legal precedent. Of course, any codification has to be interpreted. But it can clarify the basic requirements for liability. The drafting of this codification was done after cognizance had been taken of relevant judicial developments here and elsewhere. Prior to its enactment senior counsel concluded that the merit of the draft was 'that it will more or less achieve the same result as I think that our courts would achieve in the end'.

- Third parties were equally uncertain about the requirements for liability and they, too, benefit from certainty. An attempt unjustifiably to restrict professional liability at the expense of third parties would have had no chance of reaching the statute book. This measure was eventually supported by all four parties in the House of Assembly.

- In view of the greater certainty members of the profession can identify and guard against situations giving rise to potential liability. They know for instance that after the completion of their audit duties for a client they should make no express or implied representations to a third party as to the correctness of the annual financial statements – or accept the risk that they may be negligently misleading. Troublesome questions that had emerged or been recognized in other systems were avoided in the codification. It is for instance made clear that a member of the client company is a 'third party'; he is not in some vague position somewhere between the client and third parties, nor does the auditor assume a direct statutory responsibility to him merely because in terms of s 301(1) of the Companies Act the auditor reports 'to the members'.

- Another significant example is that the codification makes it clear that the requirement that an accountant or auditor 'could reasonably have been expected to know' of the reliance on his statement depends on the particular circumstances of the case; it cannot simply be inferred from his professional position as has virtually been done in some judgments.

3.5.2 Outline of effect

The codified liability to third parties for negligent misstatement is to be found in s 26(5)(b) – (8). Paragraph (5)(a), which in effect provides that there shall be *no* liability to the *client or any third party* unless malice or negligence is proved, excludes any possibility of *no-fault liability* to any person. It does not form part of the codification of liability to third parties, and is similar to the old s 26(5), which it replaced, and s 8(2) of the Companies Act.

Before a *third party* can succeed against an accountant or auditor for misstatements in an opinion expressed, statement made, etc, he will have to prove the following:

- *Negligence in the performance of duties*
  The section does not in any way change the meaning or proof of negligence. Culpa (negligence) arises if a reasonable accountant or auditor (as the case may be) in the position of defendant –
  – would foresee the reasonable possibility of his conduct causing patrimonial loss to another; and
  – would take reasonable steps to guard against such occurrence; and the defendant failed to take such steps (*Kruger v Coetzee* 1966 (2) SA 428 (A) at 430).
  Negligence is therefore always a question that depends on the circumstances of each case. However, now as formerly, standards and practices adopted by the profession to meet current circumstances provide a sound guide to the Court in determining what is reasonable.

- *Reliance by the third party on the opinion, statement, etc.*

- *Financial loss*

- *Causation*
  The third party's loss must have been caused by his reliance on the negligently made report, etc.

- That the accountant or auditor *at the time of his negligence* knew, or could in the particular circumstances reasonably have been expected to know, that –
  - the client would use the opinion, statement, etc., to induce the third party to act or not to act in some way or to enter into a transaction, or
  - the third party would rely on the opinion, statement, etc., to act or not to act in some way or to enter into a transaction,

  or

- That the accountant or auditor after he had expressed his opinion or made his report, etc., in any way represented to the third party that the opinion or report, etc., was correct, while at the time he knew or could in the particular circumstances reasonably have been expected to know that the third party would rely on his representation to act or not to act in some way or to enter into a transaction.

3.5.3 Some points of detail

A full analysis of all practical implications is obviously impracticable. However, a few matters merit comment.

- There is an obvious difference between, say, annual financial statements of a client company on the one hand and special financial statements or a prospectus on the other.

- Whether an auditor knows or ought to know that annual financial statements are going to be relied upon by a third party depends entirely on the particular circumstances. If he is asked to provide audited financial statements for a particular purpose (for instance, a loan or an acquisition of the company's shares), his risk is obviously greater. When he drafts a report forming part of a prospectus, he knows perfectly well that the very purpose of a prospectus is to induce potential investors to subscribe for the shares or other securities; if he is negligent in preparing that statement, the precariousness of his position in regard to someone who relies on that part of the prospectus in subscribing for the securities is clear.

- Subsection (6) states explicitly that the fact that a person has acted as accountant or auditor is not in itself proof that he could reasonably have been expected to know that there would be the inducement by his client or the reliance by the third party required for liability. The mere fact, for instance, that the client company's shares are listed on the stock exchange and its annual financial statements are lodged with the registrar of companies are clearly insufficient for establishing liability to a third party who has bought shares on the strength of those negligently misleading annual financial statements. More is required before the auditor can in the circumstances be reasonably expected to know of the inducement or reliance.

- Typically there is no contractual relation between the accountant or auditor and the third party concerned. In the unlikely event that there is such a contract relevant to the duties negligently performed for the client company, the codification ought not to interfere with the third party's action for breach of contract, if there is one. This explains s 26(7)(a)(i).

- Within its scope s 26(5)(b)–(8) codifies the law, and precludes reliance on the common law relating to negligent misstatement. However, statutory liability provided for elsewhere should clearly be preserved. This is done in s 26(7)(a)(ii). Probable instances are s 160 (liability for untrue statements in prospectus) and s 161 (liability of experts and others) of the Companies Act.

- The codified provision for liability does not affect a disclaimer of liability – for instance, words in an auditor's report that no liability is accepted in regard to that report. If the words used do not in fact disclaim liability, they cannot confidently be expected to have the desired effect.

- The definition of 'third party' leaves no doubt that it includes a member of any client who is a legal persona. Hence a member has to comply with the same requirements for establishing an accountant's or auditor's liability as any other third party.

3.6 Conclusion

Professional liability has become a fact of life. The moralistic counsel of perfection is never to be negligent. However, it has become particularly important to keep the liability for professional negligence to third parties within reasonable bounds. It is certainly not in the public interest that a situation should arise where professional persons of integrity will feel obliged to resort to the device of a general disclaimer in order to negate any assumption of responsibility. This is the light in which the codification should be seen.

Annexure

SECTION 26(3A) – (8) [now s 20(6) to s 20(12)] OF THE PUBLIC ACCOUNTANTS' AND AUDITORS' ACT 1951, AS AMENDED BY ACT 42 OF 1982, [NOW THE PUBLIC ACCOUNTANTS' AND AUDITORS' ACT NO. 80 OF 1991, AS AMENDED]

[Subsections (1), (2), (3), and (4) of s 26, *now s 20(1) to 20(5)*] stand unamended and are not repeated here.]

s 26(3A)(a), *now s 20(6)(a):*

If any person who was acting in the capacity of auditor to any undertaking immediately prior to its sequestration or liquidation (whether provisional or final) is satisfied or has reason to believe that at or before the date of sequestration or liquidation a material irregularity in the conduct of the affairs of such undertaking was taking place or had taken place, which had caused or was likely to cause financial loss to the undertaking or to any of its members or creditors, and such person did not comply with the provisions of subsection (3)(a), *now s 20(5)(a)* in respect of such irregularity before the said date, he shall forthwith despatch a report in writing, giving particulars of such irregularity, to the person appointed as trustee or provisional trustee, or as liquidator or provisional liquidator, as the case may be, of such undertaking, and at the same time supply copies of such report to the person in charge of such undertaking and to the board [unamended];

s 26(3A)(aA), *now s 20(6)(b)*:

If any person who was acting in the capacity of auditor to any undertaking immediately prior to its sequestration or liquidation (whether provisional or final) and who has not taken action in term of subsection (3)(a), *now s 20(5)(a)*, or despatched a report in writing in terms of paragraph (a) of this subsection, is at any time requested in writing to do so by the person appointed as trustee or provisional trustee or a liquidator or provisional liquidator, as the case may be, of such undertaking, he shall forthwith inform the person so requesting whether or not a report in writing is required by paragraph (a), *now s 20(6)(a)* of this subsection and in the event of his informing the person so requesting that such report is so required, he shall forthwith despatch the report to the person, and at the same time supply copies of such report to the person in charge of such undertaking and to the board;

s 26(3A)(b), *now s 20(6)(c)*:

The provisions of subsection (3)(c), *now s 20(5)(c)*, shall *mutatis mutandis* apply with reference to any information supplied to the board in terms of paragraph (a) of this subsection, and the provisions of subsection (3)(e), *now s 20(5)(e)*, shall *mutatis mutandis* apply with reference to any provision of this subsection;

s 26(5), *now s 20(9)*:

Any auditor or any person registered as an accountant and auditor under this Act shall, in respect of any opinion expressed or certificate given or report or statement made or statement, account or document certified by him in the ordinary course of his duties –

s 26 (5)(a), *now s 20(9)(a)*:

incur no liability to the client or any third party, unless it is proved that such opinion was expressed or such certificate was given or such report or statement was made or such statement, account or document was certified maliciously or pursuant to a negligent performance of his duties; and

s 26 (5)(b), *now s 20(9)(b):*

where it is proved that such opinion was expressed or such certificate was given or such report or statement was made or such statement, account or document was certified pursuant to a negligent performance of his duties, be liable to any third party who has relied on such opinion, certificate, report, statement, account or document, for financial loss suffered as a result of having relied thereon, only if it is proved that the auditor or person so registered –

(i), now s 20(9)(b)(i): knew or could in the particular circumstances reasonably have been expected to know, at the time when the negligence occurred in the performance of the duties pursuant to which such opinion was expressed or such certificate was given or such report or statement was made or such statement, account or document was certified –

> **(aa), now s 20(9)(b)(i)(aa):** that such opinion, certificate, report, statement, account or document would be used by the client to induce the third party to act or refrain from acting in some way or to enter into the specific transaction into which the third party entered, or any other transaction of a similar nature, with the client or any other person; or

> **(bb), now s 20(9)(b)(i)(bb):** that the third party would rely on such opinion, certificate, report, statement, account or document for the purpose of acting or refraining from acting in some way or of entering into the specific transaction into which the third party entered, or any other transaction of a similar nature, with the client or any other person; or

(ii), now s 20(9)(b)(i): in any way represented, at any time after such opinion was expressed or such certificate was given or such report or statement was made or such statement, account or document was certified, to the third party that such opinion, certificate, report, statement, account or document was correct, while at such time he knew or could in the particular circumstances reasonably have been expected to know that the third party would rely on such representation for the purpose of acting or refraining from acting in some way or of entering into the specific transaction into which the third party entered, or any other transaction of a similar nature, with the client or any other person.

s 20(9A), *no equivalent provision was contained in s 26*

Nothing in subsection 20(9) contained shall be construed as conferring on any person any right of action against an auditor which, but for the provisions of that subsection, he would not have had.

s 26(6), *now s 20(10):*

For the purposes of paragraph (b) of subsection (5), *now s 20(9)*, the fact that an auditor or a person referred to in that subsection performed the functions of an auditor or accountant shall not in itself be proof that he could reasonably have been expected to know that –

(a) the client would act as contemplated in subparagraph (i)(aa) of the said paragraph (b); or

(b) the third party would act as contemplated in subparagraph (i)(bb) or (ii) of the said paragraph (b).

s 26 (7), *now s 20(11)*:

The provisions of paragraph (b) of subsection (5), *now s 20(9)*, shall not affect –

(a) any liability of an auditor or a person referred to in that subsection which arises from –

  (i)   a contract between a third party and such auditor or person; or

  (ii) any statutory provision; or

(b) any disclaimer of liability by an auditor or a person referred to in that subsection.

s 26 (8), *now s 20(12)*:

For purposes of subsection (5), (6) or (7), *now s 20(9), 20(10) or 20(11)* –

(i)   'client' means the person for whom an auditor or a person referred to in subsection (5), *now s 20(9)*, or his firm, has performed the duties concerned;

(ii) 'third party' means any person other than the client concerned, and includes any member of a client which is a company or external company (as defined in section 1 of the Companies Act, 1973 (Act No 61 of 1973)) or which is any other juristic person.

APPENDIX 3

Specimen Deed of Transfer

DEED OF TRANSFER

in favour of

NEW OWNER

Over

ERF 498 OBSERVATORY, JOHANNESBURG

Prepared by me,

. . . .

CONVEYANCER

DEED OF TRANSFER | T 45303/2000 |

BE IT HEREBY KNOWN:

THAT . . . . (Name of Conveyancer) appeared before me, REGISTRAR OF DEEDS (*Registrar of Deeds concerned*) at JOHANNESBURG (*Situation of Registrar's office*), the said Appearer, being duly authorized thereto by a Power of Attorney granted to him/her by –

. . . .(*Name of Transferor*)

Identity Number . . . .
married out of community of property

DATED at JOHANNESBURG on the 20 day of JUNE 2002

AND THE SAID APPEARER declared that his Principal had truly and legally sold the under-mentioned property on 15 April 2000 for a purchase consideration of R400 000 (FOUR HUNDRED THOUSAND RAND), and that he, in his capacity aforesaid, did by these presents, cede and transfer, in full and free property, to and on behalf of:

. . . .(*Name of Transferee*)

Identity Number. . . . .

married out of community of property

in full and free property:
his heirs, executors, administrators or assigns:

CERTAIN Lot . . . . situated on . . . .

Street, (*Name of township*), District of (*Town*)

MEASURING . . . . square metres;

HELD BY Deed of Transfer No (*Number of former deed of transfer*) made in favour of Appearer's said Principal on the day of . . . . 20 . . . . (*year*) and the General Plan of the said Township therein referred to will more fully point out.

SUBJECT to such conditions as are mentioned or referred to in the aforesaid Deed of Transfer,

AND SUBJECT SPECIALLY to the following special conditions, namely:

(a) (*Name of township owners*) reserves to itself the right at any time hereafter to the free and undisturbed passage of electric, telegraph or telephone wires over and above any portion of any lot or lots with further right of causing them to be affixed to any building or erection at not less than three metres from the ground with access at any time to the said wires for the purpose of maintenance or removal.

(b) (*Name of township owners*) reserves to itself the right at any time hereafter to lay and maintain piping under any lot or lots and at all times access to the said piping for removal, maintenance, extension or for other purposes, as also for the construction and maintenance of waterworks, reservoirs and all machinery requisite for conserving and supplying storage water to different parts of the Township and to do all such acts and things as shall be required for the convenience of the inhabitants of this Township in regard to supplying them with water.

WHEREFORE all the right and title, which the Transferor heretofore had to the aforesaid, is renounced and, in consequence it is also acknowledged the Transferor is entirely dispossessed of, and disentitled to, the same, and that by virtue of those presents, the aforesaid Transferee now is entitled thereto, the State however, reserving its rights.

Signed, executed and sealed at JOHANNESBURG (*Registrar of Deeds*) at (*Situation of his office*)

On the . . . . day of . . . . (*Month*) 2000

. . . . (*Signature of Conveyancer*)

CONVEYANCER

q.q. His Principal

Seal of
Registrar

In my presence

(*Signature of Registrar*)

REGISTRAR OF DEEDS

Registered in the Register of . . . . TOWNSHIP,

kept at . . . . (*Deeds Registry applicable*) on the above date.

APPENDIX 4

Specimen Mortgage Bond Freehold Property

Prepared by me,

. . . . *(Signature of conveyancer)*

CONVEYANCER

MORTGAGE BOND | *Bond reference No 802.200* |

Know all Men whom it may concern:

THAT . . . . *(Name of conveyancer)*

appeared before me, ... *(Registrar of Deeds)*

he, the said Appearer, being duly authorized thereto by a Power of Attorney granted to him by . . . . *(Name of mortgagor)*

Identity Number: . . . .

dated the . . . . day of . . . . *(Month)* . . . . *(Year)* and

signed at . . . . *(Name of town)*

And the said Appearer declared his Principal(s), the said . . . .

. . . . *(Name of mortgagor)*
(hereinafter called the 'Mortgagor') to be really and lawfully indebted and held and firmly bound unto and on behalf of . . . .

. . . . *(Name of mortgagee)*

Identity Number: . . . .

(hereinafter styled the 'Mortgagee') in the sum of R. . . . .
(Amount of money advanced) (hereinafter styled '*the Capital*')

arising from and being *so much cash actually lent and advanced and to be paid to the Mortgagor on the registration of this bond and being the capital amount of the actual loan.*

Therefore on behalf of his aforementioned Principal(s), renouncing all benefits arising from the legal exceptions *non numeratae, pecuniae, non causa debiti, errore calculi, revision of account and no value received*

with the force and meaning whereof the Appearer declared his Principal(s) to be fully acquainted. And the Appearer, on behalf of his aforementioned Principal(s) hereby promises and undertakes to pay, or cause to be paid, unto the said Mortgagee or other legal holder of this Bond, *his/her/its* Order, Heirs, Administrators or Assigns the Capital, together with the interest thereon, payable . . . . *(Terms of interest payment, e.g. annually in arrears/quarterly in advance, etc.)*

at the rate of .... *(Rate)* per cent per annum, and reckoned from the .... *(Date from which interest to be paid, e.g. date of registration of this bond, etc.)*

inclusive, and to continue to be so reckoned, until such time as the whole of the Capital shall be fully paid off, which payment *he/she/it* shall be allowed, and also obliged to make.

(Special condition regarding repayment in anticipation of fixed date at mortgagor's option, e.g. interest being payable as hereinbefore set out.)

And as security for the due and punctual payment of the Capital, or any portion thereof, interest due thereon and all other sums of money which may at any time become due and owing to the Mortgagee(s) or other legal holder(s) of this Bond from any cause whatsoever in terms hereof, and for the proper fulfilment by the Mortgagor(s) of all and every term and condition of this Bond, the Appearer, *q.q.*, hereby binds as a ....
(Type of bond, e.g. 1st, 2nd or 3rd)

Mortgage the following property:

CERTAIN: .... *(Description of the property as contained in Deed of Transfer.)*

AND THE APPEARER, *q.q.*, declared to bind his Principal to the following conditions:

1. THAT all payments of Capital, Interest, and other moneys due hereunder shall be made in good, current and lawful money free of exchange at .... *(Where payment shall be made)*

    or at such other place or places in South Africa as the Mortgagee(s) or *his/her/its* Agent(s) may from time to time direct.

2. THAT his Principal shall be bound and obliged regularly and promptly to pay all Stand Licences, Government and Municipal Rates, taxes and other charges levied, or to be levied, in respect of the property hereby mortgaged, and to produce the receipts for the same to the Mortgagee(s) or *his/her/its* Agent(s) whenever the same may be demanded.

3. THAT his said Principal(s) shall keep and maintain the Buildings and Erections on the property mortgaged in good and habitable order, and insure the same, and keep the same insured in a Fire Insurance Office approved by the Mortgagee(s), for a sum adequate to cover the value thereof against risk of loss from Fire, and shall cede the Policy or Policies of such Insurance to the said Mortgagee(s) or other legal holder of this Bond, as a collateral security for this Bond and all indebtedness hereunder, and shall renew the Policy or Policies of the said Insurance (as well as any other Policy or Policies of Insurance as with the consent of the legal holder(s) of this Bond for the time being may hereafter be effected upon the Premises in addition to, or in lieu of, the aforesaid Policy or Policies) according to the conditions of such Policy or Policies,

as long as the indebtedness under this Bond, or any part thereof, shall remain unliquidated, and shall produce proof of having done so, to the Mortgagee(s) or other legal holder(s) hereof. That any moneys received under such Insurance shall, at the choice of the Mortgagee(s) or other legal holder of this Bond be wholly or partially employed either in partial or full payment of interest due, Capital and Charges which may then be due, or for the restoration, under such conditions as the Bondholder(s), or *his/her/its* Agent, may lay down, of that which has been damaged, or destroyed by fire.

4. THAT should *his/her/its* Principal(s) fail or neglect to pay the said Licences, Rates, Taxes, other Charges and Premiums, or any of them, promptly on the due dates thereof, or to keep and maintain the said buildings and erections in good order as aforesaid, the Mortgagee(s) or other legal holder(s) of this Bond may pay such moneys and do or cause the repairs to be done at the expense of Appearer's Principal(s), and to recover immediately from *his/her/it* any moneys so advanced or expended, together with interest thereon, at the same rate as is chargeable on the Capital of this Bond, as from the date on which such moneys were paid or expended by the Mortgagee(s), or other legal holder of this Bond, until such times as the same are repaid by Appearer's Principal(s); all moneys so advanced or expended being secured by and deemed to be sums due and payable under this Bond.

5. THAT any Notice or Notices which shall or may be required to be given under this Bond by the Mortgagee(s) or other legal holder(s) hereof, shall be addressed to his said Principal at. . . . . (*Address of mortgagor*) which place *he/she/it* selects as *his/her/its domicilium citandi et executandi*, for all processes to be served under this Bond.

6. THAT all future advances, debts or demands (over and above the Capital and interest thereon), which may lawfully be secured and recovered under this Bond in respect of and including any costs, charges and disbursements in having this Bond prepared and registered, in having any part payment of Capital registered and in having this Bond cancelled eventually (all of which services the Mortgagor(s) hereby agree(s) shall be rendered by a Conveyancer nominated by the Mortgagee(s), or other legal holder, of this Bond), in issuing notices and demands and in suing and taking further legal proceedings for the recovery of any sum of money due under this Bond; all moneys disbursed by the Mortgagee(s), or other legal holder, of this Bond in respect of Stand Licences, Government and Municipal rates and taxes and other charges levied in respect of the property hereby mortgaged; Premiums of Insurance and costs of Repairs and Maintenance, which interest thereon as hereinbefore stated, Bank Exchange on cheques, and generally all costs of preserving and realizing the security held under this Bond, which the Mortgagee, or other legal holder(s), of this Bond may have incurred, advanced or expended, shall be limited to a sum not

exceeding, and, in so far as they are not preferent, shall be hereby secured as preferent to the sum of .... Rand (*Amount considered necessary*) over and above the Capital.

7.   IN the event of the Appearer's said Principal(s) failing or neglecting to pay any sum or sums due and payable under this Bond promptly on the respective due dates, or to carry out any of the other conditions and stipulations of this Bond, the Capital with interest and all other sums due hereunder, shall immediately become due and recoverable without any notice (any conditions to the contrary herein contained notwithstanding).

8.   THAT the title deeds of the Property bonded shall be lodged with and remain in the custody of the said Mortgagee(s) or other legal holder(s) of this Bond during the subsistence of this Bond and the said property shall not be further burdened in any way without the consent in writing of the said Mortgagee(s) or other legal holder(s) of this Bond.

9.   THAT all rents which may from time to time be due from the present or any future tenant or tenants of the property hereby mortgaged, or any portion thereof, are hereby ceded and assigned as collateral security to and in favour of the said Mortgagee(s), or other legal holder(s) hereof; and the said Mortgagee(s), or other legal holder(s) hereof, is hereby empowered, with power of substitution, to collect, sue for and recover the said rents and to grant valid receipts for the same; but no use shall be made of the said cession of rentals unless the Appearer's said Principal(s) shall fail to pay the capital or interest upon the due date or dates thereof.

10. THAT – (*Additional clauses*).

IN WITNESS WHEREOF, I, the said *Registrar of Deeds*, together with the Appearer, *q.q.*, have subscribed to these presents, and have caused the Seal of Office to be affixed hereto.

THUS DONE AND EXECUTED at the office of ....
                                                                                    (*Location of Deeds Registry*)

On .... day of .... (*Month*) 2000

In my presence.

....   Seal of
(*Signature of Registrar*)   Registrar

         q.q

REGISTRAR OF DEEDS

APPENDIX 5

Specimen of Mortgagee Clause in Insurance Policy

'It is hereby specially agreed that this insurance as to the interest of the Mortgagee as regards the buildings, landlord's fixtures and rent insured only, shall not be invalidated by any act or neglect of the mortgagor or owner of the property insured, nor by any misrepresentation or non-disclosure by the mortgagor or owner of the property insured, at the time where the insurance is effected or renewed or during the currency thereof, nor by the alienation of the property nor by the occupation thereof for purposes more hazardous than are permitted by this policy, provided that such an act, neglect, misrepresentation, nondisclosure, alienation or occupation shall have been effected without the knowledge or privity of the mortgagee. Provided also that the mortgagee shall notify the Underwriters of the happening or existence or such act, neglect, misrepresentation, nondisclosure, alienation or occupation as soon as the same shall come to his or her knowledge and shall, on reasonable demand, pay the additional charge for any increase of hazard thereby created according to the established scale of rates, for the time such increased hazard may be, or shall have been assumed by the Underwriters, during the continuance of this insurance.'

INDEX

879